D0769110

JOHN WAYNE

JOHN WAYNE
Actor, Artist, Hero

by
Richard D. McGhee

McFarland & Company, Inc., Publishers
Jefferson, North Carolina, and London

Frontispiece: John Wayne as Captain Ralls in *Wake of the Red Witch*, 1949.

British Library Cataloguing-in-Publication data are available

Library of Congress Cataloguing-in-Publication Data

McGhee, Richard D., 1940–
    John Wayne : actor, artist, hero / Richard D. McGhee.
    p.   cm.
    Includes bibliographical references and index.
    ISBN 0-89950-501-5 (lib. bdg. : 50# alk. paper) ∞
    1. Wayne, John, 1907–1979.   2. Motion picture actors and
actresses — United States — Biography.   I. Title.
PN2287.W454M35   1990
791.43′028′092 — dc20
[B]   89-43658
                                                                    CIP

Manufactured in the United States of America

McFarland & Company, Inc., Publishers
  Box 611, Jefferson, North Carolina 28640

For Marie, as always,

our grandchildren,
Deborah and Matthew,

my mother, Golda Lucille,

and

Chu-Tak
(Judith Cochran)

Acknowledgments

I wish to thank James M. Welsh, editor of *Literature/Film Quarterly*, for permission to use a portion of my article which originally appeared in 1988 in that journal (Vol. 16, No. 1) for Chapter 9 of this book.

Many people have been involved with my work on this book, which began about ten years ago. I should like to register here my thanks and appreciation for all their help and encouragement. Bob Kruh and the Kansas State University Bureau of General Research provided financial aid along the way; my two department heads, Harry Donaghy and Robert Grindell, arranged for additional time to work on the book; especially Rob Grindell has made this project possible to complete, as he has made my professional life generally happy and satisfying. My colleagues Bill Koch and Mike Gillespie have kept my awareness of John Wayne large and alert for several years. Vera McClendon, with abundant good humor and patience, entered a longer text into the computer; she saved me more than time. My family has persevered through these many years, often putting aside other interests to allow John Wayne more time on the family television and VCR. My daughter-in-law, Janet, helped me with some Spanish translations in the film scripts, and my daughter, Beth, translated an article in Spanish on John Wayne's life. My sons, Bill and Dave, endured the trials with admirable tolerance for a subject so far from their professional interests and personal tastes.

The book is dedicated to the persons who have given me my beginnings, my bearings, and my direction.

Table of Contents

Preface

The name *John Wayne* does not recall the man whose real name was Marion Morrison, born May 26, 1907, in Winterset, Iowa, and died June 11, 1979, at the UCLA Medical Center in Los Angeles, California. President Jimmy Carter, speaking for the nation, said that John Wayne "was bigger than life. In an age of few heroes, he was the genuine article. But he was more than a hero; he was a symbol of many of the qualities that made America great."

In an essay on "The Political Theatre of John Wayne," Eric Bentley in 1972 said that "the most important American of our time is John Wayne.... In an age when the image is the principal thing, Wayne is the principal image, and if the soul of this image is *machismo* (a topic for another essay, a topic for a book, for *the* book of our time), its body is the body politic, and its name is Anti-Communism." My motives for beginning to study the films of John Wayne included one or two akin to Bentley's for writing his essay. However, my conclusions are far from what I expected, far from those Bentley drew. Our shared premise is that "the most important American of our time is John Wayne," because "in an age when the image is the principal thing, Wayne is the principal image."[1]

My book is divided into three main sections to focus on those features of John Wayne's work which make his image into a symbol of American culture. The first section concentrates on his style of work and sphere of action, as an actor: the man who works for a living, and whose work is entertainment. The actor mimics his times, works within the constraints of his immediate environment, and seeks to satisfy as large an audience as he can; if he does not, he will quickly find himself out of work. He has to be aware of his audience; he must work well with his fellow actors and actresses, directors, and producers.

There is, however, another level for the actor to aim for, a level which extends beyond the immediacy of the contemporary audience and the people with whom the actor must work; this is where the artist performs, where he lives in his art: his life is in fantasy, a realm that includes, but is not limited by, the world of the actor. In his life of fantasy, the artist subordinates himself to classic structures of scenes and stories; he disappears into his characters, expressions of deep human fears and desires. John Wayne moved quickly and easily into this realm of the artist.

Not so easily achieved, but more rewarding than the successes of actor and artist, is the realm of the hero, the artist who leaves fantasy for imagination. In this realm, reality is shaped, not abandoned, by art. The hero is the artist who enters the living experience of his audience to become a means of its self-consciousness.

Introduction

In his book about the Vietnam War, *Born on the Fourth of July* (1976), Ron Kovic refers to "the glory John Wayne war." Kovic says he went to war inspired by popular heroes of American culture: "Like Mickey Mantle and the fabulous New York Yankees, John Wayne in *The Sands of Iwo Jima* became one of my heroes." Kovic came out of the war blaming these same heroes, as in these verses:

> I am the living death
> the memorial day on wheels
> I am your yankee doodle dandy
> your fourth of july firecracker
> exploding in the grave.[2]

This is the heroic image which inspired the contempt of Eric Bentley, in his essay on "The Political Theatre of John Wayne" in 1972. Joan Didion, however, remembered a different hero in her essay for "John Wayne: A Love Song," in 1968. Bentley saw Wayne as an image of political repression in America, and he argued with the man "who put his art at the service of his beliefs." This is not the man of Joan Didion's memory; for her, the man she saw on a movie set in 1943, when she was eight, had become already the man who "rode through my childhood."

John Wayne was an image for a dream of perfect freedom: he "suggested another world . . . a place where a man could move free . . . in the early morning sun." Then, when she met the man himself, on the set for *The Sons of Katie Elder* (1965), Joan Didion and her husband had dinner with John Wayne and his wife Pilar: "For a while," Didion recalls, "it was only a nice evening, an evening anywhere. We had a lot of drinks and I lost the sense that the face across the table was in certain ways more familiar than my husband's." Then, she says, "Something happened." What happened to her is the subject of this book. "Suddenly the room seemed suffused with the dream, and I could not think why." Didion was possessed by the "dream" of John Wayne, the man who "rode through my childhood."[3]

IN EARLY MARCH, 1988, the Duke "appears" in an episode of the British Broadcasting Corporation's new series of *All Creatures Great and Small*, broadcast on the Arts and Entertainment Network. The series builds on previous programs originally aired in the United States on public television. It is based upon the books by James Herriot, with Christopher Timothy playing the role of James in the stories. This was Episode Six of the new series, entitled "Only One Woof," written by Johnny Byrne, produced by Bill Sellars, and directed by Roderick Graham. In it, James is attending a sick dog belonging to Molly Minikin (Katherine Page). James is perplexed that the dog is not improving, and more so that he cannot find exactly what is wrong with it. Molly cheers him on, despite her own pain of thinking her only companion in life may be dying.

She urges James to keep up his spirit: "You don't give up on him, do you? . . . I reckon I've got your measure, young man. Same as Sir Charles Armitage had mine, when I were convinced I'd not survive me operation years back." She points toward a table with a pair of photographs on top. James reaches over, and a close-up of the camera shows double-framed photographs. Molly explains about the photograph of Sir Charles: "He cared! You see, gave you the hope to struggle on, when others, even meself, had given up." But James is fixed on the other. Unable to restrain his curiosity, he exclaims, "John Wayne!" Molly smiles and laughs sweetly, in good-humored embarrassment, "Aye! T'other man in me life! Sir Charles, because he spoke from the heart, and John Wayne, because he's me favorite film star!" James smiles and chuckles, "It's a hard act to follow!"

IN 1969, JOHN SCHLESINGER'S *Midnight Cowboy* had a strong scene of exchange between Joe Buck (John Voight) and Ratso (Dustin Hoffman) about Joe's cowboy clothing on the streets of New York City. Joe has not been successful "hustling" rich women, and Ratso says it is because people are laughing at him. He says "that great big dumb cowboy crap of yours don't appeal to nobody except to every jockey on 42nd Street! That's faggot stuff!" Joe is choked with rage and embarrassment. He stutters, "John Wayne! You goin' to tell me he's a fag!" Joe's sense of himself, his dignity and pride, is bound by his identification with Wayne, his best defense against Ratso. This allows figurative uses of the Wayne allusion. Ratso does not have an answer for Joe, but other films would, including the popular French film *La Cage aux Folles* in 1978.

Joe Buck's identity of himself as John Wayne is pride of potency, male virility, the basis of the outrageously funny scene in *La Cage* when Renato Baldi (Ugo Tognazzi) and his gay lover Albin (Michael Serrault) try to deal with a family crisis. Renato's son has announced he is getting married. Albin threatens to kill himself, because he thinks Renato wants him out of the way. Renato chases him down to a nearby restaurant, where Renato calms

Albin. They try to think of ways to solve their problem. Albin suggests he pretend to be Laurent's "uncle." Renato proceeds to "see if we can make a man out of his dear 'uncle.'" He shows Albin how to hold a cup so his little "pinkie" finger does not rise "in the air." He must hold the cup firmly, spread his marmalade "the way a man does, a real man." Albin has a hard time responding. Then, when he goes to "freshen up a little," he walks like a woman. Renato exclaims, "Walk like that, it'll be the end of us tonight." Albin is desperate, "But what can I do?" The answer, Renato says, "Try to walk like John Wayne." Albin knows instantly who that is and how he should walk, but he can offer little more than a gay John Wayne!

The outrage of such a suggestion is an insult to masculinity so impossible to believe that it electrifies the situation of another terribly funny scene, in Alex Cord's *Repo Man* in 1983. Repo men are "always intense" anyway, and so when Miller (the yard man, play by Tracey Walter) tells his tale of meeting John Wayne in drag, he immediately sets the entire gang against him in indignant disbelief. People are ragging Otto (Emilio Estevez) about his macho image, when he comes into the yard sporting a bruise on his face. Marlene asks the cop why he doesn't do something about it. Bud (Harry Dean Stanton) explains "Repo don't go runnin' to the Man, Marlene. Repo Man does it alone." Marlene scoffs, "Just like John Wayne!" Most join in a chorus of enthusiastic, solemn affirmation: "Damn right! Just like John Wayne! What's wrong with that? Greatest American that ever lived!" Then Miller says, "John Wayne was a fag!" All, even Marlene, are startled. They protest as one: "The hell he was!" But Miller knows it is true, he saw the evidence: "I installed two-way mirrors in his pad in Brentwood. And he came to the door in a dress." The lot owner misinterprets: "That doesn't mean he was a homo, Miller! Lots of guys like to watch their buddies fuck! Don't you?"

John Wayne as the virile, courageous hero vies for dominance in the image with John Wayne as the unthinking reactionary, knee-jerk patriot. These two ways of invoking the name appear separately in *Birdy* (1984) and *Weird Science* (1985). The first, directed by Alan Parker, contains a scene in which Al Columbato (Nicolas Cage) dejectedly enters a gymnasium at the military hospital where his friend "Birdy" (Matthew Modine) is being treated as a psychiatric case (he thinks he is a bird). Al has been summoned to help Birdy's doctor, but Al is not getting through to Birdy. Al wanders away to the gym, where he watches a war veteran play basketball, alone, in a wheelchair. Al reads a large banner hanging on a wall, "WELCOME HOME SOLDIER. USA IS PROUD OF YOU." Al and Birdy are both veterans and casualties of combat in Vietnam. Al notices a legless man climbing an exercise rope, and he thinks to himself, "Funny, any other war we would have been heroes. Oh, man! We didn't know what we were gettin' into with this John Wayne shit, did we?"

John Wayne is more vital, and more complexly invoked, in John Hughes' *Weird Science*. The two teenage heroes, Gary (Anthony Michael Hall) and Wyatt (Ilian Mitchell Smith), are far from being heroic. They have created a "monster" to satisfy erotic longings: beautiful, brilliant Lisa (Kelly LeBrock), completely devoted to them. She even knows they have heroic potential. She creates a situation of danger during a wild party in Wyatt's home. She summons four party-crashing thugs and perverts, who burst through the house on motorcycles and terrorize everyone in the house, including especially the two hosts, who run to hide in a closet. Lisa tries to persuade them to come out to protect their guests. She tells them, "This is an excellent chance to prove your bravery and courage." Gary says, "Those are outdated concepts, all right?" He shuts the door, which she opens again to say, "Don't let John Wayne hear you say that!" Gary has his answer ready: "The man is dead, Lisa! O.K.?" Lisa and Gary know John Wayne stands for courage, even as Gary insists both Wayne and courage are dead and outdated. Although Lisa fails to shame the boys with the name of Wayne, she has created a situation of danger in which they eventually find courage and strength to defeat the villains. And so they discover that John Wayne is not dead after all.

Part I
John Wayne: Actor

1. "About All I Can Do Is Ride and Shoot"

Marion Morrison had little to distinguish himself as a future American hero. He was big and he had some aptitude for playing football. He had little sense of direction for his future, just as he had little sense of a past, coming from a deeply broken family. As the character he plays in *Paradise Canyon* (1935), John Wyatt, says, "About all I can do is ride and shoot." He had vigor, determination, and perseverance. They added up to "heart." These earned him the work he did in numerous low-budget films he made in the 1930s.

Wayne knew, when he made one of these pictures, he must fight. He didn't always win the fights. That is, he sometimes had to take the hard falls himself. Falling down is hard work, and it takes talent, which young Morrison had to develop if he was going to succeed as a movie star in these rough and tumble years of the 1930s. Diving from cliffs, speeding trains, motorcycles, automobiles, wagons, even from airplanes—these were daily occurrences in the life of the B-picture actor. But Wayne's specialty was to be horse riding. Most of the time he did it in the ordinary, Western way— fast and often. Sometimes he did it a harder way.

What you see is what you get, and what you see is a man hard at work. Consider an amusing scene in *The Trail Beyond* (1934) in which Wayne, as Rod Drew, must leap from a galloping horse onto a speeding wagon. He raises one leg over his horse, hurls himself at the wagon, and fails. His other foot is caught in the stirrup. The audience can witness the failure of a stunt. What happens next makes John Wayne very appealing, even if it is merely the result of an unedited action sequence: he promptly gets back onto his horse, gallops again beside the speeding wagon, and this time gets the stunt right. He completes his leap, and the plot moves along. You see perseverance and hard work, you get a determined man dedicated to the work ethic. Even if it is only "brawn, not brains," as a Wayne character in *The Lawless Nineties* (1936) puts it, the brawn is mighty impressive.

The man is the character, the character is the man. When a character works hard, one knows the man making the character is working hard as well in these films. The same is true for the films as fables: their few "tricks" are patently tricks, could fool only the people who live in the world of romances themselves. Because you see what you get, the actor is perceived to be as sincere and hard a worker as the characters he portrays.

DURING THE THIRTIES films showed troubles and trials of the times. From *Little Caesar, Public Enemy,* and *Scarface* in 1930, 1931, and 1932, to *The Thin Man* in 1934, *Bullets or Ballots* in 1936, and *Crime School* in 1938, the story of the criminal undermining of money and morals was a popular story in the movies. Prominent was the subject of militarism. The decade began with *All Quiet on the Western Front,* moved through appearances by *Duck Soup* (1933), *Grand Illusion* (1937), *The Dawn Patrol* (1938), to end with *Clouds Over Europe, Drums Along the Mohawk, Gone with the Wind.*

Social/political marks can be seen as well in John Wayne's films of these years: economic distress for individuals and financial depression for whole communities; natural disasters, particularly drought and dust; military threats; and, most frequently, criminal activity on a large scale—organized and thoroughly pervasive. These mark the films' content, and they are forces in structures of narratives. They reflect social reality historically verifiable, and they express social illusions projected as fears and wishes of audiences. They are, in any event, real fears and real wishes. Or, they are fears and wishes as producers and directors wanted, or believed, them to be in audiences, who would pay admission prices to subsidize their commercial ventures. These marks of the decade are contributing reasons for audiences' identification of Wayne's character with the roles he had to play. His character made an appeal which cut through the fable-formulas of the films, because it appealed to what concerned audiences in that special time of American history.

The actor had dirty work to do to make his living in these films. Many Americans could identify with that in those years when dust storms swept across the prairie states and threatened to destroy the agricultural economy. *Riders of Destiny* (1933) comes to a triumphant climax when dry creek beds are flushed to overflowing, providing water for a thirsty community's free use. Sandy Sanders uses his wit to find a solution to the valley's need for water, and when his scheme works, people and animals alike celebrate. To top it off, the film ends by drowning the villain who tried to deny the water. John Wayne's characters are often associated this way with fresh and flowing water.

INTEREST IN commercial possibilities for airplanes as competing industry for railroads was heightened to fever pitch by the solo flight of Charles Lindbergh across the Atlantic in 1927. One of Wayne's earliest films of the thirties is based on this public excitement. In *The Hurricane Express*

John Wayne as John Carruthers *(third from left)*, with *(left to right)* George Hayes as Sheriff Jake, Eleanor Hunt as Betty Mason, Ed Peil as Melgrove, Yakima Canutt as Danti, and Lafe McKee as Dad Mason *(on ground)* in *Blue Steel*, 1934.

(1932), public transportation systems of railroad and airplane are jeopardized by nefarious activities of a lawyer who disguises himself in masks of prominent people in the community. His aim is to destroy the economic efficiency of the railroad by random wrecks, and to undermine public confidence in air service by accusing it of masterminding attacks on the railroad. Content of the film, marketed as a serial of twelve episodes, comes clear as a pattern with a clear image of the wreck, a visual metaphor of the economic disaster that began in 1929. When Larry Baker uncovers the Wrecker, the public is saved.

More difficult to undertake is the rescue of a community under siege and threatened with starvation, a situation which occurs in two films of the same decade: *Blue Steel* (1934) and *Lawless Range* (1935). The siege aims to drive away residents, force them to sell at disastrous prices, so that gold under their land can be mined by criminal forces. The man behind the scheme in *Blue Steel* is the town merchant, Melgrove, who offers to put up capital for restocking the town if John can get a pack-train of supplies through to relieve them. Melgrove is fancy-talking and community-minded:

MELGROVE: You of course don't realize, but this town is in a most desperate state. They're without food and ammunition, terrorized by a band of murdering outlaws. Two attempts have been made now to bring supplies, only to have our men killed! And the food taken!

CHORUS OF VARIOUS TOWNSMEN: If we don't get provisions here before snow sets in we're trapped! We're trapped now! We can only last a few days longer. Let's all get out! I tell you it's the only solution. How can we get out, when our money's all gone for food . . . that we never got!

MELGROVE: Men, I have a little money—not much, but I'll do this. In order that you can get out, I'll give you a hundred dollars each for your homesteads. I'm taking a long chance of ever getting my money back, but I'll risk it.

[Townsmen murmur gratitude, such as "That's right square of you, Melgrove!"]

JOHN CARRUTHERS (Wayne): Just a minute! Don't you think before you sell your homes for a few dollars, that you should take at least one more chance at getting the provisions through?

MELGOVE: If you can get us provisions, I'll pay you well.

JOHN: Forget that! You give us an order, and we'll have the provisions back here inside of four days.

MELGROVE: Good! Then come to my ranch this afternoon, and I'll give you an order for a thousand-dollar supply.

[Townsmen cheer.]

A villain similar to Melgrove, in *Lawless Range*, is the local banker threatening to foreclose ranchers who cannot get cattle to market, and who are starved out exactly as in the earlier film. These stories portray economic disasters as the result of deliberate strategies by capitalists to rob after reducing people to desperate need and mass hysteria.

Gold and money are motives for evil and cause public unhappiness. Community economic disasters are results of capitalistic disregard for land as the source of life and happinesss. Beneath the surface of economic disaster is a source of salvation, if people will be patient and courageous to await its discovery. This is simple symbolism offered as a solution for complex reality, but that is the nature of these films, reassurances to the public, from capitalistic investors themselves. The recurring image of courage and patience is the character Wayne portrays over and over again: from Larry Baker in *Hurricane Express* to John Blair in *Winds of the Wasteland* (1936).

Winds of the Wasteland emphasizes the importance of interconnections among communities through a network of public communication and public transportation. It echoes the same subject of *The Hurricane Express* from four years earlier. But *Winds of the Wasteland* is at once a clearer and a more complex treatment of the subject. It uses subject content of the Pony Express, stagecoach lines, and telegraph systems to develop its theme of restoring a town's confidence in itself and in its ability to sustain a vigorous population of honest citizens. John Blair (Wayne) and his partner Larry

Adams start a new stage line in honest competition with an old monopolistic system, and they succeed most triumphantly when they win a federal government mail contract. Federal authenticating of private enterprise marks Wayne's character. This is a successful image in campaigns to recover public confidence in American institutions during the Depression decade.

JOHN WAYNE'S FILMS show that crime, organized on small and large scales, is a main cause of economic depression. It is a contributing factor to the erosion of public welfare: crime by an individual simply adds to the aggregate of crime as a force of social destruction. If one can catch a single criminal, then the threat to social order and public welfare is reduced a bit more. If one can catch leaders of gangs, then a larger degree of safety is assured. If whole gangs can be eliminated, preferably in one dramatic blow, in a gang-buster, then life is reconstructed and resurrected.

A parodic "Roll of Horror" appears from "out of nowhere" in *The Lonely Trail* (1936). It is hung on the wall of the villain's office, where it mocks nefarious crooks' "Roll of Honor." The "Roll of Horror" is a list of victims of carpetbagging legalized criminals in Texas during Reconstruction; it denies any "honor" to those on the official list of officers killed for "duty." With a slight turn of the point, one imagines such a "Roll of Horrors" compiled for public view from the late 1920s to the time of this film, 1936. Such a roll would include the names of "Waxey" Gordon, "Dutch" Schultz, "Legs" Diamond, Louis Lepke, and Al Capone. It has been estimated that in 1930 Capone's organizations took in $25,000,000 per year from gambling, $10,000,000 from prostitution, $10,000,000 from narcotics, and $50,000,000 from the illegal liquor trade. There was an ample number of behind-the-scenes manipulators with powerful political connections, exactly like the Adjutant General of *The Lonely Trail*.

Wayne's heroes are hard workers. Hard work is frequently a constructive violence, with moral and political sanction when aimed at elimination of crimes against the community, defenseless women and public servants. Wayne's heroes are violent, but they are crafty. He becomes, through them, an Odysseus of the American West who uses extreme methods to resolve extreme dangers. The milieu of the Depression years was well suited to receive such messages of action. The history of these films is not in their narrative structures so much as in their audiences, and in their audiences John Wayne became a part of themselves: that part which solves desperate problems as every American might wish during an era of social chaos and personal dislocation.

Heading the list of criminal activities undermining economic health are blatant thugs and thieves, of whom there are many. They rob banks, hold up stagecoaches, or rustle cattle. Sometimes these are incidental to the

real concern of the leader, as in *The Lawless Nineties*. Here robberies are
simply to raise money in a scheme to prevent voters from choosing to join
Wyoming to the Union. Usually the central motive is not so ambitious, as
in *Hell Town* (1937), where cattle rustling is paramount, or in *Lawless
Range*, where cattle rustling is a diversion from the main goal of getting land
with gold on it.

Openly operating to force out competitors are ruthless capitalists,
practicing survival of the fittest and almost surviving, such as in *The Man
from Utah* (1934), where rodeos are financial investments by the producers.
Towns are bilked of their money when the rodeo passes through; performers are bought off to throw the events; performers are maimed or killed
when they don't cooperate in gambling schemes; even the receipts are endangered by hired thugs who rob and kill the clerks. Rodeos are strongly
American figurative suggestions for all sporting events (such as boxing, or
even baseball, considering the "Black Sox Scandal" of 1919–1921).

The lawyer of *The Hurricane Express*, Stevens, a railroad attorney who
wants to control the railroad on his own, is a thorough villain who wrecks
trains, kidnaps men and women, and kills without compunction. Lawyers
cannot be trusted. Those who defend the public against thieves and
murderers must also sometimes defend it against the law itself. *The Lucky
Texan* (1934) portrays a villainous duo with government behind, using the
public assayer's office to rob and kill. They bilk an old rancher out of the
deed to his property, telling him to sign a new form of receipt for his gold
ore (actually a bill of sale). He signs because the "government" tells him to.
Trust in the government almost leads to economic disaster. To balance this,
the film also portrays the radical honesty of a town sheriff, whose integrity
survives the test of having to arrest his own son for bank robbery. But not
all citizens can be trusted to be so honest as this sheriff, even when they
are the leading citizens of the community.

Sometimes the leading citizen is simply an honest neighbor, like Joe
Dickson in *Texas Terror* (1935). He offers a confused heroine his good
counsel to distrust the man she loves and depends on to run her ranch, the
hero John Higgins (Wayne). The poor woman is nearly ruined, in body and
purse, by trusting good Joe Dickson. At other times whole communities
trust good citizens upon whose good will they must rely for financial sol-
vency, like Banker Carter in *Lawless Range*. He is a wolf in sheep's clothing,
but he is unmasked at the end. Neighbors, bankers, and merchants are
favorite roles of public trust for securing illegal advantage over people. The
merchants of *Blue Steel* and *Randy Rides Alone* (1934) are outstanding
examples. Matt Matthews is mute, and so sympathy for his affliction
strengthens trust in him, but that is a mistake, since everything about Matt
the Mute is a grotesque mask for sleek and sly bandit Marvin Black.

The summary figure of the trusted neighbor, leading citizen, is the

Chairman of the Committee for Law and Order, who appears as the villain of *The Lawless Nineties*. His targets include federal government agents who try to insure the honesty of statehood elections in Wyoming Territory, and the upright and courageous battling newspaper editor who brings his democratic convictions with him from Virginia to help civilize the new frontier. These figures anticipate something better rendered later in *Stagecoach* (1939) and *The Man Who Shot Liberty Valance* (1962), but they gather around Wayne's characters in strands that will be tied together successfully in the Ringo Kid: an outlaw whose respect for the law is learned from the wrong side, because in a world where honesty is too often a mask for dishonesty, the wrong side may be the right side.

Depression of the economy is a symptom of depression of the spirit, as these films express the temperment of the era. Widespreading disenchantment with American dreams and promises was fast turning into political discontent driven by distrust of the law and its officers, especially in *The Lonely Trail*, where government itself is guilty of stealing from citizens and killing them when they resist. The material is drawn from Reconstruction, Texas, but only a dull audience would not identify with the contemporaneity of the evil, and with the mythic solutions as well.

AS THE EX-SOLDIER in *The Lonely Trail* Wayne's character had a special appeal to veterans and their families from World War I in his audience of the thirties, particularly at risk during the Depression years, having sacrificed their youth to their country not long before. But the role of the ex-soldier, to be so beautifully realized as Ethan Edwards in *The Searchers* in 1956, was not one Wayne portrayed often in his earliest films. Surely audiences were nervous to think the solution to their economic and political problems lay in military action, however properly motivated. Using military force against civilians was too real in the thirties to make that a source of heroic character. The ex-soldier is close to the ex-outlaw, also a role Wayne does not often play in this decade.

While history provides ample evidence of outlaws turned sheriff, audiences in the thirties sympathized with a man whose basic loyalty to law was uncompromised by his violations of laws serving evil. This was the circumstance for many a bootlegger who supported families with secret distilleries during and after Prohibition. Enchantment and identification with the outlaw is an ancient audience attitude in both primitive and sophisticated art, and so the reasons for its effectiveness may lie outside the accidents of history, including those of the American Depression years. But those were years of extreme measures. Many a person who watched these films at that time was an outlaw at heart, though hoping for lawful resolutions of problems.

When Wayne plays a convicted criminal in *Sagebrush Trail* (1933), he discovers the real killer for whose crime he was falsely arrested. This is closer to his character than the reputation of a Billy the Kid. To find himself a victim of an imperfect legal system, as in this film and several later ones, puts Wayne's character in a classic Hitchcockian situation. The worlds of his survival are about as absurd and equally as sinister as those in Hitchcock's thrillers. The outlaw wrongly convicted can better serve an innocent community, then, as its agent of resistance to corrupted legal systems of commerce, industry, and police. In such a role, essential innocence of the hero is maintained even as he fights evil from outside the law corrupted by that evil. He wants for the community a fair judgment by the law to which all can freely appeal. Finally, in such films, such salvation to a community's economic, political, and even romantic problems can be found in a basic trust in the authority of law.

If this is so, then the sheriff or marshal might be a particularly good part for Wayne to enact, as he will in such films as *Rio Bravo* (1959) and *Cahill, United States Marshal* (1973). But, strangely enough, at no stage of his long career did Wayne repeat such a role many times. He was more often to the side of the law than in the law of his films. Even his character of Rooster Cogburn will serve to prove the point, for in that role he is barely legal, and not at all reputable. As a border character, in more ways than one, Rooster Cogburn much deserved to be the role that would win John Wayne his only Academy Award Oscar (for *True Grit*, 1969), because it captured long strands of character traits he had acquired from early in his career.

He is comfortable, on the other hand, as an undercover agent. He likes to play at being outlaw, while having the approval of the law for doing so. Wayne the actor could throw himself into such roles because they allowed him to play a game in which one wins even when one loses. As an entertainment, such role-playing could have beneficial effects for audiences especially in the Depression decade because it suggested (1) the possibility that appearances of triumphant evil were concealing the secret operation of good at work for everyone's eventual welfare, and (2) the notion that evil and chaos *are* mere appearances to be endured as tests of character in the game of life.

At any rate, Wayne did play many such parts in these films. Randy Bowers is a private investigator in *Randy Rides Alone,* where the source of his authority is revealed. He may be working for the government, but again he may not, which is the film's ambiguity. In *Lawless Range* and *The Man from Utah,* he is John Middleton and then John Weston, private citizens who are enlisted by government marshals to work as undercover agents. As John Middleton he is trapped to do so, after setting off to help a friend of his injured father; as John Weston, he is out of work and needs money, and again he is trapped to accept the undercover assignment. In neither case does he *want* to be a government agent.

Wayne as John Wyatt, with *(left to right)* Jim Farley as Lafe Gordon, Sheila Manners as Mary Gordon, and Frank McGlynn, Jr. as Jim Wyatt *(on ground)*, in *Westward Ho*, 1935.

The undercover man is played with relish, but the straight man with honesty written all over him is by far the most frequent Wayne has to play in these early years. He takes up the cudgels against crime for a variety of reasons, but when he does so, he throws his whole being into the battle. In *'Neath the Arizona Skies* (1934) he protects the life and property of a little girl whose Indian mother and white father have died or disappeared: as Chris Morrell he sets out to find the girl's father and ends by becoming her legal guardian. Wayne often repeats this in his career, becoming a protecting angel for children especially.

Sometimes the filial quality is more meaningful than the paternal one. Wayne's characters undertake their quests as a result of the deaths of their fathers or, more rarely, mothers. *The Hurricane Express* shows him doing private detection to find the man responsible for killing his father in a train wreck. In both *West of the Divide* (1934) and *The Dawn Rider* (1935) he is after murderers of his father. Private vengeance becomes public salvation in these films, as in *The Lawless Frontier* (1934) and *Westward Ho* (1935), where both mother and father have been murdered by roaming outlaws. In two of these he has not only a motive from the past but one for the future as well, because he is also searching for his little brother kidnapped by the murderers.

Such films sanction careers that do public good by settling private scores. *Westward Ho* justifies statewide vigilante activity and lynch-mob psychology. At a crucial point, John Wyatt encourages his men to torture a man he is interrogating for information about his parents' killers. After Wyatt has avenged his parents' deaths he disbands the Singing Riders. When the justifiable motive disappears, so does the vigilante activity.

But like Hamlet or the Boy Scouts, Wayne's private citizen must always be vigilant, remembering that "the readiness is all." He has a special responsibility because he has special talents to serve either good or evil. In *Paradise Canyon*, he is offered a job in a travelling medicine show:

> DR. CARTER: I'd like to use you with the medicine show. Yeah, you know, after what you done for us. Huh? Can you sing or dance?
>
> JOHN WYATT: Well, I'm sorry, but I'm afraid about all I can do is ride and shoot.
>
> DR. CARTER: Oh, you can shoot, can you? Now, say, say now, that gives me an idea. Yes, say, we've been needing a new act you know. . . . We'll get together a new act, feature, and call it "The Living Target."

This act is distasteful, to say the least, but it expresses the point that a person's talents, however minimal, can be put to use for larger purposes. This is reassuring everywhere and at all times. John Wayne could not sing, even as Singing Sandy, but he could ride and shoot (not an exclusive, but a very American talent).

Every person's natural talents are potential weapons against crime, and beyond crime, against the Depression itself. In *Desert Trail* (1935), John Scott is a rodeo performer whose riding skills are useful to the law for uncovering criminal schemes, and the same is true in *The Man from Utah*. Riding skill survives the march of time and industrial progress when an ex–Pony Express rider in *Winds of the Wasteland* finds a way to use those skills for commercial profit and lawful triumphs. When natural skills are combined with professional training, as in *King of the Pecos* (1936), the result can be doubly powerful: John Clayborn is both a skillful gunman and a crafty lawyer. Law sanctions a talent for violence.

IN THE ERA of these films, reaction against the costs of World War I was strong. When John Wayne began making films for his living, he found an audience conditioned to respond emotionally to the content of police and military force against civilians. One extraordinary incident in the early years of the thirties was the Bonus March of WWI Veterans on Washington in the summer of 1932. There were 25,000 veterans asking their government to pay their bonuses earlier than scheduled, since they were out of work and desperate for help. Government's answer was to send troops to drive them away. Commercial newsreels told the nation the Capital was being protected by the Third Cavalry from Ft. Myers, the First Light Tank Regiment, and the Twelfth Infantry from Ft. Washington. Then President Hoover ordered newsreel photographers to stop photographing the attack on the ex-soldiers. Still, the news was out, and sentiment was complicated, not all of it hostile to the Bonus Marchers. This disturbing episode came soon after an earlier one in Washington, in December 1931, when Hunger Marchers were routed by Capital policemen, and a more riotous one in New York City's Union Square on March 6, 1930; newsreel photographs of that attack on unemployed workers were confiscated by the city's police themselves.

Such portentous events, disturbing as they were in themselves, must have been even more disturbing to those in movie audiences who remembered other, not so distant, events when the use of military force against civilians in the United States undermined confidence in government. Throughout the decade of the twenties labor movements were harassed and intimidated by official authority, which did not hesitate to employ military force where it thought necessary. When viewers saw, as frequently they would, images of caves, tunnels, dynamite, and mining for gold, they might well recall the nationwide struggles to organize the United Mine Workers, and they might even recall more specifically the nearly legendary "Ten Days' War" in Southern Colorado in 1914.

At that time, when "Mother" Jones hastened from the East to lead the miners on their picket lines, only to be arrested herself and thus call national attention to the troubles there, miners for the Colorado Fuel and Iron Mining Company were striking against the same feudalism *King of the Pecos* describes so well in its allusive way. The company succeeded in getting the state militia to rout workers and families from tents at Forbes and Ludlow, where 52 persons were killed by the soldiers, including two women and eleven children. President Wilson sent federal soldiers to stop the civil war of Colorado.

Folk songs of the labor movement include lines that "remember Bloody Ludlow," where miners and their sympathizers sang "down with the militia, and up with the law," if they inclined still to trust the law; if they were not so inclined, they would sing "down with the militia, and to hell with the law." This is the attitude of ambivalence repeated in the Depression decade, and it is an attitude Wayne's character spoke to and sometimes resolved. The Wild West of his films was still the Wild West of Colorado, California, Oklahoma, Arizona, South Dakota, Kansas, Texas and Utah: it would continue to be the Wild West for a long while to come.

2. "Your Country Needs You"

John Wayne made 31 feature films during the 1940s. He established new directions for himself during these years: he portrayed characters from many different geographical and cultural regions; he represented people with many different livelihoods; and he again found himself taking second billing to other, more established movie stars. His image was extended to a national and international dimension, but his roles frequently made him eat humble pie.

Making connections, as a figure of imagination, is one of his main functions as a developing hero of myth. Train, airplane, and ship are as eminent now as the horse always has been. These films show him in motion, reflecting and expressing a culture in motion, a people energetic and restless. Films associating him with the West and Southwest show this, but so do others of the forties. He rides railroads and boats to Fargo, North Dakota, in *Dakota* (1945), connecting Chicago with the North Central prairies; he leads people out of the agriculture disasters of North Dakota into new farmlands of Oregon in *Three Faces West* (1940). In *Lady from Louisiana* (1941) he is a New England lawyer learning his way around New Orleans, and in *Reap the Wild Wind* (1942) he sails ships up and down the Atlantic Coast to Key West, Florida.

These films also show him as an "American" in foreign places. He is a wounded airplane pilot shot down in Nazi-occupied France, in *Reunion in France* (1942). He is in the Andes of South America in *Tycoon* (1947), in China in *Flying Tigers* (1942), in the Philippines in *Back to Bataan* (1945), a "Filipino" at heart leading Filipinos who are "Americans" at heart, and in New Zealand, Tarawa, Hawaii, and Iwo Jima in *Sands of Iwo Jima* (1949). This last film is a model of the idea that America is a family of international identities, as Wayne plays the sergeant around whom are gathered young men not only from many different places but with different cultural roots, suggested by their names: Ragazzi, Soames, Hellenopolis, Choynski, McHugh, and Stein. This film transcends boundaries of nationalism with its image of the hero as a brother to all, not merely a chauvinist patriot.

HE IS FROM everywhere, then, in the films of the forties. He is also a man who does everything. His image connects distant points into a community of shared concern, and his labors unite tasks of all dedicated to building civilization. He is increasingly everywhere and everything.

During this decade, Wayne played a combat soldier in only three bona fide World War II films. *Sands of Iwo Jima* presents the clearest picture of a professional military man who sacrifices all, including his family, for his country and for his profession; this is one of Wayne's most important as a tragic hero, to be examined in more detail later. Here it serves to show he may play the professional soldier in combat, to imitate the times, but he does it with a meaning that complicates, rather than simplifies, the call to duty. *They Were Expendable* (1945) is close to the matter of *Sands of Iwo Jima* in the sense that Wayne is a career military man engaged in modern combat action; however, there are differences, since his leadership is limited in this film, and he is relentlessly stripped of his military powers by the events of the plot (and history). The third film, *Back to Bataan*, represents heroics of a career military man also, but it must show guerrilla actions in which the American subordinates Americanism to the proud spirit of native Filipinos resisting Japanese invaders.

Wayne rarely played the professional military man in settings which celebrated virtues of military duty during WWII. He did make films which put that celebration back in the 19th century and where military life is subordinate to the health of civilization. These were the cavalry stories of *Fort Apache* (1948) and *She Wore a Yellow Ribbon* (1949), which develop ironies of focus on frontier values, as does *The Fighting Kentuckian* (1949).

The virtue of military duty is considerable, nevertheless, even in the stories which do not make the military life a focus of action. To be a veteran, an ex-soldier, is serious in some of Wayne's roles, although he does not parade military accomplishments to admire. For example, there are ex-soldiers in *Dakota* and *In Old Oklahoma* (1943; and probably in *Red River*, 1948), but *Dakota* makes little use of this information except to supply jokes and a metaphor of strategy: "When you are surrounded and haven't a chance, attack." *In Old Oklahoma* puts the value of the veteran's service to a severe test, to determine if Teddy Roosevelt's ex-sergeant is as good in civilian duty as he was in his military duty.

While it was important to make films with relevance to the military conflicts that absorbed the energies of the time, Wayne's main accomplishment was to represent a variety of livelihoods and professions. Like his representation of every place, his portrayal of all tasks was a function of his mythical stature. Even when he was a military man, he served civilians, the civilization that needed his protection. The core of his character is an essential sense of self, humanized and social. What one *is* may be expressed by what one *does*, but what one *does* is not altogether what one *is*.

Besides connecting place to place, Wayne's continuing mythic use identifies person with person through shared tasks of building, serving, and loving. That he builds is more pressing than what he builds: a railroad bridge in *Tycoon* or a steel factory in *Pittsburgh* (1942). To this must be added a sense of service. This is the focus of the military stories, but it can be seen as well in *Flame of the Barbary Coast* (1945), where the hero prevents criminal corruption of government in San Francisco after the earthquake of 1906, or in *Dakota* where he learns the virtue of unselfishness to save wheatland. The connection between building and service, through professional commitments, is made possible through love, and Wayne's films are films with love stories central to their plots. The engineer of *Tycoon*, like the miner of *Pittsburgh*, learns to serve only when he learns to love.

JOHN WAYNE became a symbol of the American trying to understand and deal with betrayals, tragedies, and triumphs in the forties. He imitated what America was at that time, or what America wanted to be, feared or failed to be. His images, subjects, and themes are reflections and expressions of events and concerns historically pertinent for audiences of that decade. It is a period dramatically defined by World War II, and the films may be viewed as imitating concerns which were pre–World War, in World War, and post–World War. This was a period when Wayne was "falling" for the forties: he fell, with the nation, into disaster, from romance into tragedy, but he also fell in love as he rose in stature.

In the earliest films of the decade, prior to the entrance of the United States into the war, there are many signs of awareness that world war is an issue. At times those signs are obvious, even to later audiences. At other times, they are more subtle signals only for those who would be concerned at the time of the films' earliest showings. This is not a new turn in Wayne's films: it is notable in several of the "Three Mesquiteer" stories. More clearly now is a prevailing concern with war and sometimes a dominating mood of darkness and foreboding, against which the hero has to battle and to which he must at times submit.

Three Faces West is one of the first of Wayne's films in the forties to express concern for the World War. Released in July 1940, it was made as "The Refugee." The story combines struggles of farmers with adversities of the Dust Bowl, including the inability of government to do much to help, and the struggles of European refugees to adjust to new life in America. Its story suggests that America's best position would be to remain a safe haven for refugees from war. The film has a message of isolationism, not of neutrality, as it expresses discontent with American politics of the time.

Discontent is a register of frustration for farmers unable to succeed in their battles with nature in the prairie states. Government efforts to save land through better conservation methods anger and then encourage farmers, as Wayne's John Phillips speaks at first on behalf of those efforts. Then, when government fails, John fails. He becomes a leader with a new mission: to leave their homes and make an exodus to better lands in Oregon. This is one of the motifs of the story echoing the story of *Grapes of Wrath* which had been turned into a film in 1940. *Three Faces West,* though less successful than *Grapes of Wrath,* is a more ambitious film in some ways. It shows a triumphant conclusion for the entire community which holds together as it searches for a new home in the West. This triumph is possible because of heroic leadership by John Phillips.

However, in another of its complicating themes, John's own heroic abilities are almost broken before they succeed. Instruction from two European refugees, Dr. Braun and his daughter Leni, keeps John intact. They teach him lessons of love and duty. They show him by their examples that Americans have a special duty to keep faith in the land and in history, because America is the hope of homeless people. If Americans begin to think of themselves as homeless, then how desperate is the condition of the world! In one of the lowest points of the story, as the citizens of Asheville Forkes prepare for their migration, Dr. Braun looks on to observe that "there must be a more tragic word for them than *refugee."* He knows coming to America as a refugee was coming to a place of promise; what do those who live in the land of promise have before them if they must leave it? The film says the promised land is always just over the horizon, somewhere in the West: America is still big enough to keep that promise alive. There are no refugees in America, as long as there is faith in America.

Wayne plays a young Swedish sailor on a tramp steamer, the *Glencairn,* in *The Long Voyage Home.* Besides picturing human community as more than a region or a language, this films shows brotherhood under attack. Like most of his films of the prewar years, this one also has ambivalences even with its clear prejudices about the war in Europe. *Three Faces West* makes a basic appeal to Americans with sympathies for Germanic culture. *The Long Voyage Home* makes its appeal to recognize the desperate plight of England and the Scandinavian countries as they faced the Nazi menace in 1940. The film started shooting in late April 1940; German armies invaded Norway beginning April 7 and seemed on the verge of overrunning Scandinavia. For Ole Olsen, then, to want to get home, and for his comrades to want to help him get home successfully, is for a man to find his country still is his home.

The Long Voyage Home contains details that mark its prewar material as a picture of the time. The ship takes on a load of explosives while in port in the United States; it is carrying them to England, where they are much needed in England's war against the Nazis. The ship is strafed and bombed as it nears port in England. The prejudice of the film is forcefully dramatized

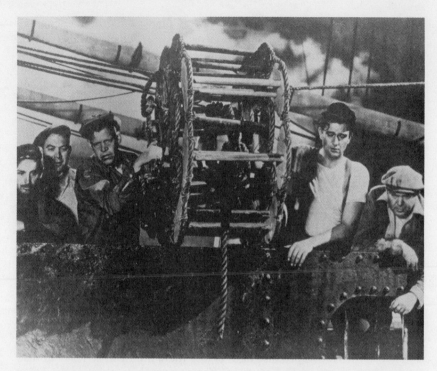

Left to right: John Qualen as Axel Swanson, Ward Bond as Yank, Jack Pennick as Johnny Bergman, Wayne as Ole Olsen, and Thomas Mitchell as Driscoll in *The Long Voyage Home*, 1940.

by the suspicions of the sailors (not including Ole) that Smitty is a "fifth columnist" (i.e., a traitor) who has signalled Germans to attack their ship: they suspect that Smitty's real name is "Schmidt." By making the mistake of misreading innocent behavior as evidence for guilt of betrayal, these comrades of Smitty show the audience how dangerous it can be to jump to conclusions about spies and traitors amongst us. The story does not attempt to explain how one does deal with the problem of spies, but it does show the tragedy of mistrust and fear (a theme more forcefully dealt with in 1943 by *The Ox-Bow Incident*). The enemy is less in another than in the darkness of one's own self.

This is certainly the point of three films from 1941–1942 which do not focus on the war even as they make verbal and thematic allusions to it. *The Shepherd of the Hills* (1941) is a parable of Christian benevolence, but it is also a story of a community trying to isolate itself from the world. The Ozark Hill country is sick, with a sick land (called "Moaning Meadows"), because it has turned itself inwards; it is made more healthy when a prodigal father returns to pay a debt he owes to his son. It is a charming film with interesting surprises for an audience which will have preconceived notions about the pastoral and about the image of John Wayne. Violence, it says, can be put to peaceful uses (a point many films of the time tried to make, as in *Sergeant York* most successfully), but here in Wayne's film that use is directed at a son by a father. Matt Matthews is taught vengeance is no answer to the problems of life, and he is taught that lesson by his father who shoots him in a pastoral, peaceful setting.

The Shepherd of the Hills says the world is too large to be shut out for long without leading to internal sickness, superstition, paralysis of will, and debilitating distrust. It makes no specific allusions to the war, but it defines an attitude of pertinence to the mood of isolationism that prevailed in America before Pearl Harbor (still a year away when this film was made). The darkness which has to be purged from Young Matt's soul is the spiritual miasma of a land and a people as well as his own. It is in the character of Jack Stuart in *Reap the Wild Wind*, a film set in the Old South and perhaps intended to capitalize on the success of *Gone with the Wind*. It is similar to *Shepherd of the Hills* when it narrates tragic consequences of betrayal and distrust. This is a story of a man who falls in love and falls from grace, but it is also a story of America fighting against threats to its merchant marine. It is a commentary in 1942 on the dangers to American shipping, from German submarines, as it is a story of 1840 salvage wreckers in the Florida Keys. The film opens with these words of narration: "America's life-lines are the sea. . . The sea and the sea alone makes America one nation." While it is an important strategic point to make to audiences in 1942, it is not a forceful point in the story itself, which has little to do with the unity of America or the dependence of that unity on the success of merchant ships that run up and down the Atlantic Coast.

DARK COMMAND (1940), the earliest of Wayne's films in this decade, is about guerrilla warfare, anticipating his war film *Back to Bataan*. In *Dark Command*, however, the setting is in the heartland of the United States and the war is the Civil War (a favorite subject of many Wayne films). Half the story describes the arrival of the hero in Lawrence, Kansas, where he meets his adversary, schoolteacher Will Cantrell (historical Quantrill). Wayne's Bob Seton opposes Cantrell in election for sheriff, and Bob wins. The rest of the story shows the consequences of this victory: increasing hostility of Cantrell, degeneration of his character, and the eruption of his evil into a destructive assault on Lawrence itself. *Dark Command* depicts an interesting phase from American history, when citizens turned against one another to fight one of the bloodiest of modern wars. Today the film seems little more. However, when it is recalled that the film was made in February 1940 and released shortly after, it is recognized as a commentary on contemporary matters.

Left to right: Roy Rogers as Fletch McCloud, Wayne as Bob Seton, and George Hayes as Doc Grunch in *Dark Command,* 1940.

Lawrence under siege is home under attack, civilization threatened, and justice endangered. These are themes not uncommon to the Western. Nor are they peculiar to the forties, though in 1940 newspapers were reporting cities and nations under attack by barbarian armies: the collapse of Poland, the pillage of cities in China, fears of imminent invasion in Belgium and France, and preparations for defense by Great Britain.

Everywhere cities and nations were under attack or threat of attack. An archetypal theme of imagination was an unmistakable actuality in the late months of 1939; Europe, Asia, and Africa were shaken, and so America itself rapidly was becoming surrounded by hostilities. Lawrence, Kansas, then, in *Dark Command,* was like America itself in those pre–World War II years. But, to make an analogy even clearer, Cantrell as a traitor to his home, undermining its defenses, and then leading an assault on its borders, is comparable to one of the most notorious traitors of history—the Norwegian Vidkun Quisling, who had met with leaders in Germany in late 1939 and whose assistance helped the Germans to begin their invasion of Norway in early 1940.

There would be many traitors like Cantrell and Quisling, unfortunately, as there would be many towns and nations under siege like Lawrence, Kansas. One of the most heartrending and dramatic would be Britain itself, and this film is prophetic in that respect. It is monitory, as it warns American audiences home is no safe haven in such times. This is the explicit "message" of *Flying Tigers*, which presents a squadron of professional fighters in China battling Japanese invaders before Pearl Harbor. Since the film was made and released after the bombing of Pearl Harbor on December 7, 1941, it could make its political message with more force than could *Dark Command*. *Flying Tigers* shows war as an opportunity for individuals to "find" themselves (it is the point explicitly stated by the wife of one of the new recruits, Blackie Bales, who needs, she says, a "second chance" to prove himself in his life), and its shows this in a traditional way—women offer their men as sacrifices for honor and pride. This is a story of tragedies, as is *Dark Command*, brought by war, but it is also a story of reluctance of men to go to war.

Now America is in the war, and there is no doubt about which side it is on. The work of the Flying Tigers has been justified by the treachery of the Japanese, and now the Tigers serve from duty, not for money. War is patriotism, not business. It is the old story of Wayne as civilian having to improvise to do a military deed. In *Pittsburgh*, he shows a new way for civilians to serve in a justified war. He is an industrialist who makes the bombers Jim Gordon did not have in *Flying Tigers*.

Pittsburgh opens on a scene of waves of planes. The camera begins to tilt downwards, and an American flag flies between the audience and the planes; the camera continues its downward movement, past the upper floors of a tall building, to the ground floor where a large sign reads "If it won't HELP WIN THE WAR, forget it." There is a voice-over, and the camera pans toward its source, on a platform before which stand plant workers assembled during lunch hour to hear exhortations to meet production quotas. The speaker reminds the audience how President Roosevelt has asked "to evolve the greatest and most efficient industrial system in history. To turn our workshops into a mighty force of war. To outbuild the aggressors." The speaker is Cash Evans, a partner in Markham and Evans Industries, Inc. The work whistle blows, and everyone returns to their jobs.

In his office, Cash (Randolph Scott) drinks a toast of success with his partners, Pittsburgh Markham (John Wayne) and Doc Powers. They raise

As Rusty Ryan in *They Were Expendable*, 1945.

their glasses to a portrait of the woman who inspired them, Josie "Hunky" Winters (Marlene Dietrich). She was the central figure in their prewar success, and she continues to be central to their wartime endeavors. When Pittsburgh and Cash allow differences to interfere with the war effort, Josie intervened to remind them:

> This is no time to think of personal feelings and personal grievances. The only emotion that should guide each of you and everyone of us today: devotion to our country, that's the one thing you should think about. [Here, when Josie says "you" and "your," she is looking straight at the film's audience, in tight close-ups of her face.] Your country needs you!

The rise and fall of a proud, talented man (Pittsburgh Markham) is enclosed by a preface and postscript that turns his career into an example for Americans in time of war.

Left to right: Jack Pennick as Doc, Wayne, Robert Montgomery as Lt. John Brickley, and Ward Bond as Boats Mulcahey in *They Were Expendable.*

The story *Pittsburgh* is a prewar narrative, told in retrospect by an observer-participant. This was one way to tell a story as relevant for contemporary audiences. *They Were Expendable* and *Back to Bataan* are retrospective, but only because they were films made after the end of the war itself. These two films were records of events imagined in "safety." They describe the sacrifices and the heroics of people who fought for a cause the audience knew had triumphed, and so the pain was more acceptable just as it was more controllable in the narratives of the films.

Understanding this, *They Were Expendable* began with prewar situations, proceeded with scenes of small victories in a larger pattern of retreat by American forces during the fall of Bataan and Corregidor in 1941. Defeat is made tolerable by the historical context of postwar production, and by the conduct of men portrayed in the story. Because Rusty Ryan and John Brickley had faith in their P.T. boats, they survived to make sure the retreats at Bataan and Corregidor would not mean defeat in the war. The story concludes with scenes of pathos, as Rusty never knows what has happened to his beloved Sandy, and as the P.T. boat squadron limps along a war-torn beach toward certain capture by the Japanese. Those men, led by

Boats Mulcahey (Ward Bond) on a crutch, watch a military transport plane
rise, carrying their hopes for the future: on board the plane are Ryan and
Brickley, who evacuate the Philippines to prepare for MacArthur's return,
as he promised when he left in those dark days of defeat.

Ryan, Brickley, and MacArthur left behind in 1941 thousands of
American prisoners in Japanese prison camps, but they also left behind a
civilian population of Philippine people who thought of themselves as
Americans. That is the view presented by *Back to Bataan*, taking up where
They Were Expendable leaves off. It is the story of Philippine guerrillas
resisting Japanese occupation, and liberating thousands of American
prisoners from Japanese captors. The film opens with a scene of liberation,
staging the scene with actors of the main story, led by Filipino Andres
Bonafacio (Anthony Quinn), as they break through a prison camp for the
escape of emaciated, wounded American soldiers and sailors. Then the film
becomes a documentary, providing close-ups with captions of "actual
American prisoners of war" just liberated from Cabanatuan on January 30,
1945. To the tune of "California, Here I Come," they march into the camera,
beginning with the happy face of Emmett L. Manson, Lt. U.S.N., Worth-
ington, Minnesota, and then the parade of liberated Americans concludes
with the beaming face of Cpl. Neil P. Loving, USMC, Chicago, Illinois.
Eleven men are identified, as typical of thousands. The film concludes with
dissolves of Bonifacio and Joseph Madden (Wayne) in the march of
liberation.

Filipinos identify themselves with America. The Japanese Homma
calls this an alienation of Filipinos from the "East Asian family" of Japan.
Back to Bataan does not ignore complications in history behind the
presence of the United States in the Philippines, but it simplifies the
idealism of that presence. When a class in history is conducted for Filipino
children (just before Japanese soldiers arrive to confiscate the schoolhouse), the teacher (an American woman) asks the children what Spain
brought to the Philippines, and the answer they give is "Christianity." Then
she asks what America brought, and the children pop up quickly with these
enthusiastic answers: soda pop, hot dogs, movies, baseball, This may be
true, but it is hardly sufficient to account for Filipino resistance to the
Japanese. The school principal, Señor Bello, who had once been Miss
Barnes' star pupil, gives the "correct" answer: "America taught us that men
are free, or they are nothing. Since then we have walked with high heads
among all men."

FOLLOWING THE DEFEAT and surrender of Germany in May 1945
and the surrender of Japan in August, Wayne starred in films with the
perspective of a great war behind them, a war fought and won. It was at first
viewed from an isolationist vantage, but it took on heroic proportions when

the Japanese attacked Pearl Harbor. After the victories, subjects of films were either retrospective, as in *They Were Expendable*, or they were prospective, as in the mood of "where do we go from here?" Reconstruction of Europe and Asia were in the background, but nearer to home were the problems of Americans themselves. They had to make many adjustments to a postwar society, not the least being the reabsorption of ex-soldiers into a peacetime economy. *The Best Years of Our Lives* in 1946 was one of the best to dramatize personal and social difficulties of making those adjustments. Wayne made films which dealt, in varying degrees, with this same subject of contemporary concern.

He portrays characters who want to get on with the business of living, of building, and moving on. His are not brooding, retrospective characters. His films in the second half of the forties portray worlds energetically in motion. Two of them, *In Old Oklahoma* and *Dakota*, use heroes who are also ex-soldiers.

Going on the attack is instinctive for Wayne heroes, never more so than in the story of a construction engineer in *Tycoon*. It has the spirit of *Dakota* and *In Old Oklahoma*, because it describes a life of building for the progress of a people. There are allusions to the rebuilding Europe (the "Marshall Plan"), though the story is not set in Europe. But Americans of enterprise working abroad is a dominant subject of these postwar films, and it will continue in Wayne's films as they take his heroes throughout the world during the fifties. He may never become cosmopolitan, but Wayne will become more and more an international traveler.

Angel and the Bad Man (1947) may seem to show little consciousness of postwar concerns. It looks like another Western, maybe even an escape from concerns of pressing reality. But it stands out from among Wayne's entire canon of work in several respects, not the least that it dramatizes the pacification of a gunman. Quirt Evans learns to be a man of peace, after a life of violence and destruction. This is not unrelated to hopes and expectations for people after the second great war. At the end Quirt gives his gun to Penny Worth, who drops it in the dirt as they ride away on a wagon. Gunman turned farmer offers hope to people who must transform soldiers into civilians.

3. "We Don't Hit the Little Guy"

A scene in *Stagecoach* shows John Wayne as lover. After the baby is delivered at Apache Wells, Dallas carries her out for the men to admire. Ringo has eyes only for Dallas. Later, he follows her into the night. He moves toward her in a nonthreatening, quiet manner. She leans on one side of a fence; he walks firmly, though gently, to the other side, leans against the fence to face her. They speak of backgrounds, and each recognizes in the other a soulmate. Dallas explains she lost her parents in an Indian massacre when she was a kid, and Ringo responds, "That's tough— especially on a girl." A line that could ring false quite easily, Wayne makes true because he makes it tender and gentle. Dallas is tough and experienced in the ways of the world; Claire Trevor plays her character with conviction. She has awakened to the possibility of tenderness from a man.

Five actresses are particularly good at evoking tenderness from Wayne in his later movies. Four appeared with him in one film each, Maureen O'Hara in five—from *Rio Grande* in 1950, to *Big Jake* in 1971. Her relationship with Wayne deserves special focus. Geraldine Page in one film was good enough to be nominated for an Oscar as best supporting actress in 1953. As Angie Lowe in *Hondo* Geraldine Page is characteristically unpretentious and strong. She moves well with Wayne through their scenes of love; they are not passionate in explosive ways. She allows his presence to dissolve her poses and to remove her masks of homeliness; she allows him to uncover warmth, courage, and confidence in her emotional capacities. Wayne shows his tenderness to her by showing respect and love for others around her. Her resistance dissolves completely when he describes his love for his dead Indian wife, in a scene that compares in setting and mood with scenes in *Stagecoach*. Wayne does not court with hands and arms. He courts with voice, eyes, and smiles, before he dares to touch.

Matched with an actress sensual rather than emotional, Wayne learns to love by retreating from physical and forceful modes of contact. In *Legend of the Lost* (1957), he is a derelict haunting the backstreets of Timbuktu before he crosses the Sahara with Rossano Brazzi and Sophia Loren. His relationship with the actress in this film is more dynamic than with

26

Geraldine Page in *Hondo.* With Sophia Loren he is crude and aggressive at first, finding courage in whiskey. But when he sees Brazzi behaving the same, he retreats to put distance between his essential self and the role of physical brute. He hurls his body about in menacing ways through much of the film, but in the last half-hour, Wayne lowers his tone, softens his voice, and restrains his hands. Sophia Loren might seem better matched with Rossano Brazzi, but in this film she turns from the sweet sexuality of Brazzi to the ironic, tender sexuality of Wayne.

When he lies with Sophia Loren under the stars of a desert night, Wayne is humbled by her integrity with the nature that surrounds them both. He bursts into action only when his whiskey bottle is shot from his hand. He cannot, despite his size and strength, force her to accept him. When he leaves off his aggression, she begins to be more receptive. Wayne knows how to make strategic retreat in courtship. He moves back, remains available as patron and protector, and he waits for her to come to him. The story of *Legend of the Lost* unfortunately requires him to continue to retreat from Sophia Loren's sensuality, until a terribly ambivalent conclusion, a pathetic role-reversal, confirms the worst fears of a masculine ego threatened by the power of a sensual woman.

The character is betrayed by the script, not by the skill of the actor, and Sophia Loren worked well with the ungainly transfigurations of Wayne's character in this film. She was everything to his Joe January that Geraldine Page was to his Hondo. Each actress was able to evoke essential tenderness from Wayne, though each was fundamentally different in character and style from the other. A pairing of contraries also occurs between Janet Leigh in *Jet Pilot* (1957) and Eiko Ando in *The Barbarian and the Geisha* (1958), a far different kind than between Sophia Loren and Geraldine Page.

Janet Leigh combines the wholesomeness of Geraldine Page with the sensuality of Sophia Loren, but she is light to Loren's dark, and she is lively to Page's demureness. She startles Wayne into attitudes of interest when he is supposed to be antipathetic to her ideologies. The film is successful if one accepts it tongue in cheek, as an exercise in irony, but *Jet Pilot* contains scenes of unusually forceful sexuality. This may be partly the result of certain settings, such as in the shopping or the bedroom scenes, but those are conventional and unexceptional without the forceful presence of Leigh and Wayne. They bring off the abstract, as in the voice-over dialogues when they fly jet airplanes together. They "make love" in disguise as airplanes. But for "electricity" between them, the early scene of her undressing for his interrogation is entertaining. She is so "hot" for him a stove is necessary to block the view of her naked body. With Janet Leigh, Wayne cannot afford to be tender as he was with Geraldine Page and Sophia Loren; he must be quick to make his strategic retreat. But, as with Sophia Loren, so with Janet Leigh: her erotic strength is greater than his ideological distrust.

Eiko Ando is an entirely different force of eroticism for Wayne, in *The Barbarian and the Geisha*. She is a gift of the local ruler, sent to please the intruding American but also to spy on him. To her, he is huge and terrifying; to him, she is delicate and demure. Eiko Ando is nonthreatening and sensuous. He responds to her without feeling need to make retreats, as with Leigh and Loren. The story of the film has an answer to this appeal of her character, since it does not allow a consummation of their loves. She disappears from his life, leaving him a mirror as an emblem of her soul. Wayne acts to Eiko Ando, then, with increasing tenderness to convince his audience that his love for her is absolute, without restraint of heart. Her withdrawal must be painful: he must be seen to succeed in the public display of his office, while he is failing in the private recesses of his heart.

Maureen O'Hara knew just when to move to Wayne's rhythm, he to flow with her energy and vitality. She gave life to his style of reserve, he gave form to her style of exuberance. She had worked for John Ford in films prior to *Rio Grande* with John Wayne in 1950, and so her successful pairing with Wayne is in part the result of Ford's genius for bringing out the the the best in Wayne. She made her first appearance with him, then, as Mrs. Kathleen Yorke, in *Rio Grande,* her second as Mary Kate Danaher in *The Quiet Man* (1952), and her third as Min Wead in *The Wings of Eagles* (1957); all were directed by Ford. Her next films with Wayne were to be *McLintock!* in 1963, and *Big Jake* in 1971, neither Ford-directed. Since there is vivacity and charm in their acting together especially in *McLintock!*, their success was not entirely the product of Ford's direction.

On the other hand, their work together in *The Wings of Eagles* was not successful, and under Ford's direction. Even in this film, however, there are moments of high spirit and at least one of quiet tenderness. When Min comes driving up in her big red convertible to meet Spig at the opening of the story, Maureen O'Hara gives the scene vivacity of spirit she so frequently brings to her work. She has a beautiful smile, a glittering eye, and a high temper; she is not hypocritical or homely, and she is capable of the vulgar without being coarse. Early in the story is an episode of pathos when the couple's baby dies; using interior framing, Ford holds Wayne in the foreground, silently surrounded by darkness, and he frames O'Hara forlornly collapsing her head on her arms in the background, bathed in an overhead light as she sits at a kitchen table, alone. As in his most successful love scenes of other films, here Wayne portrays the tenderness of his relation with a woman by quiet movement and subdued gesture.

Maureen O'Hara brought to Wayne's career a combination of the sensuous, intelligent, loyal, and loving with his unsteady need for emotional support and spiritual affirmation. In *Rio Grande*, she moves quickly into a close relationship with him though they play characters long estranged from one another; they strike up an affectionate responsiveness so quickly,

Wayne as Spig Wead *(right)* **and Louis Jean Heydt as Dr. John Keye in** *The Wings of Eagles*, **1957.**

that their estrangement is much more difficult to accept than it should be for the plot of the story. Through outlines of social stereotypes, both break through to achieve an identity of basic, honest humanity. As Mary Kate Danaher in *The Quiet Man*, O'Hara unites the bold vitality of Min Wead with the warm heart of Kathleen Yorke, and Wayne responds to meet her with one of the finest acting performances of his entire career.

WAYNE'S ACTING SKILLS meshed well with men who could share the banter of easy camaraderie. These had to be actors who could accept his crude humor and share it without seeming to compete. The best at doing this was Wayne's old acting buddy, Ward Bond. During the fifties Bond played in six films with Wayne, from *Operation Pacific* (1950) to *Rio Bravo* (1959). In *The Wings of Eagles,* as John Dodge he is to Spig Wead as John Ford was to John Wayne. Bond's most impressive parts during this time were in *The Quiet Man* and *The Searchers* (1956); in both of these films, he is a special person to Wayne's characters, a man who understands the essence as well as the surface of John Wayne. As Father Peter Lonergan, Bond shows the tact of an intimate who knows just how far he can go with horse-play before life gets serious; as the Reverend Samuel Johnson Clayton in *The Searchers,* Bonds shows the same skill for tact, knowing when to lower his voice and allow the principal characters to work for maximum effect (as in the "courtship" scene between Ethan and Martha at their final farewell).

Many times during the fifties, Wayne demonstrated greater skill and confidence with younger and older actors. With older ones, such as Victor McLaglen, Barry Fitzgerald, and Walter Brennan, he gained by the match with actors who conveyed eccentric good humor. With younger ones, such as Jeffrey Hunter in *The Searchers,* Tab Hunter in *The Sea Chase* (1955), and Ricky Nelson in *Rio Bravo,* Wayne contributed consistency and discipline to scenes which might otherwise deteriorate into sentimentality or mawkishness. But he could convey tenderness of affection for men as well as for women. Friendship is illuminated by his acting to reveal a core of love among men as well as with women, to bind all into a community of fellow creatures.

The tact of Ward Bond opened space for Wayne to fill with tenderness and affection; the quirkiness of Walter Brennan, especially in *Rio Bravo,* provoked Wayne into displays of love; and so did the impulsiveness of younger actors, as in the deadpan acting of Ricky Nelson, whose youthful ironies completed the makeup of Wayne's John T. Chance. The relationship of Ricky Nelson to John Wayne in *Rio Bravo* is a nice counterpart to that of Montgomery Clift to Wayne in *Red River:* both films, directed by Howard Hawks, provide a common denominator to point differences in the relationships. Nelson is dry as salt to Clift's sweet moisture, but for both actors John Wayne has a disturbingly deep touch of tenderness displayed most fully in moments of violence.

He is better in his films of the fifties at making persuasive love scenes. He is more often required to be an erotic hero, and when the actress can work with him, Wayne is a credible lover. His loving is, however, more tender than overwhelming, more gentle than rough. Thus he is more believable with Geraldine Page and Eiko Ando than with Susan Hayward or Constance Towers. Thus he is more moving in his work with Maureen O'Hara, combining tenderness of the lover with force of heroic action. It was a time for ironies, but Wayne turned those ironies into virtues of affection for men as well as for women. With Ward Bond he could accomplish effects with ease. With William Holden, he could not put aside the pose as he could with Pedro Armendariz. Wayne's career was more successful in the fifties because he and his colleagues understood the space he needed to establish his special rhythms. In other ways it was less successful, because he had to have space for that special rhythm, and if it was denied him by colleague, director, or script, he could be a bad actor.

THERE HAD BEEN a "red scare" or "red menace" underway in the United States long before John Wayne became associated with its slogans and symbols. People were ready to be worried about communism when the Bolshevik revolution succeeded in Russia in 1917. After the end of the First World War, the American government turned more attention to the menace at home when President Woodrow Wilson's Attorney General, A. Mitchell Palmer, and the young J. Edgar Hoover began to find evidence of Red activity under every rock in sight. By the time John Wayne broke into films at the tender age of 19, America had begun to settle into a state of chronic concern about the communist conspiracy. By the time of Wayne's first major film accomplishment in *Stagecoach*, the House of Representatives had established a special committee, the House Un-American Activities Committee, in 1938; in 1945 this became a standing committee with routine funding and routine investigations. In the meantime the Senate was not to be outdone: through its own Internal Security Committee, this body would provide the most famous of Red hunters in the person of Senator Joseph McCarthy.

Red hunting and Red baiting were not partisan political affairs. It was a popular, bipartisan effort to preserve the Republic. In 1947 President Truman issued his Executive Order for beginning a loyalty review program to uncover disloyal persons in the government. Adlai Stevenson, running for president against Dwight Eisenhower, boasted that Democrats had undertaken the hunt long before Senator McCarthy appeared on the scene; Hubert Humphrey introduced legislation to outlaw the Communist Party in America, and he was supported by the liberal Senator Paul Douglas — they proposed a provision to the McCarron Internal Security Act in 1951 which would set up concentration camps for suspected subversives. And, when the Senate considered an appropriation bill, in 1954, for continuing to fund McCarthy's investigating committee, the only vote against it was recorded by William Fulbright.

When, therefore, McCarthy delivered his infamous speech at the Wheeling Women's Republican Club in February 1950, claiming to have "in his hand" a list of "205" persons "known to the Secretary of State as being members of the communist party," the public at large and its elected/appointed representatives were well prepared to believe him. The appearance of John Wayne's *Big Jim McLain* in 1952 was hardly surprising in such a context of popular concern for the Red Menace. The really surprising thing is that Wayne had not appeared in a film of this kind much earlier. Even more surprising is to find that he was in films with distinctly anticapitalistic themes, as in, most obviously, Stagecoach.

President Truman's attorney general, J. Howard McGrath, said in a speech shortly after McCarthy's in 1950 that communists were everywhere in American society, from the factories to butcher shops. They were like "germs" spreading a terrible disease. When that germ reached the industry of filmmaking itself, the irruptions were to be foul and not forgotten to this day. Hollywood was not bashful about dealing with the issue, motivated by a keen desire to show how loyal it was to the whole enterprise of rooting out subversion. When Russia was an ally during World War II, even though it was the source of communist evil, Hollywood was bold enough to overlook Russia's faults in such films as Song of Russia (1944) and Mission to Moscow (1943). The latter was directed by Michael Curtiz, who would later direct Wayne in Trouble Along the Way (1953) and The Comancheros (1961). The "safer" course to take in those years was to focus on the war experiences of love and fighting, though some were a bit political as in Wayne's own Back to Bataan in 1945, directed by Edward Dmytryk, one of the "Hollywood Ten."

After the end of the war, Hollywood was in a rush to fill the screens with what it believed the public wanted to see: that included a flood of anticommunist movies. It is a wonder Howard Hawks had the nerve to call his film Red River in 1948. This flood included The Iron Curtain (1948), I Married a Communist (1949), The Red Menace (1949), Guilty of Treason (1949), I Was a Communist for the FBI (1951) and The Whip Hand (1951), all before Wayne's entry with Big Jim McLain. Afterwards there appeared Walk East on Beacon (1952) and My Son John (1952).

Big Jim McLain is a mild representation of the "genre." It is, nevertheless, a reinforcement of prevailing opinions and attitudes, with praise for the House Un-American Activities Committee, for the hard work of government investigators, and for the patriotic courage of people who turn against members of their own families whenever they suspect them of being communist. In this respect, Big Jim McLain anticipates the superb On the Waterfront (1954) as well as the ignominious My Son John: when Helen Hayes, as the mother of "John," fails to persuade her son to confess his guilt, she shouts for the FBI to "take him away! He has to be punished!" Terror of finding her son is a communist is the point of the drama. In Big Jim McLain an equivalent episode is much less strident, much less hysterical. In a brief episode of this episodic film, the parents of a labor union leader identify him as a communist to the HUAC investigators McLain (Wayne) and Baxter (James Arness). McLain is proud of them for having told "us something for the good of the country."

Big Jim McLain frames its story with a documentary-style picture of HUAC conducting public hearings. At the opening, which dissolves from a scene of rural thunder storm to the urban calm of Washington, D.C., a voice-over narrates the attitude that "we the citizens of the United States owe these, our elected representatives, a great debt." The audience may notice, however, a qualification: "they have staunchly continued their investigation, pursuing their stated belief that anyone who continued to be a communist after 1945 is guilty of high treason." This is a much more moderate position than many of the era; at least it does not impugn the patriotism of those who recognized the benefit of alliance with Russia during the war. The character of McLain is played for this moderation of stridency. Even in the end, when Jim has to watch again as communists are able to "go free" from prosecution as they invoke the Fifth Amendment protecting them from self-incrimination, he has to admit it proves the strength of the American system, the wisdom of the American Constitution. He is disgusted that subversives can abuse the privileges of the Constitution, but he respects the importance of those privileges the more because his partner has died to defend them for use, or abuse, by all Americans.

One of the reasons for heightened interest in communist subversion was the ten-month trial of a former State Department employee, Alger Hiss, in 1949. This followed his testimony before HUAC in 1948, when Whittaker Chambers, an ex-communist himself, accused Hiss of being a communist while he worked for the State Department in the 1930s. Then, in early 1950, a jury convicted Hiss of perjury. Two weeks later the British arrested an atomic scientist for spying for the Soviet Union; this man helped to develop the atomic bomb in the United States. By this route Julius and Ethel Rosenberg were discovered, tried, convicted and eventually executed in 1953 over the protests of thousands of people around the world. America had been betrayed, many people "knew," and so someone had to pay. The reason so many "knew" that America had been betrayed was that, amazingly, also in 1949, the Russians successfully tested their first atomic bomb. Before that, in January of 1949, Chiang Kai-shek took his people in flight from the communists to a safe haven in Formosa, leaving China to the communist hordes. The Russians with the bomb, and the communists with China: these were events requiring explanation. The convictions of Alger Hiss and the Rosenbergs were offered as part of the explanation.

Films focused sharply on shocks to national pride and security. A rash of science-fiction films dealt in popular ways with these matters, often in blatant propaganda that reinforced the public's demand for simple answers to complex questions. From *The Thing* in 1951 to *Invasion of the Body Snatchers* in 1956 to *The Blob* in 1958, Americans were treated to "scientific" explanations for their social and psychological anxieties. It is again surprising that Wayne did not find himself in science-fiction stories, and it is equally surprising that his films of the decade did not more often reflect an interest in the atomic bomb. Wayne's films were more given to pictures and themes of familiar technology, presenting mechanical problems which could be solved, rather than theoretical problems which seem beyond solution. Thus Wayne is Spig Wead who developed the "jeep carriers" for use in World War II in *Wings of Eagles,* or he is a submarine commander who helps repair torpedo duds in *Operation Pacific,* or he is an ingenious German ship captain in *The Sea Chase* who can improvise technical solutions on the run.

In *Big Jim McLain,* he accidentally encounters an ex-communist who says he has invented "a secret weapon which will make the atomic bomb an obsolete nothing, a mere child's plaything." This man is a certain Henried, played for madness by Hans Conreid. McLain patronizes the man when he realizes, quickly, that Henried is a harmless lunatic. However, the scene is interesting. It shows concern with the threat of atomic weapons. But it does so in an ambivalent, sterilizing, setting of a psychiatrist's office. Like communists generally, Henried's idea for managing the atomic threat is to make everyone look alike (sounding like the theme of *Invasion of the Body Snatchers*), so there will be no need for an atomic bomb. As Henried says, "How can you possibly fight with a fellow if he looks exactly as you do?" McLain's response is to assert his own sanity in the face of such madness; he merely laughs when Henried says he is too ugly to be a model clone.

The other shocking piece of news in 1949 that galvanized American popular opinion, the fall of China to the communists, Wayne could develop into a film story with more assurance and with more attention than he did the science of atomic weaponry. This is the subject of the story in *Blood Alley* (1955): he plays a derelict riverboat captain rescued from a Chinese communist prison to help a village escape political captivity by the communists. When the proposal is first put to him, most enticingly by Cathy Grainger (Lauren Bacall), his incredulous response is to mock, "Somebody pinned the bleeding heart of China on your sleeve, but they never got around to me." Later, after he has learned to admire the courage of the villagers, he confesses (to himself) great respect for "the bleeding heart of China! You can pin one on my sleeve, Baby!" People, not politics, shape his imagination.

When he plays one who is supposed to have strong ideological prejudices, as in *Jet Pilot,* Wayne again yields the politics to the force of person, when he surprises himself by falling in love with a Russian agent played by Janet Leigh. He tells her, in words at best laughable, "I hate your insides, and vice versa." His is a chauvinistic rather than an ideological attitude, as Shannon (Wayne) learns to ignore Anna's mind, with its twisted politics, and to enjoy her body, with its splendid beauties. Each walks a tightrope of political ambiguity in order to enjoy their physical attractions to one another. In the end the politics of both is subordinate to the appetites both have for the goods of life. Capitalism and America triumph, not as an intellectual or ideological force, but rather as a materialistic playground of mindless happiness. The Soviet Union is shown in this film to be not only an uncomfortable place to try to live, in body or in mind, but it is shown also as a place without any real power to be a threat. Politics and ideology are nonthreatening; personality, with an emphasis on love and lust, is captivating.

ONE SOCIAL ISSUE always simmering or exploding into imagery and narratives of American films is racism. The subject of relationships between the races was, by 1950, a concern in American films, often in disguise as relationships between white cowboys and dark Indians of the Old West, as in *Broken Arrow* (1950) or in Wayne's own *Searchers*. It was code any nonwhite could "stand for" blacks, insulting the integrity of the people who are "substituted" for blacks as well as blacks themselves. American films were coming round, however cautiously, to admit there was a significant *issue* worth representing in narrative terms.

It was a critical time in American social history. Black veterans of World War I did not make much progress in securing the nation's appreciation for their service in the national defense. Perhaps black veterans of the Second World War would fare better. In legal ways, they did: there was in 1948 an Army desegregation order by President Truman; in 1950 the Supreme Court banned segregation in colleges and on railroad cars; in 1954 the Supreme Court ruled that "the doctrine of 'separate but equal' had no place" in public education; in 1957 and 1960 the Congress passed significant civil rights legislation. Acceptance of such social progress in toleration was not wholehearted or entirely grateful, however.

In 1955 Rosa Parks was arrested in Montgomery, Alabama, because she refused to give up her bus seat to a white man. In 1956 University of Alabama officials expelled their first black student because her presence "threatened public order." In 1957 President Eisenhower sent Army soldiers to protect black students from white harassment when they sought entry to a previously all-white high school in Little Rock, Arkansas. And, in 1960, the "sit-in" movement began when four black students refused to leave a segregated lunch counter in Greensboro, North Carolina.

The fifties, then, was a decade of flow and counterflow in movement toward real social and political freedom for blacks in America. As in its approach to the political matters of international communism, Hollywood's approach to race matters in America was cautious, conservative, and hypocritical: such as *Pinky* (1949), *The Jackie Robinson Story* (1950), and *The Defiant Ones* (1958). Motives for such stories seemed noble, but too often the resolutions were confirmations of mainstream compromises that were fantasies of wishful thinking, that Sidney Poitier, for example, could show the way to a nice, happy reconciliation of ancient differences.

Like the powerful, invisible force of sexism with which it is often identical, racist expressions in common use of language occur in the dialogue of Wayne's films throughout his career, though in such instances as *Three Godfathers* (1949) there is a heightening awareness of the bigotry which underlies such expressions. Progress toward racial tolerance in his films is to be found in differences between *Rio Grande* and *Hondo*. In the first, Wayne justifies an illegal raid to rescue white children from ritual slaughter by drunken Indians. In the second, Wayne grows lyrical about his own Indian blood and about his love for his Indian wife: her name "means 'Morning.' Indian words mean the sound and feel of a word—'crack of dawn,' like when you get up in the first light, just two of you . . . can't say it in English, but that was her name, 'Astarte.'" Hondo is just enough Apache to keep the primitive virtues under control of the white civilized ones.

Because of the importance of China to American politics in the decade of the fifties, popular films could not well avoid subjects and images associated with Asian life and culture generally or Chinese culture specifically. It was a difficult, delicate matter to treat; it required an attitude of racial as well as political diplomacy in a context that mixed concern for a communist "takeover" with a Western (American) tradition of patronizing condescension toward Oriental cultures of all national identities. When it is recalled the Japanese were being "disciplined" to allow for their return to the decencies of civilization, a film like *The Barbarian and the Geisha* even in 1958 could strike familiar chords of popular response it tried to shape into new directions of feeling. The same could be said of *The Conqueror* (1956) and *Blood Alley*.

Big Jim McLain contains one of the most striking scenes of racism that can be found in any Wayne film until *The Cowboys* in 1972. The racism is turned against the bad guys, against the communists themselves. Obviously Americans have been vulnerable to the charge by enemies that America talks of freedom while denying it to its black citizens. This is the point of one of the questions asked of Townsend Harris in *The Barbarian and the Geisha*, a film where Wayne is involved in a complex revision of the American image he champions. When Harris answers "there are men in my country who would die to end that evil. It cannot long endure," he is marking a turn in the direction of Wayne's films away from many years of racist stereotypes and prejudices which had run through too many of his, and most Americans', pictures of American life.

The "barbarian" of *The Barbarian and the Geisha* confesses many American faults while learning much from his Japanese hosts. It is a picture of mutual tolerance, although it can be seen as simply another in many of its kind that patronize for the sake of political revisionism. For Wayne's career, it marked an achieved enlargement of vision for his film characters, but it was an achievement still in process of enlargement. His own basic instinct for human affection would find larger and larger outlets as he could escape the stereotypes of racism and bigotry, but even when it was more limited than in *The Barbarian and the Geisha*, Wayne was given an opportunity to make a "point" about racial intolerance in *Big Jim McLain*. The scene occurs when McLain bursts in on a meeting of Hawaiian communists planning disruption of the shipping industry (apparently related to the war in Korea). McLain wants to hit the man who murdered his partner Mal Baxter, but the murderer is too small for a big man like McLain to hit: "You're too small!" McLain says. "That's the difference between you people and us. We don't hit the little guy." But there is a big man among the communists, a truck driver who says, "I've had a bellyful of this East-Texas cotton-chopping jerk!"

This absurd dialogue tries to show that communist expressions of sympathy for working people are merely hypocritical and deceitful plots *against* the working people of America. McLain mocks the truck driver by asking if the man has ever chopped cotton. The truck driver's response is an amazing example of dialogue which could turn either way from an ironic edge: "No! I'm from the country-club set. That chopping cotton's for white trash and niggers!" Communists, it seems, are elitist "capitalists" who pretend to identify with the proletariat until driven to expose their true feelings. This "truck driver" *ought* (ideologically) to be mocking McLain. The issue which creates such ambiguity and ambivalence between McLain and the truck driver is the issue of black status in America. When McLain smashes the truckdriver, who is not too small to hit, he puts himself on the side of the "white trash and niggers," doing what a Wayne hero likes to do when confronted by obvious evil—punch it out.

MANY OF WAYNE'S films of the fifties show him continuing his customary existential attitude: a secular individualism, faintly irreligious and defiantly unorthodox. He may be a cynic who has to be converted to belief in something, though that "something" is not religious, as in *Blood Alley*. In *The Sea Chase* and *The Searchers*, he suffers from emptiness of soul. He finds vaguely humanized faith in persons, realizing his potenial for affection. The stories are more interesting, though, for revealing the emptiness than they are for showing how it is filled. They are stories of exile from home and society, from well-fixed structures of belief and vocation: Tom Wilder is wrenched by Chinese communists from his easy river life into a commitment for others in *Blood Alley;* Ethan Edwards is deprived of country, family, and friends before he rediscovers a capacity to love in *The Searchers;* and Capt. Karl Erlich refuses allegiance to an evil regime in Nazi Germany, accepting social and professional exile to preserve his integrity in *The Sea Chase*.

Sometimes not even nation or family suffices for self-definition, as in

Rio Bravo. As Townsend Harris in *The Barbarian and the Geisha,* Wayne represents a nation, but the character moves closer to spiritual exile as he moves closer to political success. A similar irony of movements occurs in *The Horse Soldiers* (1959), where Col. John Marlowe falls in love with his enemy the more deeply he moves into enemy territory. And Hondo is a man whose sense of direction is taken from his life among the Apaches, near extinction — "End of a way of life. Too bad. It's a good way," laments Hondo as the film concludes.

During the fifties, Wayne saw the "end of a way of life" for his characters' lost causes, their defiant individualism. Increasingly he is spokesman for present order, authority, and political conservatism. It is a role he had earlier undertaken occasionally, but always he had played it in obvious discomfort. Now he appears more comfortable, even when he uses skeptical techniques of irony, as in *Rio Bravo.*

In 1951 he launched into the new decade with a film which counterpoints the religious with the secular faith he balances more evenly in the years to follow. *Operation Pacific* shows Duke Gifford (Wayne) impressed by the religious faith of the nuns he helps to save from Japanese soldiers, though his own faith is grounded in love for his ex-wife and for the baby they lost. In this film he is "trapped" into becoming the spokesman for a religious attitude, as he had earlier in a similar scene of *They Were Expendable,* where he recited Robert Louis Stevenson's "Requiem" over the bodies of his fallen comrades. In *Operation Pacific,* he recites the "Burial at Sea" from the Navy Prayer Book, in a memorial service for his submarine commander, Pop Perry (Ward Bond). Gifford feels compelled to use religious words, even though he is not the ranking officer in the chapel: "I guess it's kind of up to me to say something," and he proceeds to recite the most specific religious words of John Wayne's career. It is a startling episode. More typical was his part in *Three Godfathers,* when he played Robert Marmaduke Hightower, religious skeptic and cynical outlaw who relives the story of the Wise Men led by a star to Bethlehem. He tosses and kicks the Bible as he stubbornly resists Biblical story. This is vintage John Wayne, not the one who in *Operation Pacific* speaks of "a sure and certain hope of their resurrection into eternal life, through Jesus Christ."

When Joe January insists at the end of *The Legend of the Lost* that he "believes in God," he is rewarded by the appearance of an Arab caravan to rescue him and Dita from death in the desert. His belief, affirmed by his voiceless prayer urged upon him by a triumphant Dita, results from desperation. The story of *The Legend of the Lost* is a "pilgrim's progress," revealing the emptiness of a religion which flaunts and imposes itself on others. The story contrasts the substance of faith discovered by social outcasts who find one another and see through the hypocrisies of an idealistic Christian.

At the center of Bonnard's supposed religious faith was his infantile trust in his father. Since this is also central to Wayne's characters, *The Legend of the Lost* is an analysis of a disintegrating force in the self-images of Wayne's own heroes. Dan Kirby's little boy in *Flying Leathernecks* (1951) made a Christmas recording for his father away fighting the Japs in the Pacific; when he is down in spirit, Kirby plays that recording to himself over and over. His little boy misses his daddy, especially when it is time to go to bed: "It's hard to say good-night when you aren't here," the boy tells his dad. "When I say good-night, I say, 'Our Father who. . . .'" The phonograph player fails again, cutting the message off at that point. Dan Kirby has become, through his absence, his son's Father as well as his father. It is a dangerous substitution, if Joe January is to be believed.

The message is interrupted, the father is eventually restored to the son, and all eventually turns out well for Dan Kirby. But heroes of culture, of popular art, might easily become godlike in their roles, exactly as Kirby became for his son. *The High and the Mighty* (1954) is an allegory, though a different one than *The Legend of the Lost*, of religious force, as Dan Roman intervenes to save his plane from airborne disaster. To do so, however, he had to lose his family. While José Locota (John Qualen) prays upon his rosary, Dan Roman looks at a photograph of his dead wife and son. He gets his strength of purpose from his loss as he brings the crippled plane to a safe landing on a runway that looks suspiciously like an illuminated crucifix.

4. "It's Going to Be All Right. Just Trust Me."

The essential strength of Wayne's acting was in his capacity to show affection and sympathy. This was most forceful when it had to be expressed through characters who resisted showing it. The buoyant happy spirit of Sean Thornton (in *The Quiet Man*) had to find its way through a mask of melancholy; love constantly fought against a strong capacity to hate in the powerful characters of Tom Dunson in *Red River* and Ethan Edwards in *The Searchers*. When stories or directors put Wayne in characters who had to be melancholy, hateful, bitter, or betrayed, his power to love was contained and controlled. This produced a tension often beautiful in expression and design. In such roles, for such films, by such directors, John Wayne achieved an artistry which surpassed mere professional competence and acquired heroic, mythic status.

Those circumstances can be understood better when Wayne's career is viewed from the perspective of his last fifteen years. The key ingredient was the presence of an analytic director: one who could, like an analyst, induce from Wayne the expression of his "repressed" capacity to live. This director had to put Wayne in situations, recreate through fantasies those critical circumstances, where Wayne's artistry could be discovered. The director who most brilliantly was able to perform this was John Ford, who may be said to have "educated" Wayne's talents in the most literal sense of the word—he led forth a spirit of comic love Wayne by culture tried to keep hidden. However, Ford did not always succeed, and he was not alone in his analytical abilities as Wayne's director. Howard Hawks first discovered the peculiar beauty possible in Wayne's acting, in *Red River*. In the final view, it is Howard Hawks who most consistently gave direction to the best performances, though he did not educe the brilliance of an Ethan Edwards or a Sean Thornton.

John Ford kept with Wayne almost to the end of Ford's professional and personal life. And Ford worked Wayne into ever more revealing portrayals. Indeed, two of Wayne's finest performances were under the direction of

John Ford at the end of Ford's career: as Tom Doniphon in *The Man Who Shot Liberty Valance* and as Michael Patrick Donovan, in *Donovan's Reef* (1963). It was fitting one should be a moody Western and the other a happy comedy, because it is in those genres that Wayne gave the best of himself for John Ford. Since those are discussed in detail elsewhere, one remaining to focus on from this period for Wayne and Ford is the episode Ford directed for the "epic" *How the West Was Won* (1962). The moodiness and irony which frame and permeate *The Man Who Shot Liberty Valance* are both present in the Ford-directed "Civil War" episode, which centers around the bloody battle of Shiloh on April 6, 1862. Everywhere there is chaos, pain, and despair typified by the hero of the film's story, Zeb Rawlings (George Peppard), who is tempted into deserting by a cynical Confederate soldier, played by Russ Tamblyn. They meet over a bloody pool of water and decide to "just leave this war to the folks that want it."

Zeb and the Confederate flee the battlefield, but on their way they overhear a conversation between two Union generals. These are Grant (Henry Morgan) and Sherman (John Wayne), who had earlier found themselves merely in the way when they inspected the hospital scene in Shiloh Meeting House, and so they have themselves retreated to an isolated spot in nearby woods. It is an odd spectacle, but the oddity is a Fordian touch. In the midst of despair and chaos is this dialogue of determination and rational optimism. At the center is a voice of resilience and resolve. The voice is that of John Wayne/General Sherman. He is chosen by John Ford to save the nation. He persuades General Grant to retain his command at a time he is near despair.

Grant, played by the unimpressive Morgan, is the character of impotence, immobility, and grave passivity. Sherman is energetic, kinetic, and elastic. Here John Wayne displays a nervous energy that becomes dramatically effective when set off against both the feckless Morgan/Grant and the two eavesdropping deserters. Although the scene is critical for its display of energy and power barely disciplined, it is also memorable for Wayne/Sherman's lines: "A month ago they were saying I was crazy! Insane! Now they're calling me a hero! Hero or crazy, I'm the same man. It doesn't matter what the *people* think! It's what *you* think, Grant!" Ford voices through Wayne's character a repetition of important themes in Ford's film career, particularly the relationship of legend and fact he had worked with in *The Man Who Shot Liberty Valance* and *She Wore a Yellow Ribbon*.

Wayne/Sherman dances about in his nervous effort to keep his temper and power under control. He stops pacing and sits beside the dejected Grant. Even seated, he moves with force in language and body signs: he shakes one of his cigars in Grant's face as he tells him a "man has the right to resign only if he's wrong! Not if he's right!" When he concludes by spitting out a bit of his cigar tobacco—even the spitting is decisive and vigorous.

As Tom Doniphon in *The Man Who Shot Liberty Valance*, 1962.

Having persuaded Grant, Sherman begins his retreat from prominence, to allow Grant to have the last word, and the last gesture: Morgan/Grant pats Sherman/Wayne's knee affectionately and says, "All right. Thanks." The little episode outlines the way Ford can take the strength of Wayne to its limits, almost cross the line of decorum, but then gently, firmly pull the power of the actor back into an attitude of submission. The restraint is impressive for its strength. In this use of Wayne, Ford may have tipped his hat to Howard Hawks, the director who showed Ford that John Wayne could really act (in *Red River*).

Perhaps, on the other hand, Howard Hawks did the first tipping, when he directed Wayne in *Hatari!* (1962), made at the same time as another characteristic film, *Man's Favorite Sport?* with Rock Hudson. Still the broad humor of Ford is well carried in *Hatari!* by the talents of Wayne as they had been often used in such films as *The Quiet Man, The Wings of Eagles,* and, later, *Donovan's Reef.* Roughhouse humor comes easily to Wayne, as both Ford and Hawks well understood (and, as later directors like Andrew McLaglen made much use of for themselves). *Hatari!*, to be looked at in more detail later, could be seen as a complement (compliment) to *The Quiet Man,* as *Donovan's Reef* might be a compliment (complement) to *Hatari!*

John Wayne is a common bond between two otherwise different *auteur* directors. Both turned to him more and more frequently as their careers drew toward conclusions. In the last ten or so years of his work, John Ford used Wayne in five of his films (including the "Civil War" episode) from 1956 to 1966, when the total number was about 12 (excluding shorts and television work). Hawks for his part used Wayne in four of his six films he directed from 1959 to 1970. Wayne gave these *auteurs* what they were looking for.

What Hawks was looking for he certainly got, and got it often, from John Wayne. The image of an American, Tom Dunson to Cole Thornton: the image of the fragile, masculine ethos that resists but needs all the feminine Eros he can find. How silly such a man can be strutting his way through life, tripping over the petticoats of destiny! John Wayne does this so well it is difficult to tell where Hawks has anything to do with it. But when Wayne as Cord McNally limps along, leaning on Amelita at the end of *Rio Lobo* (1970), he signals the touch of Hawks and no other. Cord gets the woman he deserves, crippled as he is. He is comfortable, and he can act, both he and Howard Hawks say here, as they point to the films they have made together in an artful conspiracy to define America and the American hero.

AMELIA DEDHAM refers to "the Kennedys" in *Donovan's Reef,* when she says they will "be furious" to learn she is a sister to a family of "half-caste" Polynesians. John Kennedy had been elected President in 1960, and his Boston background would be much in the mind of an audience watching this film in 1963. The fun of satirizing the Kennedys would be destroyed when the President was assassinated on November 23, 1963, but neither Wayne nor his filmmakers could have known that when they made *The Man Who Shot Liberty Valance* in the summer of 1961 and released it in the summer of 1962. Then many themes were put to the test of good humor, not the least of which was assassination itself.

Wayne portrayed an assassin in *The Man Who Shot Liberty Valance.* As Tom Doniphon, he bushwhacked the town bully and ceded the glory of the deed to Ransom Stoddard (James Stewart). Those who denounced the assassination were the evil clowns of the film, and so the moral framework of the narrative confirmed the justice in the deed. Doniphon himself had to suffer, but it was necessary for the progress of law and order. The archetypal form of the story, with roots deep in a narrative past that connect it with *Oedipus* and *Hamlet*, gives the film power of feeling and dramatic effect, but it also gives an uncanny connection with the single most traumatic event of 1963, the next year after the release of *The Man Who Shot Liberty Valance*. There had been many jokes among Americans unhappy with the election of President Kennedy, jokes of a bigoted kind, jokes of a darkly threatening kind, jokes which would come back to haunt when he was shot in Dallas on that dark November day. Here in Wayne's film career was a hauntingly dark shadow cast forward by the compromising deed of his hero Tom Doniphon, and it was no joke.

The sixties would be racked by violence, political assassinations and attempted assassinations. After the president's murder in 1963, there would be those of Martin Luther King, Jr., in April 1968, and Senator Robert Kennedy in June 1968. This list of "political" murders (i.e., assassinations) should include those of the three young men whose bodies were dug from an earthen dam near Philadelphia, Mississippi, in August 1964; James Chaney, Andrew Goodman, and Michael Schwerner had helped the Mississippi Freedom Democratic Party register voters in that state. They were three of fifteen persons murdered during the "Freedom Summer" of 1964. Malcolm X was shot to death on February 21, 1965. Later in March 1965, Mrs. Viola Liuzzo was shot to death while helping marchers during the Civil Rights pilgrimage from Selma to Montgomery.

The assassination of South Vietnamese President Diem shortly before President Kennedy was not unwelcomed by the American government at the time. It was done with motives not unlike those which justified the killing of Liberty Valance in Wayne's film. Murder for political gain was real in the world of American life, and it was imitated in the fictional world of John Wayne's films. It cost Tom Doniphon to do what he did, and so he is redeemed if not justified. After the deaths of John Kennedy, Martin Luther King, Jr., and Robert Kennedy, assassination is not again justified or redeemed in the films of John Wayne. It would not take the attempt on Governor Wallace's life in May 1972 for John Wayne to make films repudiating the violence of political murder.

This is so even in the most blatantly political of Wayne's films from the era, *The Green Berets* (1968). Here the assassins are always the enemy, Vietnamese communists, who murder teachers, professors, governors, senators, and their families; the heroine of the film, Lin, helps kidnap an enemy general because he murdered her father, a province chief. The second half of this film is an elaborate plot to kidnap General Phan Son Ti. It contrived to show that American heroes like Mike Kirby (John Wayne) do not stoop to use the hideous techniques of the enemy, including assassination. (There is an infamous scene in which Kirby exclaims that "out here due process is a bullet," after a Viet Cong spy has been tortured. Americans, however, are kept "clean" from the abuse of the prisoner; the scene of torture is not shown to the film's audience.)

Concern for justice and skeptical regard for law was frequently characteristic of Wayne's films and his portrayals of heroes' characters. In the sixties and seventies, he came close to overt criticisms of Supreme Court decisions in *True Grit* and *Rooster Cogburn* (1975). Although Clint Eastwood as Dirty Harry would seem to have taken a lock on the issues of defendants' rights and police handicaps, John Wayne had his say as well in his rowdy character of Rooster Cogburn. No one could hear Rooster's blustering defense of his unruly methods in capturing criminal suspects without hearing at the same time a criticism of recent U.S. Supreme Court decisions affecting police methods for capturing and interrogating persons suspected of criminal behavior. The drunken old one-eyed marshal shoots a rat, ranting "it's a rat-writ, writ for a rat, and this is lawful service of same." He says, "we had a good court goin' around here until them pettifoggin' lawyers moved in! The rat-catcher's too tough on the rats! Give them rats a fair show, they say!" In the year of *True Grit*'s release, the Supreme Court reaffirmed previous rulings protecting accused persons from prosecution with evidence illegally obtained (i.e., without a warrant) in *Katz v. United States*. Rooster repeats his grievance in *Rooster Cogburn*, when he is reminded by his Chinese friend Chen Lee that the judge had accused him of abusing justice. Rooster exclaims, "Abuse justice! There ain't no justice in the West no more! Men with sand in their craws bein' pushed aside by duded-up Yankee lawyers who won spelling bees back home."

By this time, 1975, American audiences would have had in their collective consciousness two infamous trials: the conspiracy trial of the "Chicago Seven" in 1969–1970, and the "Watergate" hearings and grand jury indictments against former Nixon administration staff members and campaign officials in 1974. John Wayne's Rooster Cogburn is a burlesque treatment of those who hold themselves above the law, whether they are hippies or presidents. *True Grit* and *Rooster Cogburn* establish frames of reference for laughing at Rooster, condemning his methods, but understanding his motives. To watch Rooster in the court of Judge Parker is to watch the law at its worst, making the worst case sound better in *True Grit*, and at its best, correcting abuses by the police and curtailing its zeal in *Rooster Cogburn*. The circus atmosphere of the films' courtroom scenes hardly differed from those of Judge Hoffman's Chicago courtroom or even from those of the U.S. Senate and House of Representatives investigations of the Watergate break-in, burglarly, and cover-up. Rooster Cogburn is the best and the worst of the American character, as the trials of the Chicago Seven and the administration of President Richard Nixon were expressions of the best and worst in American law. It is tempting to hear double entendres when

Rooster declares to Judge Parker, "I am re-tired, re-lieved, and re-joicin!" Richard Nixon resigned as president of the United States on August 9, 1974. Filming of *Rooster Cogburn* began in September 1974. Neither resignation, it must be noted, was voluntary.

IN *McLintock!* George Washington McLintock tells his daughter he is going to leave his land "to the nation for a park. Where no lumberman will cut down all the trees for houses with leaky roofs, where nobody'll kill all the beaver for hats and dudes, nor murder the buffalo for robes." This identifies McLintock with environmentalist positions of Theodore and Franklin Roosevelt, and also the new, young President Kennedy, who said in dedicating the National Wildlife Federation Building in March 1961, it was a national responsibility "to hand down undiminished to those who come after us, as was handed down by those who went before, the national wealth and beauty which was ours." The President also wrote a preface to Stewart Udall's book, *The Quiet Crisis,* asserting that "each generation must deal anew with the 'raiders,' with the scramble to use public resources for private profit, and with the tendency to prefer short-run profits to long-run necessities." Wayne's McLintock was affirming in his own "reactionary" way the "liberal" President's call for the first White House Conference on Conservation in 54 years.

A few years later Wayne played Chance Buckman, based upon Red Adair, internationally famed oil well firefighter. In the film *Hellfighters* (1969), Buckman takes on everything from television journalists to South American revolutionaries, with a glance along the way at the scene in Southeast Asia. At one point, Buckman joins the board of a company in the business of drilling for oil. He leaves it, however, in disgust: he cannot stand its passive and inane board meetings. He returns to the active and "meaningful" life of adventure as a firefighter. It is characteristic that he should appear as defender of the environment, protector of natural resources. Chance Buckman is so highly respected as an environmentalist that he seems to African tribesmen to be a veritable god of nature who "hung the moon" itself.

THE WAR in Vietnam was certainly a clear enough public issue in 1967–68, when *The Green Berets* was made and released. Public opposition to the war had been clear from at least 1965, when "teach-ins" were organized at the University of Michigan. Government escalation continued. On January 31, 1966, President Johnson ordered the resumption of bombing of North Vietnam, after a brief Christmas "truce." By the end of 1966, there were twice the number of American troops in-country as had been at its start, and there were five times the number of North Vietnamese regular soldiers fighting in the South. In December 1966, American bombers began to attack Hanoi itself. American demonstrations against the war escalated at the same time. In 1967 there were demonstrations for peace in New York City, San Francisco, and most spectacularly in Washington, D.C., when 75,000 people participated in the "March on the Pentagon" on October 21.

Filming of *The Green Berets* began in August 1967; the film was released in July 1968. It was in the making and appeared, then, at the height of sharpening controversy over the war. It was viewed as making a political and propaganda statement, and John Wayne would never again be free from associations with that statement, for better or for worse. The timing of the film involved several keen ironies from events which occurred during the same period. In January 1968, the Senate began televised hearings on Vietnam, to heighten and broaden the American public's focus on the issues raised by the war. On January 31, 1968, the Viet Cong launched its devastating Tet offensive, virtually the beginning of the end of the American presence in Vietnam. A film like *Green Berets* could help to satisfy a national fancy that defeats in Vietnam were only temporary in a long-term trial for the national will to win. Most darkly ironic was the episode in My Lai, on March 18, 1968, when American soldiers slaughtered a large number of people, including old and young, women and children. This was the "truth" which would destroy the credibility of *The Green Berets* and damage the reputation of John Wayne himself.

The Green Berets combines *Fort Apache* and *They Were Expendable* to produce an incoherent narrative. Its political message is grafted upon a story of the American West and World War II vintage. There is buried in it a delicious irony: the Beret's "A-Camp," dug from the jungle deep in "V-C country," is called "Dodge City" and it is "For Sale." Innocent Montagnards become the "homesteaders" of American Western stories, and the Viet Cong guerrillas become the savage, uncivilized Indians of such stories (though they rarely actually appeared as such in Wayne's own films). North Vietnamese Regulars are the film's version of savage Japanese soldiers in World War II films. Just as most Americans had a difficult time sorting among friends and enemies in Vietnam, so does *Green Berets*. It does not find it difficult, however, to explain the war is a battle against international communism, and it uses a "platform" to make that explanation.

The platform is an orientation and information center at Fort Bragg, where Green Beret spokesmen answer questions from the American press and general public at the opening of the story. Reactions to this film are complicated by its legitimate association between a "political" stand on the war and justification for it by the assassinated "liberal" President, John F. Kennedy. On a banner spread across the opening of the film, as it stretches over the platform of the orientation center, are the words "UNITED STATES ARMY JOHN F. KENNEDY CENTER FOR SPECIAL WARFARE." The "counterinsurgency" operations of the specialized Green Berets are operations the

As Colonel Mike Kirby in *The Green Berets*, 1968.

Kennedy administration fostered and encouraged to help "those peoples in the huts and villages of half the globe" secure their freedom, as the president had put it in his Inaugural Address in 1961. When John Kennedy warned, "Let every nation know, whether it wishes us well or ill, that we shall pay any price, bear any burden, meet any hardship, support any friend, oppose any foe to assure the survival and the success of liberty," he inspired both John Wayne and, eventually, the making of *The Green Berets*. Neither John Wayne nor John Kennedy could know how painfully true would the president's words be that "those who foolishly sought power by riding the back of the tiger ended up inside."

To pass "the torch" of freedom is the injunction of the president's speech, as it is the concluding message of Col. Kirby in the highly sentimental last scene of *The Green Berets*. The little Vietnamese boy, Hamchunk, grieves the loss of his friend and patron, Peter-san. It is the hard duty of Col. Kirby to try to console the boy, who is desolate, tears in his eyes. Kirby walks toward him, but the boy runs away toward the beach screaming, "No! No!" In a long shot, the boy seems even more lonely and small as he stands looking toward the horizon of the sea beyond, where the sun barely peeks through the dawn. Kirby kneels beside the boy, who asks him, "What will happen to me now?" Kirby consoles him, "You let me worry about that, Green Beret. [He has put Petersen's beret on the boy.] You're what this is all about." Then man and boy walk along the beach together at the dawning of a new day, while a chorus sings "The silver wings, on my son's vest, Make him one of America's best. He'll be a man, till then one day, Let him win the Green Beret." The sentiment and the symbols articulate the same commitment the president had made in his Inaugural Address.

PRESIDENT EISENHOWER delivered a solemn warning to Americans in his Farewell Address on January 17, 1961, against the "military-industrial complex": "The potential for the disastrous rise of misplaced power exists and will persist. . . . The prospect of domination of the nation's scholars by federal employment project allocations, and the power of money . . . is gravely to be regarded." In three of his films, John Wayne uses his popular image to communicate this warning (which he had previously done as well in *Allegheny Uprising* in 1939). Wayne's characters are especially scornful of anyone who uses patriotism to make a profit, who compromises the integrity of soldiers with the motive of money. In *Rio Lobo* Union officer Cord McNally exclaims "rotten treachery for money!" when he explains to two ex–Confederates why he can be friends with them but not with the Union soldiers who sold information to the Confederates. This sets a right tone for easy association of John Wayne with President Eisenhower's warning.

The Sons of Katie Elder (1965) turns upon unscrupulous actions of a weapons manufacturer and armaments dealer, one Morgan Hastings (James

Gregory). This villain is a caricature of the selfish weaponeer who cares nothing for principle and all for profit. John Elder repudiates the profit motive absolutely: he distinguishes himself from his brothers by his single-minded independence from interest in money, which adds to the community's distrust of him. In the end, he causes destruction of Hasting's armaments business (and Hastings along with it).

Hastings represents the "industrial" side of the complex more than the "military" one, but in *Chisum* (1970), the military side receives more emphasis. Here the local businessman villain is Lawrence Murphy (Forrest Tucker) who is determined, like Morgan Hastings, to "own a town." Lawrence Murphy wants an empire, one bigger even than John Chisum's in Lincoln County, New Mexico Territory. Murphy corrupts everything in sight, including the local sheriff and the territorial governor himself. Murphy hopes to weaken Chisum's economic and political power. He buys influence with the Army. Murphy talks with an Army Colonel alone after the Colonel has refused to give Chisum more time to deliver his cattle: "Well, Nathan, looks like we're in business. . . . After you've served your tour of duty, be an officer in the L.G. Murphy bank. Family'll like that." *The Undefeated* (1969) also alludes to the evils of military procurement and the profits made by "complexes" between civilian businessmen and military officers. Federal government agents try to cheat John Henry Thomas (John Wayne) out of a herd of horses Thomas and his men have worked to gather for sale. John's response is to punch out both of the "popinjay" American agents ("thieves," he calls them).

JOHN WAYNE'S representations of the right relationship between the races of humankind is an assertion of brotherhood. Equality before God is more consequential than equality before the law, which is too often a corruption of the heart to be much trusted for moral adjudication. While the Supreme Court decision in 1954 on school desegregation may have been responsible for putting Pompey into the classroom with whites in *The Man Who Shot Liberty Valance*, it was distinctly not related to Tom Doniphon's motive for dissolving Ransom Stoddard's school: Tom had to save the *people*, not the *students*. Prejudice obviously bothers a Wayne hero, and he demonstrates his disdain for it by dramatizing his friendships with people of various races.

In *War Wagon* and *Big Jake* race discrimination in public places of business is a matter of importance for plots and characters. In *War Wagon* (1967) Indians as a group are subjected to stereotypical treatment. Coarse comedy is made of their relationships with both Taw and Taw's Indian friend Levi Walking Bear (Howard Keel). But in this comedy is a serious point of relevance to the time, when the Indian chief tells Taw Jackson he is not welcome to stay for dinner: "Having a white man in his camp offends

Kirk Douglas as Lomax *(left)* and Wayne as Taw Jackson in *War Wagon*, 1967.

him," as Walking Bear translates. Wayne does nice acting with his face in this scene of his humiliation, then he acts as if he is "acting" in another scene, the reverse situation when a white bartender refuses to serve whiskey to Walking Bear. The Indian serves himself, and he offers a drink to both Taw and Lomax (Kirk Douglas). Lomax accepts, but Taw refuses. Walking Bear pretends to be insulted by Taw, challenges him: "You too good to drink with Indian?" Taw pretends to agree, "That's right." This begins a fight all enjoy tremendously, because it has been contrived to save Taw and Lomax from a shootout with one another.

Black Americans had been challenging the practice of segregation from whites in business establishments at least since February 1960, when a group of black college students sat down in a whites-only lunch counter in Greensboro, North Carolina. This began "sit-ins." It would eventually succeed in eliminating that pernicious practice from American public life. In the year of *War Wagon* blacks turned violently against American cities throughout the nation, from Newark to Detroit, in a reprise of the rioting that destroyed much of Watts, a section of Los Angeles, in August 1965. Though more black businesses may have been destroyed than white ones in those riots, they were a clear signal to the white community that more was required than they had received since the sit-ins began in 1960.

Big Jake has a scene of gratuitous comedy in which a hotel clerk refuses to allow Jake's Indian friend Sam Sharpnose (Bruce Cabot) to register in his hotel. It is a particularly mean-spirited refusal, since the clerk says, referring to Big Jake's dog, "The dog is all right, but we don't allow Indians." While he says that, an Oriental comes down the stairs from *his* room in the hotel. Jake is already indignant, and then puzzled when he sees that the hotel serves Orientals but not Indians. He objects, "He's with me!" This is not going to change the clerk's mind, until he sees the name of the man he is addressing on the hotel register, Jake McCandles. The clerk will make an exception for Jake, but the policy remains the same for other Indians.

Scenes of insult in *War Wagon* and *Big Jake* resonate as they do because of race issues in the sixties, but they express an attitude of values found in many of Wayne's films regardless of time and place. Refusal to treat Indians as human beings with social and economic rights would be an insult to human dignity in any Wayne film of the sixties and seventies. Segregation in schools, restaurants, or buses is an accident of environment; insult to human dignity and personal worth is a necessary result of faulty (evil) character. Social issues are vital to Wayne's heroes because they are consequences of individual, personal issues.

Chisum and *The Undefeated* present heroes who not only befriend but accept Indians as "brothers." John Chisum explains his relationship with the people once his enemies in the struggle to possess New Mexico Territory:

CHISUM: Had to fight rustlers, disease, the land itself, Indians. One Indian in particular—a Comanche chief named White Buffalo. Bravest man I ever knew.
SALLY: Dead now?
CHISUM: Might as well be. He's penned up in a piece of desert the government calls a reservation. The end of his way of life. Pretty good way, too.
SALLY: You sound as if you're sorry for him, your enemy!
CHISUM: Why, I respect him. We're brothers. As close as your father and I were. Maybe even closer.

Chisum has grown in character, become a better man than he was in his rough-hewn days of fighting the Indians. Chisum's forcing a soldier to treat the captive White Buffalo with respect is another scene of gratuity, like the hotel scene in *Big Jake*. It also is played for comic effect, as the soldier is made to swallow his pride to give the Indian back pride of his own. When Pat Garrett (Glen Corbett) explains to Sally why Chisum is different than Billy the Kid, Pat says "Mr. Chisum's changed with the times. He doesn't like to let on, but he cares. About the people here, and in town. About the Indians, and the Territory. Why he's independent, and he likes to do things his own way, but he cares." The point applies to John Wayne as well as to John Chisum.

RELAXING TENSIONS between generations is identified with dissolving tensions between races in *Donovan's Reef* and *The Undefeated*. These films, with high comic intent, aim for solutions to human frailties more sadly recognized in *The Searchers*. The potential for tragedy is always present in these themes, as in the darkly toned *Cahill, U.S. Marshal* and *The Cowboys*. In the tragedy of *The Cowboys*, a black cowboy-cook, Jebediah Nightlinger (Roscoe Lee Browne), helps young cowboys avenge the death of their "adopted" father, Will Andersen (John Wayne), a man with a lifetime of estrangement from his long-dead young sons. Nightlinger helps Will grow in his love for the young cowboys, and then he helps the young cowboys show their love for the martyred Andersen. When the boys first see Nightlinger, they are immensely curious about his "differences": he is the first black man any of them has ever seen. The episode is comic and instructive. Nightlinger teaches the point that "Black is beautiful." Nightlinger insists on his *differences* as signs of his uniqueness and personal integrity, even as he identifies with Andersen and the boys in a common social cause.

In *Cahill* the generation gap has central importance as Wayne plays an estranged father whose sons are living and rebellious. Their rebellion, however, is a protest against his absence, against his failure to show love for them. Again a figure of racial difference is used to heal the breach between father and sons. When J.D. Cahill goes to hire his tracker, Lightfoot (Neville Brand), he takes his older son Danny (Gary Grimes) with him. Danny protests he does not like dealing with Indians: "There's nothing I hate mo'n a Comanche, it's a half a one!" Cahill lets this slide by with only a mild protest, but when Danny insults Lightfoot's wife by refusing to lift his hat to her, Cahill loses his temper, knocks Danny from his horse into a mud hole, and then apologizes to her for his son: "My apologies, ma'am. Slight negligence in his upbringin'." Danny gets out of the mud, tips his hat to the woman, and adds his greeting to show he has learned a lesson in respect.

Concern for reconciliation of the generations appears in two of Wayne's last films, *The Shootist* (1976) and *Rooster Cogburn*. In *The Shootist* the hero dies instructing a young man in courage and honor. In *Rooster Cogburn*, the generation gap is less important than the racial prejudice that has prohibited an Indian from ever being a U.S. marshal. The orphaned Indian boy, Wolf (Richard Romancito), grows to admire the rough old Rooster and wants to be just like him. This pleases and surprises Cogburn. Wolf asks, "Has there ever been an Indian marshal?" and Cogburn responds, "Not that I heard tell of." This does not discourage Wolf, who says, "Well, that's what I'd like to be. A man like you." Rooster, though well pleased, objects, "You ain't aimin' your sights very high, son. But, uh, if you'd like to follow my tracks, son, I'll help you up the trail, and proud to." This may be a long way from Ethan Edwards and *The Searchers* of 1956, but it is not so far from Rod Drew and *The Trail Beyond* or Chris Morrell and *'Neath Arizona Skies*, both of 1934. To care for persons without racial prejudice, and to instruct the young in a continuity of moral tolerance, were not new to John Wayne in the sixties and seventies. The time had begun to catch up to standards he set long before.

Part II

John Wayne: Artist

5. Fables of Romance

Plots of stories in Wayne's films of the thirties are folk tales, mythic adventures, fairy tales, and sacred narratives. They are tales of fantasy. Uninhibited fancy produces highly conventionalized art. As the literary critic Northrop Frye has explained, "Removing the necessity for telling a credible story enables the teller to concentrate on its structure, and when this happens, characters turn into imaginative projections, heroes becoming purely heroic and villains purely villainous. That is, they become assimilated to their functions in the plot."[4] At the core of fiction is the romance, a form "directly descended from the folk tale," bringing us "closer than any other aspect of literature to the sense of fiction, considered as a whole, as the epic of the creature, man's vision of his own life as a quest."[5]

John Wayne's films of the thirties are movies of fancy. They show conventional structures of folk tales and romances. That makes them simple to assimilate as primitive forms of art, but it also makes them powerful in their cumulative impact. The hero is firmly subordinated to the role he plays in carrying out the narrative design. The hero is a vehicle for fancy to complete conventional designs of wishing and fearing, dreaming and dooming.

Narratives of these films are implausible and sometimes impossible. However, they are familiar forms of story-telling and ritual behavior, recalling and reenacting "once upon a time." Usual constraints of natural reality are lifted as fancy races on in an uninhibited manner that recalls childhood enthusiasms. The underlying structure is like dreaming, and a common figure of speech for going to sleep before dreaming is to "fall to sleep." This falling action is a characteristic opening for romance narratives. John Wayne's character "falls": he descends, climbs down, or dives over and over again. This is so frequent it is taken for granted, but it is an integral part of the action of romance narrative. The hero descends into a threatening world, and there he has his adventures of flight and pursuit.

Romantic heroes fall into darkness, as when they fall into caves and tunnels. This is a descent with classic predecessors: Aeneas into the Underworld, Jonah into the Whale, Orpheus into Hades, Theseus into the Labyrinth of the Minotaur. This illustrious heritage behind Wayne's films points to their shared romance structure: it imbues the hero with as much power as imagination desires when set loose to do what it wishes. Darkness is literal for the hero and symbolic for the viewer; it is bound to show up as a test of courage and intelligence at some point in the quest of the romantic hero.

Prominent actions in these stories are caused by separation from parents, death of parents, and resulting loneliness of the hero. Search for the killers of parents is a main motivation for the heroic quest. This repeats a common form of the romance structure, basic in Christian versions: Christ hunts out the killer of Adam, the first father. This is a deep-structure of these romance adventures, which simplify as they deepen toward the folktale outline.

Texas Terror (1935) is an interesting variation on this theme of loneliness after death of parents. The hero, John Higgins, suffers from anxious memories after an incident that opens the film's story. John kills his best friend during what seems to be a robbery attempt by his friend. The romance structure is complicated when this best friend is said to be "like a father" to the hero. Emotionally, he mourns the killing of his father. Because the structure is romantic, however, it can provide a solution through events of wish-fulfillment. The truth is uncovered that John did not kill his best-friend-father, and so he does not have to punish himself with remorse and alienation any longer. He can marry and renew his public duties.

IN FABLES OF ROMANCE, the hero often undergoes a change in form as he makes his descent into the lower world of adventures with evil. In a fairy tale, the metamorphosis may be literal, as a prince may turn into a frog. In the romance tales of these films, change is figurative: through changes of clothing and changes of name.

Blue Steel (1934) uses clothing to mis-identify the hero, John Carruthers, as the "polka dot bandit." For most of the story, the sheriff believes John is an outlaw, a suspicion confirmed in his mind when he finds the polka-dot neckerchief in John's possession. It is a telltale mark of identification, but in this plot it is a faulty mark the hero wears while undergoing tests of adventure. An equally simple use of clothing occurs in *The Star Packer* (1934), where John Travers tells his posse to wear white headbands to make them distinguishable from outlaws during a running gun-battle. By this mark, the hero identifies the good guys as a single community united by his magical leadership. Thus he brings a "warrant" for their use of violence by bringing them a sign of their white ideal—romantic identity.

The Hurricane Express (1932) is bound together as a community by the changing identity of the villian, Stevens, "the Wrecker." As in *Randy Rides Alone* (1934), it seems to be the villain who makes the metamorphoses, but there is a twist in this film. The villain's changes of disguise are changes of masks, appearing to be at different times as many as seven different characters. The main point is everyone is a suspect, and everyone has a touch of evil; the special twist for the hero is that he becomes a double for the Wrecker, having to bear the burden of that false identity as the Wrecker for a considerable length of time in the story. The moral monster Stevens takes Larry Baker's (John Wayne) face and clothing in the dark, leaves him as a suspect, and returns to carry him off like a demon into his den of thieves and killers. The hero, in other words, splits into a good part and a bad part, with the bad triumphant for a long while before the good can recover to battle and overcome the bad.

Becoming an "Other," a part of one's self capable of evil, is a risk the questing hero has to run, as, for example, several of King Arthur's knights found to their unhappiness in Malory's fables of their romance adventures. *'Neath Arizona Skies* (1934) is a form of this misidentification through change of clothing, in a setting that could be found in Arthurian stories of questing knights. Chris Morrell (Wayne) falls unconscious beside a stream, where his clothing is changed by an outlaw in flight, so Chris is left the suspected villian. Chris, however, has the good fortune to be found by a goodly maiden, Clara Moore, who nurses him to health with water from the stream and patiently discovers his real identity.

WHEN A CHARACTER makes a change of name, that becomes a significant metaphor. A person can be an actor can be a character *ad infinitum*, because names are promiscuous. To find the right name for the right identity is urgent business of the hero, even if the actor who plays his role can move like a bodiless essence from one name or costume to another with ease. Michael Morrison is John Wayne is the Duke is John Middleton is John Allen is not John Allen is John Middleton—all in the same story, in *Lawless Range* (1935): this sequence accurately describes the flow of name changes in the film, but it does not end, because John Middleton is the Duke is John Wayne is Michael Morrison as well, to complete the cycle and prepare for the next round.

In *West of the Divide* (1934), Ted Hayden (Wayne) is searching for the killer of his father. To carry out his mission, he seizes an opportunity to become another person, Gat Ganns, gunfighter and hired killer. This is possible because a wanted poster, accompanying a letter of introduction, is found on the body of Gat Ganns near the hero's campsite. Implausible? Of course, but right in the world of romance. The romantic point is again that the hero has taken on the taint of evil from the world of his adventures below. This cannot be escaped, because nature at the level of the quest is a fallen, tainted nature. If it were not, there would be no need for the quest. Shared identity is the means whereby the hero can pass with safety through realms of danger. It is like the magic cap of Jack the Giant Killer.

Westward Ho (1935) has a fable of irony in tension with its main fable of romance. When John Wyatt discovers his long lost brother, his brother dies in his arms. Young Jim must die, because he has lived a false identity as an outlaw. The mythic structure here is the story of Cain and Abel, long lost twins, or doppelgangers. Central to the issue of the fable is the point when Wyatt assumes the name of Allen; because the result of that decision is so ironically disastrous, the fable nearly shatters of its own internal tensions so it nearly is no romance at all. It is saved by the convention that allows a hero to do battle with his dark, shadowy double, or "Other," and after defeating him, find his way back to a life of freedom and happiness.

UNCOVERING REAL identity as a result of changing the hero's name occurs in *King of the Pecos* (1936), a patently mythic romance fable. John Clayborn (Wayne) sees his parents killed at Sweet Water. He spends his life preparing to return to Sweet Water, reclaim it, and avenge his parents' deaths. He trains as a lawyer, practices his marksmanship, and when he is ready, goes home. He introduces himself as John Clay upon his arrival, and so he conceals the fact he was *born* there. Like the pun on the name of Adam, out of red clay, so is John Clayborn's name a fixing of his nature and birthright to enjoy the sweet waters of his parents' home. He reassumes his full name when he reveals it to the diabolical Stiles at the gate locked to keep John from his home. John stands on the clay where he was born when he makes his revelation, bringing a power of conquest and promise of renewal no other name could have.

King of the Pecos is a romance of *nostoi*, fables of homecoming. Like Odysseus's journey home, it breaks false identities, recovers true identity, and scatters enemies who have usurped the hero's real name. It is a return-to-Eden fable, achieved through craft, disguise, and physical power. John Clayborn drives demons out of his Eden, sending Stiles over a cliff to his "fiery" pit. John also pursues the man who beat him as a child, a thug named Ash, up into a labyrinth of boulders in nearby hills, where John outflanks Ash, outdraws him, and kills him in a duel of quick draw. John tosses his gun alongside the corpse in a gesture of finality as he passes into his rightful inheritance of recovered identity.

Winds of the Wasteland (1936) recovers identity for a town and a man. Waste turns into energetic life processes. John is the life-bringer who makes everyone want to live. This is the character audiences were used to seeing John Wayne play in his films of the thirties. It is a role subordinate to plots of questing, of adventures in defeating powers of incredible evil, and escaping from the traps, snares, pits and tricks evil can prepare. The part calls for a romance character who can break free of ensnarements, overcome evil by craft or brute strength, and earn the rewards of a grateful community or loving woman. While most of his films of the thirties emphasize the descending movement of a hero's summons to the plains of difficulty, a few of them, like *Winds of the Wasteland* and *King of the Pecos*, celebrate his victories in forms of urgent ascent toward concord recovered.

THE PLOT of romance fables is stunningly simple, however varied from story to story. There are, however, complications that arise from any story's employment of symbolic images in its texture of telling. Films work across time through narrative rhythms and through space as patterns of pictures, images and scenes, which point outwards in a descriptive (mimetic) function, and inwards as self-reflecting symbols in the worlds of the fables. As archetypes, they are images recurrent in the history of story-telling (the romance hero himself is a symbolic image, an archetype filled out by the "content" of John Wayne).

The "face in the window" image is a variant of the Narcissus archetype. This presents self-identification, as "other," as object or illusion. The result, as for Narcissus, is usually disastrous. This image can also be a sign of separation between worlds, codes of value, order and disorder. A window, as a frame for vision, is art as a means of vision, an invitation to watch. Associated with the Narcissus theme, it produces a self-reflecting commentary by the art work on itself or in its relationship with the audience, a relationship sincerely or mockingly narcissistic.

The window functions primarily to open up spaces for vision. *The Lawless Nineties* (1936) uses windows in a way that anticipates *The Man Who Shot Liberty Valance* (1962). These films use the device for interior framing, as a repetition *in* the film of the frame which encloses the film itself. Both are means of shaping vision, and they are both conventions of the art. When the window frame of the story is a part of a newspaper office, as in these films, then the *sign* of its *sign*ificance is strongly emphasized.

The window in *The Lawless Nineties* shows a friendly face to its audience. In other films it is a face of menace, as in *The Star Packer, West of the Divide,* and *The Dawn Rider* (1935). In the first, the heroine Anita is awakened by sounds outside her bedroom. She peeks from beneath her covers to see an ugly face pressed against her window. Farther outside are three men preparing animal costumes for a show of demons. The window is a point of possible entry by the demonic into the rational and orderly. It suggests as well, since it is a bedroom window, a Peeping Tom experience which rouses fears of sexual violation. Elaborately realized, the window can even have a function of psycho-sexual meaning.

Such a scene works, as conventional and stylized action, because it offers a strong appeal of fear: abuse of privilege (the window), assault on vulnerability, reversal of vision (outside threatens inside). If the window reflects as well as mediates, it can suggest that the face in the window, distorted by the medium, is really one's own face. The ogres and demons, then, seen by Anita in *The Star Packer,* are frightening reflections of herself. She will grow in character and add a dimension of experience previously missing so long as she was innocent and helpless. Indeed, Anita finds courage to chase off her mimic demons, and the next day she announces her determination to fight for her ranch.

Use of a hole as a window smacks of spying, peeping. In romance this is necessary for survival of the hero or heroine, exactly as it was so often for Odysseus or Huck Finn, for example. But what the hero can do, so can the villain, and that makes for evil consequences. Listening and peeping through the windows in Wayne's films of the thirties reinforce themes of insecurity throughout the treacherous world of romance. In a tragic version, such as *Othello* or *Hamlet,* such spying leads to disaster; in romance, it turns out right. *Blue Steel* has a scene of spying that almost turns out wrong. The sheriff uses a knothole in the floor of an upstairs room to look down on the office of an express line. He peeps through his hole to see John Carruthers (Wayne) bent in front of an open safe, and so he concludes John is the thief. He draws an incorrect conclusion from insufficient vision—a metaphor of caution to audiences, but a fact of dubious significance to the sheriff in the story.

The same device is used in *Westward Ho,* but with a different emphasis, and with a different perspective. In this story Jim Wyatt watches through the outlaw's peephole to see John fight for a way to escape from a gang of thugs. Jim admires John's pluck and power. The peephole focuses the unknowing brother's attention, as an action of irony, but also as an excuse, or metaphor, for putting the audience in the position of the errant younger brother: both admire John at work, and both participate in guilt as they share hidden identity. It is a double speculation for looking in as well as looking out.

Randy Rides Alone uses a humorous variant of the window as peephole. When Randy Bowers walks into the massacre at Half-Way House, he notices two pictures on the wall. One is a poster of the villain Marvin Black, with its eyes shot out. Later, when John uses the poster as a target in the grotto of the outlaws, *he* puts out the eyes of the villain. A more complicated pattern connects the poster with the eyeless outlaw and the other picture John sees on the wall of Half-Way House. This is a painting, a portrait, mocking the eyeless poster of the living man-demon. This relationship suggests a mirror function, with a hint art can be used for ethical ends. The living eyes are the eyes of the heroine, who uses the picture on the wall as a cover for her peepholes looking out into the barroom. It protects her at the same time it makes her a witness to the action.

WORDS ARE COMBINED with pictures in the wanted poster for Marvin Black in *Randy Rides Alone.* This combination provides the ironic

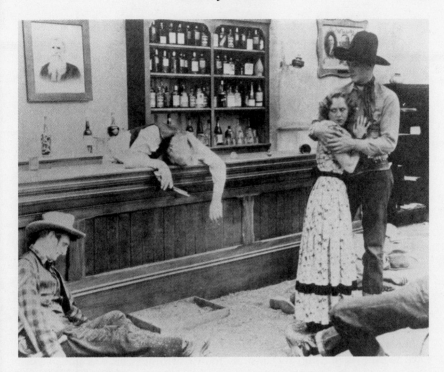

Wayne as Randy Bowers, comforting Alberta Vaughn as Sally Rogers, in *Randy Rides Alone*, 1934.

means whereby Black is undone by Randy Bowers's detective work; when the "mute" man writes to conceal his power of speech, he inadvertently marks his own uncovering. Words, written and spoken, deepen the meanings of romance narrative. They articulate the image of the hero which will endure from character to character as John Wayne passes from fable to myth.

As John may at any moment burst through a window or shatter the separation between outlaw world and world of law, he may also at any point rise above the frame of his medium to say something that breaks the boundary separating actor from character, man from audience: words and language carry the actor from entertainment toward art. When Sally Rogers comes out from behind the picture she uses for a peephole in *Randy Rides Alone*, she prefigures this transition of person from character, in a twist on the Pygmalion idea. But she does it as a purely visual gesture. John is more likely to make it a verbal one, in a "move" that speaks directly to the audience the way Woody Allen makes his hero do in *The Purple Rose of Cairo* (1985).

The knothole view in *Westward Ho* forces the audience into the same perspective as a character in the story, a perspective that focuses on the battling John. This attention is enforced by use of words, when, for example, the villain Kincaid says of Singing Sandy, "I don't like the way that fellow talks. We better watch him." Watch him is exactly what all will do in *Riders of Destiny* (1933) and in many other films as well. John Wayne, in story after story, is going on a quest. This is so obvious that one character says to John, as Rod Drew, "Oh, you're up here on a quest?" in *The Trail Beyond* (1934).

His charm is in part his ability to speak directly to audiences even as he speaks indirectly to other characters in his stories. When Ted Hayden (Wayne) hears the plan of the villain in *West of the Divide* for killing an old man to get the man's daughter, Ted says to him, "Like a dime novel, eh?" The audience knows that Ted, as John Wayne, knows this is exactly what the film as a whole is like. Again, Wayne's character signals the artificiality of his world when he tells the heroine in *'Neath The Arizona Skies*, "Some men are like books, written in a strange language." Wayne's speeches call for his character to be "read" as a figure, as an archetype.

This continues, in his ironic remarks in *Blue Steel*, when he says, as John Carruthers, "We were just playing." He has just escaped two men chasing him around a barn located on the ranch of a villain. One of these men is "killed," and the other is knocked to the ground by a bale of hay. It looks serious, and it looks dangerous. Literally, John is kidding when he says "we were just playing," because as John Carruthers he was not playing; figuratively, as John Wayne, he *has* just been playing, and this is his knowing wink at his audience.

This confidence informs the remark he makes as John Middleton in *Lawless Range* to one of the villains: "There's something bigger than this." *This* is also the film and the character as well as the scheme in the story. It is a reminder the character is also an actor who is a person bigger than the roles he plays. And he plays many parts even in this film itself. Earlier in *Lawless Range* he told a marshal who drafts him into an undercover role, "I've made a lot of changes in my life," and certainly he has, even as young as John Wayne was in 1935. He tells another law officer, in *Paradise Canyon*, "Well, this one's a new one for me," referring to yet another undercover role—to be acted out in a travelling medicine show. Once there he modestly lists his talents: "About all I can do is ride and shoot." The world of romance is impressed with these credentials. As he says in *King of the Pecos*, "I'm right at home here."

MOST OF THE ROMANCE narratives of these films in the thirties end in marriage or prophecies of marriage. That is a common feature of the conventional form. However, marriage signals the end of romance. The trick is to bring the romance to an end, and yet to leave the actor free to continue his adventures in other roles, even to "carry on" with other women without

being unfaithful to the audience's trust. He must end in marriage to fulfill
the narrative form, but he must be free at the same time to begin a new
romance somewhere else and at some other time. (Actresses who played
John Wayne's heroines in these films were nearly always different women,
even when the same cast of male actors was employed from one film to
another. The hero had to be "caught" by a woman, but the actor would be
caught by different women each time).

Marriage unavoidable, stories may conclude with the wedding
ceremony itself. Even here reluctance to end the romance is pictured in
ambivalence and ambiguity. *King of the Pecos,* which ought to end with a
return to the bliss of Eden, shows a wedding ceremony constantly interrupted by a deaf man who thinks the minister is trying to marry *him* to the
bride; focus on this conclusion shifts from the hero, rapidly disappearing
into domesticity, to the resisting man who "is not the marryin' kind." The
incomplete ceremony is a typical coda: as in *The Lucky Texan* (1934), when
the photographer gives up trying to take a picture of the wedding party. It
breaks up, having driven the photographer away, the film saying it does not
want to fix the hero in this posture of conclusion.

Most mockingly does *Desert Trail* (1935) allow a wedding to end things,
when the pseudo-minister "Rev. Smith" pretends to be marrying the hero
to the heroine, until the hero says, "I want this thing to be legal," which
breaks up the scene in most inconclusive laughter. If the marriage is actually
completed, as in *Dawn Rider,* when the bride and groom ride away from
the audience, "Just Hitched" written on a sign attached to the back of their
buggy, action is offered in a context of disturbing ambivalence: focus shifts
from the departing hero to gaze on a doctor and an undertaker, looking to
future business as they watch the newly wedded couple drive away. The
doctor expects to deliver their babies, but the undertaker is here to drive
a nail in the coffin of the romantic hero.

Making fun of marriage threatens to collapse romance structures. This
occurs often, as in the conclusion of *Paradise Canyon,* or in the opening of
Blue Steel, with its sophomoric jokes about a newly married couple staying
in the hotel robbed by the Polka-Dot Bandit. When they check in, the clerk
tells them, "Please be as quiet as you can. The man next door to you gets
up at five." Later, the new groom comes downstairs, looking befuddled and
lost. The clerk asks him what he wants. The groom says, "I can't find it."
When the clerk asks what he has lost, the groom giggles, and whispers. The
clerk takes him back up the stairs, asking as they go, "Did you have time?"
This film cannot subject its hero to the same indignity, which Mose battles
against as Mandy Lou pursues him for marriage in *The Lawless Nineties.*

THE BORDERS of romance are occasionally blurred by other forms of
satire than gentle mockery of marriage or reluctance to let the narrative end

in domesticity. Satire may be directed at the hero or at the form of the romance itself, until, if let go, hero and form would become eiron and irony. Anticipating his strongest role in a film of irony, as Tom Doniphon in *The Man Who Shot Liberty Valance,* Wayne plays remorseful, embittered ex-sheriff John Higgens in *Texas Terror,* but his humor is not so black he cannot make fun of himself even in this saddened role. Bearded and dirty, he saves the heroine from bandits, and she faints at sight of his ugly appearance. Later, when he is clean and transformed beyond her recognition, he describes himself as a "Bluebeard," and she agrees. For the young actor to laugh at himself as his character appeared to the lady is a strong performance in this film, and it is a characteristic strength of Wayne's continuing artistry.

There is hardly a film in which Wayne does not contribute modest good humor. Now and then his character is the butt of humor. He may be the straight man to others' comic antics, in scenes of low mimetic humor. In *Riders of Destiny* he must play straight to the comic team of Bert and Elmer (Al St. John and Heinie Conklin); he uses them as instruments of conquest over the villains. The situation is similar in the farce of *The Lawless Nineties,* where threat of his marriage to the heroine is translated into mockery of Mose's trembles at Mandy Lou's relentless pursuit. In *King of the Pecos,* he hands a piece of white cloth to his comic partner; this is to be tied around the arm to protect him from being shot by outlaws. As a magic charm, the device is common to romance, but as it is handled here it is again low mimetic slapstick, because it is held up to be a pair of women's bloomers.

Periodically he is a naive quester, like Percival of the Arthurian tales. As such he may well hold out a pair of bloomers, in simplicity, as his badge of protection against evil weapons in *King of Pecos.* He blushes when his little brother proposes for him in *West of the Divide,* and he would blush if he knew what he was holding up in the "theatrical" scene of *The Lucky Texan.* Here he helps dig out Jake's old costumes, and what he pulls out he does not recognize. He holds it up in vaudevillian style, modelling a bustle. But he holds it wrong, and Jake exclaims, "You durn yearling, you got it in the wrong spot." Another putdown.

The romance quester who must avoid marriage to continue his quests is in a difficult position. That Wayne was able to do it again and again is testimony to his continued success in pulling it off. Whether he is Prince Charming, Odysseus, Percival, Lancelot, or Huck Finn, he undertakes his quests with the seriousness of a true romance hero, even when he relaxes the role to sink a little for the sake of humor. When he does that, however, he blurs the edge of the romance fable, even as he broaches the boundary of his character as stereotype.

IN 1938 AND 1939 JOHN WAYNE played the role of Stony Brooke in eight "Three Mesquiteer" films. He stepped into a part played by Robert

Wayne as Stony Brooke *(center)* with two unidentified toughs in *Pals of the Saddle*, 1938.

Livingston. Wayne proved too big for the role, while Livingston was exactly fit for it. Wayne moved on to play parts which continued to add to his mythic stature, while Livingston never escaped from the primitive romance fables of B-Westerns.

One feature of Wayne's Stony Brooke missing from Livingston's requires Wayne to play many scenes alone. His Stony Brooke separates from the other two Mesquiteers. In *Pals of the Saddle* (1938) he spends most of the story as a hunted man, a disguised prospector, and an undercover government agent; in *Santa Fe Stampede* (1938) he upstages everyone during the jailhouse scene. When Livingston is put into jail, he is a helpless ninny, as in *Range Defenders* (1937), where he proves to be more of a nuisance than a service to his imprisoned brother. Here it is Tucson Smith who is the romance hero. Wayne had to leave this series because he could not fit into a middle role the way Livingston could. Wayne needed room for his character to develop, without diminishing the roles of the other two Mesquiteers. That, however, could not be sustained successfully throughout the series.

When children enter the Mesquiteer stories, as in Livingston's *Heart*

Left to right: **Tom London as Marshal, Max Terhune as Lullaby Joslin, Wayne as Stony Brooke and Ray Corrigan as Tucson Smith in** *Santa Fe Stampede,* **1938.**

of the Rockies (1937), Wayne's *Red River Range* (1938), and *Santa Fe Stampede,* contrast in their characters is at its greatest. Livingston's Stony is not comfortable with the boy Davy in his film. The boy's relationship is cultivated instead with Lullaby, who has the sympathy and understanding Livingston's Stony lacks. In Wayne's portrayals, on the other hand, Stony is beloved by children, so much so the death of the little girl in *Santa Fe Stampede* is particularly touching, because Stony is falsely accused of murdering her. When the boy in *Red River Range* first meets Stony (as "Jack Benson"), he feels instinctive trust in the big man: "He looks like a nice guy. Even if he is a dude." When Stony returns from a hard day's work in *Santa Fe Stampede* to find Julie Jane asleep with her brother and sister, he takes her in his arms and carries her to bed. These images Livingston could not match with Wayne's credibility.

Nor could many heroes of romance in the films of the thirties. Neither Gene Autry nor Roy Rogers could make the break that would have deepened and enriched their B-Western images. If Wayne had been able to sing (we remember "Singing Sandy" only with difficulty), he might have been fixed like Autry and Rogers in the roles which allowed romance to be subordinated

Advertisement for *Three Texas Steers*, 1939.

to song. If Wayne had been more suave and sophisticated, like Ronald Coleman in *The Prisoner of Zenda* (1937), or if he had been more dashing and handsome, like Errol Flynn in *Captain Blood* (1935) or *Dodge City* (1939), then he might have been locked into his image as romance hero forever, like Coleman and Flynn. If Wayne had been even more athletic, as well as more attractive, he might have been imprisoned in the romance story of the far away or long ago, as in the Tarzan stories which overcame the lesser talents of many an actor, including Weissmuller and Barker.

The Mesquiteer films are interesting as timely adaptations of contemporary concerns to the basic romance fable of the stories. They show that art swallows as much of reality as it can manage within its shaping forms. Three of these films manage the reality of drought and industrial need for water. Only one, however, makes devastation of the dust bowl a central concern of the plot, *Wyoming Outlaw*, which opens with the Mesquiteers caught in a furious dust storm in "panhandle country." They flee to an abandoned shack for refuge and there Stony Brooke finds an old newspaper reporting collapse of wheat prices after the end of World War I. Thus he concludes the cause of the country's devastation is the Great War.

Cowboy life is constantly in danger: not just the particular rancher or the particular herd of cattle. The entire way of living in accommodation with nature, with animals and with the earth, is threatened by industrialization and urbanization, as in *Frontier Horizon* (1939). Building dams was a way to control flooding in many parts of America. That in turn was a way to begin better land use programs to diminish terrible effects of drought and erosion. Dams are images of realistic concern with drought and dust in the decade of the thirties. Dams are signs of man's dominance over nature, and they are symbols of controlled power. In *Frontier Horizon* the concluding fight takes place on the newly built dam through New Hope Valley. Ranchers rush to stop the flooding of their valley (in a futile effort), and Stony Brooke makes his way to the control wheel for the dam gates. Stony turns the wheel, closes the gates, and stops the flooding. This is an important image for Wayne's continuing identity: he has superhuman power of control over nature. His heroic power is translated into social-political authority to solve the problems of the people in the story.

VARIOUS FORMS of economic pressure are thus frequent subjects in these films of John Wayne, as they are in most films of the thirties, such as in *Animal Crackers* (1930), *If I Had a Million* (1932), *It Happened One Night* (1934), *Soak the Rich* (1936), *Modern Times* (1936), and *You Can't Cheat an Honest Man* (1939). These pressures are felt at the edges, as in *It Happened One Night*, or they emphasized at the center, as in *Modern Times*. Economic problems are linked with political ones in major thematic ways, as in *Come and Get It* (1936), *Mr. Smith Goes to Washington* (1939), and *Young Mr. Lincoln* (1939). Few American films are more explicit about making this link than five of the films Wayne made in 1938 and 1939: *Santa Fe Stampede*, *Wyoming Outlaw*, *The Night Riders*, *Allegheny Uprising*, and *Stagecoach*.

These are not as subtle, penetrating, or disturbing as other films of the time, particularly some from Europe, such as Dovshenko's *Earth* (1930), the film adaptation of Shaw's *Pygmalion* (1938), or Renoir's *Rules of the Game* (1939). But Wayne's films are vehicles of romance which allow him to offer heroic solutions to social woes by means satisfying to mythic imagination. *Santa Fe Stampede* provides a romance solution to a deeply dark problem of economic exploitation by political tyranny; a town is tied up by a crooked mayor, corrupt sheriff, and decadent judge. It is a place where people are manipulated through fear and hatred, and where law is used to deceive people into thinking they are morally justified because they do things in a "legal" way.

Wyoming Outlaw is a similar situation. It has explicit connections between the poverty of the Parkers and the greed of the local politician, a "tinhorn dictator," as he is called by Luke Parker. The extent of political corruption is suggested by such references as Parker's that "there's no relief for a man that owns property," and Will's insistence that "the right of human beings to eat is higher than the right of game to live," that "the state owes its first duty to its citizens, not to animals." Stony does what he can to affect the politics, primarily by appealing to a higher political authority, where he speaks of "voters dissatisfied, not with their government, but with a man in their community appointed by you."

Over and over John Wayne is the American hero who inspires courage and confidence in the people of his fables. He urges always the principles Stony Brooke calls "freedom and fair play," and it is fair to engage in revolutionary resistance to unfair authority. This is a theme much in the films of the times, as in *The Black Legion* (1936), with Humphrey Bogart in a story of Ku Klux Klan activity; in another Mesquiteer film (without John Wayne), *Purple Vigilantes* (1938); and in an outburst of such themes in *Gone with the Wind*, *The Wizard of Oz*, and *Drums Along the Mohawk*. This last is comparable particularly with Wayne's *Allegheny Uprising* (1939), both set in colonial and revolutionary times of American battles for political independence. These carry with them echoes of Griffith's *Birth of a Nation* (1915), as do the many film versions of Zorro and the Lone Ranger made during the thirties.

Allegheny Uprising pushes the story of rebellion into prerevolutionary days, when American frontiersmen owed political allegiance to British authority, but when they were increasingly restless under it. In this way, Wayne's film is more complex than Henry Fonda's *Drums Along the Mohawk*. *Allegheny Uprising* echoes an increasing complexity of the time when military threat to civilization increased in Asia and Europe. There are enemies on two fronts in *Allegheny Uprising*, the barbaric West (the Indians) and the sophisticated East (the crooked merchants and the stupid soldiers). In between are law-abiding, independent people of the good earth, Jim Smith (Wayne) and his "Black Boys." They are so called because they smear themselves with bear-grease and charcoal when they go on nighttime raids against evil. They use the tactics of primitives to defeat the infamy of the sophisticated, because they desire the virtues of civilization.

This film attacks the stupidity of the military as well as the greed of the businessman. Leading villains are two merchants and a trader; their sentiments are well described when they ask, "What's the army for, if not to protect business?" and "What's government for, if not to protect business? Certainly not to interfere with it." These same sentiments are expressed in another Wayne film of 1939, *Stagecoach*, when the hypocritical banker Gatewood protests, "I don't know what the government has come to! Instead of protecting the businessman, it pokes its nose into business." Gatewood also protests when he loses his military protection, as do villainous Poole and Callendar in *Allegheny Uprising*. As long as they have Captain Swanson, however, they are satisfied, because Captain Swanson is a businessman's soldier.

If war is a matter of survival for civilians who have no other options left
to them, then it must be a legitimate extension of the fight for civilized
values. *Pals of the Saddle,* the first of Wayne's Mesquiteer films, shows him
in his accustomed role as an undercover agent for his government.
However, as Stony Brooke, he is a reluctant agent, blackmailed (as he was
in the earlier *Lawless Range*) into doing his patriotic duty. He does it with
enthusiasm, nevertheless, because in doing his duty he will be helping to
keep war material out of the hands of an evil foreign power. This film uses
much timely material (the Neutrality Act, embargoes on strategic goods,
and smuggling) in its romance fable, in a way familiar to romance form: to
protect romance from attacks by reality.

WHEN THE HERO of romance reaches the limits of his success, when
he cannot overcome evil on his accustomed terms, as in *Wyoming Outlaw*
and *Frontier Horizon,* then the romance structure he serves is in danger.
The hero may have to marry or make merry. He may become a comic participant in the community, rather than be a redeemer who enters and leaves
the community at need. He may remove himself to the outer limits of that
community, haunt its boundaries, become an ironic exile. Two of Wayne's
Mesquiteer films have plots which suggest the limits of the romance have
been reached. *Red River Range* and *Three Texas Steers* (1939) avoid many
of the features of propaganda which invade the other six Mesquiteer films,
as they try to keep a modicum of contemporary "realism" in their content.
Nevertheless, both use their modernity to make self-referential comments
on romantic limits. They show John Wayne as a romance hero restricting
his domain of success to narrow confines, and they show him as a hero with
definite anti-heroic potential.

Wyoming Outlaw* and *Santa Fe Stampede* show romance fables turning
in the direction of tragedy. *Three Texas Steers* and *Red River Range* suggest
an opposite movement, back toward comedy, with twists of irony and satire.
They are crumbling the romance falling away from Wayne's heroic image.
Three Texas Steers is filled with bad jokes and slapstick comic routines. As
serious ingredients of the story, they are signs of decadence in the fable that
employs them and of the milieu that enjoys them. As self-parody, they are
further evidence the romance fable has reached its limit, before it changes
into something else.

The romance of the circus cannot survive assaults by "real" evil—using
the power of economics to ruin the circus. Entertainment turns into flight
from civilization. When the Mesquiteers try to help, they prove to be fools
and befuddled antiheroes. They break the law (stealing Nancy's horse) and
end up in jail with the horse itself. Only because the silly sheriff is their
friend are they able to get the horse to the race, where they win against all
odds and generate the capital to help Nancy get her show back on the road.

The title of *Three Texas Steers* is a bizarre joke against the romance of Three Mesquiteers. This continues into *Red River Range*, where the focus is on Stony Brooke, and via Stony, on the image of John Wayne. The plot of this story is a mix of sentimentality, conventional "romance," burlesque comedy, and the romance fable itself. The result is self-parody, as the little orphan finds a new home and a "big happy family," the marriage between Tex and Jane comes as a "surprise," or trick, marriage between Stony (whose place Tex had taken) and Jane (who thought she was nursing a wounded Stony Brooke, whose name Tex had taken), and as John Wayne becomes the Dude instead of the Duke to entertain sophisticates at the Health Hacienda. When Snowflake is accused of having "seen too many movies," the film itself must plead guilty to the charge.

6. Tales of Tragedy

The range of tragic images is wide and various, from Oedipus and Antigone to Jesus and Saint Joan. Their suffering provides a glimpse of power greater than human life alone can explain; power which is God, fate, destiny, necessity, fortune, nature, nation, or history. Suffering or death of the tragic hero is payment to that power, for a fault in the hero him or herself or in the community of which he or she is a part. The pain of suffering is a measure of worth: the greater a person, more the worth and pain. Wayne is difficult to accept as a tragic hero because his characters are images of such worth, they seem incapable of suffering or perishing absolutely. They present the same problems of credibility as do gods themselves, who do not make the best of tragic personages.

IN JOHN WAYNE'S FILMS of the forties there are clear patterns of tragic experience, though Wayne is not always at the center as tragic hero. He provides a priestly function, spokesman for the community in whose service the tragic heroes suffer and sometimes perish. These films require a binary focus on victims and priestly patron together.

In *Dark Command* (1940) John Wayne is romantic protagonist Bob Seton battling with Will Cantrell: first, for the love of Mary McCarthy, then for leadership of a town, and finally for survival of that town. Will Cantrell is a good man trying to do his best, to please the women he loves most in the world—his mother and Mary McCarthy. He almost succeeds, when enters the meddlesome fool, Bob Seton, who unexpectedly defeats Cantrell in an election for sheriff and almost wins Mary away as well. Cantrell is a schoolteacher, introduced leading his pupils singing "America." He is courteous to Mary, while Bob is rude and tactless. The hero is Cantrell, and he deserves a career of romantic triumphs.

Will Cantrell, however, is too proud and too ambitious. He is not satisfied to remain only a schoolteacher. He reaches for more, and because he does not know or understand himself well enough (as his mother tries to teach him), he reaches for the wrong things to make him famous. When the Civil War begins, he dresses his gang in Confederate uniforms. He serves no state, and he pursues no cause except his own pride. Cantrell sinks into dark depths of iniquity, while Seton rises to heights of heroic leadership. Wayne here plays the role of *naif* arranger, the innocent idealist with power to expose essential character in others. In *Dark Command* he presides over the destruction of a man capable of much good, but incapable of commanding the dark powers opposed to that good in himself.

In *The Long Voyage Home* (1940) Wayne plays one of the queerest roles of his career. He is a sailor, Ole Olsen, making his last voyage before going home to Sweden and his mother whom he has not seen for ten years. Wayne is incredibly innocent and astonishingly passive. The crew is a community of men determined to preserve Ole's innocence and to protect him from corruption. The tale is a parable of the sacrificial lamb, but in this tale the lamb is rescued to reach home on behalf of the others. At the end of the tale, in a scene of desolation, two facts are revealed: Ole made it home, and Driscoll died when the *Amindra* was torpedoed at sea.

Woody Jason is the tragic hero in the story of *The Flying Tigers* (1942). Typically John Wayne makes possible the tragic action for Woody. Wayne's character of Jim Gordon attends the ritual of sacrifice made by Woody. Their plane is hit, on fire with nitro on board. Jim orders Woody to bail out with him. But Woody closes the door behind Jim, then returns to pilot the damaged plane. Jim find traces of Woody's blood on his jacket as he parachutes to safety. When the innocent lamb, or a child, is the victim, then tragedy raises a new dimension of pain, and challenges the meaning of life on a new level of suffering. Victimization can occur in the midst of impersonal disaster, as it is pictured to be in the opening of *Flying Tigers*, when a documentary newsreel shows a Chinese baby crying alone amidst bomb rubble. Here tragedy is an accident without meaning, pointing toward irony of absurd and relentless misfortune.

On the other hand, a child can be the victim of deliberate violence, and the child can redeem life for others by its death. This is the tragedy of the Greek Iphigenia at Aulis, for example, or it is the tragedy of the Passion of Christ: both models explain the tragedy found in *Back to Bataan* (1945). Before the Greek fleet could depart for Troy, its leader Agamemnon had to sacrifice his daugher Iphigenia. Once that was done, the Greeks could depart with the aid and blessing of their gods. It seems a barbarous practice, even when its like appears in the Old and New Testaments of the Bible. Nevertheless, it is a part of the folklore and ritual history of peoples around the world, and it is at the center of the tragic tale in *Back to Bataan*.

One of the schoolchildren who witnessed the shocking hanging of their principal in this film is a boy named Maximo. He is taken in by Col. Madden's guerrillas, where he continues through most of the tale. When Maximo weeps at news of his father's execution by the Japanese, Madden (John Wayne) tries to comfort the boy, saying "war hurts everybody." The time comes when such hurt becomes absolute for Maximo. He is captured by the Japanese and he is tortured to tell where Madden's guerrillas can be found. The boy is shown bloody and beaten, although the picture is naturalistically unconvincing. The *idea* of his torture, however, is powerful. Although he is assaulted here, not by his father, as Iphigenia was, Maximo is tortured by people who claim the Filipinos have "been out of our East Asian family too long."

War is a condition for universal tragedy that threatens the future as well as the present, unless the human spirit rises to powerful assertion. As propaganda, the film challenges its audience not to let the child die in vain. As tragic ritual, it shapes the environment of chaos, destruction, and death around a meaningful center in which an innocent lamb suffers to make more acceptable, if not more understandable, the darkening world around it. John Wayne's role here is again to officiate at the ritual, to give the sacrifice meaning for others, as he restores the sign of the boy's honor when he replaces the lost eagle with another. Maximo becomes the American Eagle and all its represents. The spirit of the boy, like a phoenix, endures through the eagle Madden fixes on him as his priestly blessing.

ONE KIND OF TRAGIC HERO is like Achilles or King Lear: a man of power, of compassion and energy of will, but weak at a critical point in his character. These heroes had a weakness of impetuosity, a tiny fracture in discipline, through which emotions could explode in violence of temper and deed. It is a type well illustrated as well by Oedipus, who could not yield the road to another, and so he precipitated his tragedy by killing his own father out of pride of place. Such a character John Wayne could play with credibility in several of his films of the forties. Looking over these, one can detect a pattern of increasing degree from the mildly impetuous Rusty Ryan of *They Were Expendable* (1945), to the dangerously impetuous Charles Markham of *Pittsburgh* (1942) and Jack Stuart of *Reap the Wild Wind* (1942), to the redeemably impetuous Johnny Munroe of *Tycoon* (1947).

Rusty Ryan is an interesting variation of sullen, explosive Achilles in *The Iliad*. A man who wants to fight, has a talent for war, and sulks when he does not get his way. This describes both Rusty Ryan and the mythical hero Achilles. Rusty is a proud, egotistic grouch. When finally, during the Japanese attack on the Philippines, his squadron gets an order to attack a cruiser, Rusty pays a price for his pride. He had received a minor wound to one of his fingers. He refused to take care of it, and so when times comes to enter battle, he discovers he has blood poisoning. He has to go to the sick bay while his colleagues go into action. At the hospital, he is a bully, loudly telling everyone to pay attention to him. The nurse, Sandy Davyss, strips him of his pride—she makes him remove his trousers. Another nurse describes Rusty as "tall, dark, and obnoxious."

He is rude and boorish, but he learns humility in the hospital. He falls in love with Sandy. The rest of the film shows how Rusty grows in spirit, paying for his egotism and pride of earlier days. He must learn what the Admiral explains to Brickley: "You and I are professionals. If the manager says sacrifice, we lay down the bunt and let someone else hit the home run. Our job is lay down the sacrifice." Although the metaphors are from the game of baseball, the images are from the myths of tragedy. This is a story of American retreat from the Philippines, an episode from a time when America had little reason to believe it would prevail. Because the film was made after the surrender of the Japanese to end World War II, it could open with a reference to those days as a time of "great tragedy." For others to survive, many had to perish.

Ryan was not one of those to perish. He lost his love, since Sandy disappeared when Bataan fell to the Japanese. He lost every one of the P.T. boats, and he lost men under his command. In the end he is almost as naked as a man can be—like Lear on the heath. But when he is most alone, he is at his best. Rusty works for the community now, and like Achilles, he returns to the battle on behalf of others. The irony of this conclusion disguises the tragedies of the story, because Ryan is not allowed to make the sacrifice he so instinctively would like to make. Now and then a sacrifice is wasted on egotism; the more consequential gesture is sacrifice *of* that egotism, which is the lesson of Rusty Ryan.

The lesson is not easily learned by Pittsburgh Markham in *Pittsburgh*. His ego, like Rusty Ryan's, is enormous, but it proves to be more intractable than Rusty's. The story of *Pittsburgh* is that the fate of a nation is put in jeopardy by the faults of one man. His nickname is "Pittsburgh," and so he is a city; he heads a partnership for manufacturing armaments for his nation at war, and so if he fails as a man he may weaken the security of his nation and its people. It is certainly a tale of tragic awareness, even though it is given a positive conclusion. It focuses on Wayne as the faulty, even villainous, hero. He is a lovable young coal miner with ambition. But he is also a braggart, who thinks he is every woman's object of desire and every man's superior. There are many tragic heroes like this in folk tale and literature, including King David in the Bible and the classical heroes Theseus and Jason. All are punished because each of them betrays a woman. This happens in Pittsburgh Markham's life as well.

Deliverance for Pittsburgh is World War II. In time of emergency, his spirit is roused. He goes back to work with his hands. "It is good for the soul to work with the hands," Doc says. Pittsburgh relearns the dignity of labor, of service to others, and he recovers his friendship with Doc, Cash, and Josie. But his life has shown the dangers of egotism, the darkness in a strong man, and the threat of that darkness to an entire community. There was, Doc narrates, "something bigger than yourselves" driving them through

As Capt. Jack Stuart, with Paulette Goddard as Loxi Claiborne, in *Reap the Wild Wind*, 1942.

sorrows and disappointments. Had Pittsburgh not learned to bend, finally, to the power bigger than himself, he might have perished in body before he could recover in spirit. The propaganda of the film, that "the most important word in any language is *partners,*" is a forceful message, because it explicates the mythic theme of *community* and *brotherhood.* The sufferings of tragic heroes open vision to glimpse the importance of this theme.

Whether Captain Jack Stuart (Wayne) ever has this vision is doubtful in *Reap the Wild Wind,* one of the few films in which John Wayne plays a character who dies. But this is a man who deserves his extreme punishment. Stuart is not particularly vicious; indeed, Pittsburgh Markham is more ruthless and more egotistical. But Stuart has disrupted the moral harmony of his universe. He has caused the death of an innocent young woman, and he has to pay his own life to bring the scales of justice back into balance.

Still, his tragedy is more personal than universal, even though Tolliver during the trial had argued that "this case goes far beyond the fate of one man, who betrayed his own command. We must know whether any group of men can endanger the safety of our seas by preying upon America's commerce." This set-speech reminds audiences in 1942 of the threat to shipping from Germans in the Atlantic. But it is not a point developed by the tale of the film. It remains a disaster mainly for one man, who has finally a sufficiency of vision to recognize his responsibility for others. His death is an unusual fate for a Wayne hero, but his self-punishment is consistent with the image of John Wayne as a responsible moral agent. By his death Jack Stuart delivers others to freedom of self-expression, as Loxi discovers when she accepts romantic hero Stephen Tolliver.

GIVE WAYNE'S HERO motive for revenge, but deny him an object, and he moves toward irony, as in *The Shepherd of the Hills* (1941) and *Angel and the Bad Man* (1947). The first turns upon arrival of a stranger in the Ozark hill country where Young Matt Matthews lives with an embittered family of moonshiners. They have trained him to a life of illegality and vengeance. The countryside thinks of Matt's family as the cause of everyone's troubles. Suspicion and hostility are built upon the story of Matt's birth. He is a bastard child, abandoned by his father, orphaned by the death of his mother, buried in "Moanin' Meadow." It is haunted by her ghost, which cannot be put to rest until Matt's father is killed in revenge.

The stranger is Daniel Howitt, Matt's father, though it is long before Matt learns the truth. Matt is instinctively hostile to this man. Gradually, as Howitt performs good deed after good deed, Matt comes to like him, partly at the urging of Matt's girlfriend, Sammy, who has concluded that "past and present go together." She realizes the past has returned to correct an injustice in the present. When Matt discovers his father's identity, he marches toward vengeance. They meet on "Moanin' Meadow" in a pastoral scene of natural beauty. Matt strides angrily toward Howitt, who pauses to draw a pistol at the last moment, and then he shoots his own son — to prevent the boy from doing a deed that would taint his soul forever. It is a twist on the idea of sacrifice, but sacrifice it certainly is, with innocent lambs grazing in the background. The Good Shepherd has become a father who says "vengeance is mine."

Ritual and ceremonial actions of *The Shepherd of the Hills* provide sacred justification for violence to purge Howitt's guilt and prevent the guilt of his son Young Matt. *Angel and the Bad Man* reverses this action. It uses ritual and ceremony to convert a bad man into a good one, to teach him how to grow "right side up" this time, like Young Matt, but it denies violence and eschews the use of guns except one special therapeutic occasion.

His teacher is Penelope, who does things that justify her name (as the wife of Odysseus). She works at a loom placed strategically in the bedroom where she nurses the ailing Quirt. She explains the ceremonies and beliefs of her family. He sees a motto hanging on the bedroom wall; it reads "Each human being has an integrity that can be hurt only by the act of that same human being, and not by the act of another human being." He asks, naïvely,

"Is that Quaker stuff? . . . You mean, nobody can hurt you but yourself? Well, suppos'n somebody whacks you over the head with a branding iron? Won't that hurt?"

Quirt has a distance to go. But he does reach understanding, though it takes a "miracle" to help him. Penny is near death. The doctor has given up. Her condition is the result of a fall caused by a long-time enemy of Quirt, who yields to his old instinct for vengeance. He takes off to find the villain. The doctor finds his patient well. He has no explanation, but he is too old to begin believing in miracles. The Worths prevent Quirt from killing his enemy, and in the end they drive back to the farm with Quirt aboard their wagon, about to become a gunless farmer himself.

This is a story of salvation from tragedy, because Quirt is a good man, as even the marshal admits. Had Quirt continued his life of violence, he might have followed the path of a man who betrayed his own nature. The plot for *Angel and the Bad Man* takes up at the point where most tragedies end—in the fall of the hero. Quirt takes up where Young Matt ended, and so *Angel and the Bad Man* cannot be a tragedy. It is a simple tale of irony and redemption, in contrast with the complex and confused tale of Captain Ralls in *Wake of the Red Witch* (1949), a film of flashbacks, double narrations, and histories before history begins. Underlying the complications of the narrative manner is, nevertheless, a simple tale of tragic loss.

The "angel" of this story is the hero's inspiration to dive for pearls and kill a monster of the deep. And she inspires his resurrection. He, like Young Matt and Quirt Evans, courts death, falls into delirium and needs nursing. When he comes to, he tells Angelique that "something happened to me in the water. The dark turned into light, into singing, and everything washed away. Then I heard your voice." When he came to, he believed he had found "a new world. It is you." This is a baptism and redemption appropriate to romance heroes who triumph over death. But this is not the end of this film's tale.

Ralls leaves and returns to find Angelique dying. He holds her in his arms, tells her he will take her "to a new place, a new life." Dying, she says, "This isn't the end. Only the beginning." Long after her death, Ralls sinks a ship loaded with gold—an act Sidneye believes to be revenge for Ralls's loss of Angelique. Sidneye wants to get the gold, and Ralls takes Sidneye to the site of the Red Witch, where Ralls dives again.

The ship teeters on a precipice. While Ralls removes gold from the ship's hold, a storm creates currents which disturb the wreck. A timber pins him, the hulk tips over the precipice, his lifeline breaks, and he goes down with his ship. Someone says, "She has him now." Images on the screen are a ghostly return of the Red Witch with Ralls and Angelique at the pilot's wheel, guiding it into the sky, to the words of "not an end, a beginning." It is a sentimental display of reward for the death of the hero. It is a reward because Ralls tricked Sidneye into letting his niece go free with the man she loves, so that she should not become "another Angelique." That is, however, incidental to mythical significance, as Ralls rises to his heavenly home with the woman who inspired his heroic feats.

THE COMMUNITY for which sacrifices are made is an ideal as well as an idea. Tales of films in the forties have a special challenge, even an obligation, to represent that community as well worth the sacrifices made by heroes. If community is only a collection of faulty people who use ideals of society as instruments for selfish gain, those persons must be exposed, converted, or eliminated. If the instruments of society are faulty, they must be changed or replaced. "America" is John Wayne's word for the ideal society, for the ideal of community. Sometimes America is a city, other times a state, a territory, or a colony, but always that place is a symbol for values signified by the word *America*.

What is America? It is represened by people, places, and institutions. Movies can "picture" these institutions with buildings (exteriors and interiors), with characters who serve or speak for institutions, and with language which codifies their procedures and goals. These institutions, and the images which represent them, are the ideas which together constitute the ideal of America for John Wayne's heroic sacrifices. He lives and dies for these ideas as ideal for all: he represents America wherever he goes, from New Orleans to San Francisco, from Alaska to the Philippines, from the Andes to the Rockies.

Repeatedly in his films of the forties, Wayne's heroes become involved with institutions which demand his attention. Occasionally they are targets, sometimes they are instruments of heroic action. Most general of these are family, government, police, and military. More specifically are images of social ideals, represented by banks, casinos and saloons, courts, schools, and churches. Public forms of social values imply private domestic ones of family and home, *reasons* for the public ones. Contrasting interiors of *Tycoon* show the luxurious rooms of the Alexander home versus the crude shack with barely more than a bed and a table where Johnny Munroe brings his bride Maura; the bedroom of the Worths is contrasted with the dancehall girls' bedroom in *Angel and the Bad Man*. Home is a place for feeding and breeding.

This is complicated by connections between home and office, love and work. The world surrounding home is tested, the world of work which secures the home for love. This world of "work" is the complex organization of institutional life which promises continuity and community. These work places may be temporary for individuals, but they are forms of permanence for society. They are symbols for universal values which transcend any one individual's notions of right and wrong, good and evil.

OF COURSE the saloon is a place to drink and the casino a place to gamble. They are central to many of Wayne's films. They are places of symbolic power to define the nature of community. They are retreats from domesticity, and they are diversions from work. But they are also testing places where one gambles, risks, wins and loses. They may even be emblems of tragedy—as the wheel of fortune, taking one down as well as up. In Wayne's last film, *The Shootist* (1976), such an emblem serves to summarize the career of the tragic hero.

Wayne is a gambler in several films, such as *Tall in the Saddle* (1944) and *Flame of Barbary Coast* (1945), but in each he is not *only* a gambler. Gambling is a form of self expression, a definition of relationships with fortune, time and nature. Left to itself, the casino is a useful arena for exercising power (spending money), testing skills, and defining character. But when it is manipulated, subordinated to selfish designs, misrepresenting fortune or nature, then it is a place of evil. Wayne's heroes do not condemn gambling, because for them life is a gamble—if the rules and the equipment are not interfered with. Institutions of society, like casinos and casino operators, are caretakers of nature's laws, rules of procedure by which every person has an opportunity to prove himself in competition with others or with fate itself. The rules are the law, and nature is justice.

CASINOS ARE, one might object, not places of work so much as places to play. They should, nevertheless, be taken seriously as places of recreation. They must be seriously administered and honestly proposed. Casinos as places of play, or recreation, are not limited to gambling. Usually they are saloons and dance-halls as well. Drinking and women, then, must be added to the image of the casino, and Wayne's films have a lot of both. There is nothing surprising here because his characters express joy in pleasures of the flesh. When those pleasures are forbidden, they have an even greater appeal. They become a part of his larger game of life: he dares society to open itself, to embrace rather than deny life. Handling liquor and handling women are as critical to defining character as handling a gun, handling cards, a plow, a horse, a ship, or an airplane. This is bound to offend some viewers, but the offense is surely not intended by the metaphors, which are, instead, signs of self-discipline.

Drinking and courting women, like gambling, are matters of playing the game according to rules of sincerity and honesty. Moderation for one person will be excess or insufficiency for another; no one should use personal experience to determine what is just for another. To insure that the personal measure does not become the social, tyrannical measure is the task of institutions, and protection of those institutions is ultimately the task of the hero. The hero must understand the importance of toleration, of selflessnesss, in order to serve the cause of community, but he must also be capable of enjoying the pleasures and privileges of life, by which community is justified. In tragedy, nothing would be lost if the hero did not love his life; his suffering would have no value, if he did not know the joys of pleasure.

Money and banks, gambling, drinking, and sex, are signs and images: images of capitalism, economics, recreation, and pleasure; signs of power, justice, skill, and self-expression. To be meaningful to all, they must be available to each. John Wayne's characters make that point time and again. When nature or society is threatened with imbalance, anarchy that denies the meaning of these things, as in the events of World War II, then the hero goes into action. War is an event different from other threats in degree more than in kind. Thus war may itself be a symbol of cosmic injustice, and political or criminal events may be a symbol of war.

THE BEST THING education can do in these tales is to prepare a person to use natural skills in an honest way through the game of life. Wayne's heroes rarely celebrate formalities of education, sometimes they even scoff at them. But there are occasions when even formal education is an institutional process he must defend, as in *Back to Bataan,* where the schoolhouse is a powerful symbol of human dignity. A Japanese officer tells Filipino pupils and teachers Japan will "put an end to an education intended to impress upon you a sense of inferiority." Everything the Japanese do in the story contradicts the officer's words. After the return of American forces, Bertha Barnes finds, with Dalisay Delgado, another schoolhouse in which to recommence her tasks. Barnes immediately begins clearing the blackboard. In the doorway appear, as if by instinct or by miracle, Filipino children with books and pencils, ready to take up where they left off before the Japanese invasion. And Bonifacio holds out a handful of "free Filipino soil" to his beloved Dalisay.

Maximo is not among the children preparing to recommence their school lessons. He died in heroic self-sacrifice, for the ideals he learned in his school. His death has been well worth the cost, though it has been a high price to pay. He learned his lessons not only from Barnes, but also from Col. Madden, who helped Maximo put into practice the ideals he acquired from his schooling. Madden is the teacher of life, the master of fact, while Bertha Barnes is the teacher of ideas, the mistress of ideals. Together they make a unified team, even in the jungles of occupied Philippines.

Education is of two kinds in Wayne's heroic worlds: the practical and the ideal. Both are important, but either alone is dangerous or foolish. In *The Dark Command* the schoolteacher, Will Cantrell, betrays his ideals to become a marauder. But when Bob Seton decides to run for sheriff, his first thought is to worry that he cannot read or write. He decides to go to "night school" to learn, from Cantrell. Then the "times" erupt around Bob Seton, as "bloody Kansas" begins to earn its place in American Civil War history; it is a time when reading must be secondary to doing, but it is a doing which desperately needs direction. Bob Seton's instincts for doing must be modified, be shaped by an ideal, a dream of a better world.

WAYNE'S HEROES are cowboys, gamblers, sheriffs, lawyers, sailors, soldiers, pilots, miners, engineers, and once even a pharmacist. These heroes answer the call of defense in times of crisis; even when they lose their lives, they succeed in moral victories, for themselves and for their communities. They defend people in trouble, but those people are agents of culture, society, and civilization. Col. Madden protects not the woman Mrs. Barnes so much as her *function* of teacher. When Bob Seton courts Mary McCloud he courts not only the woman but also the *culture* of the person. The world Wayne serves is America as an ideal. American faces are ideas and institutions of America—the schools, farms, ranches, and even the banks; the cities, states, and even the territories. Wayne's heroes court America as the English poet John Donne courted his lover: "Oh my America! my new-found land." Wayne's heroes say, wherever they are, in the words of the German poet Goethe, "In my house, amid my fields, among my people, I will say: *Here or nowhere is America!*"

But the design of the idea would be incomplete without one other. Without God's blessing, America might fail as the gift deserving the heroes' sacrifices. No other image is more frequent in these films of the forties than the church. It is more than a *social* institution. A hero needs to be seen against more than a secular, though universal, background. The church localizes, without containing, sacred presence. A spirit of divinity attends Wayne's heroes, as they discover a need not satisfied by secular life alone.

The church is not a building or a particular place for Wayne's heroic figure. His church is everywhere or wherever he goes. Like Cooper's Leatherstocking or Emerson's American, "the currents of the Universal Being circulate through him; he is part and parcel of God."[6] As for Emerson, Wayne's American hero "likes the silent church before the service begins, better than any preaching."[7] In *Three Faces West* (1940), a familiar pattern appears, as the minister preaches inside a building at the start, moves to the street where he blesses the exodus to Oregon, and concludes in an open field, beneath a great tree, where John Phillips (Wayne) is married to Leni Braun, the camera tilting upwards with the tree out into the expanse of the heavens above. This is where Wayne's heroes commune with God, as everyone does in both *The Shepherd of the Hills* and *Angel and the Bad Man*: in both these films people come together as spiritual community out in the openness of bluffs and groves. Granny Becky's "unveiling," the miracle of her sightedness, is located on "Flying Clouds Bluff," and the Friends' meeting to which Quirt Evans goes with the Worth family is a picnic in a park.

WAYNE IS A MAN with a child's innocence so often it is natural to see him in the company of children. As a child of nature, he is a natural companion of children. But as a man with a mission, a hero of society, he is their patron, saviour, and teacher. They sing out to him in *Dark Command*, where he feels "goose pimples" listening to children sing "America." They serve *him* in *They Were Expendable*, when he searches for relief from the pain of his men's deaths. When *he* is the child, as in *The Long Voyage Home* or *The Shepherd of the Hills*, he is in a conflict with his father or mother. This is so frequently a theme of other films of the forties it shows a paramount concern during wartime. From *Pinocchio* and *Brother Orchid* in 1940 to *The Secret Life of Walter Mitty* in 1947 and *The Sands of Iwo Jima* in 1949, films of all kinds on all subjects were concerned with the theme of generations in conflict, as if it were more critical than ever before. Issues of war sharpened the sense of its importance. It is a matter of high importance in the films of John Wayne. The future is always at stake when the hero is summoned on behalf of community, and there is no more effective a representation of that future than the presence of children.

In *Old Oklahoma* (1943) Dan Somers stands at the outskirts of a powwow between his employer Jim Gardner and the chief of Oklahoma Indians. They talk near an automobile, which Dan is leaning against in casual disregard for the chief and Gardner. His attention instead is for the play of a little Indian boy, who climbs up on the car to inspect it. Dan helps the boy, and he entertains him by honking the car's horn. This little scene, marginal to the main action, is typical of a Wayne touch. When Dan is, much to his surprise, asked his opinion about Gardner's proposition to the Indians, Dan has to say, in the only way he knows how—honestly—that Gardner would "sucker" the Indians out of their rightful profits from oil leases on their lands. This loses Dan his job with Gardner, but it wins him the trust of the Indians. His play with the boy is a sign of his instinct for honesty with people from all cultures.

He is a protector of the Worth family in *Angel and the Bad Man*, though here he learns he is an instrument of a higher will than his own. Before this lesson, he is merely a man with a reputation for being a gun. This reputation will be put to high purposes, but early on it operates in rather less impressive ways. For example, the telegrapher exaggerates the importance of his relationship with Quirt, and it leads the man into physical discomfort. A little more seriously is the impression Quirt's reputation has with the boy of the Worth family, the "angel's" little brother, Johnny. This boy, like many in Wayne's films, sees in Quirt a fascinating type of man the boy might like to become himself. Johnny asks Quirt if he will take him riding some time—past the schoolhouse where his friends can see them together. It is less important Quirt agrees than that Quirt learns from Johnny: the significance of the use of the word "thee." If this were another story,

Wayne's hero would probably teach the boy more of the "arts" of his trade, but the emphasis of this tale is for Quirt to learn humility in himself, not to teach pride of person to others younger than he.

This is a lesson in the relationship between Johnny Munroe and the boy Chico in *Tycoon*, between Joe Madden and Maximo in *Back to Bataan*. The boys look to the men as ideals of manhood and leadership. The men teach the boys values of service and sacrifice. In *Tycoon*, however, that lesson is taught in negative as well as in positive ways, because Johnny Munroe deteriorates as a hero, failing to measure up to the ideals he has represented for Chico. The faith Chico has in Johnny is, like the faith recovered by Maura, too strong to break; it is Chico who is always with Johnny, even when he has lost faith in himself. When Johnny finds no one to help him with his bridge, he retreats in despair, but Chico stays beside him and laments, on Johnny's behalf, "the men are stinkers!"

Children provide focus for Wayne's heroes when they falter, when they need a face for the future. Children are vessels of grace offered in return for the heroes' service and faith. Children are, however, not the primary or sustained focuses of Wayne's films, since he has to act in grown-up worlds (*The Cowboys* in 1976 being a major exception, where children are taught to become men in grown-ups' world of violence). The children, usually boys and young men, complete the picture for Wayne's society as a community that transcends time and place. They look to the future, linking races together into a single image of mankind: from Chico in South America, to Maximo in the Philippines; from the little Indian boy of Old Oklahoma, to the crying Chinese baby amidst the rubble of war-torn China.

8. Tales of Irony

The narrative form of irony requires a point of view that moves opposite tragedy and romance. It is a view of life as seen from "beneath." It examines human experience as a matter of survival, of uncertain destiny. It is a form which shifts with shifts in point of view. When it looks at the idealists of romance, it sees them as grotesques who do not fit into the "reality" of life. When it looks at the dreamers of tragedy, it sees them as victims or dupes of illusion. It may tend to satire, as it measures dreamers and grotesques against standards of prudence, pragmatic reality, and laws of nature. Or, it may tend to gentler irony, as it merges to identify *with* the dupes and gulls of life in a universal condition of absurdity.

Narrative irony is fully realized in the stories of *Don Quixote,* where pragmatic Sancho Panza accompanies the idealistic Don on his adventures of romance through a realistic world. When the balance is tipped in the direction of Quixote, the mode of vision veers toward romance and tragedy, as in *Oedipus the King*; when it is tipped in the direction of Sancho Panza, it veers toward satire and irony, as in Fielding's *Tom Jones,* Tolstoy's *War and Peace,* and, ultimately, Sartre's *No Exit.*

Irony and satire, then, are not exclusively the products of modern sensibility, nor are they special to the problematic perspectives of the cinema. They are in ancient literatures and folk tales with much sophistication and abundance. The ironies of, say, *Ecclesiastes* and *Job,* are as powerful as the romantic tragedies of King David and Jesus, Moses and Paul. The Athenian Greeks who lived during and after the loss of their political power to Sparta so employed the mode of irony they seem to have invented it: from Thucydides' *History of The Peloponnesian War* to Euripides' *Trojan Women,* irony shaped and preserved imaginative perceptions during a period of political stress and dislocation.

The hero of irony is a much more ambiguous character than his colleagues in romance, tragedy, and comedy. He shifts too easily within and between his forms of containment to accept easy definition. He may be at the center of the form, all knowing and disgusted by the fools who surround him, as in Alexander Pope's poetry, especially in *The Duncaid,* or in

Molière's more ambivalent *The Misanthrope* and Shakespeare's Thersites of *Troilus and Cressida*. On the other hand, he may circle experience, hovering or withdrawing to the edge of social order, like Alceste at the end of *The Misanthrope* or like Jonathan Swift's narrator in "A Modest Proposal." The view from the center is close to a comic resolution, where the hero may judge his society by a larger and better vision, as in the stories of Geoffrey Chaucer or William Faulkner; the view from the edges, on the circumference, is close to a tragic resignation, as the hero may hang on a precipice of despair at the evil and absurdity of a society that deserves no better than it has, as in the stories of Edgar Allan Poe or Franz Kafka.

THE HERO TRIES to get home, far across the ocean. Many obstacles stand in the way. Both he and his crew are distracted from their work by the beauty of a hostile woman. Such is a bare outline for the plot of *The Sea Chase* (1955). It is also an outline of the plot of Homer's *Odyssey*, Coleridge's *Rime of the Ancient Mariner*, and Joseph Conrad's *Lord Jim*. The elemental tale of endurance, trial, and alienation is potentially an outline for romance, but also for irony when romance is parodied, viewed as if from beneath. As a tale of the ironic hero, this plot emphasizes the hero as underdog in the exploits he undertakes: he is the little man against nature. If he makes a home of nature, only to find it has locked its doors, then that is a tremendous irony; however, if he, like Odysseus, opens those doors and triumphs in the end, that is ironic romance. When the hero is turned away, cannot return home after his best efforts, that is irony which hangs on the edge of tragedy.

As Capt. Karl Erlich in *The Sea Chase*, Wayne is an ironic hero who cannot get back home. He starts out from the end of the world, in Sidney, Australia. He battles his way to South America, across the Atlantic toward his home in Germany, but he disappears in stormy waters off the coast of Norway. He is, as perhaps he has always been, a man without a home. His alienation is explained as an effect of political causes: he is opposed to the rule of the Nazis, but he is loyal to his native land of Germany. In the archetypal form of such a tale, the hero is a spiritual exile, whose personal integrity is all he has to trust. For the ironist, though, even that personal integrity may dissolve beneath the pressure of an unrelenting, absurd reality.

It is not unusual to find Wayne playing such roles at several points in his career, though it is easy to find as he moves into his films of the fifties. There have been marks of it in *The Wyoming Outlaw*, *The Long Voyage Home*, and *Sands of Iwo Jima*. The war, postwar adjustments, political disillusionment, and reverse-propaganda (in which Germany and Japan become friends and brothers, while Russia and China become enemies and demons) contributed to a context in which tales of irony operate for maximum freedom of imagination.

THE HERO WHO, like Karl Erlich in *The Sea Chase*, is permanently trapped is often a victim of political tyranny, as in Orwell's *1984*, Arthur Koestler's *Darkness at Noon*, and Aldous Huxley's *Brave New World*. It is a part of his trap that he cannot compromise, that he cannot "accept internment." In the end of Orwell's story, the hero does finally yield, and indeed even Karl Erlich is prepared to yield to Napier when Karl discovers Elsa is still on board the *Ergenstrasse;* Erlich, however, unlike Winston Smith in Orwell's story, cannot save himself, or his love. The ultimate irony of Karl's situation is that he is trapped by his own ship (the "heap of scrap iron" welded by "the steel of his own character"): if he tries to leave it, he is doomed by the swirl of chaos that beats against both it and himself.

Orwell's hero provides a dark key to unlock the victim from his trap. He may find himself in a larger trap than ever, in a metaphysical or a political trap, but he is "happier" in it, because he no longer entertains an illusion of escape from it. Wayne's Karl Erlich is too stubborn of soul to recognize he had a choice other than the negative one he made; he might have chosen internment with the "good" side in the war. But to him, that would have been as dishonorable as Winston Smith's capitulation is to the reader/viewer of *1984*. The "Savage" in Aldous Huxley's *Brave New World* may have been closer to the ironic predicament of Wayne's Karl Erlich, but Winston Smith is closer to the direction Wayne's other ironic heroes move.

Brave New World and *A Clockwork Orange* are parodies (both as novels and as films) of the ironic conditions Wayne heroes deal with in his films of the fifties. Although Huxley's novel was directed at the tendency of things in the thirties, it anticipates conditions films and later novels *assume* as *givens*. These are the narrative forms which underlie rituals of irony, from Aristophanes' *The Clouds* to the film version of *A Clockwork Orange*.

Occasionally the ironic hero who tries to rebel against the trap of his world seems more absurd than those around him who resign themselves to their trap. If they do not demand a better world than the one possible to them, such heroes demonstrate strength through resignation or even acceptance. Deeper in the sliding perspective are those who think the people and the world around them are worse than they really are. Such "heroes," like Molière's misanthrope, cannot see the good in the world for the bad in their own eyes. Or, like Swift's Gulliver, they slowly yield to the standards of the world around them only to discover they are truly out of place wherever they go.

In *Trouble Along the Way* (1953), Wayne is Steve Williams, a reprobate ex–football coach who tries to make a living for his daughter and himself by gambling. He has a low opinion and a dark vision of the world around him. When Father Burke (Charles Coburn) tries to talk Williams into returning to football, Williams laughs bitterly at his friends who have recommended him for the job: "Friends who want to save my soul, and get us out

of this unwholesome atmosphere? They wouldn't let me coach at Alcatraz!
. . . Football has become an industry. The price of a good running back
often surpassed the salary of a professor. When some righteous committee
unearthed this well-known fact, it was always the coach that took it on the
chin. I just got tired of picking myself up!"

It is an impossible world in which survival seems to require compromise with integrity, to abandon ethics for combat, and to take from the
weak for the sake of the strong. The only way to win is to be strong, cheat,
and be smart enough not to get caught. It is a game and it is a gamble. When
Steve Williams tries to play, he always gets caught, and he gets caught
because he is too soft-hearted to keep up the necessary poses. His wife and
then his daughter have been the main points of his vulnerability. He cannot
accept his world, but he is willing to resign himself to it, with its faults, for
the sake of his loves. Wayne here is the ironic hero who is defeated,
humiliated, cast out, and yet keeps returning because that is the only way
he can hold on to what really counts for him.

Wayne is less believable as a man who resigns to hypocrisy, but his
medium of popular art time and again required his characters to make that
move which brings him back from the shadows of discontent into the rosy
glow of bland compromise with imperfection. In *Trouble Along the Way,*
the church and religion are made to seem allies of business in a world that
turns to a different rhythm than spiritual: standing forlorn beneath a broken
clock is exactly the right sign of the ironic hero in such a place. Later Wayne
played another character who lives in the shadows, Joe January in *The
Legend of the Lost* (1957). Here there is no child to make him vulnerable.
Nor is there a church to summon him from the shadows into the rosy glow
of social and spiritual communion.

Paul Bonnard (Rossano Brazzi) is retracing the route his father described in letters to Bonnard before he disappeared in the desert. It is a route
based upon close study of the Bible for clues, and the expedition is a
pilgrimage of faith for Bonnard. But when eventually they find the city and
the treasure, Bonnard discovers unreligious facts about his father, who had
been "courting" a native woman. In his disillusionment, Bonnard
unrestrainedly lusts for Dita (Sophia Loren) and for the treasure. Dita turns
to Joe for protection, and Bonnard flees into the desert with the treasure
and their supplies.

Dita is appalled, She says to Joe, "Poor Paul! He was so kind. How
could it happen?" Joe says, simply, "It happens." But Dita wants to understand: "But to him! He believed in God." Joe has an explanation, worthy of
an ironic hero: "I can't recite any Psalms for you, but I know about people
who believe in God. Our friend didn't. He put his faith in his father. A man.
A human being. That's an easy faith to lose. I know about that too. I'm getting pretty tired of this 'poor Paul, full of grace!' What does it take to wake

Tom Tully as Father Malone *(far left)* **conversing with Wayne, as Steve Williams,** in *Trouble Along the Way,* 1953.

you up? He didn't believe in anything but being a big shot with God as a front. I've seen these do-gooders before! Usually doing the most good for themselves. Believing in God is different than drooling over rubies and emeralds!"

Joe and Dita find Bonnard, clutching his treasure but dying of thirst. Mawkishly ironic, Joe salutes the corpse. The "lost" in the title is for the souls of the people even more than for the city of the Bible. The idealist turned cynic provides spiritual rescue for two lost souls of Timbuktu, because he showed them the emptiness of their lives. The corpse of rotting flesh is Joe's savior. He is himself without strength, wounded and thirsty, in the care of the much stronger Dita.

Together they are lost in the desert, where they seem doomed to a slow death alongside Bonnard. But the miracle of plot and film convention repeats itself in this movie just as it did in *Trouble Along the Way*. A hopeful rescue of the ironic hero is manufactured when a caravan happens along the way (it is supposed to be an ancient trade route, we should remember, and so it is often travelled). While that could be acceptable in a world of ironies, the bland glow of sentiment begins to operate here as well: Dita asks Joe

if he believes in God, and he nods silently he does. She tells him to pray
the caravan is no mirage, and he prays. His faith turns out to have substance,
as Bonnard's was exposed to be nothing. Believing in God is Joe's act of
emergency in extreme conditions.

THERE IS A kind of ironic hero who might like to "lose" himself in a
world of ruin and disconnectedness, but who cannot for various reasons *be*
lost. He would like to suspend his commitments, disappear into the fabric
of disorganized reality, and be merely a man. This is the hero who is a hero
despite himself. His ironies are potentially tragic *or* comic; his sufferings
may evoke satire or pathos; and his victories may exalt or degrade him,
depending on whether he is seen from below or from above the horizon of
his narrative.

The humaneness of the ironic hero makes him vulnerable to judgments
of pity or laughter. For example, there are occasions in Virgil's *Aeneid* when
the reader does not know whether to laugh or feel sorry for the heroic
Aeneas — usually these are occurrences in the first half of the poem, when
Aeneas is laboring without enthusiasm to lead his people to a New Troy.
He is always ready to give up the struggle, and for that we laugh at him,
because we know he is destined for loftiness he does not entirely understand yet. However, when he yearns to be dead, to lie in the rubble of his
beloved Troy with his dead wife Creusa, we feel sorrow and pity for him.
He is very human, very faulty in many ways, but he is marked to be a leader
and a hero. His supreme test, once under sail from devastated Troy, is the
love of Dido. Aeneas seems cruel when he leaves Dido behind, and he
suffers from knowing he is being cruel; however, he is also admirable for
sacrificing love, for the benefit of community and history. The ambiguous
conclusion of Virgil's story displays what the hero's trials have cost his
humanity, as Aeneas pauses for a moment before plunging his sword into
the pleading Turnus. The "romantic" Aeneas is transformed into the
"ironic" Aeneas.

Other examples of this hero would include Fielding's stories of Tom
Jones and Joseph Andrews, as well as Bunyan's allegory of *The Pilgrim's Progress*. In Bunyan's classic tale of Christian travelling from his earthly home
in "The City of Destruction" to his spiritual home in the "heavenly city of
Jerusalem" on Mount Zion, the pilgrim is forced, like Aeneas, to leave his
family behind to apparent destruction, as he sets out to find a new way of
life. His journeys take him through Vanity Fair, the Valley of the Shadow
of Death, by the Giant Despair, and through Doubting Castle. At each
crucial stage he is near surrender of his effort, when somehow he persists
and finally triumphs. This "somehow" is divine assistance, and, as with
Aeneas, Christian needs help for his puny humanity to endure. His is not,
however, like Aeneas's, a reluctance of nostalgia; rather, it is a reluctance

of the flesh. He is nevertheless a mere man who is forced to become heroic by spiritual trials.

When the instrument of enforced heroism is divine, as in *The Aeneid* and *The Pilgrim's Progress* (or the Book of Jonah and *The Divine Comedy*), the ironic episodes and ironic perspectives are made subordinate to larger (generic and archetypal) designs that are largely romantic and comic. However, when the "instrument" is a circumstance of "nature," without a discernible divinity in sight, then the design itself may incline to irony, as in *Tom Jones, Joseph Andrews,* and perhaps *Don Quixote.* In these the importance of "coincidence" is crucial for making the man into a hero, and the enforcement of the heroism is a matter of psychology, physiology, and sociology. When biology rather than theology supplies the rationale for fate, fortune, and heroism, it subjects the hero to indignities of nature of the hilarious kind Tom Jones enjoys, or the sorrowful kind Thomas Hardy's Mayor of Casterbridge suffers.

Every so often the hero must be raised above his fellows even when he prefers to be one of them; sometimes he is driven, sometimes led, and sometimes he falls into this posture. In the literature which employs this fabular form, the design may save the hero for admiration or it may condemn the hero for spiritual pride (as in stories by Hawthorne and Melville). In the tales which carry John Wayne's ironic heroes, there is not condemnation at the end, but there may be much from within the tales. He may be a foolish man made heroic by circumstance, but he usually rises to the occasion and he does not disappoint expectations in the end. He may be an ordinary man called upon to do extraordinary deeds, but he does not expect applause for them. And he may seem to others to be a fool when in fact he is an astute, self-sacrificing hero of irony.

In three of Wayne's films of the fifties, he portrays a hero who does not want particularly to be heroic. The irony of his roles in *Operation Pacific* (1951), *The High and the Mighty* (1954), and *The Horse Soldiers* (1959), is an irony of circumstance, point of view, and coincidence. In each his humanity is stressed as a mixture of weakness and strength. The model might be reluctant Aeneas rather than naive Tom Jones, but the achievements are domestic rather than imperial. The films are not the fullest realizations of the model (to be sure), as they are in *The Aeneid* and *Tom Jones,* but they take their fabular structures from the same archetype as do those classical literary tales. Though it would be unwise to argue that any of the three films is an artistic triumph, each does nevertheless contain redeeming features of interest.

"Real" heroes, *Operation Pacific* says, are "ordinary" guys who are misunderstood when they are called heroes by others. If they could escape the name or reputation of hero, they might live happy lives as real human beings. Because the film is so self-conscious, so ironic, the message itself

Left to right: John Howard as Howard Rice, Wayne as Dan Roman (holding Michael Wellman as Toby Field), John Qualen as Jose Locota and David Brian as Ken Childs in *The High and the Mighty,* 1954.

smacks of irony for an audience which knows John Wayne cannot escape the name or reputation of hero as easily as Duke Gifford wishes.

Gifford's problem is the opposite of Dan Roman's (Wayne) in *The High and the Mighty,* where he labors with the reputation of being over-the-hill, of bringing bad luck. When he is introduced as the copilot for a commercial plane enroute from Hawaii to San Francisco, he is recognized by several people in the story as too old or too guilt-ridden to be entrusted with much responsibility. A crewman says he is "the only guy I ever knew who had guts enough *not* to commit suicide." Ambiguous as this is supposed to be, certainly it indicates a potential for irony in the character of Dan Roman and in the fable of the movie. As the tale unfolds, people who seem heroic are shown to be cowards. People who seem cowardly are shown to be heroic. The more interesting heroes are those who battle with themselves, as in the characters of Sally McKee (Jan Sterling) and May Holst (Claire Trevor).

On the margin of the plot which contains these stories of individuals is the character of the sad and lonely Dan Roman. He also wrestles with himself, with his memories of the wreck that killed his wife and son, with his conscience, and with the distrust of other crew members. He is the real hero of the flight, as he keeps calm through disaster, takes charge at critical moments, and instructs the passengers in the reality of their predicament. When a passenger objects to joking about their situation, however, Dan insists "the more jokes the better." He takes an ironist's view, from the distance of experience, on all problems of a life which has lost its (romantic) meanings for him. Dan Roman is the last of the crew to leave the airfield. It is a nice, low-keyed conclusion to a story filled with anxiety and hysteria.

The third example of ironic hero as all-too-human is Colonel John Marlowe (Wayne) in *The Horse Soldiers*. In this, also an episodic tale of military bravado, Marlowe is the leader of Union cavalry raiding deep into Confederate territory. Along the way he meets a Southern lady, Hannah Hunter. They are deadly enemies, though each tries to treat the other as courteously as possible. But in the end, they fall in love despite their political differences. It is a tale that could be found in many of Wayne's films, from *Dark Command* to *Jet Pilot* (1957). There is, however, one extraordinary episode which makes it deserve special consideration.

In a hotel saloon at Newton Station Marlowe drinks as much whiskey as he can, while around him the town is burning, his men destroying track. Wounded soldiers scream during, and because of, Kendall's surgery in the back room of the hotel. It is a scene which, if it were not so degraded by a simple-minded adventure plot and overplayed character roles, would be devastating for its ironic juxtapositions. Marlowe does not want to be a main actor in the "insanity" of this war; certainly he does not want to be a *hero*, a word without meaning. It is a word twisted by circumstance of defeat or victory, since he is no "hero" to the victims of his triumph at Newton Station. Nor is he a hero to himself. He must get drunk to try to anesthetize his feelings. He is not successful, mainly because everywhere around him are signs of his success as agent of destruction and death.

Marlowe leads his men deeper into the South, into traps laid by Confederate forces. The irony is that this is their best hope for survival, as they may be able to reach friendly Baton Rouge this way. *The Horse Soldiers* concludes on a note of defeat even in victory, as Marlowe must leave Hannah behind when he rides to safety across an exploding river bridge. In this also is the ironic sorrow in all things, the sorrow that permeates the world of the ironic (Aeneas-like) hero who would be happier if his fortune allowed him to be, instead, an antihero.

H.L. MENCKEN OBSERVED, in his study of *The American Language* (1919), that "the American, from the beginning, has been the most ardent of recorded rhetoricians." He went on to elaborate that the American's "politics bristles with pungent epithets; his whole history has been bedizened with tall talk."[8] In American culture, men of letters from William Byrd (died in 1744) to John Barth have indulged in a love of language "bedizened with tall talk." Politicians from Thomas Jefferson to the Reverend Jesse Jackson have enlarged upon the American vision with an American passion for enlarged rhetoric (John Quincy Adams recorded in his *Memoirs* that "Mr. Jefferson tells large stories").[9] And America has cultivated a special brand of storyteller in the "humorist," from Benjamin Franklin and Washington Irving, to Abraham Lincoln, Mark Twain, Will Rogers, and William Faulkner. Americans have always dreamed big, and so they have always talked big—for so long they either believe in "bigness" as an end in itself, or they enjoy the pleasures of mocking themselves for this belief.

Americans may let it go in books like *Moby Dick,* where the humor is decidedly subordinate to the epic narrative, or they may express it in many a film which has been caught up in its grandiose conception of itself, as in *The Birth of a Nation* or the two *Godfather* movies. This inflation of rhetoric to match a largeness of visionary self-importance is one of the effects most noticeable in the film work of such directors as D.W. Griffith and Cecil B. De Mille. Hollywood films of the fifties were especially competitive in the attempt to make the "great American film epic": *The Greatest Show on Earth* (1952), *The Ten Commandments* (1956), and *Ben Hur* (1959) illustrate the point. When Wayne made *The Alamo* (1960), then, at the end of the decade, he was again working in a popular genre to meet his public. Any actor who worked in such self-important extravaganzas was in danger of becoming identified with the form (inflation) as much as/or instead of with the substance (vision). Charlton Heston, who appeared as a star in the fifties' films mentioned, is such an actor; because of this, he was a brilliant choice for Sam Peckinpah to cast as his star in *Major Dundee* in 1964 (three years after Heston made yet another "epic" film in *El Cid*).

Against a background of enlarged vision, of national self-importance, and heroic mission, the propensity of American rhetoric can be well understood in both its literature and its films. Is it ironic when Heston plays Moses talking with God, or when De Mille directs "the greatest show on earth?" An American audience could, given its culture, accept the rhetoric of such films as "straight" or ironic. The more distance an audience can get, the more of a sense of proportion it can manage in its view of such film prodigies. The bigger they are, the more distance required. Some which overwhelm judgment on first impression, might return with more or less force on later view.

A delayed reaction is often crucial, then, for appreciating irony, of understatement and overstatement as well. *The High and the Mighty* is an instance of the former, *The Conqueror* (1956) an instance of the latter. Watching such films on the tiny screens of television may actually improve their reputations, because the little frame enforces a vision of the disproportion between content and style. This is an aesthetic phenomenon long familiar to readers of big books, just as it must have been to the listeners of tall tales, from Odysseus narrating his harrowing adventures for the Phaikians, to the Shakespearian actors of *Huckleberry Finn*. The heroes of such ironic experience are heroes of the bombastic, of the big talk.

This kind of ironic hero makes language itself into a tool of conquest, overwhelming the enemy with talk that disintegrates common sense. The talk is a dimension of fantasy which highlights the absurdities of the fantasy itself. The hero of romance barraged by hyperbolical language is ridiculed as if he were drowned in a flood of cold water. Either the hero or his audience is "bedizened with tall talk" in "tall stories" from time immemorial to Homer, Ariosto, Rabelais, and in America to Jefferson, Lincoln, Twain, and Wayne.

In any mode of his acting, Wayne enjoyed being the American who likes to hear himself talk, even when he pretends to be modest about it (as in the role of Davy Crockett in *The Alamo*). His best roles of this kind have been the understated ones, as in *Allegheny Uprising* (where the Professor does his talking for him) and *Dark Command* (where he understates what his villainous opponent, played by Walter Pidgeon, overstates). He takes a risk, though, when he plays a role in which the language is as inflated as the character and narrative. In 1949 he played a character who harkens back to *Allegheny Uprising* of ten years earlier, John Breen in *The Fighting Kentuckian*. In this role Wayne makes transition to the hyperboles of the fifties.

John Breen wearing a beaver hat is a satire on John Wayne in a coonskin cap (*his* version of the Frenchman's liberty cap); John Wayne in the regalia of Temujin (Genghis Khan) is a mockery of John Wayne as John Breen wearing a beaver hat. One difference, for purposes of recognizing irony at work, between the satire of *The Fighting Kentuckian* and the satire of *The Conqueror* is that there is no internal norm of vision in *The Conqueror*. No one in the later film provides the commonsense, unheroic point of view in several characters of *The Fighting Kentuckian*. The ironic point of view for *The Conqueror* is the frame of the film itself—*everything* in the film is inflated: character, action, costume, and, most gloriously, language. The result is a terrible blunder in taste, or a marvelous rendition of the American tall tale.

Wayne is Temujin ridiculing the "heroism" of his enemy. The mockery of his language is the mockery of a man who is no hero, who presumed too much for himself. Buffoon and coward deserve the ridicule of language misappropriated from true heroism. When Temujin is made a captive, he is humiliated and ridiculed. He is tied to a crosstree and forced to join the oxen that pull Bortai's wagon. Derided by his captors, he is a sorry sight of a hero paraded with the cattle before his enemies. When his captors taunt him with words that echo the ones he used to torment Targutai, Temujin responds in kind: "I regret that I cannot salute as I would," he exclaims. "I am bereft of spit! As long as my fingers can grasp a sword and I have eyes to see, your teacherous head is not safe on your shoulders! Nor your daughter in her bed!" Since Kumlek has just announced his intention to subject Temujin to "the slow death" of being cut to pieces, little by little, Temujin's preposterously bold response is absurdly appropriate (as similar episodes make hilariously clear in *Monty Python's Holy Grail* in 1974, where a knight is hacked to pieces valiantly defending a stream crossing).

So it goes throughout *The Conqueror*. Boasting heroes raise language to heroic heights of whopping disproportion to actual deeds of character. Dialogue never descends from those heights — every element of experience is on the stretch. This is particularly silly in love scenes. Temujin begins his courtship of Bortai by tearing away her dress in public, and so begins his winning ways with her (in *Rio Bravo* Wayne plays out a doublecross of this relationship with Angie Dickinson). Bortai answers his boorish manners with boorish language. She tells him, "For me there is no ease while you live, Mongol." He responds, "Your future promises much discomfort!" Smiling shrewdly, he says, "You're beautiful in your wrath! I shall keep you in responding to my passion. Your hatred will kindle into love." This character can say nothing intimate, because the only language he knows is public and in rhetoric of exaggeration. He is a clown, in all senses of the word. When Wayne delivers such memorable lines as, "My blood says, 'Take her'" "Make haste, craven!" "I am bereft of spit," and "I shall keep you in responding to my passion!" he is undressing the heroic image in traditional American verbal ironies.

THE IRONIC HERO may move in the manner of the picaresque rogue, who gets the most he can out of a world bent on keeping him in line. Masterpieces of this kind are, again, *The Odyssey* and *Don Quixote*. However, more obvious are such literary pieces as *Gulliver's Travels* (especially the third book, with its satires on the "system makers") and *Brave New World* (which begins with the irony of its title, from Shakespeare's *Tempest*, and ends with the irony of its hero's desperate act of suicide). The ironic hero as rogue constantly challenges prudential society, its conventions and its ideals, as insufficient for the fullness of life he represents. He puts experience before ideas, and he mocks theory with practice. What matters is freedom for whatever chance and nature allow him to be. He does not run from life, he embraces it; he does not flee to the borders of law, government, and society, he defies all by crossing them with his exuberance and bravado. He will not be contained by other men's systems, and so his constant posture is detachment without desertion.

This is a favorite role for Wayne, especially in his films of the fifties.

Over and again he is a man who will not be contained by anyone's defini-
tions of the "good," the "right," even the "true." This Wayne-hero is almost
an anarchist in his ethic of individualism. Even in military uniform, as in *Rio
Grande* (1950), he threatens the order he serves by wearing that uniform.
The uniform is, paradoxically, a badge of his individuality. Col. Kirby
Yorke's potential for anarchy and chaos is understood by his estranged wife,
Kathleen. She recalls his interpretation of "duty" as destruction of her
family's home: "Ramrod, wreckage, and ruin!" she exclaims. "Still the same
Kirby!" His response is that of a roguish outsider: "Special privilege to
special born! Still the same Kathleen!" Yorke's uniform is the only thing that
keeps him from complete social estrangement, just as his love for Kathleen
and their son prevents him from complete spiritual alienation.

Yorke tells Kathleen "a man's word, to anything, even his own destruction, must be honored," Significance is not in the Cavalry, not in the army,
and not in the nation he serves: significance is in his *choice* to serve. It might
be service, as Kirby says, "to *anything*," even to "his own destruction." In
other words, it may be to anything — or to nothing. The origin of his meaning
is in himself, in the truth of his own integrity; its test is in the giving to
something or someone, anything or anyone. Kirby Yorke is able by his service in a distant outpost of the American frontier to detach himself from the
life of privilege his wife represents. He crosses borders between nations in
defiance of law and public policy, but he does so for the sake of life and,
to his way of thinking, for humanity. His uniform is the attachment he
chooses; inside the uniform is a man detached.

Hondo (1953) and *The Barbarian and the Geisha* (1958) are two
different ways of treating a similar ironic hero — the *ingénu*, the "newcomer"
or "outsider," simple, frank, open, and artless. The structure of the tales for
these two films is the same, to accommodate the same kind of hero: the hero
arrives from an alien society, exposes vice and faults of the host society,
seems ridiculous in his own customs, but eventually charms his hosts into
accepting him as a friend or ally. It is an ancient form of fable, found in the
drama of *The Bacchants* by Euripides in the fifth century B.C., as well as
in the cinemas *Close Encounters of a Third Kind* (1977), *Starman* (1984), and
Cocoon (1985).

Hondo is an ironic version of romantic *Shane* (1953) and *The Searchers*
(1956). Hondo Lane (Wayne) inverts the status of Shane and Ethan Edwards, primarily because Hondo succeeds in winning (being won by) the
homesteader's wife. Hondo successfully challenges the assumptions of his
host community, exposes its vulnerabilities, but he falls victim to its ac-
quisitive power in the end. When Hondo Lane walks onto the Lowe ranch,
he rouses suspicious hostility of its residents. He is met, in fact, by a woman
with a pistol. This woman, Angie Lowe, tells Hondo her husband is out
rounding up stray cattle and should be back any moment. But she is lying.

Wayne as Hondo Lane in *Hondo*, 1953.

Hondo is a man who has "got a belly full of lies." But Angie launches her most vigorous attack on his "silly ideals."

> HONDO: The truth is the measure of a man.
> ANGIE: Well, not for a woman! A man can afford to have noble sentiments and poses! But a woman can only have the man she marries. That's her truth, and if he's no good, that's still her truth! . . . You are good and fine, everything Ed could never hope to be. And out of your vanity, you want to spoil Johnny's chances and mine.

Hondo acquiesces, hugs her, mutters an Apache word for "forever," and thus finishes his "squaw-seeking ceremony." Who has overcome whom? They are, in the terms of the film, "the right two people [who] are going to meet by an arrangement of destiny," as Angie put it at the beginning of the story (though with an irony she could not have foreseen). For his own part, Hondo had early in the tale said "people learn by getting bit." Hondo has been bitten several times, and now he learns a lot. Hondo learns to lie, to live with lies, and to be a lie himself. The film has made "lie" into a metaphor for custom and myth, accommodating an alien ethos to a familiar one. The cost, however, remains a high one at the story's end: Apaches, with their good ways, are disappearing, and Hondo must take his new family to another place to keep its secrets secure.

The theme of "lying" in *Hondo* is a risk for the artist, because it confirms cynical pragmatism or rampant relativism which results from analysis of ethnocentrism. Wayne ran a similar risk when he played the role of Townsend Harris in *The Barbarian and the Geisha*, where he enters an even more alien society.

Townsend Harris stiffly forces his way into the unwelcoming arms of his Japanese hosts, who do all they can to discourage him from a long residence. Harris is the alien invader of classic tales, but he is also the big American who tries to force his will on other people (and, in the context of 1958, it is an allusion to continuing American occupation of defeated Japan). This ironic hero is prone to more buffoonery than Hondo. Harris is, like Gulliver among the Lilliputians, too big for Japan; his visual comedy is a comment on the American value system, stumbling about and around in a country whose values are real and solid but unfocused in the barbarian eyes of the hyperbolical outsider.

The ironic hero typically laughs on the outside but cries within. He may be an *ingénu*, but he is caught in a complexity of conflicting ideas and values, so he must take heroic action to resolve the contending forces around him. He is by his foreignness (his "barbarity") a detached figure; by his presence, particularly if it endures, he becomes committed to his host society. In the example of Hondo, the ironic hero is consumed by commitments until he detaches the entire community to recover his original independence. *The Barbarian and the Geisha* ends very differently, as Harris

marches *onto,* not *out of,* the host society, even though he marches with
hollow victory.

Harris is an ironic hero who suspends the conflict of ideals, values, and
cultural traditions. He becomes detached from the familiar as he commits
himself, emotionally and intellectually, to the alien; he remains committed
to his home and to his past, and so he is permanently detached from the
new and the present. This is the fate of the ironic hero as *ingénu.* If Harris
proposes a future of progress based upon continued social intercourse, he
also proposes a future which will continue to require sacrifices on both
sides, of good as well as bad. That also is ironic.

DECEPTION is natural for the outlaw who tries to keep his freedom
by outwitting the law. This puts the outlaw in the position of outsider, trying
to stay outside the "order" of law. In this he is like Karl Erlich escaping his
British pursuers, who consider him not only a political enemy but an international criminal. He may be like Joe January, who runs up a debt of unpaid
fines (bribes) to keep himself out of jail; or he is like Hondo, who seems to
be a horse thief; or he is like Steve Williams, who drops out of respectable
society to live with dignity at the edge of the law. None of these, however,
would accept the classification of "outlaw," not even Joe January, though he
takes up residence in Timbuktu jail. Nor does any of these accept his world
for what it is: not even Steve Williams, whose place in it is still uncertain
at the finish of his story in *Trouble Along the Way.*

In 1949 Wayne played in *Three Godfathers,* a tale which mixes the plot
of Bret Harte's "Luck of Roaring Camp" with the biblical story of the "Three
Wise Men." Wayne is Robert Marmaduke Hightower, a cynical outlaw on
the run. He will lie, if necessary, to keep his freedom. He allows Marshal
Sweet to think he has come to town, with his two pals, to look for a job (actually, he is looking for a bank to rob). Hightower lies to survive. On the
other hand, the marshal himself *allows* the outlaws to think they are getting
away with their lie, when in fact he suspects them to be wanted by the law.
Hightower and Sweet square off as men on opposite sides of the law. They
understand one another very well. Hightower knows Sweet will do all he
can to capture him and his friends, Sweet will trick him into captivity; on
his side, Sweet knows Hightower will use his wile to avoid capture. Theirs
is a world in which trickery, deceit, and disguise are taken for granted.

Because Hightower is a cynic who takes the world to be exactly as it
appears (duplicitous and untrustworthy), he does not expect much from it
except what he can take. His way of dealing with it is to be pragmatic, prudent, and to hold low expectations. He is not resigned; he battles against
the world of law and order. His journey is an ironic flight that turns into a
return, defiance that becomes compliance. He and his friends meet Marshal
Sweet over the marshal's picket fence, seeing the marshal at work in his

flower garden; they consider this funny and even absurd. In the end, after two of the outlaws are dead, Hightower returns to that world of the marshal's garden to become a prime candidate for rehabilitation into civilization.

The taming of Hightower is an exercise in divine irony, as the outlaw tries unsuccessfully to maintain his outsider's independence, to insist on his cynical detachment, even as he continues to play the game of flight and pursuit. In this tale, Wayne is an ironic hero who adjusts against his will to conform to the world of conventions, but it takes providential power to force that adjustment. Hightower is the happiest man in the community, which gathers to bid him a fond farewell as it sends him off to prison. This is an ironic conclusion to a fable of repeated ironies, which begin from the first moment of the film when the outlaws come upon a sign of the town they plan to rob, WELCOME, ARIZONA.

Viewed then, not as sentimental domestic romance or comedy, but rather as an ironic parody, *Three Godfathers* has a charm of detachment from the social and religious structures, the myths and fables which inform its narrative ritual. The same is true for two later, more controversial, films: *Big Jim McLain* (1952) and *Blood Alley* (1955). The story of Hightower was dressed upon a biblical fable with ancient archetypal force. These later stories are based upon romance structures of heroes who rescue communities, but they clothe themselves in political dress. To confuse the character of the hero in either of these films with the belief systems that clothe him would be as mistaken as to believe that Marmaduke Hightower fully embraces the faith of the Bible he kicks.

Big Jim McLain is an ironic hero with pragmatic sense in a world filled with traps and threatened by liars. His job is to sort through the lies, find the liars, and present them for trial. Jim does not believe in systems of intellectual abstractions. When his girlfriend Nancy Valon (Nancy Olson) offers a psychoanalytical explanation for communists, Jim impatiently interrupts: "Look, I don't know the 'why.' I've heard all the jive: 'This one's a commie because mamma won't tuck him in at night, and that one because girls wouldn't welcome him with open arms.' I don't know the *why*! The *what* I do know." Jim is an *eiron* who sees through systems as poor attempts to shield people from reality. The reality is "*what*" Jim McLain knows, and it is a reality of perpetual menace: "It's like when I was wearing a uniform. I shot at the guy on the other side of the perimeter because he was the enemy." He shrugs off rationalizations and ideals. He pulls back when he thinks he may, in explaining *his* "philosophy," be coming too close to rationalizations of his own: "Or I'll start talkin' politics!" Then he breaks into a big grin of self-awareness.

This movie contains a bizarre episode of a madman who not only provides a satire on communism as madness, but who also dramatizes the *eiron*

snared by ideological bias. Robert Henried believes in the objective reality
of his own ideals, and he is only less dangerous than communists because
he has a benign rather than a malign character. He is sorry he cannot use
Jim as the model for his scheme to make all men look alike: "You have the
right size, but your face, it seems as if you have been struck a blow on your
nose at one time or another. Your face is just not suitable, I'm afraid."
Neither John Wayne nor Jim McLain could be duplicated (cloned by communism) in any scheme to eliminate individuality.

This individuality is self consciously "conventional," the best the world
has to offer in a reality otherwise deceptive, destructive, enslaving, and fundamentally insane. Critical to McLain are not the conventions themselves
("the law," "House Un-American Activities Committee," "the Constitution"). It is important he *knows* they are conventions. The Hawaiian police
captain asks how Mal (Jim's partner murdered by communists) would feel
about "this Fifth Amendment." McLain answers, despite his hatred for all
who use the Bill of Rights to undermine it, "He died for it." As Mal died to
preserve political liberty, so Jim interprets his life's work, even when it costs
him friends and personal comforts. No ironist could do otherwise; he must,
finally, commit himself completely to the task of tolerance. Respect for a
person's right to be silent is easy for one who already believes there are too
many lies and too many words.

One way to deal with this world is to accept even its convention of
madness, the way of Tom Wilder in *Blood Alley*. He is a riverboat captain
in a communist Chinese jail, where he kept his wits by pretending to be insane. He talks constantly to an invisible person he calls only "Baby." Like
so many of the ironic heroes he plays in the fifties, Wayne's character of
Tom Wilder is trapped by an insane world. Everyone around him is a potential enemy, and so he begins with a premise of distrust, even when he is
offered an opportunity to escape jail.

His are exploits and episodes of romance, but Tom Wilder is no
romance hero. He is a scruffy reminder of the character played by Bogart
in *The African Queen* in 1951 (an equally fantastic voyage, to rescue a mis-
sionary lady who insists on attacking a giant German gunboat). Tom is an
eiron, like the Bogart character: a "little" guy against the huge giant of communist China, the *alazon* who blocks the hero from his freedom. But the
bigger they come, the better Tom likes it. In his struggle against the giant
of communist China, he discovers he is no derelict, though he is a vagabond.
He likes the escape plan because it is a skirmish with authority: "A sweet
bit of larceny," he calls it. "A whole village scratched off the Red map and
put down in Hong Kong! Wouldn't be bad, eh, Baby?" His main objection
to Chinese communists has been they wear "stinking tennis shoes." There
is no ideology in his vocabulary. He is a man who knows how to survive,
and this time he takes a whole village with him.

MANY OF THESE FILMS, such as *Blood Alley, Big Jim McLain,* and *Three Godfathers,* cannot be separated from the political and religious themes that govern their imagery and dialogue. They are as much the matter of the films as the Great Depression in the films of the thirties, World War II in the forties. So has it always been in the arts, from Guernica in the painting by Picasso, back to the struggle between Athens and Sparta in the comedies of Aristophanes. Wayne as artist, however, maintained an attitude of detachment in his films of the fifties. His characters contend with prejudices so familiar they seem like images of reality even when they are ironic parodies.

CONTEMPORARY ISSUES obscure the forms and characters of Wayne's films in the fifties. That, however, is a consequence merely of proximity. Earlier films are clearer to those who find it difficult to look past notions they associate with Wayne from films of the last 25 years in his career. Thus *Big Jim McLain* and *The Green Berets* (1968), for example, will always pose obstacles of appreciation for many. Episodes such as those in *The Quiet Man* (1952) and *McLintock!* (1963), where Sean Thornton drags Mary Kate Danaher to her brother and George Washington McLintock "spanks" Katherine McLintock, sear the memory of some to the extent they cannot separate the characters from the actor who portrays them.

Contemporary association with graphic images of imitation not only obscure judgment but also charge those images with currents of feeling that remain after accidental issues have faded from the minds of later audiences. Those same images survive to keep alive and inform feelings for as long as the art forms are encountered. If they endure, they will become conventional, stereotypical, or archetypal, depending on the artistry of the artifacts and the fashions of taste. Just as plots are conventions of mythic action, images are codes for archetypal themes.

The Conqueror is a vision of the world as carnivorous and cruel. People are lice, jackals, and vultures, if they are conquerors; if victims, they are geldings, rabbits, and sheep. Relationships implied by pairings of these animals are relationships of the film's narrative, as Temujin proves he is a conqueror, passing "up" the scale from a louse, to a jackal, to become a flying thing, a vulture. His first victim of the story, Targutai, assures Bortai that Temujin and his Mongol followers are "of no more consequence than lice on a fat gelding." After Temujin captures Targutai, Temujin asks Bortai what he should do with his captive; she answers, "What does the jackal do with the rabbit, Mongol?" Later she refuses to dance for Kasar, exclaiming, "I do not dance for jackals!" Still resisting, Bortai prophesies Temujin will never make her love him: "Before that day dawns, Mongol, the vulture will have feasted on your heart!"

The world of *Legend of the Lost* is a crawly, slinking place. Dita says

men have spent her life "crawling all over her like bugs." She is pictured
with Paul Bonnard covered by spiders. Figurative language becomes
"literal" picture. Dita sees Joe January as a bug or a pig. He sees himself as
a jackass, in a memorable scene of the film. He imitates the burro that carries their supplies, and so he comments on his own idiocy in making this
journey into the desert. But a jackass is an improvement over bugs and pigs.
When Bonnard crawls into a cave in the ruined city, his maniacal search
for treasure takes him, "blind as a bat," into a hole of iniquity and moral ruin.
He will crawl to his death at the conclusion. Dita wants to fall in defeat after
their water supply runs out. But Joe will not let her; he tells her to "stand
up and walk like a human being."

Other films of the period that present low views of life are *The Sea
Chase*, with its rats, sharks, and rotting human flesh; *Big Jim McLain*, with
its red herrings; *Blood Alley*, swarming and stinking with pigs and dogs; and
Flying Leathernecks (1951), with its turtle and chickens. While chicken con-
notes cowardice in *Flying Leathernecks*, a rooster stands for courage in
Blood Alley, where it passes from its useless function as an ornament for the
village communist's automobile, to a useful function as a timepiece for the
heroic Tom Wilder.

Association of Wayne with animals is carried to its most promising in
Hondo, where his Indian background justifies his animal propensity for
smelling people. Hondo Lane's dog Sam is an independent creature, just
like Hondo. Neither "owns" the other; each does as it pleases. But Sam is
killed by the Apache warrior Silva, in a deed of cowardice that denigrates
the Indian. Silva has killed something in Hondo himself. Killing the dog
(symbolically) transforms Hondo from his primitive, animal wildness (of independence) into a domesticated, civilized white head of family.

PEOPLE AS ANIMALS, especially as grounded or crawling ones, are
people recalled to their bestial condition. This may be a funny, comic experience, as in Shakespeare's *A Midsummer Night's Dream;* it may be a gently
ironic experience, as in Odysseus's story of his men transformed by Circe
into swine; or it may be a harshly ironic experience, as in Kafka's story of
Gregor Samsa who awoke one morning to find himself metamorphosed into
a gigantic insect. When the transformation events are episodes of romance,
as in *The Odyssey,* the hero does not fall permanent victim to his animal
nature; indeed, he learns to use it for his own ends, as Odysseus does when
he counsels the Greeks to use the horse to invade Troy, and when he clung
to the belly of a ram to escape the cannibal Polyphemos. Odysseus also once
tied himself to the mast of his ships so he could safely listen to the sweet,
dangerously seductive song of the Sirens. In this episode Odysseus also
represented the predicament of man, bound to his condition as he is, but
Odysseus was a romance hero who can use, rather than merely be victimized

by his condition of bondage. In a tragic mode, the hero in bonds is a victim of sacrifice, whether self chosen or not, as in the stories of Samson, Jesus, and Shakespeare's *King Lear* (especially in the blinding of Gloucester) and *Coriolanus*.

In an ironic mode, however, the binding of the hero hovers between laughter and sorrow, as in the ways Don Quixote is brought home when his adventures end: in Part I, he is tricked into a cage; in Part II, he is hastened to his comfortable bed, where he passes out of stubborn reality into a permanent romance of death. Don Quixote is brought down to earth many times before final domestication and death, but a central, famous episode provides one of the most significant symbols of the ironic hero bravely, absurdly battling against his bondage. Don Quixote attacks the windmills which had been, in his view, transformed from giants into illusory forms by the magician Freston. Don Quixote is a determined romantic who refuses to accept the irony of his predicament, a predicament classically represented in the tales of Ixion and Sisyphus.

For Ixion, there is no relief—his eternal condition is to revolve within his wheel, where he is, as Ovid says in *The Metamorphoses*, both "pursuer and pursued." In films Charlie Chaplin enacts the archetypal condition represented by Ixion time and again, especially in *Modern Times* (1936). The other classical type is Sisyphus, an active participant in the round of bondage, as he eternally heaves colossal rocks uphill, only to run after them when they plunged down the other side. In films Buster Keaton often enacts this archetypal condition, most forcefully in *Seven Chances* in 1925. Ixion is the eternal victim, never released; Sisyphus, however, as Albert Camus emphasized in *The Myth of Sisyphus* (1942), is the perfect ironic hero, the absurd hero, because he can triumph over his task during the pause that comes while he descends after the plunging rocks. In Wayne's films of the fifties, he is sometimes an Ixion and at other times, more happily, a Sisyphus.

In *The Wings of Eagles* (1957), Spig Wead seems at first to be Daedalus, but he turns out to be Icarus instead. When Daedalus built wings for his son Icarus, he used wax to fit the feathers, and so he warned Icarus not to fly too close to the sun. That is what Icarus did, and he fell to his doom. This archetypcal image informs the episodes of Spig Wead's downfalls. He flies high, and he falls hard. Because, however, the pattern of his life is a recurrent rising and falling, he is greater than Icarus, though less than Sisyphus. By the end of the tale, Spig Wead finally resigns himself to his bondage, no longer able to get up and start over again like Sisyphus. The last scene of his story is a sad absurdity, as he, like the encaged Don Quixote, is strapped in a chair. He hangs suspended on a rope stretched between two ships cruising side by side, an old man broken by his mortality and bound as firmly as Ixion.

Indignity of bondage is exploited again and again in *The Conqueror,*
where character after character is humiliated by captivity and enslavement.
Temujin himself is degraded by his place among the oxen pulling Bortai's
wagon. Since his escape is made possible by Bortai, his freedom is
transformed into a new bondage to her. This is like Odysseus's escape into
the arms of his Penelope. It is also Hondo Lane's experience when he is
staked to the ground by Apaches, released by mistaken identification, and
tossed in the dust as the husband of Angel Lowe. Even Kirby Yorke is
brought back on a litter dragged behind his own cavalry horse in the conclusion of *Rio Grande.*

Operation Pacific ends with Duke in the arms of Mary Stuart, but it will
begin again with Duke going back to his duty. The same cycle is only beginning for Hondo Lane when his story closes. It begins because he has found
a family to take West, but it is a cycle because he once had a family among
the Indians. Hondo is the character most like Sisyphus for Wayne's ironic
heroes, because Hondo uses a break in the circle to renew himself. He helps
soldiers and settlers escape Apaches by using a trick with their wagons: circle them and lull the pursuers into a conventional attitude, but break the
circle to burst free for a space — then repeat the strategy until they are entirely free. The circle becomes a spiral, but it remains a cycle nonetheless.

THE IRONIC HERO'S WORLD of cyclical bondages is often a sick and
giddy world as well. Such is Molière's *Le Médecin malgré Lui* (1666) and
Shaw's *The Doctor's Dilemma* (1906), or Samuel Butler's *Erewhon* (1872) and
Thomas Mann's *The Magic Mountain* (1924). Films have dealt with this in
various ironic ways, from Chaplin's *The Cure* (1917) to *The Cabinet of Dr.
Caligari* (1919) to *M* (1932), *Rope* (1948), and *Taxi Driver* (1976), where illness of mind causes or is caused by illness of the world. Universal sickness
of body suggests universal sickness of spirit, in *Nosferatu* (1922) and *Death
in Venice* (1971); a decaying body at the center of a plot may rouse or depress
the spirits of all involved in dealing with that decay, as in *Dark Victory*
(1939), *The Big Sleep* (1946), and *The Trouble with Harry* (1955). Irony is
softened from scornful resignation to stoical endurance, as in films about
atomic warfare, *On the Beach* (1949) and *Testament* (1980), where disease
is universal though manmade. Such responses by art to what Matthew Arnold called "this strange disease of modern life" are the healthiest responses
art can make. As Thomas Mann wrote in *The Magic Mountain,* interest in
disease is mainly a way of showing an interest in life itself. The critic Lionel
Trilling makes a similar point that "we are all ill: but even a universal
sickness implies an idea of health."[10]

Some of Wayne's ironic heroes of the fifties are men who recognize
with Trilling (who was following Freud), that "we are all ill." Dan Kirby tells

Carl Griffin in *Flying Leathernecks:* "Nobody chickens out on this mission because of bellyache. We're all sick." The film uses sickness to suggest something is wrong with the people who run the world where men of heroic spirit like Kirby are restrained from full expression of their resources. Kirby will not accept a psychoanalytic (i.e., abstract and intellectual) explanation of human relationships. He sees these problems as spiritual symptoms of corrupt willpower. He does not deny the symptoms, but he will not accede to the popular diagnosis. Not even Kirby, however, can find willpower enough to continue to fight when he breaks his arm.

Despite the attempt by *Flying Leathernecks* to make the best of a depressing plot, its conclusion is sad to contemplate, as Dan Kirby bids farewell to Carl Griffin. Kirby is broken in will and spirit as is his arm in flesh and bone. Equally pathetic is the conclusion of *Wings of Eagles*, where the hero has been cut down by a heart attack. He has spent his life getting back up from shocks of mortality, but this is to be the last one before death itself. Sickness of heart becomes more figurative than the film may intend, though in *Big Jim McLain* it is a sarcastic figure when Jim refers to the death of his friend Mal Baxter as the result of a "heart condition."

Big Jim McLain is a film permeated by imagery of sickness and disease, so that when Mal is murdered by communist thugs, his death is a consequence of spiritual (political) disease as much as it is a result of a drug overdose. Communists are people with sick minds; patriots, like Mal, are people with a "heart condition." The best corrective to ex-communists is to commit themselves to a life of healing, like the nurse whom Jim visits at the leper colony. Heart conditions are favorite symptoms of these films of the fifties; they are sentimental, but they are ironic features in the syndrome of a sick world. *The Sea Chase* has an old man, played by Paul Fix, who has the ever-present heart condition (as he also does in *The High and the Mighty*). This, however, is but a part of the complex disease references in *The Sea Chase*. Gangrene, which sets in to corrupt the body of the young sailor Walter Stemme, is the result of an amateur amputation performed by Erlich. Stemme kills himself, and Erlich puts his body, along with the ailing old man, in a boat to lure British pursuers into thinking Erlich's ship has sunk. The grand irony of this episode is in its parallel with Erlich's earlier use of rotting meat to lure rats off his ship.

Erlich recognizes, even helps to foster, corruption and disease, but he also has, in the words of Trilling, "an idea of health" that allows him to deal with his knowledge that "we are all ill." Erlich is not successful in his attempts to minister to a world diseased, overwhelmed as he and Elsa are in the end. In *The Barbarian and the Geisha*, Townsend Harris leads the battle to wipe out the cholera he inadvertently helped to spread though his host village. He burns the village in a desperate and ironic act which nearly destroys his hopes of diplomatic success. In *The Horse Soldiers*, Wayne plays Col. John Marlowe, who distrusts physicians and threatens to leave his wounded to the untender mercies of the enemy. He must learn to trust the military doctor Major Kendall (William Holden) before the tale is finished. *The Horse Soldiers* includes cases of malaria, gangrene, and even mumps, in addition to many scenes of suffering caused by wounds of battle. At its center is Marlowe's bitter memory of unnecessary surgery that killed his wife. Despite this, the conclusion of the film is a rousing defiance of sickness and suffering, as Marlowe gallops across an exploding bridge toward freedom, leaving behind him an ironic realm of physicians in command.

COL. JOHN MARLOWE presumably rides toward freedom as he races onto the other side of the river at the conclusion of *The Horse Soldiers*. The image that remains is ironic, an exploding bridge which separates hero from love, and the hero is ironic because he burns his bridges to find new space for freedom. The exploding bridge is a culmination of many explosions and wrecks littering the narrative of *The Horse Soldiers*. They are images with strong archetypal power to evoke feelings of dismay. They are also images which define the strategies of a hero who has to deal with a world of uncertainties, where ideals and ideologies are weapons of survival rather than goals of civilization.

Central images of power in Wayne's films of the fifties are visions of wreck, debris, and ruin. They close the forms of narratives, as in *The Horse Soldiers,* to leave impressions of ambiguity. Or they close with uncertain hope, as in *The Sea Chase,* where the floating bits of the *Ergenstrasse* remain to divide feelings, debris of shattered idealism and disillusioned patriotism. They constitute a symbolic image of the fragmented god scattered across deeps of time and space (as in the stories of Osiris and Adonis from ancient Egypt and Greece). Napier's words of hope in *The Sea Chase* expand out and away from the visible image of the floating debris; the body remains broken, the spirit struggles toward hope.

8. Comic Adventures

John Wayne was always a clown. In *Hangman's House* (1928) he is so
excited watching a horse race he beats a picket fence to pieces. He enacts
the classical comic encounter between man and matter; when confronted
with intractable matter, man is challenged to show he is more than matter
himself. Sometimes the clown outwits or evades the threatening force of his
material universe, as Buster Keaton does in *Steamboat Bill Jr.* or *The
General;* other times, the clown uses the force of matter against itself, as
Charlie Chaplin does repeatedly, as in *Easy Street* (1917) when he has to
teach the bully (Eric Campbell) "respect" for law and order, with a lamp-
post.[11]

Wayne annihilating the picket fence in *Hangman's House* shows none
of Keaton's sly ingenuity or Chaplin's knowing grace, but Wayne as clown
does show the clown's élan, that spirit of life which distinguishes him from
others. He has energy of will to survive, and, more than that, he has a will
to conquer the universe. There is more of an Aristophanic bountifulness of
comic spirit in Wayne than in either Keaton or Chaplin. This bountifulness
trips through fantastic realms in Aristophanes's plays of *The Frogs* and *The
Birds*, in which human heroes (clowns) challenge the gods themselves; they
demonstrate superior virtues of the human spirit by overcoming the laws
of nature. Matter proves to be merely a comic obstacle, not an insuperable
barrier.

This same bounty of spirit, gusto of life, drives Wayne's comic heroes
through a world whose material resistance is the main enemy. He does not
often defeat matter by annihilating it, as in *Hangman's House,* using the
physical strength of his large body to pound his way through the universe,
acting out the absurd fancies of *miles gloriosus*, braggart warrior. Since John
Wayne was a big man, he naturally had to put bigness to work, and once
in awhile he *did* simply match force against force. He might have made his
way in the absurd worlds of the Marx Brothers for zany transcendental
slapstick or he could have kept up with the comic big clowns Fatty Ar-
buckle and Oliver Hardy. Wayne had the athletic skills to put his bulk to
disciplined use in the clown's battle against matter. He used his athletic

prowess to perform his own stunts in most of his earlier films, and this same prowess served him well in his comic duels against an absurd cosmos.

Behind his romantic smile is a comic spirit. He is shy and warmly generous in *Stagecoach* (1939), though grimly egotistic in *Red River* (1948). The comic spirit lies, nevertheless, behind the faces of both the Ringo Kid and Tom Dunson; in the Kid, it is supple and widely tolerant of life; it has to force its way forward, assert itself triumphantly when Dunson finally breaks into a splendid smile after he has been knocked to his rear end. Wayne was a big man with a big spirit, but now and then he had to be put down to find which way is up in the world. Keaton and Chaplin were little men against a big hostile world, and so they were easy for audiences to identify with. Wayne had to earn that sympathy, and the way he did was to eat humble pie, *not,* as in *Hangman's House,* beat the world to a pulp in the manner of the Marx Brothers.

WHERE THE GENRES of his films overlap, John Wayne is at once a romantic hero in a tragic condition (as in *The Shootist*) or a tragic hero on a romantic quest (as in *The Searchers*): the result is a dominance of ironic mood. From *Red River* to *McQ* (1974), Wayne played characters moving at the ironic edge. All of his strong roles had in common, however, a central resource of comic spirit, surely John Wayne's basic reason for success as artist and mythic hero. This will to endure, to assert, and finally to triumph, had to be coaxed, thwarted, or contained, depending on the kind of character and the kind of film to be made. When it bursts out to triumph over all, as in *North to Alaska* (1960) and *McLintock!,* Wayne's essential self comes clean at last. Throughout his last films of the sixties and seventies, this essential, comic spirit repeatedly asserts itself in ventures of reconciliation.

Usually Wayne's heroes do not want to beat the world into submission. In fact, they will go to great lengths to avoid that solution, even in such violently explosive films as *The Sons of Katie Elder* (1965), *Chisum* (1970), and *The Shootist.* John Elder will not show himself at his mother's funeral, to avoid making trouble, in *The Sons of Katie Elder.* John Chisum evades a showdown with Lawrence Murphy out of respect for Henry Tunstall's desire for peace in *Chisum.* Even John Bernard Books, in *The Shootist,* wants to die out of sight and out of mind of his enemies. Such men, however, cannot sustain the tactic of avoidance for long, since that would constitute a denial of their hard-won identities in the worlds of romance, tragedy, and irony. In the best of his roles, Wayne plays *against* the necessity to make frontal assaults on matter and evil. He succeeds because he draws upon a rich comic reserve.

In a few of his films that reserve may be hard to recognize, or it is disguised by his romantic love, as in *The Man Who Shot Liberty Valance.*

Though this film is hardly a comic one, it contains matter of a comic kind in which the world is run by demons and grotesques. Tom Doniphon (Wayne) has little sense of humor when it comes to his "humorous" enemies, Liberty Valance and his sidekicks, Floyd (Strother Martin) and Reese (Lee Van Cleef). These three are barely human, in their caricatures of anarchy. They touch upon the comic because comedy so often denies the authority of law and order, which too frequently represses the spirit of life. Valance and his buddies might well *be* heroes of a comedy by Aristophanes or Ben Jonson, and indeed Lee Marvin is such a comic hero in *Cat Ballou* (1963) and *Donovan's Reef* (1963), along with John Wayne. However, in the *Man Who Shot Liberty Valance*, they are agents of the disorder which leads to death of spirit.

Liberty Valance is Mischief, a Lord of Misrule. He is comic adversary to the romantic hero (Ransom Stoddard) and to the ironic hero (Tom Doniphon). This is a version of the same antagonism Shakespeare pictures in the relationship of Falstaff with Prince Hal, that Milton pictured in Satan's conflicts with the Messiah of *Paradise Lost,* and it is an instance of classic encounters between buffoon, churl, and eiron. In the tradition behind the buffoon of Liberty Valance is the Devil himself, ultimate Lord of Misrule in the divine comedy of Judaeo-Christian culture.

There can be no reconciliation between the romantic hero or the ironic hero and Liberty Valance. Terms of reconciliation are, however, possible between ironic and romantic heroes, though the price paid by Tom Doniphon is ultimately his entire identity. Even in this grimly unhappy world, there is good feeling in Tom's playful affection for feckless Link Appleyard (a buffoon) and rowdy Dutton Peabody (a gentle spirit of misrule). Doniphon shares identity, not sympathy, with Liberty Valance; they are like "twin brothers" who chose different routes. Because Doniphon shares something with Valance, he can defeat him where Stoddard cannot. In Doniphon is what makes Valance a grotesque, a comic outcast, though Doniphon casts it out of himself. If Doniphon were more like the Duke of Shakespeare's *Measure for Measure,* he would liberate himself by this self-exorcism. Both Doniphon and the Duke manipulate events of their worlds. Shakespeare's play and Wayne's film share the same ironic darkness, though Shakespeare's ends with a romantic return by the Duke and Wayne's with a tragic disappearance by Doniphon. His disappearance is an invitation for renewal by those who survive him, however ironic their returns might be.

THE MAN WHO SHOT LIBERTY VALANCE is grave with irony and tragedy, but it conveys a comic spirit *even* as one of Wayne's sternest films. None other in the sixties and seventies is as grim or as dark. *Cahill, U.S. Marshal* (1973) is shaped by the comic principle of evading cruel law, however narrowly done; *In Harm's Way* (1965) shows how inadequately society accommodates the free spirit. Both center upon reconciliations of fathers and sons through understanding common frailties. Rockwell Torrey of *In Harm's Way* discovers his son Jeremiah (Brandon de Wilde) just in time to be loved, before Jerry dies in battle. Everyone who evokes the comic spirit from Torrey is sacrificed in the story. Not even Torrey himself escapes harm's way entirely. The story is a ruthless triumph over comedy, driving away energies of youth and defiance to leave compliance and mediocrity.

Cahill, U.S. Marshal concludes with the triumph of a "straight" world, represented by the law Cahill (Wayne) serves, but to which he is hardly submissive. In fact, the conclusion conveys a bit of the same grotesquerie that finds complete freedom in much comedy from Aristophanes to the Marx Brothers: evading cruel laws. Cahill does his duty to find suspects in a robbery/murder case; though he does not believe they are guilty, he binds them over to the courts for justice. Cahill suspects, but cannot prove, his sons are involved in a crime for which innocent men are about to be hanged. There is low humor in Cahill's way of dealing with his prisoners, but it is the humor of a grotesque himself: a man so obsessed with duty he diminishes his humanity by it. His sons' deviance from duty will bring him to his senses, enlarge his self-awareness, and release his diminished capacity.

Cahill flirts with a conspiracy to obstruct justice. The film is highly ambivalent on this point, as well it might be, since it seems to justify obstruction of the law by an officer of the law. This is the stuff of which much comedy has been made, from Aristophanes's *Wasps,* to Molière's *Tartuffe,* and Jonson's *Volpone;* from Chaplin's *Adventurer* (1917) to his *Modern Times* (1936) and *Monsieur Verdoux* (1947). The law is cruel, and the straight world it protects has little room for free, comic spirits who strike its citizens as diabolic and vicious.

USUALLY STRAIGHT SOCIETY, with its obstacles and blocking agents, successfully resists affronts by the comic hero, whom it forces into its fold or drives to his doom. This is endemic to comedy, not only to Hollywood films that adjust to public tastes and political platitudes. *Cahill* and *In Harm's Way* avoid distorting compromise by depicting society as "straight" only by its own internal standards, though alien and perverse by the standards of outsiders. This keeps the audience at sufficient distance to recognize the severe limitations of a society in which people are self righteous. The comic hero is the audience's touchstone for sanity, as he enters that alien world to expose its inadequacies. This is the method of *Gulliver's Travels* and *Planet of the Apes.* People in that world are made self-aware by the heroes' visits, which turn them from irony to comedy. If, however, liberation only occurs in a problematic escape by the hero, then the narrative is more ironic than comic. This is so in *The Sons of Katie Elder* and *The Undefeated* (1969).

Left to right: Clay O'Brien as Billy Joe Cahill, Gary Grimes as Danny Cahill, Marie Windsor as Mrs. Greene, and Wayne as J.D. Cahill, in *Cahill, United States Marshal,* 1973.

Comedy is contained by Katie Elder's family, sacrificed upon an altar of conventional law and order. The straight world, seized by a respectable businessman, is ordinary order threatened by the high-spirited sons of Katie Elder. Nearly every occasion when these sons are alone together is an occasion of comic revelry and lively affection; when they are drawn into the affairs of the straight world, they are eventually destroyed by that world, which cannot tolerate their happy alternatives. In a lonely cabin where their mother had lived, the four sons rediscover fun and pleasure. John Elder (Wayne) may insist his little brother Bud go to school, but not to "be rich and respectable." Although he wants Bud to learn to spell and use correct English, John prefers to have Bud with him and his brothers than let him become a citizen of Hasting's world. In *that* world a son does exactly as his father tells him, like a good little boy.

There is no *well*-ordered world anywhere in *The Undefeated*, though there are two centers of possibility. They are poles apart, yet inviting one another to unite into something new and better. The two centers are family groups: one a father-son set in which John Henry Thomas (Wayne) has an adopted Cherokee Indian son, Blue Boy (Roman Gabriel), and the other an extended family group headed by James Langdon (Rock Hudson). They are foes in the American Civil War. They are brought together after the war by a common goal, to go to Mexico. For Langdon this goal is a repetition of the American "second chance," to find a new Eden; for Thomas, to find a better market for his horses. Thomas and Langdon find between themselves a better, happy, and comic society than any before or behind. They return to the United States from a Mexico more divided than their own nation had been when they left it, but they take back hopes for a radiant, joyful community.

Before that can happen, the two groups must undergo many tribulations, but they frolic together in a fine comic adventure. On the Fourth of July, Southerners invite Northerners to camp for celebration. Here is a bacchanalian feast of joy, from the basest slapstick of McCartney's adventures in eating, to the brawling fun of "the manly art of self defense," to the pastoral ease of Short Grub reluctantly joining the brawl with his equally reluctant Confederate fishing partner. A rifle shot in the air by Ann Langdon puts an end to the revelry. Sprawled on the ground, John Henry makes his silly smile of approval for Ann, as Langdon quips, "Well, that's civilization for you."

John Henry knows Ann has an instinctive desire, like himself, to be free from civilization. He once had a wife who fled the West for a secure life in Philadelphia, and so John Henry responds to Langdon's remark, "Not like Philadelphia." If he and Ann get together at the end, and it seems likely they will, they will not be heading to Philadephia. Their idea of the good life is in Oklahoma Territory, where he will be free to do the things his wife had disapproved: "When I want to go huntin' and fishin', I *go* huntin' and fishin'!" But his wife "didn't like *that* any more than she liked Indian country, which she hated. And I wanted children, and she didn't like that either." John Henry asserts the erotic interests of his comic spirit.

RAUCOUS COMIC JOY in being alive marks the center of *The Undefeated*. It is a buoyant Aristophanic comedy John Wayne plays to the hilt, even if it is contained by straight societies to which the hero must yield. When those straight folks dominate comic possibilities, they require darkly ironic interpretation. The vigor and gusto of the comic scenes in *The Undefeated*, which reveal essential John Wayne, cannot be long contained in his films of the sixties and seventies. He has short shrift with ironic comedy represented by *The Sons of Katie Elder*. He is on his way out of the alien world of the "new" Mexico at the end of *The Undefeated*, characteristic of the films of this era in which Wayne's comic spirit is twisted by ironic circumstance. He just gets away from the "legal" world of the "straight," in the same manner Don Quixote tries to get away.

Like Don Quixote, such a hero will seem grotesque to those in the world of the ordinary real, even as *they* are grotesque to him with his larger comic vision. Brannigan leaves behind a London awfully twisted to the

American's foreign vision. In the end of *El Dorado* (1967), Cole Thornton limps alongside J.P. Harrah, who is urging Cole to leave El Dorado now that it is once again safely in Harrah's sobered hands. There is little gusto in either film, where society demands too much energy, leaves little for comic expression. The happiest thing the heroes can do in both films is to get out of town.

The same is true for Cord McNally in *Rio Lobo* (1970) and Jake Cutter in *The Comancheros* (1961), characters with élan to make them comic, but in worlds of dominating grotesques, unable to do much to change those worlds. They flee what they cannot redeem, though to say Cord McNally "flees" is stretching the point. He limps away from a community he has helped to save, but its order is not for him; he tells Phillips and the others they can have their town back. Cord McNally's relationship with Rio Lobo is a visitor, as was Cole Thornton in El Dorado. In Howard Hawks's trilogy, the hero's relationship with the town is increasingly distanced, from John T. Chance as sheriff of Rio Bravo, to Thornton as the sheriff's ally in El Dorado, to McNally as enemy to the sheriff of Rio Lobo. The further away he is thrust from the center of the community, the more free the Wayne-hero becomes to indulge in a comic opposition to it.

His comedy must, however, be ironic because the hero does not fit into the town. He works for it, he serves it, but he is not *of* it: even in Rio Bravo, John T. Chance has to give up his place as servant to become a lover — of an outsider. And *Rio Bravo* (1959) is the most inviting of the films' three towns. In *El Dorado*, J.P. Harrah disinvites Thornton and in *Rio Lobo* McNally "gives" the town back to the good guys before he limps away with Amelita, who has a wound to share with him. All three films are marked by a sense of comedy as the hero gets the girl in romance style, with comedic effect.

WAYNE PLAYS various comic roles very effectively, including the buffoon, as in *True Grit* (1969). Rooster Cogburn is, however, educated by his affection for Mattie Ross until he is rejuvenated to become a romantic hero. The romantic youth, La Boeuf, has to be eliminated; otherwise, comic convention in the romance myth would require that La Boeuf not only rescue Mattie but marry her as well. The film belongs to John Wayne's Rooster Cogburn, though, and so he draws renewal from symbolic displacement of youthful La Boeuf. Rooster is too old for Mattie, and it is this disparity of their ages which gives *True Grit* a deeply comic quality.

It is a strange feature of *True Grit* that Mattie Ross seems to be a little girl much of the time, and yet at other times she is a young woman. She is both sexually attractive (to La Boeuf) and matronly distanced (in her business dealings, for example). This ambiguity of sexual status allows the film to develop an ambiguous relationship between Mattie and Rooster, who is like her lover and father at once. As a father, Rooster is a *senex iratus,* irate old man, who stands in the way of young men who court the young women in his care. This is a comic role John Wayne plays to the hilt, and as he gets older, it is a role he plays with increasing gusto.

A number of his films of the sixties and seventies group themselves into a set of plots moved by Wayne as *senex iratus,* and they work out the ambiguities of the father/daughter relationship to channel energies of affection toward socially acceptable objects of desire. One group includes *War Wagon* (1967), *Chisum, Circus World* (1964), and *Hellfighters* (1969). Beginning with Taw Jackson in *War Wagon,* Wayne plays an older man who shows little or no interest in women, young or old, though his role promotes the normalizing courtship by young Billy Hyatt (Robert Walker). In *Chisum,* he plays John Chisum, who sacrificed romance and now protects the happiness of his niece Sally Chisum (Pamela McMyler). There is an "advance" from Taw Jackson to John Chisum, who has a larger concern for the stability of happy society.

In both *Circus World* and *Hellfighters,* the *senex* figure is sustained, even more emphatically, but it is also complicated because it is doubled and coupled. Matt Masters and Chance Buckman (Wayne) have father roles to play. They spend much energy protecting their young wards from romantic attacks, but they are involved in romantic quests of their own. Hence, the plots are doubled by old people repeating the courtships of young people in their charge. The comic emphasis of these plots is made clear by the presence of yet another set of blocking agents in each film, as Cap Carson (Lloyd Nolan) is *senex* to Matt Masters, as Matt is *senex* to Chance Buckman as Buckman is to Greg Parker (Jim Hutton).

In the normal world of comedy, blocking figures of the older generation may represent the law and order which sustain the society of their generation, as in much of Shakespeare's romantic comedy, with Baptista and Vincentio for examples in *The Taming of the Shrew;* in classic film comedy, ritual order shapes Buster Keaton's *The General* (1926) where Johnny Gray overcomes the opposition of "patriotic" father and brother to win Annabelle Lee. Though less common in Chaplin's comic plots, it does appear in *Tillie's Punctured Romance* (1914), *The Adventurer* (1917), *Sunnyside* (1919), and *The Idle Class* (1921) and *The Circus* (1927).

W.C. Fields and the Marx Brothers depend on such a comic plot as a conventional norm to attack in such films as *The Bank Dick* (1940) and *A Night at the Opera* (1935). Wayne's blocking figures rarely propose staunch defenses of the established order of things; indeed, they would rather like to join the assaults with Fields and Groucho. Wayne finds it hard to block access for healthy youth, the way Shylock does in *The Merchant of Venice,* and so he cannot be the buffoon who must be removed by comic action, for the good health of a renewed society. Wayne more often serves as the blocking agent for an alternative society, and so he can be at once a defender and an attacker: he is an ironic outsider to the straight society, but he is romantic patron for a counterculture. His comic roles are therefore of an ambivalent kind, related to the troubling ones played by Chaplin in *The Great Dictator* and *Monsieur Verdoux*.

CIRCUS WORLD AND HELLFIGHTERS are instances of what Stanley Cavell has called "the Hollywood comedy of remarriage." Although Matt Masters (Wayne) was not literally married to Lili Alfredo in *Circus World*, the formula of "remarriage" underlies the soapy version the film gives of marital infidelity and personal disasters. It is tribute to the film that it could so successfully mask tawdry infidelity behind sentimental romance of "remarriage." Matt and Lili *should* have been married in the first place, because they were in love; they should have *re*married when they are reunited with Toni's blessing. It is easy to forget they were never married in the first place, there really was a traumatic event of dramatic suicide in public, and they are not yet married even by the end of the film.

Hellfighters offers no such legerdemain of romance. It is a straightforward comedy of remarriage, in which Chance Buckman has separated (several times, lately for a long time) from his wife Madelyn (Vera Miles). Chance never stopped loving Madelyn, as she never stopped loving him during their separations. Their daughter, Tish (Katherine Ross), however, has grown up without understanding that her parents always have been in love. In *Circus World* Matt Masters protects Lili's daughter as if he were Toni's father, and Matt will not be united in love with Lili until Toni is reconciled to the past. In *Hellfighters* Chance Buckman protects his daughter Tish by remaining at a distance from her, and he will not be reunited with Madelyn until Tish has been reconciled to her father.

Both films are basic melodrama, but this is what happens to ordinary comic plots when they pass from irony into romance. Lovers are separated, engage in sports of courtship, and are united/reunited to begin a happier life in a reordered society. These two films add a dimension of theatricality to give them self consciousness *as* entertainments. *Circus World* suggests the circus is the right location for romantic comedy, and *Hellfighters* shows crowds of mindless spectators watching the dangerous work of oil-well firefighters. The efficiency of the circus and the firefighters depends on comic resolutions of sexual needs.

Hero/heroine leave a straight world, enter an alien one, then return to enliven the straight one, having brought back the magic of the green world. John Wayne plays the role of the "green" man whose proper medium is the magic world of romance (like Circus World, or the Buckman Company). His comedy occurs at the level of the slapstick clown when he has to leave that world for the straight one. Chance Buckman makes an effort to impress

Madelyn and enter her world to be with her. He tries to disband his own company. Then he joins the board of directors of Jack Lomax's oil company, but he cannot abide the inanities and trivialities of that life. As comic hero, he is out of place in an executive boardroom.

On the other hand, when he returns to the dangerous world of firefighting, he ceases to be funny. Then he becomes a romance hero, with smiles of contentment to replace laughter of disturbance. The clown may disappear in the success of the alternative happy community, but the comedy is disclosed in the triumph of sexual love. The *senex iratus* is transformed by this triumph into a happy juvenile, fixed by the frame ending of the film into a permanent principle of joy.

AT THE END OF ROMANCE is comedy; at the heart of comedy is romance. In his comic films, Wayne displays romance as Eros, passion liberated to transform the ordinary world into an extraordinary one. Wayne's hero moves from one region into the other with values gained by the hero for his community. In *Circus World* and *Hellfighters,* movements through wastelands are threatening and heighten the value contained by the circus *in* such a waste and by the Buckman Company *in* such a world that needs its services; happy communities represented by the circus and the company are vulnerable to corrupting influences from wastelands which surround them.

There are a few films of this period, however, when Wayne's hero moves with much greater freedom from worldly corruption. These are the films of his rollicking green world at its happiest. From within such films as *North to Alaska* and *Donovan's Reef,* one looks outwards with contentment. At the center is uninhibited good fun. There is a bit of "drama" in each, with obstacles to be overcome, enemies to be defeated, and happiness to be recovered or discovered as a reward. But there is never any real doubt the hero will be joyously happy. Even in his battles, he fights with good will and spreads cheer for all to share. This is the narrative form Shakespeare found so congenial to his work: the romantic comedy.

This formula idealizes the desires of humanity as happy ones. Its underlying ritual theme is the triumph of life and love over death and fear. It unveils the reality of happiness *in* liberty, tending toward anarchy of spirit in which individuals play out their wildest fantasies without fear of doing harm to anyone else. Triumph requires something or someone over which to rise from conflict. In the idealized world of these comic films, triumph proceeds with smiling, laughing celebration throughout; it is a movement in which all of humanity reaches the shrine of its pilgrimage, where enemies are welcomed back into the fold to share in the feast of life. In *McLintock!* and *North to Alaska,* the villains are more playfully than painfully disposed; indeed, heroes and heroines are dragged through about as much "degradation" as villains. But grand comic visions recognize all are human together: shared vulnerability.

Vulnerability is a capacity for hurt and shame, but in comedy it is a wound of joy when the heroes turn it from weakness to strength. The triumph of the comic hero is a triumph for community and for humanity, throwing away its fear of death by accepting its fundamental weakness of the flesh. To make a ritualistic "carrying out of Death" in comedy is to cast off fear of mortality, to embrace the pleasures of flesh and all that flesh is heir to. Triumph in this ritual progress is really a birth, or a rebirth, of the life that drives all together, but especially the comic hero. Generally a woman embodies this life-force which seeks birth/rebirth in the hero: she is (in mythic terms) the earth-mother and he the sky-god, Venus and Adonis, Diana and Apollo. More commonly, she is the beloved and he the courting lover; she may be the object or the product of his sexual desire, wife/lover or daughter.

This describes adventures in *McLintock!*, *North to Alaska*, and *Donovan's Reef*, though *McLintock!* is especially interesting as another version of the comedy of remarriage. Women who enter the worlds of these films renew the life of their communities though the comic heroes played by John Wayne. They are among the most important of Wayne's "mythic" heroes in this period as well, and so more detailed analyses of them are made in other sections of this book. They can stand here, meanwhile, as satellite examples of variations on a form which makes *Hatari!* (1962) a successful comic film for John Wayne—the form of ideals made "real."

Hatari! ("Danger!") is set in the veldt of Africa. Difficulties of pursuing animals, to capture them alive and in good health, are not matters of much interest. They add local color and "romance" of the exotic. Location is divided into three: the compound-headquarters for the hunting company, the surrounding open space of the veldt, and the distant town. These identify traditional regions of romance and comedy, town and country, desert and forest, civilization and wilderness. While the town has importance in *Hatari!*, it is strongly subordinated to the veldt and the compound. The veldt, in turn, is subordinate to the compound. Both the town and the veldt are frames, circumferences enclosing a center, the compound, which is the heart and soul of the film.

If action occurs in the town or upon the veldt, it is rapid and intense, but at the heart, in the compound, it is slow and easy. Comedy varies with the location as well; it inclines to be slapstick in town, coarse on the veldt, and lovingly sentimental in the compound. The film opens with intense and rapid movement, as the "catching truck" pursues a rhino on the veldt of Tanganyika. Indian (Bruce Cabot) is wounded and has to be rushed to a hospital. Then the story slows down when Indian is safe. Everyone gets drunk, they ride home together, and reach the compound in happiness. A strange woman is discovered in the hero's bed, to begin the romantic comedy at the center of the film's adventure.

The central, normal world of the compound is, then, the comic green world itself; the world outside is only normal to those who accept greater limits on happiness and freedom. In this center is much erotic play and social activity. It is a tight but complex little community of six men and two women. Playing at the edges of the human community are many animals which live in the compound, to provide disturbing irony that animal play is mimicked by human play, and therefore that all are "trapped" together. Happiness in the compound depends on keeping distance from the straight world of the town as well as retreating from the open world of the veldt. The ideals of the compound as a green world are possible, but only temporarily (in the sure rhythms of nature) as a compromise between the town and the wild. The compound is therefore marginal even as it is central. It is an oasis of spirit to which a retreat is necessary in the cycles of life.

WHILE ROWDY GUSTO and boisterous vitality mark the comic world of many Wayne films, especially when they are driven by Eros, the heroes who make their ways through that world are often making journeys of particular and special discoveries. These journeys are narrative devices for expressing mythic form to a search for identity. In comedy the search is fun even when it is difficult, and its conclusion is triumphantly happy. In the continuing spirit of reconciliation, Wayne's films of the sixties and seventies frequently show him on a comic adventure of questing for a son, finding him, and renewing himself in that discovery. This is a most pleasing comic form, enclosing many of the themes of imagination in our culture, from the *Odyssey* to the Bible to the *Divine Comedy*.

Comedy of this kind comprehends irony and tragedy as it employs romance to reach fulfillment. Largeness and vitality of heart are most compelling—to make for a magnanimity that embraces wide differences without compromising the life of spirit. Time and again Wayne's films work for this conception of heroic endeavor. In the pathos of *The Cowboys* (1972) is a structure of this kind, a journey to reconciliation and self discovery, with tolerance and love essential to make the journey successful. The end of that journey was tragic in the sacrifice of the hero, but it was comic in its renewal of spirit that identified the hero with nature itself. The sadness of *The Cowboys* is so strong its comic intent is almost lost even as it brings father and sons together at last. This also informs *The Green Berets*, where the orphaned boy Hamchunk "adopts" Sgt. Petersen (Jim Hutton), but in the end has to be adopted instead by Col. Kirby (John Wayne). There is less of tragic loss in *The Green Berets* than in *The Cowboys*, partly because John Wayne's character survives to promise a new life but also because Jim Hutton's character is comic buffoon, wily and clever in the tradition of Odysseus.

As Rooster Cogburn in *Rooster Cogburn,* 1975.

This Odyssean quality makes *Rooster Cogburn* (1975) and *Big Jake* (1971) into comic films that use the journey to formulate their narrative themes, with Rooster and Jake as versions of the Odyssean hero of survival and return. In Homer's epic story the wandering hero is allied with his searching son to defeat their enemies and establish happy order at home. This is a significant feature of both of Wayne's films.

Both Rooster and Jake have Odyssean qualities, to the point of sharing the special trait which identifies Odysseus as *odyssean:* loosely translated, it means "trouble maker," one who causes pain and is willing to do so. Such a person is comic in the special sense that makes W.C. Fields the comedian who never gives a sucker an even break. This comic hero exposes himself, and others, to injury, but for the significant purpose of finding identity, earning recognition, and asserting selfhood. The odyssean troublemaker stirs things up, keeps life going, and drives for identity though a hostile universe. It is comic because it is a victory for human spirit over inhuman matter.

There can be little doubt Rooster Cogburn is a troublemaker. He enforces law with a vigor of independence that makes him a liability to the law itself. He acts with "excessive zeal," as Judge Parker says. The proof is in the episode which precedes the courtroom scene, a prologue to show Rooster blowing a gang apart during an arrest. This is very odyssean, especially if compared with the massacre of the suitors that concludes *The Odyssey*.

Rooster Cogburn is a linear movement of hero from home to adventure and back again to home. In this it is less like *The Odyssey* than Fielding's *Joseph Andrews* and *Tom Jones,* clear variants of Homer's poem. Rooster moves from a "home" in disorder (both the court and the room shared with Chen Lee), to a home destroyed (the Mission, where he finds Eula Goodnight and the Indian boy Wolf), through a forest of ogres and along a river of monsters, to a conclusion which is a return to home, now reordered and submissive to the comic spirit. In two crucial acts of recognition, Rooster discovers his essential identity: he accepts Wolf as his adopted son who will follow in his footsteps as marshal; he learns to accept Eula Goodnight (Katharine Hepburn) for what she is, while earning her love and respect in return.

Eula and Rooster part company though their parting is really a climactic recognition scene. Eula takes a "sip" with the old reprobate, and she starts to ride away in farewell. Suddenly, she stops, turns, and rides back to this dumpy-looking old codger and blurts out, "Reuben, I have to say it! Livin' with you has been an adventure any woman would relish for the rest of time!" She is proud to have him for a friend who is "a credit to the whole male sex." She is absolutely right. Rooster has a "shining eye" that beams from his dumpy figure. He in turn admires Eula's spunk and gets the last word in the film even as he says, happily, "I'll be damned if she didn't get the last word in again. Welllll— —!" This concluding "welll!" is Rooster Cogburn's "yielding," that reenacts the way Homer's poem ends, as Odysseus yields to Athena, "and his heart was glad." Both heroes yield to the woman's call for peace at the end of a lifetime of trouble.

The return of Jake McCandles to his family in *Big Jake* is another episode in the odyssean, troublemaking, wanderings of Wayne's comic hero. Jake is a loner with a reputation for making trouble, for himself, for his family, and for anyone who gets in his way. In the film's opening he is unable to avoid trouble when he sees a sheepherder about to be lynched, but Jake just can't stay out of trouble—so he ambles down to stop the lynching, and reassert his identity. The episode introduces a refrain for the film, as the leader of the lynchers expresses surprise to find out Jake McCandles is still alive—"I thought you was dead!" The odyssean spirit keeps coming back, keeps returning to life.

This particular hero is an Odysseus with many sons, and his journey will take him on a search for his grandson (really, Wayne's youngest son, John Ethan). Martha is the Penelope who does not yearn for her wandering husband so much as to summon him home: the one man who is "harsh and unpleasant" enough to deal with a dangerous mission. There is more self-conscious manipulation of folk ritual in this story than in *Rooster Cogburn*, where animal names and fantastic adventures are more secure and self-confident expressions of folk imagination. The dialogue and framing introductions of *Big Jake* create the effect of a tall tale for the story of the film as a whole. It is a yarn to entertain exactly in the spirit of Odysseus telling his tales of danger and escape to the overcivilized Phaiakians in *The Odyssey*.

Structures here are journeys of turning and returning, until disorders are ordered and reordered. The happy societies which benefit from these journeys of comic hero are societies which contain him at the same time they lose him. When Rooster finds Eula, or when Jake returns to Martha, the hero comes upon a scene of frightening disorder, though his own world seems beyond or behind him. The larger visions of the narratives in these films contain the films themselves, as the hero bursts into the frames to make them subordinate to his ordering prowess, of crafty energy in the service of free society (free from evil, free for love). This larger vision makes the narratives more pensive than the rollicking, smaller ones of such films as *Hatari!*, but all move with the archetypal force of a returning husband/father/lover who redeems/rescues society/nature when he finds his wife/son/beloved.

THE TRAIN ROBBERS (1973) is an odyssean adventure, with a hero more worthy of the wily Odysseus than any other played by John Wayne. Lane plays more tricks than, flirts with as many disasters as, any other Wayne character in his films of the sixties and seventies. Lane is, however, a special comic hero. He shows his age more than most (more like the characters of the Hawks trilogy), and he shows the comic consequences of being both wrong and stubborn at the same time. In his hero, then, Wayne portrays an Odysseus going to seed, moving through a world of troubles that seem never to end, and always having to adapt to new and trying circumstances. This is the man of "many turns," as Homer calls Odysseus, *Polytropos*.

This comedy is hurtling toward irony. The society of its vision is not only free, it is free to a fault. The name of the town is "Liberty," blown to pieces to show consequences of anarchy. Romantic comedy inclines to show a pairing of couples who wander off to private niches of happiness; *The Train Robbers* shows a breaking apart of the happy society formed only for the occasion, not for eternity. The men summoned together by Lane include some rejoining him, and so their action repeats a basic narrative form of comic experience: a nostalgic return to society. This society of men serves a woman, survives her temptation to fight over her, but in the end falls victim to her deceit.

Lane tries to keep his world free of Eros, a disaster for more than Lane alone: it is a mistake for all of society. And so the final fall of this film is to show the witty triumph of Eros, denied and repressed until it flies away with Lilly (formerly known as Mrs. Lowe) and the darkly leering Pinkerton Man (Ricardo Montalban) laughing at Lane and his men in hot pursuit. If Lane had been less patronizing or more erotic, he and his men would be, if not less foolish, at least more wealthy. Yet the comic spirit does not want to be satisfied with the world. It prefers, like Lane, to run off on yet another mad adventure as the happiest way of the world after all.

JOHN WAYNE PLAYS comic buffoons so often that even hardened Wayne-haters should be mellowed by these performances. Inability to separate the character of, say, Rooster Cogburn from the actor who plays Ethan Edwards or Col. Mike Kirby, prevents a full pleasure of recognizing a classic comic spirit at work. Rooster is surely a fine embodiment of the European folk clown, Punch, a knockabout hero of cartoon violence. Rooster is to be appreciated as such a character in an ancient tradition of "the physical violence and horseplay of the Old Comedy," in the words of Francis Cornford. It may be, as the Judge tells him, that Rooster has "gone to seed," but he is destined in the end to be reborn yet again from his adventures with Eula Goodnight and the young Indian boy Wolf: "gone to seed" or not, Rooster, like Punch, is a crude expression of the phallic sources for comedy itself.

Again and again Wayne portrays the knockout clown with phallic energy, from Sam McCord in *North to Alaska*, George Washington McLin- tock in *McLintock!*, "Guns" Donovan in *Donovan's Reef*, to Rooster Cogburn, "gone to seed." The heroes of Wayne's last fifteen years are rowdies in extravaganzas of narrative action with little plot, apart from mak- ing opportunities for the hero to display gifts of survival in an obstinately adversary world. But, it would seem, "plot" is not the most important feature of comic form. As Francis Cornford observed, "the proper term for the comic plot is not *mythos*, but *logos*. The term seems to mean the 'theme,' or 'idea,' of the piece."[12] The image of Wayne-as-Punch may, then, be the major organizing idea/theme of these films.

The character of the clown emerges from encounters with objects in the world of his adventures: these are objects of fictional "reality" in the film experience (real for the hero, fictional for the audience which observes them) and sometimes they are "subjects" of imaginative perception for the hero himself (conceived through language rather than perceived through action). Governing the images of these objects/subjects is a principle of op- position between *order* and *disorder* in the comic rhythm, which Suzanne Langer compared with "the basic biological pattern" of "struggles to retrieve original dynamic form by overcoming and removing obstacles."

The "fabric of comedy," she said, lies in the pattern of "upset and recovery of the protagonist's equilibrium."[13]

Vital to Wayne's comic action is an image Ralph Waldo Emerson proposed as the "highest emblem in the cipher of the world"—the circle/arc. Emerson stressed the dynamic quality of life as a process of "self-evolving circles" in which "permanence is a word of degrees." In Wayne's films circles expand as they evolve, within and between films, to display thematic progression of enlargement, toleration, and loving reconciliation. As Emerson put it, "each new step we take in thought reconciles twenty seemingly discordant facts, as expressions of one law. . . . We can never go so far back as to preclude a still higher vision."[14] Circles of expanding vision reconcile facts which had seemed discordant, fragmentary arcs of experience. Comic heroes can be agents for reconciling arcs of experience into circles of vision.

RHYTHM between the order of games and the disorder of explosion is obvious and basic to the story of *Hellfighters*, where games of cards and billiards provide ordered rests from dangerous duties of oil-well fighters. The rhythm of this narrative is complicated, however, because explosions are necessary to restore order to burning oil wells. New and better degrees of order follow from skillful opposition by controlled disorder. This rhythm of alternating disorders produces a human community of emotional order and happy reconciliations.

Dynamite explosions are used in the Hawks trilogy of *Rio Bravo, El Dorado,* and *Rio Lobo* in ways paradoxically constructive. The number of Wayne's films which conclude with explosions of evil and old disorder is impressive. Besides the Hawks trilogy, so do *The Comancheros, The Sons of Katie Elder, War Wagon, Hellfighters, The Train Robbers,* and *Rooster Cogburn. Chisum* ends with a purging of Lincoln County by, appropriately enough, a cattle stampede; even this was initiated by Billy's intention to steal dynamite from John Chisum's merchandise store.

The power and desire to blow things up with dynamite or nitroglycerin, to burn and rebuild, are so frequent and so dominating they suggest symbolic force as much as narrative device. they are expressions of infantile, primal urges to destroy opposition, force surrender, and reshape reality. This power is not always in the service of a stronger will to create, as in *Hellfighters;* occasionally it is merely defensive and barely survivable, as in *The Train Robbers.* But it is always a dramatic way to clear out the old, to make space for new starts.

Breaking down beds is a repeated image in these films, almost a counterpoint to breaking glass and breaking out of jail. Sometimes the bedroom scenes are less "explosive," but just as suggestive, as in the risque episode of *Rio Lobo,* when McNally holds the unconscious Shasta DeLaney in his arms, asking rather pathetically, "What'll I do with her?" then carries her up to a bedroom where Cordona has been "sleeping" with another woman; they toss for the privilege of undressing Shasta, put her in bed, and wait for her to awaken—in the (symbolic) nude. Rooster Cogburn sprawls out on his ragged bed of decadence, unable and uninterested in female companionship. But the most delightful of such jejune bedroom humor is in the more ambivalent images of the broken beds in *The Quiet Man, Hatari!*, and *Circus World*. These are hints of disaster at the heart of creativity, breaking before making.

As bedroom vitality explodes, so does graveyard solemnity force a pause in narrative action. In *The Searchers* and *Chisum*, Wayne plays a man impatient with rituals of death. In *The Sons of Katie Elder* and *Donovan's Reef*, monuments to the dead are significant motives for heroic action. But the most comic adventure of graveyard antics occurs in *Cahill, U.S. Marshal:* here "ghosts" ride in slow motion to frighten children, but spirit is brought down to earth in a forceful way when both ghosts are thrown from their horses and one breaks his leg. Cahill has to walk, leading his horse with the wounded Indian until Cahill buys a mule for himself later on.

Even the mule bucks and poor Cahill is again humiliated, or better, humbled, by the facts of his heavy mortality. Wayne is repeatedly put through this ritual of humility, either bucked from his horse or forced to ride the lowly mule. Besides *Cahill*, this occurs in *The Comancheros, Big Jake*, and *The Train Robbers,* with a variant in *Circus World*. Such episodes are images of the clown brought down to earth, of the hero submitting to his mortality. Breaking of will and pride keep the spirit flexible and elastic, springing back to reassert discipline and restraint time and again.

Counter rhythms of discipline and disaster, restraint and collapse, are developed in group actions of dancing and brawling, both ancient traditions of folk comedy. The rowdy hijinks of *The Undefeated* mix dancing and brawling with feasting to create a milieu of high, good humor in the story's growth toward revived brotherhood and national identity. The accelerating chaos of *Chisum* is barely restrained by courtesies of dancing; indeed, the dancing itself contains the seeds of chaos, as John Chisum inadvertently introduces Billy the Kid to his niece at his welcome-home dance for her. Scenes of tenderness are captured by images of dancing in both *Hatari!* and *Circus World*. In *Hatari!* especially the intimate, happy dancing of the hunters at home is often counterpointed with energies unleashed in fights and hunting.

Whatever disordering process he passes through, Wayne's hero must make that journey, as he ventures from one level or circle or order into another. This passage is ritualistic in its conventions of form, and it is purgatorial in its form of significance. It occurs in many settings and it employs many images of communication, from shattering glass to broken beds, from bucking horses to barroom brawls. When the hero rises from his fall, he is like Antaeus, a new Adam on his way to fresh adventures and renewed dedications.

TO BE ALWAYS on the move, pausing for rest, to collect strength and wit, and then pressing ahead: this is the nature of the American hero, driven by his comic vision and romantic optimism to overcome and outwit the obstacles of an ironic world with tragic faults. This hero must keep in mind the counsel of Ralph Waldo Emerson, that "everything is medial" for one who knows that life "is a self-evolving circle." When he pauses, the hero must be careful his circle does not harden into a prison; he must keep his soul "quick and strong to burst over that boundary on all sides and expand another orbit on the great deep," again as Emerson put it. To such a person, who is the American hero, "the only sin is limitaton."[15]

John Wayne's heroes are, in their vigor of self reliance, constantly testing the Emersonian thesis. Wayne's heroes know the difficulty of maintaining this vigor, that it involves much falling, some sliding, and a steady press against the tightening circles of society and nature. The imagery of circles is put to severe testing in Wayne's later films, because these are stories of reconciliation. The test is in the temptation to interpret reconciliation as resignation or surrender, rather than a coming together. This "coming together" is to make, figuratively, a new circle, one larger than anyone alone can make. Evolution proceeds through reconciliation, breaking old circles, merging new ones, and enlarging human spirit through the communion that makes community. The hero has to recognize "the only sin is limitation," old circles must be broken because "everything is medial," and become himself the means to enlargement.

Emerson wrote that "the eye is the first circle; the horizon which it forms is the second." Close-up shots establish the first circle with monotonous frequency, and so do long shots, especially of Western landscapes, establish the second even more tediously. However, of special interest is the unusual attention given to the Wayne hero whose eyesight is threatened by old age in *Big Jake*, and whose horizon is blurring around him in *The Undefeated* and *Chisum*.

BREAKING CIRCLES are complex statements in *War Wagon* and *The Train Robbers*, which saves most of its breaking for an apocalyptic conclusion, when Lane and his gang blow up the train-stop town of Liberty. Most everything is annihilated, including a pair of rocking chairs and a windmill. Grady and Jesse (Rod Taylor and Ben Johnson) are happy to follow their friend Lane on these adventures, because they want to be saved from the fate of old age represented by the empty rocking chairs. Like Jake Cutter of *The Comancheros*, these men in *The Train Robbers* must keep moving or they will be fixed by time and nature until they die. The heroic spirit will

not let them rest; the comic heroic spirit will not let them die of boredom.
They cannot escape the wheel itself, but they do all they can to keep it
turning.

War Wagon is replete with circle emblems, from the racing wheels of
the war wagon itself to the glass wheel of fortune broken in a barroom
brawl. A gun turret tops the war wagon, and barrels of flour conceal stolen
gold. The gun turret is a secret addition, its building a rhythmic event of
the narrative until it is rolled out in its intimidating power. Comically, it is
to be broken apart on its only mission. This breaking is the work of a prudent comic hero, who has put together a comic crew of villains to do this
deed of larceny and justice. Taw Jackson (Wayne) needs all his Emersonian
prudence to make his gang work together and accomplish its mission of
destruction and retrieval.

A last "circle" of the Emersonian hero is in the formal relationships of
conversation. Although, Emerson wrote, "silence is better," discourse is
good. It is a "game of circles" in which "each new speaker strikes a new
light" to free himself from the smaller "circle" of the last speaker. Much in
the character of the Western hero is an affirmation of Emerson's point,
especially about the preference for "silence." The laconic Westerner is
legendary, and Wayne's characters have contributed much to the legend.
The hero knows the proper rhythm, knows when to be silent, when to talk,
and when to listen: this is in accord with his principle of prudence. At the
right moment the virtue of silence "expresses" itself as the virtue of speech;
communion of spirit becomes communication.

These moments are special in Wayne's films, especially in this last era
of his career. They are insights into the paradox of the American, Emersonian character: it is self-reliant, independent, and silent, yet there is at its
center an emptiness, a longing for fulfillment through others. Friends and
family satisfy this longing, though service to the nation is a frequent abstract
expression of the need. More interesting, as more demanding, are satisfactions of fighting and reconciliation with enemies. A worthy adversary can
be as appealing for companionship as a sympathetic friend or family.

In *Cahill, U.S. Marshal*, Cahill teaches his son the respect he must have
for all human beings, and Cahill himself learns how to reach out to find the
family he has almost lost through his devotion to duty. In a tender moment
of conversation that expands the spirit of a Wayne hero, Cahill talks with
his son Danny while they wait anxiously to learn if the little boy Billy Joe
is going to live:

DANNY: Pa! You ain't never around.
CAHILL: You're dead right, Daniel. I can't argue that. I been gone a lot
of times when you kids really needed me. And I've missed a lot. . . . I
don't want what I'm saying to sound like I'm making excuses. There's
no excuse for negligence! No excuse for a man ignorin' his duty either.

Your mother, God bless her, when she was dyin', the last thing she said on earth was, "go get 'em, J.D.!" And I been goin' and gettin' 'em ever since, till it's no longer just my job. It's part of my life. And that's what I want you to try to understand son. Your old man's life. You give it a try?

DANNY: Yeah, Pa. I'll try.

CAHILL: I'm glad. Cause even grown men need understanding.

The essence of silence emerges because it is talk of reconciliation and confession of need, understated in subdued tones of humility. The camera angle and distance on Wayne/Cahill's face in tilted profile, tight closeups, mark a man bent to learn, and learn he does even as his sons learn through him. They learn together through many, sometimes vicious, mistakes. Cahill's friend/foe, the Indian Lightfoot, articulates their learning. He tells Cahill, afraid he has lost his sons because he has failed them, "There ain' *nothin'* too late! If you love it."

Circles of conversation expand the spirit not only in *The Undefeated* and *Cahill*. They stretch out across these films toward audiences then and now, as Wayne the actor determined to bridge gaps of division within America, between himself and those in his audience who distrusted or disliked him and what he stood for. The artist in the man used techniques of tone and scene to establish moments of intimacy with audiences of the films as well as in the films—techniques which, at their best, identify the wisdom of silence with the form of utterance. Wayne was drawing yet a new circle in these films, hoping for that sign of growth marked by Emerson long ago: "A man's growth is seen in the successive choirs of his friends."

Part III
John Wayne: Hero

9. "The Hero with a Thousand Faces"

John Wayne is, in the words of Joseph Campbell, a "hero with a thousand faces."[16] He has spoken to cinema audiences around the world; he has articulated a mythic adventure with universal appeal. The faces of John Wayne are heroic characters he created. Wayne's was a persistence of character from film to film. This gave an *essence* to his identity, a continuity which made him transcend his films. Wayne is distinguished by dexterity of adaptation without abandoning his essential core of identity. John Wayne remained himself even as he changed roles, but when he changed roles, he grew in character and enlarged his identity. In this cumulative force acquired through his career lies the mythic dimension of the name "John Wayne." The star's name keeps the hero alive, while the man's name (Marion Michael Morrison) has largely disappeared with his death.

From role to role John Wayne takes his continuing image, growing as he changes "faces" to create, finally, a monomyth: the hero moves from alienation through trial to victory and return. The myth of John Wayne is larger than any single role in any single film. As a whole, out of time, his films constitute not only a canon of accomplishment, they also compose themselves into a mythic *pattern* that marks them, and his career, as the matter of folklore and folk art.

The appearance of the "star" is an aesthetic experience of essence incarnated. Successive reappearances are successive reincarnations, transfigurations of the archetypal figure. Like divine heroes of old, popular movie stars move through myth-making adventures which fulfill ancient patterns. The star becomes hero of comedy, romance, irony, and tragedy, whenever he descends to make presence visible. Because he *will* return in another role, the experience of tragedy (in which the hero disappears), then, is his least remarkable achievement.

THE MOST FULLY REALIZED of Wayne's romance-heroes is Ethan Edwards, mysterious avenger in *The Searchers* (1956). Ethan's search is a quest for a girl kidnapped by Indians. She is his niece, but he denies kinship. Ethan plans to kill Debbie. His quest, then, is a purification by destruction;

it becomes, in the end, however, a baptism of his own soul when he embraces Debbie and reaffirms his kinship with her. In returning her to the white community, Ethan confirms its cultural identity and integrity, even though he continues to feel excluded from it.

In films of this kind, Wayne's heroic task is to undertake and complete a quest: this displays features Campbell outlined as a "call to adventure," "refusal of the call," "crossing of the first threshold," and "victories of initiation." Northrop Frye's analysis of the romance myth is similar: the quest is a perilous journey, a crucial struggle, and an exaltation of the hero.[17] The peril of Ethan's journey is dramatized several times: from the Indians' trick to lure the Rangers and Ethan on a futile search, to the final, successful attack and rescue mission.

The relationship between Martin Pawley (Jeffrey Hunter) and Ethan Edwards is as much a perilous struggle as the one between Ethan and Chief Scar (Henry Brandon). Plot is complicated by this double set of adversary relationships and the quest is correspondingly enriched. Towards Scar, Ethan is protagonist, but increasingly Scar seems more victim than criminal. Inversion of protagonist-antagonist in such films as *Stagecoach* and *Red River* marks those films as thoughtful and humane. Like Dunson and Garth, Martin and Ethan struggle in *The Searchers*. The perilous journey is a continuous struggle between these two. Ethan's ambivalent attitude toward Martin is a reprise of Dunson's toward Matthew in *Red River*. The ambiguous relationships in these pairings suggest cosmic as well as psychological adversaries that need to be reconciled before order can be assured. Cruel father must be opposed by romance hero to rescue fair maiden. Ethan and Dunson become villains while Martin and Matthew become heroes.

The ambiguous relationship between Ethan and Martin reflects a larger ambivalence in *The Searchers*. Dark strife between races sets humankind against itself, brought to focus by the brooding hostility of heroic Ethan Edwards. In *Stagecoach* the evils of discord are social and economic. In *Red River* they are psychosocial. All are disturbing and challenging to the integrity of the romance-hero, but none is as powerful as this between Ethan Edwards and Martin Pawley. For Ethan to accept Martin would be for Ethan to cleanse himself of racial prejudice. The conclusion of the film troubles this point: Ethan walks away as a door closes him out once again.

The Searchers opens with the return of the hero, and it closes with his departure once again. Its opening moves into the realm of romance, in the spirit of comedy's joyful reintegration with society; its close sends the hero back out, on yet another departure. The poignancy of the closing door, blocking access to this threshold, has the force of tragedy, and so *The Searchers* sends Ethan off alone like Oedipus at Colonus or Lear and Gloucester

As Ethan Edwards in *The Searchers*, 1956.

into the dark heath. The fine quality of this film's mythic power, in its opening and close, is comparable with two other powerful Westerns: *High Noon* and *Shane,* in neither of which is the opening a *return,* or the close a *separation* as well as departure. *The Searchers* closes from romance to become an opening for tragedy.

THE ROLE of tragic protagonist is infrequent for John Wayne, even though one was his last, as John Bernard Books in *The Shootist* (1976). His characters closest to romance, yet tragic, are Capt. Ralls (*Wake of the Red Witch,* 1949) and Col. David Crockett (*The Alamo,* 1960): these emerge barely into tragedy because of sacrificial deaths of the heroes. Their "sources of dignity are courage and innocence," and especially Ralls experiences "the tragedy of innocence in the sense of inexperience." Their loss of life is loss of innocence and idealism.

Most of Wayne's tragic heroes, however, lean from romance toward irony. These include Wedge Donovan (*The Fighting Seabees*, 1944) and Sgt. John M. Stryker (*Sands of Iwo Jima*, 1949). Each completes his task, but he does so through the "defeat" of his sacrificial death. While these characters have flaws in their psychological or moral natures, those flaws are not emphasized so much as the strengths which devote them to idealistic goals. More obviously flawed characters of tragedy are Capt. Jack Stuart (*Reap the Wild Wind*, 1942) and Lt. Lon McQ (*McQ*, 1974), in both of whom "the ironic element increases as the tragic decreases." Indeed, McQ is a decadent tragic hero, experiencing "the tragedy of lost direction and lack of knowledge."

The character who most confounds is Will Andersen of *The Cowboys* (1972). This role, forcefully and tenderly created, carries quest themes of romance in a tragedy where "a strong emphasis is thrown on the success or completeness of the hero's achievement."[18] Andersen's cattle drive succeeds (as in romantic *Red River*), at the cost of Andersen's own life (death is *logical* for Tom Dunson as well). He is a teacher-father to a new generation that carries on the duties of civilization. As tragedy, Andersen's death is required to expiate his failures toward his dead sons. Andersen suffers no loss of direction. He finds it as he loses his life.

Will Andersen is focal as the tragic hero John Wayne best embodies — one who dies to enrich the lives of a new generation. As an older hero Wayne best enacts the tragic myth. When death is sacrificial, as in *The Cowboys* or *The Alamo*, the films barely seem tragic. When the creativity is in the character rather than in the narrative, as in *The Cowboys*, then the films are darker, veer toward irony.

Where there is balance between narrative and character, as in *Sands of Iwo Jima*, the mode is romantic tragedy. When the character is too tragic for the action of the plot (in which the "quest" is completed), mode touches upon irony and satire, as in *McQ*, where the tragic hero does not die, though he loses nearly everything that matters to him. Between clear tragedy in the death of Sgt. Stryker and ambiguous tragedy in the death of Will Andersen, there is a more complex one that includes and transcends the categories of tragedy. The death of John Bernard Books in *The Shootist* shows that tragedy is "a mimesis of sacrifice."[19] *What* Books achieves, however, is less certain than the splendor he gains in the style of his loss.

The body of the tragic hero is divided for communion to insure continuity of civilization through new life. In these roles, Wayne develops an acting style which opposes the wrathful power of fate, nemesis, nature, to affirm the dignity of the single, solitary individual spirit and to confirm the dignifying power of the community that endures. The star who transcends the roles he plays "belongs" to audience and posterity (a "wrathful power") in ways more important than does the body of his characters sacrificed in his films.

The end of *The Shootist* is, like the end of *The Cowboys*, a bloody division of the hero's body. Such violent episodes offend many who approve the more stylized and patriotic violence that concludes *The Alamo, The Fighting Seabees*, and *Sands of Iwo Jima*. The ambivalence of the story in *The Cowboys* complicates response to that film, though the character of Andersen is applauded. The ambivalence of character in *The Shootist* makes more demanding experience of art, attributable to the enriched acting John Wayne brings to his creation of John Bernard Books.

The drama of an old man's coming to a strange place to die befits the autumnal experience of tragedy. John Books is in significant ways like Oedipus who comes to Colonus to find hospitality and then to die out of sight. When Books enters Carson City, he is framed in the spokes of a turning wagonwheel, first of several images for the wheel of fortune. Here is a man brought to his necessary end just as inevitably as the earth turns and time ticks away. The last face of John Wayne as actor is the dying face of John Books: he looks in pain at his audience, and at the boy Gillom, with sorrow and gratitude. He is sorry his death has caused the young man to kill, but he is also grateful Gillom has felt affection for him. Books' is the face of tragedy redeemed by new life. Wayne as Books bids a mute farewell to his audience, fittingly made to a young man upon the threshold of adulthood. This is the archetypal form of John Wayne's achievement: to induct the young through ritual (art) and example (acting) into responsibilities of maturity.

AT THE NADIR of descent through the tragic phase Campbell calls "the mythological round," the hero "undergoes a supreme ordeal." This climaxes his journey in a turning point on the circle of his career. The hero triumphs and he returns whence he came, with springtime, to restore life and community; he brings back an "elixir" of life. This constitutes the mythic action of comedy, but between the return and the descent must occur the ambivalent phase Frye calls "ironic."

Its hero is the "eiron," a trickster (like Odysseus) who hovers on the border of uncertainty between good and evil, light and dark. As he is tainted by the evil he battles, the eiron is tragic; on the other hand, his goodness makes him comic. He risks his life and his good name to "steal" the elixir. The touchstone for Wayne as eiron is Tom Doniphon, in *The Man Who Shot Liberty Valance* (1962), but he worked toward this achievement in earlier roles as Capt. Kirby York, in *Fort Apache* (1948), Capt. Nathan Brittles, in *She Wore a Yellow Ribbon* (1949), Dan Roman in *The High and the Mighty* (1954), Townsend Harris in *The Barbarian and the Geisha* (1958), and John T. Chance in *Rio Bravo* (1959).

He had done the shadowy part of this role in other films with more romance-or-tragic-actions, such as Ethan Edwards (in the ambush of Futterman, for example), or Lon McQ (who breaks laws to enforce them à la Dirty Harry), and James Brannigan (who "knocks" after he enters). In these roles, however, the hero only approaches the threshold of civilization or operates entirely outside its moral boundaries. As eiron, the hero makes it possible for civilization to endure and renew itself. In irony, however grim, is a clear vision of the "green world" of comedy, even if not for the ironist himself.

The Man Who Shot Liberty Valance tends toward satire in its caricatures: the helpless, cowardly, mooching town marshal; the drunken newspaper editor, and the equally drunken town doctor; the outrageous villainy of Liberty Valance and his two cronies; the pompous two-bit politicians who meet to elect a representative to Congress. The principle of survival is "first of all to keep one's eyes open and one's mouth shut."[20] This Ransom Stoddard has to learn and Tom Doniphon has to teach. These men are two types of the eiron who deprecates himself to protect his integrity in a crazy world of Cassius Starbuckles, Link Appleyards, and Liberty Valance.

The eiron, as Frye describes him, is "entrusted with hatching the schemes which bring about the hero's victory." This is the function of Tom Doniphon, as it is of Kirby York (for Owen Thursday), of Nathan Brittles (for Flint Cohill), of Dan Roman (for the pilot Sullivan), of John T. Chance (for Dude), Cole Thornton (for Harrah), and Cord McNally (less emphatically, for Phillips and Tuscarora). Tom Doniphon manipulates events to insure the victory of Ransom Stoddard (James Stewart), at the cost of losing Hallie. He goes so far to deprecate himself he attempts suicide. Tall and strong, he is reduced to a helpless drunk, rescued by his alter ego, Pompey (Woody Strode).

At last Tom is diminished to a shabby, unshaven nondescript walking lonely away from the hall where Ransom Stoddard strides confidently in new innocence to accept nomination as the "man who shot Liberty Valance." Tom Doniphon as eiron is a "plain, commonsense, conventional person who is a foil for the various *alazons* [impostors, pretenders] of society," like Liberty Valance and Link Appleyard. Doniphon's commonsense is conventional frontier ethos, symbolized by the gun. But Doniphon fades into anonymity as Stoddard emerges to take over the role of the eiron himself, whose new commonsense will be the convention of a new ethos, the conventions of order based on law. The eiron figure who stands in the shadows to shoot down the unsuspecting Liberty Valance is not out of place in low-norm satire where "the *alazon* is a Goliath encountered by a tiny David and his sudden and vicious stones, a giant prodded by a cool and observant but almost invisible enemy into a blind, stampeding fury and then polished off at leisure."[21]

Wayne's bulk makes it difficult to accept him in the role of an under-dog–David, and so when he is accepted as such, then indeed he has accomplished something extraordinarily difficult. This is the comic point behind such episodes as the fight with the giant Samurai in *The Barbarian and the Geisha*, and the capture of Cord McNally by the bandit–Confederates in *Rio Lobo*. The more significant function, however, Frye describes thus: "the figure of the low-norm *eiron* is irony's substitute for the hero, and when he is removed from satire we can see more clearly that one of the central themes of the *mythos* is the disappearance of the hero."

John Wayne as eiron carries out the corpse of the heroic past into mythic anonymity: thus Tom Doniphon, and Nathan Brittles who "retires" into the sunset of *She Wore a Yellow Ribbon*, Dan Roman who whistles his way into the dark end of *The High and the Mighty*, and Cole Thornton who hobbles through another town where his gun has restored precarious order. Wayne's ironic heroes clear a space for more life, or new life, or better life. They allow, by their own fading disappearances, heroes of the next generation to continue their work with authority earned by sacrifices of previous generations. Legends have the force of facts in a world that respects facts more than legends. This is the world of Ransom Stoddard, purchased at the price of Tom Doniphon's world.

As eiron, John Wayne shows he need not fill frame space to make his characters work. He could play roles of support in *Fort Apache* and *The High and the Mighty*, where Henry Fonda and Robert Stack have the distinction of dubious limelight, or in *The Man Who Shot Liberty Valance*, where Wayne's character is present through absence, where he is diminished in importance as Stewart's character is enhanced, and then where his value is most realized in images of a burned-out house, a shortlived cactus rose, and a plain wooden coffin. As the character of Doniphon and his world of absurd villains recedes, the world of Stoddard's minimal and unearned normality emerges. This is a world, ironically, of talk and words that take themselves awfully seriously. It is a world where language and talk are substitutes for heroic action and unrestrained passion. John Wayne's face as ironic hero is set against such a world.

IN HIS COMIC ROLES, John Wayne is a romantic hero of life triumphant. He combats manners which interfere with frank expression of Eros and passion, and he battles those who substitute language and talk for action and love. Comedy is a happy genre for this ungainly champion of masculine energy, because comedy celebrates the triumph of sexual power as life renewed. Wayne courts the scorn of viewers who take no pleasure from rough masculine triumphs over grateful women, but he brings gusto and joy to his comic roles, as in *North to Alaska* (1960), *Donovan's Reef* (1963), and *McLintock!* (1963), where brawling is a prelude for loving. The same could be said for Wayne's most winning comic role, as Sean Thornton in *The Quiet Man* (1952), except in this Wayne developed more depth of character from his ability to play slapstick.

In earlier films Wayne provided comic romance for two major stars of Hollywood films: Jean Arthur in *A Lady Takes a Chance* (1943) and Claudette Colbert in *Without Reservations* (1946). In the first, he is a cowboy teaching the Easterner how to make love without reservation, and in the second he discovers for himself how to take a chance on love. In neither film is Wayne completely at ease, but the models for his later successes are there: the independent cowboy who will not rope nor be roped, and the good-natured Marine aviator who demands passion, not ideas from his women.

The Quiet Man is a classic of romantic comedy, conducted throughout in springtime abundance of flowing water and profusion of flowers. It opens with the arrival of a stranger in Castletown, Ireland, to the words of Father Peter Lonergan (Ward Bond):

> Well, then, now, I'll begin at the beginnin'. A fine soft day in the spring it was, when the train pulled into Castletown, three hours late as usual, and himself got off. He didn't have the look of an American tourist at all about him, not a camera on him, and what was worse, not even a fishin' rod!

The stranger is Sean Thronton, returning to Innisfree, the home of his childhood. Magically, mysteriously, as if by providential design, there appears an impish little man to take Sean in hand and lead him home. This little man is the local drunk, oddsmaker, matchmaker, Michaeleen Flynn (Barry Fitzgerald). As they ride a horse-drawn cart towards Innisfree, the train pulls away, leaving Sean Thornton in this pastoral land he has come to call "heaven."

The plot of *The Quiet Man* has the structure of Greek New Comedy, like Shakespeare's *Taming of the Shrew*. A young man wants a young woman, his desire is resisted, but in the end, he will have desire fulfilled. Red Will Danaher (Victor McLaglen), Mary Kate's brother in *The Quiet Man*, refuses Mary Kate's dowry. Money withheld is power denied; her dowry denied, Mary Kate (Maureen O'Hara) cannot allow her marrige to be consummated. This symbol of social value that interferes with honest sexual expression is frequent in comedy. The absence/presence of money makes possible the courtships of both *A Lady Takes a Chance* and *Without Reservations;* in the first money is a gift of fortune, not something the hero spends energy to acquire; in the second, the heroine learns to depend on the hero because she is without access to money and social identity. In his later comedies, Wayne's hero is above money because it is secondary to his force of character, although the "myth" of his industry accounts for ways he acquired social power to match his sexual power in *North to Alaska*, *Donovan's Reef*, and *McLintock!*

In Wayne's comic world it is possible, even necessary at times, for violence to be part of a constructive re-ordering process. Removal of obstacles involves exercise of force, not cunning, in his drive to the new life of comedy. Violence clears away obstacle after obstacle in the heroes' paths, though in the end there is a promise of violence-free society with the women of his love, as in *Donovan's Reef* and *The Quiet Man.* In this film violence is in the service of *re*construction, as when Sean Thornton goes into epic battle with his brother-in-law. This is the festive ritual that signals the appearance of a new society in Innisfree, when the brothers-in-law appear at the end, worn out in body, dizzy from drunkenness, but revived in spirit and in heart. They are welcomed home by a happy wife and sister. Everybody is happy with the new arrangements of society, made possible by Sean's return home.

Sean Thornton removed a disguise hiding him from others and from himself, when he found a constructive purpose for his physical strength. This channeling of sexual potency into building civilization is the process of comedy, which makes a green world of happy conclusions. This is the transcendent message of John Wayne's career through all his roles as hero. Even in *Without Reservations* when Rusty Thomas gives in to the wiles of Kit Madden, he is "coming home" with power to make her dreams of a better society into reality. In other Wayne comedies, hero rescues heroine from decadence to vitality, as in *A Lady Takes a Chance* and *North to Alaska,* or he welcomes her into his own decadent community revived by love (*Donovan's Reef*), or by the return of prodigal love (*McLintock!*). Wayne's comic hero does not trick society into reform, as do his ironic ones; nor does he sacrifice himself to community or to fate as do his tragic ones. Wayne's comic hero always returns, or welcomes back the prodigal love, to celebrate new life in the end, after long wandering and many battles of separation.

10. "Romantic Heroes"

John Wayne made approximately 65 films, including *The Big Trail* in 1930, before he played the Ringo Kid in *Stagecoach* in 1939. By the time of his last romance hero, Brannigan in 1975, he made about 84 more films, and after Brannigan he would live to make only another two. Although he had 75 percent of his professional years left to him, he had completed almost half of the number of his pictures by the time of *Stagecoach*. In his history of mythmaking, he had by 1939 established a well defined romance-mode of heroism in his films.

This is a major reason for his easy identification with American audiences, who see themselves as "romantic" people. Film art is fundamentally a fantasy, in which the human is all it wishes to be. One of the most frequently recurring themes in romance is, therefore, "innocence," yearning for untrammeled romantic adventure. This is what Wayne's heroes had been offering in his films up to 1939. When he delivers the Ringo Kid, he confirms an identity nicely anticipated by Breck Coleman in *The Big Trail*. His romantic hero was long in the making and easily accepted.

Breck Coleman: *The Big Trail* (1930)

In April 1930, shooting began for *The Big Trail*, directed by Raoul Walsh. Its star was young John Wayne, not yet 23 years old. He was to play a role the producers hoped would be taken by Gary Cooper, fresh from his triumphant part in *The Virginian* (1929). Wayne was virtually snatched from carrying props to carrying a big film. The character of Breck Coleman moved Wayne toward heroic status. *The Big Trail* is a beautiful cinematic experience, and Breck Coleman is a romance hero with youthful vigor, spirited optimism, and, best of all, openness of heart. Breck Coleman is a young man who has nothing to hide and everything to offer. He has a duty to revenge the murder of his best friend, but he does it without guilt, without deceit, and as he says to the settlers, without "hatred in my heart." With another actor, another character, this would not be credible. Wayne as Coleman is, however, convincing when he claims innocence of motive.

This is the way of the hero whose strength is in his innocence. Where

144

he gets that innocence, or why he should be so innocent, is a mystery, since he has the skill of a killer, the fortitude of a wild animal, and the cunning of an Indian warrior. His reputation precedes him. Flack asks Lopez if he knows who this "young buck" is, this boy "with no hair on his face." Lopez replies that "he come from the plains, the mountains, he live with the Indians. He can throw a knife through the heart in twenty feet. He is the best shot in all this country. He knows everything." This introduces a special champion, the hero of romance, who *is* an innocent *and* who *does* "know everything." At least he knows everything that matters, though he does not know evil or guilt in himself.

D.H. LAWRENCE, in his *Studies in Classic American Literature*, makes penetrating observations on American character and American ideals. He had lived in Taos, New Mexico, from late 1922 to late 1925, when he published his *Studies* in 1923. He liked much that he saw in American character and culture. However, as a European he could recognize features Americans themselves might ignore or deny. He was examining the living, struggling, boastful and yet insecure generation of Americans which included John Wayne. Lawrence saw that "somewhere deep in every American heart lies a rebellion against the old parenthood of Europe. Yet no American feels he has completely escaped its mastery." Americans boasted of liberty, but it was a "thing of sheer will, sheer tension," and America was consequently "a vast republic of escaped slaves."[22]

Breck Coleman is a voice of this liberty. He speaks from the American heart, and he speaks of "a rebellion against the old parenthood of Europe." Breck, however, speaks to draw strength from that rebellion, to inspire a determination in the settlers of the wagon train:

> We can't turn back! We're blazing on a trail that started in England. Not even the storms of the sea could turn back those first settlers. And they carried it further. They blazed it on through the wilderness of Kentucky. Famine, hunger, not even massacres could stop them! And now we've picked up the trail again. And nothing can stop us—not even the snows of winter, not the peaks of the highest mountains! We're building a nation! And we've got to suffer! No great trail was ever blazed without hardship. And you gotta fight! That's life! And when you stop fightin', that's death! What're you going to do? Lie down and die? Not in a thousand years! You're going on with me!

Needless to say, the settlers respond with renewed energy to persevere.

Breck draws upon America's idea of itself as a goal to be reached by suffering, combat, and finding a "trail" away from "the old parenthood of Europe." The *tradition* of America is a trial of exodus and rebellion. Its leaders, like Breck Coleman, must have vision to know where America is heading, but they must also be pure of heart so their rebellions against the past are not compromised. To feel guilt in rebellion would be to create "a

As Breck Coleman, with Marguerite Churchill as Ruth Cameron, in *The Big Trail*, 1930.

vast republic of escaped slaves," and this Breck Coleman is intended to prevent, as characters like Bill Thorpe are intended to encourage.

Fighting is "living," then, for Breck Coleman. His governing metaphors are the figures of struggle, combat, and aggression. Nevertheless, he's a man with peace in his heart, because he is a creature of "nature" itself. This is another feature of the American romantic hero, long a fixture in American literature and folk tale, especially marked in James Fenimore Cooper's Natty Bumppo, known as Deerslayer, Leatherstocking, or Pathfinder. The virtue and appeal of this character is in his mythic force. He is a fellow of the Indians, in friendship or enmity, but he is at the same time a European gentlemen. Natty Bumppo is Cooper's dream of the American at home in the new land. So is Breck Coleman such a dream.

The Big Trail is one of many "tributes" to its predecessor of 1923, *The Covered Wagon*, directed by James Cruze. Both films are derivatives from a firmly engrained sense of self, place, purpose that Americans had well in their collective minds by the time of movie invention. Besides the trapper-scout who finds and shows the way to a hidden valley of happiness, there was the larger image of a whole community on the move, from Europe itself, as Breck Coleman properly recalled. The odyssey of a people was of ancient vintage with prototypes in narratives by Homer and Moses.

The occasion of these films throughout the twenties, and on into the thirties as well, is more than a dramatic public consciousness about self identity, economic insecurities, or political instabilities. The films gave mythic denial to the argument of Frederick Jackson Turner, who had in a year of financial panic, 1893, asserted "the closing of a great historical movement" with the disappearance of the frontier in the American West. His thesis, in "The Significance of the Frontier in American History," could never be accepted by a deeply American consciousness, however forcefully his argument and his facts might be. There would always be a need for a "new frontier" to make the "great society." American national politicians must find "new deals" and "new ideas" to keep that "frontier" in view.

D.H. Lawrence understood this better than Turner did. But Lawrence also believed it was a signal fault of American culture and character. The notion of the frontier was a beckoning to continue the rebellion, to tempt the European spirit to endure even as it sought to escape its past. The *image* of a frontier implies a clear line of separation into duality for the American. Lawrence believed this duality was dramatized by the American's ambivalance toward Indians: "There has been all the time, in the white American soul, a dual feeling about the Indian. . . . The desire to extirpate the Indian. And the contradictory desire to glorify him. Both are rampant still, today."[23] Today—that is, in 1923. And it could still be seen in 1930, or in 1956 in *The Searchers,* or in 1973 in *Cahill, United States Marshal*—to name only a few of Wayne's own films treating the point.

Breck Coleman is an expression of the American desire for unity and innocence. Breck comes out of a dim, obscure region, vaguely associated (by Lopez) with Indians who have taught him their "ways." Breck himself explains this to a group of children just before he leads the wagon train west to Oregon. Breck is confronted by a group of small boys, eager to know his Indian days. One asks him, "Did you ever kill a dead Indian?"

> BRECK: No, I never killed a *dead* one.
> ANOTHER BOY: Before they was dead, did ya?
> BRECK: You see, the Indians was my friends. They taught me all I know about the woods. They taught me how to follow a trail by watching the leaves, how to cut your mark on a tree so you won't get lost in the forest, and they taught me how to bury in the snow so you won't freeze to death in a storm, and they taught me how to make a fire without even a flint! And they taught me how to make the best bow and arrows too.

Sincerity of speech, honesty of emotion, and ease of delivery suggest an integrity which comes from shared identity with the Indians who taught Breck how to survive in a hostile environment. But they taught him how to be more.

BRECK COLEMAN'S "negative ideal of democracy," his insistence on
private justice, rebellion against evil, is absorbed in his discovery that a
large goal can be served by a narrow end. Breck must learn to commit personal virtue to public good. He knows, in the language of D.H. Lawrence,
how to "obey from within." He has to find others who will follow and find
in him how *they* can also obey "some deep, inward voice of religious belief."

Obedience to a shared principle, experienced under conditions of
community struggle, and recognized in a narrative of mutual regard: these
are the qualities Breck Coleman clarifies in the settlers' vision, the vision
of the film itself. When a person can feel "the superior of most men," as
Lawrence put it, that person is prepared to participate in the only
democracy that counts, the democracy of shared essential being. This
Breck Coleman represents. Throughout his career John Wayne would
depict its appeal, sometimes mistaken for a political rather than an existential point.

Coleman cannot feel the superior of others on account of family. He
does not have money or property, and so he cannot feel superior on account
of wealth. His only education is from the Indians who shared their ways of
surviving the wilderness, and so he cannot feel superior for intellectual
achievements of scholarship and erudition. The John Wayne hero, beginning with Breck Coleman, is no high-brow. Could his superiority come in
the pride of beauty? This is more arguable, since the early image of young
Wayne is an attractive one.

The essential being of Breck Coleman shines through Wayne's
representation. It is best understood as "beauty," though it is no mere static
image. It is a beauty of dynamic grace, what Walt Whitman meant when
he sang "the body electric." This youth of 22 years had much to learn, but
there is more than potential demonstrated by his work in *The Big Trail*.

Breck Coleman shows self confidence throughout the film. Only occasionally does he stumble, and those are scenes when his dialogue is either
badly written or he is left to improvise. Even in his set speeches, as in the
scene of his introduction, Wayne/Coleman conveys a posture of physical
relaxation between person and setting. This comes from, and communicates, what Lawrence looked for to complete the American character:
"natural superiority," felt in each person's self regard. It is a superiority in,
simply, "myself." This is felt in situations of challenge, when another brings
his sense of superiority to a level of meeting with *my* superiority: "He is a
man and I am a man. We are ourselves. There is no question between us."
This is Whitman's American "song of myself."

Breck Coleman makes one feel what Whitman sang and what Lawrence
described as the real democracy, which does not look back to rebellions or
put ideas of education and wealth between persons who meet in common-
ness of being. Breck is not a perfect representation of this "natural

superiority," however, because Breck has a beauty to distinguish him from, at least, the villainous Red Flack, though his physical beauty is not greater than that of the equally villainous Bill Thorpe. Breck also has the "manly strength" Lawrence denied as a basis for superiority, though it is nothing Breck asserts unless he is challenged. He is at ease with his physical and intellectual virtues; there is none of the "tension" in him Lawrence found to fault in most Americans of his time. Breck is, with a simplicity both Whitman and Lawrence hoped for, superior "in himself."

THE HEROINE OF THE STORY is a daughter of the Old South. She is Ruth Cameron (Marguerite Churchill), travelling with her brother Dave and her little sister, Honey Girl. She is vulnerable to the wiles of slick con-man Bill Thorpe. She resists his insistent courtship, until she meets the temptation of Breck Coleman. This is an ancient story, and an imitation of *The Covered Wagon.* It is an analysis of passions which educate the hero. Ruth is another innocent, a special target for the melodramatic villain, gambler and sneak, Bill Thorpe. But she understands Breck Coleman is the most serious threat to her integrity, so much so she practically rushes into the arms of the man she repelled.

Breck wins Ruth's love, finally succeeding in making her want him more than she understands. He completes in himself the sense of superiority that makes a genuine democracy of human community: he has put himself to the test of a woman's love, and because he survives it with his integrity intact, he earns her gift of self. That he has already made a gift of himself, constantly offered and diminishingly refused, is the point of the sentimental but necessarily conventional conclusion of the film.

FULFILLMENT OF THE HERO, strong but incomplete without a woman's love, is a goal of romance adventure. Sometimes woman's love is the last temptation in the way of a hero's completed mission, and sometimes it is the reward. It can even be reward and temptation at once, if the hero knows how to preserve his integrity in the face of temptation. The structure of the relationship owes much to courtly love conventions developed and elaborated in Medieval European allegories of romance: allegories because they narrated religious themes or doctrines in human adventures. More is owed, however, to the archetypal forms of sacred texts themselves, as in the stories of Adam and Eve, Samson and Delilah, David and Bathsheba.

Ralph Waldo Emerson, in "Self Reliance," beautifully articulated a point central to the American circle of identity. His words anticipate D.H. Lawrence's observations on American character and culture: "To believe your own thought, to believe that what is true to you in your private heart is true for all men — that is genius. Speak your conviction, and it shall be the universal sense; for the inmost in due time becomes the outmost." Emerson provided the text for understanding the character of John Wayne's romantic heroes, including the rough, hard side of those heroes: "Your goodness must have some edge to it—else it is none. The doctrine of hatred must be preached, as the counteraction of the doctrine of love, when that pules and whines."[24]How Laurentian! and, more to the point, how like John Wayne!

When heroines "pule and whine," heroes must put "some edge to it—else it is none." This is Emerson's response to sentimentality, "the doctrine of love." Breck Coleman has not hatred in his heart when he strikes out in revenge, but he does know how to put "some edge" on his goodness when he meets the romantic resistances of the woman he loves, who pleads with him not to do "this awful thing," not to leave her alone. Emerson explained that "to be great is to be misunderstood," to find one's goal is to follow "a zigzag line of a hundred tacks." "Genuine action will explain itself." To be "genuine" may appear selfish, unfeeling, perhaps even cruel and merciless. But Breck Coleman is none of these, even as he insists on his duty to do.

Breck never agonizes over the choice he must make, between the woman and the mission. He has a clarity of purpose which makes him seem simple, even as he seems hardheaded if not hardhearted. He is at ease with himself, so much so he has no need to plea for help from anyone, from anywhere. Breck knows instinctively he is Emerson's "self-reliant" American. He is not among those who lift up prayers in *The Big Trail.* Bascom does the praying for the community, sometimes in gratitude for the deeds of Breck Coleman himself. Little Honey Girl is shown once saying an evening prayer, asking God to look after her sister Ruth and her brother Dave; Ruth asks her, when she has finished, if she is not going to ask God to look after Breck: "Aren't you going to ask God to take care of Breck Coleman?" Honey Girl responds as if she thinks Ruth is a simpleton, not to know what Zeke had pointed out to Honey Girl already: "Breck Coleman can take care of himself."

Emerson said, "as soon as the man is at one with God, he will not beg. He will then see prayer in all action." The beauty of Breck Coleman's character is in this confidence, ease, and self reliance. There is little evidence of misunderstanding about him in the film, apart from Ruth Cameron's innocent failure of vision, which produces the only significant test of Breck's heroic stature. John Wayne the actor might not be so fortunate, since throughout his career there would be those without understanding who would question his greatness, especially when he was successful in creating the image of the self-reliant American romantic hero.

Another actor of Wayne's generation, Gary Cooper, had similar tests of his "greatness," as he had similar opportunities to create images of the American romantic hero. They would come in such films as *The Plainsman* (1937), *Sergeant York* (1941), *High Noon* (1952), and *The Court-Martial of*

Billy Mitchell (1955). Most appropriately to the context for the *The Big Trail,* however, was Cooper's image of the Western hero in *The Virginian,* a film released in 1929. Tied closely to Owen Wister's enormously popular novel, the most trying experience of the hero is also the most obsessive theme of the story: his response to what Emerson called "the doctrine of love."

COOPER'S VIRGINIAN is a different American hero, though he is intended (as in the novel) to represent the doctrine of "inequality" D.H. Lawrence identified in genuine American democracy, and which Breck Coleman expressed through his easy self-confidence. However, the Virginian, as Owen Wister conceived him, is a man of aggressive, competitive skills put to the service of a propertied society. Law is an instrument of power to protect property. The Virginian is ready to lynch his best friend because that friend helped to rustle cattle. He fails a crucial test set by Emerson: "the reliance on Property, including the reliance on governments which protects it, is the want of self-reliance."

The Virginian of the film is not an innocent, like Breck Coleman. Instead, he is coarse, sexually bold, and cocky—all features he shares with the villain, Trampas (Walter Huston). The Virginian is a skilled cowboy working for a large cattle ranch, and so he is from the outset a spokesman for business interests, for the stability of property. His friend Steve is a reminder of his earlier days when they had fewer social commitments, when they were loners. But then they were not mature, the film is quick to show. Maturity is measured by responsibility for the management of property.

It is also measured by ease of relationships with women, and for a mature man in the West, that means to be a woman's master. Cooper is equally cocky with women as with men, a point that distinguishes him from Wayne's Breck Coleman. At the opening of the film, the Virginian rides into town where he sees Steve lounging in front of a saloon. In this reunion Gary Cooper shows how different is his rendition of the Western American hero from Wayne's at an early age. The Virginian is unsteady in his motion, not smooth and graceful like Breck Coleman—on a horse or off, the Virginian leans and bobs, shuffles and weaves, as if he were subject to wind and horse alike, rather than the master of both, like Coleman. Cooper's Western drawl is forced and frequent, unlike Wayne's crisp, economical expression in *The Big Trail.*

The Virginian "wins" a contest with Steve for a bargirl, and he is about to enjoy his conquest, when Trampas joins the competition. The Virginian warns Trampas off. Trampas responds, "Whenever I want to know anything from you, I'll tell ya, you long legged son of a — — — —!" The Virginian pulls his gun, puts it in Trampas's belly, and says, "If you want to call me that — — — — smile!" Trampas knows when to retreat, lifts his eyebrows, shows

his teeth through a forced smile, and says, "With a gun against my belly, I
— — — — always smile." He laughs and strolls away.

Cooper's Virginian leers at the bargirl, as Wayne's Breck Coleman
could never leer at anything. And Cooper's Virginian tries to be as cocky
with the innocent Eastern schoolteacher Molly Stark Wood (Mary Brian)
as he had been with the less innocent bargirl. To him a woman is a woman
is a woman, and all are proper prey (i.e., property) for the survivor in the
struggles of the "fittest." The only real test of Molly's love for this uncouth
champion of Western civilization in *The Virginian* comes when he risks
ruining their wedding ceremony to meet Trampas in a duel "before sun-
down." Molly cannot accept the personal ethos of her hero, as Ruth can of
Breck Coleman. For Molly, the Virginian is about to "kill in cold blood." She
distinguishes the duel with Trampas from the lynching of Steve, which had
been "a public duty to law and order." This duel is to be done "just to satisfy
a personal grudge." She claims his life is no longer his own: "You've given
it to me. Don't take it away." And then she threatens, in a scene that anticipates *High Noon,* "If you do this, there'll be no tomorrow for you and
me."

Ruth meets Breck Coleman on superior grounds of being, where self
yields to what is superior in the other. Molly claims in the Virginian what
he claims in all things, that the other is property. But the Virginian is no
one's property, though he makes others respect his claims to it. He pushes
Molly back, firmly, though he duels less firmly with Trampas: he is shifty,
stalking and being stalked. He kills Trampas, and he claims his prize, as the
much relenting Molly runs to embrace him. Intercuts of the scene, and the
words of the heroine, contrast sharply with the quiet solemnity that concludes *The Big Trail,* where there is no property to be claimed, only "gifts"
of presence. It is an auspicious contrast for the American hero: Cooper's
Virginian or his Sergeant York is a hero of "ownership," Wayne's Breck
Coleman or *his* Sergeant York is a hero of "stewardship."

The Ringo Kid: *Stagecoach* (1939)

In 1939 audiences could see three of America's most prominent film
actors in important character roles: Clark Gable as Rhett Butler in *Gone
with the Wind,* Henry Fonda as Abraham Lincoln in *Young Mr. Lincoln,* and
John Wayne as the Ringo Kid in *Stagecoach.* The actors are about the same
age, though Wayne is the youngest; in 1939, he was 32, Fonda was 34, and
Gable 38. Wayne and Gable had broken into films with bit parts in 1927 and
1924 respectively, Fonda not until 1935.

Fonda as young Lincoln gives a performance of shy, shrewd, and
neighborly Americana; his features are ungainly imitations of Lincoln portraits, and his speech is slightly "Southern." Gable as Rhett Butler is
dashing, also shrewd, far from shy, and unmannerly; his features are sensual,

dark physical strength, and his speech is as "Southern" as Gable could make it. The Ringo Kid is also strong and agile of body, but he is mild of manner and sensuous rather than sensual. Ringo is a blend of Lincoln's friendly manners and Butler's courteous masculinity. Both Rhett and Ringo are "notorious" and both endear themselves to their communities, overcoming social prejudices. In this they acquire applause that Lincoln receives when he defends his clients against mob and state.

The Ringo Kid, however, is more innocent and pure even than Fonda's Lincoln, and certainly more than Gable's Rhett Butler. One of the more implausible points in *Stagecoach* is that Ringo could be so sexually innocent. One of the pleasing surprises is to realize this boyish Ringo Kid is played by a man 32 years old. His unselfish innocence in sexual relations remains with Ringo throughout the film. Whether Fonda's Lincoln can be said to have the same is more difficult than to make the contrast with Rhett Butler. Lincoln courts Anne Rutledge to open the story, he courts Mary Todd through the remainder, and he distributes compliments to the ladies of the Clay family as he manages the defense of their case.

The Ringo Kid is out to avenge the murders of his father and brother, and he undertakes his mission with a spotless heart. Lincoln is also an avenging angel, as defense attorney for the wrongly accused innocent and as the one who discovers the guilty. The Kid has the same virtues as Lincoln, with the difference that Ringo is outside the law even as he is comfortably within a "higher" morality. In this Ringo is more like Rhett Butler, whose unmannerliness and frank criticism of Southern codes make him seem outside that society; ultimately, however, Rhett proves to have a larger vision than those within the small society he shuns, and his larger vision almost rescues the heroine.

The Ringo Kid is not as reflective as Lincoln, nor is he as detached as Rhett Butler. Ringo *feels* what is right and wrong, rather than think or say it, like Lincoln and Butler. Ringo's strength is, like Galahad's, as the strength of ten, and his strength comes from his uncorrupted vision of love and justice. His motives are his strength: avenge the deaths of father and brother, defend the honor of outcasts, and love the unloved. As a lawyer, Lincoln has a similar set of motives, but one special peculiarity distinguishes Fonda's role from Wayne's: Lincoln is mama's boy, and Ringo is a daddy's boy. Lincoln is entangled by memories of his mother and dead beloved Anne Rutledge. This film cultivates the "feminine" strengths of Lincoln even as it compensates with masculine feats of splitting rails and chopping firewood, but it cannot strike the balance.

The entrances of Lincoln, Butler, and Ringo in their stories make for interesting comparisons. Lincoln leans back in a chair against a porch post, rising slowly to make his first speech of the movie; he introduces himself as "plain Abraham Lincoln," and he talks with his head down, hands in pockets. Rhett Butler is leaning against a balustrade on a stairway in the mansion at Twelve Oaks; he is looking up as Scarlett O'Hara looks down at him. Rhett's stare makes the women feel as if he is undressing them. By contrast, the Ringo Kid halts a stagecoach and grows large as the camera zooms in on his startling interruption. He is a personification of tightly disciplined energy. This drama and visual excitement disappear from the same episode of the 1966 version of *Stagecoach*.

WE KNOW SOMETHING ALREADY about the Ringo Kid long before we meet him on the trail. From early in the film's story, we know he has escaped prison, a posse is looking for him, he is looking for the killers of his father and brother, and he has a large reward on his head. He must be a dangerous man, dangerous to the state as well as to the persons in it. We are led to expect a dangerous man. We meet a determined youngster, friendly to acquaintance and stranger alike but stern in his quest for vengeance. He is tempted to abandon his quest when he falls in love with the fallen woman Dallas. But he is a man destined for something else, and so he continues with the stage. His spirit cannot be imprisoned any more than his body had been before, and his talent is too valuable for the society of passengers for him to remain in shackles. When the stage reaches Lordsburg, the stage is being driven by Ringo.

The Kid's courage is never doubted, his strength is never overwhelmed, and his innocence is vindicated even as he carries out his vengeance against the Plummers. What is "realistic" about his character is the motive he has for revenge; what is romantic is the uncorrupted innocence he sustains throughout. Like his heroic predecessors in romantic myth and legend, the Ringo Kid is a servant as he is an agent of a force larger than he is alone. This force is, as a matter of art, in the structure of romance itself.

That Ringo becomes useful in the defense of the stagecoach is almost an accident of the quest adventure; it is only an episode, not the main action, of his journey. Crucial to the plot, however, is the way of Ringo's participation in the journey. He becomes a litmus test for character in the other passengers, as he accepts people for what they are: from Doc Boone to Dallas to Hatfield. All the characters of the stagecoach, including Buck and Curly, change by the time they reach their destination. Most of them grow, even Hatfield, and one of them, the banker Gatewood, is shown for the cowardly hypocrite he is.

These changes in character owe much to Ringo's presence. Whether Doc's sympathy for Dallas could have restored her dignity to her is doubtful; certainly it is restored by Ringo's courtesy and love. This particular change is at the heart of the story's development, and in it Ringo is crucial. He is not on the stagecoach at the start of the journey. He interrupts its progress, and he becomes a passenger who must sit on the floor betweeen the seats. But he, the man without a home and without a horse, gradually rises in the action to the top of the stage, to become the riding guide on the lead horse, and then finally to be the driver of the stagecoach itself when it rolls into Lordsburg. This progressive move to leadership and control is a part of the revelation of his character.

When Ringo takes Dallas across the border to his special place, he takes her back into Eden, the ultimate destination of romance heroes. To get there he has to leave a land of discontent, darkness, and "social prejudice." He leaves behind a place the better for his having been there, but it is still a place the romance hero cannot call his home. The Ringo Kid is neither a Fonda-like farmer who takes a wife along the Mohawk Valley, nor is he a Rhett Butler who can leave his woman to her own devices with the parting words, "Frankly, my dear, I don't give a damn." Even *Gone with the Wind* could not leave it so, allowing its audience to believe with Scarlett that "after all, tomorrow is a better day." That better day is what romances offer, and must continue to offer, or they would turn into another story altogether.

When Ringo crosses the border he is translated into a new realm of being, taking his beloved with him. As we have seen in many of Wayne's earlier films, this is the usual conclusion to Wayne as romance-hero. We are usually not allowed to follow him into paradisal retreat, and when we are, it is with a reluctance that makes us guilty along with the film itself. In that place of happiness the romance hero becomes something else: either he will be a dowdy family man, or he will be a god who may return again whenever the lower world needs his attention. The Ringo Kid will always be the latter, with features that associate him with divinity and myths of godlike heroes of legend.

RINGO IS ONLY A NICKNAME. He says "Right name's Henry." The name has a history with special meanings. By the way of French, it comes from the German words *Heinrich* and *Haganrich*, literally the *ruler* of an enclosure. In Ringo's case, he must be Ringo in the world of romance adventures, but he is "rightfully" *Henry*, ruler of a distant place, across the border somewhere. In his rightful name, then, Ringo is heir to another country, as are all men victorious in the lower world of trouble and romance.

The plot of the narrative plays upon the name of *Henry*, since Gatewood's name is also Henry. But he proves to be a false ruler, in contrast with Ringo the true one. Another name in the circle is Hatfield's, which has associations with Gatewood's, and also with Ringo's (as a range, or enclosure). Hatfield is the romance-double to Ringo, though he is a contrary to Gatewood's contradiction. Hatfield stands between Ringo and

Gatewood, since Hatfield is a man at the edge of the law, a prodigal son, but one redeemed by his love of Lucy Mallory (perhaps his sister). Ringo works from above the law, while Hatfield works below it; Ringo redeems through love, while Hatfield is redeemed by it. And so Hatfield has to die, not only of thematic purposes, but also for satisfaction of the romance structure, where the dark double is left behind when the hero makes his ascent to a higher world.

Which brings us to the fundamental, underlying structure of the story of the Ringo Kid in *Stagecoach*. With his innocence, his power to love, his risk of self sacrifice, his temptations to waver, his battle with powers of darkness, and his ultimate translation into a new "kingdom," the Ringo Kid is a humanized recreation of Christ. While Ringo has other associations, with the Greek avenger Orestes, for example, Ringo moves through a paradigm of action which underlies the Christian as well as certain classical stories of antiquity. As Orestes, he is out to avenge the death of his father, and also as Orestes, Ringo finds his justification by law (Curly) at the end. His torment is not, however, made tragic like Orestes'. On the other hand, he is mysteriously powerful like Christ. His mystery is in his innocence, and it is in the paradox of his outcast social status from which he lifts society by his heroic deeds. His power is in his love for the outcasts and misfits of life, as well as in his justice for all—both the lawful and the lawless.

The Ringo Kid is not, of course, Jesus Christ any more than he is Orestes. However, all cling to a central pattern of heroic character, at its deepest or at its highest a pattern of mythic proportions, where signs of human experience reach through archetypal symbols to dreams of divine purpose. It is, for the culture in which John Wayne and the Ringo Kid live and move and have their being, a pattern traced by the journeys of Christ: a pattern that took him through a society with types like those who rode in the stagecoach from Tonto to Lordsburg, a pattern which concluded with the journey to Emmaus as narrated in Luke 24 of the Bible. On this journey, the last of the several made by Jesus, he appears mysteriously to accompany two others who have "their eyes opened" to his identity. In a similar way, with different substance, the story of the Ringo Kid is a journey to Emmaus.

Tom Dunson: *Red River* (1948)

Nine years after the Ringo Kid rode out of Lordsburg with Dallas into the sunrise, Tom Dunson left his love behind to start a new life in Texas. Tom at the opening of *Red River* is about the age of Ringo, and Tom has the same opportunity for erotic happiness Ringo had. But Tom chose what Ringo turned from doing after seeing Indian signals at Apache Wells; Tom left the wagon train and his love, Fen, to go south into Texas, but he also left his love to her fate at the hands of murderous Indians. The tale of Tom Dunson is a tale of tragic possibilities, as he suffers tribulation from his stubbornness, and as he carries a burden of guilt for his betrayal of romance. However, the story is a romance after all, because the hero carries on with his mission, and fulfills the goal of heroes of romance: he overcomes villainy, he clears a space for civilization, and he repays the debts of love.

The story has many surprises when measured against the formula Western, because it shares a romance-structure. For example, Indians attack a wagon train twice: at the beginning and at the end. The formula Western is satisfied with one attack, but this story has doubled the quality, without doubling the cost. When Tom and Groot notice smoke from the wagons, Groot asks, bitterly, why Indians always have to burn good wagons. In the second attack, looking at the attack of Tess Millay's wagon train, Buster asks also with bitterness, why Indians always have to yell like that. These questions express audience boredom with narrative conventions of formula Westerns.

Wayne's Tom Dunson contributes enriching details of realism. Gestures of body, particularly hands and face, as well as tones of voice are expressive means the actor employs to create in Tom Dunson his most complicated and most convincing character so far considered. After the dissolve from 1851 to 1865, Tom is bent over the ground between Matt and Groot; Matt stands with one leg on a rock beside Tom, who when he rises puts one hand on Matt's leg to use as a support for getting on his feet. It is understated mutuality. Wayne works with his face in a later scene of this same episode, when he listens patiently to Groot (Walter Brennan) mock him into accepting Groot as cook on the drive. Tom submits in loving silence, and when Groot concludes with his finger in Tom's face, Tom nods his head firmly to put a period on it.

SUCCESS OF THE FILM and of the character of Tom Dunson are marks of Wayne's professionalism, because they show he can adapt to the needs of his art. What may astonish is the apparent ease with which he makes this transition from the primitive romances of the thirties, culminating in the clean innocence of the outlaw Ringo Kid, to the making of Tom Dunson, almost beaten by the errors of his life, but finally larger than anyone thought he could be. It is instructive to compare Tom Dunson with John Higgins in *Texas Terror* (1935), a character also ridden by guilt like Tom Dunson. The differences are not only accountable to the increasing skill of the actor to be convincing, nor are they only the results of better direction and higher production values; they are differences as well between a primitive romance and a sophisticated one, to which the actor must adapt his natural skills in educated ways.

In 1948 appeared a Hitchcock film starring James Stewart, *Rope*. Here

Wayne as Tom Dunson, with *(from left to right, standing)* John Ireland, Hank
Worden, Montgomery Clift and Ray Hyke in *Red River*, 1948.

is a different vehicle, a murder thriller, also stylish in its undertones, though
more obvious in its use of psychology than is to be found in *Red River*.
Stewart's cynical Rupert Cadell is comparable with Wayne's Dunson.
Rupert has much to learn about himself, to take responsibility for his past
mistakes, and restore order to a world threatened by disorders of his own
making. Rupert is a romance hero, though that point could not be pushed
before it would dissolve into tragedy and irony.

In the climax of *Rope*, when the plot is being untied in the sarcastic
manner of a sly Hitchcock story, Rupert has to find out if his suspicions are
correct about Philip and Brandon. He returns to their apartment after the
party, where he is made to realize the horrible truth it is *he* who is responsible

Wayne slugging Montgomery Clift (as Matthew Garth) in *Red River*.

for this ugly murder. His voice rises to a shrill, screeching curse against the young men, "You're going to die." One wonders who is mad, or more mad, in this scene, as Rupert gestures wildly with eyes, eyebrow, and arms, until he fires a pistol out the window, and then collapses in a chair beside the trunk, with his back turned to the film audience.

A scene with similarities in *Red River* occurs when Matt takes command of the drive from his foster father Dunson. Tom sits leaning against a wagon while Groot nurses his leg. Valance rides in with the quitters, and Tom quietly tells them he is going to hang them. Matt says he won't. The father is displaced, disgraced, and dismissed. He is made helpless by his wound, by his drink, and by his men. His growing realization of helplessness does not express itself in shouting or wild gesticulation. He submits, biding his time for vengeance. Matt approaches in his manner of gentleness as he prepares to tell Tom farewell; Tom is leaning against his horse, looking off into the distance—*not* at Matt. He tells Matt, in effect, "You're going to die," but he does it so quietly the audience might not hear it, and he does it mainly looking away from Matt and the film audience.

For a similar theme, of father as obdurate-hero, in conflict with his son, an audience in 1949 could have looked at *All the King's Men* for comparisons with *Red River.* Broderick Crawford portrays a deteriorating Willie Stark (a role reportedly first offered to Wayne), against Jack Burden and Anne Stanton, both played by stars from *Red River,* John Ireland and Joanne Dru. Again Wayne's Tom Dunson stands out for power from restraint, when compared with Crawford's frenetic Willie Stark.

A fairer context is made by recalling *The Virginian* had appeared in yet another remake in 1946, with Joel McCrea in the title role, or by recalling that Robert Mitchum acted in a Western film released the same year as *Red River,* a *film noir* called *Blood on the Moon* (also including Walter Brennan in a supporting role and a murderous stampede at the center of its plot). In the stories of both these films, the actors employ styles of understatement, like Wayne's in *Red River.*However the characters they portray are overwhelmed by the plots of their films. As good as Mitchum might be, he could not survive the burden of complications in this story, and as appropriate as McCrea's bashful style might be to the tale of the Virginian, he could not match the tough innocence of either Gary Cooper or Wayne's Ringo Kid, much less measure up to the versatility of Wayne's Tom Dunson.

The greatest challenge for comparison is the style of Humphrey Bogart, perhaps *the* actor of the forties in American films. In 1948 he appeared in the classic *Treasure of the Sierra Madre,* as Fred C. Dobbs, on a quest for the self respect he never finds. He is a romance hero who fails in his quest, and whose weaknesses of character overwhelm his pitiful gestures of defense. Like Dunson, he has beside him an old man, Howard, and a young man, Curtin. Also like Dunson, Dobbs has a face-off with the young man, but Dobbs kills his man—or he thinks he has. Like Dunson, Dobbs finds his fortune in the earth, climbing high on a mountain of gold and falling low in blinding greed. Dobbs sinks into a degradation from which he cannot rise, while Dunson sinks only until he accepts the embrace and rescue of his son. Again there is a marvelous difference of style. The saturnine qualities of Bogart are famous. On the other hand, when Wayne adds darkness and brooding to his characters, as in Dunson or Ethan Edwards, he does it in the way of romantic hero—as a low point in his quest, as a state of being, not as a fixture of character. Dobbs sinks to a dark ending, while Dunson falls into a dusty redemption.

WHEN TOM GIVES WAY to Matt in the meeting with Tess Millay, he repeats an old requirement of romance, as when Lancelot gave way to his son Galahad. Neither Tom nor Lancelot is pure enough to find the Grail, but they make possible the success of the quest in the next generation. A similar transfer of power was necessary in Virgil's *Aeneid,* as the reluctant hero Aeneas undertook his mission with unheroic energies. Tom Dunson is like Aeneas in special ways that lift his character toward mythic stature: both he and Aeneas leave women behind to disaster, both are haunted by guilt, and both pursue their destinies as mediators between past and future. Tom has Groot to point his past, and Matt his future; Aeneas had Anchises and Ascanius. As Dido, Tess Millay has a happier role than Virgil's love-sick queen, because Tess fulfills as well as tempts the heroes in their quests.

The theme of conflict between generations structures story after story in classical mythology. In Greek stories, adopted by Romans, Saturn feared usurpation by his sons, and so he did all he could to prevent it until Jupiter succeeded in taking his father's place. Then Jupiter feared the same for himself, tormenting Prometheus to learn secrets that would preserve his sovereignty. Battles between parents and children, between the fathers and the sons of gods, continue throughout the stories of ancient peoples around the world. Tom Dunson's relationship with Matthew Garth is a similar battle of generations in conflict, resolved in romance fashion. This can be compared with Hebraic narratives of the Old Testament, where father-son conflicts abound in the cycle of stories that provide the typology for the New Testament.

Tom and Matt and Cherry Valance are to one another as Adam to his sons. Tom also has the stern features of Moses during the Exodus, as both leaders sacrifice something of the future because of their special strengths from the past. The stories of Jacob/Joseph and David/Absalom have conflicts similar to *Red River*. Most telling, however, is the story of Abraham and Isaac, beginning with God's promise that "I will make of thee a great nation," and His delivery to Abram when He showed him the promised land, in words echoed by Tom Dunson when he finds his land in Texas:

> Lift up now thine eyes, and look from the place where thou are northward, and southward, and eastward, and westward.
>
> For all the land which thou seest, to thee will I give it, and to thy seed for ever. (Genesis 13: 14–15)

This story comes to a climax when God renamed Abram as Abraham, "father of many nations," and then father of Isaac, a child God instructs Abraham to sacrifice to His name. This is the relationship between Tom Dunson and his "son" Matthew Garth, whom Tom is willing to sacrifice in his zeal to complete his mission, but who is delivered, like Isaac to Abraham, as a reward in the end.

Ethan Edwards: *The Searchers* (1956)

Ethan Edwards is heir to the riches of Wayne's previous romance heroes. He has the outline of Wayne's earliest lone (and lonely) cowboy, the adventures of his earliest questing redeemers, and the ambiguities of his earliest timid lovers. Because Wayne raised that archetypal form of the romance hero above the constraints of fable in the characters of the Ringo Kid and Tom Dunson, he makes of Ethan Edwards a richer portrayal of the mythic hero. In Ethan are the Wayne-created ancestors. Wayne is the energy carrier of a genetic code for an evolutionary process that passes from any number of heroic "Johns" in the B-films of the thirties, to the youthful power of an essentially innocent Ringo Kid, through the versatile maturity of Tom Dunson, to this fulfillment in Ethan Edwards.

Ethan has the gentle, courteous manners of the Ringo Kid. When Ethan returns to his brother's home at the opening of the story, he rides slowly, with ceremonial solemnity. He dismounts quietly, shakes hands with his brother, and then he walks gracefully to Martha. He removes his hat, and then he kisses her on the forehead. Like the Kid, Ethan is courteous and kind toward women. He has, however, severe limits on his patience. His curt judgment is a sign of something deeper in Ethan than in the Kid. It is a tiny opening into a darkness always in Ethan Edwards, even when he is most gracious. It explodes into madness before the story is half over. Ethan has no tolerance for white women who have been "tainted" by Indians.

The Kid is never tested in this way. His world is limited to few women. Ethan encounters several different women in different social contexts. But, even as Ethan descends into the darkness of his hatred, he does not lose the control which underlies his mannered relationships with women. He frightens Martin in the buffalo shooting episode, he shoots eyes out of a dead Indian, and he scalps Chief Scar, but when it comes to women, even Indian women, he retains marks of his courtesy. Toward Look, Ethan is condescending and amused, but he understands her in ways Martin cannot. When Ethan finds Look's body, he shows his respect for her innocence and dignity, silently taking her beloved hat and gently removing the dust from it, while Martin merely condemns the soldiers who did the deed.

The most severe test of Ethan's courtesy occurs with white women who have lived with Indian captors. He hates and fears the taint of contact between white women and Indian men. This is not abnormal in his world. Nearly ever other character shares this attitude, with the outstanding exception of Martin, who is one-eighth Cherokee. Toward Martin, Ethan has ambivalent feelings, which undergo complex changes. When, however, everyone realizes little Debbie has become a squaw of the Indians, all freely express the very prejudice against which Ethan struggles so bitterly. The pain of irony is obvious, though not to the characters in the story, blinded as they are by social prejudices deeper and darker than any Dallas and Doc Boone had to suffer in Tonto.

Consequently, when Debbie is embraced by Ethan and then by the Jorgensons, a profound victory for tolerance is celebrated. But, before anyone can enjoy spiritual liberation, Ethan has to descend deep into the blackness of hatred within himself and his culture. Like the Ringo Kid, Ethan is mannered even at his worst. When he and Martin ride to the Army post for evidence of Debbie, Ethan has to inspect rescued white captives, including two girls of about Debbie's age. He hates the sight. His brooding, dark face as he looks at them is one of the most formidable of Wayne's career. It is conveyed, however, in a silence of restraint that lends power to his expression.

Blackness of hatred makes Ethan Edwards more complicated than the Ringo Kid, who had the motives for hatred but did not let them darken his personality. Ethan is, in this respect, more like Tom Dunson. Both grow darkly, and both learn from passages through darkness. Ethan learns tolerance when he shows love, though his education does not restore him to society as does Tom's. Wayne's hero is at the same time more romantic and more ironic in Ethan than in Tom.

Irony is in Ethan's return to a roaming existence, a borderland from which he emerges and toward which he returns. Shadows of guilt are not sufficiently driven away for Ethan to find permanent peace. A romance hero saves community from evil and barbarism, restores precious objects and persons to it when they seem lost, and enjoys the gratitude of community in the end. Ethan Edwards does these things, but he does not follow his people into the safe confines of their homes at the end. Ethan does not carry away his love, like the Kid, nor does he return to her like Breck Coleman, nor does he remain with her, like Tom Dunson. *Stagecoach* and *The Big Trail* show the hero nearest an ideal model for romance, *Red River* exhibits him approaching comedy, and *The Searchers* shows him turning into the ways of irony.

The goal of the Kid's journey is, like Breck Coleman's, vengeance as justice. The Kid succeeds, and he has the reward of love. He carries away a precious "vessel" because he had the heart to carry out his mission of duty. Ethan Edwards' motive is the same, but his goal is different: to purge corruption from the "blood." When Ethan reaches his goal, he betrays it: first, when he aims to kill Debbie at the stream, where she is shielded by Martin, in a betrayal of the higher law of love; second, ironically, when he catches up to Debbie, could kill her, but does not, in a "betrayal" of his original intention, which turns into a ritual ceremony of love instead.

The goal of Tom Dunson is to carry precious goods, the herd, to a magic place, the market. The property of Dunson is an emblem of duty. More important is the bracelet, a "ring" of love. To bring them together is his spiritual mission, and to do that he requires the mediation of his foster son Matt. Ethan Edwards also requires a mediating influence, from his foster nephew Martin. These young men enrich the quests of these later heroes, since the Ringo Kid (and, to a lesser degree, Breck Coleman) is himself a mediator and heir to the world of an older generation. Ethan learns to love more generously, and to forgive, because he learns to love the young man who accompanies him. Ethan is, however, more complicated than his heroic predecessors, because Ethan cannot embrace his "son" as

Tom Dunson does his. Ethan has only himself to embrace. He steps aside
to let Martin take his proper place in the society of men and women. Ethan
opens doors for other outsiders, but he does not enter to remain with
them.

ETHAN EDWARDS had not only the heritage of Breck Coleman, the
Ringo Kid, and Tom Dunson to enrich his character as a mythic hero. He
had a contemporary company of film heroes gathering romance to a focus.
In the Western alone there appeared in 1950 *Wagon Master* and *Winchester
'73*, *Johnny Guitar* in 1954, *Johnny Concho* in 1956, and *The Left-Handed
Gun* in 1958. These films express a special theme of menace, of dark powers
lurking behind the most common experiences of life. This was the era of
"psychological" Westerns, to which *The Searchers* makes a contribution, as
do other Wayne movies of the same period: *Hondo* in 1953, and, more con-
sequentially, *Rio Bravo* in 1959.

The company of heroes who most enrich the mythic context of Ethan
Edwards are Will Kane (Gary Cooper) in *High Noon* (1952), Shane (Alan
Ladd) in 1953, John J. Macreedy (Spencer Tracy) in *Bad Day at Black Rock*
(1954), Johnny of *The Wild One* (Marlon Brando, 1954), and Jim Stark
(James Dean), *The Rebel Without a Cause*, in 1955. Each is a hero of the
romance fable, though Will Kane is a special one for later comparisons in
viewing Wayne's *Rio Bravo*. The others, however, are considered here, not
only because of the film context they create for *The Searchers*, but also
because they signal new demands on romance heroes.

The influence of Shane is weighty. His adventure is archetypal
throughout. He descends from a mountain at the beginning, enters a home
and society in jeopardy, raises hearts in love and courage, educates a boy,
purges civilization of evil, and rides back up into his mountain heights,
wounded, to end the story. Few of Wayne's romance heroes are so completely realized. Although there are obvious points of resemblance between
Shane and Ethan Edwards, differences are significant. Shane attempts to
change his role, becoming a farmhand, and so change his identity; Ethan
makes no such attempt, as he knows he cannot when he tells Clayton he
can swear only "one oath at a time," and he swore his long ago. Shane learns
he cannot change, Ethan already knows what he is: *what* he is, however,
is not the same as *who* he is. Shane is more like Breck Coleman or the Ringo
Kid—a naive, innocent man of mystery, an alien wishing to be a part of society. Ethan knows his place, and he knows his place is lost: Ethan has to learn
he has resources of love to endure his loneliness. There is never any doubt
about Shane's capacity to love. About Ethan there is increasing doubt.

There is more barbarity as there is more darkness in Ethan Edwards
than in Alan Ladd's Shane. This releases Shane from the interior struggles
of Ethan, freeing Shane for a messianic role. The same is true for the

character Spencer Tracy plays in *Bad Day at Black Rock*. John Macreedy is a one-armed veteran of World War II who comes into a western town suspicious of strangers, finds no friendly family to welcome him, and has to fight for his life to escape. The plot reflects the long-ranging influence of *High Noon*. The absolute goodness of the hero prevails over the absolute evil of the villains, and along the way some goodness is released in a few of the townspeople, such as Doc Velie (Walter Brennan) and Tim Horn (Dean Jagger). Macreedy shares Ethan's cynicism: he only intended to pass through Black Rock on his way "out of the human race." But he leaves Black Rock a better man than he came.

Villainous Reno Smith (Robert Ryan) protests that Macreedy is "like a case of the smallpox, carrying disease" into town. Macreedy *is* a foreign substance, creating disease in the parent body, making the host inhospitable. He is an "outside agitator." The dis-ease of Ethan Edwards is a deepening understanding of himself, though he has been, and will again be, the means of reshaping the society he serves. Wayne's Ethan is more convincing as a man who gradually uncovers horror in himself than Tracy's Macreedy is as a man who gradually discovers humanity in himself. Ethan dramatizes the darkening of character Macreedy is already supposed to have when he steps off the train at Black Rock.

The topicality of *Bad Day at Black Rock*, a romance with political sermon, is comparable with *The Wild One*, a romance with a political lesson, but a romance so distorted it makes a clear example of the way society kidnaps romance forms to serve ideological ends. Will Kane and John Macreedy reject the values of their towns, even as they preach their messages of conservative or liberal politics. Johnny, on the other hand, really wants to be a part of the town against which he rebels. Johnny is a more acceptable romance hero: exchange his motorcycle for a horse, and he could ride with Shane himself.

At the end of *The Wild One* Johnny returns to "apologize" and say "thank you." He is unable, however, to say anything. He shuffles restlessly. Then he leaves, after placing the "Second Place" motorcycle trophy on the cafe counter. This is a gesture of "pure" romance, in both the senses of the word *romance*: Johnny "makes love" through this token, and he delivers the "chalice" of the questing knight. But the gesture is debased like the trophy itself, because neither Cathy nor Johnny knows where to go. She stays behind, and he rides out to rejoin his weekend rebels. Brando's Johnny is an impotent romancer. Ethan Edwards is very potent. He makes new life for the future of a better civilization in the way of a mythic father: he finds and restores children to their rightful homes. This cannot be said of Johnny in *The Wild One*, a film which leaves its world a little the worse for its hero's adventures.

The same can be said of *Rebel Without a Cause*, which makes the romance hero a caricature of myth. In fact, it makes myth into a bad word. James Dean himself is no lie, though he serves one in the kidnapped romance of this film. As in *East of Eden* and *Giant*, he is searching for a father, the father Wayne's characters often provide. Jim Stark moves into a new town, quickly identifies with the kids who have the same family problems he has, and he becomes a hero to them. To Buzz he becomes a brother, to Plato a father, and to Judy a husband. They offer a vision of change, or real growth. But the film makes Buzz and Plato into villains, so it can recapture the potency of Jim and Judy for its own social confirmations. Ethan is a "rebel" with a lost "cause" of the American Civil War. That rebellion and that cause are emblems of Ethan's integrity: bonds of his loyalty to the best of the past without blindness to the worst. Jim Stark lacks what Ethan Edwards has to offer: a vision of integrity, a model of humanity which can inform and restore society to lost wholeness.

ETHAN EDWARDS explores, as a mythic hero, cultural darknesses. He is an investigation into ideas of the Nietzschean "superman," because Ethan places himself above another race, to his discredit. He is an experiment in understanding what happens to idealists of a lost cause, of a lost battle, of the defeated. Thus are many romantic heroes, from Aeneas to Robin Hood. Ethan Edwards is heir to Wayne's romance heroes, and, behind them, to all who have surrendered personal happiness for the sake of larger social and spiritual well being. This makes for his mythic stature, and this raises him above the plot of his story. Ethan is an American culture hero. He is identified with the cause of the Confederacy, without making him a spokesman for its politics. His name is a combination of American heroic associations: Ethan Allen of Revolutionary fame, and Jonathan Edwards, of prerevolutionary colonial fame. He continues the practice of Wayne's romance heroes: to identify with the destiny of the nation, its tribulations as well as its triumphs.

The film opens with its theme song, "What makes a man to wander?/What makes a man to roam? What makes a man abandon all,/And turn his back on home?" When myths are stabilized, when there are complete cycles for imaginative growth, through romance to comedy and through tragedy to romance, then answers come clear: a man must wander because he is Adam, a child of Adam, looking for lost perfection and lost innocence. Like Cain, he is burdened by guilt of pride, and so he roams and wanders in his constant purgation. But "what makes a man abandon all,/And turn his back on home?" If he wanders farther from the ideal of his lost perfection, he will be abandoned. If he carries a vision of perfection to be recovered, then he only seems to abandon all and only seems to turn his back on home.

Ethan Edwards has associations with numerous mythic heroes. Theseus rescued maidens from the Minotaur in the Labyrinth of Crete. Perseus saved Andromeda from the sea monster. Hercules went down into the kingdom of death to carry back Alcestis. More especially Ethan is Orestes, the archetypal avenger: he undertakes his quest driven by Furies of guilt, until he submits to a judgment which vindicates his integrity.

Ethan Edwards is John Wayne's highest achievement in the romance form. He gathers the light of previous portrayals, he keeps faith with the romance, and he enriches it with a specifically American myth, a general Judeo-Christian one, and a deeply archetypal Classical one as well. He rises clear of temporal realities without abandoning them, and he raises the structure of his fable to mythic dimensions without betraying its debts to primitive imagination.

Reuben "Rooster" Cogburn: *True Grit* (1969)

"Reuben" is a name for the first born son of the patriarch Jacob, who laid a terrible curse on his son: "Reuben, thou art my firstborn, my might, and the beginning of my strength, the excellency of dignity, and the excellency of power: Unstable as water, thou shalt not excel; because thou wentest up to thy father's bed; then defiledst thou it" (Genesis 49: 3–4). As the name of John Wayne's character in *True Grit*, then, Reuben is a name of profound ambivalence. In the later story of *Rooster Cogburn* (1975), he is pressed by Eula Goodnight (Katharine Hepburn) to confess his Christian name: "My baptized name is Reuben. But I ask you not to repeat that to nobody." Eula is surprised: "Why not? It is a name of which to be proud! Reuben led the foremost tribe of Israel." Rooster responds, "Well, it hit rock-bottom with me."

Reuben Cogburn is like Reuben son of Jacob. Both have various excellencies of strength, power, and even dignity. But they are both "unstable as water" in some fundamental way which prevents them from excelling. Rooster tells Eula his tail feathers droop and his waddles show. His strength is in decline, though his pride in that strength remains high: "I can still out-crow anything in the barnyard." The rock-bottom is deep within, or pushed far back, in his life, concealed by the new and preferred name he bears.

Reuben Cogburn has not retreated so far from his given name in *True Grit* as in *Rooster Cogburn*. More characters of the earlier film know his name, though they also know him as "Rooster." Reuben has no "real" family—he lives with Chen Lee and an itinerant cat by the name of General Stirling Price, whom he introduces to Mattie Ross as his "father" and his "nephew." They are all the family he has, and while they may constitute a family satisfying enough to Rooster Cogburn, they are not a family of the sort Mattie expected to meet. Later Mattie will get Rooster to confess more about his personal life to her, but until that remarkable scene, the "family" of Chen Lee and Stirling Price must do.

Reuben Cogburn lives barely within the confines of social order. He is a hunter of men, and his respect for his prey is purely that of a hunter. He hunts for pay and booty. He expects to find his prey will be "rats." Mattie is impressed with his credentials as a man who can be relied upon for getting tough with the killer of her father. However, she has mixed feelings about Rooster and Rooster's "ethics" when she sits with him in his lodgings. Reuben has become so alienated from ordinary human society he has come close to losing his inheritance as a human being altogether.

Rooster has respect for his prey when that prey earns it, as in the case of Ned Pepper. This, however, is not much: it is still the respect of a rat-catcher for his rats. Rooster's physical features are expressions of his inheritance, not only the consequences of his aging. Rooster is a slob, a drunk, a boor, and a menace to life itself. No wonder, then, Stonehill tells Mattie he would not want to sleep with Rooster, and certainly it is no surprise that neither would Mattie. She will change her mind by the end of the film, when she invites Rooster to lie with her in eternity — if not in Arkansas. That moment of the story identifies Rooster as the outcast who has a home in heaven if not on earth. There he recovers his mythic identity, lost as his name of Reuben the disinherited one has suggested.

GIVEN THE AMBIVALENT reasons for his disinheritance or alienation as Reuben, what comes into better focus with clearer reasons is his name of "Rooster." Eula says, in *Rooster Cogburn*, "Why should you be called Rooster? I never heard a man called that before." Rooster replies, "Well, I guess in the old days I was cocky. Kind of a struttin' bird." He can still crow because he can still "outdo" the other creatures in the barnyard. He has pride in his physical courage, more than a mere compensation for being a social outcast. He is like the outlaw heroes of romance, like the Ringo Kid, Robin Hood, and the Scarlet Pimpernel.

Rooster reveals to Mattie in his "confession" he *has* been an outlaw. When LaBoeuf needles Rooster about riding with Quantrill, Rooster tenses at the accusation Quantrill's raiders killed women and children in the notorious raid on Lawrence, Kansas. Rooster did ride with Quantrill, whose "soldiers" were possibly murderers and thieves, just as LaBoeuf says they were. Whether they were so, depends on "your point of view," which turns them into patriots for the Confederacy as Rooster would call them. They were criminals only because they were on the losing side. In this shadowy realm, Rooster does not like to move any more: he warns LaBoeuf to "let it alone."

The borderline of ethics, defined by a mysterious past during the American Civil War, marks Rooster's personal history. It associates him with other Wayne characters from John Ashley in *The Lonely Trail* (1936) to Ethan Edwards in *The Searchers* (1956). In the "old days" of self-certain

Top: With Kim Darby (as Mattie Ross). *Bottom*: Wayne and Darby admiring H.W. Gim's (as Chen Lee) cat in *True Grit*, 1969.

commitment to a clear-cut ideal of some kind, the hero could be "cocky." Now, in the present of *True Grit*, however, that calling is less clear and those ideals are less assuring. The old cock of the walk is bedraggled in ethics as well as in body; his vision is blurred by uncertainty (and drink), and it is constrained by alien laws and customs (as by the loss of one eye).

Mattie is a Red Riding Hood wandering through a forest of cops and criminals. She is gathering details of an unsavory fellow when she asks about this Rooster Cogburn. The sheriff in Fort Smith tells her Rooster is the "meanest" of the federal marshals in town; her landlady tells her she has "heard some terrible things" about Cogburn; Stonehill says "most people here have heard of Rooster Cogburn, and some people live to regret it." Stonehill asks her, "How did you light on that greasy vagabond?" Mattie herself calls Rooster a "sorry piece of trash." This is not a promising description of a romance hero.

Rooster is a hero in an animal fable. *True Grit* is filled with the liveliness of animality. It is an animal farm that includes the cat, the rat, a turkey, a horse compared to a sheep, a character named LaBoeuf, and another name Finch. Into this barnyard comes evil in all human shapes but also in the most sinister of animal shapes, rattlesnakes in the pit where Mattie Ross falls and where Rooster descends to rescue her. This use of animals, animal names, and animal images, is an ancient storytelling technique in folklore and sophisticated narratives alike. It is obviously substantial in Aesop's *Fables* and Orwell's *Animal Farm*. It is a little less obvious, but just as important, in the works of such modern and sophisticated writers as W.B. Yeats, D.H. Lawrence, Dylan Thomas, and Ted Hughes.

True Grit is not an Aesopian fable, but it draws its imaginative power from that tradition, as well as from a Christian tradition that incorporates folklore and animal imagery. Rooster Cogburn is guardian of a barnyard where his crow warns against lions and foxes, just as the medieval English poet Chaucer described Chauntecleer (which Chaucer "borrowed" from many preceding tales of the Cock and the Fox). The Rooster crows also to announce the rise of the sun, the new day of safety after a night of danger. Such natural action is the stuff of many a symbolic tale, as in the story by D.H. Lawrence, "The Man Who Died," originally called "The Escaped Cock." This is the story of Jesus, who is in Christian iconography represented by the rooster crowing at dawn. Christ warned, in the gospel of Mark, "Watch ye therefore: for ye know not when the master of the house cometh, at even, or at midnight, or at the cockcrowing, or in the morning" (13: 35). When Rooster climbs down to help Mattie out of the snake pit, he enacts a Christian archetype of heroic descent — the rooster destroying the serpent. His "grit" is not only the gravel of earth that makes a rooster's digestion work, nor is it only the courage of the human hero: it is also the essence of the redeemer, which is the "truth" of true grit.

Wayne, Darby, and Glen Campbell (as LaBoeuf).

Rooster is not only an old cock whose feathers drag. He is also cockeyed, looking the way a rooster will, from off to the side, tipping its head to get its focus. John Wayne is such a rooster in this tale, creating rooster-like attitudes in head and body. Rooster Cogburn has to cock his eye, because it is the only one he has. The one-eyed man is cockeyed because he is so eccentric, so intimidating to his brethren, but also because he is like those ancient outcasts, the Cyclops—giants with one eye. They are monsters in the stories of Homer, divine instruments of providence in Hesiod's verses. Cockeyed Cogburn is a social monster who acquires spiritual grace from his rescue of the innocent girl Mattie Ross. He is even Polyphemus, who fell in love with Galatea in Ovid's *Metamorphoses;* like that Cyclops, Cogburn is a little ridiculous as he serves his ladylove.

At the end, when Mattie invites him to take the place of her dead father in her heart and life, she warns Rooster not to jump his new horse over the four-rail fence: "You're getting too old and too fat to be jumping over fences." But Rooster knows better, as he tells her, "Come see a fat old man sometime." He leaps toward heaven like the good romance hero he is. His ascent is captured in a still shot held beneath the concluding credits of the film: an emblem of his apotheosis.

AT THE CENTER of *True Grit* is a special feature of romance, the "confession." If this were a tale of the Middle Ages, it would be a confession by the knight during his retreat to a local monastery while on the way to his next adventure with evil. (Thus did Ingmar Bergman employ the convention in his allegorical film of *The Seventh Seal* in 1957.) Naturalistically, it

Rooster Cogburn (1975), six years after *True Grit*.

is set in the darkening landscape where Rooster and Mattie wait for Ned Pepper's gang at the dugout. Mattie questions Rooster about his background. The old man tells "tall tales" to the little girl. Rooster relaxes, becomes grandfatherly.

As a convention, however, the scene is also a repetition of the spiritual confession which, say, Dante makes to Matilda and Beatrice at the end of his purgatorial journey in the *Divine Comedy*. The "priest" is not a man, not even a woman, but a girl. This is even better for the convention than in *Rooster Cogburn*, where the confession is made to a mature, though still virginal, woman, Eula Goodnight. Rooster needs a situation of unquestioned innocence, of uncorrupted integrity, and unstained frankness, which he has in the person of Mattie Ross.

Their discussion proceeds thus:

> MATTIE: How'd you lose your eye?
> ROOSTER: It was in the war. Lone Jack. Little scrap outside Kansas City.
> MATTIE: What'd you do after the war?
> ROOSTER: I robbed me a federal paymaster and went to Cairo, Illinois, and bought a eatin' place there called "The Green Frog" and married a grass-widow. Place had a billiard table.

MATTIE: You never told me you had a wife!

ROOSTER: Oh, well, I didn't crave their so-ci-ee-ty, so she up and left me and went back to her first husband who was clerkin' in a hardware store in Paducah. "Goodbye, Reuben," she says. "The love of decency does not abide in you." That's a divorced woman talking for you — 'bout decency! Well, I told her, I said, "Good-bye, Nola, and I hope that nail-sellin' husband makes you happy this time."

MATTIE: Did you have any children?

ROOSTER: Oh, there was a boy. Nola taken him with her. He never liked me anyway. A clumsier child you'll never see than Horace. I bet he broke forty cups.

MATTIE: Never did get you . . . for stealin' that money?

ROOSTER: I didn't consider it stealin'!

MATTIE: Didn't belong to you.

ROOSTER: I needed a road-stake. Like that little high-interest bank in New Mexico. Needed a road-stake, and there it was. I never robbed no citizen, takin' a man's watch!

MATTIE: Its' all stealing.

ROOSTER: That's the position them New Mexicans took. I had to flee for my life. Beau was a young colt then, no horse could ride 'im into the ground. When that posse thinned out, I . . . I turned old Beau around, and takin' them reins in my teeth, I charged them boys firing two [laughs with pleasure of the memory] . . . They must've all been married men that loved their families, 'cause they scattered and run for home!

More of the story about his "disinheritance" comes clear. The loss of his eye becomes a badge of his courage. It is a sign of his lost vision, lost innocence, as it may be a sign for the nation he served then, or for the one he now serves. He took his wartime ethics into the peacetime society that triumphed, and there he found himself permanently out of place. He is a servant, though not a part, of society. He now serves the federal government (even its carpetbagging Judge Parker) he once fought against and once robbed, but he serves at the price of his alienation from it.

At the end of his confessional, he rises to his tale of two-gun assault on a New Mexico posse, a high point in his career which gives him joy to remember. His telling is a prophecy of a repetition audiences of *True Grit* enjoy as well as he does telling it to Mattie. But, in a moment of tenderness, Mattie sees through his gusto of storytelling. She asks, or asserts, quietly, "You don't have any family, do you? Except Chen Lee, and that lazy cat?"

This is the insight of the innocent, and old Rooster is taken aback. Mattie is right. Rooster does *not* have a family. Whether a romance hero *can* have a family is at the heart of the nature of romance. He cannot have a family, except as it is the family of man, of all life. And so Rooster answers, "Oh, General Price don't belong to me. Cats don't belong to nobody. He just rooms with me." There can be no "belonging" anywhere, of anyone by anyone, in the romance world. Rooster teaches as he confesses. He says, finally, "Course I depend on him." In the style of its acting, Rooster does not let it become sentimental. He will make a greater family for himself, so he does not have to depend only on a cat. He becomes Mattie's spiritual father as he has been Chen Lee's "spiritual" son.

ROOSTER COGBURN is an excellent example of Wayne's heroic image accommodating change: in his age, features, public, and competition. Kept within romance narrative, relationships of love are distanced, without diminishment, from the sexual to the social. This is a commentary on Wayne's star relationship with his audience over the decades. He became more avuncular or patriarchal, but his image continued to be heroic and his service of imagination continued to be messianic.

This was a decade when the best popular films glorified outlaws: *Bonnie and Clyde* (1967), *Butch Cassidy and the Sundance Kid* (1969), and *Dr. Zhivago* (1965). Some celebrated the loner in familiar romance structures: *Lawrence of Arabia* (1962), *Tom Jones* (1963), *Lord Jim* (1965), *The Graduate* (1967), and *Easy Rider* (1969). Wayne's Rooster Cogburn is at home in his decade, as Wayne always was in his romance roles. Films edged into irony, as in *Psycho* (1960), *Hud* (1963), and *Harper* (1966); into satire as in *Lolita* (1962), *Dr. Strangelove* (1964), and *The Pink Panther* (1964); into parody as in *Batman* (1966) and *Barbarella* (1968). Romance is their point of departure. This was to be the decade of irony, one might say, and as such, John Wayne made his adaptations to it in such films as *The Man Who Shot Liberty Valance* (1962) and *El Dorado* (1967). Rooster barely survives the temptations of irony, because he can make his confession to Mattie and because he can still ride his winged Pegasus toward the heavens.

That is a considerable accomplishment for Wayne's heroic image, because it had to compete with talented and demanding new actors. These were Paul Newman, Warren Beatty, Steve McQueen, and especially Clint Eastwood, who was beginning to challenge Wayne on Wayne's own turf (the romance Western). Eastwood was even pushing that challenge into new territory, as in *Coogan's Bluff* (1968). This film, with others such as *Bullitt*, present a direction Wayne tries in *Brannigan* and *McQ*. Just as Tarzan finally went to New York in 1942 and Sherlock Holmes to Washington, D.C., in 1943, so the Western cowboy had to go to the City in *Coogan's Bluff*.

Eastwood's Coogan shows the self parody of Wayne's Rooster Cogburn, as he shows the same explosive impatience. Coogan returns to Arizona without lessons of self sacrifice Rooster learns, even though Coogan also rises in ascent. Rooster waves his hat in farewell to the girl Mattie, and Coogan kisses goodbye to the woman Julie. Coogan uses sexual charm as a tool of his trade. He seduces Julie for information about Linny Raven, and he seduces Linny for information about Jimmy Ringerman. Like Eastwood's other romance heroes, Coogan moves toward deeper isolation of satiric irony than Wayne's. The title of the film is a symbol of Coogan's existential loneliness; he has "locked the world out," just like Mrs. Coogan at Coogan's Bluff.

None of Wayne's romance heroes does this, even at their worst. Rooster, not the worst, retreats, from women and the world, but he always comes back out to learn he cannot remain in retreat permanently. It may take a child to lead him, but he follows the lead and he puts limits on the extent he allows anyone to cross the line of social decency. Rooster does things Coogan would do, such as kicking a prisoner, but he will work for a girl as he says he would not work for a woman. He will live in love and friendship with a Chinese, talk with cats, and enjoy the trust and confidence of Indians in Indian Territory. These are touches of the Wayne hero Eastwood must acquire to enrich his own heroes of later films.

Younger heroes of romance in the sixties mounted a campaign to usurp the place of John Wayne, only to find themselves outdone and upstaged. Older ones were still in abundance and making Westerns in the modern ways at the same time as Wayne's Cogburn films. There were *Lonely Are the Brave* (1962, with Kirk Douglas), *Ride the High Country* (1964, with Randolph Scott and Joel McCrea), *Will Penny* (1968, with Charlton Heston), and in the year of *True Grit* there was *The Wild Bunch* (with William Holden and Robert Ryan, among others). Some aimed for the difference of psychological analysis, others for social analysis, that came with changing times and changing values; some were movements toward tragedy, like *Lonely Are the Brave*, others toward irony, like *The Wild Bunch*. All were cast from the same mould of romance, as in the curious Western of *The Misfits* (1961).

The Misfits identifies three men and Roslyn Taber (Marilyn Monroe) with a herd of wild horses in the mountains. The title is an emblem for the alienated souls of modern culture. Sadly the most misfit is Gay Langland, still trying to be Clark Gable, as Gable was in *Gone with the Wind* and many other films in between. The way Gay courts Roslyn, trying to compete with two younger men, dramatizes limitations on the romance hero as an old man. Wayne's way, as Rooster Cogburn in *True Grit*, is not only more credible but, more importantly, it is also more honorable.

Honor is in the faith *True Grit* has in its basic romance form, and it is in the joyous fidelity John Wayne has in his romance role, even as a fat old man. If he chased a girl half his age, as Gay chases Roslyn, Rooster would be little more than a seedy, dirty old man in the farce of January and May. He would betray not only the romance tradition, he would also betray the Wayne myth. As Rooster, he is true to both.

James Brannigan: *Brannigan* (1975)

After 45 years of success as a hero of romance, Wayne made yet another stab in *Brannigan*. Wayne is 67 years old when he makes this film, and he is required by the plot and the romance conventions to play a part which should be done by someone half his age (or by Clint Eastwood, 44 in 1974). Nevertheless, John Wayne can pull it off simply because he is a man of myth, and his myth adds meaning to his character Wayne could not otherwise have given at the time.

For example, Wayne could survive a paternalistic relationship with women because he has become a father figure in his mythic image. He would need to survive in a somewhat decadent film during an era dominated by the *Godfather* films, by the *Dirty Harry* films, and by the two versions of *The French Connection*. In all of these the value of a woman is hardly flattering to the integrity of women as real human beings. This was the decade the United States Congress passed the Equal Rights Amendment (1972—never to be ratified by the states, however). It was a period when women themselves felt increasingly vulnerable in the competition for equal rights; Clare Booth Luce lamented in an essay she published in 1973, "The Technological Castaway," that "male supremacy is the most obvious and massive fact in our society."[25]

It is an "obvious and massive fact" in *Brannigan* in ways to surprise the viewer of Wayne as a hero of romance. He had been attentive to women in old-fashioned ways that verged on the godfatherly in his romance roles, on the macho in his comic roles, but he worked within well-established conventions as he did so. That included his innocent pursuit of the virgin in *The Big Trail*, his loving, tolerant treatment of women in *Stagecoach*, his learning from mistakes in *Red River*, his learning tolerance in *The Searchers*, and his self parody as a seedy misogynist in *True Grit* and *Rooster Cogburn*. This is a role developed brilliantly by Clint Eastwood, and it is a role Wayne found comfortable in his later films.

But it does not ring true in *Brannigan*. The women of this story are little more than "technological castaways." They are, in "ascending" order of importance: a parade of women through Piccadilly Circus; a screaming barmaid; a thieving girlfriend, Miss Rook; a prostitute; a lonely, love-hungry landlady, Mrs. Cooper; and a sweetly innocent guardian, Jenny Thatcher, who works for Scotland Yard.

The prostitute serves the special tastes of the assassin Gorman. In the conventional image of woman's degradation, the nameless prostitute displays her charms of legs and breasts for the camera long before the arrival of Gorman. This woman is allowed one bit of self respect when she protests against Gorman's mixing pain with sexual pleasure: "Nice and gentle, love!" she says while he puts his hand around her throat. "I'm not kinky!" But Gorman makes the conventional response, "You are what you're paid to be."

Certainly Brannigan would not do this. He is at the opposite end of the spectrum of values represented by Gorman. But Brannigan moves through a world where women have little more value than the prostitute. In his own apartment building Brannigan is the object of seduction by his landlady, Mrs. Cooper. She gives him her best smile, waves her fingers coyly in greeting, and after his "wc" blows up, she invites him to stay in her apartment. This is the film's contrast with Gorman, but it nevertheless betrays the romance hero's higher ideal of courtly manners when it allows Commander Swann to accept Mrs. Cooper's invitation to "coffee" immediately after Brannigan refuses her.

Coffee is about all Brannigan shares with a woman in the story. He and Jenny ride cars together, eat together, and confront Gorman together in two particularly violent scenes. Jenny is a thin version of the constant companion to a romance-hero. She is not even much of a sex object for Brannigan, apart from lame jokes about Yanks from World War II who were "overpaid, over-sexed, and over here." She chauffeurs Brannigan, and as such she almost loses her life. She is played for a woman-as-man, exposed to violence because she has stepped out of the conventional role of woman as sex object.

Within the world of the police, Jenny is assigned the "gentle" jobs. This is despite the fact she was transferred from assignment to "vice." It is part of a pattern of relegating women to their "proper" places, and Jenny's usual, if not proper, place is in Vice. It is inconsistent with the role of the character in the main plot; it is a part of the aroma of the film in its decadence, rather than in the focus of the film as a romance adventure. Sir Charles Swann, a decadent of the British aristocracy, is a gentleman of sorts. When he receives the amputated finger (from Larkin's third finger, left hand), Swann nervously finds an excuse to get Jenny out of the room, before he shows the finger to Brannigan (but not to the audience). The connection of sex and violence is obvious to Swann and Brannigan, and it ought to be routine for an officer from Vice, but Jenny must be excused when men deal with the realities of life.

WHAT MAKES the romance hero's adventures acceptable is the broad humor of the style. Brannigan suggests the "terminal" qualities of Wayne's Stony Brooke in the "Mesquiteer" films. This is an end of the line for the romance hero, who looks like a bull in a china shop. The film plays against the roles of similar characters in other popular films of the time, as it plays against the reputation of John Wayne himself. In this self-conscious way it becomes an entertaining performance—as a hero in decline.

The humor echoes films Wayne made for John Ford, with lines of division between women and men. When those lines are crossed, comedy or tragedy results. *Brannigan* tries to keep the lines distinct in unsuccessful ways, even as it blurs the focus on places for women. One place not for women is in the bar where Brannigan meets Drexel—that is, except as a

servant of the men, like the barmaid who screams a lot in the scene. Here
is broad humor and self-conscious parody. Drexel, a pathetic and minor
character, invites Brannigan to his apartment for a drink. Quite implausible,
but who cares? The invitation once made will help advance the plot only
somewhat, but the real point is to give Brannigan one more slapstick opportunity: he grabs a bottle of whiskey raised in the air by one of the fighting
men in the pub. At Drexel's, he will be praised as an American "who thinks
big."

The comic sequence does not end with the macabre killing of Drexel.
Brannigan spots and pursues the suspected killer in the customary romance
way. But this is a city story, in the era of *Bullitt* and *The French Connection*.
It has a spectacular jump on Tower Bridge, which marks its generic class
(nothing really new in it, if one recalls how often Wayne jumped his horses
in dangerous spots throughout his films of the thirties). The difference is the
humor of the chase, as Keystone Cop Brannigan confiscates a citizen's new
car for the purpose. He puts the owner in a frenzy. The final touch occurs
when Swann informs Brannigan he owns the car he wrecked so dramatically,
but which took neither him nor the story any closer to an objective.

Such adventures pump a little life into a tired convention. The energy
of the hero is, however, almost as tired as the rest of the film. Brannigan
does have some gusto at times, as in the brawl in the pub. Usually he is sitting, merely standing, or even lying on the ground, when he is not in a car.
He needs a lot of help to keep going. There is something sad about the use
of slow-motion shots in the two violent action sequences. They punctuate
the condition of this romance hero as a man who has slowed down.

Brannigan does the things a romance-hero is supposed to do. He goes
through deadly adventures to overcome obstacles in the way of his goal. He
is on a quest of vengeance. Brannigan's personal motive is more "professional" than most have been in Wayne's career or romance-heroes: his partner has been killed by Larkin, and Brannigan feels responsibility, though
he disliked the partner. Professional pride is more important than emotional and moral outrage. Even here is a touch of parody, and a self-
referential statement about what happens to an actor whose mythic stature
is too large for a single role any longer.

This turns it into a theatrical joke. Brannigan is on a lark when he pursues Larkin. He meets a Jenny, then a Swann; his landlady is a Cooper, and
the pathetic city clerk is a Rook. Everyone is a bird. They flit across and
around Mel Fields, and the action is propelled by the husk of a man that
is Brannigan. These are characters gone to seed, Wayne's Brannigan not the
least. From grit to bran is not so great a distance, after all.

WAYNE'S BRANNIGAN mirrors, as a distortion, fads of the time. *Brannigan* has similarities with *Coogan's Bluff*, given the plot of extraditing a

criminal, the journey by the hero to an alien environment of law enforcement where he has few if any legal justifications for personal violence, and the lessons to be learned in humility by both parties. Both take an uncomplimentary attitude toward women, and in Brannigan's case the best he can do to compete with Coogan is to "use" Jenny as his chauffeur—not a serious competition after all is said and done. Brannigan's return to Chicago is as conventional as Coogan's return to Arizona, when it is viewed as a way to bring the romance structure to an end; it is, however, hardly as "romantic" in the erotic sense.

Since Eastwood plays Coogan tongue-in-cheek anyway, there is not much to be gained by parody, except to say "I can do that too." On the other hand, Brannigan becomes more of a commentary as a character compared with Eastwood's Dirty Harry and with Gene Hackman's Popeye Doyle. In the case of Popeye, two films were necessary to round out the romance structure of *The French Connection* (1971, same year as *Dirty Harry;* and 1975, same year as *Brannigan*). Popeye Doyle is a disreputable, small-time drug buster for the New York City Police. His reputation has been tainted by a past which includes the killing of a fellow officer, and it will be more deeply tainted when Popeye accidentally kills the federal officer Bill Mulderig. When Popeye discovers he has shot Mulderig instead of Charnier, he has not a second thought, much less regret, as he disappears into the decaying rooms of the final setting in *The French Connection I.*

Popeye Doyle is a mindless, sexually perverted and obsessive instrument of the law. He is a commentary on law and its enforcement practices. He can only be made into a romance hero as such a hero merges with the *eiron,* the outsider in irony, where the world of the ironist is strongly corrupted by the world he observes. However, when Popeye is taken to Marseilles to complete his pursuit of Charnier in *The French Connection II,* he is redeemed as romance hero. The system becomes the target, rather than persons in the system. Although Brannigan never becomes, nor could he become, such a scapegoat as Popeye in Marseilles, Brannigan is an agent of his own police chief, who sends squad cars of Chicago police to pick up Brannigan. Even though Brannigan is a loner with "unconventional" methods of law enforcement, he is not a threat to the system or to his superiors in the system, the way Popeye Doyle is to become by the end of *The French Connection I.*

Brannigan in London becomes a representative of American ideals of justice, not a critic of those corrupted ideals, as Popeye does in Marseilles. Brannigan is father of a son who is assistant district attorney in Cook County. Thus Brannigan, who insists there will be no more policemen in his family, marks a progressive transition toward law and order of a just and equitable kind. He kills a demon, just as Popeye does: both use weapons illegally in a host country, and both shoot their victims in harbors. Popeye

has nowhere to go at the end of *The French Connection II*, while Brannigan
has a home to which he returns.

The French Connection inspired the crazy scene by Brannigan across
the Tower Bridge, as *Bullitt* had inspired *The French Connection*. They
share romantic conventions of flight-and-pursuit. Both *Bullitt* and *The
French Connection* films have an ingredient missing from *Brannigan*,
however: the patent political message. To survive, Popeye lives and works
outside the system he serves. In his first film, this is suggested by his personal life style and by his reputation for inept work; in the second, by his
enforced drug addiction. The first was mainly careful not to accuse
establishment figures; it is a Hitchcockian thriller which opens the seams
of a clean exterior to let vermin crawl forth. The second, however, is filled
with blatant social and political criticism.

Brannigan could so the same. At times it seems to be answering *The
French Connection II*. Except in *Brannigan* the criticism is directed at the
reputation of English, not American, law and law enforcement. Things go
wrong in London that Swann cannot believe possible, and they are not all
caused by the introduction of an alien guest (as in *Coogan's Bluff*). Brannigan does the job in London which Coogan could not do in New York City,
and Brannigan does his job in a way that is successful as it could not be for
Popeye Doyle in Marseilles.

That way is made clear by comparing Brannigan with his close
kinsman, "Dirty" Harry. Interconnections between Wayne and Eastwood
are many. Between these two films is a wave of recognition. Harry Callahan
uses the expression (referring to working overtime), "That'll be the day!"
This echoes Ethan Edwards in *The Searchers*, as does Harry's reputation for
racial bigotry. On the other hand, *Brannigan* opens on images of a police
gun and a policeman's badge, in imitation of *Dirty Harry's* opening over the
badge of a San Francisco police officer. When Brannigan makes his first,
spectacular, entrance on the counterfeiter, he is repeating the ironic
episode of *Dirty Harry* when Harry breaks open the door of Scorpio's lodg-
ing: this was a mistake in law by Harry, while it is a habit of Brannigan (to
enter before knocking). Brannigan holds an unloaded weapon to bluff the
counterfeiter to surrender; this repeats the trick Dirty Harry uses to open
and close his story, "Russian roulette" on his captives—one wins, the other
loses.

When Popeye Doyle uses such methods, he is vulgar and not even
effective. When Dirty Harry uses them, he is slick, effective, and cynical.
But when Brannigan uses them, he is crude, effective, and idealistic. Dirty
Harry takes shortcuts to law enforcement and runs up against his mayor,
played by John Vernon; Brannigan takes a long trip to enforce the law and
runs up against Ben Larkin, played by the same John Vernon. Brannigan
defies the Popeye Doyles and the Dirty Harrys of the world, just as he defies

both the London Police and the Chicago Police. The world suffers even when Harry and Popeye succeed, but it benefits when Brannigan goes to work.

His mythic stature is suggested when Jenny meets Brannigan at the airport in London. She had been instructed to look for someone "only slightly smaller than the Statue of Liberty." To the thugs Brannigan is a "big Irish bastard," but to others Brannigan is a statue of Liberty, a hero of romantic myth. That raises him above politics and propaganda, above the vulgarity of materials mimicked in his own film or imitated by Dirty Harry and Popeye Doyle.

11. Tragic Heroes

The pressure of World War II and the preeminence of the United States in world affairs produced much imagery and many themes in Wayne's films of the forties. Playing at war had suddenly become real life. Then it could be turned again into playing at war, with a new level of significance for the actor/artist and for his audience which felt the mythic power of his image as a hero.

Wayne's heroes of tragedy are motivated by ideals of love and patriotism in *The Fighting Seabees* (1944), *Sands of Iwo Jima* (1949), and *The Alamo* (1960). Wedge Donovan learns as he makes mistakes; he rises in spirit as he drives himself to atone for errors of arrogance and ignorance. Sgt. John M. Stryker, mythic in the role of selfless leader, lives for his men. Stryker is an instance of the hero who sublimates passion into discipline of service, passes on his powers of leadership to a younger generation, then fades into nature and society when he dies in an unheroic manner.

After *Sands of Iwo Jima*, Wayne's hero of tragic myth takes on the challenge of shaping history for contemporary expression. Clearly so in *The Alamo*, it was also true of *The Fighting Seabees* and *Sands of Iwo Jima*, where the "history" was too recent to seem "historical." Wedge Donovan and John Stryker are less historical than Davy Crockett only because their settings are more familiar in audience imagination of war. Wayne's heroes move from story as propaganda to story as history. With *The Alamo*, movement regresses as history becomes story and propaganda as well, while the hero of history becomes a hero of myth.

The Cowboys in 1972 and *The Shootist* in 1976 mark distinctive turns from history and propaganda. These present men as heroes without large public identities and without reputations for public service. These heroes and films are conventional instances of the Western, just as *The Fighting Seabees* and *Sands of Iwo Jima* are conventional types of the war film. On the other hand, all are unconventional developments of John Wayne's career as a hero of tragic myth.

Will Andersen in *The Cowboys* is a different man than Donovan, Stryker, or Crockett. Andersen is private, reticent, and humble. His band

182

of men are not construction workers, soldiers, or frontiersmen. They are boys who look for him to teach and lead, to love and respect them. Will learns from the boys that he can still give of himself, even unto death. His tragedy is that he had to lose so much before he realized what he had to give. Andersen's is the tragedy of a private man, whose death drives boys to a violent outburst of bloody vengeance.

John Bernard Books also involves youth in a bloody conclusion to *The Shootist*. Books' heroism is quite different, though no less powerful than Andersen's. Books has lived by the gun and chooses to die by it. His act of choice, not his habitual courage, makes the man heroic. He is an *essential*, not existential hero. He recognizes the worth of others, sharing himself with them to his end.

John Wayne brought the same skills of acting style in challenging, interesting, and artful ways to all these characters. The more able he was to display an essential tenderness for life, the more painful it may be to accept the need for violence in the acts of heroes. Both the tact of the actor and the decorum of the genre are needed to create effective art especially in tragic forms. They come together in *Sands of Iwo Jima*, *The Shootist*, and perhaps in *The Cowboys*. The other films establish a norm for the actor's work in the genre, by which his artistic successes are seen more clearly.

Wedge Donovan: *The Fighting Seabees* (1944)

John Wayne could play the hero who makes an act of self sacrifice that results in his death, as in *Reap the Wild Wind*, two years before *The Fighting Seabees*. Susan Hayward appears in both films, though in the first she is paired with the "good" villain played by Robert Preston. In *The Fighting Seabees* she falls in love with two heroes at once: one must die for her to be happy. In both films John Wayne dies. He is more heroic and tragic in *The Fighting Seabees*. Wedge Donovan is a great man made small by forces greater than he. Action subordinates character to circumstances of history. In other times, other places, Wedge Donovan would have lived and thrived. Because he is valuable, he is precisely the sacrifice required in tragic action. He, like heroes in stories since Achilles, could have chosen to stay at home and live a long life, or leave home and find glory in a short life instead. He chose the glory.

The plot of events is nicely symmetrical in *The Fighting Seabees*. The first half shows the moral decline of skillful leader whose physical courage rises paradoxically to its highest at the same time. The second half pictures moral ascent to reenforce the physical courage already demonstrated. Together moral and physical courage produce spiritual triumph in tragic, dramatic splendor.

Wedge Donovan heads a company building Navy bases on islands in the Pacific during early days of World War II. Wedge leads workers in heroic march, some driving bulldozers, to confront the dastardly enemy. They will show that Americans can fight as well as build. In a huge tragic irony, not only are they no match for trained soldiers well armed, they are a threat to success of American military plans. The result is carnage, for soldiers and civilians alike. The cost to Americans is high indeed. The voice of reality begins to be heard in Donovan's begrudging admission of defeat. His construction crew was about as equal to the Japanese as a junior-high football team would be against the Chicago Bears. Their combat is a scene of embarrassing ineptitude. They were lucky Marines were nearby, but they were unlucky to expose the Marines in the first place. Their unluckiness will prove, however, to be their salvation.

RETURN to Washington marks the beginning of the second stage of tragic rhythm. Donovan relearns the meaning of courage. He learns only "a fool wouldn't obey orders." The Navy, with its tradition and authority, speaks for the necessary discipline of a nation fighting for survival. Wedge Donovan must learn to serve tradition and authority in ways which enhance rather than jeopardize the battle. Behind the picture of Navy, then, is nation, and behind the nation is a people and culture (names of the men in Donovan's construction crew suggest an international community).

Scenes of training and discipline balance earlier ones of careless and cocky efficiency. The men learn use of weapons, condition their bodies, and march in harmony under military command. They train to be citizen soldiers, who embody the truth of their new name and insignia. The motto of the Seabees is "Construimus Batuimus" ("We are Builders, We are Fighters"). Donovan's men, old workers and new recruits, are the builders Americans know themselves to be. Now they learn to be fighters as well, not the fighters of brawls and boxing, but the fighters of war and powerful weapons.

Donovan yearns to fight the way he works: with his hands and his heart, but heart is his vulnerability. He must pay for his pride, for his sentimentality. He lets love for his men interfere with duty to his mission; he allows his heart to rule his head, and so here is to be the consequence. The enemy closes in on outlying oil tanks, which they could explode and incinerate Donovan's battalion. Wedge, however, has a plan. He can explode one of the furthermost tanks and drive the Japanese back into a crossfire. He attaches a "thermite bomb" to a bulldozer, and drives it into the nearest oil tank. Before he can leap from the dozer, he is shot. He is still on the dozer when it goes up in the explosion of the oil tank. Wedge Donovan dies, but the enemy is defeated.

TO HIS MEN Wedge Donovan is "a mighty man" who "makes work a joy." Or he is a crazy fool. Donovan can be both because he is always the same: essentially loyal and loving, existentially elastic. He can learn from mistakes because he feels, with his heart, the losses his decisions exact upon his crew. At the center of the story, standing in a hospital tent, surrounded by his wounded men, he is a defeated hero. His pride is now a vice, an obstacle to success, when always before it had been a virtue, a service to his profession. He needs a new opportunity to express his essential character. This comes in an ancient way: he will fall in love.

Donovan's character continues in its essence the same. By accepting Connie's love, he extends his commitment to duty. When his oldest and best friend Eddie Powers is killed, Donovan cracks again, but he is better prepared to atone for his weakness of heart. This makes his final sacrifice tragic. He has shown his willingness to give up personal happiness for another. Now, when he dies in the explosion that will save his men, he merely repeats in a physical way what he had already demonstrated in a moral way. The episode shows the grit of a mighty man who has made choices with consequences he accepts, who has made mistakes from which he has learned, and who has grown in spirit before he offers up his life.

The communion which underlies community is portrayed in ritual action. The Seabees parade to honor the units led by Wedge Donovan. Lt. Commander Yarrow reads a presidential citation for the men who defended the fuel station. They are honored for their "courage and heroism" displayed in June 1942, in action that will be a "memorial on which is inscribed in blood and fire, their own immortal challenge," the motto of the Seabees, "We build for the fighters, and we fight for what we build."

Those sacrifices are celebrated as if they were the body and blood consumed for spiritual nourishment, uniting the entire body of mankind, "from the shores of the Pacific to the Arctic, from Europe to Asia." If the bodies of heroes are sacrifices to nourish the spiritual body of the community, they are also debts paid to some higher, stronger force than the human community itself. That is history, fate, or providence. It is enduring and transcendent. Therefore, the more valuable the life of the hero who is sacrificed, the more honor paid. Connie tells Bob Yarrow she loves both him and Wedge Donovan. She and Bob together call Donovan "a great guy, one of the best." Ancient Greeks called the *best* by the word *arete*, spiritual aristocracy, heroic spirit. The best must be offered as gifts to the gods in myths of tragic triumph.

In the early forties American films did not offer many competitors for tragic hero. The political atmosphere and the star system prevented a significant perception of tragedy. There were, however, two films which courted tragic possibility and one which realized it in their treatments of war subjects between 1940 and 1945: these were *Sergeant York* in 1941, *Casablanca* in 1942, and *To Have and Have Not* in 1944, the same year as *The Fighting Seabees*. None has quite the courage of Wayne's to make a

sacrifice of its hero. None of the four has, on the other hand, the darkness
that sometimes breaks through in power of tragic action, as do *The Ox-Bow
Incident* in 1943 or *The Seventh Cross* in 1944.

Sergeant York (winner of an Academy Award for Gary Cooper) shares
a subject with *The Fighting Seabees:* war and the battles of war. It puts
World War I to an emotional and propaganda use on the eve of American
entry into World War II. Its theme of *conversion* draws it even closer to
Wayne's film. Cooper is a rowdy, fun-loving young country boy from Ten-
nessee, a heavy drinker and godless fellow who is converted to a deep
religious faith and simple commitment to the Ten Commandments. He
believes the Bible is literally true in its texts and tales, and so when he is
called to military duty he resists as a conscientious objector.

Sergeant York presents itself as a piece of history. It dedicates itself "to
the many heroic figures still living, who have generously consented to be
portrayed in its story." It also draws upon heroes long dead, Daniel Boone
in particular, to enhance the virtues of its hero Alvin York. Its fantasies are
disguised as history, and it employs the romance structure to shape those
fantasies. Alvin is called to the house of God where he is converted from
an aimless life to one of service. He is pressed to extend that service when
he goes forth to save his nation in its "struggle for freedom."

Alvin York is an elemental force of nature, coarse and rough, but he
is skillful even when he is drunk. His story is one of pacification and dedication to "somethin' a heap bigger than I be." Wedge learns by making
mistakes, not by divine guidance. Differences between their stories is a key
to differences between romance and tragedy: in one the hero is rewarded
with love and land, in the other the hero is repaid with loss of life.
Something is wrong with the end of *Sergeant York*, however. The reward
is too palpably of this world; York learned the best service he could render
was spiritual, and yet he lives to enjoy the best he can imagine in the world
of "Caesar." It is a vulgarizing of the romance, and it is a "tragedy" only in
its willingness to compromise the cost of sacrifice. This Wedge Donovan
does not do. Wayne's heroes are at their most convincing when they can
say, with Wedge Donovan, "I'm never one for sitting on fences."

Stripped to its essentials, *The Fighting Seabees* is a glimpse of the heroic
ideal illustrated by Samson in the Bible, by Ajax or Achilles in stories by
Homer and Sophocles. It is a film with its patent vulgarisms also, perhaps
an inevitability when rare (aristocratic) qualities of character are celebrated
on behalf of a democratic culture. But Wedge Donovan displays a touch of
greatness in his pride that *will not* yield, even to the "order" of the State.
In Donovan is a touch of defiance almost, though not quite, a rebellion
against reason altogether. The heart of the man is too large for the world
he serves. There can be no question of reward for him, as for Alvin York,
from a world which cannot contain his pride and spirit.

York's spirit is broken by his religion and by his patriotism. Underlying both is the power of women: his mother sends his little brother to bring him home, humiliating him before his peers; his chase through life is interrupted and aborted by Gracie Williams. Cooper plays a man tamed by the "Eternal Feminine." When Alvin York bends for his mother to sew a tear in his overalls, he humbles himself to go a courting Gracie. Energies of nature, turned from destructive to creative tasks, are sublimated by religion and war until put to the service of procreation in *Sergeant York*. The contrast with *The Fighting Seabees* is instructive. Donovan does not submit to be led nor does he bend before the sovereignty of the Eternal Feminine, though he is tempted mightily. Instead he denies the power of woman, yields it to another, and drives his ego to a last superb deed.

While Humphrey Bogart may not seem a likely candidate for milksop, he plays the role of a hard-bitten, cynical and self-serving man (as usual) who turns into a patriotic pussycat in *To Have and Have Not*. Again the film romanticizes a hero who tries to resist efforts to bend his will to the ways of the world. There is no question here of Harry Morgan being turned by religion to a life that will bring him worldly rewards. But Morgan's head is turned by "Slim" so he is willing to make a radical change in his life, from a "have not" to one of the "haves." Slim has the toughness and dignity Morgan cannot resist, in a man or (especially) in this woman. She is the providential power that delivers Morgan to the French Resistance Movement. She comes out of nowhere to change his life, and so she is the "grace" suggested by Alvin York's girlfriend. Morgan learns to assert himself in new ways, new deeds of courage, mainly becaue he courts this woman best in those ways. In the end, Harry Morgan leaves with his woman and his best friend for a new life of service to democracy and freedom.

Again, the contrast with Wayne's heroes of the forties is striking. Wayne's characters cannot match the steamy sexuality of the Bogart for Bacall match, but neither is Wayne's hero converted to politics by lust. When Wayne plays in a situation like this, as in *Pittsburgh*, he bungles and almost destroys himself as well as everyone around him. Harry Morgan has a shell of cynicism that crumbles when attacked by Eros. Wedge Donovan constructs defenses against attack, until his ego is protected not only by cynicism in love but also, and even, by patriotism in politics.

Bogart's character who matches, and exceeds, Wayne's Donovan is Rick Blaine in *Casablanca*. Rick runs from his past, finding his escape in the stoical pose of a self-serving tough man of the world. Unlike Donovan, Rick does not take joy from his world, but Rick has a romantic past missing from Donovan's. Rick denies and represses history, while Donovan directs and expresses it. When Rick's past catches up to him, in the shape of Ilsa Lund, he is healed by his confession of love. When history becomes destiny, Wedge Donovan is sacrificed to it by his denial of love. Rick and Wedge are alike in the crucial and climactic deeds of their lives: each tells a lie to his love, each yields that love to another. In each instance, love is a private affair compromised by public expressions. It is a tragedy of loss for both Wedge Donovan and Rick Blaine, though Wedge dies to pay the cost and Rick departs for romantic horizons to confirm its value.

THE FIGHTING SEABEES has mythic dimensions in words as well as deeds. Connie mocks Donovan's confidence that he can do anything: "You do things easily, Mr. Donovan, by just a wave of the hand! Who was it flung seeds on the earth and saw furrows of armed men rise from them between sunset and sunrise?" One was Cadmus, founder of the tragic family of Oedipus. Cadmus killed a sacred serpent and invoked the wrath of the war god Ares. Cadmus was rescued by Athene, who commanded him to plough the earth and sow the teeth of the serpent. Armed men arose from those teeth, and immediately began to fight. Another was Jason, who sailed in search of the Golden Fleece. He required the help of Medea to perform impossible tasks set by her father, including the taming of frozen hills, ploughing with them, and planting teeth from a serpent. Again, from that planting arose a crop of armed men.

With his Irish view, Eddie Powers said it was St. Patrick, the patron saint of Ireland, who charmed the serpents into following him to the sea where they drowned. Like St. Patrick, Irish Donovan led the conversion of his people. He turned them from coarse, though talented, civilian workers into disciplined, tough soldiers held together by their faith in him, and through him in the Navy they served. Wedge Donovan is a union of worker and soldier, Cadmus and Jason, leader and martyr, lion and lamb.

Sgt. John M. Stryker: *Sands of Iwo Jima* (1949)

The concluding scene of *Sands of Iwo Jima* is a portrayal of the flag-raising memorialized in the statue near Arlington National Cemetery. Five Marines plant the flag of the United States on Mt. Suribachi in Iwo Jima on the morning of February 23, 1945. Sgt. John M. Stryker summons men from the "First Squad." Three of them *are* those very men: Rene A. Gagnon, Ira H. Hayes, and John H. Bradley. Other men of Stryker's squad remain with him to watch with pride. Stryker says, "I never felt so good in my life." He offers cigarettes and falls dead from a sniper's bullet through the heart. Corporal Al Thomas finds an unfinished letter by Stryker to his son. Thomas reads it, and Pfc. Pete Conway says he will finish writing it. Their eyes lift to see the flag raised (to the music of the Marine's battle hymn), the camera rising with their gaze to focus on the banner waving in the wind. Conway looks down and the camera looks with him: there is the dead sergeant, face down, back to the camera. His name is stencilled across the shoulders of his shirt, JOHN M. STRYKER, and a large stain covers the left side behind his heart. Conway calls out, "Saddle up! Let's get back in the war." The men follow him into a mist that moves across the mountain.

This is an epiphany of tragic experience. It reveals the power embodied in tragic action. It is also an artful identification of that power with the sacrificed hero, with the will of those who survive him, and with the audience privileged to witness the scene. If this were a religious story, the epiphany would also be an apotheosis, or transfiguration of the human into the divine, as the spirit of the dead man would rise to reveal itself to his witnesses as a holy spirit of a god. As a secular story, it uses religious iconography for patriotic meanings.

The art of the experience is an illusion that depends upon the audience's recognition of the flag-raising memorial. So art employs art to recreate a spiritual experience of victory out of death. "Something" takes charge of matter, drives the view of the camera-audience as it presents the imagery in that view. It passes from Stryker the moment he falls from the sniper's bullet. It charges the energies and expressions of his men who are gathered around him: it asserts itself in the fury of Charlie Bass's vengeance; it expresses itself in the words of the letter, where Stryker "becomes" Thomas; and it completes itself in the promise by Conway to complete the letter. The energy of this "something," the heroic spirit, also communicates itself through the emblem of the flag. The flag is moved by the wind whose power is also the spirit which makes the flag emblematic. This same power moves the mist that moves the men through the mist.

STRYKER IS TRANSFORMED into the American flag, into the men who are his witnesses, into the mist which embraces all at the end. He is also transformed into the audience which hears and sees. The plot produces his transformation through double action: training and combat, retraining and renewed combat; learning and testing, relearning and retesting. The two subplots, taking the squad from New Zealand to Tarawa, from Hawaii to Iwo Jima, generate preliminary sacrifices, before the climactic primary sacrifice and passage into community.

The plot is a circle with two semicircles (further divided, to produce four quadrants) moving around the stationary figure of Stryker. Men move within the quadrants of action, and the closer they get to Stryker the more open to vision they become. Contact is painful but redeeming. If they make it through all quadrants, they are in a position at last to carry on from where he falls. A succession of characters comes into contact with the tragic hero, beginning with the least and ending with the most resistant.

The brute with physical courage is also a man with an inner calm which commands and directs that courage: this is Stryker in the first half of the story. His patience and insight with Choynski are added to calm courage with Thomas, who hates Stryker's guts. Theirs is a complicated relationship

Left to right: **Richard Jaeckel as Frank Flynn, Wayne as Sgt. John M. Stryker, Bill Murphy as Eddie Flynn and John Agar as Peter Conway in** *Sands of Iwo Jima,* **1949.**

with previews in New Zealand. There Stryker gets drunk, not the first time. Bass looks after Stryker, especially when he does not get a hoped-for letter from his young son. He never will get it. Mail call is a crisis for Stryker, particularly if he gets leave to town. Thomas and others come across Stryker, stumbling alone, dead drunk, and likely to be picked up by passing Shore Patrols. Thomas, even though he has his chance to get revenge on Stryker, chooses instead to protect him from arrest.

THOMAS IS REWARDED when he reads Stryker's unfinished letter to his son. The greatest privilege is reserved for Pete Conway, who will finish the letter and who will assume the authority of the dead hero. Conway is to be the son Stryker never knew.

Stryker saves Conway from a grenade during retraining in Hawaii. Conway begins to confide in the Sergeant, responding to Stryker's desire for friendship. Both know it is important for the identity of the Colonel to be passed on: through Stryker, to Conway, and then to Conway's own son, whom he will name Sam also. The continuity was not to be there for Stryker himself, since he lost his family when he chose his military career. Conway accepts his place, as a foster son of the spirit, when Conway confides his fears to Stryker, and finally when he saves Stryker's life. The concluding scene is finished appropriately, then, by Pete Conway, who best knows how to finish Stryker's letter to his son, having earned that knowledge as a son and then as a father himself.

Fatherhood is essential to Stryker's function as a sacrificial hero. At the same time, he must be no father at all, because his ties must be broken for him to host redemption for others. He has to be without a family, but he must understand what it means to have a family so that he knows the value of what he has sacrificed. Stryker is in agony for the loss of his family, waiting to hear from the son he never knows. His need is greater because it is unsatisfied. If there were not such a place of emptiness, of lacking, then the hero would be fulfilled in himself, not available to serve the needs of others.

During the episode of the "pick-up" by the young mother Mary in Hawaii, she tells him "I'll pray for you, Sergeant." He responds, "let's not get religion." Characteristic of the American hero as John Wayne portrays him, he is not easy with religious sentiment. Stryker does not need religion; he already has it. He does not call upon God or Church to guide him. He is a medium of the Spirit served by all religions. When Sid Stein falls, dying, during the assault on Mount Suribachi, he mutters a prayer in Hebrew, calling to Adonai as Stryker bends over him. Stryker finishes the prayer with a whispered "Amen." The scene virtually identifies Stryker as "Adonai."

He proceeds from this ritual to incarnate many cultures and national backgrounds. The surnames of his men suggest the breadth of that community. Stryker's unfinished letter to his son, to his audience, is a challenge to improve this film's definition of that community for which he has died. In the words of his letter, "Always do what your heart tells you is right. Maybe someone will write you some day and tell you about me. I want you to be like me in some things, but not like me in others, because when you grow older and get to know more about me, you'll see I've been a failure in many ways. This isn't what I wanted. Things just turned out that way. If there was only more time, I'd. . . ."

FRAMING *Sands of Iwo Jima* in 1949 are two American films based upon World War II combat: *Battleground*, 1949, and *Halls of Montezuma*, 1950. Each offers a vision of courage and leadership different than Stryker's. Neither film, though classics of their kind, matches the power of *Sands of Iwo Jima* for delineating the essence of American tragic heroism. *Halls of Montezuma* looks like Wayne's film, and Richard Widmark plays Lieutenant Anderson like Wayne's Stryker. But Anderson is a neurotic who suffers from "psychological migraine," a symptom of displaced fear. Anderson's drug dependence was the consequence of an unresolved personality disturbance.

Sgt. John M. Stryker.

His is a story of discovering courage, resolving his fears, and dispensing with his pills.

Widmark is always grimacing, anxious with guilt and pain; Wayne is typically changing from comedy to irony to sentiments of romance. When Anderson has to deal with the personal problems of Conroy, he does not put the youth to a test of physical courage, as Stryker does Choynski. Anderson teaches Conroy, first, to overcome his problem of stuttering by doing mental exercises, and then to overcome fear of combat by remembering that lesson of verbal will power. Intellect over matter, for Anderson; emotion over matter, for Stryker. Anderson is sure he is going to die, and so he has to learn a lesson of life; it is his men who die, and when they do, he is hit by an anxiety attack. On the other hand, when Stryker's men die, Stryker immediately turns his attention to problems of the living. Stryker never speaks of fate, yet he is marked by fate on Mt. Suribachi.

Stryker is not invited to the church for Conway's wedding, and he tells Mary, "Let's not get religion," though he finishes a prayer for Stein. Refusal to be fixed by religious dogma separates *Sands of Iwo Jima* from sanctimonious blessings in *Halls of Montezuma*, with its echo of Stryker's unfinished letter. "Doc" Jones knows Anderson is befuddled by the war, not able to accept his own life while his men die around him, and so "Doc" leaves a message to console his guilt-ridden survivor: "Our faith in the Supreme Being" answers the question why some must live. "Our country was weak," he says of America unprepared for Pearl Harbor, and so "we will not forget what we saw. We must keep our country strong. We are on God's side." Anderson is healed when he accepts God's decision he must live. His fate is to live while others must die.

In *Halls of Montezuma* the American soldiers discover the Japanese are human, but they have a religion of death no good American can accept. In Wayne's film, the hero sees battle in emotional and physical terms exclusively. There are no attempts to understand the enemy, important only to test heroic character. The enemy is impersonal for Stryker, and so it needs no explanation as in *Halls of Montezuma*. Trying to be more "realistic," Widmark's film is less efficient than Wayne's. The character of the hero dissolves beneath the pressures of realism in *Halls of Montezuma*.

Dissolution of the hero is the point of ironic *Battleground*. A tough sergeant, Kinnie (James Whitmore), is not given credit he deserves for holding his men together. The same is true for the actor, because Whitmore's name appears well down the list in the roll of credits. The star actor is Van Johnson, but his character, Holley, is peripheral. This film makes a point about impersonality, absence of heroism, and so it diminishes even its stars. *Battleground* turns men into things and drains them of identity. Home and family are not important, and Holley's idea of emotion is to seduce the women and steal their eggs.

This story decentralizes meaning and denies heroic personality. It also, like *Halls of Montezuma*, seeks religious sanction for its cynical antiheroism. On Christmas a chaplain gathers the men together as the Germans close in. His sermon is an answer to the question, "Was this trip necessary?" He begins by saying, "Let's look at the facts." The logic of his sermon is directed at reasons to oppose Nazism, a "force dedicated to a 'super-race,' 'super-idea,' or 'super-anything.'" The film cannot concede a super-man without jeopardizing the logic of *its* sermon.

This was a strong sentiment of postwar America and Europe. It intensified through the fifties into the sixties. *Battleground* and *Halls of Montezuma* express postwar cynicism and ironic defensiveness about heroism. They represent a context in which Wayne's heroes were viewed with skeptical hostility by some, zealous loyalty by others. This context was not limited by films in America. Indeed, the most powerful were European, extending the frames of *Battleground* and *Halls of Montezuma,* such as *Paisan* (1946) and *The Third Man* (1949).

THESE TWO FILMS use the subject of Americans in Europe to examine the hero—during the war in *Paisan,* after the war in *The Third Man.* The Italian film employs a technique of semidocumentary to tie together separate stories of Americans in the push from Sicily to Naples, Rome, Florence, into the Po Valley, from the summer of 1943 to the winter of 1944. Its technique is its point about ironies and incoherences of war, disasters of war, and emptiness of heroism. *Paisan* diffracts heroism and dissolves community exactly as Italian society had been. The final story is the most grim, as Italian partisans are drowned by German captors in the Po River, and OSS men are shot when they protest.

One victim of postwar cynicism was religious faith. *Sands of Iwo Jima* conveys religious feeling without institutional identity. *Paisan* includes in its stories one of three American chaplains visiting a Francescan monastery at Romangna. The monks are hospitable, gracious, and selfless. But they are also superstitious, bigoted, and spiritually selfish, when they discover one of the chaplains is Jewish and the other a Protestant, bearing "the heresies of Luther." This episode forces the question of the significance of the war into deeps of spiritual darkness.

Even deeper is the darkness of *The Third Man,* as it explores the decay of postwar, black-market Vienna during occupation by Allied powers. Major Calloway's (Trevor Howard) heart is hardened or atrophied. He cannot do what he feels, because he has little feeling left to guide him. He can, however, do his duty, because he can see what his duty is: to police the ruins of Vienna for the lowlife feeding on its decay. Calloway is English; the woman of romance, Anna, is a Czech posing as an Austrian. Calloway loves no one, though he uses the suffering of children to tug at the heart of Holly Martins; Anna loves deeply, but the man she loves is a piece of vermin who dies appropriately in the sewers below the city. One American is a "romantic" who writes paperback westerns in the "tradition" of Zane Grey; he begins to imagine himself as one of his own heroes, a character out of his book called *The Lone Rider of Santa Fe.*

This American writer, Holly Martins, is a character common to

American fiction—the naive romantic American visitor to corrupt, dark Europe. Holly is dragged into the pit of infamy where he finds his schooltime friend Harry Lime is well entrenched. The reward for Holly's faith in his friend is that he will have the privilege of shooting Harry, a mercy to Harry as well as to everyone else. The reward for Holly's love for Anna is that she refuses to be the price of his education: in the fine scene that ends the film, Anna walks past waiting Holly, never turning her head or breaking her stride.

Harry Lime is a test of atmosphere in postwar Europe. Overlooking the city from a carnival lift, Harry and Holly confront each other with their American ideals and illusions. Holly cannot understand how Harry could have betrayed those ideals, and Harry responds: "Oh, Holly, you and I aren't heroes! The world doesn't make any heroes, outside of your stories." Harry points below to people walking in the streets. To him they are merely "moving dots." From his elevated point of view, he can see human beings as they really exist, (merely) for governments and ideologies: "Nobody thinks in terms of human beings. Governments don't. Why should we? They talk about the people and the proletariat. I think about the suckers and the mugs. It's the same thing." Holly is appalled. He exclaims, "You used to believe in God."

The hero must believe in something, that dying makes life worth living. Wayne's heroes of the forties sustain this belief, at first to make the war effort endurable, then to check the tendency toward cynicism when selfishness seemed to be the only reasonable motive for living. To prevent people from becoming merely "moving dots" is the ethical motive for his heroes in later decades; in the thirties and the forties it is hardly conceivable as a problem. Wayne's heroes have a simple trust in "heart," a capacity to express love as physical and moral courage.

Wedge Donovan makes choices, and mistakes, which drive him toward the decision which will destroy him. Stryker made a choice long before his story begins; everything in *Sands of Iwo Jima* is an extension of consequences from that choice, so that he is an instrument of grand design, of some continuing spirit which uses him even as he may seem unaware. Such heroes are Aeschylus's Prometheus, Homer's Achilles, Milton's (and the Bible's) Samson, and Sophocles's Philoctetes. All are heroes of suffering, and they are heroes of patience, waiting for the call which summons them to service. Stryker may not shout from the ramparts and scatter his enemies, nor might he bring down the temple of his tormenters, but he does embody passion to articulate a community of communion between the past and the future.

Col. David Crockett: *The Alamo* (1960)

The Alamo has been described as an epic story comparable with *The Battleship Potempkin, Alexander Nevsky,* and *The Seven Samurai.* Certainly

the film has epic ambitions. Its subject is an episode of American history
which doubtless contributed to the self image of a nation fulfilling goals of
Providence, of "manifest destiny," as it swept across the continent. The
defense of an outpost by a small detachment of men, doomed but willing
to give up their lives for a sacred cause: this is the stuff of romance, tragedy,
and epic, from Thermopylae in 480 B.C. to Dien Bien Phu in A.D. 1954.

When *The Alamo* was made, September to December 1959, American
audiences were enjoying television shows about Davy Crockett and Daniel
Boone. They also had seen Fess Parker in two movies put together from
Disney productions made for television: *Davy Crockett, King of the Wild
Frontier* (1955), and *Davy Crockett and the River Pirates* (1956). These are
unabashedly fantastic in the "tall-tale" tradition of American folk story.
They were also enormously popular recreations of a legendary superhuman. If one wanted something more authentic, one could have turned,
also in 1956, to a new biography, *David Crockett: The Man and the Legend*,
by James A. Shackford. But Wayne's characterization of Crockett is neither
the Disney fantasy nor the scholar's fact. His Crockett is a hero of moderation, balance, and cool sanity. This hero is an answer to extremism of all
kinds, in all modes of vision.

This was a particularly appropriate interpretation for the time, as was
the challenge of presenting heroism in the midst of defeat. Wayne had done
this in *Back to Bataan* (1945) and *They Were Expendable* (1945), accounts
of American surrenders at Corregidor after the disaster at Pearl Harbor.
They were opportunities to celebrate courage and pay tribute to the
sacrifices of men and women who turned those defeats into victories. They
were models of inspiration as well as interpretations of history and human
destiny.

So too is the story of *The Alamo*. Here also is an initial defeat which
leads, paradoxically, to an ultimate victory; here also is physical disaster and
spiritual triumph. This message might be well received by American audiences in 1960. The "police action" to defend South Korean democracy
from North Korean communist aggression turned into a military disaster
when the Chinese drove United Nations forces back toward the sea in 1950
and 1951. The best Americans could see in that adventure was a compromise in the ceasefire of 1953, and the best they could foresee in 1960 was
repetition of Korea in South Vietnam where, since 1954, a similar separation of North from South was being tested in military actions. Like his films
of 1945, *Back to Bataan* and *They Were Expendable*, *The Alamo* in 1960 looked back in order to look ahead.

WAYNE PORTRAYS David Crockett as a man between extremes: between Jim Bowie, impulsive and quick-tempered, and Will Travis, cool and
over-disciplined. This also describes the relationships of Crockett with

Wayne as Col. David Crockett.

Wedge Donovan and Sgt. John Stryker. Donovan was a man whose tragic flaws drove him to imprudent actions; he had to learn to overcome mistakes, but in the end he paid with his life. He was a civilian turned soldier, a builder defending what he built. Donovan made choices which turned him from private happiness to public honor. This also describes Jim Bowie (Richard Widmark) in *The Alamo*. Like Donovan, Bowie is a man of instincts and action; he has a reputation for building, and he has personal stake in the political succes of his military adventures.

Opposite Bowie is Col. William Travis, like Wayne's Sgt. John Stryker. His weakness is his strength of discipline. He is rigid, lives by rules, puts

With Linda Cristal as Flaca in *The Alamo*, 1960.

manners above spontaneity. Travis's early encounters with Bowie are tensely potent with danger. He refuses to tell Bowie the truth of their situation or the reason for their strategy at the Alamo; he does not trust Bowie, as man or soldier. Travis is elitist, distrustful of civilians and volunteer soldiers.

Travis is a man of reason and duty, versus Bowie, a man of feelings and instincts. Bowie says, "Travis, you can't help being you, and I can't help being me." Men are fated to be what they are. Something is needed to prevent their mutual destruction. When Wayne played one of these types, in Wedge Donovan, he followed the logic of the character to its tragic conclusion; in the other, as Sgt. John Stryker, he followed it to its fateful end in tragic irony. In *The Alamo* he mediates the two types. The man of duty and discipline dies first, breaking his sword—a gesture of finality. The man of instinct and easy living dies last, his newly freed slave across his lap. He dies, powerless to defend himself. Crockett, hero of compromise and moderation, is the second to die.

THE "REAL" ENEMIES of the story are in the main characters. Bowie has to learn to calm down, to submit to authority. Travis has to learn to put people before plans, to trust his fellow man, and to realize that noble ends do not justify ignoble means. Crockett exemplifies the wisdom of these lessons, and he does it in his relationships with women and children. He has Travis's manners and Bowie's feelings for women. Crockett walks with Flaca along a lovely river bank and explains why he stays to fight in Texas. His speech is a formal, disguised confession of love. There are no strong embraces, searing kisses, quick breaths. Their relationship is passionate without animality, ideal and conventional.

They stand beneath a giant tree, whose beauty inspires Crockett: "It's green, and growing! Like those 'green pastures' they talk about. Lord above! That's one beautiful tree! This tree must have been growed before man put his first dirty footprints on this prairie. Kind of tree Adam and Eve must have met under. You know something, Flaca? I guess I saw who knows how many trees before I ever took a long thoughtful look at one." Their gaze rises with the camera to the height of the tree. Then the camera looks down at Davy and Flaca from above the tree. They are Adam and Eve. Davy says he has found a way to be useful. Flaca is Crockett's sacrifice of love, to live for the future as he prepares to die in the present. A tree burns to complete the statement when the Alamo falls.

Crockett's devotion to women and children is typical of Wayne's heroic image. Rightful, then, is the conclusion. Mexican soldiers storm a supply room, uncover three cowering people hiding there, and are prepared to kill them in the general slaughter. They are Mrs. Dickinson, her daughter Angelina, and a young black servant. The screen blanks. Then Smitty (Frankie Avalon) appears on the ridge overlooking the Mission fortress. Back in the Mission, Mrs. Dickinson is seen walking alongside a mule carrying Angelina and led by the black youngster. They pass between ranks of Mexican soldiers, who come to attention and salute as Santa Anna himself removes his hat to her and these children. They are the future, they join their new protector Smitty on the ridge, and they disappear over the horizon. Wayne's heroes die for people, not for ideas, though he identifies ideas *as* people in his imagination.

As Davy Crockett John Wayne balances the extremes of previous roles. Saying goodbye to Flaca, Crockett explains why he fights at the Alamo:

When I came down here to Texas I was looking for something. I didn't know what. It seems like you'd added up my life, and I'd spent it all either stompin' other men, or in some cases gettin' stomped. Had me some money, and had me some medals. But none of it seemed a lifetime worth the pain of the mother that bore me. It was like I was empty. Well, I'm not empty anymore. Tha's what's important—to feel useful in this old world.

He is speaking as much for John Wayne the actor as for Davy Crockett the heroic character. Wayne uses the legend of Crockett to resolve divisions in his own image, life, and reputation.

IMPORTANCE OF FAMILY was the target of bitter irony in a film of contrary spirit, *Paths of Glory,* three years before *The Alamo.* In this story of World War I carnage, General Mireau (George Macready) occasionally tours the trenches under his command. He is accustomed to greeting his soldiers with the same question, "Are you married, soldier?" If the soldier says he is, the General says his wife must be proud of him; if the soldier says he is not, the General says his mother must be proud. Then he asks, "Ready to kill more Germans?" This film debunks heroic military motives as hypocritical self-glory. Officers are interested in their reputations, at any cost, especially of their men's lives. Mireau balked at the orders he received from General Broulard to take a particularly difficult German position on the "Ant Hill." Mireau claimed he would not risk his men's lives for that, but when Broulard suggests there might be a promotion in it, Mireau begins to praise his units for their skills and dependability.

He uses pride of family to motivate his men, and he tries to use pride of patriotism to motivate his chief officer, Colonel Dax (Kirk Douglas), but Dax responds with a quotation from Samuel Johnson, "Patriotism is the last refuge of a scoundrel." Dax is pathetically ineffective. He sends men to their deaths, and he fails at law to save them from their executions. Everyone is expendable, except one's self. There is no heroism in the deaths of these soldiers in combat; they are animals doomed to early deaths from monstrous impersonal forces of "war." There are no minds behind these forces, and there is little sign of heart. Dax has a sense of decency, fair play, and some power of reason: none operates well against the madness of war. He does not fight for country or for family; he does what he can, however little, to keep his men together, alive as long as possible. He is ordered to select three men for trial.

Their executions could make meaningful what would have been merely absurd if they *had* taken the Ant Hill. But socially undesirable Ferol turns out to be a whimpering coward (exactly as charged); rational atheist Arnaud is knocked unconscious trying to attack a priest; and proud Corporal Paris breaks down begging for life. Ferol dies whimpering. Arnaud is propped on a litter against the execution post, shot while unconscious. But then Paris walks proudly to his execution, forgives the Captain who chose him, and refuses the blindfold. Here is the candidate for tragic hero—a man shot by his own commander as an example to others who refused, or failed, to glorify the commander's reputation. Paris finally saw the light of religious faith, and he is thinking of his family when he marches to death.

Paths of Glory aims to indict war, the military, and perhaps all human behavior as hypocritical masks for selfishness. But it produces a tragic hero after all, insignificant Corporal Paris, who dies for God and family, if not for country and commander. This neutralizes the execution scene as a satirical parody of Christian Golgotha with its three crosses and "social undesirable" placed in the middle position. The film itself is a hypocritical treatment of hypocrisy, suggesting there are no heroes and no ideal motives for sacrifice, but concludes with exactly those motives to create the heroism it denies. These motives are virtually the same as in *The Alamo*, except that Davy Crockett excludes religious belief from his heroic motives.

When the Parson asks him if he ever prays, Crockett responds: "I never found the time!" Then he stalks away. When Gambler asks Crockett what he is thinking about on their last evening, Davy tells him, "Not thinkin'! Just rememberin'." Earlier, when Smitty finally delivered his message to General Houston, the General told his officers he hoped all the new recruits would remember what their friends, neighbors, and fellow Texicans were doing for them in the Alamo: "I hope they remember. I hope Texas remembers." Thus John Wayne offers his film and hero "in remembrance." Crockett looks back to what is real and important in his life to give meaning to existence; what is now, is the consequence of what he has been, not the promise of what he might be through faith. Crockett is "rememberin'" his life of service. His courage has been paid for as a gift to others.

Courage is a kind of madness when detached from largeness of vision, or abstracted from life's pressing immediacy. Used by ego, it may serve tyranny and cruelty. Bowie and Travis could pervert the virtue; Crockett knows the vice as well as the virtue. An epic story of heroism enlarges the issue to national and cultural levels of courage or cowardice, over great space and through great time. Rarely questioning courage, faith, and vision, Wayne's films present heroes who are products of traditional answers. The time of *The Alamo* was a period when films searched frequently to find those traditional answers in epic proportions. Wayne acted in many of these American productions, from *The Conqueror* in 1956 to *The Greatest Story Ever Told* in 1965. These stories try, without success, to adjust individual needs to transcendental designs of religious and political ideals.

British director David Lean consistently aimed high for such adjustments, as in *The Bridge on the River Kwai* in 1957, *Lawrence of Arabia* in 1962, and *Doctor Zhivago* in 1965. The first, appearing in the same year as *Paths of Glory*, also contributed like that one to the context of ironic treatments of military heroism. But it contains a less bashful picture of the possibilities for meaningful sacrifice. *The Bridge on the River Kwai* marks two men of balance and integrity: the British doctor, Major Clipton (James Donald) and the American "Commander," Shears (William Holden). These men are boundaries to the "visions" of two career officers: the Japanese commander of a prison camp, Colonel Saito (Sessue Hayakawa), and the British Colonel Nicholson (Alec Guinness). Shears also complements British Cambridge-don-turned-professional saboteur, Major Warden (Jack Hawkins). Like Davy Crockett, both Clipton and Shears are the world's hope of sanity out of madness of war.

Shears is the film's ethical center. He keeps true to his instinct for survival, for enjoying life in the moment, for loyalty to people, not to institutions. Shears reminds those around him that their endeavors are for greater life, not for death. When Warden is wounded and insists on being left behind in the jungle, Shears delivers a set speech which could easily be delivered by Crockett to Travis and perhaps even to Bowie:

> You make me sick with your heroics. There's a stench of death about you. Explosives or "L-Pills," they go together, don't they? ["L-Pills" are for suicide.] And with you, it's just one thing or the other—destroy a bridge or destroy yourself. This is just a game, this war! You and that Col. Nicholson, you're two of a kind! Crazy with courage! For what? How to die like a gentleman! How to die by the rules! When the only important thing is how to live like a human being.

One does not let abstractions rule behavior without regard for concrete realities. One does not let ideas usurp emotions. Life itself is the goal of life, even when sacrificed in a last resort to preserve it for others. Shears, who pretended to be an officer, to be sick, to be unheroic, is in the end better than his officers, healthier than most, and more heroic than he could have admitted to himself. The only survivor from the group of central characters is Major Clipton. At the film's conclusion, Clipton walks aimlessly toward the ruins of the bridge, muttering, "Madness! Madness!" *The Alamo* does not allow its tragic heroes to succumb to madness, cynicism, compromise or even religious martyrdom, as other films of the time were inclined to do.

Will Andersen: *The Cowboys* (1972)

Will Andersen is 60 years old (John Wayne is 65) in the story of *The Cowboys*. Before Will leaves on his last cattle drive, he revisits the graves of his sons. One marker reads, "Lucius Andersen, 1837–1858"; the other, "Matthew Andersen, 1836–1858." That both his sons died in the same year is one of the somber facts of this solemn story. The name Matthew is one of several connections between *The Cowboys* and *Red River*, made 24 years earlier.

The Cowboys explores the tragic possibilities of *Red River*. The most serious enemy Tom Dunson had to meet was himself, and so his story is rich with the complexities of psychological conflicts. The most dire enemy Will Andersen has to encounter is "Long Hair." Because Will's enemy is another being, his battle seems less subtle than Tom's. Long Hair is so evil and sinister that his combat with Will Andersen is a battle of darkness against light, absolute evil with conditional good. It lacks the ambiguities of *Red River*. It has the moving and instructive power of melodrama. Will Andersen's story is a coming to terms with his own nature, so he can be prepared to oppose absolute evil when the time comes. He must be able to recognize the evil for what it really is. His entire life has been a training in recognition. *The Cowboys* compresses Will Andersen's life into its journey as a pilgrimage to ultimate recognitions.

LONG HAIR IS PLAYED by Bruce Dern, who is able to insinuate madness with a smile. The casting of the role is crucial to secure immediate distrust of Long Hair. He makes a serious mistake when he lies to Will. "I've been caught at it, haven't I? Mr. Andersen, I'm sorry I lied to you. I got all them names right out of the Stockman's Association Brand Book. You see, we're fresh out of jail." Will tells him, "I don't hold jail against you." But Will Andersen "hates a liar." Long Hair observes, "You're a hard man, Mr. Andersen." Will responds, simply, "It's a hard life."

Long Hair is a devil in his ways. He and his men shadow the cattle drive. Eventually Will notices them, though he does not at first recognize who they are. He does, however, suspect they intend to rustle his cattle. When dark comes, Will and his young cowboys are visited by Long Hair, at last revealing himself to them. It is an appropriate setting. He hails them from the darkness, walks into the light of a burning fire, and taunts Will mercilessly. He asks, in his customary coarse and brutal manner, where the "nigger driver" might be. Then he drags out the boy Weedy, to show Will the boy did not succeed in getting to Nightlinger. Weedy is bruised from a beating. A deadly encounter has begun.

Long Hair whines, "Do I look like the kind of man that would beat an innocent boy?" Will responds, "You look like the vermin-ridden son-of-a-bitch you are!" Long Hair kicks Weedy away, sneering as he notices poor Dan. He pulls the unfortunate boy close to his face, asks his age, and tells him he had killed his first man by the time he was 13. The he gives his fullest attention to Will, who insults Long Hair for picking on children. This begins the episode of Will's murder.

Evil seems triumphant in the death of Will Andersen. Worldly goods are taken as booty, and the villains slink back into the night. The young cowboys vow to finish the job, and so they pursue the rustlers, stalking them as they had been stalked. The cowboys have reason on their side, as Nightlinger provides counsel and guidance. Boys have become men, not just because they successfully use force against force in scenes of bloody violence,

As Will Andersen in *The Cowboys*.

but mainly because they use reason, craft, and guile against powers of madness. Evil cannot cope with an alliance of force, reason, and justice. The rustlers are outwitted, and so they are undone.

The old enemy, Long Hair, has one last opportunity to show how despicable he is. He is lured into the final trap by the bait of Nightlinger. Long Hair drags the man, insulting him again as "nigger," toward a tree where he plans to lynch him. Again Nightlinger outwits the adversary. He asks permission to "atone to his Maker." Long Hair cannot resist this appeal to reverence; he lowers his head, takes off his hat, and hears Nightlinger begin his prayer. This mockery of sanctity is Long Hair's final undoing.

Long Hair cowardly shoots his own men to escape, but he is pinned beneath a horse, whining for help with a broken leg. The boys free one leg, leaving the other caught in a stirrup; Cimarron takes out his gun, as if to shoot Long Hair, but instead he fires it into the air. The horse (of the Apocalypse) gallops off, dragging Long Hair into oblivion, screaming as he disappears from the screen and from the story.

THE MURDER OF WILL ANDERSEN by this depraved agent of evil is a tragic death with the power of classical tragedy behind it. Will is a good and strong man, but he must die an unnatural death. This scene, violent and graphic as any Wayne ever made, is a climax to the action and a consummation of the hero's life. His audience for the film is represented in the film by the audience of boys who watch in horrified disbelief as they share the agony of their hero, falling before this incredible madness. The boys, as characters, are privileged to witness this tragedy, because they are to be its beneficiaries; as audience they are instructed in greatness, as spiritual victory emerges from physical defeat.

Will Andersen is a model for masculine ethos as father and teacher. He tells the boys, at his second visit to the schoolhouse, to "come with grit teeth. 'Cause, gentlemen, that's when school really begins." Their lessons in the ways of the world, where life is "hard," are hard lessons indeed. Andersen is a hard taskmaster, as the men who previously worked for him knew. In words echoed by the boys later, one of the previous cowhands accuses Will of working them "like dogs night and day, and Christmas too." The boys have reason to expect a rough relationship, and they get it.

Dying, Will Andersen tells the boys, "Every man wants his children to be better than he was. You are." After Nightlinger has seen to Will's burial, he speaks words of comfort to the boys as they stand over Will's prairie grave:

> This may seem a lonesome place to leave him. But he's not alone. Because many of his kind rest here with him. The prairie is like a mother to Mr. Andersen. He belonged to her. She cared for him while he lived and she is nursing him now, while he sleeps.

Like most of Wayne's heroic characters, Will Andersen is a hero of nature. His is an identification with the best in nature, both human and nonhuman. Thus, when Cimarron says of himself that he is a "mistake of nature," he is pleading for someone to correct that "mistake," which is exactly what Will Andersen does.

Nightlinger wins the boys' respect with kinship and with difference. He has imagination, courage, skill, and greatness of heart. In him Will Andersen meets a match to complement his own rough character. Nightlinger speaks words over Will's grave as Will had spoken them over Charlie Schwartz's grave; Will Andersen buries a courageous Jewish youth, and

Top: In mortal conflict with Bruce Dern (as Long Hair) in *The Cowboys*. *Bottom*: with Roscoe Lee Browne as Jebediah Nightlinger.

Will Andersen is buried by a courageous black man. Here is an image of continuing importance for Wayne's heroic type, who comprehends all people from all cultures in all colors. Will Andersen tells the truth of color when he identifies evil in Long Hair and good in the black man. This is a demythologizing of the bigotry rampant in America throughout Wayne's career. The survival of Nightlinger to lead the boys into their deserved manhood is, in the symbolism of the film, the reincarnation of the dead Andersen's own heroic spirit.

THE KIND OF MAN he has been is well understood by the time Will Andersen confronts Long Hair in his last battle. Will is hard, expecting others to be hard as well. He works hard and he wants others to join him in the same hard work. He needs and loves his wife. He still grieves the loss of his two sons, almost 20 years after their deaths. He hates liars, and he deplores the disappearance of loyalty. He distinguishes the world of women from his own world of men, as when he tells the schoolteacher he wants to talk only to the boys in her class: "I have nothing to say to young ladies," and she responds by saying, "Then we bow to the fact that it's a man's world and leave it to you."

Most of all Will Andersen is a proud man. Anse tells him, "If your neck was any stiffer, you couldn't even bend over to pull your boots on." From Ajax to Achilles, to King Lear and Captain Ahab, pride is an essential ingredient of tragic heroes. It is not necessarily his flaw, though many have followed Aristotle in thinking so. A proud man may have difficulty bending, but the virtue of his pride is that he can bend and still be proud: unlike Lucifer, whose pride disappears in shame, as in Long Hair.

At the center of Will's pride, where his power of will originates, is a point of uncertainty and self doubt: his grief for his lost children. Without this, he could not be a great man, as he could not be a man of heart. His death is a ritual occasion to test the meaning of his pride, as self-destructive or self-liberating. Long Hair orders Will to give up his gun. Will does so, and then he is ordered to drop his belt. Will does that also. Finally, Long Hair tells him to bring the belt to him, but this Will does not do: he won't bend over. Long Hair pulls out his gun, points it at Will as if to shoot him, but instead turns it away and says, "Pride! Stubborn pride! I admire that. It truly is an admirable quality. To tell you the truth, I wouldn't 'a picked it up either."

Will has this in common with Long Hair: pride destructive rather than redemptive. But Will Andersen has been learning to bend, from the moment he decided to enter the schoolhouse to learn the most critical lessons of his life. He was reminded by Anse of his own youth, and that set Will on the spiritual pilgrimage that fulfills itself in this ordeal with Long Hair. In this he defines pride as self esteem, not vanity and arrogance. This pride

comes from surviving tests of probation—to find probity of soul. The audience for Will Andersen's tragedy witnesses a lesson in this probity.

The shooting, long and tortured, finally ends. Will lies on his back,
arms extended in cruciform attitude, surrounded by the young cowboys.
There is a spot of blood over his heart. Will Andersen's last lesson to his boys
is that they can find courage in passive resistance to evil, more redeeming
than a victory of direct assault. Will fought his battle in the ways he knew:
prudence, pride, passion, and then, triumphantly, with fortitude of passive
indifference to personal danger. This is high tragedy. It raises the spirit of
the suffering hero to new levels of insight, for himself and for the audience
he invites to his scene of suffering.

JUST BEFORE HE DIES Will tells Nightlinger, "summer's over." Fall
uncovers tragic experience. *The Cowboys* says "summer's over," as it
describes the world of heroic action and heroic suffering when, as Will's
wife had said to him, "it's a different day." Wayne's character of Will
Andersen is no more hard-bitten than several others he had portrayed in
earlier movies, than Tom Dunson or Ethan Edwards, for example. The
world of Will Andersen is not any more violent in its ways than that of
Wayne's 1930s B-Westerns. But the violence is bitter, perhaps more irrational, and it is more urgent as it strikes a dark note of disillusionment. The
truth of this film is, finally, a complicated truth: violent yes, but senseless no.

To make sense out of violence, betrayal, madness ever lurking at the
edges of sanity: these are challenges to art always, from Homer and
Euripides to Hawthorne and Faulkner; from *The Book of Job* to *The Death
of a Salesman*. In 1972, American popular films found the challenges more
urgent in more graphic ways. In that year appeared, for example, *The
Assassination of Trotsky, Deliverance, Slaughterhouse Five*, and *Godfather
Part One*. It was to be a decade of disillusionment expressed in these conventions of graphic violence, from *Patton* in 1970, to *Jaws* in 1975, to *The
China Syndrome* and *Alien* in 1979.

In 1971 appeared a story of small-town Texas during the 1950s, *The Last
Picture Show*. This tale of dreary disillusionment suggests how difficult it
was for fiction to be tragic, and how much easier it was to be ironic. The
same is true for a blockbuster movie which appeared in the same year as
The Cowboys. In *Godfather Part One* there is the same grim picture of ironic
tragedy as in *The Last Picture Show*. They offer, however, contrasting approaches to the problem of tragedy in popular American film. With a little
license, one could call *The Cowboys* Wayne's own version of a "godfather,"
and with no need for license, one may recall that the last picture show in
The Last Picture Show is Wayne's own *Red River*.

The closures of all three films create symmetries of form in all three
stories. *The Last Picture Show* reverses the movement of the camera, from

left to right, coming back to where it began with a still shot of the, now closed, ROYAL picture show house. Little has changed in the physical appearance of the place; there might never have been a picture show, for all the effect it has had on the community. The movement of the picture back to its starting point does not recover spiritual significance from the events of the story. If anything, the town is less meaningful than it was in the beginning. This cannot be said of the conclusion of *Godfather Part One,* which imitates the end of *The Searchers* with its closing-door sequence. In *Godfather Part One,* however, the person closed out has no place to go, not even into the expanses of a limitless desert as in *The Searchers.*

Kay Corleone has just been reassured by her husband, the new Don, he had nothing to do with killing his brother-in-law. He puts Kay in her place, outside the sanctum of his study. She is a helpless, pathetic victim of the world where those who seem to pull the strings (of business, of politics, of law enforcement) are themselves merely puppets on disappearing and invisible strings. The final resting point of the scene identifies audience with the Godfather again, as in the opening. Plunging back into darkness, this closure suggests that conventional values have been displaced by new, darker ones. The occasion for the closing door is a deception of wife by husband, of life by death (murder). To be where we are at the end is to find ourselves a party to that deception.

Deception breaks apart in *The Cowboys,* as evil is seen for what it really is, and good is seen for what it can really be. Seeing is important for all, as the attention to Dan's glasses suggests. When Long Hair puts on the empty frames, he can see no better than ever before. But Dan, whose vision has been sorely tested, sees deeper and wider than any child can do without turning into a man. Will Andersen hates a liar more than he hates a man who has been in jail; indeed, he does not hold it against a man for being in jail. But a liar is like a cancer that turns a healthy body politic into a mass of corruption. If a person's word cannot be trusted, in the simplest as well as in the greatest of things, then little can be expected from the institutions which come from those persons and are preserved by their words. When Will Andersen dies, then, he dies for honesty as well as for loyalty. *The Godfather Part One* can understand death for loyalty, but it has a hard time with death for honesty.

The Cowboys moves to close from a focus on the tombstone of Will Andersen: "Beloved Husband and Father." The camera moves up and away from the stone, to gaze across the prairie which is Will's grave and mother. This reverses the movement of *The Godfather Part One,* appropriately marking a difference between films of strong views. When the camera rises to withdraw from Will's grave, it enlarges to a view of the mountains and the heavens in the background. As in the conclusion to *Sands of Iwo Jima,* the spirit of the dead man rises with the camera to merge with the enlarged scene before the camera's view. Then, if one is steady in one's view, one can see a movement of figures at a distance, coming from out of the frame on the left and moving toward the center on the right. These are the cowboys going home, repeating the movement of action which opened the film: moving in the right way, keeping the world of their new understanding well in balance.

MATTERS OF VIOLENCE call for special consideration in the three films. It is not more frequent in films (or other arts) of the sixties and seventies than at any other time in the history of popular art. But in a survey of Wayne films, one is struck by intensifying attention to details of violence: from images of blood to obscenities of language. These three films of 1971–72 use violence to present narrative visions of a world which is fraught with danger, and vicious in its pursuit of power.

There is plenty of ferocity in *The Last Picture Show*, though its violence is less physical than moral. On the other hand, it is frequent, physical, and moral in *The Godfather Part One*. Artfully introduced in a succession of episodes which heighten action, scenes of brutality intercut scenes of festivity and ritual. Baptisms of babies counterpoint assassinations, marriages mirror contracts for terror. This creates dazzling uncertainty about relationships between ceremony and civilization, contracts and killing. Words of loyalty lead to deeds of terror, feelings of love lead to words of duplicity. The order of this world requires the disorder of violence to endure. Santino ("Sonny," James Caan) is murdered because he impetuously rushes out unprotected to help his sister.

While the murder of Sonny is deliberate and calculated, it is impersonal; he might as well be a fish. He is butchered in a hail of bullets. It is a scene without passion, which is the real substance of Will's death scene in *The Cowboys*. (Little Charlie's death beneath cattle hooves is more akin to the killing of Santino.) Will and Long Hair are almost as bloody as Santino, but they wear their blood as badges of conflict in a battle of furious good and evil. Passion may not justify violence in *The Cowboys*, but it motivates spiritual and emotional growth. Passion *is,* these films suggests, violence: it is an energy of expression, a means of being, not an end in itself and not a value by which to measure ends.

John Bernard Books: *The Shootist* (1976)

The Shootist was John Wayne's last film. It portrays a man legendary in his time. It appeals to the legend of the actor himself: it introduces the hero with scenes from *Red River, Hondo, Rio Bravo,* and *El Dorado.* He is presented as an aged Tom Dunson, Hondo Lane, John T. Chance, and Cole Thornton. The hero is thus a summary, archetypal character embodied in John Wayne himself. As John Bernard Books, Wayne enacts the tragic

With James Stewart *(right)* **as Dr. Hostetler in** *The Shootist.*

conclusion to a career of romance adventures. It is an essay on the meaning of violence in that career.

To recall merely the ten years of films released before and after *The Shootist* in 1976, one notices, first, shortly before its appearance, such films as *The Wild Bunch, The Exorcist,* and *Jaws.* In these, violent deaths of human beings are considered normal and routine. Whether any of these could be called "tragic," however, is debatable. They were representations of *disaster,* without doubt. Indeed, one sign of the times was the obsessive attention given to mass disasters in movie stories, as in *The Poseidon Adventure* in 1972. After 1976 appeared *Looking For Mr. Goodbar, Dressed to Kill,* and *Caligula.* There is something representative about *Caligula;* its search for novelty of violence conveys a decadence not only of Imperial Rome.

John Wayne's films of the seventies are not unusual when they represent brutality in graphic detail. They present characters who use violence to assert themselves in a violent world, as do characters played by William Holden, George C. Scott, Burt Lancaster, and Frank Sinatra in films of the same era. Their films are, like his, studies in the problems of an aging hero. Such a hero interests because his life has been burdened by countless deeds of violence, legitimate and illegitimate, moral and immoral. The line which

separates good from evil, moral from immoral, even legitimate from illegitimate, is difficult to locate.

A CHARACTER like William Holden's Pike Bishop in *The Wild Bunch*
has difficulty finding that line, but so does the audience which accepts the
point of view of the film. The code of "The Wild Bunch" may lack the
legitimacy of the military code in *Patton*, but it does not prevent its heroes
from performing deeds of valor, courage, and even honor as admirable as
one looks for in the military lives of *Patton*. Such films work their effects in
a mode of irony rather than tragedy or romance. Moral and legal definitions
shift with shifting points of view into a kind of relativism. For Wayne's
heroes, there is little difficulty in knowing right from wrong, although Ethan
Edwards, or Tom Dunson, or Tom Doniphon might take his private "right"
so far that it becomes a public "wrong." Even those characters, however,
know or come to know they are in the wrong.

Later tragic heroes of Wayne's career, like Will Andersen and John
Bernard Books, are men whose visions of right and wrong remain steady to
the end. They are tragic because their worlds are too small for them. The
people who surround them are too weak or too narrow and dim-sighted to
honor and accept them or their visions. Nevertheless, when those heroes
die, they leave behind some of the light their lives have borne through the
general dark, or grayness, of the world. The young cowboys carry on for
Will Andersen, and Gillom Rogers carries light from John Books.

This passing of the torch by heroes of tragedy is conventional. It
relieves the pain of their deaths. Out of the awful events of *Agamemnon*
emerges a grand idea of justice for Orestes, son of the murdered Agamemnon and murderer of his mother Clytemnestra. The dreadful discoveries of
Oedipus Rex precede solemn sanctification of the tormented hero in
Oedipus at Colonus. In those ancient trilogies, present disaster yields future
tranquility to heirs of the tragic heroes. These heirs, like Gillom Rogers, are
witnesses privileged to learn from the sufferings of great people.

What they learn the audience can learn as well. Tragedy is a lesson of
enlightenment as well as a purgation of emotions. To understand what the
hero is, what his life means, and how his death is a proper conclusion—
these are the lessons of imaginative enlightenment. One need not feel pity
or fear to be moved by enlightenment from Orestes in *The Eumenides*,
Oedipus in *Oedipus at Colonus*, or Samson and Jesus in the Bible. Such
heroes, in their passions and sufferings, in their triumphant powers of will,
are profoundly tragic nevertheless.

The heroism exhibited by Orestes among the Areopagites, Oedipus at
Colonus, Samson among the Philistines, and Jesus in Gethsemane, is
heroism of submission, of self sacrifice. Their battles are battles of will
power, of spiritual strength. The violence of their lives and deaths proclaims

spiritual strength and power. When the violence is an instrument of divinity, it is condoned and sanctified by purposes beyond the ken of ordinary mortals, sometimes beyond the understanding of heroes themselves. The people who execute those purposes are themselves victims of violence. They are heroes because they choose to surrender themselves to fulfill large patterns of meaning. In their choice is an understanding of the price they must pay to fulfill such purposes. The price is suffering, sometimes death.

This is the tragic hero John Wayne portrays in the character of John Bernard Books. He is a hero of sacrifice, what the Greeks called a *pharmakos*, the victim whose death is the medicine of healing. The tragic pattern is a ceremony of ritual, designed to insure spiritual sanction of the violence necessary to carry out the sacrifice. It is not the kind Euripides shows in his *Bacchae*, where Pentheus is torn apart by ecstatic women (including his own mother) who worship the god Dionysus. Rather, it is the kind Nietzsche distinguished from the Dionysian as *Apollonian:* disciplined, solemn, and illuminating. With tense awareness of the dangers involved, the hero goes to his doom in a ceremonial manner solemn, dignified, and eloquent.

This is necessary to contain the central, climactic event that consummates the ritual, violent act of the sacrifice itself. If one considers the root meaning of the word *violent,* as coming from *vis/vim,* one appreciates the necessity for the violence: energy is released by the sacrifice (the energy of "vim and vigor"). It *must* be violent, an explosion of atoms themselves, transforming matter into energy of spirit. The ceremony creates a pattern of intention for directing this energy, so that it does not merely dissipate or disappear into a random disarray of particles (as in a mere accident or mass disaster). The *plot* of a story with a tragedy of sacrifice is itself the ceremony of the ritual.

In the ritual of the pharmakos is a tearing apart of the victim. This was the *sparagmos* of Greek ceremony; it frightens and alarms, raising emotion to heights of terror, as it ought, or it would not carry the ominous significance the sacrifice intends. One does not enjoy this spectacle with any more pleasure than one might in contemplating the imminent explosion of an atomic bomb over one's own household. The violence is to be as convincing as it can, since the deed is a communication with powers which bind and loose the universe itself. Because the victim submits to the binding which will result in a loosing, the victim is a "religious" hero — as the word *religion* implies in its root meaning that combines *re-* with *ligion:* a "tying back."

The cultural tradition behind *The Shootist* includes not only Greek tragic forms, but also Hebrew and Christian ones. The Bible is a crucial source for understanding the significance of violence in ritual sacrifice. The

Bible is a continuous narrative of sacrifice, culminating for Christians in the crucifixion of Jesus on Calvary. Although John Books is not an allegorical type of Jesus, Samson, Oedipus, or Pentheus, he moves through a mythic plot of purification and ritual sacrifice. The persons are not the same, but the myths are always the same.

BIBLICAL SACRIFICES include the ones which led to the first murder—when God preferred the animal sacrifice of Abel to the vegetable sacrifice of Cain. The blood of the sacrifice suggests a preferred kind of "vim," or violence. A grand displacement occurred when "God did tempt Abraham" and commanded him to take his son Isaac "and offer him for a burnt offering." When Abraham showed he was willing to obey God, an Angel appeard to substitute a ram for the child. When God renewed his Covenant, he included in his commandments this one: "All that openeth the matrix is mine; and every firstling among thy cattle, whether ox or sheep, that is male." This was to include "all the firstborn of thy sons" as well. Again, however, there was to be a merciful substitute, as He commanded the first-lings to be redeemed with a lamb (*Exodus* 34: 19–20).

Most exemplary are Samson and Jesus. They enact, in old and new ways, rituals ordained by the priests of *Leviticus* and foretold by the prophet Isaiah. In *Oedipus at Colonus,* a vital component of the ritual is washing to purify the polluted soul. Dante is cleansed by river passages in the *Divine Comedy.* Jesus is baptized in the Jordan, reenacting the passage of the priests with the Ark of the Covenant in *Joshua* 3: 15: "And as they that bare the ark were come unto Jordan, and the feet of the priests that bare the ark were dipped in the brim of the water." Jesus later in his ministry, at his Last Supper on Passover, washed the feet of his disciples: "If I then, your Lord and Master, have washed your feet; ye also ought to wash one another's feet" (*John* 13: 1–14).

Instructions for cleansing of lepers are guidelines for purification, though in the blood of a lamb. The priest is to slay a lamb as a sin offering, then "take some of the blood of the trespass offering . . . put it upon the tip of the right ear of him that is to be cleansed, and upon the thumb of his right hand, and upon the great toe of his right foot" (*Leviticus* 14: 8–14). Later in *Leviticus* is a description of the procedure for sacrifices to atone for sins of a whole people. This is the ritual involving the scapegoat. One goat is slaughtered for its blood of purification (the Greek *sparagmos*); another carries sins into a wasteland. Perhaps this is a ritual basis for mythic narratives which divide tragic sacrifice in drama and fiction: one hero dies, and another survives to carry on burdens of conscience. When Horatio survives to tell the story of Hamlet, he carries the conscience of that sweet prince. When Theseus survives to witness the secrets of Oedipus's death, he carries on the mysteries of justice for Athens. And when Gillom Rogers survives his witness of John Books's death, he carrries away in solemn ceremony the lessons of justice he learned from that violent deed.

The stories of Samson and Jesus, like the story of Oedipus, are narratives of ritual purification leading to sacrifice. Samson's self sacrifice is a sacrifice of his enemies as well. The story of Jesus follows a pattern of temptations which climax in Gethsemane: "And he went a little farther, and fell on his face, and prayed, saying O my Father, if it be possible, let this cup pass from me," according to *Matthew* 26: 37. In *Luke,* Jesus needs an angel to strengthen him: "And being in an agony he prayed more earnestly: and his sweat was as it were great drops of blood falling down to the ground" (22: 43–44). Matthew uses imagery of ripping, renting, tearing to narrate Jesus' crucifixion as a painful, but apocalyptic, scene of suffering. The victim's clothing is torn by soldiers, the body of God is ripped, and the whole earth is broken by shuddering quakes. *Sparagmos* is a cosmic event.

WHILE IT CANNOT BE SAID that John Books' death scene is cosmic, it can be understood as a climax to ritual purification. Like Biblical Job, J.B. Books is tested in these, his last days of pride. Dr. Hostetler says, before examining him, that Books has the constitution of an ox, but afterwards he says, "even an ox dies." Books asks the doctor if he can't cut the cancer out, and Hostetler exclaims, "I'll have to gut you like a fish." The man has been reduced to his animal status, but it is a status of high symbolic value: oxen were favored animals of sacrifice in Greek and Hebrew ritual, and the fish is an emblem of sanctity in Christian ritual and iconography.

The victim's mood of mind as he approaches sacrifice is all-important. It should be a mood of humility, particularly difficult for one who has been proud all his life. To be reduced to animal status is an early phase of the humbling process. When Hostetler tells Books to take off his clothing, to bend over the examination table, and put his "trap door down," he is preparing the victim for intensifying humility (to do it without humiliation challenges physician and priest alike).

Dying on his birthday is a rounding of the hero's circle, as the plot is rounded from Monday to Monday. Coming to Carson City to see Hostetler is also a rounding, a return to the place Books received his first and only wound. This is ritual purification, as the victim prepares to go back whence he came into life. These days of return are passages across thresholds, marks of division between what Books has been and is becoming. The most consequential threshold is at the Metropole, whose name has special significance as a "mother city." It is the sacred place of communication between life and death. After Books's death, Gillom walks out of the casino, through the swinging doors, past the mysterious, quiet presence of Hostetler. In this completion of the ritual, the Doctor is, as the priestly physician, in attendance for a new life as well as for the end of an old one.

The most meaningful actions of his purification ritual are related to Books' bathing and clothing himself. He begins by having to disrobe for the doctor. He is shown to his room by Bond, who points out the bathroom and says, "We do have running water." When he and Bond go riding together, they ride alongside a beautiful mountain lake, and they stand beside it to talk. After the nighttime massacre in his bedroom, Books rolls up his bedclothes for Bond to clean. He gives Bond his suit for cleaning before visiting a barber on Saturday. On Sunday, he bathes, suffers a sharp attack of debilitating pain, and he has to be helped from the bathroom by Bond. Finally, he is thoroughly clean and freshly groomed for his deathday, so that Bond exclaims at "how grand you look!"

BOOKS' RITUAL OF PURIFICATION is counterpointed by the *sparagmos* of his body and identity. People are rending him asunder as he begins to falter and fall. The process begins even before Books enters town. Books takes charge when he arranges the shootout. He submits to death, but on his terms. When he walks into the Metropole on his birthday, he finds his enemies surrounding him, like Samson. He does not change his identity even as he offers himself for sacrifice. He is still the "shootist" he has always been. He is shot many times, bloodied even before the bartender ambushes him. The ritual and symbolic importance of his blood is strong enough that the film is right to show it in abundance. However, the tearing apart of the body which would occur in "reality" from two shotgun blasts at short range the film does not attempt to imitate. That might be dramatically appropriate as an image of *sparagmos,* but it would not allow for the dignified salute of honor by Gillom as he bids farewell to the dying man. He must be seen intact, because he is an example of integrity: whole in spirit, torn in body.

This is not allowed the "shootists" of two films released during the same time as Wayne's last movie. In *The Missouri Breaks* (1976), Marlon Brando portrays a "regulator" hired to protect cattle from rustlers. He is the perfumed psychotic Lee Clayton, as opposite to J.B. Books as could be imagined. Clayton arrives hanging behind his horse, frightening unsuspecting Jane Braxton. He lifts a corpse from its casket of ice, in a mockery of resurrection and introduction to death. He bathes himself in a luxury of soap bubbles. But his purification cannot succeed. Lee Clayton tears people apart, and when Tom Logan (Jack Nicholson) comes to get him (in the bathtub), Tom turns away in disgust, observing, "My God! You ain't even there!" An observation about Clayton's sexuality, it is more seriously a comment on his spiritual identity—of which Clayton has none. He deserves the indignity of his death: he wakes from a happy sleep to find his throat cut.

The sick shootist of *The Missouri Breaks* can bear no one's sins, because he has no conscience, no respect for life. He has no soul to be purified. On the other hand, in a story with a ritual pattern like *The Shootist,* Steve McQueen played a famous gunman in his last days in *Tom Horn* (1980). He is a "stock detective." The betrayal of Horn by those who preyed upon his skills and reputation for violence is comparable with episodes of *The Shootist.* There is dignity in the character of Tom Horn. It comes from exhaustion, however, rather than from discipline. Like Wayne in *The Shootist,* McQueen shows the effects of an illness which eventually killed the man, but he was playing a character who, also in 1901, had worn out his role in history.

Horn is trapped, tricked into his death. He has little dignity in his going, though it is great indeed when compared with Lee Clayton's. Horn does not define himself in his own terms, as does John Books; but Horn does not have his throat cut in his sleep either. The trial and execution of the shootist Tom Horn is a ceremony of innocence in which he is a scapegoat victim of sacrifice for the sins of the community which has used him. But Horn is pathetic, not tragic. His spirit is wrung from him, and he seems unaware of the price is he paying. He is Christlike in his innocence, but he is hardly Christlike in his understanding. Some dignity comes to him in death, which echoes Herman Melville's story of Billy Budd. Tom Horn is allowed to hang himself, because no one will accept responsibility for springing the trap on the gallows. It is a torture of time lengthened out by trickling water before Tom Horn drops into oblivion. His dignity is that he "keeps his nerve" when no one else can.

Tom Horn is an ironic, and *The Missouri Breaks* a cynical, treatment of violence and scapegoats. A more conventional romance form of the gunman appeared also in 1976 in Clint Eastwood's film of *The Outlaw Josie Wales,* a vindication of the uses of violence in violent times. None of these, however, has the solemnity and richness of *The Shootist,* which allows its hero a fullness of identity as he answers for his life in the best way he knows. Tom Horn is befuddled in death. Lee Clayton is astonished and surprised by it. Josey Wales loses his identity to stay alive and free. Only John Books understands, controls, and knows who he is when he walks through the doors of the Metropole on his 58th birthday.

12. Ironic Heroes

Wayne made opportunities for excellence in the ironic mode because he established himself in romance early and triumphantly. His heroes of irony have a sharper, bitter, edge to them, because they measure the failures of a world which does not deserve heroes at all—especially heroes like the Ringo Kid, Tom Dunson, and Ethan Edwards. When Kirby York abets the romantic myth of Col. Owen Thursday at the end of *Fort Apache* (1948), York is John Wayne putting an edge on the outline of his own romance heroes. When Nathan Brittles visits the graves of his wife and children at the end of *She Wore a Yellow Ribbon* (1949), he is John Wayne paying his respects to his romantic past. Both characters are sentimental, but they are ironists in control of that sentimentality.

As John T. Chance in *Rio Bravo* (1959) and Cole Thornton in *El Dorado* (1967), Wayne turns irony from sentiment to cynicism, from pathos to ethos. Hawks elaborates *Rio Bravo* into a parody of the western genre, and *El Dorado* into a parody of *Rio Bravo,* while Wayne sophisticates his characters' self awareness in both films. Hawks uses his parodies to analyze ethical relationships between people with little moral certainty. Wayne is able to act on the surface so well his characters seem to have no ethical center. The irony of his roles produces confusion of surface seeming with central realities, of dislocated actions with essential principles.

As hero victimized by sentiment and sacrificed to cynicism, Wayne is the consummate *eiron* Tom Doniphon in *The Man Who Shot Liberty Valance* (1962). Other ironic heroes find ways to accommodate their worlds, however irrational and unstable. Doniphon cannot make that accommodation, even as he sacrifices himself in the attempt. The finest irony of this character is that he triumphs in his defeat, and he disappears in his triumph. Wayne preserves through Doniphon a glimpse of integrity otherwise shattered in a world without direction. Wayne's final ironic hero is a fitting one to end with because Lon McQ (1974) is squeezed by such a world to abandon more and more of what he values, until he has nothing left to work for and perhaps nothing in himself to believe.

Capt. Kirby York: *Fort Apache* (1948)

Although John Wayne gets top billing in the credits for *Fort Apache*,
he does not seem to be the major character. That honor seems to go to
Henry Fonda, as Lt. Col. Owen Thursday, lately assigned to command the
regiment at Fort Apache, Arizona Territory. The main plot seems clear by
the time the new commandant has taken his command: he must bring
discipline to a remote outpost guarding the frontier of the nation. It will be
thankless duty, and to be effective it will have to be done without glory or
personal reward. Thursday is to be one of the many nameless men who
bring civilization to the wilderness. The subplot reflects this: his daughter
Philadelphia (Shirley Temple) will be courted by young Lieutenant
O'Rourke (John Agar), and their marriage will domesticate the wilds of the
frontier. It is a romantic story. But it is also a comedy, carried by a team
of four burly sergeants. They are big, rough, and tough, but they are
buffoons as well, especially in their liquor. Slapstick prevails when they take
over.

It is a class-conscious romantic comedy, focusing on Col. Thursday,
Philadelphia, Lieutenant O'Rourke, and the four sergeants. Thursday's
class consciousness is strong. He wants officers and men to act according
to their separate places in the organization of the Army, a picture of the way
the world is or ought to be for Col. Thursday. It is an artificial set of distinc-
tions, and it is un–American. By the time Thursday breaks in on the
O'Rourke household to stop Philadelphia's courtship, he is out of place. The
tyrant father must be removed for love to triumph. Where in all this action,
it may be asked, is the "star" of the film?

FIRST SEEN, CAPTAIN KIRBY YORK is one of several officers dancing
to celebrate the birthday of George Washington, which Thursday interrupts. York stands beneath the portrait of George Washington and he keeps
the festivity going when he asks Philadelphia to dance. Thursday does not
know it is Washington's birthday. He is trapped, not knowing what to do.
The dance is to honor the father of his country. Capt. York saves the occasion and rescues the Colonel.

York is little more than a foil to the foolishness of the Colonel. York is
the comic servant who helps a romantic hero get his girl. York is repeatedly
put down, in his place. Thursday learns O'Rourke is riding with
Philadelphia. He uses O'Rourke as bait in a trap for the renegade Apaches.
York is appalled, but he obeys his orders. The trap works, and Thursday
captures the renegades. With York's guidance, Thursday discovers
Meacham has been selling rotgut whiskey to the Indians, hidden in crates
marked "Bibles." York explains why Cochise broke the treaty and fled to
Mexico: he "wanted to live here in peace, and did—for two years. And
then," York goes on,

As Capt. Kirby York, with *(from left)* Grant Withers as Silas Meacham, Victor McLaglen as Sgt. Mulcahy, Henry Fonda as Lt. Col. Owen Thursday, George O'Brien as Capt. Sam Collingwood, and Miguel Inclan as Cochise, in *Fort Apache*, 1948.

Meacham here was sent by the Indian Ring. The most corrupt political group in our history! And then it began: whiskey but no beef, trinkets instead of blankets, the women degraded, the children sickly, and the men turning into drunken animals. So Cochise did the only thing a decent man could do—he left, and took most of his people and crossed the Rio Bravo into Mexico.

Thursday only objects to Meacham's methods of administration, though Thursday is not above twisting rules to serve his own ends. Thursday is a man for appearances, York for realities; Thursday for legal and physical order, York for moral and spiritual order. But York remains subordinate, a pawn for his commanding officer.

York volunteers to seek out Cochise. Cochise trusts him. York enters into ceremonies of greeting and negotiation with Cochise and Geronimo. York knows what real courtesy and discipline are. But he is a tool of deceit even as he sincerely offers trust and confidence to Cochise. York returns to interrupt the noncommissioned officers' annual dance, in a reprise of the opening. The film accelerates to reveal its radically ironic form.

Thursday must, by ceremony of tradition, participate in a closing of the gap between officers and noncommissioned soldiers. He carries on

Fonda, O'Brien, Wayne and Withers in *Fort Apache*.

beautifully. But he is too happy to break up the dance the moment York
returns. Thursday does what York would not do at the birthday dance: he
halts the festivity. He does so to betray a trust. York protests: "Cochise'll
think I've tricked him!" Thursday agrees, "Exactly!" York, appalled, says, "I
gave my word to Cochise! No man is going to make a liar out of me, sir."
But that is exactly what Thursday proceeds to do, as he denies there can
be any "question of honor" between an American officer and "a breech-
clouted savage, an illiterate, uncivilized murderer and treaty-breaker" like
Cochise. York's last words are, "There is to me, sir."

THE FILM SHOWS the fall of a fool in Colonel Thursday, crossed by
the rise of a hero in Captain York. New ironies develop as York watches in
disbelief while Thursday rides to glory. York watches helplessly as the
Apaches sweep with no resistance over the encircled position of Thursday
and his tiny group of survivors. One of the Apaches grabs a pennant of Company B as the Indians sweep through the circle.

York and his handful of men wait for the Apaches to attack them. The
din of horses' hooves fills the air. Then the Apaches do the unexpected—
they halt. The warrior carrying the pennant rides out alone; York drops his
weapons, walks out to meet the single Apache. They are seen at middle
distance. The Indian plants the captured pennant alongside York, wheels his

horse, and rides away. York is caught in a strong scene of irony: the Apaches ride away, kicking up a massive cloud of dust, concealing the lonely figure of York beside the pennant. He is diminished by the distance, obscured by the dust.

As the dust settled from the end of the last battle, the scene dissolves from the beclouded ironic hero to a comfortable office of the new commander of Fort Apache. The camera retreats to show the pennant standing in a place of honor in the new commander's office. Beside it is a portrait of Colonel Thursday, dressed in lavish cape and stunning uniform. The voice of Kirby York is heard: "However, gentlemen, I warn you, this may be a long campaign. It may be weeks before you have any headlines for your newspapers." York, talking to newspaper reporters, sounds like Thursday. One of them says, "If we catch Geronimo, that'll be headline enough, *Colonel* York." Another reporter, "And more glory for your regiment."

This is the grandest irony of the film, as Captain York has "become" Colonel Thursday all over again. Is this a defeat for honesty and honor? York agrees Colonel Thursday was "a great man," a "great soldier." He says, "No man died more gallantly, nor won more honor for his regiment." A reporter asks if York has seen the famous painting of "Thursday's Charge." York replies he saw it "when last in Washington." The reporter describes the painting: "That was a magnificent work. There were these massed columns of Apaches, in their war paint and feathered bonnets, and here was Thursday leading his men in that heroic charge." York, the man who earlier told Thursday, "No man is going to make a liar out of me," now says, "Correct in every detail." York looks out a window, as if to a vision, reflected in the glass: a parade of the living dead, glorious heroes of the romantic army of the U.S. Cavalry. He describes what he sees: "Faces may change, names, but they're there, they're the Regiment."

What is "really" out there, in the scene beyond the window, beneath the image of art, is the same dirty truth, where soldiers have to leave their families, ride through dust, and risk their lives and honor for a country that needs romance, legends, and heroes. Colonel York's new truth is that people need to believe in something more than dirt-reality. His most compelling service is to keep alive a hope for a romantic future, even if it costs a lie about the realistic past. This is the fate of an ironic hero, to turn a lie into a legend (myth) as a weapon of civilization.

IN 1946 HENRY FONDA *had* been the star of *My Darling Clementine*. He was Wyatt Earp, driving a herd of cattle with his brothers near Tombstone, Arizona. Wyatt becomes marshal to find the killers of his brother. When he has his legal revenge against the Clantons, Wyatt rides away from Tombstone leaving behind "his darling" Clementine.

Fonda is playing a standard romance hero like Hondo or Shane. Unlike

Colonel Thursday in *Fort Apache,* Wyatt Earp is loose and easy, though tough and determined. When he goes for a shave, he stops a drunken Indian's shooting spree before he can finish his "tonsorial": he asks repeatedly, "what kind of a town is this?" This sounds like the question of a naïve Easterner (like Ransom Stoddard in *The Man Who Shot Liberty Valance*). But this is a man accustomed to law and order based upon raw force. Wyatt proceeds to demonstrate his prejudices. He drags Indian Charley from a saloon to the grateful citizens of Tombstone. Again he asks "What kind of town is this?" but he adds, ". . . selling liquor to Indians?" He tells Charley, "Indian, get out of town and stay out!" Doc Holliday (Victor Mature) throws out a crooked gambler. However, Holliday is no racist like Earp. Holliday mocks Earp as a puritan—"You haven't taken it into your head to deliver us from evil?" he chides.

In romances this is exactly what the hero does—he delivers from evil. But Fonda is still the straight man, just as he was to be in *Fort Apache.* Doc Holliday is the ironic hero in his film, as York is in his. Holliday has mysteriously given up love, comfort, and culture, to disappear into pseudonymity. His ability to complete a soliloquy of Hamlet identifies him as Hamlet-like himself. He is a good man who has found evil out. He is a realist with few illusions; Earp is a sentimental romantic who dreams of goodness right through the thick of evil. The story of Doc Holliday gives *My Darling Clementine* its significant texture, lifts it from a routine story into meaningful art. The same is true of Kirby York in *Fort Apache.*

York is the ironic hero as survivor, Holliday the ironic hero as sacrifice. York moves from the circumference of a marginal man, to assume the central role that gives continuity to his story. Holliday appears out of central darkness, briefly challenges the romance hero, but then disappears back into the shadowy heart of things. Holliday is a good man wasted by a discontented imagination, destroyed by the reality to which Earp is brutally callous: neither is redeemed by his imagination. On the other hand, York learns to adapt to his world of realities, though the price of his adaptation is to learn to be an actor—the very thing Holliday could, but chose not to, do (he knew the lines, but he refused to act them). York is the ironist who is heroic in his self consciousness: reality requires not compromise, but irony—saying more or less than one knows. Holliday knows this, but he could not bear it; York knows it, and he bears it.

Victor Mature's Doc Holliday is an enrichment, but he sinks into the nothingness against which Earp contends; Wayne's Kirby York never sinks, always contends, and returns his story to a new level of insight. This he achieves because his able to detach himself and then reattach himself at crucial points of necessity. Holliday can only be detached, which is his tragedy as it is his irony he cannot see as largely as he can see deeply.

WITHOUT HENRY FONDA to supply the limited romance of illusion, *Wagon Master* (1950) presents a trio of heroes who together give what Fonda could mark alone. Wiggs (Ward Bond) has a temper and an itch for fighting, but he struggles (successfully) to suppress his propensity for violence—he knows himself and his limits. Travis (Ben Johnson) is hard-bitten and capable of cheating anyone. But Travis is, way down deep, a sentimental man, even though he knows a snake when he sees one (and he can kill a man who shows himself to be a snake). Travis's buddy, Sandy (Harry Carey, Jr.) comes closest to the Fonda-romantic, as he supplies naïveté to the trio. It takes all three, however, to complete the complexity of either Owen Thursday or Wyatt Earp.

The same is true when they are compared with Wayne's Kirby York. Wiggs knows when to lie, when to say something different than he knows. Wiggs is also basically decent and courteous to others. All three demonstrate this in their characters when they dance well together with strangers, including Indians. This identifies them (in a John Ford way) with Kirby York, and it should identify them with Thursday/Earp. However, Thursday only dances out of necessary formality. Earp surprises himself and everyone else when he submits to love and moves ungainly with Clementine across the unfinished church floor in Tombstone. Wiggs/Travis/Sandy dance with joy and ease of community. Kirby York does the same.

LIKE MOST AMERICAN WESTERNS *My Darling Clementine* and *Wagon Master* are best understood as romances with romance heroes triumphant. *Fort Apache* is different, and that difference is the difference of irony, which wrinkles the face of the film, refusing to let it say everything it knows. This difference is created by John Wayne as Kirby York, who puts up with Owen Thursday because he knows something is true in the man's vision even as he also knows there is something shabby and hollow in the man. Wayne's Kirby York sympathizes and yet distances himself in an elaborate "dance" with Thursday. He fills the space created by Thursday, but he is bigger than Thursday in vision as well as in bulk. York's vision is ample because he observes himself playing a role: he sees the difference between what he is and what he is supposed to appear to be.

The actor preserves a saving distance between himself and his character, as he creates an image of freedom. This "freedom" to move from edges and boundaries to the center and then back again prevents Wayne from being trapped and contained by stereotypes and conventions. His triumph in this mode is that he can be hero and antihero at the same time: the space between is his region of existential license. In this he recreates the experience of classical comedy, from Aristophanes to Molière, from Chaplin to Kurosawa.

The *eiron* of classic Greek comedy is usually an ordinary citizen who

outsmarts a boastful public hero, the *alazon*. Because the eiron must, to survive, pretend to say more or less than he means, he *uses* language as a tool
or weapon. He is ironic because he seems to be less important than he really
is; his adversary, the alazon, is ironic because he seems to be more important than he really is. The ironic hero exposes and defeats the boastful,
hyperbolical character.

Whether it is Aristophanes or Plautus, the comic writer may need an
eiron to unmask the dangers of ego in positions of leadership. As the issues
of life and death become more desperate, comedy may turn dark, but the
eiron still serves his purpose, whether in Shakespeare's pairing of Prince
Hal with Falstaff, or Hamlet with Polonius. It is the basis for Chaplin's pairing of the little barber with the dictator Hynkel in *The Great Dictator*
(1940), as it is the basis for Kurosawa's characters played by Toshiro Mifune
and their adversaries in *The Seven Samurai* (1954), *Yojimbo* (1961), and *Sanjuro* (1962). Mifune is a superior eiron, capable, like Wayne, of playing
against his heroic reputation. Chaplin, Mifune, and Wayne find aesthetic
freedom in detachment: essential to the actor who wants to keep imagination alive in himself as well as in his audience.

Captain Nathan Brittles: *She Wore a Yellow Ribbon* (1949)

THE CONCLUSION of *She Wore a Yellow Ribbon* bears away from the
endings of *Fort Apache* and *Rio Grande*. In the last Yorke is brought back
to his fort, wounded, on a litter drawn by his horse; he recovers to join his
General and his wife on a reviewing stand for the "coda" of the film—a
tribute to the integrity of the nation. Yorke's reunion with his wife is the
emblem for a nation reunited, he the Union, she the Confederacy. There
is also a coda to *Fort Apache*, raising the plot to ironic heights, in which a
faulty hero as apotheosized and the future of the nation is assured by the
continuity of family and faith. In both stories the hero played by Wayne is
returned to a central place of authority. Something similar seems to occur
in the coda of *She Wore a Yellow Ribbon*.

The story appears to end when Brittles completes his career in the
Cavalry. It is just past midnight on the last day of his professional life. He
bids his colleagues farewell, turns his horse and rides off a civilian. The
voice-over narration:

> So Nathan Brittles, ex–Captain of Cavalry, U.S.A., started westward for
> the new settlements in California. Westward toward the setting sun,
> which is the end of the trail for all old men.

Not only are cliches rounded into this, they defy the logic of the action, as
the new civilian rides towards a setting sun just a few minutes after midnight. But this is a mythic, not a realistic, conclusion, where time disappears
at the end of one cycle and recommences at the beginning of a new one.
Brittles crosses the threshold from an old to a new existence. There is a

tension of contradiction: "westward for the *new* settlements," and "westward toward . . . the end of the trail for all *old* men." Realistically, Brittles is going to a new life in the West; metaphorically, he is going to his death. These also are clichés, though they contain imaginative truth.

The solitary figure on horseback, riding across a forlorn desert, toward the "end of the trail for all old men," is a visual cliché working with the verbal ones. None of this is simply the result of careless direction, editing, or writing. It is all part of the self-conscious parody of conclusions audiences expect. Most of all it is a parody of a John Ford Western, which is why the next sentence of the voice-over is, "But the Army hadn't finished with Nathan Brittles—it sent a galloper after him. That was Sergeant Tyree's department."

Tyree (Ben Johnson) indeed gallops across the screen, across the desert, to catch Brittles. He delivers a letter to Brittles, who puts on his glasses to read it. He lets out a whoop of happiness when he reads he has been appointed Chief of Scouts with the rank of Lieutenant-Colonel, endorsed by Phil Sheridan, William Tecumseh Sherman, and President Ulysses Simpson Grant. He returns with Tyree to Fort Stark, where he is met with formal dignity of a ritual welcome by the troop in dress uniform. They are gathered to dance in his honor. This is the cliché Ford conclusion to a Western film. Olivia asks Brittles to join the dance, but he says he must "make my report first." He revisits the graves of his long-dead family (a wife and two daughters). He goes out into the twilight to sit besdie his wife's grave, as he has been accustomed to do the past nine years. Then does it seem the film can end. Again a voice-over narration as the graveyard dissolves into a new scene, as the waltz music of the dance dissolves into the theme music of the film:

> So here they are, the dog-faced soldiers, the regulars, the fifty-cents a day professionals, riding the outposts of the nation. From Fort Rio to Fort Apache, from Sheridan to Stark, they were all the same—men in dirty blue and only a cold page in the history books to mark their passing. But wherever they rode and whatever they fought for, that place became the United States.

It has started over again, the parade of life, as the scene is a company of cavalry on patrol, led by Chief Scout Lt. Col. Nathan Brittles. The cycle has gone round and begins again. This is the "real" end of the story—at least until the opening of *Rio Grande*.

The "recall" of Nathan Brittles to rejoin his comrades on a new tour of duty is a figurative translation of his identity into a new realm of being—like reaching the "end of the trail" and finding it is home after all, like finding "new settlements" in "old" territory. When Nathan asked Major Allshard to tell Abby good-bye for him, Abby overheard and protested, "You'll do no such thing, Nathan Brittles. 'Good-bye' is a word we don't use in the cavalry!" As she kisses him, she says tenderly, "To our next posting, dear." The coda of the film confirms Abby's insight, as Nathan Brittles finds himself again with his friends together on his "next posting."

WHILE THE CODA OF *She Wore a Yellow Ribbon* does not have the irony of hyperbole, exaggeration, and extension, of *Fort Apache*, it does have the irony of metaphor that turns back on itself, of repetition. When Brittles turns to return, he repeats the pattern of irony at its most dramatic: the hero is bound to the turning wheel of Ixion, is trudging back up the hill as Sisyphus. Within the parodic form of the coda, Nathan Brittles happily returns to do again what he has been doing all his life. The happiest irony of this conclusion is to recall what Nathan had said to Chief Pony-That-Walks: "We are too old for war. But old men should stop wars." Perhaps this is to be his new mission as Chief of Scouts—to "stop wars" at the head of the *Paradise* River Patrol.

One of the most unfair ironies of movie history is the popular (mis)conception of John Ford and John Wayne as militarists, as Indian-killers. *She Wore a Yellow Ribbon* (and not it alone) should correct such a view, for in it the old warhorse John Wayne is dedicated to stopping, not starting, wars, and he is, just as he was in *Fort Apache*, a friend, not a foe, of the Indians. *She Wore a Yellow Ribbon* could be called John Ford's "paean of peace," and John Wayne's Nathan Brittles could be called a blessed peacemaker. This accounts for much of the poignancy in the film.

Brittles tells his men to "shoot over their heads," during a crucial scene of Indian attack. Nathan can barely be heard above the noise of the action, but that is the order he gives, and that is exactly what his troopers do. They do not shoot, wound, or kill any of the pursuing Indians, who turn and ride away to leave Quayne to give his report. What makes this remarkable is that the pressure of the situation is to kill as many Indians as possible: Custer has been massacred; many of Nathan's own friends have been killed in that massacre; the Army Paymaster was killed; and a brave man, Corporal Quayne, near death from Indian attacks.

Later Nathan leads his column back to the fort away from the scene of massacre at Sudrow's Wells. Tyree reports he has spotted Rynders trading with Red Shirt and his renegade Indians. Nathan takes Tyree and Lt. Pennell (Harry Carey, Jr.) for a closer look. They see a stupid Rynders trying to cajole Red Shirt into paying a high price for his guns. Rynders (Harry Woods) relies on his pal (Paul Fix) to interpret for him. Red Shirt has little to say; "fifty dollars is too much." Then he casually shoots an arrow into the heart of a surprised Karl Rynders. Red Shirt's braves then proceed to torture Rynder's partner, dragging him through a campfire to burn him alive.

Meanwhile Brittles, Tyree, and Pennell are watching from a concealed position in the rocks above. They hear the screams of the man dragged back and forth through the fire. Brittles stops Tyree from an impulse to help. Brittles does not move to interrupt the torture. Ford repeats this scene with Wayne in *The Searchers*, when Ethan Edwards tries to prevent his two young companions Martin Pawley and Brad Jorgenson (Harry Carey, Jr., again) from attacking Indians who hold his nieces captive. Ethan has an ambivalent attitude for the audience to deal with: he wants to let the girls die, and he does not want to risk the lives of his companions. Nathan also has ambivalent motives: he wants to let the Indians work their will on the corrupt whites (as a form of justice), and he does not want to risk the lives of his companions (including two women under his protection).

But Nathan Brittles is different than Ethan Edwards. At worst, Nathan permits the scene to "play itself out" in the education of his young lieutenant, Ross Pennell. The lesson for Pennell is that his enemies are capable of savagery, of doing deeds which can turn the stomach of a civilized person. Does Pennell have the stomach to deal with such enemies? Nathan pushes him, offers him a chaw of tobacco. Pennell knows he is being tested, and he takes the chaw. He demonstrates he is Army material after all, he can stomach brutality.

In a third episode Nathan rides with Tyree to a council with the Indians. He has defied Major Allshard's orders to leave his men to take care of themselves and to go into retirement. He chose instead to rejoin the men he left as a rearguard during his retreat to the Fort. Although he is wearing his civilian jacket, he is still technically in the Army. He writes out an order for Lt. Cohill (John Agar) to protect the young lieutenant in event of a court martial after this episode. Then he and Tyree ride out on a mysterious mission. It is a repetition of York's journey to confer with Cochise in *Fort Apache*.

But it is a different kind of conference in *She Wore a Yellow Ribbon*. It will indulge some humor in the "Christian" sentiments of Pony-That-Walks, and it will exploit ironies of age beset by youth. Nathan must deal with the hostility of Red Shirt, who rides defiantly past him as he enters the camp. Nathan dismounts to show his peaceful intent, but also to show Red Shirt he does not fear him. In response, Red Shirt shoots an arrow at the feet of Nathan. While Red Shirt sits astride his horse, ready to shoot again at the slightest sign of aggression, Nathan calmly but firmly bends to pick up the arrow. He looks closely at it. Then he snaps it into two parts, spits on it, and tosses it back at the startled Red Shirt. Nathan proceeds to his fruitless, though humorous, conference with Pony-That-Walks.

When Nathan Brittles startles Red Shirt he does not startle the audience, because we know John Wayne as hero is capable of courage. However, when Nathan breaks the arrow he does a very significant thing: he is saying not only that he has no fear of Red Shirt, but he has contempt for war itself. This is the passionate irony of the story and of the character. While walking into the camp, Nathan had whispered to Tyree to look out for the location of the Indians' ponies. Later, after they have returned to the patrol on the river, we discover why.

He leads his troopers toward the Indian camp under cover of darkness. They attack the unsuspecting Indians. But they do not shoot anyone, even though several of the Indians try to shoot them. Instead, they stampede the Indians' ponies through the village. The ruse works. When it is finished, Lt. Cohill reports there have been no casualties. Nathan is pleased. He says,

> No casualties. No Indian war. No court martial. You will have your soldiers follow the hostiles all the way back to the reservation. You will follow a mile behind 'em. Walkin' hurts their pride. Your watchin'll hurt it worse.

What kind of man is this, then, who refuses to shoot his enemies? For one thing, he is a man who likes to teach lessons. He used the scene of torture to test and teach young Lt. Pennell. Then he reversed the direction of instruction when he explained to Cohill that "watching will hurt [the walking Indians'] pride worse." He uses occasions of spectating to teach moral lesons. He is the artist who stands in detachment to inform audience imagination. More importantly, he is the *eiron* who takes such stances to deal with a world of brutal realities. Nathan Brittles is an ironic artist at work.

TWO YEARS AFTER *She Wore a Yellow Ribbon,* Charles Chaplin made *Limelight,* a film also of retirement, aging, recall, and instruction. These themes shared by both films made at about the same time invite comparisons between them and their star actors, even though they are obviously unlike in significantly fundamental ways. *Limelight* story focuses on consequences rather than anticipation of retirement, and it focuses on the pathos more than the ethos of the hero. It is a melodrama with touches of black humor, while *She Wore a Yellow Ribbon* is a Western with ripples of slapstick. Both, however, develop portraits of an aging hero who learns how to translate experience into vision, and vision into prophecy.

Calvero (Chaplin) finds out the heroine (Claire Bloom) is a dancer who suffers from hysterical paralysis of her legs. She finds out he is a once-famous clown afraid to risk his reputation. Calvero coaxes and cajoles Terry back into walking, then dancing; she loves and strokes him back to the stage. At the end Calvero sacrifices himself for the success of his patient-pupil. She dances to glory while he dies of heart failure, watching her from the wings.

Calvero's way of instruction is to entertain, crack jokes, be a clown. Terry's way of repaying him is to perfect her own talent. Calvero also guides Terry, as Nathan does Olivia, toward a proper lovemate. Both Calvero and Nathan use their professional skills to give their pupils this instruction.

Calvero jumps with joy when his pupil succeeds. During the benefit performance at the end, Terry will repeat that jump when she hears the audience applaud Calvero's performancs. They exchange roles.

Nathan Brittle does not leap with joy (not his style), but he gives a whoop of pleasure when he receives his appointment as Chief of Scouts. He has not exchanged places with the young lieutenants, but he has given them his former place, and he has been recalled from oblivion to play out a benefit performance of his own. When Nathan returns to rejoin the command at Fort Stark, to repeat his ritual of visiting his family in their graves, he does for his career what Calvero does when he joins with his friend (Buster Keaton) in their marvelous "musical satire." Nathan Brittles and Calvero repeat, in a finer tone, their professional lives in tribute to their audiences, the community which has made them what they are.

Calvero had to discover he could not perform successfully again unless he could perform under his old name. The audience's identification of him with his reputation was an important ingredient in his final success. The old man cannot start over again by renouncing his past; he has to affirm it, extend it, and repeat it. This is, fundamentally, what Nathan Brittles does when he rides back to Fort Stark and revisits the graves of his wife and daughters, as well as when he once again leads the troop out on patrol. As Calvero tells Terry, "Nothing's gone. It only changes." So had Brittles answered Quincannon: when the sergeant insisted "the Army will never be the same when we retire," Brittles responded, "The Army is always the same. The sun and the moon change; the Army knows no seasons."

NATHAN BRITTLES AND CALVERO both stand at a distance from the scenes of youthful drama involving their pupils. They are watchers as well as instructors, but they are "trained" spectators, because they have spent their lives being watched by others: one as entertainer, the other as leader. In their detachment, both are ironists able to disengage temporarily from the delusions and illusions of others.

Both films concern heroic confrontations with failure. *She Wore a Yellow Ribbon* makes this central to its plot, as Nathan Brittles spends his final days in a failure of his last official mission; *Limelight* converts the failures of a man and a woman into the triumphant success of art and artists, as it shows how failure in life (to find "meaning") can become a source of success in art (to create "form"). The two films produce, then, different textures of experience, but they do it out of the same materials of life's problems.

Lately the life of Nathan Brittles is filled with little failures. True, he does not manifest it like Calvero in drunkenness — Nathan gave up drinking nine years ago when his family died. But he has a patient tolerance for those who do enjoy a drink, like his sergeant, Quincannon. Most things going wrong in Nathan's life are the results of a failing nature, not a failing character. His hair is going white. His joints are stiff. His eyesight is beginning to fail (he blushes when he takes out his spectacles). There have been great failures as well: his family is dead, his friends have been killed with Custer, and the fragile peace of the territory has been broken to make it unsafe even for picnics.

Most pressing is failure of peace in the territory. This is not his responsibility alone, nor does he make it so. But he has a responsibility to his conscience if not to his command, to do what he can to prevent a massacre of the soldiers he left behind to guard his retreat. Because he manages to save those soldiers, just as his time runs out, he saves the peace of the land. His limited objective, personal honor, achieves broad success of social peace. He turns failure into success, making all failures into versions of the fortunate fall. Nathan Brittles embodies the power to exploit failure, to convert it to good fortune. He knows the horse soldier must walk as often as he rides to get his job done. His profession is a dialectic of war and peace. The war is a sign of failure, the peace a sign of success. Life is filled with the failures of nature, and it needs the artist-soldier's dedication to convert those failures into an order of peace. To observe Nathan Brittles is to watch that artist at work.

John T. Chance: *Rio Bravo* (1959)

Before the story of *Rio Bravo* can be resolved, John T. Chance must suffer a climactic, humiliating fall. He rushes down Carlos's Hotel (called "The Alamo") stairs, trips over a rope at the bottom, and lies unconscious while his friends are captured by Burdette's hired guns. His fall is an epitome of this ironic hero's career: he is bursting with viciousness, righteous indignation, but he is hemmed in by the facts of life, denied means of explosive self-expression, and finally captured by the woman who missed her stagecoach.

John T. Chance is such an ironic hero. His story could be a likely plot for comedy or romance. His world of authority is small, but even there his power is limited and constrained on all sides at all opportunities. That he holds his prisoner in a jail under siege is almost a metaphysical fact. The circle narrows as if it were a noose, and even after release is gained by a series of dynamite explosions, the real victim turns out to be the sheriff, tied by the charms of Feathers (Angie Dickinson) triumphant.

THE OPENING EPISODE is filled with hints of irony and ambiguity. Chance is knocked down for his service to Dude (Dean Martin), who is beaten for his gesture of defiance. An innocent bystander is murdered casually by vicious Joe Burdette when the man makes a gesture of interfering with the beating of Dude. Then, when Chance staggers into the Burdette saloon to arrest Joe, Chance himself is surrounded by Burdette men. But behind the Burdette men appears Dude himself, to rescue Chance from further violence. The ironies and ambiguities of the opening have produced a murder and pain for innocents and the law, while the pathetic victim whose degradation was the cause of it all turns out to rescue his rescuer.

This is not the only occasion Chance's good intentions lead to greater danger for Dude. The chase for Pat Wheeler's killer also puts Dude in physical and moral danger, though it also ironically gives Dude his first taste of renewed power and pride. But it is in the final sequence of action that Dude is most in jeopardy, when he is kidnapped by Burdette's men after Chance's grand fall down the hotel stairs. In this concluding episode, Dude manages his own affairs, even baffling Chance as he does so.

Chance's failures expose Dude to the final capture, but Dude let himself fall victim. When Chance seems at a loss what to do, Dude suggests he take the thugs to the jail and let Joe out—knowing Stumpy (Walter Brennan) will shoot them and Colorado (Ricky Nelson) is there to help. Finally, in a scene of great irony heightened by Wayne's acting, Chance agrees in a daze to lead the thugs away to the jail. When Chance returns to help Dude, he finds him gone—a prisoner of Nathan Burdette. Chance sends Carlos to Nathan to arrange a talk, but Nathan refuses (again Chance is frustrated). Chance then agrees to an exchange of prisoners, but it happens that Dude has another idea—he tackles Joe, recaptures him, escapes from Burdette, and helps Chance out of a mess at the end.

There is a double irony in this. First, the immediate consequences of deliberate and impetuous actions by the hero plunge the community into danger; second, the patron repeatedly falls from authority into a final domestication, while the ward repeatedly escapes from jeopardy to final independence of authority. (That Dude learns to forget the woman who "ruined" him is set against the fact that Chance is falling for Feathers.) A hero cannot exist in this world, he only makes things worse if he tries to help others. Individuals can, nonetheless, escape degradation, if they have patience and resilience. The key item of character is patience rather than aggression, impulse, or impetuosity. Dude learns that "the readiness is all." Chance fails when he is moved by immediate motives rather than submit to the "providence" of occasion, or, ironically, of "chance."

CHANCE TRIES TO HELP another person and he endangers a whole community. Dude helps himself and thereby helps Chance. Those who look after themselves seem more ethical, then, than those who help others. (Socrates, in Plato's *Republic*, called this a matter of "justice," which he defined as "minding one's own business.") If, alternatively, one manages to help oneself, one might ironically be of assistance to others. This is parodied

Ricky Nelson *(left),* **as Colorado Ryan and Wayne as John T. Chance blaze away in** *Rio Bravo.*

by the impotence of the Nathan/Joe relationship. Nathan tries to help his brother, and he makes things worse; Joe does absolutely nothing to help himself, and so he helps no one at all. This is a demonic reflection of the Chance/Dude relationship.

The Pat Wheeler/Colorado Ryan relationship provides a parody of a different kind. Pat (Ward Bond) is the victim of a paid killer. That drives Chance into yet another impulse of rage. Pat's young ward, Colorado, is the opposite of impulse. Colorado is all patience: careful and observant. He helps himself, and he becomes a major help to Chance. When Colorado

Nelson, Angie Dickinson as Feathers, Bob Terhune as Nesdon Booth, and Wayne in *Rio Bravo*.

joins the "team" at the jail, he joins a circle that includes Stumpy and Dude—but puts John T. Chance on the outside (illustrated by the beautiful irony of the song sequence, when all sing except Chance).

Colorado submits to circumstance, because he knows that readiness is all. He does not put himself in jeopardy, but ironically because he does not, he is blamed by Chance for the death of Pat Wheeler. When he is not so emotional, Chance admires Colorado for being "smart," i.e., taking care of himself. Just as there must be a turning point for Dude (his conversion), when he moves from shame to pride, so must there be one for Colorado, when he decides to help someone other than himself. Ironically, it happens when he seems to act impulsively: Chance is in danger outside the hotel, separated from his rifle and confronted by three gunmen. When Feathers throws a pot through a window, Colorado coolly kills two gunmen and tosses a rifle to Chance at the same time. Colorado puts himself on a "side." Colorado is supposed to be entirely selfish in his behavior ("smart"), like the professional whose integrity is in his skill and whose pride is in his independence. There seems to be no one reason, no clear motive, for Colorado to help Chance. It is irrational, though Colorado is reason itself when it comes to matters of means and ends.

Rio Bravo is permeated by the irrational. Causes do not always produce expected results. John T. Chance is an emotionally impulsive man who seems cool and in control, but he has deep inside him a strong need for love and friendship that gets him into trouble as a professional. Colorado Ryan is a self-centered, smiling young man cool as can be way down deep, but even he cannot control everything within or about him. For whatever reason, Colorado at least does not make a commitment on account of friendship. That is what killed Pat Wheeler, and that is what makes it hard for Dude to survive. Neither family nor friendship is a sufficient bond to justify interference in the state of self reliance.

CHANCE HELPS ANOTHER FRIEND, Carlos (Pedro Gonzalez-Gonzalez), which gets that friend in trouble. It is not serious trouble, and it is trouble Carlos can handle, because he "knows women." But Chance gets into trouble himself when Carlos displays scarlet bloomers he has ordered for Consuela (Estelita Rodriguez), and holds them up for Chance to admire. Feathers enters and sees John T. Chance "modelling" the scarlet bloomers. She observes, "Those things have great possibilities, but not for you!" Chance is not amused, but he is embarrassed, as he will be time and again when he is with Feathers. This is what helping a friend can do in *Rio Bravo*, but it also, in its typically ironic way, introduces the heroine and hero to one another.

Chance helps Carlos, and he finds himself embarrassed. Chance asks Carlos to help get Feathers on the stage, which earns a black eye for Carlos. At another time Carlos wants to help protect Chance while he sleeps in Carlos's hotel, but Chance refuses. Ironically, however, that refusal opened the possibility for Feathers to show her interest, and so she stood "guard" over Chance all night. Carlos is tied up and unable to help Chance in his time of greatest ignominy, the fall down the stairs. But at the end, when Chance and Colorado are attacking the Burdette gang at the warehouse, Chance goes to warn Stumpy, leaving Carlos to carry on with the attack against the Burdettes. They seem, by the end of the story, to be of one kind, as Carlos becomes the gunman taking Chance's place at the window and Chance becomes the messenger Carlos volunteered to be.

This merging of identities between Carlos and Chance leads to the final union between Chance and Feathers, as it has been foreshadowed by the relationship between Carlos and Consuela. In fact, Consuela stands at the door of Feathers' room when Chance arrives to see her for the final episode of the film. Consuela inducts Chance to his bower of bliss with a significant gesture of her waving hand (it will be a "hot" encounter).

Feathers (Angie Dickinson) successfully seduces John T. Chance. He suspects her of cheating, of being an accomplice to a gambler wanted for cheating, and of being a hooker. Feathers exists to show how mistaken John

T. Chance can be. He picks up signs of evidence, but he misjudges them.
She repays his suspicions by falling in love with him, standing guard while
he sleeps, and helping to save his life. She knows him so well by the end
that she knows exactly how to pin him in place; she puts on a very brief
black "tight," says she is going to wear it while she "sings." He finally blurts
out he will "arrest" her if she goes out in that "thing." He tosses the garment
out the window, to be picked up by a passing Stumpy.

Feathers and Stumpy have much in common: both talk a lot (they go
on and on, overwhelming the taciturn Chance); both love Chance; but
neither ever meets the other. The closest they come is in this final scene.
The tossing of the "tights" is a transfer of identity between Stumpy and
Feathers. One of Wayne's warmest gestures of acting occurs when Chance
kisses Stumpy on the top of his head in the jail (a reprise of similar scenes
in *Tycoon*, 1947, when Johnny kisses Pops, and in *The Searchers*, 1956, when
Ethan kisses Martha on the forehead). This is a sign of the bond between
Chance and Stumpy, signifying *in* Stumpy something *in* Chance.

Stumpy represents, as guardian of justice, an objectification of
something in Chance. That is a set of values crippled, like Stumpy, by a
sterility of the purely masculine relationship. Stumpy completes the circle
of men without women around Chance: from Pat to Dude to Colorado, they
constitute a "family." Stumpy allows Chance affection otherwise unper-
mitted, because Stumpy is crippled and condemned to his station. Chance
moves back and forth between the jail and the hotel between Stumpy and
Feathers, until he chooses Feathers and the hotel over Stumpy and the jail.
This has the immediate effects of (1) liberating Stumpy, who now walks the
streets of joy, and (2) imprisoning Chance, who yields to the domesticating
embrace of Feathers. Stumpy's new partner is Dude, walking alongside to
patrol the streets of Rio Bravo in their new life together.

WAYNE AS JOHN T. CHANCE is an ironic hero par excellence. His
ironic status is the comic kind in which love triumphs to promise a new
beginning. Chance disappears from the heroic life and Dude takes his
place. *Rio Bravo*, it turns out, has little to do with the excitement of a battle
between good guys and bad guys, where a hero emerges to save the community from evil. It is really about the ironies of heroic action, about the
disappearance of heroes, and it is about the emergence of the anti-hero(es).

High Noon (1952), on the other hand, was about the emergence of a
hero in the person of Will Kane (Gary Cooper). *Rio Bravo* was said by
Howard Hawks to be his "answer" to *High Noon*. Amy Kane (Grace Kelly)
is a pure-minded Quaker anxious to get her new husband Will Kane out of
town as quickly as possible, to find a place of peace and quiet away from
guns and violence. Helen Ramirez (Katy Jurado) is the Mexican woman
lusted after by Harvey Pell (Lloyd Bridges), and she is the former girlfriend

of the villain Frank Miller as well as Will Kane—Helen also wants Will to get out of town because she does not want him dead. In Feathers is a combination of Amy and Helen, to produce the ambiguous, sensual woman who overwhelms John T. Chance—trying to get *her* out of town.

At each point of character and action, *Rio Bravo* counters *High Noon*. Harvey Pell is answered by Colorado Ryan, as both are the youngsters good with their guns. Pell is selfish like Colorado, but Pell tries to sell his guns to Kane in return for a recommendation to be the new marshal of Hadleyville. Colorado Ryan "minds his own business" until he saves Chance. When Chance says it is "nice to see a smart kid for a change," he in effect rebukes Harvey Pell as he compliments Colorado Ryan; in *High Noon*, Joe the barkeep notices Harvey isn't wearing his deputy's badge and says, "It takes a smart man to know when to back away."

There is even a Stumpy in *High Noon*. In fact, Stumpy seems to be a joke in bad taste, seen as a counter to ex-marshal Mart Howe (Lon Chaney, Jr.), to whom Will goes in desperation for help. Low-keyed and cynical, Mart tells Kane, "I couldn't do nothin' for you." Then he holds out his hands, warped by arthritis and busted knuckles. They are "stumps." The justice of the peace, on the run, tries to teach Will a lesson in history and civics: people cannot be trusted to do what is "right," and "nothing that happens here is really important" anyway. Will Kane refuses to believe it, but *Rio Bravo* assumes this as basic to its view of reality.

People slink away and betray Will Kane, until only his Quaker wife (who shoots a man in the back) is left. People gather in loyalty around Chance, though he discourages or refuses their help. When Will decides to confront Frank Miller, Amy exclaims, "Don't try to be a hero! You don't have to be a hero, not for me!" Will responds, "I'm not trying to be a hero. If you think I like this, you're crazy!" He may not like it, but he *is* trying to be a hero. By the end of the story, Will Kane is a triumphant hero who saves himself *and* the town that does not deserve him. Although *High Noon* is built of ironies in its incidents, showing disparities between expectations and realities, it is not finally a film of irony, because it raises its hero to heights of approval. Will Kane is a romance hero in a world of ironies, while John T. Chance is an ironic hero in an ironic world.

John T. Chance does not expect much from people, and so he gets a lot more. He is played with ease and versatility by Wayne, moving the character through difficulties of feeling and action with impressive skill. In scenes with Angie Dickinson, he shows bafflement and timidity, in degrees to make it convincing. At first, he approaches her with firmness to force her out of town, but he does not get rough, though he has reason to be irritated with the woman who ridiculed him modelling the scarlet bloomers. Gradually, Wayne retreats before the barrage of Dickinson's coy talkativeness. In the end he asserts his authority as a lawman, to conceal his

submission as a man. Wayne carries a sleeping Dickinson up stairs for a
night of loving but he also falls heavily down them to help a woman in
distress.

There are few tricks of camera in *Rio Bravo,* movement and angles to
manipulate the meanings of the actors' gestures, as in *High Noon.* Long
shots do not make people seem small and lonely as they do in *High Noon;*
pictures do not retreat or rush forward, to create a sense of uncertainty in
the relationships of people as in *High Noon.* The camera angle, except for
the parody of high and low angle to open the film, and the camera distance
remain steady and predictable in *Rio Bravo.* This puts the weight of meaning in the film on the actors and actresses, more than it does in *High Noon.*
Wayne makes his steady world more easy by his acting, while Cooper
makes his unsteady world more firmly so by his.

THE SHAPING OF THE WORLD as viewed through the eye of the
camera is more obvious in *High Noon* than in *Rio Bravo,* though the extraordinary angle that introduces John T. Chance suggests intense self-
consciousness in *Rio Bravo.* This tilting of view, to create unusual long shots
or unusually tight close-up shots, marks the exaggerated style of *Touch of
Evil* in 1958, the year before *Rio Bravo,* six years after *High Noon. Touch of
Evil,* like *Rio Bravo,* shows the world as a "border" condition. All three films
narrate the test of a lawman's ability to uphold the law, when the community
seems to be indifferent to his real worth. The irony of *Touch of Evil* is,
however, that the lawman, Hank Quinlan (Orson Welles), is corrupt to the
core: he plants evidence to justify arrests of suspects, and his conviction rate
is high. The indifference of Quinlan's community is not to his skill, but to
his corruption. The final twist is that his suspects probably *are* guilty.

Quinlan is an ironist appropriately undermined by "straight" Vargas
(Charlton Heston). The angular camera view in *Touch of Evil* is Quinlan's
view. He makes his way through the nightmare of a world where the center
has failed. Quinlan "helps himself," as Chance chooses to do and as Kane
is forced to do, but Quinlan finally hurts himself most of all. Vargas has just
got married at the opening of *Touch of Evil,* like Will Kane, and Vargas ignores his new bride to pursue a professional interest, again like Kane. Both
are made upright and "pure" by their women, but not without exposing
them to corruption. By contrast, Chance keeps his woman at a distance
from his professional life, and it is she who "corrupts" him.

Hank Quinlan is a bloated, vengeful man who dies on a garbage dump
to float down a river like a rat at the end of *Touch of Evil;* he is a sick man
in a sick world. While *High Noon* would concur that the world is sick, it
denies that men of health and integrity can do little about it. Indeed, *High
Noon* offers, with its long shot of Kane moving alone down the street of
Hadleyville to meet his destiny, a visual metaphor of David moving to meet

Goliath, and like David, he wins. *Rio Bravo* keeps its adversaries in medium shots, or it shows its heroes behind buildings, being prudent, and using dynamite to defeat enemies: in this world, even the bad guys are rational — they get paid to be "bad," or they are motivated by brotherly love. The sickness of *Rio Bravo* is shame, a consequence of too much self awareness.

Self awareness leads some heroes into madness, like Quinlan in his obsession for vengeance. Dude could be obsessed in the same way, but he suffers from delirium instead, as he attempts to repress a memory of betrayal. Finally there are no obsessions in *Rio Bravo*, as people behave for prudent reasons in an imprudent world. Another film of 1958, Alfred Hitchcock's *Vertigo*, narrates the fall of yet another lawman, forced to retire from the San Francisco police force after his vertigo caused the death of a fellow officer. James Stewart as "Scotty" Ferguson, like the other lawmen of these films, decides midway through his story to take things into his own hands, to do something for himself, when he remakes the girl Judy into the woman of his obsession, Madeleine. Scotty produces disaster for Judy and for himself, as he forces her to reenact the falling death of Madeleine Elster.

Vertigo makes the human eye into an image of vertigo, a madness which takes possession of a person, pushes away every other consideration, and drives all reality into the vortex with (or within) himself. What had been tilting, angulation, and distortion of perspective for thematic purpose in *High Noon*, for ironic adjustment in *Rio Bravo*, and for metaphysical assertion in *Touch of Evil* becomes in *Vertigo* the subject as well as the object, the matter as well as the form of the film. Gary Cooper is the aging, good man whose ideals see him through the pitfalls of an ironic, un-ideal world. Orson Welles is an aging, corrupt man whose sickness of mind has made him successful in a sick world; Charlton Heston is a young alien whose ideals mislead him in the sick world of Hank Quinlan. James Stewart is an innocent middle-aged man who goes mad when he falls in love, and whose madness sucks all reality after him into the vortex of his distorted perceptions.

Romance, comedy, and even tragedy all seem futile forms of expression in these films. Only irony could deal with their outrageous worlds, provide human orientation. Hadleyville is not saved, nor is it worth saving. The towns on the Mexican-American border in *Touch of Evil* are beyond saving, as Quinlan knew and Vargas has to learn. The city of *Vertigo* is an illusion, or delusion, of the protagonist's madness. In *Rio Bravo*, on the other hand, there is little to save, but Wayne's John T. Chance saves that little because he expects so little from it. This makes him a bigger man than Cooper's Will Kane, Welles's Hank Quinlan, Heston's Vargas, or Stewart's Scotty Ferguson.

Tom Doniphon: *The Man Who Shot Liberty Valance* (1962)

The Man Who Shot Liberty Valance is a troubling, sometimes poignant, often sentimental, essay in the ironies of modern American heroism. It was a peculiarly appropriate way to begin the decade of the sixties, as a retrospective on the legends and realities of political power in America. It was also a welcome to the future as a bastard child of the past. The film retains a power to disturb easy judgments and facile characterizations of John Wayne's image.

As in *Fort Apache,* Wayne's character does not appear until late into the development of the story of *The Man Who Shot Liberty Valance.* More teasingly than in *Fort Apache,* he makes his mark emphatically by his *absence.* The signs of his absence are lovingly put on display as a Senator and his wife arrive in Shinbone to pay tribute to a man unknown even to the eager local editor of *The Shinbone Star.* The plain, rough hewn wooden coffin in a back room of the undertaker/carpenter/wheelwright shop; the missing gunbelt and boots—these are the signs of something amiss, something awry. They are the emblems of a man but also of a past so distant now that it is, quite emphatically, a mythic past. The film begins as a meditation on death, on disappearances, on featureless origins whose consequences are pieces of the past, mockeries of life, and insults against honor.

Before Senator Stoddard (James Stewart) and Hallie (Vera Miles) visit the carpenter's shop to pay their respects, ex-marshal Link Appleyard (Andy Devine) drives Hallie in a buggy out into the desert to look for cactus flowers. He takes her where he knows she wants to go, though she never says so. They drive to a site of ruin, where a house once stood. Now it is a pile of stones, charred wood, and covered with prickly cactus, though some are in bloom. Hallie admires one, Link digs it up for her. This is a crucial symbol, setting tone and dominant theme for the story: it is a sign of general ruin, but it is also an emblem of specific disappointment—the home, family, love, all displayed in empty, painful beauty.

THE MAN WHO SHOT LIBERTY VALANCE offers several levels of meaning: political, social, psychological, and, holding all together, mythical. As a political story, it focuses on the character and fate of Ransom Stoddard, so that Tom Doniphon can function as the marginal, ironic hero in the shadows of political reality. As a social analysis, the (political) story focuses on Hallie and Pompey, at the expense of the narrative heroes Ransom and Tom. The psychological dimension of the film pulls attention to Liberty Valance. At a mythical level of "deep structure" Tom Doniphon is essential and central, whereas he is marginal at more superficial levels. Those superficial levels are where legends operate as facts; the deeper level is where facts *are* legends.

Because it is a retrospective, told to a small audience sitting around a stove in the carpenter's shop, the story-within-the-story must be recognized as made by Ransom Stoddard. Politics is thus a simple matter of good people triumphant over bad ones, good ideas over bad ones. Law and order, served by the editor Dutton Peabody and by the new lawyer from the East, Ransom Stoddard, prevail over anarchy and brute power, served by Valance and Starbuckle on behalf of cattle owners opposed to federalism. Law and order are matters of ideological conditioning.

The lesson in political science is that it is a management of public opinion through institutionalized education and control of the media of communication. (Ransom works for the editor of the *Shinbone Star* while he teaches the townsfolk how to read and write.) This part of the lesson is of little or no interest to the audience for Senator Ransom—that is, for the modern-day editor of the *Star*, Maxwell Scott, for his young reporter Charlie Hasbrouck, and the modern-day mayor Winder. What they hear in the tale is only the startling confession about who shot Liberty Valance. That should not surprise, since they are heirs to the ideology embodied by the institutions which created Senator Stoddard, their "hero." It will take the audience *for the film* to recognize the powers of ideology in the political design not only of Stoddard's tale but of the film's (total, formal) narrative as well.

THE ROLE OF TOM DONIPHON in the making of Stoddard is central in truth but marginal in legend. Tom is more prominent in the film's sociology, where he is the displaced lover. He is courting Hallie, even building a new room onto his house for her. His courtship is threatened and then destroyed by the arrival of the stranger from the East, Ransom Stoddard. In this romance-triangle, Tom provides the straight man to Ransom's winning ways.

Ransom wins Hallie because he is weak, not because he is strong. Tom loses her because he is strong, and because he misreads the signs of her relationship with Ransom. These are ironies of melodrama, but they are also ironies of the film's social meanings. They turn upon the conception of woman as little more than sexual object or nursing mother.

Ransom wins the contest for Hallie because he offers himself as victim. He identifies with Hallie's weaknesses. Both Hallie and Nora are kitchen workers who are busiest when they are taking care of their customers, the weekend drunks who crowd the restaurant demanding big steaks, potatoes, and deep-dish apple pie. There are not even any bedrooms in this society—the only bed is in the kitchen, and Ransom monopolizes that. Even sex is subordinate to eating. Women have no role in the political process. They are relegated to bystanders proud of their men going off to do important business. There is no more equality between the sexes than there is between the races.

There is no real society in *The Man Who Shot Liberty Valance*, not even the happy homes of dancing domesticity often found in films directed by John Ford. The only home is a burned-out shell of a house. The rest is a mix of restaurant, kitchen, saloons, newspaper office, and darkened streets. The social emptiness of the film is akin to the political impotence of the women, the Spanish-Americans, the children, and the one black person in it. The death of Tom Doniphon which surrounds the narrative conveys more than the disappearance of heroism, strength, and integrity. It puts forth a view of reality sterile and hopeless for all who draw identity from false premises.

THE BLANK SOCIAL TEXTURE and the cynical political gestures of the film provide threadbare integuments to a melodramatic and sentimental plot. The psychological message is a central concern. Tom Doniphon *as* Ransom Stoddard and *as* Liberty Valance becomes intelligible. The archetypal relationships of these three derive from the literary device of the "double," or "doppelganger." From Biblical stories of brothers (Cain and Abel, Jacob and Esau, Reuben and Joseph, Moses and Aaron) to Kurasawa's film of *Kagemusha*, doubles provide psychological analyses of character and cosmos. They denote neurotic symptoms of disturbed personalities (as in Dostoevsky's story of "The Double"), signs of ethical structure (as in Edgar Allan Poe's story of "William Wilson"), or techniques for spiritual renewal (as in Henry James's "Jolly Corner" and Joseph Conrad's "Secret Sharer"). Doubles operate with the force of primitive power in sophisticated forms.

They are found in the earliest films, as in *The Cabinet of Dr. Caligari* (1919), and in the latest, as in *True Confessions* (1981). In the work of Hitchcock, doubles are virtually a *sine qua non:* from *The Lodger* (1926) to *Frenzy* (1972). For Hitchcock's films, the metaphysical nature of the world is expressed in the psychological implications of double symmetries in narrative. Something of the same applies to the psychological structure of *The Man Who Shot Liberty Valance*.

Narrative structures with doubles respond to the psychological experience of "the uncanny." This is the feeling of déjà vu, recognition of the familiar in the strange. Something repressed returns to confront its repressor; something the conscious mind does not want to face returns in disguised form. If it is confronted, embraced, and accepted ("worked over"), the ghostly repressed is conquered and reintegrated into the fractured psyche. If it is denied, it continues to haunt its repressor, crippled by continued denials.

Ransom Stoddard, in telling his tale, is like a patient on the couch. His narrative is a return of the repressed. A confession, it is also an analysis of his own psyche, of the collective psyche expressed in political ideology. Liberty Valance and Tom Doniphon are the doubles into which Ransom's mind (character) splits. All three are one. To become a politically healthy person, Ransom had to overcome something within himself as well as in the community he serves. How he did that is the substance of his narrative. That he has kept secret (from his constituents and maybe even from his wife) the means of his victory over Valance is, in psychological terms, a repression of guilt which expresses itself in neurotic ways (as, for example, in his "poke-chop money" to Pompey). Before Ransom can be free of guilt, he must be freed from the threat of Liberty Valance. His way will be found by Tom Doniphon.

TOM DONIPHON IS A POWERFUL authority figure for Ransom Stoddard. In psychoanalytical terms, Tom is a father figure for Ransom, and so the deep structure of this narrative confession is determined by the classic Oedipus project: son desires mother and fears punishment from father. Ransom cannot openly court Hallie, though it is obvious he is attracted to her. The assaults by Liberty Valance are punishments for guilty desires. Ransom will need help to eliminate his impulse to self punishment, and where should he get it but from the father figure himself?

John Wayne as Tom Doniphon is, then, a "father" once again. In the broadest of terms, Tom is the father (origin) of Ransom's sexual identity as well. Symbols here are multiple expressions of sex and politics. Hence, Hallie is not only a sex object (in whom the mother is always involved), she is also the West itself (the "virgin land"). Liberty Valance is not only the shadowy id, unregulated instinct of death and destruction, he is also the radical (neurotic/psychotic) ideal of absolute individual liberty associated with the frontier of the American West. Tom Doniphon is the crucial symbolic expression for self and for nation.

He represents the potential for a conservative identity. As a father figure, authority with mastery of weapons and command of resources, Tom represents the best of what has been achieved in the building of home, in the adaptation of instincts to environment, and affection well expressed through work and love. His relationships with others in the story suggest he is the happy solution which escapes Ransom Stoddard.

As the "other" self, Tom Doniphon is the wasted possibility for a more healthy order of life, while Ransom Stoddard is the realized possibility of a neurotic, spiritually impotent way life has taken in the world of today. Tom Doniphon sacrificed himself twice to save Ransom Stoddard. He had tried to force Valance to a showdown over Ransom in the restaurant, but Ransom aborted that. He had tried to teach Ransom how to use a gun, but Ransom proved inept. At that point, when Tom shot the paint can to spill on Ransom, Tom "adopted" the man. The promise of civilization as sublimated instinct, of community as homoerotic, seduces the strength of Doniphon from his commitment to more primitive, aggressive forms of society. He becomes the ironic hero *par excellence,* as he emerges from darkness, takes on full glare of recognition, and then gradually moves back into increasing darkness until he disappears altogether in death.

As a confession, then, Ransom's narration exposes the guilt he has repressed in taking credit for Tom's successes. The community, represented by his audience, refuses to accept the consequences of Ransom's self analysis. It could not be what it is if it denies its origins in the myth of Ransom Stoddard's victory over Liberty Valance. Modern community ensues from the unattractive, though victorious one represented by neurotic Stoddard, "heartless" Hallie (she has left her heart behind in the coffin, in the West), feckless Appleyard, invisible Pompey, and, most of all, the annihilated Doniphon. The result is a spiritless machine that runs on the ghosts of those sacrificed in the past.

THE MAN WHO SHOT LIBERTY VALANCE is not, however, merely a record of psychoanalysis. Nor is it a political manifesto or sociological report. As art it draws upon all resources of human culture. The film teases analysis, partly because it seems to say more than it really does say; its subtexts make it feel more profound than its surface text says. This develops from the peculiar status of John Wayne in it. He is the heart and soul of the film, but he is not, one might say, the body of it.

This absence/presence of Wayne-as-Doniphon contributes to the structural and thematic tensions of the film, because audiences expect him to be more aggressive and physically victorious than he is here. To see him as nothing, contained by a crude wooden coffin, is deeply affecting. In Stoddard's story, told by an actor well known for his ability to communicate neurotic experience, the behavior of Wayne-as-Doniphon is strangely quiet. This suggests that Stoddard is, in his telling, distorting the reality of Doniphon, diminishing the force of the hero, and doing to the image of Doniphon what Stoddard knows has been done to himself, i.e., making it impotent.

Doniphon is invoked by Stoddard as a summons to the repressed, but he is summoned so he can be put back down again. If Stoddard represents the view and voice of triumphant modernism, then it is the film's way of passing judgment on that modernism. The price of the modern, with all its machinery and order of law, is the vigor and independence of Tom Doniphon. The image of Doniphon-Ransom-Valance as distinct functions of a single mind becomes larger in a wider context of referents, including the intertextual one of the movie stars themselves. In this context the image of Doniphon-as-Wayne conveys the popular nostalgia for something in American history that could have been better than it has become. Doniphon-as-Wayne is a lost hope for a better America.

This context expands further to become mythic, where the tale is a fable of cosmic agents in universal history. *The Man Who Shot Liberty Valance* draws from the winter season of this universal history, when the community is visited by a divine outsider, as in romance, saved from a demon of dark menace, but has its heart taken away in return for safety and material prosperity. Ransom is this alien redeemer, champion of life, who has won the fair maiden as his reward for his courage in battle with the old dragon. The tale as seen from Ransom's point of view is a structure of classical romance, but its victorious conclusion and enclosing frame of personal success for the hero are darkened by a mood of futility.

The divine agency of reason, in Ransom, appears to bring the deliverance of reason to a community which has been at the mercy of diabolical powers of darkness. He finds a maiden bound in the darkness of ignorance (as Perseus found Andromeda bound to a rock in the ocean), he frees her and wins her. This should be a happy fairy tale. It is not, because the myth is a false one (a "legend"). Outsider has taken credit due insider; the alien divinity has usurped the identity of local heroes. Here is the sadness of a myth when seen from the point of view of the defeated gods, as in Richard Wagner's *Ring* cycle of operas (particularly in the last, *Gotterdammerung*). The redeemer (Ransom) is a false god, and the true one (Doniphon) cannot be resurrected. The price of rational achievement is the loss of wisdom.

THE CYNICISM OF THE MODERN EDITOR Maxwell Scott has a special resonance when set against the cynicism of E.K. Hornbeck (Gene Kelly) in *Inherit the Wind*, released two years before *The Man Who Shot Liberty Valance*. Hornbeck is, it turns out, a villain in the story of the infamous "Monkey Trial" of 1925. He is introduced in a close-up shot eating an apple. Though he assures Rachel Brown (Donna Anderson) he is not Satan, he is clearly just that in this film which exploits the ironies of the historical scene by using them to retell the fable of the fall of man.

The Man Who Shot Liberty Valance accepts the necessity for myth (call it "legend"), though it deplores the sacrifices required for it. *Inherit the Wind* sacrifices honesty and integrity to resist this necessity, casting out the devil of cynicism (a characterization of H.L. Mencken, who reported the Scopes trial) and championing the sentimental atheist who secretly believes in God (a characterization of Clarence Darrow, played by Spencer Tracy as Henry Drummond). *Inherit the Wind* deals with several subjects taken up by *The Man Who Shot Liberty Valance*, including the ones of journalism, politics, education, and rights of women. In the name of "truth," *Inherit the Wind* attacks a bigotry and superstition that separates children from parents, women from men, and reason from heart in every person. The film claims the troubles which divide the national house are troubles of religious myth; however, its answer lies not in the cynical reason of E.K. Hornbeck.

The "answer" of *Inherit the Wind* is in the character of Henry Drummond, hired to defend the schoolteacher Bertram Cates (i.e., Scopes, played by Dick York) from prosecution for teaching Darwin's theories of evolution. This splitting of the institutions of law and education is balanced by a splitting of education and politics in the character of Matthew Brady (i.e., William Jennings Bryan, played by Fredric March). However forceful the resulting drama may be, where institutional interests collide, the effect is to mitigate the ambiguity and complexity which inheres when *The Man Who Shot Liberty Valance* identifies all of these in a single character.

Stoddard is a painfully ambiguous product of institutional and ideological interests combined to be a single identity. His divisions are denied in character as repressions of ambivalent fears and desires. Against his chaiacter of compromise and popular success is set the character repressed and denied, Tom Doniphon. There is more richness of character in either and both of these than in any of the characters of *Inherit the Wind*. The greatest irony of Kramer's film is that the schoolteacher who represents what Drummond calls "the right to think" is driven to a point where he does not know what to think, to a point of such disillusionment he becomes what Hornbeck calls a "little hero." This is comparable with what happens to Tom Doniphon as an ironic hero, but *Inherit the Wind* makes Cates more "little" than "hero."

For Stoddard to become a popular hero, a real hero has to be sacrificed. For Henry Drummond to become the hero of *Inherit the Wind*, a popular hero has to be humiliated. Here is the "liberal" intent of Kramer's film, to expose the errors and weaknesses of the "conservative" position represented by Matthew Brady. Drummond represents the position of the victorious illusion some might call rational liberalism or intellectual humanism — an illusion because he does not acknowledge the real sources of his strength in the repressed, or defeated, blind instincts. Stoddard represents a version of the same position, though he *does* confront the origin of his victory, to make that the real focus of narrative. Tom Doniphon is more than blind instinct, warm heart, and anti-intellectual passion (Matthew Brady). Tom is the complication, the pain and guilt, the price of progress championed by rational liberalism, though that does not make him simply a defeated conservatism or exposed irrationality (like Matthew Brady). In *The Man Who Shot Liberty Valance*, the melodramatic simplicities of *Inherit the Wind* are made complex and poignantly dramatic.

Cole Thornton: *El Dorado* (1967)

There is much ritual cleansing in *El Dorado*, reflecting and refracting a key episode of *Rio Bravo*. Because Dude took a bath, withdrew from the circle of defense, the circle was weakened and vulnerable: in that moment of weakness, John T. Chance was tricked, humbled, and overcome by the enemy. In *El Dorado,* Cole Thornton will also be overcome by the enemy and he will also be humbled, but he will not be tricked and he will not be the victim of another man's moral weakness (or, "uncleanness").

Cole Thornton tries to keep himself clean throughout, as in the opening of the film. It is particularly appropriate, then, that Cole should be joined by "Mississippi" (James Caan). Thornton is constantly presented in conjunctions with water. The plot turns on the conventional struggle by villain Bart Jason (Edward Asner) to seize control of water rights from a hardy, honest family of good people (the MacDonalds—R.G. Armstrong plays Kevin MacDonald, head of the clan). Cole becomes a "guardian" of the water in the film.

Dude's bath took place behind a closed door in an upstairs room of a hotel; there the vulnerability of a person, represented by nudity and ritual, is exploited by evil. At the opening of *El Dorado,* the possibility of its repetition is represented by Cole's encounter with Harrah in the washroom. It is not "fair" to be accosted while doing what everyone needs to be civilized—such as bathing. Because Cole Thornton and J.P. Harrah recognize one another as civilized, subject to reason by ritual, the scene does not conclude in disaster, as in *Rio Bravo.* (Hitchcock made the most famous modern use of the conventions here in the shower scene of *Psycho,* and Arthur Penn plays with the same conventions in the bathtub scene between Marlon Brando and Jack Nicholson in *The Missouri Breaks;* Hawks varies the idea in the barbershop scene of *Rio Lobo,* a later "remake" of *Rio Bravo/El Dorado.*)

THE IDEA OF THE EXPERT PROFESSIONAL, frequent in films directed by Howard Hawks, is important in *El Dorado,* as it is in *Rio Bravo.* In both films, however, it is set in contexts of ironic limitations on it. *Rio Bravo* is a story of rehabilitation for a professional, *El Dorado* of professional deteriorations: the skills, both expert and not-so-expert, of professionals are sources of chaos and devastatingly empty of meaning, either personal or social.

One looks in vain to find competent professionals in *El Dorado.* When Cole Thornton rides to Bart Jason's ranch, he looks in disgust at Jason's men. They are not even tough enough to "stomp a stringy jack rabbit." Their skills are little more than accidents of nature. Perhaps Nelse McLeod (Christopher George) is the real professional with potency in the story? His men also prove to be of little skill. When Mississippi confronts Charlie Higgin, McLeod scoffs at Charlie for needing four men to kill one: "it shouldn't 'a taken four of you." When Charlie's pals gang up on Mississippi, Cole intervenes as McLeod observes, disgusted, that it "always seems to take more than one, don't it?" Cole responds, "That's because they're no good."

McLeod ought to be the worthy adversary of Thornton and Harrah.

As Cole Thornton in *El Dorado*, 1967.

The plot forces a confrontation between "top guns." But when that comes, the climax is undercut by an obvious impotence in both Thornton and Harrah. Thornton is suffering from paralysis, and Harrah is hobbled by a wound. But they manage to fulfill their appointments with destiny. When Cole asks McLeod to extend him "professional courtesy," to let him have time to get down out of the wagon, McLeod agrees. Thornton counts on McLeod's "courtesy" to disarm him, take him off guard, so Thornton can kill him. Dying, McLeod objects, "You didn't give me any chance at all, did you?" Cole replies, "No. I didn't. You're too good to give a chance to." McLeod grimaces in shame, "Yeah. I let a one-armed man take me."

A parody of the classic shootout, this scene mocks the professional, whose weakness is his pride and code of honor. The real winners are the cheats, the double-dealers, the counter-agents, like Thornton himself. McLeod's professionalism is a vulnerability. His ethos of loyalty to his employer proves to be weaker than Thornton's ethos of guilt. McLeod is a means to another man's end; Thornton uses any means to serve his own end. His end is a private, personal one of paying a debt to the MacDonalds. His debt of guilt justifies dishonorable means and betrayal of "class."

Thornton is a seriously flawed hero, as he is a disreputable professional. When he "kills" the boy Luke MacDonald, Thornton shows himself an expert man of violence. Justice strikes back when Joey MacDonald bushwhacks Cole at the very place he shot Luke. This attack is typical of *El Dorado:* exploit the professional's sense of security, use nature against the artifice of ethic, and subordinate means to immediate ends. Joey is good, though not quite good enough. Cole must be shot, because he abused his professional ethic when he shot the boy. He is a guilty man, driven by pride to atone; he time and again violates conventional codes to do so. Cole smears his blood on Joey's shoulder, passing on his identity as an avenger in guilt. She has to pay her debt to him, complicating the network of guilt and dishonor. At the end Joey kills Bart Jason to save Cole and thus balance the ledger, while Thornton rescues Joey's brother.

Driven by ethical relativism and spiritual pragmatism, *El Dorado* climaxes with the shooting of Cole Thornton by Mississippi. It is, as everything finally is, simply an accident. Mississippi's sawed-off shotgun symbolizes the scattergun pattern of meaning in the film as a whole. Cole takes yet another crippling wound in the moral and physical deterioration of *El Dorado.* It is appropriate he suffer unintended violence.

JOEY MACDONALD MIRRORS Mississippi, as a perversion of conventional sexual roles. In *El Dorado,* men generally are pusillanimous. Where they are not, as with Thornton and McLeod, they are ironically vulnerable to weaker forces of nature. McLeod, killed by a one-armed cripple, is weak from his own code of honor. Thornton is powerless through patronizing innocence about women. He should be wounded by a woman, even if she is mistaken for a man. Relationships in *El Dorado* derive from ancient archetypal ones in which heroes are undone by women: Adam by Eve, Samson by Delilah, Aeneas by Dido, Don Quixote by Dulcinea, and Tom Sawyer by Becky Thatcher.

In *El Dorado* the eiron is the norm, not an abnormality. Thornton is such, but he is an old man to Joey's youth. Thornton and Harrah represent the generation to be displaced by Joey and Mississippi. Thornton can find his complement, only within his own age group, where he is yoked with J.P. Harrah (symbolically Thornton's double) and conventional saloon woman,

With Robert Mitchum (as J.P. Harrah).

Maudie (Charlene Holt). Both Harrah and Thornton are "drawn" to Maudie, who tells them, "I'm girl enough for both of you."

Harrah needs a companion of his own, as all the main characters pair off to end the story. Harrah urges Bull to stay with him. "Bull, I need you," he implores. They return to their old ways as Thornton and Mississippi choose new ways and new identities. El Dorado is a place where men must be men, women should be women, and each sex ought to go its separate way. Ironically, this does not mean the sexes are conventionally defined in El Dorado. They are equal in value and equal in functions—hence, Maudie can have two lovers at once if she pleases, Joey can ride, shoot, and dress like a man if she wants, and men can bathe in full view of women without embarrassing the women. El Dorado is a place of sexual equality, at the price of sexual distinction. To change roles to a conventional relationship is to take people outside the town, outside of El Dorado.

This threat to sexual difference is (comically) suggested by the character of Mississippi, whose "real" name is Alan Bourdillon Traherne. He is a man without a gun, cannot even handle a shotgun; he wears a silly hat; he needs to be with someone stronger and more skilled than he. Such a man is "abnormal": he is a man in search of a woman. He is liable to confuse the sexes (as when he fights with Joey). He fires his shotgun and hits a street sign which reads "DRESSMAKING."

The point of Mississippi is that he is like a woman, so he will be an appropriate match for Joey MacDonald, who is like a man. Their union will either restore conventional roles, or it will heighten the abnormal ones they have already indulged. The direction of the story of the film suggests they will, by their courtship, exchange roles and "find" normal identities, as a parallel with the pairing of Thornton and Maudie. Within the world represented by El Dorado, however, Thornton's sexual identity is threatened by his companionship with Mississippi. In their "man's world," they confuse sexual roles when they are together.

IN THIS WORLD of ethical relativism, nothing holds together. Thornton can be tamed from his soulless energy of violence, released from his contract of guilt, and restored to some norm of social order, but he will have to be taken from Harrah and Mississippi for that to happen. El Dorado is an idea of social and ethical chaos, in which normality is abnormality. In contrast with Rio Bravo, where everyone stays where he or she is supposed to be, where roles and stations are fixed and well understood, here in El Dorado, lines are easily crossed, barriers fall and identities are fluid. It is a place of perversity and ironic individuality.

The name of the town, the title of the movie, is taken from a poem by Edgar Allan Poe, quoted twice by Mississippi and once by Thornton. In the conclusion to Poe's poem, the Shadow tells the Seeker to look for Eldorado somewhere else than in life or on earth. The film says the heroes are no longer really looking for Eldorado anymore. The second stanza of Poe's poem is ignored (unquoted) in the film:

> But he grew old—
> This knight so bold—
> And o'er his heart a shadow
> Fell as he found
> No spot of ground
> That looked like Eldorado.

Thornton is obviously this knight who has grown old looking for El Dorado.

Ironically he has been searching for something that mocks him with its in-substantiality, until he finds it perverting and distorting his entire life. The "shadow" that falls across his path is perhaps Mississippi, threatening to mislead Thornton further astray by his sexual confusion (when romantic heroes devote themselves to dreams of masculine power and individualism). Or perhaps the "shadow" is Maudie, who falls across Thornton's heart to rescue him from the spiritual emptiness of El Dorado.

EL DORADO IS A DREAMLAND of failed idealism, ethical relativism, and ironic antiheroism. Thornton is well adapted to his place, because he is a man without strong commitments, almost without moral principles. What is right for Cole is survival first of all. He cannot be a "hero" unless he can keep some distance from the claims of others. As a hero, Cole rejects both Bart Jason and Nelse McLeod. He is also an antihero because he cannot openly and frankly ally himself with the beleaguered J.P. Harrah or the Mac-Donald family. Until, that is, he shoots the MacDonald youth "in the gut."

In *Will Penny* (1968), a friend of Will Penny (Charlton Heston) shoots himself in the gut fighting the evil family of Preacher Quint (Donald Pleasence). This friend is one "Dutchy" (Anthony Zerbe). Here also is bare-faced irony, in the accident and in the attitude all take toward the wound. The emphasis on the prolonged suffering, on the casual hopelessness, and the insensitive "reality" of men resigned to death gives the experience a "naturalistic" interpretation. The ultimate irony of the episode is that *because* Will Penny was so resigned, so hardened, and so hopeless, his friend actually does survive.

The naturalistic treatment of a gut wound in *Will Penny* contrasts with the stylized treatment in *El Dorado,* as Will Penny himself contrasts with Cole Thornton. Charlton Heston is playing a man too old to be much good as cowboy any longer, and in the end he is no good as husband or father either. Cole Thornton is an old man who proves he can still survive, even if he must break his own rules to do so. The antihero Will Penny turns into a hero of domestic romance, while the heroic Cole Thornton turns into an antihero of domestic irony. When Cole finds the boy Luke shot in the gut, he does not save him, but he does not surrender responsibility like Will Penny. Neither does Cole escape the consequences, for he continues to pay a debt of conscience and pain. On the other hand, Will Penny not only aban-dons hope but is rewarded, by the plot, for that hopelessness. Wayne's film may be ironic and even cynical at its center, but *Will Penny* is dishonest and cynical toward its audience. The suicide of Luke MacDonald is an ironic consequence of ignorance and thoughtless instinct; the survival of Dutchy is an ironic result of ignorance and moral resignation. *Ed Dorado* deplores what Will Penny celebrates, and that is the difference between ironic ethos of moral responsibility and one of moral irresponsibility.

THE DIFFERENCE BETWEEN *Will Penny* and *El Dorado* is fundamentally a difference of sentiment. *Will Penny* offers to be a story of "realistic" truth about the troubles of an aging cowboy who falls in love too late to support a family; however, it proves to be a sentimental melodrama that has Will Penny singing Christmas songs with a woman who makes him bathe more than nine times a year. Just as they are about to kiss (after many weeks together), in bursts the insanely evil Quint family to ruin the holidays for everyone but themselves. In such a story, irony is merely a tease, used to serve self-righteous melodrama. *El Dorado* works on exactly the opposite frequency. It puts self righteousness to ironic tests it fails; self-righteousness is found as much in the hero himself as in the cowardly villain whose greatest strength is that he is innocuous.

El Dorado remade *Rio Bravo* by turning its antihero inside out, and putting him outside as well. It also remade the romance Western in the image of its era, of *Major Dundee* (1964), *For a Few Dollars More* (1966), *The Wild Bunch* (1969), and *Butch Cassidy and the Sundance Kid* (1969). In none is the Western more sentimentalized than in *Butch Cassidy and the Sundance Kid*. It is difficult to imagine any hero less like John Wayne than either Paul Newman as Butch Cassidy or Robert Redford as the Sundance Kid. What else, one might ask, could John Wayne do in such company (successful company, it should be added) than to be ironic? As in *Will Penny*, the ironies of *Butch Cassidy and the Sundance Kid* are vehicles for sentimentality, even when the two heroes are supposed to be antiheroes.

El Dorado is conscious of itself as a Western, as a "remake" of *Rio Bravo*, but it has none of the self celebration or cinematic narcissism of *Butch Cassidy*. There is no serious probing of heroism in this popular film, with its beautiful people vindicating the use of violence for the sake of irresponsible lives. When Butch and Sundance violate codes and principles, they enjoy the violation for its own sake. They look for the dreamland of Eldorado which Poe's poem and Cole Thornton's career deny as anything but a delusion. When the Kid complains about Bolivia, Butch promises something better than the dirty, squalid village they find; they try to turn the reality of that squalid condition into a fantasy of private happiness for themselves, at the cost of everyone else's happiness. To the end, Butch and the Kid refuse to give up their dream of an "Eldorado." They call it "Australia" and charge into a barrage of gunfire as the film saves them in a nostalgic freeze-frame of their glory.

This refusal by the film to accept the consequences of its own conventions or even its own ironic point of view is, finally, a contribution to sentimentality and dishonesty. Against this Wayne as Cole Thornton and Hawks as director of *El Dorado* set themselves and their art. Such a difference implies a greater respect not only for the "rules" and conventions of film as art, but also for audience intelligence. At the time, *Butch Cassidy and the Sundance Kid* may have seemed closer to the "truth" of American experience. It caught, in a mimetic way, the air of youth rebellion and social protest more joyously than Wayne or *El Dorado* could possibly claim. However, Wayne's film retains interest in serious ways the more glamorous film cannot, because Wayne's film has a concern that always makes art vital even when it treats life and the "rules" of life in an ironic manner.

A more serious film than *Butch Cassidy* was *Bonnie and Clyde*, which appeared in the same year as *El Dorado*. The frivolity of *Butch Cassidy* was a subject of enquiry in *Bonnie and Clyde*, but it was so violent a treatment of frivolity that the later *Butch Cassidy* seems a deliberate attempt to rescue it. Both are social-protest films, though neither is an earnest criticism of the capitalism which underlies the social organizations satirized and mocked in both. Each is a Black Mass inversion, rather than subversion, of capitalistic endeavor. In this respect, *Bonnie and Clyde* at least dramatizes how the dream of economic success can become a nightmare of violence and distrust. *Butch Cassidy* merely disguises the common interests of outlaws and lawful forces by focusing on the lives of the beautiful people.

El Dorado may be a sometimes humorous treatment of capitalistic motives, such as the individual's struggle to survive, trust in self alone, and defiance of community to maintain integrity. In these terms, not only does Cole Thornton represent the best of this ethos, but so do J.P. Harrah, Mississippi, and even Maudie and Nelse McLeod. *El Dorado* exposes the weaknesses of capitalism as a cause of tragedy; however, because the strengths of capitalism are fundamental to the strengths of the individualistic ethos, weaknesses are understated in the mode of irony rather than disguised in the tones of sarcasm and sentiment.

Lon McQ: *McQ* (1974)

McQ inverts the romantic form of *Brannigan*. However creaky, *Brannigan* confirms the successful quest of a romance hero, and it puts its hero in the service of a social order. *McQ* parodies the quest, allowing the hero to unravel the mysteries of his professional life while unraveling his personal life in the process. In both films, the hunter becomes the hunted, and in both the hero is able to complete a circle that makes a trap of detection. Brannigan's circle, however, is one of wit and violence; McQ's has little wit, much violence, and more fatality. Brannigan's is a trap for the forces of evil, moral idiots caught in his larger circle of understanding. McQ's is a diminishing one, throwing out suspects and victims as it grows smaller, until McQ is left virtually alone, trapped himself in a circle of which he is both center and circumference. Brannigan triumphs over machine and technology, while McQ is reduced by both.

THE NARRATIVE WHICH CARRIES the theme of McQ's disillusionment is a complication of ironies unfolding themselves to audience and McQ simultaneously. It is a densely misleading story of the kind many popular mystery and detective stories often are—false clues, false suspects, even false crimes. In McQ, however, the deceptions of plot are worked upon the hero as well as upon the audience; for the hero *in* the story, deceptions are in the nature of things, of his reality. This narrative has nonetheless an economical, clearly focused architectural structure to it even as its details confuse and betray. This structure is a simple, elegant movement of changes in the identity of McQ himself. These changes are marked by his transitions from policeman, to private detective, to private citizen. The more discoveries Lon McQ makes about the nature of reality, the more private and individual he becomes.

The first third of the story gathers around Lon McQ as police detective. His partner Stan Boyle is one of three policemen shot during a night of murder. Lon searches compulsively for the killer. He "knows" Manny Santiago, the biggest drug dealer in Seattle, is behind it. He follow Santiago everywhere, turning into a murderous machine. He tortures his suspect, badgering him with false information, and behaving in an unprofessional way. He may be more direct than his Captain (Eddie Albert), but Lon is no more effective than Kosterman in getting at the truth. He smashes Santiago's face into a mirror, and then throws him into a urinal.

We are shown, then, a man shedding a role and some identity as he moves from efficient policeman to clumsy avenger. His passions are under control when he shoots a gunman on the dock, where he exercises proper judgment throughout. His essential tenderness is exposed by his regard for the pain of his friend's wife in the hospital, though she is manipulating him without his understanding. His passion is aroused, but it is merely irritated by the interference of the "official" suspects at police headquarters. Indeed it is also aroused, more seriously, by Kosterman's warning to lay off the case. He is driven by emotion to follow his professionally trained instinct toward the drug dealer Santiago.

News of Stan's death triggers an explosion of passion that leads directly to Lon's resignation from the police force. He cannot contain his emotional pains of loss, of love, within his role as impersonal law. However, even as he resigns on impulse, he perceives an intolerable irony at work around him: he believes the police itself (the law, the community, all social authority) is protecting the master criminal (the lawless, the business community, the rugged individualists, the "real" anarchists). He cannot any longer identify with such an organization of authority. The irony of this is that Lon is wrong (in specific identifications), but he is also right (in general suspicion). Until he *knows* where he is wrong and why he is right, he will be more a victim than avenging angel.

IN THE NEXT PHASE of Lon McQ's transformation he is in a twilight zone of identity: he is a private citizen, but he is also a detective. This zone is along a border that separates the private from the public, personal emotion from legal authority. He wants the advantages of both roles, both identities, but he will have to deal with the disadvantages as well. Pinky Farrow (David Huddleston) tries to alert Lon by telling him that "a lot of bad cases are carrying your bruises" out on the streets. Lon's response is, "That's a part of the bundle." He discovers in his new role that his work, as a private detective, exposes something frightening in his nature, that he is a little bit "crazy."

Lois invites Lon to "do something crazy" with her. He will, but not with her, not right away. He gets money from Walter, information from Rosey, then from Myra, and finally he understands the connection between the police murders and the drug deals. He understands that drugs are being stolen from the police department itself, and he understands they are stolen while the drugs are transported from police headquarters to unspecified locations for burning. Lon spies and follows the law, the "state" itself. It is one of many strands of irony in the film that everyone spies on everyone else: Lon spies on Santiago and here on the State Bureau of Narcotics, while J.C. is spying on Lon, and someone unknown is spying on everyone else.

Lon follows the state truck to a hospital (another irony), where he tries to follow the officers into the basement furnace room. A security guard, however, stops him. By the time Lon outwits the guard, the drugs have already been stolen. He suspects the white uniformed attendants who push out carts of laundry. Then begins his wild pursuit after the laundry truck through busy streets and highways of the city. When he dashes to his car in a hurry, he is frantic to catch the truck; he backs his car dangerously out of the parking lot, almost colliding with a car carefully trying to exit. The woman driving the car stops, gets out, and shouts after him, as he roars off, "Are you crazy?"

Lon follows and stops the wrong laundry truck. Its driver gets out, frightened but angry. Lon asks him why he drove through three stop signs to try to escape, and the driver quite rationally explains, "The way you were chasin' me, I though you were some kind of a nut." This makes the point of the theme brutally clear, and it dramatizes the way Lon has, as a private detective, become a public nuisance. He is misreading signs and endangering public order. Though crazy as a public man, as a private individual Lon is beginning to understand himself and his predicament. He responds to the frightened laundry-truck driver, "Well, maybe I am!"

Opposite top: **Wayne as McQ "interrogating" Al Lettieri as Santiago.** *Bottom*: **Wayne as McQ, "avenging angel," with Diana Muldaur as Lois.**

KOSTERMAN THROWS MCQ OUT of the police offices, takes his gun permit from him, and yells him, "You're out!" This is an emphatic ejection, putting Lon further away from the institutional authorities for whom he has given his professional life. This distancing of the hero from his society, from all that has given him his identity and sense of purpose, continues through the last third of the plot. There is a twist, however, which says, in effect, the further Lon is distanced from the law, the further he finds himself in the "right." This continues with deepening irony and darkening sarcasm until it can go no further without tainting McQ with the evil he combats. When he begins to seem the same as Santiago, then things have gone too far and a reversal must occur. Otherwise, war is peace and evil is good. That is a conclusion no Wayne hero can accept, however ironic he becomes.

Everyone associated with the police is now suspect, including McQ's dead partner Boyle. Rosey bursts out at McQ, "If anybody was dirty, you ought to know." Lon assumes that Rosey means Boyle, and he threatens to kill Rosey if he repeats the accusation. This continues the identification of Lon McQ as a criminal, but at the same time it reminds that McQ is fiercely loyal to friends. When he talks to Myra just before she is murdered, McQ teases her, saying "I'm a tired man." He is being drawn thin, and his emotions are being pressed toward an explosion that may finish him. Myra affectionately calls him "a liar," but again the dialogue contains more than it seems. The ironic hero may use deceit to operate in a deceitful world, but in the world of *McQ*, the only source of truth finally lies in the alienated, tired, and emptied McQ himself.

His distancing is not complete until he is separated from his car. Several thematic motifs are brought together when massive trucks pound away at McQ in his "Green Hornet." They trap him in his machine to create an archetypal predicament of the ironic hero caught in the bind of his absurd existence. Separated from his car, McQ has completed the process of alienation from his past, without accepting the anarchy of criminal outsiders. When he refuses a wheelchair after the car-crushing episode, McQ is also refusing to be "crippled" as an outsider. He has to purge himself now of suspicion as a drug thief. He crashes a police car into a fiery explosion, to effect another "separation" of his identity, another phase of his purgation.

Clean of all taint, clear in his own understanding, he finds Lois, and reveals his knowledge of the entire plot. He admits that "Stan was dirty," and that he feels "kind of silly acting like an avenging angel all that time." Lois accepts that information, but she defends Stan as having engaged in "the new national sport, called 'grabbing.'" But McQ does not "grab." He is still an "avenging angel," though now his own integrity is to be avenged and recovered. He forces Lois to admit her part in the crimes, that she and an "insider" have stolen the dope, murdered Stan, and used McQ himself.

At first she tells him, in a familiar refrain, "You are crazy!" But it is the world, *her* world, that is crazy—not McQ. In his new-found sense of certainty, McQ moves with dispatch and force.

He exits the main highway to locate a favorable site for the final confrontations. He chooses a borderline, the beach, for his showdown. He kills Lois's partner, Frank Toms, whom Lon calls "servant of the people." Then he drives Lois's car in flight from Santiago's gang. The high shots of this episode establish a visual metaphor of the hero's border-existence, exploding in a violent gun-battle he wins with his superior (illegal) automatic weapon. When Santiago calls to Lon to "stop the nonsense, shake hands on an agreement," he invites McQ to join the "establishment" of "grabbers." But Lon kills Santiago and his thugs, kicks open the suitcase of drugs, and leaves them to drift to destruction. He kicks away the venality of his society though he accepts its violence.

The concluding scene is troubling. Kosterman and J.C. join Lon after taking Lois into police custody. Outside the law, McQ has purged the law. They, on the other hand, inside the law, have compromised it. All have suffered failures of judgment, of understanding, and of vision. They need one another to repair the damage and to recover themselves. McQ especially needs to make a return to social order, or he will dwindle further into nihilism. He has gone as far as it is possible to go without disintegration.

Kosterman is the *deus ex machina* of the plot when he holds out the badge McQ threw away. J.C. apologizes to McQ and explains why he spied on him. Lon, in disgust, says, "Yeah! It's your job! Lousy, damned. . . ." He is on the point of damning the "job," but he pauses to substitute "junk" as he turns to look back toward the beach where he kicked open the suitcase. This gesture equates the "job" with the "junk." It is not, however, McQ's final judgment. He snatches the badge from Kosterman and then he says, "There's a bar over there. Let's get a drink." The job may be junk, the law is fallible, and men are frail, but that is in the nature of things. To recover his lost identity, Lon McQ must accept the badge. He does it on his own terms, terms which will purge the past with the drink that "purifies."

THE SUBJECTS OF MCQ had strong topical relevance. Corruption of social order by the poison of narcotics (as fact and as symbol) was the concern of *The Panic in Needle Park* (1971), *The French Connection* (1971 and 1975), and *The Godfather* (1972 and 1974). The special corruption of police power was acute in *The French Connection* and *Godfather* movies, and central to *Serpico* (1973), a referent for several later films, including *McQ*. Disillusionment with law enforcement and the attraction of the hard-boiled but decent private detective were popular themes, though they were modified with more cynicism than the romantic Bogart films of *The Maltese Falcon* (1941) and *The Big Sleep* (1946). Revisionary Raymond Chandler characters appeared in *The Long Goodbye* (1973) and a remake of *The Big Sleep* in 1978 with Robert Mitchum in the Bogart role. Social alienation of the private eye was taken to nihilistic and amoral extremes, which McQ refused to follow, in such films as *Chinatown* (1974) and *The Long Goodbye*. These themes were reduced to comic absurdities in the *Pink Panther* movies renewed from the original of 1964 in the same period as *McQ* (*The Return of the Pink Panther* in 1975, *The Pink Panther Strikes Again* in 1976).

McQ may be impulsive, but he is always forceful and usually efficient. When he makes mistakes, as when he follows the wrong laundry truck, he does so from the evidence of appearances. He is not a bungler, and he is not a fortunate fool like Clouseau. McQ is a man in transition; his role is a compromise between tradition and fad. Wayne has to protray the hard-boiled detective with a past connection and loyalty to the police, but also the private citizen-avenger disillusioned by the corruption of everyone around him, including especially the police. The challenge of this role is better appreciated by examining it in the line of descent from Humphrey Bogart's Philip Marlowe in *The Big Sleep* of 1946 to Robert Mitchum's remake in 1978.

Bogart set the standard for the *film noir* hero with his renditions of Sam Spade in *The Maltese Falcon* (1941) and Frank McCloud in *Key Largo* (1948), among many others, including his Marlowe in *The Big Sleep*. His hat set aslant his head, Bogart's Marlowe moved beneath a shadow of ambiguity as the brim shaded one of his eyes—even inside the many shadowy rooms of his story. Other special gestures include a tightly receding upper lip that reveals his teeth when he smiles and talks. This creates a sexually sinister effect which makes Bogart's Marlowe menacing and honest at once. His innocence comes through as well when he pulls his ear lobe, usually in moments of sexual unrest around Vivian. His vulnerability is suggested by his size ("You're not very tall, are you?" taunts Carmen on their first meeting), but also by his habit of putting his thumbs inside his trousers and belt. Bogart is a very active actor as Marlowe; he is nervous with energy and intense with detection. When he asks Vivian, "What's Eddie Mars got on you," he asks because he loves her.

When Mitchum asks the same question of Charlotte Regan (Sarah Miles), he asks because he wants to solve the case for his client General Sternwood. There is no sexual power in Mitchum's Marlowe. He tells Mrs. Regan, "Kissing is nice, but your father didn't hire me to sleep with you. I'm a detective! I work at it, lady, I don't play at it." This Marlowe loves his job, not the women involved in it. When Mitchum puts his hands in his pockets, he makes the gesture of a casual observer, uninvolved in the lives of those around him. When Bogart's Marlowe puts his hand in his pocket, he barely contains the energy of his personality, in a calculated distancing of himself from others. Mitchum brings strong credits to his own portrayal of the *film noir* hero (*Out of the Past*, 1947, for example), but in 1978 he has to emphasize one special characteristic Wayne has to emphasize as well: the ironic detachment from everything, including particularly women.

The ages of the actors are relevant, of course. But the differences in ages from Bogart's 46 in *The Big Sleep,* Mitchum's 61 in 1978, and Wayne's 67, are less important than the differences in style that determine meaning and point of view for their respective films. Bogart reeks of romance, and Mitchum insists on purity of purpose; Wayne is in the middle as McQ, using sexual appeal to solve his mysteries (somewhat like Clint Eastwood's police detectives). How each does this defines the significance of each. Their entrances and exits provide clues to their styles of representation. Bogart's Marlowe is literally foreshadowed in silhouette (with Vivian) beneath the opening title and credits, and the film opens onto him only after he has announced himself to the Sternwood butler from behind a slightly opened door. He never shows himself fully until he gives his name and is admitted, taking off his hat (a rare gesture) and thrusting one hand into a trouser pocket as he enters. He is an outline to be filled in, an opening for opportunity. He is easy and interested in what lies ahead of him.

Mitchum's Marlowe, on the other hand, takes command of audience perspective. He fills in everything, sometimes in advance, through a voice-over narration. He also is withheld in body for a few minutes during opening titles and credits. However, he enters the Sternwood mansion with full identity and disinterested professional observation. He hands the butler his card to establish that identity as a professional on duty. He goes inside to gaze at a portrait of the General. The gaze of Mitchum's Marlowe establishes a special, primary relationship with his client the General. When Camilla enters, she varies the line used to introduce Bogart as short by observing to Mitchum, "Tall, aren't you!"

Wayne's McQ has neither the shadowy ambiguity of Bogart's Marlowe nor the self-assured detachment of Mitchum's. McQ enters his film late into the action of the plot, after Boyle has committed two murders and been fatally shot himself. The point of view of *McQ* is limited neither to the third person of Bogart's *Big Sleep* nor to the first person of Mitchum's. McQ is more the victim than the controller of information in his story. McQ is awakened on his boat by the horn of his telephone. He gropes for the receiver, at last reaches it, emerges from the cabin finally to be seen, and then answers his call—but the telephone is not plugged in. The slapstick of this episode, which reduces his stature in sight as well as in idea, portends the struggles of the character throughout his story. He adjusts quickly, but he is constantly caught off guard. His entrance, then, is ambivalent rather than ambiguous, personal rather than professional.

When McQ exits his story, he invites Kosterman and J.C. to join him for a drink at a nearby bar. The shot cuts to the bar itself. The angle of the camera is across the highway from the bar. Between the gaze of the camera-audience and the image of the bar pass several people enjoying their leisure on the beach, oblivious to the violence and betrayals which seek resolution in the bar. McQ disappears at the end of his story. He dissolves into compromised anonymity, behind the aimless crossing of people without significant purpose. This exit is in strong contrast with Bogart's Marlowe, who makes meaning for himself and Vivian as he rearranges truth to fit his purposes. Vivian tells him, "You've forgotten about me." He responds, "What's wrong with you?" and she assures him, as police sirens are heard in the background, "Nothing you can't fix." On this last word the film ends appropriately.

There *is* nothing Bogart's Marlowe can't fix. On the other hand, Mitchum's Marlowe in 1978 does not even try to fix things. In episodes closer to the plot of Raymond Chandler's novel, *The Big Sleep* of 1978 concludes with a lecture by Marlowe to Charlotte in her cavernous bedroom. He rejects her offer of money to be silent, and she is astonished. He explains that his "itch" for money is satisfied by his hard work as a detective. He stands with hands in pockets, she sits defeated on her canopied bed, and the distance grows between them until Marlowe turns to leave her alone, tiny, sinking into insignificance. As he walks out of the mansion, he thinks (through voice-over narration) of "the big sleep." All three detective heroes succeed in their service to clients. Mitchum's is the General, virtually death itself; Bogart's is Vivian, certainly the power of Eros and romantic love; but Wayne's McQ worked for himself alone — as he told Pinky, he would be his own client. Bogart makes the world over for his love, Mitchum turns his back on it for his work, and Wayne disappears into it to start over again.

13. Comic Heroes

Comic heroes affirm the joy of living, assert the importance of society, and celebrate the vitality of sex which binds men and women together in harmonious community. From Duke Hudkins in 1943 to George Washington McLintock in 1963, Wayne portrayed heroes who made love the purpose of their lives; they recognize that erotic love is the same as social love. They show increasing maturity and responsibility, without losing their comic joy and sense of humor.

Duke Hudkins and Rusty Thomas are rogues of the road. They pursue and are pursued by heroines until they accept social responsibility for "romantic" satisfaction. Duke Hudkins, in *A Lady Takes a Chance*, is least settled of the comic heroes; he seizes his heroine to take from the Eastern city to more liberty in the wide open West. Rusty Thomas, in *Without Reservations* (1946), leaves his life of wandering, turns from a Marine life of heroic adventure, to accept the happiness of civil domestication, represented by a woman with progressive ideas of social reform.

Sean Thornton, in *The Quiet Man* (1952), is among the restless ones: he leaves his home in America to search for something more satisfying in Ireland, where he was born. He is, therefore, eager to settle even as he cannot escape an unsettling past. He falls deeply in love with pastoral Mary Kate Danaher. She is his salvation, and their love renews an entire community.

Thornton is a self exile who finds childhood paradise because he learns how to love. Other Wayne heroes are already in paradise, but they have to discover paradise is incomplete without erotic love. *North to Alaska* (1960) shows Sam McCord turning his land of gold into a land of love, and *Donovan's Reef* (1963) shows "Guns" Donovan transmuting wealth of money into happy love and tender joy. Both heroes, like Sean Thornton, must struggle to adjust pleasures of masculine independence with responsibilities of loving a woman, and so their stories are also tales of power and politics. This is a larger theme of *McLintock!* (1963), which makes a fable of politics in America through the power of George Washington McLintock, whose reunion with his wife is a Fourth-of-July celebration of erotic love in America.

Duke Hudkins: *A Lady Takes a Chance* (1943)

A Lady Takes a Chance is a nostalgic look back to good times, before World War II brought wartime shortages to America. The story is set in 1938, "when there were more fellows around than girls." It was a time when "everybody was having a good time without knowing it." The film hopes for a "quick tomorrow" when those good things will be once again, "only better." *A Lady Takes a Chance* is a fantasy trip back in time to an era of plenty, and it is a fantasy trip way out West to a place of high spirits and bouncing energy.

Molly Truesdale *is* the East. She is America without direction, without the energy to enjoy its blessings in 1938. She needs to be awakened: to her good fortune, and to a sense of purpose. Molly rides a luxurious bus through town and country along America's highways, through a land of abundance and beauty. But she is not aware of much in it. She sees her reflection in the window of the bus more than she sees America through it. These scenes draw attention to Molly *as* the America whose images are superimposed by her own, and they picture her as self absorbed, alienated in her social plenty.

Duke Hudkins captures her entire being. He is her attendant spirit, her Peter Pan, her pied piper. She has been looking for him even as she has not known it. She is typically alone in a crowd watching rodeo events at Fairfield, in the Great American West, a highlight of the Rainbow Bus Tours. She takes pictures, moving closer and closer to the front of the arena until suddenly a man comes flying straight at her, knocking Molly on her back and breaking her camera. The man is Duke Hudkins, rodeo performer.

Molly Truesdale needs a man in the purest of comic impulses. She is America, she is the East, but she is most of all a lonely and bored young woman restlessly searching for sexual awakening. Duke Hudkins makes her understand what she is looking for, what she needs. And so he is her West, her destiny, the man who will satisfy her sexual instincts. A bucking horse throws him into her life, as nature drives the instinct of sex in violent and dramatic ways. They "fall" in love, though it will take most of the film's narrative to make them both understand fully what has happened to them.

DUKE HUDKINS IS SIMPLE and naïve. He thinks horses are more important than women, though he plays around with women a lot. He thinks he can do what he pleases, ride through life without real commitments, and never be "roped" himself. He is a classic comic character–type, especially in films popular in the American thirties, such as *It Happened One Night* (1934), *Twentieth Century* (1934), *Go West Young Man* (1936), *Nothing Sacred* (1937), and *Holiday* (1938). These are "screwball" comedies, which sometimes take a special, populist direction in the films of Frank Capra,

As Duke Hudkins *(center)* with Jean Arthur as Molly Truesdale in *A Lady Takes a Chance,* 1943.

such as *Mr. Deeds Goes to Town* (1936) and *Mr. Smith Goes to Washington* (1939), both of which starred Jean Arthur. Duke Hudkins is neither a Mr. Deeds (Gary Cooper) nor a Mr. Smith (James Stewart), though Duke does go to New York City just long enough to rescue his damsel in distress. Duke Hudkins has little energy to waste on things political, like Deeds and Smith. All Duke's energy is gathered for horses and women.

The film plays to a wartime audience starved for the good things of material comforts, but it also plays to a timeless audience that dreams of happiness for men and women who need one another through times good and bad. It is a simple want simply expressed, but its simplicity is its strength. The most basic want is most difficult for the films to show, namely, sexual desire. The screwball comedies found various angles to express sexuality when moral codes dictated narrow paths for films to deal with the forbidden subject. *A Lady Takes a Chance* is virtually a program of procedure for indirect ways to deal with sexuality in movies. Duke Hudkins is a phallic hero, so crude, naïve, and awkward that he is honestly expressing the most repressed, hypocritically denied instincts of human endeavor.

WAYNE IS PLAYING horse opera for all it is worth, and he does it well. He really seems to care more for the horse than for the woman. Jean Arthur's Molly is convincing in her perplexed responses to this strange behavior, but Wayne's Duke makes his behavior seem more natural than strange. He has told her he will not be roped, and he will not rope his horse. She has found a way to cripple both him and his horse, and he knows it; she is dangerous, though she does not realize what her danger is. Waco recognizes the danger of the "eternal feminine," warning Duke to stay away from this one — she is too serious for the easy life style he enjoys with Duke.

Molly threatens natural freedom and careless energy when she sickens the horse. There is no question of compromise for Duke. He simply puts her aside, out of mind, and gives his entire attention to the sick horse. His victory over feminine containment cannot last any more than she can destroy the commitment represented by the horse. Molly, as America and the East, has to understand what is at stake here, that there is more to America than cabs and fruit baskets, and that it is endangered by the very civilization America aspires to achieve. Waco has decided "East is East and West is West, and never the two shall meet." But the film asserts they *must* meet, somehow and sometime, or Molly and America will be buried in the boring banalities of the urban East.

Duke "divorces" Molly, as he gives his entire attention to the horse. Molly's fantasies about the dream-horse Gwendolyn have little force to resist when confronted by the reality of this emergency. Waco advises Molly to "go home." He says "love is the best thing there is, but you're barking up the wrong cowboy." She refuses to accept that advice: "any fella that can love a horse can love a girl." Losing Duke to the horse alerts Molly to what is best in the man, to what is generous and impulsive, committed to energies of nature itself. She realizes what she has been looking for. "I was right about him!" she asserts to Waco. "He's the most unusual man I ever met."

THROUGHOUT THE FILM, Wayne is supposed to be a lecherous Don Juan who pursues women, conquers their resistance, has his will, and abandons them carelessly. They are supposed to be grateful for whatever attention he gives them, making no trouble for him when he happily leaves them behind. His only real commitments have been to his horse and his sidekick Waco, who now warns Duke he is heading for something more serious in pursuit of Molly Truesdale. He reminds Duke of his frequent observation about women, that they are "like socks — you got to change 'em regular." Duke has not changed Molly yet, because he has not yet had his way with her completely.

One character John Wayne does not play convincingly is just this. He is not a heartless lecher, and little he does or says makes him seem like one in this or any other film. The story calls for one, and he gives it his best shot, as the innocent virgin rescues the careless sensualist. The climax is the most banal of clichés, as Molly finds her way to his heart through Duke's stomach. She prepares a grand meal for him, seduces him with the comforts of an efficient domesticity, and he falls for it. The banquet of Eros must proceed, however. It is the best scene for Wayne to show his slapstick talents, as he gulps, grimaces, and gripes about the dinner Molly has prepared: from the tomato cocktail to the sticky dessert. His surprise at the cocktail (he says "to-may-to" to her "to-mah-to") is simply a preliminary to his astonishment that she has served him dainty little lambchops instead of his accustomed big beefsteaks. It is a nice scene of comedy for putting rough Duke in his human place.

Duke does not overwhelm with the force of his mind, with the sharpness of his logic, and this scene is a powerful demonstration of that. Like Odysseus charmed by Circe, Duke is mindlessly led "by the nose" to sit at Molly's tidy little table; there he is a ridiculous sight, a big man surrounded by tiny furniture and tiny food. Molly has him drunk on her, and she takes him to the slaughter with her specialty, lamb chops. He tries to squirm out of the situation by suggesting, gauche as it is, they go somewhere for a steak. Molly drops her head to pout, Duke relents, and bashfully insists he never eats lamb chops because he doesn't like them. Molly asks why; he says, because he never eats them. She is more downcast, and he seeks to mollify her by taking a tiny little bite.

Now Molly has him where she wants him. She serves dessert, a fluffy, sticky, gooey mound called "Sunset in the Desert." Duke is doubtful, but he plunges in, and promptly has his teeth stuck together. He is grateful when Molly releases him (from her "charm"), and he submits helplessly to her manipulations for cleaning the dishes. She does to him what no woman before has ever managed to do—she "ropes" him, as she puts an apron around his paralyzed body. He moves toward the kitchen like a zombie, until he passes a mirror. He awakens from his daze, throws off his apron, curses himself for being "drunk," and hurries out of the cabin.

The supper is a comic feast of love, a banquet of sensuous delights that runs a classic course of near disaster, then great success, with final catastrophe. Man, natural energy, and the raw West are embodied in Duke Hudkins brought to the table of manners and civilization, formality and elegant East. But he sees himself made ridiculous, as the mirror reflects to him what the film shows to its audience. He will not be tamed so easily, and so he stalks out, jeopardizing civil order but saving natural energy. As he leaves, Duke exclaims, "I got my own way of living," and he adds, "I don't want to get hooked!"

SUCH A COMEDY requires, however, that the couple be united in the end. To bring this off without compromising the hard-won integrity of the barely escaped Duke is the challenge of the film's narrative. At the conclusion of the unhappy supper, Molly has won the battle but she has lost her man. She cannot believe she has failed, even as she reluctantly boards her tour bus to return to the East. She looks all around for Duke, believing he will show up at the last moment to save her after all. But he does not. She journeys back to where she began.

There she is met by her trio of unappealing Eastern lovers, less desirable than ever. She has been dreaming of some ideal, Edenic love, and now she awakes to find life more dreary. Her lovers lose themselves in argument, jostling, and clumsiness to get her attention. It is intolerable, but it is the way of life in the real world of the East. She leaves with the motley crew, captured like the Lady by Comus at last.

But comic heroes do not fade away to disappear so easily. Comic heroes are unbound by banal reality. They leave their fantasy existence to rescue ladies in distress of reality. Duke Hudkins bursts through the doors of the bus terminal, carrying Molly away from the terrible city and the more terrible lovers. He vanquishes all, and she is now his captive completely. He takes her to the bus about to return on yet another "tour" of the West, she yielding completely, though he promises (for the censors perhaps) he has a "job" for her, since he has now "divorced" Waco.

This is the "real" John Wayne as hero, bursting out of fantasy to make reality seem negligible. He is the *deus ex machina* of ancient Greek and Roman melodrama and timeless myth. The heroine finds him in the West of romantic enchantment, and he finds her in the East of cynical mayhem. The thematic strands may not be neatly tied together by the narrative, but they work to reassure Americans theirs is a land of happy rescues by romantic heroes and comic (cosmic) forces.

SUCH A VIEWING OF *A Lady Takes a Chance* is extravagant. The film is claustrophobic as a result of studio shooting, unconvincing special effects, and poor editing. Close-up scenes of Wayne and Arthur yield what virtue it has, a comic romance of intimacy and charm. Lying together on a stack of hay, exchanging dreams, or eating dinner by dim light, hero and heroine find sentimental happiness amidst aimless monotony. They are not zany enough to be screwballs. They are too "serious," the fate of Wayne as a comic hero in this and other films that try to make him a zany simpleton like Stan Laurel (whom Wayne can resemble when he chooses). Wayne is too big for such a confined film, though the character he plays is conceived appropriately enough. He is supposed to break through the forms of urban frustrations to release inhibited spirits, as he does to end the story. He is supposed to carry reality off into romance, and he is supposed to impress jaded spirits with nervous energy. He is a comic hero in search of a better, larger romantic form.

A Lady Takes a Chance looks back at an era of uninhibited romantic comedy, produced and enjoyed before the grim years of World War II. But there were in those years some bitter satire of the values which look attractive in the retrospect of *A Lady Takes a Chance*. One particularly strong satire was *Nothing Sacred* (1937), in which Fredric March plays a bigtime New York City newspaper reporter, Wallace Cook. He desperately tries to save his job by exploiting sentimental possibilities from mortally ill Carole Lombard as Hazel Flagg, dying of "radium poisoning." Reporter Cook goes from hypocritical New York to search for the dying Hazel in curt, suspicious Vermont; he finds her despite the hostility of her fellow townsfolk, and he falls in love with her even as he exploits her mortality.

The sex roles are reversed from *Nothing Sacred* to *A Lady Takes a Chance*, from male cynical urbanite to female bored urbanite, from simple village girl to simple rural cowboy, but in both the ancient comic pattern is fundamental. *Nothing Sacred* is an extraordinarily sophisticated satire of all human foibles, though it focuses on urban ennui and Eastern American hypocrisy. It nevertheless resolves differences in a romantic manner, while exposing the rotten center of social pleasures. Its solution is to escape responsibility as it permits Cook to disappear with Hazel Flagg into the tropical South Seas of marital bliss and primitive alienation. Hazel tells a lie in her last lines to protect her anonymity, and so the film ends on the same cynical note with which it begins, subverting the premise on which romantic escape is founded. *A Lady Takes a Chance* is more "heroic" in its resolution and more optimistic in its conclusion.

A Lady Takes a Chance rescues American ennui with American élan. The West liberates the spirit of the repressed East. John Wayne embodies the promise of those values, though he has to be educated by love. He inclines, as Duke Hudkins, to pervert them into selfish narcissism as he tries to seduce the vulnerable Molly Truesdale. The same "education" occurs in the romance of *Nothing Sacred*. Both films, however, propose that love cannot survive unperverted in societies represented by metropolitan America. Both contend that love must find a less restrictive, more honestly physical, environment in which to flourish. That environment is more emphatic in *A Lady Takes a Chance* than in *Nothing Sacred*, and John Wayne is a more positive expression of it than either Carole Lombard or Fredric March.

Duke Hudkins is intended to "correct" a character played by Gary Cooper in *The Cowboy and the Lady*, released in the very year of 1938 which *A Lady Takes a Chance* is recreating. Bashful Cooper is pursued by sophisticated Merle Oberon. The working title for *A Lady Takes a Chance* was *The Cowboy and the Girl*.

The Cowboy and the Lady (directed by H.C. Potter) has a Capra-esque quality in its aim to "convert" show-horse high society into work-horse cowboy populism. A spoiled rich girl ("lady") runs from self-centered politician father who is converted to rural simplicities by the honesty and plain good sense of humble-pie Stretch Willoughby (Cooper). Stretch is a rodeo cowboy whose main value is work (a "work horse" is preferred to a "show horse," and people are brought down from their "high horse"). He scorns money and high society for a life of personal commitments and hard work.

He even has a fond relationship with a housekeeper "mother," Ma Hawkins (Emma Dunn), anticipating Cooper's sentimental Sergeant York and *his* mother in 1941. Wayne's Duke Hudkins may have to be weaned and seduced away from his horse, but Cooper's Stretch Willoughby will never be taken far away from his Ma Hawkins. Indeed, Stretch builds his new house just a few steps down the path from Ma's own house on the ranch in Montana. Duke is far more emotionally independent than Stretch.

Duke would never preach to politicians the way Stretch does. *The Cowboy and the Lady* is a revision of *It Happened One Night,* proposing the frank populism of rural simplicities to solve the economic blight of super-sophisticated and abstract urban selfishness. *A Lady Takes a Chance* virtually ignores the importance of money to substitute play for work, as *The Cowboy and the Lady* substituted work for frivolity. Wayne's cowboy enjoys life more than Cooper's. Duke Hudkins is far less burdened by awareness of economic oppression than he is by suppression of spirit in a society of empty formalities.

Duke is narrow but deep in his love for Molly, blindly pursuing what he wants as if the rest of the world did not exist. His heroism is highly romantic in its individualism, but is equally comic in its disregard for the constraints of society. This is not the comedy of manners; instead, it is the comedy of character. Duke is a future of fun, better than Stretch's past of purity; he is the "quick tomorrow" the film hoped for in its beginning, when everybody can have "a good time without knowing it." A comic hero can never be completely independent of social complications, but Duke Hudkins is a modest proposal for happiness with a minimum of deference to social constraints. He is a youthful, happy clown in cowboy clothes, not the sad, jaded clown of Gary Cooper; he is a comic spirit of Eros, not the jaded, cynical comedian of Fredric March.

Rusty Thomas: *Without Reservations* (1946)

Without Reservations is, self-described, a "reactionary" film. It opposes its hero, Marine flyer Captain Rusty Thomas, to "progressive" novelist Christopher (Kit) Madden (Claudette Colbert). *Reactionary* is meant to be a generous and aggressive opposition to narrow, abstract and generally withering notions about life. At a central point of the film, the heroine is advised to enlarge her experience of life before she attempts a philosophy of reconciling "ideals" with "love." Her advisor is a man of passionate experience himself. Kit protests that "to live appears to be full of confusion, and very little else." Ortega (Frank Puglia) agrees: "Confusion, yes! But it is better to live and to make the confusion than to burrow and not to live." To passionate, but pragmatic Ortega, the reality of life is more important than ideals which attempt to make order and sense of it. Love is not, Ortega insists, a matter of gentility, consideration, and dignity, as Kit had thought it should be: love is, instead, "brutal, selfish, and turbulent." It is "the primitive urge of conquest."

This is love "without reservations." This is what reactionary Rusty Thomas teaches progressive Kit Madden. The ideal of the film is, then, presented as the reality, in a reversal of terms no less contradictory and confusing than the American romanticism of the conquering heroes, Rusty Thomas and Dink Watson (Don DeFore). They are supposed to embody the power of "brutal, selfish, and turbulent" love. Their primitive natures propel them toward "conquest" of all women who attract their easily aroused "glandular" attention. The plain truth is, however, there are no such heroes in this film. Heroic passion falls short of its goal, though modest gains are made for it when Kit finally succeeds in driving Rusty to desperate measures of jealousy.

Nothing in *Without Reservations* is quite as funny as the scene of Duke Hudkins' fighting agianst lambchops in *A Lady Takes a Chance*. However, Rusty Thomas had a stubborn, narrow-minded character much in common with Duke Hudkins, and Rusty is vulnerable to the same educational ridicule as Duke. Most of the time Rusty is upstaged for comic effects by the antics of his sidekick, Dink, a version of the classical tricky slave (*dolosus servus*) or scheming valet (*graciosos*). Wayne will be teamed with comic sidekicks in much better films later, *North to Alaska* (1960) and *Donovan's Reef* (1963), when he will be less restrained from mastery of the comic spirit, from manipulation of the comic community. As Rusty Thomas, however, he is distinctively repressed by boorish Dink and coyly clever Kit Madden.

Without Reservations is designed for the stardom of Claudette Colbert. Nevertheless, the best scenes of the film involve Wayne. When Rusty finally realizes "Miss Klotz" is really Christopher Madden, Wayne reveals his strength as a comic actor. He sets his jaw to restrain his anger and disappointment, and just as he is about to walk out of her life, his iron jaw is suddenly seized and turned to sharp profile for the camera. A close-up frames his now-distorted profile into a pose of ridicule, as Henry Baldwin (Thurston Hall) has been impressed with Rusty's potential for screen stardom. In this climactic scene, producer/director Baldwin has his first opportunity to meet this potential leading man. Thus he grips Rusty's jaw in his hand, holding Rusty for the camera and eagerly anticipating the time when he can give Rusty a screen test: "We're going to make a test with you, son. You should look wonderful in Technicolor."

His face twisted into a grimace of anger and surprise, disappointment and wonder, Rusty presents a grotesque figure. Wayne is put in his place, made a prisoner of Hollywood. Here also is capture of the comic spirit, distorted by forces of entertainment and torn from the happy life of carefree nature. The scene is funny because Rusty's (Wayne) face is compelled to be comic when it intends to be tragic, and because his essential purpose is misused and abused by people he trusted. Rusty is trapped and shown up as a fool when he thought himself a knowing, careless man of the world. Dink blurts out, "They're trying to make an actor out of you!" Nothing worse could happen to this man of nature and natural expression than to be reshaped by the artifices of Hollywood. Rusty/Wayne indignantly exclaims, "An actor! Come on, Dink!"

THE COMIC HERO is retrained to find his proper place in civilized community. As the film is a commentary on the insufficiencies of ideals and illusions, reason and order, so also it exposes and corrects ideas of heroism. The most prominent image of the hero is conquering warrior, valiant soldier marching home after victories abroad. Soldiers, sailors, and marines are presented *en masse* as prey for eager, hungry women. The knowing men, like Dink and Rusty, keep their distance from such women as Connie, calling them "beetles" who "worry" their men until they cannot do their duties (i.e., fly their planes). Kit herself becomes a beetle, successfully worrying her man Rusty until she grounds him permanently.

The hero must be "worried" into emotional commitments, domestic responsibilities, because those are more important to a community in time of peace than detached, careless self sacrifice is in time of war. It is a difficult proposition, especially so close to the end of World War II, but *Without Reservations* does exactly that as it ridicules the military hero and transforms him into a peacetime lover. Dink and Rusty have been through a hospital just before they meet Kit. They have been prepared to undergo the process of "healing" before re-entering a peacetime society. They are a threat to that society as long as they continue to behave as recklessly as they do on and off the train. Their behavior is fundamentally antisocial, and it is undesirable when it disrupts fundamental rules of order (leading to their ejection from the train in La Junta, New Mexico).

Bogus heroes and fictional heroes are complementary if not the same. Both are illusions, and both need the fleshing out of *Esquire* (which Rusty read in hospital) to become real and significant. Comic heroes are often tricksters in classic comic actions, from Aristophanes to Shaw. They are, however, not at home as tricksters. Their tricks are means of getting home (like Odysseus, Sancho Panza, and Yossarian in *Catch 22*). When they get home, they no longer have a need for tricks. To get home is what this film is designed to do for its hero and heroine, to break down the fence that divides them, to dissolve the need for tricks and allow the spirit of relaxation to prevail, without reservations.

RUSTY THOMAS IS MORE a plain dealer than *eiron*. When he is tainted by tricks, it is from his involvement with Dink more than an expression of his character or methods. More plainly his style is his dismissal of Kit's novel as "silly" or his chagrin at her deception. His main purpose in the story is to provide Kit with a humanizing purpose to her life; he is the opportunity for her to follow Ortega's advice, "to live and make the confusion," not "to burrow" out of the way of life with all its wonderful confusions. It is a simplistic pattern, Kit's intellectual ideals and Rusty's passionate turbulence. Together they will be whole, apart each is merely a fragment.

Rusty's purpose is to offer Kit a path from office to bedroom, from books to orchids, from East to West. Kit "fulfills" herself in this way without compromising her integrity as an artist, because she has accepted the truth of Rusty's love. He is Kit's opportunity to enlarge her vision of reality, free her self from misty ideals of imposture, and clear her view of herself. Most of the narrative is, then, a sequence of episodes which center on Kit's education and self discovery. Her ordeals are escapades of passionate and fleshly entanglements with Rusty and Dink.

Rugged individualism is Rusty's entire "philosophy," which he explains by contrasting the present tendencies with the struggles of America's founding fathers: "Did they have insurance for their old age, for their crops, for their home? They did not! They looked at the land, the forests, and the rivers. They looked at their wives, their kids, at their houses, and they looked up at the sky, and they said, 'Thanks, God. We'll take it from here.'" Dink is impressed: "They were rugged fellas!" Rusty corrects Dink, "They were *men!*" This is the answer to Kit's questions about life: she needs such a man and she will be happy. The only society that really matters unites man and woman, their children, and the elemental forces of nature.

Rusty and Dink hardly measure up to their own conceptions of the rugged men they admire as "real heroes" from American pioneering history. But it is their ideal answer to Kit's socializing progressivism. Rusty must therefore show Kit the possibilities of a primitive spirit. Kit is thrown off the train in New Mexico, where she is joined by Rusty/Dink. They test rugged individualism on the road in American open spaces. Rusty courts Kit in a hayfield under the moon. The scene echoes *It Happened One Night,* but it lacks that film's strong social consciousness. In fact, *Without Reservations* offers the "primitive" alternative to Capra's folksy moralisms. The alternative is itself pretty mild stuff, as Rusty tries to seduce Kit from her seat of hay bales to the nearby bed of a soft haystack. Here is the union of the human and the natural which Peter Warne (Clark Gable) described for Ellen Andrews (Claudette Colbert) in *It Happened One Night.* Rusty does

not merely describe the mixture of the elements, he tries to make the
elements mix when he repeatedly kisses away Kit's resistance. In the end,
he fails with her as Kit cannot yet yield her "yakkitty yakkitty" to his fleshly
confusions.

Kit is close to losing her opportunity now. It will take Ortega and the
pleasures of his family, especially his comely daughter, to bring Kit back to
her proper place with Rusty. She sees how Dolores captures Rusty's attention with music, food, and a generous body. When Ortega tells her "love
and violence go hand in hand," Kit is inspired, tells him that Rusty and Dink
are not really Marines, that they have stolen the uniforms they wear. This
so angers the fierce patriot he takes his gun after the two. They flee
Ortega's, and along the way Rusty shows that finally Kit has learned an important lesson, because she has acted from passion and jealousy. He pins
his airman's wings on her as his woman.

Although there are still ordeals ahead for Kit, including her night in
jail, the focus of the narrative shifts from her to Rusty, as he learns to deal
with the deceptive woman who took his wings. He has served his purpose
for making Kit into a primitive, into a reactionary—she revises the script
for the movie of her book. Rusty must experience the same jealousy he inspired in Kit, so they can be united in a happy ending for the film. Their
picturesque journey brings both to a reconciliation of ideals with reality,
from newsreel to filmland, from impostures to revelations.

IN 1934 A YOUNGER AND LIVELIER Claudette Colbert had played
her delightful role as the rich brat Ellen Andrews, running from a protective
father in Miami to a playboy husband in New York City. In that part Colbert
had to be educated in the ways of the world, as does Kit Madden. Ellen Andrews's instructor was yakkitty-yakkitty Clark Gable as star reporter Peter
Warne. John Wayne in *Without Reservations* plays against the image of
Clark Gable in *It Happened One Night,* whose picaresque road adventures
Wayne's film imitates to revise the education of the heroine.

Without Reservations cannot compete well with the earlier film, whose
vitality makes it a special film achievement of the time. That time was also
special, prewar and mid-depression, when the issues seemed more immediately pressing and more soluble by Americans themselves. When
Peter Warne subordinates hunger to imagination, he challenges Americans
to solve social problems through greater faith in mind and heart. When Rusty
Thomas ignores intellectual abstractions to pursue, first, fleshly and then
emotional delights, he challenges America to recall its pioneering spirit of
rugged individualism. *Without Reservations* had actually the more difficult
challenge, judging from the films which appeared during the years when it
was made.

In 1944 Colbert had a prominent role in *Since You Went Away,* a sentimental story of the tribulations suffered by an American family during the war. The year of *Without Reservations* saw *The Best Years of Our Lives*, with its biting analysis of civilian life ill-prepared to accommodate returning heroes. In a similar, though more tragic vein, *All My Sons* in 1948 exposes the dark center of American patriotism as a pitiful greed of ego and materialism. Howard Hawks's satire of postwar dislocations and social confusions, *I Was a Male War Bride*, in 1949, would display the muddle and absurdity into which even male/female relationships had fallen during and after the war.

These muddles and confusions are the target of *Without Reservations*, which prefers the old relationships and the old ideals to all the new plans for a new America. Only when the liberal intellect begins to make abstract demands on conservative nature does life seem, or become, confused. What is confusion to the intellect is gusto and adventure to passion. Intellectual confusion is comic clarity. When America attacked ideological "confusion," as in its awkward rapprochement with Soviet Russia during the war, it left much to be desired in clarity of purpose itself. This was the difficulty of much social commentary in the arts during the war, as represented by the social comedy of *The Male Animal* in 1942, where Henry Fonda is a college professor who discovers there is even in his civilized soul an animal spirit.

The resolution of problems in *The Male Animal* is a plea for tolerance, though emptied of political responsibility. Fonda's Professor Turner has to deny he has any political interests when he reads, defiantly, the moving letter of Bartolomeo Vanzetti that upset the fascist college trustees. Compared with the delicate and difficult balancing acts such films as this one had to do to be serious in social comedy, a film of the thirties had an easy time of resolving its thematic problems. *It Happened One Night* virtually ignores the difficulties of the times, in the shorthand ways of the screwball comedies, although it puts responsibility for wealth in the persons of Ellen Andrews and her father. The ethics of this responsibility, however, are plainly less complicated than they are for Professor Turner. *It Happened One Night* proposes that a selfless, chaste, and hard working young man who refuses to exploit opportunities for wealth can expect to be well rewarded by those who enjoy the advantages of wealth for themselves. Peter Warne, like Professor Turner, denies political or ideological interests; he only wants to do his job the best way he can, and along the way he falls in love with a wealthy woman. Colbert is like America itself, as in a fairy tale, testing the virtues of a young knight who proves his worthiness by respecting her chastity.

This kind of thing John Wayne's comic heroes generally resist. Both Duke Hudkins and Rusty Thomas frankly admit their fleshly lusts and desires for the pleasures of life. They pursue their women as objects of prey; they are frankly "male animals" trying to be honest about their natural selves in a hypocritical and muddled world. Their successes are conquests of passion over intellect, flesh over fantasy. At least that is what they offer as comic spirits.

Rusty Thomas does not, like Peter Warne, hang blankets between himself and his woman. He does not create the delight of social comedy that thrives on wit and stratagem in the bedroom. Rusty is an enemy to yakkitty-yakkitty, while Peter Warne is a professional talker/writer. John Wayne is laconic and easily insulted as a hero of honest deeds; Clark Gable is a ruthless chatterer and virtually impervious to insults. Claudette Colbert could hardly have found two more different comic heroes to court her on the open roads of America. She may be taken as a test of what is possible to bring out in the comic spirit of John Wayne, though she is a decade older when she acts with Wayne than when she did with Gable.

She gives Gable the opportunity to talk his way into her heart; she talks Wayne into abstracted distance he cannot overcome with ease. Wayne's set speeches in *Without Reservations* carry messages which contradict the means of their expression. As Rusty Thomas he is not reluctant to be political, but he is reluctant to talk about it. He prefers to kiss than to talk, to love than to act. When he invites himself to visit Kit in her Hollywood home, he takes her off screen and off the newspapers from between both Stalin and MacArthur. His politics are, finally, neither "progressive" nor "reactionary." They are, instead, quite blatantly and without reservations, firmly sexual.

Sean Thornton: *The Quiet Man* (1952)

The Quiet Man is a film of classic form containing primitive forces barely held in restraint by a will to hope. When Sean Thornton tries to explain why he wants to purchase the cottage where he was born, White of Morning, he says the town of Innisfree "has become another word for heaven for me." Longing for heaven inspires the film, longing for home informs it with archetypal shape. The happiness of going home, recovering paradise, and realizing the dream of Eden is identical with the happiness longed for in great comic literature. Sean Thornton comes home to take possession of his ancestral home and, in doing so, he takes possession of himself.

The film glows with the soft lights of Fordian sentiment, and so it has an aura of crude daydreaming. It is commercial art that panders to the easy emotions of vulnerable people, but it is also folk art with strong kinship to Homeric poetry. It is a layered experience of emotional richness, and it is a crosswork of archetypal narrative structures. At its center is Sean Thornton, whose heroic strength is in his will to find purpose in a world without order. This is one of John Wayne's most moving of portrayals, shaped by the direction of John Ford and informed by classic motives. In this role, Wayne must resolve classic complications of Old and New Comedy, integrate the naïve and comic lover with the forceful power of impersonal nature itself.

Barry Fitzgerald *(left,* as Michaeleen Flynn) makes his point with Wayne, as Sean Thornton, in *The Quiet Man,* 1952.

He is the mysterious stranger whose arrival reshapes a community, renews its vigor, and is himself renewed by it. He is a man of sorrows who finds joy for others when he discovers happiness for himself.

SIGNS OF DISORDER and disorientation abound in the world of *The Quiet Man.* Trains do not run on schedule, directions are confused, men talk of treason, priests spend their time fishing and playing tiddlywinks, taverns are more patronized than churches. Most disturbing, lovers are kept apart by meaningless formalities and impostures of form. Sean Thornton arrives to a chorus of misdirections when he asks the way to Innisfree. He sees a beautiful young woman, Mary Kate Danaher (Maureen O'Hara), herding sheep in a dreamscape of pastoral loveliness; he is stunned, asks "Is that real?" In the ideal comic world such beauty *is* real, but to the unimaginative denizens of the "real" world it is only a "mirage," as Michaeleen Flynn (Barry Fitzgerald) insists to Sean. Michaeleen goes further, to say what Sean has seen and felt was only "brought on by your terrible thirst." Innisfree is missing the power of love to rescue it from its tawdry social and spiritual disorders.

Innisfree suffers symptoms of an empty heart. The yearnings of Mary Kate and Sarah Tillane express this emptiness waiting to be filled. Red Will cannot see how to do what his heart tells him, until he is forced by the arrival of the stranger Sean Thornton. In the classic plot of New Comedy, young lovers are thwarted by family from marriage and must remove all obstacles to realize their love. In tragedies this can be done only at the cost of life, often their own lives (as in *Romeo and Juliet*), sacrifices to redeem the community of its faults. But in the joy of comic action, this can be done to make happy everyone who has stood in the way as well as the comic hero and heroine themselves.

Sean Thornton is the young naif, quietly searching for himself and his home, awakened by his vision of love, and driven by that love to a new life of energy and commitment. When he arrives on the train, he drops the window of his compartment and signals his intent to remove barriers. When he is surrounded by the confusion of conflicting directions on the road to Innisfree, he stands quietly bemused until mysteriously, strangely he is summoned by a quiet little man to follow him to the land of his heart's desire. It is a dreamlike experience, which suggests the source of Sean's strength—his quiet resolve, his submission to instinct.

He is rewarded by his vision of Mary Kate amidst her sheep. That determines his destiny. He becomes the comic hero of courtly romances; through him operates the springtime deity of Eros bringing new life. Sean is a phallic hero bound to be educated by the ways of the world, but he will assert the primacy of his will even as he deals with the challenges of his erotic education. First he exercises restraint, subduing his spirit to the forms necessary to fit into this alien community, even though he occasionally makes a mistake here and there—as in the episode of the holy water. When he offers his hand as a basin for her to use, Mary Kate is startled by what Sean has done; but she yields to *her* best instinct and takes the drops of water as his holy gift of love. Sean seems to break up a holy ritual, but in fact he revitalizes it through his naïve and simple act of love. He would like to be more bold in his courtship, but he continues to restrain his impulses (recalling the sorrow of his dark deed when he did not).

He sends the matchmaker to begin courtship of Mary Kate, even as he orders his "Homeric" bed. He appears dutifully in his formal attire (including hat) bearing flowers to his love, but he disbelievingly departs when Red Will rudely refuses to permit the courtship. Sean really cannot believe all these formalities are important, and he is right in some respects. The test is to be the matter of the dowry. Sean had told Flynn Mary Kate could come to him naked if she pleased; he did not expect, did not wish for, a dowry. All he wanted was her love. But she knows more is necessary, that she must have something to offer in the match besides herself, something that is her claim on the community and on history—her dowry.

This is a difficult problem for the film as well as for Sean Thornton, who must at the same time reject and accept the dowry if he is ever to find his happiness with Mary Kate. Like America itself, Sean must find a way to incorporate the past of history into the present of boundless opportunity. Until that way is found, the present will be incomplete and the future cannot promise the unlimited happiness longed for by hero and heroine. The phallic hero cannot be a comic hero until he accepts the terms of the community and thereby transforms it with his fresh energies of enriching love.

Red Will relents, allows the courtship to begin, and Sean settles back into the formality of tradition. His sexual energies are given respectability by these formalities, and he works hard to keep them under restraint. But he is an innocent (an American) abroad, not completely understanding what all the formality is about, but knowing what the end of it is to be. He rides the jaunting car with Mary Kate under the public eye of Michaeleen Flynn, and he keeps his spirit contained in unnatural silence until even Michaeleen cannot endure it any longer. He permits the lovers to walk ahead, without patty-fingers.

They walk together demurely for a while. Then Sean sees a bicycle. They break away and escape their guardian. Mary Kate removes her shoes and stockings to cross a brook; Sean removes his hat and, with a whoop of glee, tosses it across the hills into meadows beyond. They become one in their separateness as they (symbolically) remove their clothing, pass back through time (figuratively, through an ancient cemetery) into the ruins of an ancient chapel where they are spiritually united.

When Sean tosses his hat away he exults in his natural and sexual spontaneity. Mary Kate responds, and they are honestly united by nature and Eros. They are married but they are not happy, on account of the withheld dowry. She will not sleep with him, locks herself in their bedroom, and he breaks down the door. As sexual hero, Sean could "take" his woman exactly as Flynn will believe he has at sight of the broken bed. But Sean is not a ruffian of old, though he does break down the door. Mary Kate is startled but also impressed. Sean leaves her alone on the bed, goes to his sleeping bag in the outer room, and they spend their wedding night apart in their own house.

Flynn observes the broken bed the next morning, draws the wrong conclusion, leers and exclaims, "Impetuous! Homeric!" The scene is a sadly amusing comment on the catastrophe of the sexual hero. His phallic sleeping bag has been transformed into a sign of sexual dissatisfaction, and the broken bed must be restored to make paradise possible after all.

SEAN PULLS HIS WIFE from the train, and drags her across fields and pastures, pursued by delighted neighbors. He confronts Red Will at his threshing. This episode is a happy parade of rustic energies, central to comic action from Homer to Aristophanes, from Punch and Judy to *Adam's Rib*, from the Old Testament to *The Taming of the Shrew*. It is like the ritual of *Komos* that involves the entire community in celebration of marriage and the triumph of Eros. The comic spirit emerges in Sean Thornton, now fully given over to impetuosity—which means, he has become the nature god, Pan, and Bacchus, and Phales—whoever embodies the *force* of nature that drives man and beast in triumphant life.

This force makes the figure epic; its subservience to the ends of Eros makes it comic. The community of observers, men and women both, is delighted by the scene, though the participants are grim and full of pain. It is a complex event which demands comic vision as well as an aesthetic distance of impersonal detachment, represented by the much amused people of Innisfree. Sean hurls Mary Kate at the feet of Red Will. It is a delicate moment, capable of tragedy and cynicism. But the audience does not believe it—the audience knows it is a glorious comic moment, what it has been waiting for, forever and always.

Red Will throws his sister's dowry at Sean, who strides silently with it to the threshing machine. Mary Kate is no longer ashamed; she is filled with pride and purpose, as she dashes to open the door to the boiler of the machine, knowing instinctively what is to happen. Sean throws the dowry money into the machine and resolves the problem it posed: it has been forced from the villain, drained of power to divide Sean from Mary Kate. Comedy arises from the triumph of spirit and will over money and matter. Mary Kate proudly marches home, telling her husband she will have supper waiting for him when he gets there himself. She knows, the community knows, and so should all audiences, the affair is not yet concluded, though Mary Kate's interests are now completely satisfied.

The phallic hero has conquered, nature is satisfied, and love awaits the renewal of new life. But first something more, the battle of spring and winter, young and old, to make the *Komos* complete. Sean fights Red Will with gusto and joy, for himself and Red Will as much as for the indomitable Irish audience. This battle sustains life, pushes it into new directions. This fight endears the combatants, does not divide them (as in the boxing for money, or in the contempt of courage). Again Flynn can exclaim, "It's Homeric!" It is a successful realization of ancient comic action, and it is a graduation of the comic hero from his education.

Sean is put down as much as he gains the top. Men are fools in fact, and much of the fight scene shows this elementary truth. But they triumph together as they share the pain and the pleasure of battle. Mary Kate is at home, happily oblivious to the epic fight because it is insignificant to her; she knows they will come home happy, because she is fully comic herself. Indeed, her husband and brother troop in together, drunk and joyful, though they are humble in the region of her domestic authority. Here is the paradise sought for, celebrated in drinking and eating, loving and fighting, where one's adversary is one's friend, where fighting does not hurt, and where love sanctions all.

THERE ARE COMEDIES WITHOUT "HEROES" as there are "heroes" who have no comedy in their souls. John Wayne made comic heroes like Sean Thornton; he did not only, or merely, make comedy, such as some appearing at about the same time as *The Quiet Man.* Two classic French films will illustrate. *La Ronde* appeared in 1950, and *Mr. Hulot's Holiday* in 1953. They surround the point of *The Quiet Man* in more than time, because they are at structural and thematic extremes from *The Quiet Man.* Both assume a distance from their stories that is alien to Wayne's film, asserting themselves as "art," with intellectual and even emotional detachment. *La Ronde* is introduced by a master of revels, a figure of many disguises (played by Anton Walbrook) who tells the audience, "I am you," a "personification of your desires to know everything." He claims to "see from every side," and he takes the film back "in the past" of old Vienna—a nostalgia trip like Sean's, but without the complicated motives of Sean Thornton. Then begins the "merry go round" of the film's title, as life is set to turning through eight little episodes of "love."

La Ronde purports to have the comic vision of, say, Boccaccio or Chaucer, on themes of love, but its stories are bound by one narrow view, that love is selfish and little more than carnal. The story that begins the film centers on the "itch" of a prostitute (Simone Signoret) for a passing soldier. The film ends by claiming to be "the story of everybody;" it returns to the prostitute again, now without desperation as she lies in bed watching a drunken Count come to consciousness on the floor beside her, not knowing if they did "it" or not. The notion of love is as cynical as the dog which passes by the merry-go-round to end the film. It is more concerned with the status of art than it is with the complicated experiences of love.

The Quiet Man offers itself as a story with a hero, as an adventure of fantasy with emotional consequences for those who will give themselves to it. It is, certainly, a "story with a hero," as *La Ronde* cannot bring itself to be, unless the narrator himself is to be taken as such. *La Ronde* debunks heroes, shows up soldiers especially to be puny bundles of nervous twitches, but generally that men are, in the words of the film itself, "disgusting." This is comedy of a sort, and it is significant comedy which exposes the hypocrisies and pretensions of humankind. But it is not high comedy, and it is not comedy with heroic dimensions.

Neither is Jacques Tati's *Mr. Hulot's Holiday,* which dares the audience to make a plot out of the film at all. There is definitely a rhythm that gives lovely form to *Mr. Hulot's Holiday* and there is an archetypal form that emerges from that rhythm, though it is not the same as *The Quiet Man.*

Mr. Hulot tries to escape from the banality of modern life; he takes a holiday
on the seacoast, where he finds the other guests on holiday (especially the
English ones) do not wish to be disturbed from their customary banal preoc-
cupations. Hulot tries to do some things similar to Sean's painting his cottage "emerald green," as when Hulot plays tennis or goes hiking or pony
(donkey) riding on the beach. A holiday should be an escape into the security
of conventional playtime, but Hulot has a difficult, almost impossible, time
trying to play.

A hero in the mold of Chaplin or Keaton, Hulot is diminished by his
world by achieving even the ends of Chaplin, which are usually decisions
to banish the world itself when it proves unreceptive. Hulot may have the
elasticity of Keaton, the pertinacity of purpose, but he does not have the
opportunities of Keaton to be the genius of *The General* or the pilot of
Steamboat Bill, Jr. Which is to say that Hulot is not a hero in fact. He is an
ironist who exposes the inadequacies of his humorless, joyless world. Hulot
tries to have fun in a world without a sense of humor, and the result is the
admiring sadness felt in the end of a Chaplin adventure. The comedian's
spirit triumphs *over* his world, does not reform and renew it.

Sean Thornton is a comic hero, not a mere comedian; his spirit works
to reform and renew Innisfree. There are comedians in the story, characters
played by actors with strong reputations for "types," such as Michaeleen
Flynn played by Barry Fitzgerald, Dan Tobin played by the irrepressible
Francis Ford, and Feeny by Jack McGowran. But these characters are
vehicles for moving the hero, instruments for his desires, servants of his purposes. The comic hero is not only fun or merely funny; he is a force for happiness and joy in being, for others as well as for himself. Hulot is a picture
of the possibility for fun and joy, but he fails to deliver others to that condition. Unlike Keaton, Hulot does not get the girl of his desire, though in *Mr.
Hulot's Holiday* the "girl" seems interested enough in him. His film is
nostalgic in a sad sense, that it longs for a love no longer attainable in the
world of modern art.

The Quiet Man denies that, shows how love can be attained and satisfies
the longing for happiness from such love. Between the cynicism of *La
Ronde* and the sad clowning of Mr. Hulot, there would seem to be little
room for a film like *The Quiet Man* in the decade of the fifties. Are there
any comic heroes to compete with the likes of Sean Thornton? In America,
always confident and always romantic, there should be many companions
for Sean Thornton and John Wayne in the time of 1952.

What one finds, however, are films of social purpose and artful self consciousness, sometimes successful and more often not. As for comic heroes,
they are rare even in America, where perhaps John Wayne could after all
assert himself without much competition even in that kind of role. Nearby
the date of *The Quiet Man* are three films offering to fill the void that

surrounds Wayne's film and buffer it from the French failures of comic nerve.

CONSIDER FIRST a monument to human idiocy, *Bedtime for Bonzo* (1951), a smarmy story that belittles human intelligence and insults the comic spirit. A chimpanzee makes people look like monkeys, especially college professors, and it takes a chimpanzee to show men and women what real love is. The dialogue is peppered with such terms as "inverted psychological domination," "Gestalt theory," and "sublimation," but they are meaningless except as easy targets for low humor. It is a love story—of sorts. It panders to coarse tastes and produces bad jokes from a situation where a chimp is treated as a child. Priorities are lost and values obscured in a film that offers itself as mere entertainment while trying to make a "significant" point about the importance of a "good environment."

The plasticity of environment, without its obduracy as in *Mr. Hulot's Holiday*, is taken by the American spirit to be important for molding human character in defiance of ideas about genetic destiny. A good person is the product of a good environment, regardless of genetic history. *The Quiet Man* challenges the simplistic optimism (or is it pessimism?) of propositions found in *Bedtime for Bonzo*. There is no confusion of human and animal, no reduction of spirit to nervous reflex, and no psychological pabulum of that sort in *The Quiet Man*, where anyone like Professor Peter Boyd (Ronald Reagan) would get short shrift from people to whom "aggressiveness" could never become "an aberration" (as Boyd suggests in his "experiment" to turn Bonzo into a virtue-loving creature). Comedy of joy demands recognition of the aggressiveness that characterizes life, a source of the heroism of Wayne's Sean Thornton.

There is no hero in *Bedtime for Bonzo*, because there is no reality or truth to the proposition of the film's postulates. Even if there were, who among the characters might compete for the status of hero? It should be Peter Boyd, but he is both stupid *and* naive; he is blind to love, and he is self absorbed. The doddering old laboratory scientist, Hans (Walter Slezak), is little more than a zoo attendant. It could be Jane Linden (Diana Lynn), who learns to care for Bonzo as if the chimp were a child, but Jane is a helpless youth whose main resource is tears. The only real hero of this film is Bonzo, the chimpanzee, who shows intelligence, resourcefulness, good taste, and love.

The absurdity of such a proposition is the subject and theme of a much more consequential film of the time, Howard Hawks's *Monkey Business* (1952). It may have been a mere coincidence this film came out so soon after *Bedtime for Bonzo*, but it was nevertheless a serious treatment of a similar theme. The professor of this film, Professor Barnaby Fulton (Cary Grant) is turned, not into a monkey, but into a child (almost an infant) by a monkey.

The animal in human beings is released by base motives (greed, acquisitiveness, ambition, better jobs, etc.), until the virtues of the human are lost in the vices of uninhibited and undirected energies. Hawks's film shows the low humor of *Bonzo* to be unworthy of human consideration, the product of the worst in human nature.

Monkey Business, however, is trapped by its own intentions, so that it has little room in which to show what is good in human nature, only what can go wrong with it. While *The Quiet Man* is a search for the good which succeeds through love and aggression, *Monkey Business* is a regression from the good to viciousness in aggression. Barnaby never treats his wife, Edwina (Ginger Rogers) quite like the mate of a caveman, but *Edwina* treats Barnaby in just such a fashion. In a typically Hawksian inversion, Barnaby is the victim of his wife's aggression and even finds himself wearing her clothing in his absurdity. *The Quiet Man* uses the aggressiveness of humanity to establish community, to motivate love. *Monkey Business* undermines community with aggression, showing that without love it is only a destructive power of hostility.

Sarcasm and cynicism threaten to strangle the comic spirit during the time of *The Quiet Man.* An exception for hope of happy companionship may be *Adam's Rib* (1949). Here was a mature social comedy of manners with an important theme about the equal rights of women in a world where men needed some comeuppance to set things, really, right. The wit of the film begins with the title and carries through with the energies of Tracy and Hepburn as they reenact the ancient ritualistic struggles of Punch and Judy (alluded to in the framing of the film's credits and titles, by a newspaper cartoon of the two protagonists, and by Adam [Tracy] himself when he accuses Amanda [Hepburn] of turning a court of law into a Punch-and-Judy show).

It is a strange figure to organize the film, Punch and Judy, since the theme is a denial of the charm and attraction of the Punch-and-Judy tradition. But probably its point is supposed to be ironic, in the sense that men have made marriages into the Punch-and-Judy relationship, while they have denied to women any power to reverse the roles, as if in a Punch-and-Judy relationship any difference could result from a reversal of roles. That seems, finally, to be the real point of the film, because when the roles *are* reversed, by Doris Attinger (Judy Holliday) shooting her husband (Tom Ewell), or Adam Bonner "shooting" his wife, there is little difference after all. The real problem with this film (a serious problem since the film is still popular, even cultist) is that violence (both "real" and "pretended") is shown to be—not hostile to happiness, as in *Monkey Business,* not happily in the service of Eros, as in *The Quiet Man*—but ironically irrelevant.

When aggressiveness is subordinate to love, it can be fun and liberating as *The Quiet Man* shows. When it is superior to love, it is ugly and destructive, as *Monkey Business* shows. But when it is denied, pushed aside as a deviation and maybe even irrelevant to serious concerns with life (of the intellect?), it is trivialized and, though *Adam's Rib* does not intend this, it is most dangerous. This film disguises its hypocrisy as comedy (in the tradition of Oscar Wilde), producing a bitter aftertaste to the laughter it excites. Adam and Amanda really *are* Punch and Judy, really are the romping children Howard Hawks had revealed in *Monkey Business*, but they do not seem to know it, or, if they do, they choose to ignore it and thus doom themselves to a destiny of blitheful enslavement to their own animal natures. His jealousy, her competitiveness, and their violence are conjured away with the magic of pretense that they do not exist unless one notices them. But when Adam strikes Amanda's rear while "massaging" her, she knows, as Dr. Johnson knew when he kicked the stone, that aggressiveness *is* real and that it is painful—especially when it is denied.

The triumph of *The Quiet Man* is, in part, that it makes a place for human aggression without reducing it to animal brutality. This it does because it makes aggression only one of the traits of humanity, and not a major one at that. Major characteristics are, in priority of well ordered society, love between the sexes, love of fellow humankind, neighborliness, pride of place, honesty with one's self, and pride of origin; aggression is a tool of asserting values, not an end in itself in *The Quiet Man*. The hero is the man of heart who knows, or learns, how to use his aggressiveness (now call it physical strength) to acquire, hold, and protect his values which give purpose to his life and to the life of his human community.

Sam McCord: *North to Alaska* (1960)

As Sam McCord, John Wayne carries *North to Alaska* by mere strength of character. He is not surrounded and buttressed with the fine clowns he enjoyed in *The Quiet Man*. Instead he is the unequivocal clown of the narrative, stronger and more impressive than any of the other actors who move in the wake of his Rabelaisian spirit. Sam McCord is a free spirit who learns that love is more liberating than lust, and John Wayne gives one of his best comic performances in creating the gusto of Sam McCord. The thin narrative of the film is subordinate to the star's performance, though the narrative is a significant vehicle because it derives from classic comic form that makes education and marriage central to a hero's development.

Wayne is a heavy hero, puffing through difficult physical routines, some done by doubles, as in the pole-climbing contest. He makes much joyful humor out of this heavy work, and so he continues to show his ability to make a little go a long way in his acting, as when he trudges through the mud to chase after Angel at the end. Because he is heavy, he has a hard time getting through the mud, which shows how determined he is to overcome his nature in his capitulation to love—at last. Wayne uses his big body over

Wayne as Sam McCord, Stewart Granger as George Pratt, and Capucine as Angel in *North to Alaska*, 1960.

and over to communicate the earthiness of the character, but more marvelously he uses his mobile facial expressions to communicate the dawning of a spirit from that earthy body.

Wayne must be a clown, clown around a lot. He is a sacrifice to nature, though certainly not in any tragic sense. He loves to fight, to feel the power of physical contact, as in the opening sequence, when he, George Pratt (Stewart Granger), and Billy Pratt (Fabian) brawl to defend the "honor" of one Jenny Lamont. This fight proceeds to the rhythms and music of a calliope, started by a man's body set flying from a blow to the face. The bartender wears a bowler hat that rises to ring a bell each time he is punched in the nose. Beer spews from barrels all over the room, filling the screen with spray and dousing the performers with happy brew. Sam loves it, even when he is knocked silly. The brawl finishes only because the men lose their interest in it; they hear the cry of "Girls!" and all rush out to "see" the "new" girls who have arrived for their entertainment in Nome, Alaska, 1900. Sam is as gleeful as the others, joining in the joyful cry of "Girls!"

Burlesque action also marks the final sequence. It is a superb street fight between good guys and bad guys. The fray is peppered with a bucking mule, butting goats, a Salvation Army band, a text that invokes love for one's fellow man, an applauding and snorting seal, falling buildings, to the tune of "The Saints Go Marching In." It is a Dionysian rout and spiritual celebration, as the cynical Frankie is buried in mud and his loutish partner has his bell rung. Out of this mêlée, a rout of physical disorder and joyous destruction, emerges a new birth of love. Sam McCord pursues the retreating Angel who will not stay until he confesses what he really feels for her. It takes more spirit than Sam McCord has ever known to say, finally, what he has fought against thoughout his life, that he loves a woman enough to marry her. His confession of love delivers him from a bondage he did not know existed when he thought Alaska was the last frontier of freedom because "matrimony hasn't hit up here yet." Angel is the "real gold mine" he has spent his life to find. The spiritual triumph of the scene is not in the cliche of the theme. Rather, it is in the spectacle of defiant flesh, stubborn pride yielding to honest emotion.

SLAPSTICK, PARODY, AND BURLESQUE raise the spirit of Sam McCord to high levels. Comedy drives toward inevitability of marriage, to delight the rowdy community that watches its hero confess his humanity. But the milieu of the film's world is frankly sensuous and sensual; physical appetites are enormous, and Sam McCord's are the most enormous of all. This is the world of the flesh, to be enjoyed and to give joy; it is to be indulged, not repressed; its aim is to implement, not inhibit or prohibit, the rush of Eros. From Aristophanes to Ben Jonson to Nikos Kazantzakis, this is a comic experience with rich pedigree, and it is no less appealing to something important in the American spirit than it was, with wonderful effects, to Rabelais in sixteenth-century Europe. When Sam McCord is called "the Paul Bunyan of pole-climbers," he is identified as an American Gargantua.

The Renaissance Gargantua of Rabelais was a venting of colossal desire for life and for the freedom to enjoy life's pleasures and material rewards without fear and guilt. Paul Bunyan and Gargantua aspire to uninhibited happiness of mastery over nature. This is vital in American optimism, and central to the charcter of Sam McCord. Alaska is a utopia, though not one made by imagination as in Aristophanes's Cloud-Cookoo-Land of *The Birds*. It is instead more like Thomas More's Utopia, a haven of nature itself. On the other hand, Alaska is governed by a rule of living which could have been taken directly from Gargantua's ideal retreat, the abbey Theleme, whose motto was "DO AS THOU WILT." Here was to be perfect liberty for the members to marry honestly, enjoy wealth and live in perfect freedom. Members were to be men who are handsome, athletic, and personable; women who are beautiful, shapely, and pleasing in nature.

While Sam McCord's Alaska cannot honestly claim its inhabitants are only men who are handsome and personable, they are "athletic," and all the women are beautiful and shapely. Doing what they wish, a crude variant of Plato's idea of Justice in *The Republic,* "Minding one's own business," does produce anarchy and licentiousness in all who live there, though some (mainly the outsiders, like Frankie, who do not really belong there) try to take advantage of liberty to ruin it for others. The gusto for life, the liberty of choice and taste, are defined by the compatible ideals of friendship, chastity, and trust—even in Alaska, Billy Pratt is 17 and still a virgin, though he much wishes not to be. George Pratt is well into adult maturity, but he has "saved himself" for three years, waiting to marry the woman of his dreams, Jenny Lamont. George trusts his friend Sam McCord to deliver his fiancée "intact." While that trust is severely tested by the reversals of the story, it survives because it is based upon something even more important to the order of Alaska—friendship.

Friendship is the bond of spirit that preserves the integrity of this ideal land. It is sufficient to contain the animal gusto of rough people, who brawl and drink and lust without any other restraint than to mind their own businesss. When in Seattle, Sam is disgusted with the selfish priggishness of the women who initially object to Angel at the loggers' picnic. The women relent and finally welcome Angel, but Sam registers his discontent with the difference between Seattle and Alaska: "What I can't stand is when people look down on others who aren't doin' 'em any harm." Angel is amused by this idealism: "Oh, Sam, you cannot change the world! And, it . . . it's so nice here. And that's enough." But it is not enough, as Angel has already shown when she decided to accept Sam's invitation to go to Alaska, where a gold mine awaits her: "Instead of jumping into the bay, I'm going to jump into a gold mine! And, Mister, am I going to jump!"

The gold of Alaska, more specifically of Sam and his friends, is a symbol of natural power, but it has been sanctified by friendship. Sam explains to Angel the gold was actually found by George and that Sam's life was saved by George. Their friendship, then, established the little community of worthy men into which they now invite worthy women. Their virtues are not limited to their elite community of self interest, however, for they share their bounty with all who enjoy their company. This takes the form of great drinking and rough brawling together. In the end, then, when Frankie is exposed and humiliated in the muddy street of Nome, the entire community cheers.

More momentously, when Angel forces Sam to confess his love for her, the entire community cheers and celebrates the triumph of Eros by tramping into the nearby Palace Saloon to drink the good health of the loving couple. Thus the plot of the story rounds itself out, returning where it began, in an atmosphere of rowdy comradeship, now raised to a higher pitch by the promise of marriage. Angel turns out to be a "real Venus" (as Frankie had ironically observed), a proper match for the "Mars" who is Sam McCord. She is the "breath of spring" George felt her to be, and she melts away the last snows of resistance to an eternal Eden of the heart for Sam McCord. Such are the cosmic forces which move through comic heroes and heroines.

NORTH TO ALASKA derives from Charlie Chaplin's *The Gold Rush* (1925). Wayne's film suffers considerably when compared with its classic predecessor, but it also shows some individual strengths. *The Gold Rush* is mournful and satiric, *North to Alaska* buoyant and celebratory. Chaplin's film is an exercise in heroic suffering and individual pride, Wayne's in heroic action and community joy. There is little of the Rabelaisian in Chaplin's film, which develops instead the more bitter Swiftian satire (of everything except its own sentimentality). *North to Alaska* extends the successful and happy conclusion of *The Gold Rush*, while a later film, Nicolas Roeg's *Eureka* (1984), extends the bitterness of the satire in *The Gold Rush* into a vision of terror and corruption.

Chaplin's film stresses the waste and destructiveness of (notions like) utopia, using the setting to highlight the reality of heart in human character. The hero does not settle in the utopia of Alaska, like Sam McCord; instead, the Lone Prospector sets sail away from the place as quickly as he has the means to do so. How he gets there, what in the world he is doing there, and how he gets about while he is there, are all matters left unanswered, as if "nowhere" is the place of everyone's common existence — a testing ground of the spirit. Wayne's film makes far less use of the frozen, wasted, and threatening possibilities for Alaska; indeed, it offers some strikingly beautiful scenes of the landscape to suggest the potential for harmony and happiness there.

Sam and George have been in Alaska for at least three years when the story opens, and they show every intention of staying at the end. For Angel, Alaska represents an opportunity for a new and meaningful life, a real utopia of happiness. Alaska in *The Gold Rush* is a condition of brutality and degradation, against which the human spirit battles for survival and integrity. In *North to Alaska*, it is a second chance, a new frontier of honesty and love. Wayne's film asserts the continuing ideal of America's history and destiny, while Chaplin's questions its value in the modern world of materialistic and competitive reality.

Sam McCord has love of friends and lust of women; he has to learn that love of women can be more. Sam's hunger is a matter of the spirit, not the flesh. His huge appetite is a sign of his potential for loving in spirit as well as in body. The Lone Prospector of *The Gold Rush* is a sad "little fellow," but he also has a huge appetite, a consequence of desperation rather than potential. Chaplin's film indulges the comic motif of eating, to

point out the cannibalistic nature of man and man's society. The hunger of
the Lone Prospector is also a metaphor of sexual appetite, indicated by the
dream sequence in Hank Curtis's cabin, which includes the wonderful
dance of the dinner buns.

Sam McCord is much like the local Don Juan of *The Gold Rush,* Jack
Cameron (Malcolm Waite), who is surrounded by the women of the dance
hall. But Sam is Jack Cameron with a difference; he wins the heroine
because he bends for her, to combine heartful Charlie and powerful Jack.
Chaplin's Lone Prospector does not "grow" in any significant way; he merely
survives, and not mainly because he has special heroic skills (as, say, would
a hero of Buster Keaton's). In this respect, Sam McCord is more suggestively
human — if being more fully human is a matter of change, development, and
growth. Things both good and bad come to the Lone Prospector; Sam
McCord makes things, mainly good, happen. Charlie Chaplin shows, as the
Lone Prospector, what it really means to speak of an "art of *re*acting," while
John Wayne, as Sam McCord, shows once again that his essential style is
an art of *act*ing.

IN SAM MCCORD'S UTOPIA of Alaska the law is minimal, but when it
makes its presence known — to interfere in the private affairs of honest
men — it is barely suffered by the comic hero, who is no champion of law.
The order of comedy is much more likely to be the product of passion and
desire, and so it is usually in conflict with the order of reason upon which
social reality depends. When Frankie Canon uses Breezy to file a counter-
claim on Sam's and George's goldmine, the law intervenes to suspend all
operations pending a determination of ownership. This is rational and it is
in accord with social order, but it is contrary to the pressures of passion in
Sam McCord. He is caught at just the wrong (or is it the right?) moment
when soldiers appear to occupy the mine. Sam is caught at the moment
when he has been raised to the highest pitch of love and jealousy he has
ever experienced. In this state of passionate indignation, he runs afoul of
the law and finds himself its prisoner. The soldiers take him to court where
he calms himself just long enough to understand the proceedings, and then
he rushes to confront the man representing Breezy.

Sam finds this man, one Duggan, in a barber's chair. Here is an episode
of outrageous brutality and torture, in any kind of setting than a comic one.
But in comedy of the Punch-and-Judy kind, or of the kind Jonson and
Molière employed, Sam's "torture" of Duggan is a fair and just means to a
fair and just end — it is passion's way of expediting the aims of reason. Sam
holds a kettle of boiling water over the helpless Duggan. When he refuses
to tell Sam what he wants to know, Sam pours scalding water over the
screaming victim until Sam hears what he wants. Moreover, Sam does not
merely pour the water over his victim, he pours it over his groin, the point

of passion's aim. The question of potency, powers, fertility, and honesty is raised by the deed, as Eros uses passion to restore justice to those who best fulfill the goals of love.

This scene is troubling, no doubt, to many. But it has a proper function in the world of *North to Alaska* as it should not in a less coherent form of life. Alaska is Utopia and it is a *comic* utopia, where Dionysus prevails over the rule of Apollo. That America seemed, in fact, to be a land of Dionysian revel was a view taken by Chaplin in *A King in New York*, released just three years before *North to Alaska*. This film, Chaplin's last to star in, takes up an issue Chaplin had stressed in the voice narrative of his re-released *Gold Rush:* the definition of "utopia" which becomes in 1957 a "real" place, not the "nowhere" of Alaska in *The Gold Rush.*

Chaplin's last film is a bitter denunciation of America, which seems to welcome victims of political oppression in flight from tyranny—even when they are apparently thieving monarchs driven from their tyrannic thrones. When, therefore, King Shahdov (Chaplin) expresses his gratitude to America, "wonderful America! Its youth, its genius, its vitality," he speaks as a deposed monarch who has (he also thinks) supposedly escaped with a fortune robbed from his own rebellious people. A reflection upon this discovers that America, in fact, does welcome even the villainous tyrants and dictators when they flee communism. It takes a while for the King, and possibly the film's audience, to see just where this is going to go in the narrative, but in the end it will be brutally clear that America is blinded by its passions, by its selfish and paranoid prejudices, and that its "genius" is Dionysus indeed—dancing in a frenzy of fear.

The law and order of America no longer makes sense, at least not to a benevolent monarch like King Shahdov. He in fact was deposed because his people wanted him to use atomic power to make bombs, not to provide peaceful energy for the utopia he intended to fashion. He has come to America with the offer of his blueprint for "nuclear plans that will revolutionize modern life and bring about utopia." When he discovers he has no wealth at all, barely has the money to pay his hotel bill, he pins all his hope on acceptance of his "atomic plan." While he waits, the King begins a tour of New York City, and when he cannot stand the noise and rout of the streets, he seeks refuge in a cinema. The satire is indeed heavy, as the "coming attractions" show America's love of violence and pleasure in chaos (a chaos of sexual confusion), but the thematic point is worth emphasizing here as the King has to wait and then make his way through a horde of girls dancing in the aisle of the theatre, to the beat of a so-called "rock and roll" band. One of the girls, in her ecstasy, even bites the King as he tries to get to his seat. This is what the rule of Dionysus looks like to Chaplin, the comic genius in exile from America.

Chaplin's Apollonian comedy is incompatible with Wayne's more

Dionysian kind, and the contrast between the themes and styles of their films and their acting is instructive in the differences between the comic traditions. Wayne's comic heroes use disorder to liberate themselves and their communities from hypocrisies and dishonesty; Chaplin's use disorder to suggest a state of reality in need of a better way, in need of reason's light. This is forcefully, though not most happily, rendered in the climactic scene of *A King in New York*, which may be contrasted with the courtroom scene of *North to Alaska*.

The King has given refuge to a victim of American tyranny, a little boy named Rupert Macabee (the heavy hand of the film shows even in the names; the little boy is played by Michael Chaplin). The boy's parents have been cited for contempt of Congress because they refuse to inform a panel of the House Un-American Activities Committee the names of their colleagues in the Communist Party. Since the boy is tainted by his parents' guilt, so is the King when it is discovered the boy has been with him in his rooms. Although it strikes Shahdov that a communist king is an absurd impossibility, he is nevertheless caught in the American net of suspicion and summoned to appear before the House Committee.

Sam McCord protested angrily, stalked out of the courthouse immediately to do what the law could not get done in less than two months, and brought the entire community of Nome back into happy celebration in less than a day. Sam unleashed Dionysus to serve Eros well. In Chaplin's film, the King is tricked by his vanity into accepting a subpoena before the House Committee. His frightened and fawning lawyer joins him in a slapstick routine that will resolve the complication of the film's narrative — they are tangled in a firehose the King carries with him before the Committee. When he raises his hand to be sworn in, he has to lift the nozzle of the firehose in such a manner as to seem a finger of obscene insult to the Committee. The King does all this in innocent fear of the Committee's power, not at all in conscious defiance of its authority. But Chaplin's reaction to the viciousness of American disorder is an appropriate response of order and decency to expose the corruption of American society. Everyone in the hearing room is doomed to be doused by the firehose, which does its best, in a very symbolic manner, to purge the place of spiritual filth.

By submitting, then, the King exposes vice to its own inadequacy. This leads to little more than a resignation, however, because the end is the most bitter part. The King is allowed to leave America (he is glad to), but first he visits his little friend, Rupert Macabee, who has been taken into custody by federal agents. The purging of America is not complete without the tears of a defeated child. The King discovers Rupert has been "tortured" into giving the evidence his parents refused — he told the names of the colleagues he knew were his parents' communist friends. Rupert is humiliated, the King is appalled, and the film is dismaying as it comes to an end. America is no utopia, and it wishes to have nothing to do with the King's plans for utopia. There is little to be done for America, and better to be well out of it. While the little boy weeps in shame, the King flies away to his Queen in Paris. He leaves with the observation that it is "too crazy here."

INTELLECTUAL AND EMOTIONAL TORMENT of children is a symptom, *King in New York* asserts, of American cultural illness in the 1950s. Chaplin's film shows a disillusioned view of the utopia America has always been in the best sense of itself. It is shrewd of Chaplin to focus his analysis of the American malaise through the eyes of the alien, especially trained on the behavior of America's children. Time and again John Wayne's films were structured around his role as biological father of his children, spiritual father of his nation, of his culture. Although this role will again come to prominence in *Donovan's Reef* and *McLintock!*, it has not been significant in the comic films so far examined for his heroic status, from *A Lady Takes a Chance* through *Without Reservations,* to *North to Alaska.* Not even the family-oriented *Quiet Man* gives fatherhood a strong function; in that film, the hero's own past, his own childhood, has to be recovered and mastered before he can become the adult and husband who can give promise of a future with children.

North to Alaska is insistently a film without children. The only child in it is the 17-year-old Billy Pratt, played by one of the pop singers whose pale renditions of rock-and-roll are satirized in *A King in New York. North to Alaska* defines utopia as a place without children, without the distractions and encumbrances children would be to a life of uninhibited freedom and pursuit of erotic satisfactions. Yet children were becoming, just as Chaplin protested, the heroes of American culture. They are not merely the promise of the future, of new life to be shaped and directed by heroes like John Wayne—they are the heroes themselves, shaping, and directing the adults who have borne them and failed them. This is the theme of a strong domestic comedy of 1958, *Houseboat.*

It is an apt theme, expressing the rosy celebration Chaplin saw through dark glasses of vision. From *Bedtime for Bonzo* (1951) to *Teacher's Pet* (1957), value is determined by children's standards. It makes one think the otherwise mature science-fiction story of *The Incredible Shrinking Man* (1957) might be somewhere in its depths a satire of the child as (America's, technology's) hero. One of the most successful comedians of the time was the ever-childish Jerry Lewis.

What is supposed to be a celebration of the Dionysian spirit which drives American anarchy, as in *North to Alaska,* becomes instead a deflection from seriousness of joy to sad pleasure in sobriety among children. This is what happens in *Houseboat,* where the widowed father of three young children must learn responsibility and happiness from the instruction of his

children. Tom Winters (Cary Grant) is a government lawyer who lives in
Washington, D.C. This blatant symbol of American power takes his family
to live on a houseboat (on the Potomac?) to find its own little utopia of order
and happiness. The key relationship is that happiness comes only from
order, though the film is ambiguous and even misleading on this relationship. The family spends much of its time making the houseboat look much
like a suburban cottage, though it is supposed to be finding itself and its
direction independently of the modern world.

The sad thing about the film is that, although it mates primitive Cinzia
with stiff, abstracted Tom Winters, it does so by cutting Eros down to
childish size. Cinzia must learn, right along with Tom, that the children are
the real powers and the real arbiters of what is good. One of the striking
features of the film, in this respect, is that Tom has been sleeping with his
daughter, Elizabeth (about 11 years old), to protect her from fear of thunder
and storms. But he sleeps with her even when it is not thundering and
storming, so that Elizabeth comes to think of herself as her father's bed-
mate. Thus, when Elizabeth discovers Cinzia may be her father's lover, she
is jealous and worries about losing her place beside her father. Elizabeth
quizzes Cinzia: "Do married people sleep together?" Cinzia gives the snappy
answer, "In America sometimes, in Italy all the time." Cinzia finally wins
Tom's heart and takes Elizabeth's place in Tom's bed.

Houseboat might well be a satire of what is happening to America life,
but it is more a criticism of what has not happened to America—that it has
not centered children sufficiently in its vision of maturity. Chaplin's film
says that such a centering has perverted American values and American
political judgment, turning children into guilty monsters or mindlesss
machines while it has destroyed American openness to experience and
diversity of values. *Houseboat* could be a significant critique of the drifting
of American culture, the despiritualizing of intellectual experience in
America. But it does not. Instead, it turns the houseboat into a child's version of American modern life, taming European passion and deflecting
political awareness to concentrate on fishing and learning to swim.

The hero of *North to Alaska* could never be captured and tamed by
children, like the hero of *Houseboat;* nor could he ever be dismayed by the
spectacle of raucous good fun like the hero of *A King in New York.* Sam
McCord's only politics is to be anti-wife, and even that is taken from him
by his love for Angel. In McCord's Alaska, politics is interference in individual happiness (judges, soldiers), and so when Sam agrees to marry
Angel, perhaps he is admitting that politics can be fulfilling as well as interfering. Angel raises Sam's level of vision at the same time he frees her
from the decadence of an aimless life. Angel is redeemed as well as redeeming, Sam is liberated and liberating, Alaska itself is all the better for Sam's
angelic happiness.

"Guns" Donovan: *Donovan's Reef* (1963)

The island paradise of Manulani is far more hospitable to ideas of utopia than Alaska, and *Donovan's Reef* is a film with a larger notion of what utopia ought to be. It is a more ambitious film than *North to Alaska*, aiming to give a more complicated texture to the images of happiness, to draw those images from legends and tradition, to celebrate them in solemn festivals of high comedy, and to draw the human community together in a great reconciliation. Organizing these themes is the image of the family. Of course, the family has at *its* center the joys and problems of raising children.

Sam McCord's Alaska was utopian for uninhibited brawling and lovemaking, *and so* there could be no children of his world, or his heroic spirit could not have the expanse it required for full expression. Sean Thornton's Ireland was utopian for reconciliation of brawling with lovemaking, its children little more than a twinkle in the eyes of the hero. It is difficult to conceive of a comic paradise where children can have meaningful existence *as* children; they get in the way of essential happiness, as W.C. Fields so often discovered. One reason children are obstacles to comic fulfillment is that children are superfluous in the paradise of comedy.

Comedy reaches for a paradise of fulfillment and perfection. Children are undeveloped, and so they cannot *as* children be fulfilled or perfect. Not even the Romantic poets considered children as images of perfection; to them, children are symbols of the innocence and openness lost or repressed by adult experience. There is an agreeable logic to the banishment of children from paradise, where in its ideal state of unqualified happiness, paradise makes children of all its inhabitants.

Children, then, are different creatures in paradise than in the natural (or "fallen") world of reality, where they are merely promises of the future. In paradise there is no future, only an eternal present. To bring children into Manulani is to aim for comic fulfillment, but it is also to jeopardize the images of perfection that make up its paradise.

Donovan's Reef is built upon obvious religious images and ideas which strengthen and weaken the film, depending upon how much importance is attached to them. There is a trinity of heroes who saved the island from the Japanese during World War II — Guns Donovan, Boats Gilhooley (Lee Marvin), and Dr. William Dedham (Jack Warden). That was in the "past." Now there is a trinity of children who are the offspring of Dedham and the mysterious hereditary princess of the island, now dead. These three children, Lelani, Sally (Sarah), and Luki, duplicate the trinity which gives Manulani its sacred richness. They combine East and West, pagan with Christian, flesh with spirit.

ADULTS BREAKING DECORUM, departing from restraints of ceremony to affirm independent spirit—these are the norms of paradise.

Wayne as Michael Patrick Donovan, spanking Elizabeth Allen (as Amelia Dedham) in *Donovan's Reef,* **1963.**

The reason there are "really" no children in paradise is there are "really" no adults in paradise either: adults *are* children and, in a more difficult equation, children *are* adults. There is not much detail in the film to describe the lives of the children, apart from their lessons, their music, and a little bit of their play. The two younger children most enjoy the spectacle of adults at play, especially their play at fighting. Children like to fight, and in a world where the adults are children, naturally they like to fight too. The brawl that opens the story, when Boats Gilhooley returns again to celebrate Guns Donovan's birthday, is a happy communal ritual as essential to paradise as the two more solemn ceremonies at the center of the narrative. The joy of the children watching the fight is shared by all in the village, including priest, governor, merchants, and even the policeman (Mike Mazurki).

This play of fighting is the frame of the film, which opens when Gilhooley has to knock out a ship's bully to escape onto Manulani. The rhythm of the narrative is governed by this motif of fighting, coming to conclusion through Donovan's reconciliation with Amelia in the dusty street of the village. There too is some fighting, another enactment in Wayne's career of the Punch-and-Judy show. Amelia is dumped into the street from a passing, bumping jeep. She and Donovan engage in a verbal fight of love. They abuse one another into marriage while walking in front of the saloon Donovan has given to Gilhooley as a wedding present. In the closing moments of the film, Donovan and Amelia celebrate their engagement together on the rim of a fountain in the square: he pulls her across his knees and spanks her, like a child, and then they kiss, like adults.

Surrounding the courting couple of the film, then, is another courting couple. While the main narrative line is to bring Donovan together with Amelia Dedham, a secondary and reflecting line is to marry Boats Gilhooley to Miss Lafleur. Their marriage is an epitome of the paradox that marriage blesses and makes sacred the most profane of people, because Gilhooley is little more than an adolescent in mind and body—a state of confusion, and Miss Lafleur is little more than a fading flower of passion, innocence in a far-from-innocent body of delight. She loves the idea of marriage, and perhaps she loves even more the ceremony of marriage, since it will give her an occasion to wear the wedding dress she has dreamed of owning all her life. Gilhooley, meanwhile, is blessedly unaware of his impending marriage, since he is entranced by the toy train Amelia has given to him to play with at Christmas. Gilhooley's train and Miss Lafleur's dress (also a gift from Amelia) together represent the film's idea of marriage as sacred play.

Although Donovan's gift, the saloon (i.e., "Donovan's Reef"), has made it easier for Amelia to accept him as her husband, that saloon remains at the center of the life of the island and proves to be no "reef" of danger to anyone. The joy of drinking and brawling that go on there is the joy of, once again, Dionysus, a divine agent of comedy. At the back of the saloon, where Donovan lives, resides the other god of comedy, Apollo, where lessons are learned, Mozart is played, and the garden is neat and trim. Donovan is making a sacrifice of his saloon when he gives it to Gilhooley, but the sacrifice is, like most things lost in paradise, a gesture of individual surrender to community happiness.

The courtship of Guns Donovan and Amelia Dedham is familiar for John Wayne in his comic roles. It allows him to show love and affection, to enjoy human community, and to have fun in being alive. His pranks and rowdiness are the expressions of a childish spirit uninhibited from fear of really hurting anyone. In the scheme of the film's plot, his rowdinesss is important for attracting the love of a woman whose life has been withered, almost ruined by the joylessness, hypocrisy, and greed of a society as far from paradise as Boston is from Manulani. The kinds of fighting Boston sanctions are fights in the darkness of the heart, not in the bright light of the spirit as in Manulani. Amelia is saved from spiritual death to enjoy life fully with her father, family, friends, and lover on Manulani. Donovan and Amelia are children again, and that is their comic salvation.

THE BRAWLING AND DRINKING of *Donovan's Reef* are features of ceremony which make one kind of rhythm in the film; they are counterpointed by the singing, dancing, praying, and parading features of ceremony which make for another, complementary rhythm. These rhythms contain the energy of life and give it the comic shape it needs for its fulfillment. They are the systole/diastole of Dionysus and Apollo, of life itself. Each rhythm uniquely contributes to the shape of life, and either apart from the other (the film seems to say) might be damaging, even destructive, without the other. John Wayne's heroic image has little to do with the Apollonian, much with the Dionysian orders of ceremony.

Michael Patrick Donovan knows the difference between Mozart and Chopin (he corrects Amelia when she thinks she hears Chopin's music), runs at least two business operations (the saloon and a shipping company), helps the doctor and the priest, and once helped to protect the natives from invading soldiers. He is a person of adult responsibility, then, even though his identity is in his joy of play. He fights with Gilhooley, likes Miss Lafleur though he has no lust for her, boats, swims, drinks, fights the "Limey" Australian soldiers (whose leader is played by Wayne's son Patrick), and attends to details of the children's Christmas celebration. He takes them to find their Christmas tree, goes out into the storm to get Luki's baseball hat, and lets the Chinese merchants play with his slot machine. He is never drunk and he never hurts anyone in his fights. When, on the other hand, he courts, he does it with strength of purpose, intimidating the more "romantic" Marquis and awakening the erotic powers of Amelia Dedham (who tells him she did not know what a kiss was until he kissed her). Donovan is at his ease in rhythms of this kind of action, and he is clearly the heroic mover in it.

This is not so in other ceremonies of the film. Two set pieces lie at the narrative heart: the Christian celebration of Christmas in the leaky chapel, and the Polynesian ritual of honoring the traditional island princess. In the Christmas scene, Donovan sits quietly back in the audience as the priest conducts a service and others parade in a recreation of the story of the Magi. In his one noteworthy act of the scene, Donovan moves from his back chair to a front one to sit beside Amelia. This is at the prompting of Eros or Dionysus, but not certainly the Apollonian dignity more appropriate to the occasion (however compromised by its peculiar interpretation of the legend of the Magi). Donovan is observer, not participant in such ceremonies as these.

The same is true the next day, when Lelani is carried solemnly to her throne of state, where guests and dignitaries are greeted as they pay their ceremonial respects. Donovan is again at a distance. After Amelia has made her public gesture of recognition, loving her father, brother, and sisters, she immediately breaks away from the well-ordered group to find Donovan alone in the garden behind his saloon. She confronts him with the truth he had concealed from her. She is indignant he has been an instrument in her deception, and he is amused at how far she has come to fulfillment—even in this passionate outburst. He explains with a smile that he has "made a human being of her" in the process, and he is right. She may sputter at being called an old "maid," but she knows Donovan is essentially right. She shows it by beating him over the shoulders with her parasol and then pulling up her skirts to fume out of sight. The Polynesian ceremony has unveiled the truth of Amelia's kinship. In that, her eyes are opened to the truth of her attraction to Donovan himself.

Donovan's place is not in a church, leaky or otherwise, and it is not in the solemn ceremonies of royalty. His place is in gardens, saloons, bedrooms, mountain valleys, ocean bays, and flowered pools. Donovan is an expression of the "life force," the pandemic god whose medium is the elemental force of nature. When he and Amelia conclude their marriage vows to one another, it is appropriate they do it in the dusty street, covered with the earth itself, and on the rim of a public fountain, where instead of water there spreads out around the loving couple a great green fern, emblem of the life they affirm together.

IN 1963 THE ACADEMY AWARD for Best Picture went to *Tom Jones* (and to Tony Richardson, its director, for Best Director). With a large cast of successful and popular actors and actresses, this film roared to heights of sustained applause in the same year *Donovan's Reef* was greeted with disappointment and dismay even by admirers of John Ford. Youthful Albert Finney (age 27 at time of film's release) romped through the film with convincing lust and moral innocence as the bastard hero Tom Jones. He had a great script to work with, made by John Osborne, in an adaptation from the classical novel by Henry Fielding. And, just as important for his success, Finney had a clever director with epic ambitions in film art. It was a big film and a big event to start the decade.

Nevertheless, *Tom Jones* cannot survive the trials of time for a variety of reasons, some being the very ones which gave it initial popularity. The novel is a triumph of literary art universally agreed to. The film is great entertainment and technically versatile, but both its entertainment value *and* its technical versatility are borrowed from the story and style of the novel. More significantly, the film loses the novel's complication of thought and reflective power of strong intellect.

A splashy and noisy success, then, like *Tom Jones* will probably, maybe inevitably, diminish in interest and value for succeeding audiences, when a more quiet, less ambitious and certainly less commercially successful film like *Donovan's Reef* may increase in value and perhaps in interest. Both are comic films with comic heroes, but a comparison reveals how different comedy can be. Tom Jones is a youthful rogue on the road learning as he lives and survives, Guns Donovan an aging reveler well settled after a life of adventure and learning. Both have good hearts, make lasting friends, and triumph in their main affairs of love. Both actors perform their roles by strategies of "reaction" to events around them, but Wayne's Donovan does more than react to the threat of Amelia's invasion—he reorganizes society on the island, orchestrates its movements, and makes it possible for Amelia to become "a better human being" as a part of it. Finney's Tom Jones organizes nothing, much less reorganize a well established society to accommodate his youthful energies. The difference is important, because Donovan proves to be a persuasive comic hero, while Tom Jones is no more than Fielding had shown him to be in the novel, a parody of the hero, subject to comic correction as he learns to fit into a prearranged order of things.

Donovan shows how scheming can be put to comic and happy uses, turning a narrow-minded bigot into a tolerant, large-hearted human being. Tom Jones shows how a warm-hearted young man with natural passions (in the eyes of some, "polymorphous perversities") is to be knocked and tricked into shape, to fit into a society which will not be changed from its coarse, crude, even selfish and bigoted ways, a society which does not expand to accept the new but instead rejects the rebel or tightens the noose to make him fit in.

There is much rowdiness and love of drinking in *Donovan's Reef*, to create its atmosphere of feasting and community. The same is true of *Tom Jones*, but the differences are large. The big scenes of *Tom Jones*, in the country or in the city, in the fields or in the bedrooms, display a vulgarity and brutal interpretation of gusto, of Dionysian joy. One of the most lovable of the characters, Squire Western (Hugh Griffith) is also one of the most brutal and coarse; he is what Tom could easily turn into if he is not rescued by warm-hearted Sophie Western (Susanna York). The scene of the hunting, a sport in which women as well as men take delight, is "great fun" (as reviewers of the film called the film as a whole): the hounds' pursuit of the deer, men and women following close behind, climaxes in a bloody dismemberment of the deer. Consistent with the film's cynical parody of censorship, the hounds ravage the deer in a thicket to conceal details of the slaughter from direct view. However, when the hunters arrive to wrestle the carcass from the hounds, the blood and gore are held up for clear view. Hunters are identified with hounds, to expose the brutality of human nature in general, but particularly when it claims heroic status.

Tom Jones panders to audience tastes for such bloody adventure, just as it does for lascivious and sexually obscene ones. *Donovan's Reef* has adventures, even a hunt of a kind, but in none of its rituals of the chase does it pander or condescend to coarsen the pleasures of comedy. The "hunt" in

Donovan's Reef is to find a Christmas tree; Amelia's journey to Manulani is also a figurative "hunt" for her father. The violence of *Donovan's Reef* is not brutal, bloody, or even (paradoxically) insensitive. In the barroom brawl with the Australian honor guard, the sensitivity of the brawlers is emphasized by their courtesy of codes, fair play, and relaxation. It yields to the order of tolerance and generosity. The brawling of *Tom Jones* is mean spirited, intense, and desperate, yielding to an order of force, selfishness, and hypocrisy. *Tom Jones* makes fun of the way things are, not only of what they may have been in Fielding's novel or in Fielding's time. *Tom Jones* therefore comes to a depressing conclusion in its twisting of the comic spirit to serve ironic principles: it sacrifices its joyous, uninhibited hero to a joyless, much inhibited world of social reality.

THE ACADEMY AWARD WINNER for Best Picture in 1964 was *My Fair Lady*, which also picked up Best Actor award for Rex Harrison, and the Best Actress award went to Julie Andrews in *Mary Poppins*. Both of those films can still be seen on a regular basis on a number of occasions on American television, and both surely are in the genre of comedy, with a good deal of help from music to make them sparkle. Both are "uplifting" and maybe even "educational." Though Shaw's bite in *Pygmalion* has been blunted considerably in the happiness of *My Fair Lady*, the film does retain the point of complementary educations for both hero and heroine, which makes it a little more complicated than the vastly simple lessons of *Mary Poppins*.

Mary Poppins is designed for children's tastes and it panders to childish imagination. *My Fair Lady* is designed from an adult comic drama, but it also does a good deal of pandering to childlike tastes and imagination. As a story of educating and cultivating, *My Fair Lady* (like *Pygmalion*) uses a thematic point to reverse romantic conventions of courtship. This is an attitude typical of comedies directed by Howard Hawks, whose film of *Man's Favorite Sport?* also appeared in 1964, in which the "professional" sportsman, Roger Willoughby (Rock Hudson) is taught his own sport, fishing, by the amateur, Abigail Page (Paula Prentiss). The stories of all three films make more of the comic heroines than of the comic heroes, especially and absurdly in *Mary Poppins*, but more interestingly and revealingly in *Man's Favorite Sport?*

The question of the title is answered in the lyric of the theme song which introduces, in its bubbly, bouncy way, the titles and credits of *Man's Favorite Sport?* "That's the way it's been since the world began, /The favorite sport of men is girls!" However, in many delightful reversals and double entendres, the film shows the really more important fact is that "the favorite sport of women is men." From the moment of the opening when Abigail takes Roger's parking place, to the close when he climbs into her

sleeping bag to float off to a very wet paradise, Abigail shows Roger for the
fraud he is, in his claim to knowledge and in his claim to masculinity. She
turns him into a fisherman and into a man.

The comic effects of Hawks's films derive from an underlying assump-
tion shared with *Donovan's Reef*, that men are aggressors made vulnerable
by their pride in aggression, that women are equally aggressive but less
vulnerable and therefore more proud as they are more powerful. *Man's
Favorite Sport?* emphasizes the female aggression to humiliate the male.
Donovan's Reef emphasizes the female pride to justify the male aggression.
Whether one or the other is "right" or "wrong" is less important than how
each employs the conventions of such attitudes to develop the image of the
comic hero. When Donovan meets Amelia, she falls immediately—into
water and then in love, much later. When Roger meets Abigail, he falls up-
side down trying to get into her car, and only much later does he fall in love
with her. Donovan is aggressive even when he does nothing, Roger is
foolish when he tries to be aggressive. When Roger finds Abigail soundly
asleep in his bed, he is wild with anxiety and runs for a sleeping bag for protection; when Donovan finds Miss Lafleur in his bed, he heaves her out the
window into a fish pond. When Roger finally kisses Abigail (insisting he
"hates domineering females!"), she swoons (as Hawks intercuts with a scene
of colliding locomotives), but Roger thinks she doesn't like it. When
Donovan kisses Amelia, she confesses it is the best of all possible kisses.

George Washington McLintock: *McLintock!* (1963)

McLintock! is a film with many themes and many scenes, many
characters and many stories, but they all gather around a single image, a
single character, George Washington McLintock, who is himself virtually
a tribute to the heroic image of John Wayne. At the time of this film, Wayne
was undergoing some of the most difficult days of his life. He was trying to
recover from financial reverses after production of *The Alamo*, he was griev-
ing for the deaths of several good friends (including Ward Bond and Grant
Withers), and he was beginning to realize how mortal even he could be,
since he was feeling some of the pains diagnosed in 1964 as cancer of the
lung. He was a man besieged, an actor criticized, and a hero in doubt.

As George Washington McLintock he asserts a vigor of body and spirit
to defy the doubt, answer the critics, and break the siege. Here is a character
who takes the name of America's foremost, almost legendary, national hero.
McLintock is, like George Washington, the founder of a country (helped to
tame the Mesa Verde, built a town named after him). Wayne has gathered
around him in the making of the film many members of his family (son
Michael produced the film, son Patrick acts a main role in it, daughter Aissa
appears in it, and brother Bob worked as production supervisor); he has also
with him many of his professional family including the director Andrew

McLaglen, son of his friend and colleague, Victor (who had died in 1959), Bruce Cabot, Bob Steele, Chuck Robertson, and, of course, Maureen O'Hara. He has surrounded himself with friends and family, and he produced a community of feeling based on his presence, proud and vital.

When Bunny Dull (Edgar Buchanan) observes, "I can see you're in good health," McLintock responds, "Never felt better! Contrary to what you may hear!" This is early in the film, in its second scene, set as a notice to the film's audience as much as it is for the characters in the film's story. Indeed, the film may overdo the insistence on McLintock's vigor and energy, subjecting the hero to many a fall and tumble as it does. Wayne actually did hurt himself in one of the stunts, though obviously he does not do all the hardest ones used in the film. The falls are important, however, because the hero is not a cowboy romantic so much as he is a cowboy clown who sometimes rises to be a comic hero.

THE FACTS OF FAMILY AND FRIENDS in the film's production are imaged in the film as characters who carry the critical theme of reconciliation, so important to the films of Wayne's last years in his career. This theme, related to the genre which has been called "comedy of re-marriage,"[26] is emphatically represented by the story of McLintock's reunion with his wife, Katherine (O'Hara). Secondary episodes which reinforce this theme involve the courtship and engagement of Becky McLintock (Stefanie Powers) and Devlin Warren (Patrick Wayne), Louise Warren (Yvonne De Carlo) and Sheriff Lord (Chuck Roberson). Further out from the center are the affairs of Ben Sage (Bruce Cabot) and his son Young Ben (Edward Faulkner), who stands for an unstable variable in matters of love (he disapproves his sister's friendship for an Indian, and he endangers the Indians' lives when he keeps a Sooner's daugher out overnight). Finally, to set the mark for domestic insipidity is the family of Matt Douglas (Gordon Jones)—the land agent whose silly son, Junior (Jerry Van Dyke) tries to woo Becky McLintock herself.

The theme of family unity is bound with the larger theme of national identity, in which problems of politics and race are posed for solution by McLintock and friends. The key figure to make McLintock's family concerns into a symbolic image for national ones is the governor of the territory, Cuthbert H. Humphrey (Robert Lowery), who has his eyes on McLintock's wife, his mind on McLintock's property, and his hands on the bureaucratic reins of power. Governor Humphrey is a bumbling fool, like all the bureaucrats in the story, including especially the Indian agent, Agard (Strother Martin), who has much difficulty seeing (as he is constantly losing his glasses) and cannot even ride a horse properly. The only government official who has any sense is the sheriff, who shows a proper respect for McLintock by calling him "mister," to the irritation of Douglas. The most

This time as George Washington McLintock administering a spanking to Maureen O'Hara, as Katherine McLintock, in *McLintock!*, 1963.

serious threats to McLintock's family reunion and reconciliation are from Douglas's son Junior and from Governor Humphrey whose formal office has temporarily dazzled Katherine's eyes for social importance.

The film's narrative, however, is too slapstick and too episodic to keep a serious tone in dealing with these threats, and it is too interested in watching the character of McLintock himself to develop any single theme with focused and sustained attention. As soon as Katherine returns to rejoin her husband in McLintock, after a two-year separation, the power of his presence overwhelms all her determination to leave again, diminishes the stature of the governor, and conquers Katherine's will to resist McLintock's coarse but real charm. As for daughter Becky, whose return home from school is the occasion for Katherine's return as well, this young woman has genuine education to undergo when she comes home to the substantial West after a sojourn in the unsubstantial East. Becky is much taken with what she and her mother call "style," a word used to describe what is really pretentiousness, affectation, shallowness, and snobbishness—all represented by Junior Douglas and Governor Humphrey. Like her mother, Becky has to be won from her emotional estrangement.

Conflicts of manners with morals, education and experience, and liberty with law are reflected in most scenes of the film. All drive toward resolution in two highlights of the narrative: Dev's spanking of Becky, and McLintock's spanking of Kate. The first climaxes exposure of Junior's unworthiness, the second climaxes exposure of Kate's emotional honesty. Neither scene will entertain an audience offended by stereotyped images of male dominance, brute power, and sexual politics, because such images are offensive to serious minds concerned with real problems in the real world. But these are images of comic gusto, subordinate to comic harmony, and instruments of the comic spirit.

BEHIND THE SPANKING SCENES is an "ethos" of power which asserts the primacy of energy in affairs of sex and love. It is not a completely attractive notion, but it is an ancient one which gives particular shape to comic experience as a happy use of such power to punish dishonesty, purge hypocrisy from social relationships, and create harmony in human community. Tragedy befalls those who misuse or abuse this ethos, but happy comedy rewards those who understand its purposes and apply it with proper restraint. This is the way of George Washington McLintock, who will not use power against others unless they first insult him or those he loves; nor will he use it to keep those he loves, unless they drive him to it, as Becky had Dev and as Kate does him.

He does not understand why Kate has left him; she angrily walked out without explaining, some two years earlier than the opening of the film's story. He is puzzled and vulnerable in his ignorance of her motives, though in the real world he should have had plenty of clues. In the comic world, his vulnerability to Kate is in his ignorance of women generally; he has to learn to understand his wife better, if he is to become a better human being himself. He is a symbol of sexuality, and as such he is attractive to all the women of the film. Many images are employed to make this identity clear and strong. The bull of his weathervane is a symbolic image of his character: he tosses his hats with unerring accuracy to top the bull on his roof, and it is not only when he is drunk that he can do it so well. Kate's admiring words at the end are a double entendre for the deed itself: "Three hundred and

ten times! Without a miss! That's a record!" In the first scene a bull passes
by McLintock when he comes out to greet the day and the children line up
to race for his hat; the bull is a pet that grazes right up to the front porch.
So as not to relax the identification, the film makes an emphatic, though
somewhat obscene, pun when McLintock later invites Ben Sage to "a few
hands of stud," while in the background a bull is mounting a cow in the
stockyard corral.

McLintock is a fertility figure, even though his mate has left him
without explanation. When the explanation finally does come, it is far from
surprising and it is consistent with the comic figure of the sexual hero—
Kate was jealous at the sight of lipstick on the hero's shirt. Various scenes
show he has not been wanting for female companionship during his wife's
absence, but most important is the appearance of his relationship with his
new cook, Louise Warren. On the evening when Louise wants to tell him
she is to marry Sheriff Lord, McLintock makes her get drunk with him (or
more drunk with him) under the eyes of a comically furious Katherine.
McLintock tries to do the gentlemanly thing and escort wobbly Louise up
the stairs when both take the first of several tumbles. With Louise dazed
on top of him, drunken McLintock tries to ward off the "suspicious" eyes
of an inquiring Kate: "Now, Katherine, are you going to believe what you
see,—or what I tell you?"

Before the slapstick is finished in the scene, all three fall down the
stairs again, and the hero gives up entirely as the heroic wife carries the
cook up to bed on her own shoulders. It is a funny reversal of heroic roles,
balancing the epic chase of the conclusion. In that episode, emerging from
the holiday festival of Independence Day celebrations, Kate McLintock
leads her husband on a merry chase until he catches her, spanks her, and
leaves her to pursue him most honestly at last. It is a reprise of the conclusions Wayne had enacted in *North to Alaska, Donovan's Reef,* and with
Maureen O'Hara herself in *The Quiet Man,* but it is special for its greater
burlesque of the more "serious" scene in *The Quiet Man* and for its greater
complication than the one in *North to Alaska* with Capucine as Angel.

Celebrating the Fourth of July, the community of McLintock dissolves
into riotous, chaotic laughter as an audience for its hero's triumph over its
heroine's stubborn pride. The crowd has gathered and enjoys this as the
grandest scene of the day's festivities. The odyssey begins with increasing
energy of pursuit; this is the race that really matters, the man's race for his
woman, the husband's trial of courtly worthiness—as determined by Pan
and Dionysus, rather than by mannered Apollo. Kate leads her man on a
merry chase indeed: from the haystack, across picnic tables, up a ladder,
into a horse trough, through a mud puddle, until she is caught, given her
spanking, and left to make a great decision—to run after and now chase
McLintock himself. She pursues him all the way home to make their peace

where erotic comedy properly comes to an end, in the bedroom. The good humor of the scene, an American Western version of the Roman Saturnalia and Carnival, is pointed by the almost muted "threat" Kate hurls at McLintock as he begins to "raise his hand" on her now exposed posterior: she tells him he will "rue the day," an expression Wayne's own heroes have used many a time in previous films.

THE HAPPY PUBLIC FESTIVAL of the conclusion is a proper comic end for the main plot of the story, as McLintock wins his wife back by the only means she would ever accept. It is, however, not the only point made in the film that Eros and Hymen are happily gratified by ritualized and stylized violence. This is a chaos which confirms a spiritual harmony threatened by a more sinister force because it is a more dishonest one. That force is the consequence of moral dishonesty and social pride, represented in the many stereotypes of the film's cast of characters. The blatant use of stereotypes, to buttress the stylized clowning of Wayne and O'Hara, is a mark of the film's self-conscious artistry and thematic assertiveness.

These stereotypes express McLintock's insistence on clarity of values, honesty of motives, and openness of intentions. Even the problems between Kate and McLintock occurred because Kate was not forthcoming about her reasons for leaving him, and Becky's willful blindness to Junior's silliness could have ruined her life in a world of greater "reality," of stylish sophistication and selfish pleasures. Where stereotypes are conventions of public significance, images of honest prejudices, they are instruments of real communication and can be forces of genuine integrity. There is artistic ingenuity behind the absence of subtlety, because the images and traits which together make up stereotypes are nothing more than the generalizations which are necessary for civilized communication. They can be abused, they can be untrue, and they can be misunderstood, even in this film.

But when the Chinese cook, Ching (H.W. Gim), waves a meat cleaver at McLintock and others, threatening to kill himself because McLintock has hired a new cook to replace him, the image of the Oriental in American is not divisive because it is a stereotype in the film. There is racism only if the aim is to separate, dehumanize, and alienate the persons represented by the image. It is dangerous to use, but the comedy of *McLintock!* risks the danger to make a more generous point: all people are one family. Ching feels his honor is at stake when McLintock brings Mrs. Warren to cook; he says, "I kill myself!" as McLintock searches for the right thing to say, to reconcile the man: "I'm not talkin' about firin' you! I'm retirin' ya! You've been rustlin' food for us for thirty years. We're going to put you out to pasture. All you have to do is give advice. Be one of the family." This may not be the most diplomatic way to make the point, but motive and consequence are the same: "Be one of the family." Ching relents in the face of Drago's childish threat to cut off Ching's pigtail: "All right! All right! I be one of the family," even as he insists this is a "pretty crummy family."

The epic mud-hole fight at the center of the film is a great put-down of civilized white America, as all except the Indians fall unceremoniously into the mud to the amusement of the stereotyped Indians. Their dignity is compromised, however, even as they are generally represented as more civilized and more restrained than the whites. The Indians are exaggerated in the character of the chief victim himself, old Running Buffalo, who cries out his refrain of "More whiskey!" They all turn to leave when Running Buffalo tells McLintock, standing soaked in mud as he is, that it has been a good "party," but since there is "no whiskey," they will leave the whites to their muddy mess. Several points of ambivalence are raised by this figure of Running Buffalo, a pitiful relic of the past (he had once been an honorable adversary, as both McLintock and Drago reveal), but there is no ambivalence or ambiguity in the point that the plight of the Indians, including Running Buffalo, is a consequence of white intolerance and selfishness, not a natural condition of their debased humanity.

The point has been made again and again in Wayne's films, though it has not so often been a subject of his comedies as in *McLintock!* The Indians are sterotyped for the message of comedy, that human beings are mortal together and together they can transcend their mortality. In the meantime, between the time of ignorant division and the time of enlightened community, many characters are twisted and made grotesque, like Running Buffalo and Ching, the Chinese cook.

MCLINTOCK, explaining his way of life to Becky while he tells her what he is leaving to her in his will, says, "I work for everybody in these United States." It is an assertion John Wayne could be making for the benefit of all his audience, then and now. McLintock is a stereotype of the cowboy, the range master, the American macho individualist, the bully with a great heart, and so forth, but the stereotype is charged with a special energy of meaning when it is aimed at an audience for which George Washington is also a "stereotype" especially appropriate to be noticed on the Fourth of July. It is, as Drago says during the chase scene in the end, "A great day!" because it is a day of independence through community, and neither the independence nor the community is possible without the images of identification which are sometimes called "stereotypes." One image which asserts both the individuality of independence and the sociality of community is the image of the hero, who is uniquely comic because he is both one and many at the same time. The romance hero wanders alone, the tragic hero is sacrificed alone, and the ironic hero is alone in detachment: only the comic hero, fully realized, is both himself and all others, single in his integrity and multiple in his identity, atypical only because he is so completely typical.

The sixties was a decade of parody, mockery, and increasingly dark satire, and so it was a time for streaks of comedy in popular film. Wayne's own career had been marked by mockery, self parody, and sometimes even dark irony and some satire, but generally in his later comic films there is little tendency to be ironic and much impulse to be magnanimous. In films like *North to Alaska, Donovan's Reef,* and *McLintock!,* with unique exceptions, even the opponents of the hero enjoy the fun of the fights; the exceptions are Frankie Canon in *North to Alaska* and the territorial governor in *McLintock!* Everyone, without exception, on Manulani enjoys a part in the community of *Donovan's Reef.* Frankie Canon is still able to crack a joke about his cigar, though soaked with mud and thoroughly humiliated (repudiated). The silly governor of *McLintock!* suffers only in his pride, punished only with (rotten) egg in his face. There are a couple of "goats" to be marked for exile from the happy community, but they are marked with a sign they share with the heroes themselves: the bond of a common nature ties Sam McCord with Frankie Canon, and G.W. McLintock with Governor Humphrey, though the heroes affirm it and the villains deny it.

Generic conventions and stereotypes make them easy to imitate, and easy to mock. If other films parody from respect, they affirm a common identity with the predecessor or model film, somewhat as the comic hero mocks the comic villain in a generous way: to acknowledge a common identity endangered by misunderstanding. In the case of films parodying with respect, the parody aims at loving correction with artistic tribute. Stereotypes of charcter, plot, and theme provide a continuity of identity from one genre to another, from an original to a parody. When the product of the performance of the stereotype is lifeless, mechanical, and unselfconscious, then it is in danger of decay into mere machinery, mere distraction. Some comic films, like some comic heroes, try to rescue the original spirit of comedy endangered by mechanical performances of stereotype; other films, less comic and more ironic, aim to destroy the machinery itself, banish the culprits into outer darkness.

Ready for a searching self-examination in the sixties, popular film could look back to what Jacques Tati had been doing in his work of comedy, from *Jour de Fête* in 1948 to *Mon Oncle* in 1958. Both of those films marvelously continued the generous styles of great clowns like Buster Keaton, and especially *Mon Oncle* put to searching comic analysis the alienating effects of urban living in the mid-twentieth century. By 1967, with *Playtime,* Tati had pressed that analysis toward a limit which touched upon darkness, an emptiness in lives crushed and squeezed by the gadgetry of a mechanical civilization. Character struggles to survive in *Mon Oncle* and perhaps fails to survive in *Playtime;* in these films, the distinction between stereotype and character has been lost. When a person tries to find character in a world of machines and stereotypes, that person is alone and the world is lost. Tati's

John Wayne, shortly before his death.

characters, like Chaplin's, never give up trying to be a part of that world, though the more they try, the more desperate they become, and the more distant they move away from it.

The aesthetic experience that matters for the audience of a film is to realize it is itself the target, so that it is awakened from its own machinelike, stereotyped existence to make a place for the spirit of the comic hero. The satire of such experience is a therapeutic weapon against irony of division and detachment. Tati's heroes are themselves stereotypes, categories of convention, and emblems of ideology, but they are distinguished from those who deny them by their strong self-awareness *as* stereotypes in need of company. This qualitative difference of self awareness saves them as heroic models, and it differentiates affectionate parody from hostile satire. As the films of Tati illustrate, the affection can, over time, turn into hostility as the self awareness of the hero turns into desperate alienation.

A feature *Jour de Fête, Mon Oncle,* and *Playtime* have in common is that they target American culture, its machinelike efficiencies and unselfconscious aggressiveness, as objects of laughter. At the same time, they confess attraction to the objects they satirize. This is a forceful point of parody, the attraction to imitate while displaying a difference for room to "improve." Film artists, including directors as well as actors, generally outside America could exploit the advantage of their natural distance from it to make America, its culture and its art, objects of parody and satire, *for* an American popular audience. All of the genre films of Hollywood invite such responses, especially the detective films (of Bogart) in France, the zany comedy (Jerry Lewis), again in France, and the western romances, virtually everywhere in the world.

The Japanese films of Akira Kurosawa particularly made a mark on American self-examination in the sixties, the time of John Wayne's own best comic era and also the time of his most ambiguous reputation for Americans. The man had become identified with his image as actor, and that image had been reduced to a stereotype, but it was a stereotype which had a powerful impact upon many, especially foreign, audiences. Directors and artists might increasingly target or use the Wayne-image-stereotype to their own purposes, but Kurosawa showed more generally how the principle of such use could be put to artistic purposes at the same time he showed respect for the American culture whose stereotypes he used.

Yojimbo (1961) is a timely, classic instance. Kurosawa has often been quoted as acknowledging his obligations to the films of John Ford, and Toshiro Mifune could just as well have acknowledged some obligation to the stereotyped image of John Wayne, some of whose gestures and expressions are present in Mifune's characters. Sanjuro the unemployed samurai (Mifune) enters the frame of the film in a manner like Shane (Alan Ladd), confronts villains in the main street like Gary Cooper in *High Noon* (1952), and cleans up a town like Henry Fonda in *My Darling Clementine* (1946), but none of these actors had the swagger of Sanjuro/Mifune, the arrogance of confidence he shows by turning his back, not only to the brutes and thugs of the story, but to the camera itself. He walks like a machine, almost lurches in his movements, and yet he has a grace to redeem it all. These are characteristics much more those of John Wayne than Alan Ladd or Henry Fonda, but they are characteristics which have made Wayne more often the target of criticism than the model for praise.

Until, it should be argued, the foreign directors and actors took it up. Then critics, like Pauline Kael, for example, could appreciate the art which had looked like natural awkwardness in the home-grown products. *Yojimbo* was, to such American critics, wonderfully boisterous, even in its obsessive focus on violence, which could be dismissed as a "satire" with tongue-in-cheek gusto. The violence of *Yojimbo* may be exuberant, while it is boring (to such critics) in *McLintock!* Nevertheless, *Yojimbo* represents what the foreign view can do to make Americans aware of their own lives, as the stereotypes which represent those lives in their films. Wayne might be doing the same thing, but he could only act against his own reputation for it to be recognized, and too much of that merely created yet another stereotype. But when someone like Mifune does it, swaggers with a swivel at his hips, and then pauses to scratch (the fleas in?) his hair, the stereotype suddenly leaps out for detached inspection — and appreciation.

McLintock is a "boss" who does not exploit his community, though his opponents would like to have others think so. He is set against their motives of division, because his impulse is comic rather than ironic. His is what W.B. Yeats describes in his *Autobiography* as the "imperious impulse [which] held all together." When this is turned to ironic effect, it will produce a Mel Brooks kind of a boss in *Blazing Saddles* (1974), where the satire is acidic and the parody is alienating: the genre and its stereotypes completely collapse in *Blazing Saddles*, whose conclusion is a chaos because there is no "imperious impulse" to hold it all together any more. Whether characteristic of the time or merely characteristic of its director, *Blazing Saddles* does show what can happen when American art turns against its own stereotypes.

On the other hand, more immediate to *McLintock!*, Sergio Leone began to parody American stereotypes and values by mediation. He looked at American culture through Kurosawa's film of *Yojimbo* and produced the wonder of *Fistful of Dollars* in 1964. The result is to recreate the heroic, alienated cowboy-gunman, but with a new difference, which catapulted the career of Clint Eastwood, whose career has been a logical succession to John Wayne.

There is little fun to the rituals of *Fistful of Dollars*, where the humor is in the exaggeration of events more than of characters. There is even respect for machinery in the film, expressed through the "exuberance" of its display. A heavy hand employs the machinery of *Fistful of Dollars*, in style as well as in theme, and the best example is in the Stranger's making armor for his "heart" while convalescing from his beating. This might not be noticeable at all, in the world of generic stereotypes, unless contrasted with the same episode *it* imitates in *Yojimbo*, where Sanjuro "plays" with a dagger and a floating leaf for his target. There is no play in the Stranger's convalescence. *Fistful of Dollars* recognizes the American stereotypes because they have been isolated by *Yojimbo*. *Fistful of Dollars*, however, uses them as weapons of criticism and satire against American culture, while *Yojimbo* makes them into expressions of affection for the weaknesses of American culture as well as for its strengths. That affection of respect and admiration, critical esteem and keen-eyed regard, has been earned especially by the heroic image of John Wayne in comedy, irony, tragedy, and romance.

John Wayne Filmography

Primary sources for this filmography are the credits appearing in the films themselves. In addition, the sources listed at the end of the filmography have been consulted.

Brown of Harvard (MGM, 1925). ¶*Cast:* William Haines; Jack Conway; Francis X. Bushman, Jr.; Mary Brian. **John Wayne** doubled for Francis X. Bushman as football player; Wayne not billed.

Bardelays the Magnificent (MGM, 1926). ¶*Cast:* John Gilbert. **John Wayne** as a spear-carrying guard.

The Drop Kick (British title **Glitter**; First National, 1927). ¶*Director* Millard Webb. ¶Richard Barthelmess in starring role. Also Barbara Kent, Dorothy Revier. **Wayne** is a member of the football team from University of Southern California shown playing a game in the film. **Wayne** is unbilled. ¶Released September 25.

Mother Machree (Fox, 1928), 75 min. ¶*Director* John Ford; *scenarist* Gertrude Orr, *from novel by* Rita Johnson Young; *photographer* Chester Lyons; *editors and title-writers* Katherine Hilliker, H.H. Caldwell. ¶Belle Bennett (Ellen McHugh); Neil Hamilton (Brian McHugh); Philippe De Lacy (Brian, as child); Pat Somerset (Robert De Puyster); Victor McLaglen (Terrence O'Dowd); Ted McNamara (Harpist of Wexford); John Mac-

Sweeney (Irish priest); Eulalie Jensen (Rachel van Studdiford); Constance Howard (Edith Cutting); Ethel Clayton (Mrs. Cutting); William Platt (Pips); Jacques Rollens (Signor Bellini); Rodney Hildebrand (Brian McHugh, Sr.); Joyce Wirard (Edith Cutting, as child); Robert Parrish (Child). **Wayne** is unbilled. ¶Released October.

Four Sons (Fox, 1928), 100 min. ¶*Director* John Ford; *scenarist* Philip Klein, *from the novel Grandma Bernie Learns Her Letters by* I.A.R. Wylie; *photographers* George Schneiderman, Charles G. Clarke; *music arranger* S.L. Rothafel; *theme* "Little Mother" *by* Erno Rapee, Lee Pollack; *editor* Margaret V. Clancey; *title writers* Katherine Hilliker, H.H. Caldwell. ¶Margaret Mann (Fraue Bernle); James Hall (Joseph Bernle); Charles Morgon (Joann Bernle); George Meeker (Andres Bernle); Francis X. Bushman, Jr. (Franz Bernle); June Collyer (Annabelle Bernle); Albert Gran (Postman); Earle Foxe (Maj. Von Stomm); Frank Reicher (Headmaster); Jack Pennick (Joseph's American friend); Archduke Leopold of Austria (German Captain); Hughie Mack (Innkeeper); Wendell Franklin (James Henry); August Tollaire (Mayor); Ruth

Mix (Johann's girl); Robert Parrish (Child); Michael Mark (Von Stomm's orderly); L.J. O'Conner (Aubergiste). **Wayne,** whose presence is uncertain, is unbilled. ¶Released February.

Hangman's House (Fox, 1928), 80 min. approx. (6,430 ft.). Silent. ¶*Director* John Ford; *scenarist* Marion Orth, *from story by* Donn Byrne *adapted by* Philip Klein; *photographer* George Schneiderman; *editor* Margaret V. Clancey; *title writer* Malcolm Stuart Boylan. ¶Victor McLaglen (Citizen Hogan); Hobart Bosworth (James O'Brien, Lord Chief Justice); June Collyer (Connaught O'Brien); Larry Kent (Dermott McDermott); Earle Foxe (John Darcy); Eric Mayne (Legionnaire colonel); Joseph Burke (Neddy Joe); Belle Stoddard (Anne McDermott); **John Wayne,** as racetrack spectator, is unbilled; Jack Pennick. ¶Released May 13.

Words and Music (Fox, 1929), 81 min. Sound; also in a silent version. ¶*Director* James Tinling; *associate* Frank Merlin; *writer* Andrew Bennison, *from a story by* Frederick Hazlitt Brennan, Jack McEdwards; *cinematographers* Charles G. Clarke, Charles Van Enger, Don Anderson; *musical director* Arthur Kay; *editor* Ralph Dixon; *executive producer* Chandler Sprague. ¶Lois Moran (Mary Brown); David Percy (Phil Denning); Helen Twelvetrees (Dorothy Blake); William Orlamond (Pop Evans); Elizabeth Patterson (Dean Crockett); **Duke Morrison** (Pete Donahue); Frank Albertson (Skeet Mulroy); Tom Patricola (Hannibal); Eddie Bush, Paul Gibbons, Bill Seckler, Ches Kirkpatrick (Biltmore Quartet); Bubbles Crowell (Bubbles); Ward Bond (Ward); Richard Keene, Dorothy Ward, Collier Sisters, Muriel Gardner, Dorothy Jordan, Helen Parrish, Jack Wade, Vina Gale, Arthur Springer, Harriet Griffith, John Griffith, Helen Hunt, Charles Huff (bits). ¶Released August 18.

Salute (Fox, 1929), 86 min. Sound; also in a silent version. ¶*Director* John Ford; James Kevin McGuinness, *from screen story by* Tristram Tupper, John Stone; *dialogue* James K. McGuinness; *photographer* Joseph H. August; *editor* Alex Troffey; *titles* Wilbur Morse Jr. ¶George O'Brien (Cadet John Randall); Helen Chandler (Nancy Wayne); Stepin' Fetchit (Smoke Screen); William Janney (Midshipman Paul Randall); Frank Albertson (Midshipman Albert Edward Price); Joyce Compton (Marion Wilson); Cliff Dempsey (Maj. Gen. Somers); Lumsden Hare (Rear Adm. Randall); David Butler (Navy coach); Rex Bell (Cadet); John Breeden (Midshipman); Ward Bond, **John Wayne** (Football players). ¶Released September 1.

Men Without Women (Fox, 1930), 77 min. ¶*Director* John Ford; *stage director* Andrew Bennison; *scenarist* Dudley Nichols, *from the story* "Submarine" by Ford, James Kevin McGuinness; *photographer* Joseph H. August; *music* Peter Brunelli, Glen Knight; *editor* Paul Weatherwax; *art director* William Darling; *associate producer* James Kevin McGuinness. ¶Kenneth MacKenna (Chief Torpedoman Burke); Frank Albertson (Ensign Price); Paul Page ("Handsome"); Pat Somerset (Lt. Digby, R.N.); Walter McGrail (Cobb); Stuart Erwin (Jenkins, radio operator); Warren Hymer (Kaufman); J. Farrell McDonald (Costello); Roy Stewart (Capt. Carson); Warner Richmond (Lt. Comdr. Bridewell); Harry Tenbrook (Dutch Winkler); Ben Hendricks, Jr. (Murphy); George Le Guera (Pollock); Charles Gerard (Com. Weymouth); **John Wayne** (bit, as sailor carrying messages); Robert Parrish. ¶Premiere January 31, released February 9.

Rough Romance (Fox, 1930). 55 min. ¶*Director* A.F. Erickson; *writers* Elliot Lester, Donald Davis (dialogue), *from the story* "The Girl Who Wasn't Wanted" by Kenneth B. Clarke; *cinema-*

tographer Daniel B. Clark; *editor* Paul Weatherwax. ¶George O'Brien (Billy West); Helen Chandler (Marna Reynolds); Antonio Moreno (Loup La Tour); Roy Stewart (Sheriff Milt Powers); Harry Cording (Chick Carson); David Hartford ("Dad" Reynolds); Eddie Borden (Laramie); Noel Francis (Flossie); Frank Lanning (Pop Nichols); **John Wayne,** billed as Duke Morrison. ¶Released June 15.

Cheer Up and Smile (Fox, 1930), 76 min. ¶*Director* Sidney Lanfield; *writer* Howard J. Green *from the story, "If I Was Alone with You,"* by Richard Connell; *cinematographer* Joseph Valentine; *editor* Ralph Dietrich; *associate producer* Al Rockett. ¶Dixie Lee (Margie); Arthur Lake (Eddie Fripp); Olga Baclanova (Yvonne); "Whispering" Jack Smith (Himself); Johnny Arthur (Andy); Charles Judels (Pierre); John Darrow (Tom); Sumner Getchell (Paul); Franklin Pangborn (Professor); Buddy Messinger (Donald); **John Wayne,** as college student—billed as Duke Morrison. ¶Released June 22.

The Big Trail (Fox, 1930), 158 in., (70mm Grandeur); 125 min. (35mm standard); 99 min. Great Britain. ¶*Director* Raoul Walsh; *story* Hal G. Evarts; *screenplay* Jack Peabody, Marie Boyle, Florence Postal, Fred Sersen; *art director* Harold Miles; *incidental music* Arthur Kay; *song* Joseph McCarthy and James F. Hanley; *sound* Donald Scott, George Leverett, Louis Witte; *assistant directors* Ewing Scott, Sid Bowen, Clay Crapnell, George Walsh, Virgil Hart, Earl Rettig; *wardrobe* Earl Moser; *makeup* Jack Dawn, Louise Sloane; *camera (35mm)* Lucien Andriot, Don Anderson, Bill McDonald, Roger Sherman, Bobby Mack, Henry Pollack; *Grandeur camera (70mm)* Arthur Edeson, David Ragin, Sol Halprin, Curt Fetters, Max Cohn, Harry Smith, L. Kunkel, Harry Dawe; *editor* Jack Dennis; *production manager* Archibald

Buchanan. ¶**John Wayne** (Breck Coleman); Marguerite Churchill (Ruth Cameron); El Brendel (Gussie); Tully Marshall (Zeke); Tyrone Power, Sr. (Red Flack); David Rollins (Dave Cameron); Ian Keith (Bill Thorpe); Frederick Burton (Pa Bascom); Russ Powell (Windy Bill); Charles Stevens (Lopez); Louise Carver (Gussie's Mother-in-Law); William V. Mong (Wellmore); Dodo Newton (Abigail); Ward Bond (Sid Bascom); Marcia Harris (Mrs. Riggs); Marjorie Leet (Mary Riggs); Emslie Emerson (Sairey); Frank Rainboth (Ohio Man); Andy Shuford (Ohio Man's son); Helen Parrish (Honey Girl); Jack Peabody (Bill Gillis); Gertrude Van Lent, Lucile Van Lent (Sisters from Missouri); De Witt Jennings (Boat Captain); Alphonz Ethier (Marshal). ¶Premiere October 24, released November 1. ¶German version, **Die Grosse Fahrt,** filmed with German-speaking cast. French version, **La Piste des Geants,** made and directed by P. Couderc.

Girls Demand Excitement (Fox, 1931), 69 min. ¶*Director* Seymour Felix; *writer* Harlan Thompson; *cinematographer* Charles Clarke; *editor* Jack Murray. ¶Virginia Cherrill (Joan Madison); **John Wayne** (Peter Brooks); Marguerite Churchill (Miriam, Joan's friend); William Janney (Freddie); Martha Sleeper (Harriet Mundy); Helen Jerome Eddy (Gazella Perkins, college instructress); Eddie Nugent (Tommy); Winter Hal (The Dean); Addie McPhail (Sue Street); Ralph Welles, George Irving, Marion Byron, Jerry Mandy, Ray Cooke, Emerson Tracy (bits). ¶Released February 8.

Three Girls Lost (Fox, 1931), 80 min. ¶*Director* Sidney Lanfield; *writer* Bradley King *from a screen story by* Robert D. Andrews; *cinematographer* L. William O'Connell; *editor* Ralph Dietrich. ¶Loretta Young (Noreen McMann); **John Wayne** (Gordon

Wales); Lew Cody (William Marriott);
Joyce Compton (Edna Best); Joan
March (Marcia Tallant); Catherine
Clare Ward (Mrs. McGee); Paul Fix
(Tony); Bert Roach. ¶Released April 19.

Men Are Like That (Columbia, 1931);
British title **The Virtuous Wife**. 70 min.
(First reviewed under the title of
Arizona). ¶*Director* George B. Seitz;
writers Robert Riskin, Dorothy Howell
(continuity), *from the play, Arizona, by*
Augustus Thomas; *cinematographer*
Teddy Tetzlaff; *editor* Gene Milford.
¶Laura LaPlante (Evelyn Palmer);
John Wayne (Lt. Bob Denton); June
Clyde (Bonita Palmer); Forrest Stanley
(Col. Bonham); Nena Quartaro (Con-
chita); Susan Fleming (Dot); Loretta
Sayers (Peggy); Hugh Cummings
(Hank). ¶Released June 27.

The Deceiver (Columbia, 1931).
¶*Director* Louis King. ¶Ian King as
Thorpe; **Wayne** as the corpse of
Thorpe. The main actors, Lloyd
Hughes and Dorothy Sebastian.

Range Feud (Columbia, 1931), 64
min. ¶*Director* D. Ross Lederman;
writer Milton Krims; *cinematographer*
Ben Kline; *editor* Maurice Wright.
¶Buck Jones (Sheriff Buck Gordon);
John Wayne (Clint Turner); Susan
Fleming (Judy Walton); Ed LeSaint
(John Walton); William Walling (Dad
Turner); Wallace MacDonald (Hank);
Harry Woods (Vandall); Frank Austin
(Biggers). ¶Released December 1.

Maker of Men (Columbia, 1931), 71
min. During production, called **Yellow**.
¶*Director* Edward Sedgwick; *writer*
Howard J. Green, *from screen story by*
Howard J. Green, Edward Sedgwick;
cinematographer L. William O'Con-
nell; *editor* Gene Milford. ¶Jack Holt
(Dudley); Richard Cromwell (Bob);
Joan Marsh (Dorothy); Robert Alden
(Chick); **John Wayne** (Dusty); Walter
Catlett (McNeill); Natalie Moorhead

(Mrs. Rhodes); Richard Tucker (Mr.
Rhodes); Ethel Wales (Aunt Martha).
¶Released December 25.

The Voice of Hollywood. Second
Series, No. 13 (1932, Tiffany), 12 min.
¶*Director* Mack D'Agostino. ¶John
Wayne as announcer introducing
movie stars in the radio background:
George Bancroft, El Brendel, Jackie
Cooper, Gary Cooper, Lupe Velez.

Shadow of the Eagle (Mascot, 1932).
¶A serial in 12 episodes: (1) "The Car-
nival Mystery"; (2) "Pinholes"; (3) "The
Eagle Strikes"; (4) "The Man in a
Million Voices"; (5) "The Telephone
Cipher"; (6) "The Code of the Car-
nival"; (7) "Eagle Vulture"; (8) "On the
Spot"; (9) "When Thieves Fall Out";
(10) "The Man Who Knew"; (11) "The
Eagle's Wings"; (12) "The Shadow Un-
masked." ¶*Director* Ford Beebe;
writers Ford Beebe; Colbert Clark,
Wyndham Gittens; *cinematographers*
Ben Kline, Victor Scheurich; *editor* Ray
Snyder; *producer* Nat Levine. ¶John
Wayne (Craig McCoy); Dorothy
Gulliver (Jean Gregory); Edward
Hearn (Nathan Gregory); Richard
Tucker (Evans); Lloyd Whitlock
(Green); Walter Miller (Danby); Ken-
neth Harlan (Ward); Edmund Burns
(Clark); Pat O'Malley (Ames); Little
Billy (Midget); Ivan Linow (Strong-
man); James Bradbury, Jr. (Ventrilo-
quist); Ernie S. Adams (Kelly); Bud
Osborne (Gardner); Yakima Canutt
(Boyle); Billy West (Clown). ¶Released
February 1.

Texas Cyclone (Columbia, 1932), 63
min. ¶*Director* D. Ross Lederman;
writer Randall Faye, *from a story by*
William Colt MacDonald; *cinematog-
rapher* Ben Kline; *editor* Otto Meyer.
¶Tim McCoy (Pecos Grant); Shirley
Rey (Helena Rawlins); Wheeler
Oakman (Utah Becker); **John Wayne**
(Steve Pickett); Wallace MacDonald
(Nick Lawlor); James Farley (Webb

Oliver); Harry Cording (Jake Farwell); Vernon Dent (Hefty); Walter Brennan (Lew Collins); Mary Gordon (Kate). ¶Released February 14.

Two Fisted Law (Columbia, 1932), 64 min. ¶*Director* D. Ross Lederman; *writer* Kurt Kempler, *from a story by* William Colt MacDonald; *cinematographer* Benjamin Kline; *editor* Otto Meyer. ¶Tim McCoy (Tim Clark); Alice Day (Betty Owen); Wheeler Oakman (Bob Russell); Tully Marshall (Sheriff Malcolm); Wallace MacDonald (Artie); **John Wayne** (Duke); Walter Brennan (Deputy Sheriff Bendix); Richard Alexander (Zink Yokum).

Lady and Gent (Paramount, 1932), 80 min. Before release, known as **The Challenger.** ¶*Director* Stephen Roberts; *writers* Grover Jones, William Slavens McNutt; *cinematographer* Harry Fischbeck. ¶George Bancroft (Stag Bailey); Wynne Gibson (Puff Rogers); Charles Starrett (Ted Strever); James Gleason (Pin Strever); **John Wayne** (Buzz Kinney); Morgan Wallace (Cash Enright); James Crane (McSweeley); William Halligan (Doc Hayes); Billy Butts (Ted, aged 9); Joyce Compton (Betty); Frank McGlynn, Sr. (Principal); Charles Grapewin (Grocer); Frederick Wallace (Watchman); Lew Kelly (Coroner); Sid Saylor (Joe); Russell Powell (Second bartender); Frank Darien (Jim); Hal Price (First bartender); A.S. Byron (Judge); John Beck (Workman); Tom Kennedy (Small arena fighter); Frank Dawson (Minister). ¶Released July 15.

The Hurricane Express (Mascot, 1932). ¶A serial in twelve episodes: (1) "The Wrecker"; (2) "Flying Pirates"; (3) "The Masked Menace"; (4) "Buried Alive"; (5) "Danger Lights"; (6) "The Airport Mystery"; (7) "Sealed Lips"; (8) "Outside the Law"; (9) "The Invincible Enemy"; (10) "The Wrecker's Secret"; (11) "Wings of Death"; (12) "Un-

masked." ¶*Directors* Armand Schaefer, J.P. McGowan; *writers* George Morgan, J.P. McGowan, *from a screen story by* Colbert Clark, Barney Sarecky, Wyndham Gittens; *cinematographers* Ernest Miller, Carl Wester; *editor* Ray Snyder; *supervising editor* Wyndham Gittens; *sound engineer* George Lowerre; *producer* Nat Levine. ¶John Wayne (Larry Baker); Shirley Grey (Gloria Martin [Stratton]); Tully Marshall (Mr. Edwards); Conway Tearle (Stevens); J. Farrell MacDonald (Jim Baker); Matthew Betz (Jordan); James Burtis (Hemingway); Lloyd Whitlock (Walter Gray); Joseph Girard (Matthews); Edmund Breese (Stratton); Al Bridge (Carlson); Ernie S. Adams (Barney); Charles King (Mike); Glenn Strange (Jim); Al Ferguson (Sandy). ¶Released August 1.

The Hollywood Handicap (The Thalians Club, Bryan Foy; distributor, Universal, 1932). Two-reeler. ¶*Director* Charles Lamont. ¶John Wayne a guest in this comedy series; other guests were Anita Stewart, Bert Wheeler, Dickie Moore, and Tully Marshall. ¶Released August 10.

Ride Him Cowboy (British title, **The Hawk;** Warner Brothers, 1932), 56 min. ¶*Director* Fred Allen; *writer* Scott Mason, *from a story "Ride Him Cowboy"* by Kenneth Perkins; *cinematographer* Ted McCord; *editor* William Clemens; *producer* Leon Schlesinger. ¶John Wayne (John Drury); Ruth Hall (Ruth Gaunt); Henry B. Walthall (John Gaunt); Harry Gribbon (Deputy Sheriff Clout); Otis Harlan (Judge Jones); Charles Sellon (Judge Bartlett); Frank Hagney (Henry Suggs); Duke, the "Devil" Horse. ¶This is a re-make of **The Unknown Cavalier** (1926), in which Ken Maynard played John Drury. ¶Released August 27.

The Big Stampede (Warner Brothers, 1932), 54 min. ¶*Director* Tenny

Wright; *writer* Kurt Kempler, *from a screen story by* Marion Jackson; *cinematographer* Ted McCord; *editor* Frank Ware; *producer* Leon Schlesinger. ¶**John Wayne** (John Steele); Noah Beery (Sam Crew); Mae Madison (Ginger Malloy); Luis Alberni (Sonora Joe); Berton Churchill (Gov. Lew Wallace); Paul Hurst (Arizona); Sherwood Bailey (Pat Malloy); Duke, the "Miracle" Horse, Frank Ellis, Hank Bell, Lafe McKee. ¶This is a re-make of **Land Beyond the Law** (1927), in which Ken Maynard played John Steele. The film was re-made again in 1936 as **Land Beyond the Law,** with Dick Foran as John Steele. ¶Released October 8.

Haunted Gold (Warner Brothers, 1932), 58 min. ¶*Director* Mack V. Wright; *writer* Adele Buffington; *cinematographer* Nick Musuraca; *editor* William Clemens; *associate producer* Sid Rogell; *producer* Leon Schlesinger. ¶**John Wayne** (John Mason); Sheila Terry (Janet Carter); Erville Alderson (Benedict); Harry Woods (Joe Ryan); Otto Hoffman (Simon); Martha Mattox (Mrs. Herman); Blue Washington (Clarence); Slim Whitaker. ¶This is a re-make of **The Phantom City** (1928), in which Ken Maynard played the Wayne character, but under the name of Tim Kelly. ¶Released December 17.

The Telegraph Trail (Warner Brothers, 1933), 55 min. ¶*Director* Tenny Wright; *writer* Kurt Kempler; *cinematographer* Ted McCord; *editor* William Clemens; *producer* Leon Schlesinger. ¶**John Wayne** (John Trent); Marceline Day (Alice Ellis); Frank McHugh (Sgt. Tippy); Otis Harlan (Zeke Keller); Albert J. Smith (Gus Lynch); Yakima Canutt ("High Wolf"); Lafe McKee (Lafe—oldtimer); Clarence Geldert (Cavalry commander); Duke the "Miracle" Horse, Slim Whitaker, Frank Ellis. ¶Some film footage used from **The Red Raiders** (1927). ¶Released March 18.

The Three Musketeers (Mascot, 1933). ¶A serial in twelve episodes: (1) "The Fiery Circle"; (2) "One for All and All for One"; (3) "The Master Spy"; (4) "Pirates of the Desert"; (5) "Rebels' Rifles"; (6) "Death's Marathon"; (7) "Naked Steel"; (8) "The Master Strikes"; (9) "The Fatal Cave"; (10) "Trapped"; (11) "The Measure of a Man"; (12) "The Glory of Comrades." ¶Reissued (in 1946) by Favorite Films as **Desert Command** (60 min. version). ¶*Directors* Armand Schaefer, Colbert Clark; *writers* Norman S. Hall, Colbert Clark, Wyndham Gittens, Ben Cohn, Ella Arnold (dialogue), *from the novel by* Alexandre Dumas; *cinematographers* Ernest Miller, Ed Lyons. ¶**John Wayne** (Tom Wayne); Ruth Hall (Elaine Corday); Jack Mulhall (Clancy); Raymond Hatton (Renard); Francis X. Bushman, Jr. (Schmidt); Noah Beery Jr. (Stubbs); Creighton Chaney [Lon Chaney, Jr.] (Armand Corday); Al Ferguson (Ali); Hooper Atchely (El Kador); Edward Piel (Ratkin); George Magrill (El Maghreh); Gordon DeMain (Col. Duval); William Desmond (Capt. Boncour); Robert Frazer (Major Booth); Emile Chautard (Gen. Pelletier); Robert Warwick (Col. Brent); Rodney Hildebrandt (Demoyne). ¶Released April 7.

Central Airport (Warner Brothers, 1933), 71 min. ¶*Director* William A. Wellman; *writers* Rian James, James Seymour, *from a story by* Jack Moffitt; *cinematographer* Sid Hickox; *editor,* James Morley. ¶Richard Barthelmess (Jim); Sally Eilers (Jill); Tom Brown (Neil); Harold Huber (Swarthy man); James Murray (Eddie); Grant Mitchell (Mr. Blaine); Claire McDowell (Mrs. Blaine); Willard Robertson (Havana Manager); Arthur Vinton (Amarillo Manager); Charles Sellon (Man in wreck); **John Wayne** (non-speaking bit, as injured co-pilot). ¶Released April 15.

Somewhere in Sonora (Warner Brothers, 1933), 57 min. ¶*Director* Mack V. Wright; *writer* Joe Roach, *from a magazine story and the novel, Somewhere South in Sonora by* Will Levington Comfort; *cinematographer* Ted McCord; *editor* William Clemens; *producer* Leon Schlesinger. ¶John Wayne (John Bishop); Henry B. Walthall (Bob Leadly); Shirley Palmer (Mary Burton); J.P. McGowan (Monte Black); Ann Fay (Patsy Ellis); Frank Rice (Riley); Billy Franey (Shorty); Paul Fix (Bart Leadly); Ralph Lewis (Burton); Duke, the "Miracle" Horse. ¶Remake of **Somewhere in Sonora** (1927) with Ken Maynard in the starring role. ¶Released June 7.

His Private Secretary (Showmen's Pictures, 1933), 60 min. ¶*Director* Philip H. Whitman; *writer* John Francis Natteford, *from a screen story by* Lew Collins; *cinematographer* Abe Schultz; *editor* Bobby Ray; *supervisor* Al Alt. ¶Evalyn Knapp (Marion Hall); John Wayne (Dick Wallace); Alec B. Francis (Doctor Hall); Reginald Barlow (Mr. Wallace); Natalie Kingston (Polly); Arthur Hoyt (Little); Al St. John (Garage owner); Hugh Kidder (Butler); Mickey Rentschler (Boy); Patrick Cunning. ¶Released June 10.

The Life of Jimmy Dolan (Warner Brothers, 1933; British title, **The Kid's Last Fight**), 89 min. ¶*Director* Archie Mayo; *writers* Erwin S. Gelsey, David Boehm, Bertram Milhauser, Beulah Marie Dix, *from a story by* Bertram Milhauser, Beulah Marie Dix; *cinematographer* Arthur Edeson; *editor* Bert Levy. ¶Douglas Fairbanks, Jr. (Jimmy Dolan); Loretta Young (Peggy); Fifi D'Orsay (Budgie); Aline MacMahon (Aunt); Guy Kibbee (Phlaxer); Lyle Talbot (Doc Wood); Harold Huber (Reggie Newman); Farina (Sam); Dawn O'Day [Anne Shirley] (Mary Lou); David Durand (George); Shirley Grey (Goldie); Mickey Rooney

(Freckles); Arthur Hohl (Malvin); Arthur Dekuh (Louie Primaro); George Meeker (Magee); John Wayne (Smith). ¶Remade in 1938 as **They Made Me a Criminal.** ¶Released June 14.

Baby Face (Warner Brothers, 1933), 76 min. ¶*Director* Alfred E. Green; *writers* Gene Markey, Kathryn Scola, *from a screen story by* Mark Canfield (Darryl F. Zannuck); *cinematographer* James Van Trees; *art director* Anton Grot; *editor* Howard Bretherton. ¶Barbara Stanwyck (Lily—Baby Face); George Brent (Trenholm); Donald Cook (Stevens); Arthur Hohl (Sipple); John Wayne (Jimmy McCoy); Henry Kolker (Carter); James Murry (Brakeman); Robert Barrat (Nick Powers); Margaret Lindsay (Ann Carter); Douglas Dumbrille (Brody); Theresa Harris (Chico); Renee Whitney (The Girl); Nat Pendleton (Stolvich); Alphonse Ethier (Cragg); Harry Gribbon (Doorman); Arthur De Kuh (Lutza). ¶Released July 1.

The Man from Monterey (Warner Brothers, 1933), 57 min. ¶*Director* Mack V. Wright; *writer* Lesley Mason; *cinematographer* Ted McCord; *editor* William Clemens; *producer* Leon Schlesinger. ¶John Wayne (Capt. John Holmes); Ruth Hall (Dolores); Luis Alberni (Felipe); Francis Ford (Don Pablo); Nina Quartaro (Anita Garcia); Lafayette McKee (Don Jose Castanares); Donald Reed (Don Luis Gonzales); Lillian Leighton (Juanita); Charles Whitaker (Jake Morgan); Duke, the "Devil" Horse. ¶Released July 15.

Riders of Destiny (Lone Star/ Monogram, 1933), 58 min. ¶*Producer* Paul Malvern; *director-story-screenplay* Robert North Bradbury; *cinematographer* Archie Stout; *editor* Carl L. Pierson; *technical director* E.R. Hickson; *recorded by* John A. Stransky, Jr. ¶John Wayne (Singin' Sandy

Saunders); Cecilia Parker (Fay Denton); George "Gabby" Hayes (Sheriff Denton); Forrest Taylor (Kincaid); Al St. John (Bert); Heinie Conklin (Pete, the Stage Driver); Earl Dwire (Slip Morgan); Yakima Canutt (Stunts); Lafe McKee (Sheriff); Fern Emmett (Farm Woman). ¶Released October 10.

College Coach (British Title, **Football Coach;** Warner Brothers, 1933), 75 min. ¶*Director* William A. Wellman; *writers* Niven Busch, Manuel Seff; *cinematographer* Arthur Todd; *editor* Thomas Pratt. ¶Pat O'Brien (Phil Sargent); Ann Dvorak (Claire Gore); Dick Powell (Coach Gore); Hugh Herbert (Barnett); Lyle Talbot (Buck Weaver); Arthur Byron (Dr. Philipi Sargent); Guinn Williams (Matthews); Nat Pendleton (Petrowski); Philip Faversham (Editor); Charles C. Wilson (Hauser); Donald Meek (Spencer Trask); Berton Churchill (Otis); Arthur Hohl (Seymour Young); Harry Beresford (Professor); Herman Bing (Glantz); Joe Sauers [Sawyer] (Holcomb); Philip Reed (Westerman); **John Wayne** (bit, with one line); Ward Bond. ¶Released November 4.

Sagebrush Trail (Lone Star/ Monogram, 1933), 55 min. ¶*Director* Armand Schaefer; *writer* Lindsley Parsons; *cinematographer* Archie Stout; *technical director* E.R. Hickson; *recorded by* John A. Stransky, Jr.; *editor* Carl Pierson; *producer* Paul Malvern. ¶**John Wayne** (John Brant); Nancy Shubert (Sally Blake); Lane Chandler (Bob Jones); Yakima Canutt (Ed Walsh); Wally Wales (Deputy Sheriff); Art Mix (Henchman); Robert E. Burns (Sheriff Parker); Henry Hall (Dad Blake); Earl Dwire (Blind Pete). ¶Released December 15.

The Lucky Texan (Lone Star/ Monogram, 1934), 56 min. ¶*Director/ writer* Robert North Bradbury; *cinematographer* Archie Stout; *editor*

Carl Pierson; *technical director* E.R. Hickson; *recorded by* Dave Stoner; *producer* Paul Malvern. ¶**John Wayne** (Jerry Mason); Barbara Sheldon (Betty); George Hayes (Jake Benson); Lloyd Whitlock (Harris); Yakima Canutt (Cole); Gordon DeMaine (Sheriff); Edward Parker (Sheriff's son); Earl Dwire (Banker). ¶Released January 22.

West of the Divide (Lone Star/ Monogram, 1934), 55 min. ¶*Director/ writer* Robert North Bradbury; *cinematographer* Archie Stout; *technical director* E.R. Hickson; *recording engineer* Dave Stoner; *producer* Paul Malvern. ¶**John Wayne** (Ted Hayden); Virginia Brown Faire (Fay Winters); Lloyd Whitlock (Gentry); George Hayes (Dusty Rhodes); Yakima Canutt (Hank); Billy O'Brien (Spud); Lafe McKee (Winters); Blackie Whiteford (Hutch); Earl Dwire (Red); Dick Dickinson (Joe). ¶Released March 1.

Blue Steel (Lone Star/Monogram, 1934), 54 min. ¶*Director/writer* Robert North Bradbury; *cinematographer* Archie Stout; *editor* Carl Pierson; *technical director* E.R. Hickson; *recorded by* J.A. Stransky, Jr.; *producer* Paul Malvern. ¶**John Wayne** (John Carruthers); Eleanor Hunt (Betty Mason); George Hayes (Sheriff Jake); Ed Peil (Melgrove); Yakima Canutt (Danti, the "Polka Dot Bandit"); George Cleveland (Innkeeper, Hank); George Nash (Bridegroom); Lafe McKee (Dad Mason); Hank Bell (Stagedriver); Earl Dwire (Henchman). ¶Released May 10.

The Man from Utah (Lone Star/ Monogram, 1934), 55 min. ¶*Director* Robert North Bradbury; *writer* Lindsley Parsons; *cinematographer* Archie Stout; *editor* Carl Pierson; *recorded by* J.A. Stransky, Jr.; *producer* Paul Malvern. ¶**John Wayne** (John Weston); Polly Ann Young (Marjorie Carter); George Hayes (George Higgins);

Yakima Canutt (Cheyenne Kent); Ed Peil (Barton); Anita Campillo (Dolores); Lafe McKee (Judge Carter); George Cleveland (Sheriff). ¶Released May 15.

Randy Rides Alone (Lone Star/ Monogram, 1934), 53 min. *¶Director* Harry Fraser; *writer* Lindsley Parsons; *cinematographer* Archie Stout; *technical director* E.R. Hickson *recorded by* J.A. Stransky, Jr.; *editor* Carl Pierson; *producer* Paul Malvern. ¶**John Wayne** (Randy Bowers); Alberta Vaughn (Sally Rogers); George Hayes (Matt the Mute); Yakima Canutt (Spike); Earl Dwire (Sheriff); Tex Phelps (Deputy); Arthur Ortega (Hench man). ¶Released June 5.

The Star Packer (Lone Star/ Monogram, 1934), 54 min. *¶Director/ writer* Robert North Bradbury; *cinema tographer* Archie Stout; *editor* Carl Pierson; *technical director* E.R. Hickson; *recorded by* J.A. Stransky, Jr.; *producer* Paul Malvern. ¶**John Wayne** (John Travers); Verna Hillie (Anita); George Hayes (Matlock, alias "The Shadow"); Yakima Canutt (Yak, the Indian); Earl Dwire (Mason); Ed Parker (Parker); George Cleveland (Pete); Tom Lingham (Sheriff); Arthur Ortega (Deputy); Davie Aldrich; Tex Palmer (Stagecoach driver). ¶Released July 30.

The Trail Beyond (Lone Star/Monogram, 1934), 55 min. *¶Director* Robert North Bradbury; *writer* Lindsley Parsons, *from the novel, The Wolf Hunters, by* James Oliver Curwood; *cinematographer* Archie Stout; *art director* E.R. Hickson; *editor* Charles Hunt; *recorded by Ralph Shugart; producer* Paul Malvern. ¶**John Wayne** (Rod Drew); Noah Beery (George Newsome); Noah Beery, Jr. (Wabi); Verna Hillie (Felice Newsome); Iris Lancaster (Marie); Robert Frazer (Jules LaRocque); Earl Dwire (Benoit); Eddie Parker (Ryan, the Mountie); James Marcus, Reed

Howes. ¶An earlier version, in 1926, was called **The Wolf Hunters.** A later release, in 1949, also **The Wolf Hunters,** based on same source with different writer and Lindsley Parsons as producer. ¶Released October 22.

The Lawless Frontier (Lone Star/ Monogram, 1934), 54 min. *¶Director/ writer* Robert North Bradbury; *cinematographer* Archie Stout; *editor* Charles Hunt; *art director* E.R. Hickson; *recorded by* Ralph Shugart; *producer* Paul Malvern. ¶**John Wayne** (John Tobin); Sheila Terry (Ruby); George Hayes (Dusty); Earl Dwire (Zanti); Yakima Canutt (Joe); Jack Rockwell (Sheriff); Gordon D. Woods (Miller). ¶Released November 22.

'Neath the Arizona Skies (Lone Star/ Monogram, 1934), 52 min. *¶Director* Harry Fraser; *writer* B.R. (Burt) Tuttle; *cinematographer* Archie Stout; *film editor* Charles Hunt; *art director* E.R. Hickson; *recorded by Ralph Shugart; producer* Paul Malvern. ¶**John Wayne** (Chris Morrell); Sheila Terry (Clara Moore); Jay Wilsey [Buffalo Bill, Jr.] (Jim Moore); Shirley Ricketts (Nina); George Hayes (Matt Downing); Yakima Canutt (Sam Black); Jack Rockwell (Vic Byrd); Phil Keefer (Hodges); Frank Hall Crane (Express Agent). ¶Released December 5.

Texas Terror (Lone Star/Monogram, 1935), 58 min. *¶Director/writer* Robert North Bradbury; *cinematographer* William Hyer; *editor* Carl Pierson; *technical director* E.R. Hickson; *recorded by* Dave Stoner; *producer* Paul Malvern. ¶**John Wayne** (John Higgins); Lucille Brown (Beth Matthews); LeRoy Mason (Joe Dickson); George Hayes (Sheriff Williams); Buffalo Bill, Jr. (Blackie); Bert Dillard (Red); Lloyd Ingraham (Dan). ¶Released February 1.

Rainbow Valley (Lone Star/Monogram, 1935), 52 min. *¶Director* Robert

North Bradbury; *writer* Lindsley Parsons; *cinematographer* William Hyer; *editor* Carl Pierson; *technical director* E.R. Hickson; *producer* Paul Malvern. ¶**John Wayne** (John Martin); Lucille Brown (Eleanor); LeRoy Mason (Rogers); George Hayes (George Hale); Buffalo Bill, Jr. (Galt); Bert Dillard (Spike); Lloyd Ingraham (Powell); Lafe McKee (Storekeeper); Frank Ellis, Art Dillard, Frank Ball (Townsmen). ¶Released March 15.

The Desert Trail (Lone Star/ Republic, 1935), 54 min. ¶*Director* Cullen Lewis; *writer* Lindsley Parsons; *cinematographer* Archie Stout; *editor* Carl Pierson; *technical director* E.R. Hickson; *recorded by* J.A. Stransky, Jr.; *producer* Paul Malvern. ¶**John Wayne** (John Scott); Mary Kornman (Anne); Paul Fix (Jim); Edward Chandler (Kansas Charlie); Carmen LaRoux (Juanita); Al Ferguson (Peter); Lafe McKee (Sheriff Barker); Henry Hall (Banker). ¶Released April 22.

The Dawn Rider (Monogram/ Republic, 1935), 56 min. ¶*Director/ writer* Robert North Bradbury, *from a story by* Lloyd Nosler; *cinematographer* Archie Stout; *editor* Carl Pierson; *technical director* E.R. Hickson; *recorded by* D.S. Stoner; *producer* Paul Malvern. ¶**John Wayne** (John Mason); Marion Burns (Alice Gordon); Yakima Canutt (Barkeep); Reed Howes (Ben McClure); Denny Meadows [later, Dennis Moore] (Rudd Gordon); Bert Dillard (Buck); Jack Jones (Black); James Sheridan. ¶Released June 20.

Paradise Canyon (Monogram, 1935), 52 min. ¶*Director* Carl Pierson; *writers* Lindsley Parsons, Robert Emmett, *from a screen story by* Lindsley Parsons; *cinematographer* Archie Stout; *editor* Gerald Roberts; *technical director* E.R. Hickson; *recorded by* D.S. Stoner; *producer* Paul Malvern. ¶John

Wayne (John Wyatt); Marion Burns (Linda Carter); Earl Hodgins (Doctor Carter); Yakima Canutt (Curly Joe Gale); Reed Howes (Trigger); Perry Murdock (Ike); Gordon Clifford (Mike); Gino Corrado (Rurale Captain); Tex Palmer. ¶Produced under title, **Paradise Ranch.** ¶Released July 20.

Westward Ho (Republic, 1935), 60 min. ¶*Director* Robert North Bradbury; *Vice President in charge of production* Trem Carr; *writers* Lindsley Parsons, Harry Friedman, Robert Emmett, *from a screen story by* Lindsley Parsons; *cinematographer* Archie Stout; *editor* Carl Pierson; *continuity* Harry Friedman; *technical director* E.R. Hickson; *recorded by* Dave Stoner; *producer* Paul Malvern. ¶**John Wayne** (John Wyatt); Sheila Manners (Mary Gordon); Frank McGlynn, Jr. (Jim Wyatt); Jack Curtis (Ballard); Yakima Canutt (Red); Bradley Metcalfe (Young John Wyatt); Hank Bell (Mark Wyatt); Mary McLaren (Hannah Wyatt); Jim Farley Lafe Gordon); Dickie Jones (Young Jim Wyatt). ¶Released August 19.

The New Frontier (Republic, 1935), 59 min. ¶*Director* Carl Pierson; *Vice President in charge of production* Trem Carr; *writer* Robert Emmett; *cinematographer* Gus Peterson, Harry Neumann; *editor* Gerald Roberts; *technical director* E.R. Hixon [for Hickson?]; *recorded by* J.A. Stransky, Jr.; *producer* Paul Malvern. ¶**John Wayne** (John Dawson); Muriel Evans (Hanna Lewis); Murdoch MacQuarrie (Tom Lewis); Alan Cavan (Padre); Warner Richmond (Ace Holmes); Al Bridge (Kit); Sam Flint (Milt Dawson); Glenn Strange (Norton); Earl Dwire, Mary McClarie, Theodore Loran, Phil Keefer, Frank Ball, Jack Montgomery. ¶Released October 5.

The Lawless Range (Republic, 1935), 59 min. ¶*Director* Robert North Bradbury; *writer* Lindsley Parsons; *cinema-*

tographer Archie Stout; *editor* Carl Pierson; *supervisor,* Paul Malvern; *technical director* E.R. Hickson; *recorded by* Dave Stoner; *production* Trem Carr. ¶**John Wayne** (John Middleton); Sheila Manners (Anne); Earl Dwire (Emmett); Frank McGlynn, Jr. (Carter); Jack Curtis (Marshall); Yakima Canutt (Burns); Wally Howe (Mason). ¶Released November 4.

The Oregon Trail (Republic, 1936), 59 min. ¶*Producer* Trem Carr; *supervisor* Paul Malvern; *director* Scott Pembroke; *story* Lindsley Parsons, Robert Emmett; *screenplay* Jack Natteford Emmett Parsons; *camera* Gus Peterson; *editor* Carl Pierson. ¶**John Wayne** (Captain John Delmont); Ann Rutherford (Anne Ridgley); Yakima Canutt (Tom Richards); Ben Hendricks, Jr. (Major Harris); Joseph Girard (Colonel Delmont); Frank Rice (Red); E.H. Calvert (Jim Ridgley); Harry Harvey (Tim); Jack Rutherford (Benton); Roland Ray (Markey); Edward J. LeSaint (General Ferguson); Octavio Giraud (Don Miguel); Fern Emmett (Minnie, Old Maid); Marian Farrell (Sis); Gino Corrado, Forrenza (Californians' Leader). ¶Released January 18.

The Lawless Nineties (Republic, 1936), 55 min. ¶*Director* Joseph Kane; *writer* Joseph Poland, *from a screen story by* Joseph Poland, Scott Pembroke; *cinematographer* William Nobles; *film editor* Lester Orlebeck; *supervising editor* Joseph H. Lewis; *sound engineer* Terry Kellum; *supervisor* Paul Malvern. ¶**John Wayne** (John Tipton); Ann Rutherford, (Janet Carter); Harry Woods (Plummer); George Hayes (Major Carter); Al Bridge (Steele); Lane Chandler (Bridger); Snowflake [Fred Toones] (Mose); Etta McDaniel (Mandy Lou); Tom Brower (Marshall); Cliff Lyons (Davis); Jack Rockwell (Smith); Al Taylor (Red); Charles King (Hartley); George Cheseboro (Green); Tom Lon-

don (Ward); Sam Flint (Pierce); Earl Seaman (T. Roosevelt); Tracy Lane (Belden); Philo McCullough (Outlaw Leader); Chuck Baldra (Tex); Jimmy Harrison (Telegraph Operator). ¶Released February 15.

King of the Pecos (Republic, 1936), 54 min. ¶*Director* Joseph Kane; *writers* Bernard McConville, Dorrell McGowan, Stuart McGowan, *from a screen story by* Bernard McConville; *cinematographer* Jack Marta; *supervising editor* Joseph H. Lewis; *film editor* Lester Orlebeck; *sound engineer* Terry Kellum; *supervisor* Paul Malvern. ¶**John Wayne** (John Clayborn); Muriel Evans (Belle); Cy Kendall (Stiles); Jack Clifford (Ash); Frank Glendon (Brewster); Herbert Heywood (Josh); Arthur Aylsworth (Hank); John Beak (Clayborn, Sr.); Mary McLaren (Mrs. Clayborn); Bradley Metcalfe, Jr. (Little John Clayborn); Yakima Canutt (Smith). ¶Released March 9.

The Lonely Trail (Republic, 1936), 56 min. ¶*Director* Joseph Kane; Bernard McConville, Jack Natteford, *from a screen story by* Bernard McConville; *cinematographer* William Nobles; *editor* Robert Johns; *supervising editor* Murray Seldeen; *sound engineer* Terry Kellum; *technical supervisor* Harry Grey; *producer* Nat Levine; *supervisor* Paul Malvern. ¶**John Wayne** (John); Ann Rutherford (Virginia); Cy Kendall (Holden); Bob Kortman (Hays); Snowflake (Snowflake); Etta McDaniel (Mammy); Sam Flint (Governor); Denny Meadows [later, Dennis Moore] (Terry); Jim Toney (Jed); Yakima Canutt (Horrell); Lloyd Ingraham (Tucker); Bob Burns (Rancher); James Marcus (Mayor); Rodney Hildebrand (Captain of Cavalry); Eugene Jackson (Dancer); Floyd Shackelford (Armstrong); Jack Kirk, Jack Ingram, Bud Pope, Tex Phelps, Tracy Layne, Clyde Kenney (Troopers); Leon Lord (Blaine). ¶Released May 25.

Winds of the Wasteland (Republic, 1936), 57 min. *Producer* Nat Levine; *supervisor* Paul Malvern; *director* Mack V. Wright; *story/screenplay* Joseph Poland; *music supervisor* Harry Grey; *camera* William Nobles; *editors* Murray Seldeen, Robert Jahne. ¶John Wayne (John Blair); Phyllis Fraser (Barbara Forsythe); Yakima Canutt (Smoky); Douglas Cosgrove (Cal Drake); Lane Chandler (Larry); Sam Flint (Dr. Forsythe); Lew Kelly (Rocky); Bob Kortman (Cherokee Joe); Ed Cassidy (Dodge); W. Merrill McCormick (Pete); Bud McClure, Jack Ingram (Guards); Charles Locher [Jon Hall] (Pete); Joe Yrigoyen (Pike); Chris Franke (Grahame); Jack Rockwell. ¶Released July 6.

The Sea Spoilers (Universal, 1936), 63 min. *Director* Frank Strayer; *writer* George Waggner, *from a screen story by* Dorrell McGowan, Stuart E. McGowan; *cinematographer* Archie Stout; *editors* H.T. Fritch, Ray Lockhart; *music director* Herman S. Heller; *producer* Trem Carr. ¶John Wayne (Bob Randall); Nan Grey, (Connie Dawson); William Bakewell (Lt. Mays); Fuzzy Knight (Hogan); Russell Hicks (Phil Morgan); George Irving (Commander Mays); Lotus Long (Marie); Harry Worth (Nick Austin); Ernest Hilliard (Reggie); George Humbert (Hop Scotch); Ethan Laidlaw (Louie); Chester Gan (Oil); Cy Kendall (Detective); Harrison Green (Fats). ¶Released October.

Conflict (Universal, 1936), 60 min. *Director* David Howard; *writers* Charles Logue, Walter Weems, *from the novel, The Abysmal Brute, by* Jack London; *cinematographer* J.A. (Archie) Stout; *editor* Jack Ogilvie; *music director* Herman Heller; *supervisor* Paul Malvern; *producer* Trem Carr. ¶John Wayne (Pat); Jean Rogers (Maude); Tommy Bupp (Tommy); Eddie Borden (Spider); Frank Sheridan (Sam); Ward

Bond (Carrigan); Margaret Mann (Ma Blake); Harry Woods (Kelly); Bryant Washburn (City Editor); Frank Hagney (Malone). ¶Previously made under title of **The Abysmal Brute** in 1923, with Reginald Denny. ¶Under production, September; released November 29.

California Straight Ahead (Universal, 1937), 67 min. *Director* Arthur Lubin; *writer* Scott Darling, *from a screen story by* Herman Boxer; *cinematographer* Harry Neumann; *art director* E.R. Hickson; *editors* Charles Craft, Erma Horseley; *musical director* Charles Previn; *associate producer* Paul Malvern; *producer* Trem Carr. ¶John Wayne (Biff Smith); Louise Latimer (Mary Porter); Robert McWade (Corrigan); Theodore von Eltz (James Gifford); Tully Marshall (Harrison); Emerson Treacy (Charlie Porter); Harry Allen ("Fish" McCorkle); LeRoy Mason (Padula); Grace Goodall (Mrs. Porter); Olaf Hytten (Huggins); Monty Vandergrift (Clancy); Lorin Raker (Secretary). ¶Released May 2.

I Cover the War (Universal, 1937), 68 min. *Director* Arthur Lubin; *writer* George Waggner, *from a screen story suggestion by* Bernard McConville; *cinematographer* Harry Neumann; *art director* E.R. Hickson; *editor* Charles Craft; *associate producer* Paul Malvern; *producer* Trem Carr. ¶John Wayne (Bob Adams); Gwen Gaze (Pamela); Don Barclay (Elmer Davis); Pat Somerset (Archie); Major Sam Harris (Col. Armitage); Charles Brokaw (El Kadar — Muffadi); James Bush (Don Adams); Arthur Aylsworth (Logan); Earl Hodgins (Blake); Jack Mack (Graham); Franklyn Parker (Parker); Frank Lackteen (Mustapha); Olaf Hytton (Sir Herbert); Keith Kenneth (Sgt.-Major); Abdulla (Abdul). ¶Released July 4.

Idol of the Crowds (Universal, 1937), 60 min. *Director* Arthur Lubin; *writers* George Waggner, Harold Buckley,

from a screen story by George Wagg-
ner; *cinematographer* Harry Neumann;
art director Charles Clague; *editor*
Charles Craft; *associate producer* Paul
Malvern; *producer* Trem Carr. ¶**John
Wayne** (Johnny Hanson); Sheila
Bromley (Helen Dale); Charles Brockaw
(Jack Irwin); Billy Burrud (Bobby);
Jane Johns (Peggy); Huntley Gordon
(Harvey Castle); Frank Otto (Joe
Garber); Russell Hopton (Kelly);
Virginia Brissac (Mrs. Dale); Clem
Bevans (Andy Moore); George Lloyd
(Spike Regan); Hal Neiman (Squat
Bates); Wayne Castle (Swifty); Lloyd
Ford (Hank); Lee Ford (Elmer).
¶Released October 10.

Adventure's End (Universal, 1937),
60 min. ¶*Director* Arthur Lubin;
writers Ben Grauman Kohn, Scott
Darling, Sid Sutherland, *from a screen
story by* Ben Ames Williams; *cin-
ematographer* Gus Peterson; *editor*
Charles Craft; *associate producer*
Paul Malvern; *producer* Trem Carr.
¶**John Wayne** (Duke Slade); Diana Gib-
son (Janet Drew); Montagu Love
(Capt. Abner Drew); Moroni Olsen
(Rand Husk, mate); Maurice Black
(Blackie); Paul White (Kalo); Cameron
Hall (Silvers); Patrick J. Kelly (Matt);
George Cleveland (Tom); Oscar W.
Sundholm (Chips); James T. Mack
(Hooten); Glenn Strange (Barzeck);
Wally Howe (Kierce); Jimmie Lucas
(Flench); Ben Carter (Stantul); Britt
Wood (Hardy). ¶Released December
5.

Born to the West (Later reissued as
Hell Town; Paramount, 1937), 59 min.
¶*Director* Charles Barton; *writers*
Stuart Anthony, Robert Yost, *from the
novel, Born to the West, by* Zane Grey;
cinematographer J. Deveraux Jennings;
editor John Link. ¶**John Wayne** (Dare
Rudd); Marsha Hunt (Judith Worstall);
Johnny Mack Brown (Tom Fillmore);
Monte Blue (Bart Hammond); Syd Say-
lor (Dinkey Hooley); John Patterson

(Lynn Hardy); Nick Lukats (Jim
Fallon); Lucien Littlefield (Cattle
Buyer); James Craig (Buck Brady); Jack
Kennedy (Sheriff Stark); Alan Ladd,
Jennie Boyle, Lee Prather, Jack Daley,
Vester Pegg. ¶Made earlier as **Born to
the West,** in 1926, with Jack Holt as
Dare Rudd. ¶Released December 10.

Pals of the Saddle (Republic, 1938),
55 min. ¶*Director* George Sherman;
writers Stanley Roberts, Betty Bur-
bridge, *based on characters created by
William Colt MacDonald; cinematog-
rapher* Reggie Lanning; *editor* Tony
Martinelli; *music director* Cy Feuer;
production manager Al Wilson; *unit
manager* Arthur Siteman; *associate pro-
ducer* William Berke. ¶**John Wayne**
(Stony Brooke); Ray Corrigan (Tucson
Smith); Max Terhune (Lullaby Joslin);
Doreen McKay (Ann); Josef Forte
(Judge Hastings); George Douglas
(Paul Hartman); Frank Milan (Frank
Paige); Ted Adams (Henry C. Gordon);
Harry Depp (Hotel Clerk); Dave
Weber (Russian Musician); Don Or-
lando (Italian Musician); Charles
Knight (English Musician); Jack Kirk
(Sheriff). ¶Released August 28.

Overland Stage Raiders (Republic,
1938), 58 min. ¶*Director* George Sher-
man; *based on characters created by*
William Colt MacDonald; *story* Ber-
nard McConville, Edmund Kelso;
screenplay Luci Ward; *cinematog-
rapher* William Nobles; *editor* Tony
Martinelli; *production manager* Al
Wilson; *unit manager* Arthur Siteman;
associate producer William Berke.
¶**John Wayne** (Stony Brooke); Louise
Brooks (Beth Hoyt); Ray Corrigan
(Tucson Smith); Max Terhune (Lullaby
Joslin); Frank LaRue (Milton); Fern
Emmett (Ma Hawkins); Anthony Marsh
(Ned Hoyt); Gordon Hart (Mullins);
Ralph Bowman [later, John Archer]
(Bob Whitney); Roy James (Harmon);
Olin Francis (Jake); Henry Otho
(Sheriff); George Sherwood (Clanton);

Archie Hall (Waddell); Yakima Canutt (Bus Driver); Slim Whittaker (Hawkins). ¶Released September 20.

Santa Fe Stampede (Republic, 1938), 56 min. ¶*Director* George Sherman; *writers* Luci Ward, Betty Burbridge, *from a screen story by* Luci Ward, *based on characters created by* William Colt MacDonald; *cinematographer* Reggie Lanning; *editor* Tony Martinelli; *music* William Lava; *production manager* Al Wilson; *associate producer* William Berke. ¶John Wayne (Stony Brooke); Ray Corrigan (Tucson Smith); Max Terhune (Lullaby Joslin); William Farnum (Dave Carson); June Martel (Nancy Carson); LeRoy Mason (Gil Byron); Martin Spellman (Billy Carson); Genee Hall (Julie Jane Carson); Walter Wills (Harris); Ferris Taylor (Judge); Tom London (Marshal); Dick Rush (Sheriff); James F. Cassidy (Newton). ¶In production, October; released December 8.

Red River Range (Republic, 1938), 56 min. ¶*Director* George Sherman; *writers* Stanley Roberts, Betty Burbridge, Luci Ward, *from a screen story by* Luci Ward, *based on characters created by* William Colt MacDonald; *cinematographer* Jack Marta; *editor* Tony Martinelli; *music* William Lava; *production manager* Al Wilson; *associate producer* William Berke. ¶John Wayne (Stony Brooke); Ray Corrigan (Tucson Smith); Max Terhune (Lullaby Joslin); Polly Moran (Mrs. Maxv. ell); Lorna Gray [later, Adrian Booth] (Jane Mason); Kirby Grant (Tex Reilly); Sammy McKim (Tommy); William Royle (Payne); Perry Ivins (Hartley); Stanley Blystone (Randall); Leonore Bushman (Evelyn Maxwell); Burr Caruth (Pop Mason); Roger Williams (Sheriff); Earl Askam, Olin Francis. ¶In production, November; released December 22.

Stagecoach (Walter Wanger Productions/United Artists, 1939), 97 min. ¶*Director* John Ford; *producer* Walter Wanger; *based on the story "Stage to Lordsburg" by* Ernest Haycox; *screenplay* Dudley Nichols; *music director* Boris Morros; *music adaptors* Richard Hageman, W. Franke Harling, John Leipold, Leo Shuken, Louis Gruenberg, from 17 American folk tunes of the early 1880's; *art director* Alexander Toluboff; *set decorator* Wiard B. Ihnen; *costumes* Walter Plunkett; *assistant director* Wingate Smith; *second unit director* Yakima Canutt; *special effects* Ray Binger; *photography* Bert Glennon, Ray Binger; *editorial supervisor* Otho Lovering; *editors* Dorothy Spencer, Walter Reynolds. ¶John Wayne (The Ringo Kid); Claire Trevor (Dallas); John Carradine (Hatfield); Thomas Mitchell (Dr. Josiah Boone); Andy Devine (Buck); Donald Meek (Samuel Peacock); Louise Platt (Lucy Mallory); Tim Holt (Lieutenant Blanchard); George Bancroft (Sheriff Curly Wilcox); Berton Churchill (Henry Gatewood); Tom Tyler (Luke Plummer); Chris-Pin Martin (Chris); Elvira Rios (Yakima, Chris's wife); Francis Ford (Billy Pickett); Marga Daighton (Mrs. Pickett); Kent Odell (Billy Pickett, Jr.); Yakima Canutt (White Scout); Chief Big Tree (Indian Scout); Louis Mason (Sheriff); William Hoffer (Sergeant); Harry Tenbrook (Telegraph Operator); Jack Pennick (Jerry the Bartender); Paul McVey (Wells Fargo Agent); Walter McGrail (Captain Sickels); Brenda Fowler (Mrs. Gatewood); Florence Lake (Mrs. Nancy Whitney); Cornelius Keefe (Captain Whitney); Vester Pegg (Hank Plummer); Bryant Washburn (Captain Simmons); Nora Cecil (Dr. Boone's Housekeeper); Billy Cody, Buddy Roosevelt (Ranchers); Chief White Horse (Indian Chief, Geronimo); Duke Lee (Sheriff of Lordsburg); Mary Kathleen Walker (Lucy's Baby); Helen Gibson, Dorothy Appleby

(Saloon Girls); Joe Rickson (Ike Plummer); Ed Brady (Saloon Keeper); Robert Homans (Editor in Lordsburg); Franklyn Farnum (Deputy); Jim Mason (Jim, the Expressman); Artie Ortega (Barfly in Lordsburg); Merrill McCormick (the Ogler); Steve Clemente, Theodore Lorch, Fritzi Brunette, Leonard Trainor, Chris Phillips, Tex Driscoll, Pat Wayne, Teddy Billings, Al Lee, John Eckert, Jack Mohr, Patsy Doyle, Wiggie Blowne, Margaret Smith, Si Jenks (other Bits). ¶Produced November-December. Location filming at Kernville, Dry Lake, Fremont Pass, Victorville, Calabasas, Chatsworth—all in California; at Kayenta, Mesa, and Monument Valley, in Arizona. ¶Released March.

The Night Riders (Republic, 1939), 58 min. ¶*Director* George Sherman; *writers* Betty Burbridge, Stanley Roberts, *based on characters created by* William Colt MacDonald; *cinematographer* Jack Marta; *editor* Lester Orlebeck; *music* William Lava; *production manager* Al Wilson; *associate producer* William Berke. ¶John Wayne (Stony Brooke); Ray Corrigan (Tucson Smith); Max Terhune (Lullaby Joslin); Doreen McKay (Soledad); Ruth Rogers (Susan Randall); George Douglas (Pierce Talbot, *alias* Don Luis De Serrano); Tom Tyler (Jackson); Kermit Maynard (Sheriff Pratt); Sammy McKim (Tim); Walter Wills (Hazelton); Ethan Laidlaw (Andrews); Edward Peil, Sr. (Harper); Tom London (Wilson); Jack Ingram (Wilkins); William Nestell (Allen); Francis Sayles (President Garfield); and Yakima Canutt, Bud Osborne, David Sharpe, Glenn Strange. ¶Produced, from mid–February, as **Lone Star Bullets.** Released April 12.

Three Texas Steers (British title, **Danger Rides the Range;** Republic, 1939), 57 min. ¶*Director* George Sherman; *writers* Betty Burbridge, Stanley

Roberts, *based on characters created by* William Colt MacDonald; *cinematographer* Ernest Miller; *editor* Tony Martinelli; *music* William Lava; *production manager* Al Wilson; *associate producer* William Berke. ¶John Wayne (Stony Brooke); Ray Corrigan (Tucson Smith); Max Terhune (Lullaby Joslin); Carole Landis (Nancy Evans); Ralph Graves (George Ward); Roscoe Ates (Sheriff); Collette Lyons (Lillian); Billy Curtis (Hercules); Ted Adams (Steve); Stanley Blystone (Rankin); David Sharpe (Tony); Ethan Laidlaw (Morgan); Lew Kelly (Postman); Naba (Willie the Gorilla); John Merton (Mike Abbott); Ted Mapes. ¶In production, April; released June 19.

Wyoming Outlaw (Republic, 1939), 57 min. ¶*Director* George Sherman; *writers* Betty Burbridge, Jack Natteford, *from a screen story by* Jack Natteford, *based on characters created by* William Colt MacDonald; *cinematographer* Reggie Lanning; *editor* Tony Martinelli; *music* William Lava; *production manager* Al Wilson; *associate producer* William Berke. ¶John Wayne (Stony Brooke); Ray Corrigan (Tucson Smith); Raymond Hatton (Rusty Joslin); Donald Barry (Will Parker); Adele Pearce (Irene Parker); LeRoy Mason (Balsinger); Charles Middleton (Luke Parker); Katherine Kenworthy (Mrs. Parker); Elmo Lincoln (U.S. Marshal); Jack Ingram (Sheriff); David Sharpe (Newt); Jack Kenny (Amos); Yakima Canutt (Ed Sims). ¶Released June 27.

New Frontier (Television title, **Frontier Horizon;** Republic, 1939), 57 min. ¶*Director* George Sherman; *writers* Betty Burbridge, Luci Ward, *based on characters created by* William Colt MacDonald; *cinematographer* Reggie Lanning; *editor* Tony Martinelli; *music* William Lava; *production manager* Al Wilson; *associate producer* William

Berke. ¶**John Wayne** (Stony Brooke); Ray Corrigan (Tucson Smith); Raymond Hatton (Rusty Joslin); Phyllis Isley [later, Jennifer Jones] (Celia); Eddie Waller (Major Broderick); Sammy McKim (Stevie); LeRoy Mason (Gilbert); Harrison Greene (Proctor); Reginald Barlow (Judge Lawson); Burr Caruth (Doc Hall); Dave O'Brien (Jason); Hal Price (Sheriff); Jack Ingram (Harmon); Bud Osborne (Dickson); Charles Whitaker (Turner). ¶Released August 10.

Allegheny Uprising (British title, **The First Rebel**; RKO Radio, 1939), 81 min. ¶*Director* William A. Seiter; *writer* P.J. Wolfson, *based on the novel, The First Rebel, by* Neil H. Swanson; *cinematographer* Nicholas Musuraca; *art directors* Van Nest Polglase, Albert D'Agostino; *dance director* David Robel; *editor* George Crone; *music* Anthony Collins; *Miss Trevor's wardrobe by* Earl A. Wolcott; *set decorations* Darrell Silvers; *recorded by* Earl A. Wolcott; *assistant director* Kenneth Holmes; *producer* P.J. Wolfson. ¶Claire Trevor (Janie McDougle); **John Wayne** (Jim Smith); George Sanders (Captain Swanson); Brian Donlevy (Trader Callendar); Wilfrid Lawson (McDougle); Robert Barrat (Magistrate Duncan); John F. Hamilton (The Professor); Moroni Olsen (Tom Calhoon); Eddie Quillan (Will Anderson); Chill Wills (M'Cammon); Ian Wolfe (Poole); Wallis Clark (Sgt. McGlashan); Monte Montague (Morris); Eddy Waller (Jailer); Clay Clement (Governor John Penn); Olaf Hytten (General Gage); Charles Middleton (Doctor Stokes); Douglas Spencer (Prisoner in irons). ¶Released November 10.

The Dark Command (Republic, 1940), 94 min. ¶*Director* Raoul Walsh; *writers* Grover Jones, Lionel Houser, F. Hugh Herbert, *from a novel by* W.R. Burnett, *adaptation by* Jan Fortune;

second unit directors Yakima Canutt, Cliff Lyons; *cinematographer* Jack Marta; *art director* John Victor Mackay; *supervising editor* Murray Seldeen; *editor* William Morgan; *music* Victor Young; *production manager* Al Wilson; *costumes* Adele Palmer; *associate producer* Sol C. Siegel; *stunts* Yakima Canutt, Cliff Lyons. ¶Claire Trevor (Mary McCloud); **John Wayne** (Bob Seton); Walter Pidgeon (William Cantrell); Roy Rogers (Fletch McCloud); George Hayes (Doc Grunch); Porter Hall (Angus McCloud); Marjorie Main (Elizabeth Adams [Mrs. Cantrell]); Raymond Walburn (Judge Buckner); Joseph Sawyer (Bushropp); Helen MacKellar (Mrs. Hale); J. Farrell MacDonald (Dave); Trevor Bardette (Mr. Hale); Harry Woods (Dental Patient); Al Bridge (Slave Trader); Glenn Strange (Yankee); Jack Rockwell (Assassin); Ernie S. Adams (Townsman); Edward Hearn (First Juryman); Edmund Cobb (Third Juryman); Hal Taliaferro (Vigilante); Yakima Canutt (Townsman); Ben Alexander (Sentry); Tom London (Messenger); John Merton (Cantrell Man); Dick Rich, Harry Cording. ¶In production, February; released April 15.

Three Faces West (Republic, 1940), 79 min. ¶*Director* Bernard Vorhaus; *writers* F. Hugh Herbert, Joseph Moncure March, Samuel Ornitz, Doris Anderson (uncredited); *cinematographer* John Alton; *art director* John Victor Mackay; *supervising editor* Murray Seldeen; *editor* William Morgan; *music* Victor Young; *production manager* Al Wilson; *wardrobe* Adele Palmer; *special effects* Howard Lydecker; *associate producer* Sol C. Siegel. ¶John Wayne (John Phillips); Charles Coburn (Dr. Braun); Sigrid Gurie (Leni Braun); Spencer Charters (Dr. "Nunk" Atterbury); Roland Varno (Dr. Eric Von Scherer); Trevor Bardette (Clem Higgins); Helen MacKellar

(Mrs. Welles); Sonny Bupp (Billy Welles); Wade Boteler (Harris); Russell Simpson (Minister); Charles Waldron (Dr. Thorpe); Wendell Niles (Radio Announcer); Dewey Robinson (Bartender). ¶Filmed under title of The Refugee. ¶Released July 12.

The Long Voyage Home (Walter Wanger/United Artists, 1940), 105 min. ¶*Director* John Ford; *producer* Walter Wanger; *scenarist* Dudley Nichols, *from one-act plays, "The Moon of the Caribbees," "In the Zone," "Bound East for Cardiff," "The Long Voyage Home,"* by Eugene O'Neill; *photography* Gregg Toland; *art director* James Basevi; *set decorator* Julia Heron; *music* Richard Hageman; *music conducted by* Edward Paul; *sound* Jack Noyes; *production assistants* Wingate Smith; B.F. McEveety, Lowell Farrell; *editor* Sherman Todd; *sound editor* Robert Parrish; *special effects* Ray Binger, R.T. Layton. ¶Thomas Mitchell (Aloysius Driscoll); John Wayne (Ole Olsen); Ian Hunter (Thomas Fenwick, "Smitty"); Barry Fitzgerald (Cocky); Wilfred Lawson (Captain); Mildred Natwick (Freda); John Qualen (Axel Swenson); Ward Bond (Yank); Joe Sawyer (Davis); Arthur Shields (Donkeyman); J.M. Kerrigan (Limehouse Crimp); David Hughes (Scotty); Billy Bevan (Joe, Limehouse Barman); Cyril McLaglen (Mate); Robert E. Perry (Paddy); Jack Pennick (Johnny Bergman); Constantin Frenke (Narvey); Dan Borzag (Tim); Harry Tenbrook (Max); Douglas Walton (Second Lieutenant); Raphaela Ottiano (Daughter of the Tropics); Carmen Morales, Carmen d'Antonio (Girls in canoe); Harry Woods (Captain of "Amindra"); Edgar "Blue" Washington, Lionel Pape, Jane Crowley, and Maureen Roden-Ryan. ¶Filming begun in April; released October 8.

Seven Sinners (Universal, 1940;

reissued 1947 in Britain as Cafe of the Seven Sinners), 87 min. ¶*Director* Tay Garnett; *writers* John Meehan, Harry Tugend, *from a story by* Ladislas Fodor and Laslo Vadnai; *cinematographer* Rudolph Mate; *art directors* Jack Otterson, Martin Obzina; *editor* Ted J. Kent; *music* Frank Skinner, Hans Salter; *songs* Frank Loesser, Frederick Hollander; *producer* Joe Pasternak. ¶Marlene Dietrich (Bijou); John Wayne (Lt. Dan Brent); Albert Dekker (Dr. Martin); Broderick Crawford (Little Ned [Edward Patrick Finnegan]); Anna Lee (Dorothy Henderson); Mischa Auer (Sasha); Billy Gilbert (Tony); Richard Carle (District Officer); Samuel S. Hinds (Governor); Oscar Homolka (Antro); Reginald Denny (Capt. Church); Vince Barnett (Bartender); Herbert Rawlinson (First Mate); James Craig, William Bakewell (Ensigns); Antonio Moreno (Rubio); Russell Hicks (First Governor); William B. Davidson (Police Chief). ¶The same story used for new screenplay in film called South Sea Sinner (not with Wayne) in 1949; released in Britain as East of Java. ¶Filming in August; released October 25.

Melody Ranch (Republic, 1940), 84 min. ¶*Director* Joseph Santley. ¶John Wayne is said to have done the stunt for the car trolley crash scene. The film is a musical Western starring Gene Autry, Jimmy Durante, and Ann Miller. ¶Released November 4.

A Man Betrayed (Television Title, Wheel of Fortune; British title, Citadel of Crime; Republic, 1941), 80 min. ¶*Director* John H. Lauer; *writer* Isabel Dawn, *from a story by* Jack Moffitt; *adaptation by* Tom Kilpatrick; *cinematographer* Jack Marta; *art director* John Victor Mackay; *supervising editor* Murray Seldeen; *editor* Charles Craft; *music director* Cy Feuer; *associate producer* Armand Schaefer. ¶John Wayne (Lynn Hollister); Frances Dee (Sabra

Cameron); Edward Ellis (Tom Cameron); Wallace Ford (Casey); Ward Bond (Floyd); Harold Huber (Morris Slade); Alexander Granach (T. Amato); Barnett Parker (George, the Butler); Ed Stanley (Prosecutor); Tim Ryan (Mr. Wilson); Harry Hayden (Langworthy); Russell Hicks (Pringle); Pierre Watkin (Governor); Ferris Taylor (Mayor). ¶Filmed as **Citadel of Crime** from January to February. ¶Released March 7.

Lady from Louisiana (Republic, 1941), 82 min. ¶*Director* Bernard Vorhaus; *writers* Vera Caspary, Michael Hogan, Guy Endore, *from a screen story by* Edward James, Francis Faragoh; *cinematographer* Jack Marta; *art director* John Victor Mackay; *supervising editor* Murray Seldeen; *editor* Edward Mann; *music director* Cy Feuer; *production manager* Al Wilson; *wardrobe* Adele Palmer; *associate producer* Bernard Vorhaus. ¶**John Wayne** (John Reynolds); Ona Munson (Julie Mirbeau); Ray Middleton (Blackie Williams); Henry Stephenson (General Mirbeau); Helen Westley (Mrs. Brunot); Jack Pennick (Cuffy); Dorothy Dandridge (Felice); Shimen Ruskin (Gaston); Jacqueline Dalya (Pearl); Paul Scardon (Judge Wilson); Maj. James H. MacNamara (Senator Cassidy); James C. Morton (Littlefield); Maurice Costello (Edwards). ¶Filmed as **Lady From New Orleans** in March-April released April 22.

The Shepherd of the Hills (Paramount, 1941), Technicolor, 98 min. ¶*Director* Henry Hathaway; *writers* Grover Jones, Stuart Anthony, *from a story by* Harold Bell Wright, *based on his novel, Shepherd of the Hills; cinematographers* Charles Lang, W. Howard Greene; *art directors* Hans Dreier, Roland Anderson; *editor* Ellsworth Hoagland; *music* Gerard Carbonara; *color art director* Natalie Kalmus; *color art associate* Henri Jaffa; *sound recording* Harold Lewis, John Cope; *producer* Jack Moss. ¶**John Wayne** (Young Matt Matthews); Betty Field (Sammy Lane); Harry Carey (Daniel Howitt); Beulah Bondi (Aunt Mollie); James Barton (Old Matt); Marjorie Main (Granny Becky); Samuel S. Hinds (Andy Beeler); John Qualen (Coot Royal); Marc Lawrence (Pete); Tom Faddon (Jim Lane); Ward Bond (Wash Gibbs); Dorothy Adams (Elvy Royal); Olin Howland (Corky, the Storekeeper); Fuzzy Knight (Mr. Palestrom); John Harmon (Charles, the Deputy); Carl Knowles (Revenuer); Fern Emmett (Mrs. Palestrom); Vivita Campbell (Baby Royal); William Haade, Robert Kortman, Henry Brandon, Jim Corey (Bald Knobbers); Doctor (Selmer Jackson). ¶A remake of the 1927 **Shepherd of the Hills**, with John Boles as Young Matt Matthews. ¶Filmed from October to November; released July 18.

Lady for a Night (Republic, 1942), 87 min. ¶*Director* Leigh Jason; *writers* Isabel Dawn, Boyce De Gaw, *from a screen story by* Garrett Fort; *cinematographer* Norbert Brodine; *art director* John Victor Mackay; *supervising editor* Murray Seldeen; *editor* Ernest Nims; *music* David Buttolph; *production manager* Al Wilson; *musical direction* Cy Feuer; *associate producer* Albert J. Cohen. ¶Joan Blondell (Jenny Blake); **John Wayne** (Jack Morgan); Ray Middleton (Alan Alderson); Philip Merivale (Stephen Alderson); Blanche Yurka (Julia Alderson); Edith Barrett (Katherine Alderson); Leonid Kinskey (Boris); Hattie Noel (Chloe); Montagu Lover (Judge); Carmel Myers (Mayor's Wife); Dorothy Burgess (Flo); Guy Usher (Governor); Ivan Miller (Mayor); Patricia Knox (Mabel); Lew Payton (Napoleon); Marilyn Hare (Mary Lou); The Hall Johnson Choir; Dewey Robinson. ¶Filmed October-November; released January 5.

Reap the Wild Wind (Paramount, 1942), Technicolor, 124 min. ¶Director

Cecil B. De Mille; *writers* Alan LeMay, Charles Bennett, Jesse Lasky, Jr., Jeanie Macpherson (uncredited), *from a Saturday Evening Post story by* Thelma Strabel; *2nd unit director* Arthur Rosson; *cinematographers* Victor Milner, William V. Skall, Dewey Wrigley (underwater); *art directors* Hans Dreier, Roland Anderson; *editor,* Anne Bauchens; *music* Victor Young; *associate producer* William H. Pine; *Technicolor color director* Natalie Kalmus; *special photographic effects* Gordon Jennings, Al Pereira, Farciot Edouart; *sound recording* Harry Lindgren, John Cope; *costumes* Natalie Visart; *makeup supervisor* Edwin Maxwell, Phyllis Loughton; *marine advisor* Capt. Fred F. Ellis; *producer* Cecil B. DeMille. ¶Ray Milland (Stephen Tolliver); **John Wayne** (Capt. Jack Stuart); Paulette Goddard (Loxi Claiborne); Raymond Massey (King Cutler); Robert Preston (Dan Cutler); Susan Hayward (Drusilla Alston); Lynne Overman (Capt. Phillip Philpott); Walter Hampden (Commodore Devereaux); Louise Beavers (Maum Maria); Elisabeth Risdon (Mrs. Claiborne); Janet Beecher (Mrs. Mottram); Hedda Hopper (Aunt Henrietta Beresford); Martha O'Driscoll (Ivy Deveraux); Victor Kilian (Nathias Widgeon); Charles Bickford (Captain of the "Tyfib"); Oscar Polk (Salt Meat); Ben Carter (Chinkapin); Wee Willie (William) Davis (The Lamb); Lane Chandler (Sam, Philpott's Mate); Lou Merrill (Captain of the "Pelican"); Frank M. Thomas (Dr. Jepson); Keith Richards (Capt. Carruthers); Victor Varconi (Lubbock [Cutler's Henchman]); J. Farrell MacDonald (Captain at Conference); Harry Woods (Mace, [Cutler's Henchman]); Raymond Hatton (Master Shipwright); Milburn Stone (Lt. Farragut, Claiborne Lookout); Tony Patton (Cadge); Barbara Britton, Julia Faye, Ameda Lambert (Charleston Ladies); D'Arcy Miller, Bruce Warren (Charleston Gentlemen); Byron Foulger (Bixby, the Emissary); Frank

Ferguson (Cutler's Co-Counsel); William Haade (Seaman in First Wreck); Stanley Andrews (Jailer); Davidson Clarke (Judge Marvin); Frank Lackteen (Cutler Henchman); George Reed (Servant at Mottram House); and bits by following: Nestor Paiva, Emory Parnell, Monte Blue, George Melford, Forrest Taylor, John Sainpolis, Stanhope Wheatcroft, Ed Brady, Frank C. Shannon, Buddy Pepper, Tom Chatterton, Frank Richards, Hayden Stevenson, William Cabanne, Mildred Harris, Hope Landin, Claire McDowell, Dorothy Sebastian, Jack Lyden, Ottola Nesmith, Max Davidson, Gertrude Astor, Maurice Costello. ¶Produced June to August, 1941; released March 1942.

The Spoilers (Charles K. Feldman Group/Universal, 1942), 87 min. ¶*Director* Ray Enright; *producer* Frank Lloyd; *associate producer* Lee Marcus; *based on the novel by* Rex Beach *and the play by* Beach and James MacArthur; *screenplay* Lawrence Hazard, Tom Reed; *art directors* Jack Otterson, John R. Goodman; *music* Hans J. Salter; *music director* Charles Previn; *costumes* Vera West; *camera* Milton Krasner; *editor* Clarence Kolster; *assistant director* Vernon Keys; *set decorations* R.A. Causman; *special photographic effects* John P. Fulton; *dialogue director* Gene Lewis; *musical director* Charles Previn; *musical score* H.J. Salter; *sound director* Bernard B. Brown; *technician* Robert Pritchard. ¶Marlene Dietrich (Cherry Malotte); Randolph Scott (Alex McNamara); **John Wayne** (Roy Glennister); Margaret Lindsay (Helen Chester); Harry Carey (Dextry); Richard Barthelmess (Bronco Kid Farrell); George Cleveland (Bantry); Samuel S. Hinds (Judge Stillman); Russell Simpson (Flapjack Simms); William Farnum (Wheaton); Marietta Canty (Idabelle); Jack Norton (Mr. Skinner, the Drunk); Ray Bennett (Clark); Forrest Taylor

(Bennett); Charles Halton (Struve); Bud Osborne (Marshal); Drew Demarest (Galloway); Robert W. Service (Himself, the Poet); Charles McMurphy, Art Miles, William Haade (Deputies); Robert Homans (Sea Captain); Irving Bacon (Hotel Proprietor); Robert McKenzie (Restaurateur); Chester Clute (Montrose); Harry Woods (Complaining Miner); William Gould (Marshal Thompson); Willie Fung (Chinaman in Jail); Lloyd Ingraham (Kelly). ¶Previously filmed with same title in 1914, with William Farnum as Roy Glennister; again in 1923, with Milton Sills as Roy Glennister; again in 1930, with Gary Cooper as Roy Glennister. Later filmed with same title in 1955, with Jeff Chandler as Roy Glennister. ¶Filmed January–February; released May 8.

In Old California (Republic, 1942), 88 min. ¶*Director* William McGann; *writers* Gertrude Purcell, Frances Hyland, *from a screen story by* J. Robert Bren, Gladys Atwater; *cinematographer* Jack Marta; *art director* Russell Kimball; *supervising editor* Murray Seldeen; *editor* Howard O'Neill; *music* David Buttolph; *associate producer* Robert North. ¶**John Wayne** (Tom Craig); Binnie Barnes (Lacey Miller); Albert Dekker (Britt Dawson); Helen Parrish (Ellen Sanford); Patsy Kelly (Helga); Edgar Kennedy (Kegs McKeever); Dick Purcell (Joe Dawson); Harry Shannon (Mr. Carlin); Charles Halton (Mr. Hayes); Emmett Lynn (Whitey); Bob McKenzie (Mr. Bates); Milt Kibbee (Mr. Tompkins); Paul Sutton (Chick); Anne O'Neal (Mrs. Tompkins); Frank McGlynn. ¶Filmed March–April; released May 31.

Flying Tigers (Republic, 1942), 102 min. ¶*Director* David Miller; *writers* Kenneth Gamet, Barry Trivers, *from a screen story by* Kenneth Gamet; *cinematographer* Jack Marta; *art director* Russell Kimball; *editor* Ernest Nims;

music Victor Young; *set decoration* Otto Siegel; *musical director* Walter Scharf; *wardrobe* Adele Palmer; *special effects* Howard Lydecker; *technical assistance* Curtis-Wright Corporation, William D. Pawley, co-founder of The American Volunteer Group; *associate producer* Edmund Grainger. ¶**John Wayne** (Jim Gordon); John Carroll (Woody Jason); Anna Lee (Brooke Elliott); Paul Kelly (Hap Davis); Gordon Jones (Alabama Smith); Mae Clarke (Verna Bales); Addison Richards (Col. Lindsay); Edmund MacDonald (Blackie Bales); Bill Shirley (Dale); Tom Neal (Reardon); James Dodd (McIntosh); Gregg Barton (Tex Norton); John James (Selby); Chester Gan (Mike); David Bruce (Lt. Barton); Malcolm McTaggert (McCurdy); Charles Lane (Airport Official); Tom Seidel (Barratt, a New Flyer); Richard Loo (Doctor); Richard Crane (Airfield Radio Man); Willie Fung (Jim, the Waiter). ¶Filmed May–July; released October 8.

Reunion in France (British title, **Mademoiselle France**; Metro-Goldenn-Mayer, 1942), 104 min. ¶*Director* Jules Dassin; *writers* Jan Lustig, Marvin Borowsky, Marc Connelly, Charles Hoffman (uncredited), *from a screen story by* Ladislas Bus-Fekete; *cinematographer* Robert Planck; *art director* Cedric Gibbons; *editor* Elmo Vernon; *music* Franz Waxman; *set decoration* Henry Gray; *special effects* Warren Newcombe; *recording director* Douglas Shearer; *producer* Joseph L. Mankiewicz. ¶Joan Crawford (Michele de la Becque); **John Wayne** (Pat Talbot); Philip Dorn (Robert Cortot); Reginald Owen (Schultz [Pinkham]); Albert Bassermann (General Hugo Schroeder); John Carradine (Ulrich Windler); Ann Ayars (Juliette); J. Edward Bromberg (Durand); Moroni Olsen (Paul Grebeau); Henry Daniell (Emile Fleuron); Howard Da Silva (Anton Stregel); Charles Arnt (Honore); Morris Ankrum (Martin); Edith Evanson (Genevieve);

Ernest Dorian (Captain); Margaret Laurence (Clothilde); Odette Myrtil (Mme. Montanot); Peter Whitney (Soldier). ¶Filmed as **Reunion**. ¶Filmed July–September; released December.

Pittsburgh (Charles K. Feldman Group/Universal, 1942), 91 min. ¶*Director* Lewis Seiler; *writers* Kenneth Gamet, Tom Reed, *with additional dialogue by* John Twist, *from a screen stroy by* George Owen, Tom Reed; *cinematographer* Robert De Brasse; *art director* John Goodman; *editor* Paul Landres; *music* Frank Skinner, Hans J. Salter; *special photographic effects* John Fulton; *set decorations* R.G. Gassman, Ira S. Webb; *dialogue director* Paul Fix; *sound director* Bernard B. Brown; *technician* Paul Neal; *musical director* Charles Previn; *music* Frank Skinner, H.J. Salter; *gowns* Vera West; *assistant director* Charles Gould; *associate producer* Robert Fellows. ¶Marlene Dietrich (Josie "Hunky" Winters); Randolph Scott (Cash Evans); **John Wayne** (Charles "Pittsburgh" Markham); Frank Craven ("Doc" Powers); Louise Albritton (Shannon Prentiss); Shemp Howard (Shorty the Tailor); Thomas Gomez (Joe Malneck); Ludwig Stossel (Dr. Grazlich); Samuel S. Hinds (Morgan Prentiss); Sammy Stein (Killer Kane); Paul Fix (Burnside, the Mine Operator); John Dilson (Wilson); William Haade (Johnny, a Miner); Charles Coleman (Mike, the Butler); Nestor Paiva (Barney, the Restaurateur); Harry Cording (Miner); Douglas Fowley (Frawley, Josie's Escort); Ray Walker (Wise-guy Reporter); Charles Arnt (Building Site Laborer); William Gould (Burns, the Production Manager). ¶Filmed September–October; released December.

A Lady Takes a Chance (RKO Radio, 1943), 86 min. ¶*Director* William A. Seiter; *writer* Robert Ardrey, Garson Kanin (uncredited), *from a screen story by* Jo Swerling; *cinematographer* Frank Redman; *art directors* Albert S. D'Agostino, Alfred Herman; *editor* Theron Warth; *music* Roy Webb; *associate producer* Richard Ross; *special effects* Vernon Walker; *set decorations* Darrell Silvera, Al Fields; *gowns* Edmund Stevenson; *musical direction* C. Bakaleinikoff; *recorded by* Roy Meadows; *re-recorded by* James C. Stewart; *assistant director* J.D. Starkey; *producer* Frank Ross. ¶Jean Arthur (Molly Truesdale); **John Wayne** (Duke Hudkins); Charles Winninger (Waco); Phil Silvers (Smiley Lambert); Mary Field (Florrie Bendix); Don Costello (Drunk); John Philliber (Storekeeper); Grady Sutton (Malcolm); Grant Withers (Bob); Hans Conreid (Greg); Peggy Carroll (Jitterbug); Ariel Heath (Flossie); Sugar Geise (Linda Belle); Joan Blair (Lilly); Tom Fadden (Mullen); Ed Waller (Bus Station Attendant); Nina Quartaro (Carmencita); Alex Melesh (Bartender); Cy Kendall (Gambling House Boss); Paul Scott (Second Bartender); Charles D. Brown (Dr. Humbolt); Mysty Shot (Sammy, the Horse); Butch and Buddy, The Three Peppers. ¶Originally intended to be called **The Cowboy and the Girl**. Filmed March–April; released August 19.

In Old Oklahoma (Reissued as **War of the Wildcats**; Republic, 1943), 102 min. ¶*Director* Albert S. Rogell; *writers* Ethel Hill, Eleanor Griffin, *from adaptation by* Thomas Burtis *of his story*, "War of the Wildcats"; *cinematographer* Jack Marta; *art director* Russell Kimball; *editor* Ernest Nims; *music* Walter Scharf; *sound* Dick Tyler, Howard Wilson; *set decorations* Otto Siegel; *costumes* Walter Plunkett; *special effects* Howard Lydecker, Jr.; *associate producer* Robert North. ¶**John Wayne** (Dan Somers); Martha Scott (Catherine Allen); Albert Dekker (Jim "Hunk" Gardner); George "Gabby" Hayes (Desprit Dean); Marjorie Rambeau

(Bessie Baxter); Dale Evans ("Cuddles" Walker); Grant Withers (Richardson); Sidney Blackmer (Teddy Roosevelt); Paul Fix (The Cherokee Kid); Cecil Cunningham (Mrs. Ames); Irving Bacon (Ben, the Telegraph Operator); Byron Fougler (Wilkins); Anne O'Neal (Mrs. Peabody); Richard Graham (Walter); Robert Warwick (Big Tree); Stanley Andrews (Mason, the Indian Agent); Will Wright (Doctor); Harry Shannon (Charlie Witherspoon); Emmet Vogan (President Roosevelt's Aide); Charles Arnt (Joe, the Train Conductor); Edward Gargan (Kelsey, the Waiter); Harry Woods (Al Dalton); Tom London (Tom); Dick Rich, Charles Whittaker, LeRoy Mason, Lane Chandler, Arthur Loft (Other Men on Train); and (perhaps) Rhonda Fleming. ¶Filmed August–September; released December 6.

The Fighting Seabees (Reissued in Ireland as **Donovan's Army;** Republic, 1944), 100 min. ¶*Director* Edward Ludwig; *writers* Borden Chase, Aeneas MacKenzie, *from a screen story by* Borden Chase; *2nd unit director* Howard Lydecker; *cinematographer* William Bradford; *art director* Duncan Cramer; *editor* Richard Van Enger; *music* Walter Scharf; *"Song of the Seabees," music by* Peter De Rose, *lyrics by* Sam M. Lewis, *sound* Tom Carman, Howard Wilson; *set decorations* Otto Siegel; *gowns by* Adele; *special effects* Theodore Lydecker; *technical advisors* Lt. Cmdr. Hubert Hunter, USNR, Lt. Cmdr. William A. McManus, USN; *associate producer* Albert J. Cohen. ¶**John Wayne** (Wedge Donovan); Dennis O'Keefe (Lt. Commander Robert Yarrow); Susan Hayward (Constance Chesley); William Frawley (Eddie Powers); Leonid Kinskey (Johnny Novasky); J.M. Kerrigan (Sawyer Collins); Grant Withers (Whanger Spreckles); Paul Fix (Ding Jacobs); Ben Welden (Yump Lunkin); William Forrest (Lieutenant Kerrick); Addison

Richards (Captain Joyce); Jay Norris (Joe Brick); Duncan Renaldo (Juan); Tom London (Johnson); Hal Taliaferro (Seabee); Crane Whitley (Officer In Charge of Refueling); William Hall, Charles D. Brown, Roy Barcroft, Chief Thundercloud. ¶Produced September–December, 1943; released March 10, 1944.

Tall in the Saddle (RKO Radio, 1944), 87 min. ¶*Director* Edwin L. Marin; *writers* Michael Hogan, Paul P. Fix, *from a magazine story, later novel, by* Gordon Ray Young; *cinematographer* Robert De Grasse; *art directors* Albert S. D'Agostino, Ralph Berger; *editor* Philip Martin, Jr.; *music* Roy Webb; *associate producer* Theron Warth; *producer* Robert Fellows. ¶**John Wayne** (Rocklin); Ella Raines (Arly Haroldday); Ward Bond ("Judge" Garvey); Audrey Long (Clara Cardell); George "Gabby" Hayes (Dave); Elisabeth Risdon (Miss Martin); Russell Wade (Clint Haroldday); Don Douglas (Mr. Haroldday); Frank Puglia (Tala); Emory Parnell (Jackson, the Sheriff); Raymond Hatton (Zeke); Paul P. Fix (Bob Clews); Harry Woods (George Clews); Cy Kendall (Cap, the Bartender); Bob McKenzie (Doc Riding); Wheaton Chambers (Ab Jenkins); Walter Baldwin (Stan, at the Stage Station); Russell Simpson (Pat); Frank Orth (Ferdy Davis); George Chandler, Eddy Walker, Frank Darien, Clem Bevans, Erville Alderson, Russell Hopton. ¶Filmed April–June; released September.

Flame of the Barbary Coast (Republic, 1945), 91 min. ¶*Director* Joseph Kane; *writer* Borden Chase, *from a story by* Prescott Chaplin; *cinematographer* Robert DeGrasse; *art director* Gano Chittenden; *editor* Richard L. Van Enger; *music direction* Morton Scott; *associate producer* Joseph Kane. ¶**John Wayne** (Duke Fergus); Ann Dvorak (Flaxen Terry);

Joseph Schildkraut (Tito Morell); William Frawley (Wolf Wylie); Virginia Grey (Rita Dane); Russell Hicks (Cyrus Danver); Jack Norton (Byline Conners); Paul Fix (Calico Jim); Manart Kippen (Doctor Gorman); Eve Lynne (Martha); Marc Lawrence (Joe Disko); Butterfly McQueen (Beulah); Rex Lease (Collingswood, the Headwaiter); Hank Bell (Hank); Al Murphy (Horseshoe Brown); Adele Mara (Marie); Emmett Vogan (Rita's Agent). ¶Filmed July–August; released May 28.

Back to Bataan (RKO Radio, 1945), 95 min. ¶*Director* Edward Dmytryk; *writers* Ben Barzman, Richard H. Landau, *from a screen story by* Aeneas MacKenzie, William Gordon; *cinematographer* Nicholas Musuraca; *art directors* Albert S. D'Agostino, Ralph Berger; *editor* Marston Fay; *music* Roy Webb; *musical director* C. Bakaleinikoff; *special effects* Vernon L. Walker; *set decorations* Darrell Silvera, Charles Nields; *recorded by* Earl A. Wolcott; *gowns* Renie; *assistant director* Truby Rosenberg; *re-recording* James G. Stewart; *technical advisor,* Colonel George S. Clarke, USA; *associate producer* Theron Warth; *executive producer* Robert Fellows. ¶John Wayne (Colonel Joseph Madden); Anthony Quinn (Captain Andres Bonifacio); Beulah Bondi (Bertha Barnes); Fely Franquelli (Dalisay Delgado); Richard Loo (Major Hasko); Philip Ahn (Colonel Kuroki); Lawrence Tierney (Lt. Commander Waite); Leonard Strong (General Homma); Paul Fix (Jackson); Abner Biberman (Japanese Captain at Schoolhouse; also, as Elder Japanese at Conference); "Ducky" Louie (Maximo Cuenca); Vladimir Sokoloff (Senor Buenaventura J. Bello, School Principal); J. Alex Havier (Sgt. Biernesa ["Skinny"]); John Miljan (General at Headquarters); Harold Fong (Prince Ito); Bentson Fong (Officer Making Broadcast). ¶Filmed as **The Invisible Army,** November, 1944–March, 1945;

released May 31.

They Were Expendable (Metro-Golden-Mayer, 1945), 136 min. ¶*Director* John Ford, Captain, USNR; *writer* Commander Frank Wead, Comdr., USN (Ret); *from the book by* William L. White; *2nd unit director* James C. Havens (*rear projection plates by* Robert Montgomery); *assistant director* Edward O'Fearna; *cinematographer* Joseph H. August, Lt. Comdr., USNR; *art directors* Cedric Gibbons, Malcolm Brown; *set decorators* Edwin B. Willis, Ralph S. Hurst; *editors* Frank E. Hull, Douglass Biggs; *music* Herbert Stothart; *recording director* Douglas Shearer; *special effects* A. Arnold Gillespie; *makeup created by* Jack Dawn; *2nd unit director* James C. Havens, Captain, USMCR; *associate producer* Cliff Reid; *producer* John Ford. ¶Robert Montgomery (Lt. John Brickley); **John Wayne** (Lt. Rusty Ryan); Donna Reed (Lt. Sandy Davis); Jack Holt (General Martin); Ward Bond ("Boats" Mulcahey; also called "Irish"); Marshall Thompson (Ens. "Snake" Gardner); Paul Langton (Ens. Andy Andrews); Leon Ames (Maj. James Morton); Arthur Walsh (Seaman Jones); Donald Curtis (Lt. Shorty Long); Cameron Mitchell (Ens. George Cross); Jeff York (Ens. Tony Aiken); Murray Alper ("Slug" Mahan); Harry Tenbrook ("Squarehead" Larsen; also called "Cookie"); Jack Pennick (Doc Charlie); Alex Havier (Benny Lecoco); Charles Trowbridge (Admiral Blackwell); Robert Barrat (The General [MacArthur]); Bruce Kellogg (Elder Tompkins); Tim Murdock (Ens. Brant); Louis Jean Heydt ("Ohio," the flyer in the hospital); Russell Simpson ("Dad" Knowland, chief of shipyard); Vernon Steele (Army Doctor); Robert Emmett O'Connor (Bartender); William B. Davidson (Bar Proprietor); Tom Tyler (Officer on Plane); Lee Tung Foo (Oriental Bartender); Wallace Ford. ¶Location filming in Florida. ¶Filmed March–June; released December 20.

Dakota (Republic, 1945), 82 min. ¶*Associate producer-director* Joseph Kane; *story* Carl Foreman; *adaptor* Howard Estabrook; *screenplay* Lawrence Hazard; *art directors* Russell Kimball, Gano Chittenden; *set decorators* John McCarthy, Jr., James Redd; *music director* Walter Scharf; *choreography* Larry Ceballos; *song* Andrew Sterling and Harry Von Tilzer; *assistant director* Al Wood; *sound* Fred Stahl; *special effects* Howard and Theodore Lydecker; *camera* Jack Marta; *2nd unit director* Yakima Canutt; *editor* Fred Allen. ¶John Wayne (John Devlin); Vera Hruba Ralston (Sandra "Sandy" Poli Devlin); Ward Bond (Jim Bender); Walter Brennan (Captain Bounce); Mike Mazurki (Bigtree Collins); Hugo Haas (Marko Poli); Ona Munson (Jersey Thomas); Paul Fix (Carp); Nicodemus Stewart (Nicodemus [Mose]); Olive Blakeney (Mrs. Stowe); Robert Livingston (Lieutenant); Robert H. Barrat (Anson Stowe); Pierre Watkin (Wexton Geary); Olin Howlin (Devlin's Driver); Grant Withers (Slagin); Selmer Jackson (Dr. Judson); Claire Du Brey (Wahtonka); Jack LaRue (Slade); Jonathan Hale (Colonel Wordin); Roy Barcroft (Poli's Driver); Larry Thompson (Poli's Footman); Sarah Padden (Mrs. Plummer); George Cleveland (Mr. Plummer); Houseley Stevenson (Railroad Clerk); Bobby Blake (Boy); Paul Hurst (Captain Spotts); Dorothy Christy (Nora); Michael Visaroff (Russian); Victor Varconi (Frenchman); Paul E. Burns (Swede); Linda Stirling (Girl); Eddy Waller (Stagecoach Driver); Cliff Lyons, Fred Graham. ¶Filmed July–September; released December 25.

Without Reservations (RKO Radio, 1946), 107 min., ¶*Director* Mervyn LeRoy; *writer* Andrew Solt, *from the novel, Thanks, God! I'll Take It From Here, by* Jane Allen, Mae Livingston; *cinematographer* Milton Krasner; *art directors* Albert S. D'Agostino, Ralph Berger; *editor* Jack Ruggiero; *music*

Roy Webb; *special effects* Vernon L. Walker, Russell A. Cully, Harold Stine; *set decorations* Darrell Silvera, James Altwies; *production assistant* William H. Cannon; *musical director* C. Bakaleinikoff; *sound* Clem Portman, Frances M. Sarver; *Miss Colbert's clothes by* Adrian; *montage* Harold Palmer; *assistant director* Lloyd Richards; *producer* Jesse L. Lasky. ¶Claudette Colbert (Christopher [Kit] Madden); John Wayne (Rusty Thomas); Don DeFore (Dink Watson); Anne Triola (Connie [Consuela Callaghan]); Phil Brown (Soldier); Frank Puglia (Ortega); Thurston Hall (Henry Baldwin); Dona Drake (Dolores); Fernando Alvarado (Mexican Boy); Charles Arnt (Salesman); Louella Parsons (Herself); Cary Grant (Himself); Jack Benny (Himself, the Autograph Hunter); Dolores Moran (Herself); Charles Williams (Louis Burt); Charles Evans (Philip Jerome, the Publisher); Frank Wilcox (Jack); William Benedict (Telegram Boy); Harry Hayden (Randall, Hotel Clerk in Albuquerque); Ian Wolfe (Gibbs, the Reporter); Robert "Bob" Anderson, Marvin Miller (Radio Announcers); Esther Howard (Women in the Book Club); Raymond Burr (Paul Gill); Griff Barnett, Will Wright (Ticket Collectors); Sam McDaniel (Train Porter); Houseley Stevenson (Jailer); Cy Kendall (Lawyer); William Challee (Flyer who advises the Train Porter). ¶Filmed as **Thanks God, I'll Take it From Here,** October 1945–January 1946; released May 1946.

Angel and the Badman (Republic, 1947), 100 min. ¶*Producer* John Wayne; *director-screenplay* James Edward Grant; *second unit director* Yakima Canutt; *music* Richard Hageman; *music director* Cy Feuer; *songs* Kim Gannon and Walter Kent; *assistant director* Harvey Dwight; *production designer* Ernest Fegte; *set decorators* John McCarthy, Jr., Charles Thompson; *sound* Victor Appel; *special camera* *effects* Howard and Theodore Lydecker; *cinematographer* Archie J. Stout; *editor* Harry Keller; *costumes* Adele Palmer; *makeup supervision* Bob Mark; *hair stylist* Peggy Gray. ¶John Wayne (Quirt Evans); Gail Russell (Penny Worth); Harry Carey (Marshal Wistful McClintock); Bruce Cabot (Laredo Stevens); Irene Rich (Mrs. Worth); John Halloran (Thomas Worth); Lee Dixon (Randy McCall); Tom Powers (Dr. Mangrum); Stephen Grant (Johnny Worth); Paul Hurst (Frederick Carson); Olin Howlin (Bradley); Joan Barton (Lila Neal); Craig Woods (Ward Withers); Marshall Reed (Nelson); Hank Worden (Townsman); Pat Flaherty (Baker Brother). ¶Filmed as **The Angel and the Outlaw,** April–July, 1946; released February 15, 1947.

Tycoon (RKO Radio, 1947), Technicolor, 128 min. ¶*Director* Richard Wallace; *writers* Bordon Chase, John Twist, *from the novel by* C.E. Scoggins; *cinematographers* Harry J. Wild, W. Howard Greene; *art directors* Albert S. D'Agostino, Carroll Clark; *editor* Frank Doyle; *music* Leigh Harline; *Technicolor color consultant* W. Howard Greene; *Technicolor color director* Natalie Kalmus; *associate color director* Morgan Padelford; *musical director* C. Bakaleinikoff; *orchestral arrangements* Gil Grau; *special effects* Vernon L. Walker; *set decorations* Darrell Silvera, Harley Miller; *makeup supervision* Gordon Bau; *hair stylist* Hazel Rogers; *assistant director* Grayson Rogers; *sound* John L. Cass, Clem Portman; *gowns by* Michael Woulfe; *men's wardrobe* Dwight Franklin; *production assistant* Edward Killy; *producer* Stephen Ames. ¶**John Wayne** (Johnny Munroe); Laraine Day (Maura Alexander); Sir Cedric Hardwicke (Frederick Alexander); Judith Anderson (Miss Braithwhaite); James Gleason (Pop Mathews); Anthony Quinn (Ricky Vegas); Grant Withers (Fog Harris); Paul Fix (Joe); Fernando Alvarado (Chico, the Boy); Harry Woods (Holden); Michael Harvey (Curly Massinger); Charles Trowbridge (Senor Tobar); Martin Garralaga (Chavez); Nacho Galindo, Eduardo Noriega. ¶Filmed February–May; released December 27.

Fort Apache (RKO Radio, 1948), 127 min. ¶*Producers* John Ford, Merian C. Cooper; *director* Ford; *based on the story "Massacre" by* James Warner Bellah; *screenplay* Frank S. Nugent; *music* Richard Hageman; music director Lucien Cailliet; *art director* James Basevi; *set decorator* Joe Kish; *costumes* Michael Meyers (Men), Ann Peck (Women); *assistant directors* Lowell Farrell, Jack Pennick; *2nd unit director* Cliff Lyons; *makeup* Emile La Vigne; *choreography* Kenny Williams; *technical advisors* Major Philip Keiffer, Katherine Spaatz; *costume researcher* D.R.O. Hatswell; *sound* Frank Webster, Joseph Kane; *special effects* Dave Koehler; *camera* Archie Stout; *editor* Jack Murray; *production manager* Bernard McEveety. ¶**John Wayne** (Captain Kirby York); Henry Fonda (Lieutenant Colonel Owen Thursday); Shirley Temple (Philadelphia Thursday); John Agar (Lieutenant Michael O'Rourke); Ward Bond (Sergeant Major O'Rourke); George O'Brien (Captain Sam Collingwood); Victor McLaglen (Sergeant Mulcahy); Pedro Armendariz (Sergeant Beaufort); Anna Lee (Mrs. Collingwood); Irene Rich (Mrs. Mary O'Rourke); Guy Kibbee (Dr. Wilkens); Grant Withers (Silas Meacham); Miguel Inclan (Cochise); Jack Pennick (Sergeant Schattuck); Mae Marsh (Mrs. Gates); Dick Foran (Sergeant Quincannon); Frank Ferguson (Newspaperman); Francis Ford (Shotgun Guard, Bartender); Ray Hyke (Recruit); Movita Castenada (Guadalupe); Mary Gordon (Ma, the Trading Post Owner); Mickey Simpson (Officer at Dance); Hank Worden (Hick Recruit); Archie

Twitchell, William Forrest (Reporters); Cliff Clark (Stagecoach Driver); Fred Graham (Cavalryman); Philip Keiffer; Ben Johnson (Wayne's Stunt Double). ¶Filmed as **War Party**, August–September, 1947; released March 9, 1948.

Red River (Monterey/United Artists, 1948), 125 min. ¶*Producer-director* Howard Hawks; *based on the novel* Blazing Guns on the Chisholm Trail *by* Borden Chase; *screenplay* Chase, Charles Schnee; *art director* John Datu Arensma; *music-music director-song* Dimitri Tiomkin; *assistant director* William McGarry; *makeup* Lee Greenway; *sound* Richard DeWeese, Vinton Vernon; *special effects* Donald Steward; *special photographic effects* Allan Thompson; *camera* Russell Harlan; *editor* Christian Nyby; *2nd unit director* Arthur Rosson *(credited as "co-director")*; *executive producer* Charles K. Feldman. ¶**John Wayne** (Tom Dunson); Montgomery Clift (Matthew Garth); Joanne Dru (Tess Millay); Walter Brennan (Nadine Groot); Coleen Gray (Fen); John Ireland (Cherry Valance); Noah Beery, Jr. (Buster McGee); Chief Yowlachie (Quo); Harry Carey, Sr. (Melville); Harry Carey, Jr. (Dan Latimer); Mickey Kuhn (Matthew — as a boy); Paul Fix (Teeler Yacey); Hank Worden (Simms); Ivan Parry (Bunk Kenneally); Hal Taliaferro (Old Leather); Paul Fiero (Fernandez); William Self (Wounded Wrangler); Ray Hyke (Walt Jergens); Tom Tyler (A Quitter); Shelley Winters (Dancehall Girl); Lane Chandler (Colonel); Glenn Strange (Naylor); Dan White (Laredo); Lee Phelps, George Lloyd (Gamblers). ¶Location shooting at Elgin, Arizona. ¶Filmed September–November 1947; released September 17, 1948.

Three Godfathers (Argosy Pictures/Metro-Golden-Mayer, 1948), Technicolor, 106 in. ¶*Director* John Ford; *based on the story by* Peter B. Kyne; *screenplay* Laurence Stallings, Frank S. Nugent; *art director* James Basevi; *set decorator* Joe Kish; *music* Richard Hageman; *assistant director* Wingate Smith, Edward O'Fearna; *camera* Winton C. Hoch, Charles P. Boyle *(second unit)*; *editor* Jack Murray; *Technicolor color director* Natalie Kalmus; *associate color director* Morgan Padelford; *arranger and conductor* Lucien Cailet; *costume research* D.R.O. Hatswell; *men's wardrobe* Michael Meyers; *women's wardrobe* Ann Peck; *makeup* Don Case; *hair dresser* Anna Malin; *sound* Frank Moran, Joseph I. Kane; *sound effects* Patrick Kelley; *special effects* Jack Caffey; *properties* Jack Golconda; *set decorator* Joe Kist; *production manager* Lowell Farrell; *producers* John Ford, Merian C. Cooper. ¶Dedicated "To the Memory of Harry Carey, 'Bright Star of the early western sky...'" ¶**John Wayne** (Robert Marmaduke Sangster Hightower); Pedro Armendariz ("Pete" [Pedro Roca Fuerte]); Harry Carey, Jr. (William Kearney [The Abilene Kid]); Ward Bond (Perley "Buck" Sweet); Mildred Natwick (Mother); Charles Halton (Mr. Latham); Jane Darwell (Miss Florie); Mae Marsh (Mrs. Perley Sweet); Guy Kibbee (Judge); Dorothy Ford (Ruby Latham); Ben Johnson, Michael Dugan, Don Summers (Patrolmen); Fred Libby, Hank Worden (Deputy Sheriffs); Jack Pennick (Luke the Train Conductor); Francis Ford (Drunk); Richard Hageman (Saloon Pianist); Cliff Lyons (Guard at Mojave Tanks). ¶Previously made in 1919 as **Marked Men**, with Harry Carey as Marmaduke Hightower; again in 1930, as **Hell's Heroes**, with Charles Bickford as Hightower; again in 1936, as **Three Godfathers**, with Chester Morris as Hightower. ¶Filmed May–June, 1948; released January 14, 1949.

Wake of the Red Witch (Republic, 1949), 106 min. ¶*Director* Edward

Ludwig; *writers* Harry Brown, Kenneth Gamet, *from the novel by* Garland Roark; *cinematographer* Reggie Lanning; *art director* James Sullivan; *editor* Richard L. Van Enger; *music* Nathan Scott; *orchestration* Stanley Wilson; *sound* J.A. Carman, Howard Wilson; *costumes* Adele Palmer; *special effects (underwater sequences)* Howard and Theodore Lydecker; *set decorations* John McCarthy, Jr. *George Milo; makeup supervision* Bob Mark; *hair stylist* Peggy Gray *optical effects* Consolidated Film Industries; *associate producer* Edmund Grainger. ¶John Wayne (Captain Ralls); Gail Russell (Angelique Desaix); Gig Young (Sam Rosen); Adele Mara (Teleia Van Schreeven); Luther Adler (Mayrant Ruysdaal Sidneye); Eduard Franz (Harmenszoon Van Schreeven); Grant Withers (Capt. Wilde Youngeur); Henry Daniell (Jacques Desaix); Paul Fix (Antonio "Ripper" Arrezo); Dennis Hoey (Captain Munsey); Jeff Corey (Mr. Loring); Erskine Sanford (Doktor Van Arken); Duke Kahanamoku (Va Nuke); John Wengraf (Prosecutor); Henry Brandon (Kurinua, a Native); Myron Healey (Seaman on "Red Witch"); John Pickard (Second Diver); Harlan Warde (Seaman Handling Diving Line); Fernando Alvarado (Maru); Jose Alvarado (Taluna); Carl Thompson (Hekkim, the Cabin Boy); Mickey Simpson (Second Officer); Grant Means (Dirk); Jim Nolan (First Diver); Harry Vegar (Jarma); David Clarke (Mullins); Fred Fox (Ship's Surgeon); Al Kikume (Native Servant); Leo C. Richmond (Native Priest); Harold Lishman (Kharma); Fred Libbey (Sailor—Lookout); Robert Wood (Young Sailor); Fred Graham (Sailor in Fight); Rory Mallinson (Officer); Norman Rainey (Lawyer); Wallace Scott (Sailor); Kuka Tuitama, George Pliz (Natives). ¶Filmed July–November, 1948; released March 1, 1949.

The Fighting Kentuckian (Republic, 1949), 100 min. ¶*Director* George Wag-

gner; *writer* George Waggner; *cinematographer* Lee Garmes; *art director* James Sullivan; *editor* Richard L. Van Enger; *music* George Antheil; *orchestration* R. Dale Butts; *sound* Dick Tyler, Howard Wilson; *gowns designed by* Adele Palmer; *uniforms by* D.R. Overall Hatswell; *set decorations* John McCarthy, Jr., George Milo; *special effects* Howard and Theodore Lydecker; *makeup supervision* Bob Mark; *hair stylist* Peggy Gray; *optical effects* Consolidated Film Industries; *producer* John Wayne. ¶John Wayne (John Breen); Vera Ralston (Fleurette DeMarchand); Philip Dorn (Colonel George Geraud); Oliver Hardy (Willie Paine); Marie Windsor (Ann Logan); John Howard (Blake Randolph); Hugo Haas (General Paul DeMarchand); Odette Myrtil (Mme. DeMarchand); Grant Withers (George Hayden); Paul Fix (Beau Meritt); Mae Marsh (Sister Hattie); Jack Pennick (Captain Dan Carroll); Mickey Simpson (Jacques, the Wrestler); Fred Graham (Carter Ward); Mabelle Koenig (Marie); Shy Waggner, Crystal White (Friends); Hank Worden (Announcer of Wrestling Contest); Charles Cane (Band Leader [Knot Brown]); Cliff Lyons, Chuck Roberson (Driver). ¶Filmed as **A Strange Caravan,** March–May; released September 15.

She Wore a Yellow Ribbon (Argosy Pictures/RKO Radio, 1949), Technicolor, 103 min. ¶*Director* John Ford; *based on the magazine stories,* "War Party," *and* "The Big Hunt," *by* James Warner Bellah; *screenplay* Frank S. Nugent, Laurence Stallings; *Technicolor consultants* Natalie Kalmus, Morgan Padelford; *music* Richard Hageman; *music director* Constantine Bakaleinikoff; *orchestrator* Lucien Cailliet; *art director* James Basevi; *set decorator* Joe Kish; *costumes* Michael Meyers, Ann Peck; *assistant directors* Wingate Smith, Edward O'Fearna; *2nd unit director* Cliff Lyons; *sound* Frank

Webster, Clem Portman; *special effects* Jack Caffee; *camera* Winton Hoch; *2nd unit camera* Charles Boyle; *editor* Jack Murray; *assistant editor* Barbara Ford; *associate producer* Lowell Farrell; *producers* John Ford, Merian C. Cooper. ¶John Wayne (Captain Nathan Brittles); Joanne Dru (Olivia Dandridge); John Agar (Lieutenant Flint Cohill); Ben Johnson (Sergeant Tyree); Harry Carey, Jr. (Lieutenant Ross Pennell); Victor McLaglen (Sergeant Quincannon); Mildred Natwick (Mrs. Abby Allshard); George O'Brien (Major Allshard); Arthur Shields (Dr. O'Laughlin); Francis Ford (Barman); Harry Woods (Karl Rynders); Chief Big Tree (Pony That Walks); Noble Johnson (Red Shirt); Cliff Lyons (Trooper Cliff); Tom Tyler (Quayle); Michael Dugan (Hochbauer); Mickey Simpson (Wagner); Fred Graham (Hench); Frank McGrath (Trumpeter); Don Summers (Jenkins); Fred Libby (Colonel Krumrein); Jack Pennick (Sergeant Major); Billy Jones (Courier); Bill Gettinger and Post Park (Officers); Fred Kennedy (Badger); Rudy Bowman (Private John Smith); Ray Hyke (McCarthy); Lee Bradley (Interpreter); Chief Sky Eagle (Chief Sky Eagle); Paul Fix (Rynder's Partner); Dan White. ¶Location filming at Monument Valley. ¶Filmed November–December, 1948; released October, 1949.

Sands of Iwo Jima (Republic, 1949), 100 min. ¶*Director* Allan Dwan; *writers* Harry Brown, James Edward Grant, *from a screen story by* Harry Brown; *cinematographer* Reggie Lanning; *art director* James Sullivan; *editor* Richard L. Van Enger; *music* Victor Young; *sound* T.A. Carman, Howard Wilson; *costume supervision* Adele Palmer; *set decorations* John McCarthy, Jr., Otto Siegel; *special effects* Howard and Theodore Lydecker; *makeup supervision* Bob Mark; *hair stylist* Peggy Gray; *optical effects* Consolidated Film Industries; *associate producer* Edmund

Grainger. ¶John Wayne (Sgt. John M. Stryker); John Agar (Pfc. Peter Conway); Adele Mara (Allison Bromley); Forrest Tucker (Corporal Al Thomas); Wally Cassell (Pfc. Benny Ragazzi); James Brown (Pfc. Charlie Bass); Richard Webb (Pfc. Dan Shipley); Arthur Franz (Corporal Robert Dunne); Julie Bishop (Mary); James Holden (Pfc. Soames); Peter Coe (Pfc. George Hellenopolis); Richard Jaeckel (Pfc. Frank Flynn); Bill Murphy (Pfc. Eddie Flynn); George Tyne (Pfc. Harris); Hal Fieberling (Pvt. "Ski" Choynski); John McGuire (Captain Joyce); Martin Milner (Pvt. Mike McHugh); Leonard Gumley (Pvt. Sid Stein); William Self (Pvt. L.D. Fowler, Jr.); Don Haggerty (Colonel in Staff Car); Col. D.M. Shoup, Lt.-Col. H.P. Crowe, Capt. Harold G. Shrier, Rene A. Gagnon, Ira H. Hayes, John H. Bradley (Themselves). ¶Filmed July–August; premier in San Francisco, December 14; general release March 1, 1950.

Rio Grande (Argosy Pictures/Republic, 1950), 105 min. ¶*Director* John Ford; *based on the story* "Mission with No Record" *by* James Warner Bellah; *screenplay* James Kevin McGuinness; *art director* Frank Hotaling; *set decorators* John McCarthy, Jr., Charles Thompson; *music* Victor Young; *songs,* "My Gal Is Purple," "Footsore Cavalry," "Yellow Stripes," *by* Stan Jones; "Aha, San Antone," *by* Dale Evans; "Cattle Call," *by* Tex Owens; *and* "Erie Canal," "I'll Take You Home Again, Kathleen," "Down by the Glen Side," "You're in the Army Now," *sung by* The Sons of the Pioneers; *2nd unit director* Cliff Lyons; *camera* Bert Glennon; *2nd unit camera* Archie Stout; *editor* Jack Murray; *assistant editor* Barbara Ford; *producers* John Ford, Merian C. Cooper. ¶John Wayne (Lieutenant Colonel Kirby Yorke); Maureen O'Hara (Kathleen Yorke); Ben Johnson (Trooper Tyree); Claude Jarman, Jr. (Trooper Jeff Yorke); Harry Carey, Jr. (Trooper Sandy

Boone); Chill Wills (Dr. Wilkins); J. Carrol Naish (General Philip Sheridan); Victor McLaglen (Sergeant Major Tim Quincannon); Grant Withers (Deputy Marshal); Peter Ortiz (Captain St. Jacques); Steve Pendleton (Captain Prescott); Karolyn Grimes (Margaret Mary); Alberto Morin (Lieutenant); Stan Jones, Jack Pennick (Sergeants); Fred Kennedy (Heinz); The Sons of the Pioneers—Ken Curtis, Hugh Farr, Karl Farr, Lloyd Perryman, Shug Fisher, Tommy Doss (Regimental Singers); Chuck Roberson (Indian); Patrick Wayne (Boy); Cliff Lyons (Soldier); and Tommy Doss. ¶Filmed, as **Rio Bravo**, June–July; released November 15.

Operation Pacific (Warner Bros., 1951), 111 min. ¶*Director* George Waggner; *writer* George Waggner; *cinematographer* Bert Glennon; *art director* Leo K. Kuter; *editor* Alan Crosland, Jr.; *music* Max Steiner; *sound* Alan Crosland, Jr.; *set decorations* Francis J. Sheid; *makeup artist* Gordon Bau; *special effects* William M. Gann (Director), H.F. Koenekanp; *technical advisor* Vice-Admiral Charles Lockwood, USN (Ret.); *orchestration* Murray Cutter; *producer* Louis F. Edelman. ¶John Wayne ("Duke" Gifford); Patricia Neal (Mary Stuart); Ward Bond ("Pop" Perry); Scott Forbes (Larry); Philip Carey (Bob Perry); Paul Picerni (Jonesy); William Campbell (The Talker); Kathryn Givney (Commander Steele); Martin Milner (Caldwell); Cliff Clark (Comsubpac); Jack Pennick (The Chief); Virginia Brissac (Sister Anne); Vincent Forte (A Soundman); Lewis Martin (Squad Commander); Louis Marconi (Radarman); Sam Edwards (Junior); James Flavin ("Mick," the Shore Patrol Commander); Harlan Warde (Admiral's Aide); Carleton Young (Instructor); Harry Lauter (Freddie). ¶Filmed September–November, 1950; released January, 1951.

Flying Leathernecks (RKO Radio, 1951), Technicolor, 102 min. ¶*Director* Nicholas Ray; *writer* James Edward Grant, *from a screen story by* Kenneth Gamet; *cinematographer* William E. Snyder; *art directors* Albert S. D'Agostino, James W. Sullivan; *editor* Sherman Todd; *music* Roy Webb; *Technicolor color consultant* Morgan Padelford; *production supervisor* Cliff P. Broughton; *musical director* C. Bakaleinikoff; *set decorations* Darrell Silvera, John Sturtevant; *sound* Frank McWhorter, Clem Portman; *technical advisor* Col. Richard Hughes, USMC; *makeup artist* Mel Berns; *hair stylist* Larry Germain; *producer* Edmund Grainger. ¶John Wayne (Major Dan Kirby); Robert Ryan (Capt. Carl Griffin); Don Taylor (Lt. "Cowboy" Blithe); Janis Carter (Joan Kirby); Jay C. Flippen (Master Sgt. Clancy); William Harrigan (Lt. Commander Curan); James Bell (Colonel); Barry Kelley (General); Maurice Jara (Shorty Vegay); Adam Williams (Lieutenant Malotke); James Dobson (Pudge McCabe); Carleton Young (Capt. McAllister); Steve Flagg (Lieutenant Jorgenson); Brett King (Lieutenant Ernie Stark); Gordon Gebert (Tommy Kirby); Dick Wessell (Mess Sergeant); Gail Davis (Virginia Blithe); Milburn Stone (Ground Control Officer); Keith Larsen, Mack Williams. ¶Filmed November, 1950–February, 1951; released August 28.

The Quiet Man (Argosy Pictures/Republic, 1952), Technicolor, 129 min. ¶*Director* John Ford; *producers* Ford, Merian C. Cooper; *Scenarist*, Frank S. Nugent, *from the story,* "Green Rushes," *by* Maurice Walsh; *photography* Winton C. Hoch; *2nd unit photography* Archie Stout; *art director* Frank Hotaling; *set decorators* John McCarthy, Jr., Charles Thompson; *music* Victor Young; *songs* "The Isle of Innisfree," *by* Richard Farrelly; "Galway Bay," *by* Dr. Arthur Colahan, Michael Donovan;

"The Humor Is on Me Now," by Richard Hayward; "The Young May Moon," by Thomas Moore; and "The Wild Colonial Boy," "Mush-Mush-Mush"; editor Jack Murray; assistant editor Barbara Ford; second unit directors (uncredited), John Wayne, Patrick Ford; Technicolor color consultant Francis Cugat; sound T.A. Carman, Howard Wilson; costumes Adele Palmer; set decorations John McCarthy, Jr., Charles Thompson; assistant director Andrew McLaglen. ¶John Wayne (Sean Thornton); Maureen O'Hara (Mary Kate Danaher); Barry Fitzgerald (Michaeleen Flynn); Ward Bond (Father Peter Lonergan); Victor McLaglen (Red Will Danaher); Mildred Natwick (Mrs. Sarah Tillane); Francis Ford (Dan Tobin); Eileen Crowe (Mrs. Elizabeth Playfair); May Craig (Woman at Railroad Station); Arthur Shields (Reverend Cyril Playfair); Charles Fitz-Simmons (Forbes); Sean McClory (Owen Glynn); James Lilburn (Father Paul); Jack MacGowran (Feeney); Ken Curtis (Dermot Fahy, ballad singer); Mae Marsh (Father Paul's mother); Harry Tenbrook (Policeman); Maj. Sam Harris (General); Joseph O'Dea (Guard Maloney); Eric Gorman (Railroad conductor, Costello); Kevin Lawless (Fireman); Paddy O'Donnell (Porter); Webb Overlander (Railroad Station Chief); Hank Worden (Trainer, in flashback); Harry Tyler (Pat Cohan, the Barman); Patrick Wayne, Michael Wayne, Elizabeth Jones, Antonia Wayne, Melinda Wayne. ¶Filmed June–August, 1951; released August 1952.

Big Jim McLain (Wayne-Fellows/ Warner Bros., 1952), 90 min. ¶Director Edward Ludwig; writers James Edward Grant, Richard English, Eric Taylor, from a screen story by Richard English; cinematographer Archie Stout; art director Alfred Ybarra; editor Jack Murray; music Emil Newman, Arthur Lange, Paul Dunlap; production mana-

ger Nate H. Edwards; assistant director Andrew McLaglen; set decorations Charles Thompson; sound Tom Carmen; makeup artist Web Overlander; hair stylist Fae Smith; wardrobe Geneva Bourne; producer Robert Fellows. ¶Quotes from The Devil and Dan'l Webster, by Stephen Vincent Benet. ¶John Wayne (Big Jim McLain); Nancy Olson (Nancy Vallon); James Arness (Mal Baxter); Alan Napier (Sturak); Veda Ann Borg (Madge); Gayne Whitman (Dr. Gelster); Hal Baylor (Poke); Robert Keys (Edwin White); Hans Conreid (Robert Henried); John Hubbard (Lt. Commander Clint Grey); Mme. Soo Yong (Mrs. Namaka); Dan Liu (Chief of Police); Vernon (Red) McQueen (Phil Briggs); Paul Hurst (Mr. Lexiter); Sara Padden (Mrs. Lexiter); Peter Brocco (Mr. Nash); William Forrest (McLain's Superior); Gordon Jones (Olaf); Peter Whitney (Truck Driver); Harry Tyler (Waiter). ¶Filmed as **Jim McLain** May–July; released August 30.

Trouble Along the Way (Warner Bros., 1953), 110 min. ¶Director Michael Curtiz; writers Melville Shavelson, Jack Rose, from a screen story by Douglas Morrow, Robert Hardy Andrews; 2nd unit director David C. Gardner; cinematographer Archie Stout; art director Leo K. Kuter; editor Owen Marks; music Max Steiner; sound C.A. Riggs; dialogue director Norman Stuart; set decorator William Wallace; technical advisors Jeff Cravath, Father Louis V. Pick; wardrobe Moss Mabry; makeup artist Gordon Baer; assistant director Russ Saunders; orchestrations Murray Cutter; producer Melville Shavelson. ¶John Wayne (Steve Aloysius Williams); Donna Reed (Alice Singleton); Charles Coburn (Father Burke); Tom Tully (Father Malone); Sherry Jackson (Carole Williams); Marie Windsor (Anne McCormick); Tom Helmore (Harold McCormick); Dabbs Greer (Father Mahoney); Leif

Erickson (Father Provincial); Douglas Spencer (Procurator); Lester Matthews (Cardinal O'Shea); Chuck Connors (Stan Schwegler); Bill Radovich (Moose McCall); Richard Garrick (Judge); Murray Alper (Bus Driver); James Flavin (Buck Holman, the Coach); Ned Glass (Pool Player); Phil Chambers (Bishop); Frank Ferguson (Mike Edwards, Store Proprietor); Howard Petrie (Polo Grounds Manager); Renata Vanni (Italian Mother); Tim Graham (Bill, Team Manager); Robert Keys (Joe, Team Manager). ¶Filmed as **Alma Mater** October–December, 1952; released April 4, 1953.

Island in the Sky (Wayne-Fellows/ Warner Bros., 1953), 109 min. ¶*Director* William A. Wellman; *writer* Ernest K. Gann, *from his novel; cinematographer* Archie Stout; *aerial cinematographer* William Clothier; *art director* James Basevi; *editor* Ralph Dawson; *music* Emil Newman; *producer* Robert Fellows. ¶John Wayne (Capt. Dooley); Lloyd Nolan (Stutz); Walter Abel (Col. Fuller); James Arness (McMullen); Andy Devine (Moon); Allyn Joslyn (J.H. Handy); James Lydon (Murray, the Navigator); Harry Carey, Jr. (Hunt); Hal Baylor (Stankowski, the Engineer); Sean McClory (Frank Lovatt, the Copilot); Wally Cassell (D'Annunzia, the Radioman); Gordon Jones (Walrus); Frank Fenton (Capt. Turner); Robert Keys (Major Ditson); Sumner Getchell (Lt. Cord); Regis Toomey (Sgt. Harper); Paul Fix (Miller); Jim Dugan (Gidley); George Chandler (Rene); Louis Jean Heydt (Fitch); Bob Steele (Wilson); Darrly Hickman (Swanson); Touch (Michael) Connors (Gainer); Carl Switzer (Hopper); Cass Gidley (Stannish); Guy Anderson (Breezy); Tony DeMario (Ogden); Ann Doran (Moon's Wife); Dawn Bender (Murray's Wife); Phyllis Winger (Girl in Flashback). ¶Filmed at Donner Lake, Truckee, California. ¶Released September 5.

Hondo (Wayne-Fellows/Warner Bros., 1953), WarnerColor 3-D, 93 min. ¶*Director* John Farrow; *based on the story, "The Gift of Cochise," by* Louis L'Amour; *screenplay* James Edward Grant; *music* Emil Newman, Kugh Friedhofer; *art director* Al Ybarra; *camera* Robert Burks, Archie Stout; *editor* Ralph Dawson; *2nd unit director* Cliff Lyons; *some sequences directed, without credit, by* John Ford; *special effects* Al Gonzalez; *script supervisor* Sam Freedly; *sound dialogue recording,* Nicolas de la Rosa; *stills* Don Christi; *production manager* Nate H. Edwards; *unit production manager* Andrew McLaglen; *assistant director* Nate Gauraca; *property master* Joseph La Bella; *wardrobe* Carl Walker; *makeup artist* Web Overlander; technical advisor Major Philip Kieffer; *producer* Robert Fellows. ¶John Wayne (Hondo Lane); Geraldine Page (Angie Lowe); Ward Bond (Buffalo); Michael Pate (Vittorio); James Arness (Lennie); Rodolfo Acosta (Silva); Leo Gordon (Ed Lowe); Tom Irish (Lieutenant McKay); Lee Aaker (Johnny Lowe); Paul Fix (Major Sherry); Rayford Barnes (Pete). ¶Remade in 1966 as **Hondo and the Apaches** by John Wayne's production company, Batjac/Fenady Associates, as a pilot for TV series, with Ralph Taeger as Hondo. Subsequently developed into a TV series. ¶Location filming at Carmago, Mexico. ¶Filmed June–August; released November 27.

The High and the Mighty (Wayne-Fellows/Warner Bros., 1954), CinemaScope, WarnerColor, 147 min. ¶*Director* William A. Wellman; *assistant director* Andrew McLaglen; *writer* Ernest K. Gann, *from his novel; cinematographer* Archie Stout; *aerial cinematographer* William H. Clothier; *art director* Al Ybarra; *editor* Ralph Dawson; *music* Dimitri Tiomkin; *song "The High and the Mighty," music by* Dimitri Tiomkin, *lyrics by* Ned Washington; *production manager* Nate

H. Edwards; *production director* Andrew McLaglen; *camera plane pilot* Loren Riebe; *technical advisor* William H. Benge; *sound recording* John K. Kean; *technical advisor* USCC, Lt. Commander Robert M. Cannon; *script supervisor* Sam Freedle; *set decorations* Ralph Hurst; *property man* Joseph La Bella; *special effects* Robert Mattey; *wardrobe designer* Gwen Wakelung; *hair stylist* Margaret Donovan; *makeup artists* Web Overlander, Loren Casand; *technical advice from* Transocean Air Lines, Oakland, California; *producer* Robert Fellows. ¶**John Wayne** (Dan Roman); Claire Trevor (May Holst); Laraine Day (Lydia Rice); Robert Stack (Sullivan); Jan Sterling (Sally McKee); Phil Harris (Ed Joseph); Robert Newton (Gustave Pardee); David Brian (Ken Childs); Paul Kelly (Flaherty); Sidney Blackmer (Humphrey Agnew); Julie Bishop (Lillian Pardee); Gonzalez-Gonzalez (Gonzalez); John Howard (Howard Rice); Wally Brown (Lenny Wilby, the Navigator); William Campbell (Hobie Wheeler); Ann Doran (Mrs. Joseph); John Qualen (Jose Locota); Paul Fix (Frank Briscoe); George Chandler (Ben Sneed); Joy Kim (Dorothy Chen); Michael Wellman (Toby Field, the Boy); Douglas Fowley (Alsop); Regis Toomey (Garfield); Carl Switzer (Ensign Keim); Robert Keys (Lt. Mowbray); William DeWolf Hopper (Roy); William Schiallert (Dispatcher); Julie Mitchum (Susie); Doe Avedon (Miss Spalding, the Stewardess); Karen Sharpe (Nell Buck); John Smith (Milo Buck); Robert Easton, Philip Van Zandt. ¶Filmed November, 1953–January, 1954; released July 3.

The Sea Chase (Warner Bros., 1955), CinemaScope, WarnerColor, 117 min. ¶*Director* John Farrow; *writers* James Warner Bellah, John Twist, *from the novel by* Andrew Geer; *cinematographer* William Clothier; *art director*

Franz Bachelin; *editor* William Ziegler; *music* Roy Webb; *sound* Francis J. Scheid; *set decorator* William Wallace; *wardrobe* Moss Mabry; *special effects* H.F. Roenerkamp; *makeup artist* Gordon Bau; *orchestrations* Maurice de Packh, Leonid Raab; *assistant directors* Emmett Emerson, Russell Llewellyn; *producer* John Farrow. ¶**John Wayne** (Capt. Karl Ehrlich); Lana Turner (Elsa Keller); David Farrar (Commander Napier); Lyle Bettger (Kirchner); Tab Hunter (Cadet Wesser); James Arness (Schlieter); Richard Davalos (Cadet Walter Stemme); John Qualen (Chief Schmitt); Paul Fix (Max Heinz); Lowell Gilmore (Capt. Evans); Luis Van Rooten (Matz); Alan Hole (Wentz); Wilton Graff (Hepke); Peter Whitney (Bachman); Claude Akins (Winkler); John Doucette (Bos'n); Alan Lee (Brounck); Adam Williams (Kruger, the Wireless Operator); James Lilburn, Gavin Muir (British Officers); Anthony Eustrel (British High Official); Tudor Owen (Trawler Survivor); Jean de Briac (French Governor); Patrick O'Moore (Warship Officer); Gail Robinson, Gilbert Perkins. ¶Location filming at Hawaii. ¶Filmed September–December, 1954; released June 4, 1955.

Blood Alley (Batjac/Warner Bros., 1955), Cinemascope, WarnerColor, 115 min. ¶*Director* William A. Wellman; *writer* A.S. Fleischman, *from his novel*; *cinematographer* William H. Clothier; *art director* Alfred Ybarra; *editor* Fred MacDowell; *music* Roy Webb; *production manager* Nate H. Edwards; *unit production manager* Tom Andre; *assistant director* Andrew V. McLaglen; *sound* Earl Crain; *script supervisor* Sam Freedle; *orchestrations* Maurice de Packh, Gus Levens; *set decorator* Vincent Gangelin; *property master* Joseph LaBella; *costumes designed by* Gwen Wakeling; *men's costumes* Carl Walker; *hair stylist* Margaret Donovan; *makeup supervisor* Web Overlander, Norman

Pringle. ¶**John Wayne** (Wilder); Lauren Bacall (Cathy Grainger); Paul Fix (Mr. Tso); Joy Kim (Susu, Cathy's Maid); Berry Kroger [or, Kroeger] (Old Feng); Mike Mazurki (Big Han); Anita Ekberg (Wei Ling); W.T. Change (Mr. Han); George Chan (Mr. Sing); Henry Nakamura (Tack, the Engineer); Walter Soohoo (Feng's No. 1 Nephew); Eddie Luke (Feng's No. 2 Nephew); Victor Sen Yung (Cpl. Wang); Lowell Gilmore. ¶Location filming at San Rafael, California. ¶Filmed January–March; released October 1.

The Conqueror (RKO Radio, 1956), Cinemascope Technicolor, 111 min. ¶*Director* Dick Powell; *writer* Oscar Millard; *2nd unit director* Cliff Lyons; *assistant director* Edward Killy; *choreography* Robert Sidney; *cinematographers* Joseph LaShelle, Leo Tover, Harry J. Wild, William Snyder; *art directors* Albert S. D'Agostino, Carroll Clark; *editorial supervision* Stuart Gilmore; *editors* Robert Ford, Kennie Marstella; *sound* Bernard Freericks, Terry Kellum; *music* Victor Young; *music director* Constantin Bakaleinikoff; *photographic effects* Linwood Dunn, Albert Simpson; *orchestrations* Leo Shuker, Sidney Cutner; *set decorations* Darrell Silvera, Al Orenbach; *sound effects* Walter Elliott; *script supervisor* William Hole, Jr.; *choreography* Robert Sidney; *assistant director* Edmund Kelly; *Miss Hayward's costumes* Michael Woulff; *men's costumes* Yvonne Wood; *makeup artist* Mel Berns; *hair stylist* Larry Germain; *associate producer* Richard Sokolove; *producer* Dick Powell; *a Howard Hughes Presentation.* ¶**John Wayne** (Temujin); Susan Hayward (Bortai); Pedro Armendariz (Jamuga); Agnes Moorehead (Hunlun); Thomas Gomez (Wang Khan); John Hoyt (Shaman); William Conrad (Kasar); Ted de Corsia (Kumlek); Leslie Badley (Targutai); Lee Van Cleef (Chepei); Peter Mamakos (Bogurchi); Leo Gordon (Tartar

Captain); Richard Loo (Captain of Wang's Guard); Ray Spiker (A Guard); Sylvia Lewis (Solo Dancer); Jarma Lewis, Pat McMahon (Girls in Bath); George E. Stone (Sibilant Sam); Phil Arnold (Honest John); Torben Meyer (Scribe); Pat Lawleer, Pat Tiernan (Wang Khan's Wives); John George (Drummer Boy); Weaver Levy (A Mongol); Michael Granger (1st Chieftain); Fred Aldrich (2nd Chieftain); Paul Hoffman (3rd Chieftain); Lane Bradford (4th Chieftain); Carl Vernell (Merkit Captain); Fred Graham (Subuya); Gregg Barton (Jalair); Ken Terrell (Sorgan); Jeanne Gerson (Hochin); Michael Wayne, Norman Powell (Mongol Guards); Members of the Chivwit Indian Tribe (Mongolian Warriors). ¶Location filming in Escalante Desert, near St. George, Utah. ¶Filmed May¶August, 1954; premiere in London, February 2; released February 21.

The Searchers (C.V. Whitney Pictures/Warner Bros., 1956), Technicolor, VistaVision, 119 min. ¶*Director* John Ford; *based on the novel by* Alan LeMay; *screenplay* Frank S. Nugent; *color consultant* James Gooch; *music* Max Steiner; *title song* Stan Jones; *orchestration* Murray Cutter; *art directors* Frank Hotaling, James Basevi; *set decorator* Victor Gangelin; *assistant director* Wingate Smith; *special effects* George Brown; *camera* Winton C. Hoch; *2nd unit camera* Alfred Gilks; *editor* Jack Murray; *production supervisor* Lowell Farrell; *sound* Hugh McDowell, Howard Wilson; *men's wardrobe* Frank Beetson; *women's wardrobe* Ann Peck; *makeup* Web Overlander; *hair dresser* Fae Smith; *special effects* George Brown; *properties* Dudley Holmes; *script supervisor* Robert Gary; *associate producer* Patrick Ford; *executive producer* Merian C. Cooper; *producer* C.V. Whitney. ¶**John Wayne** (Ethan Edwards); Jeffrey Hunter (Martin Pawley); Vera Miles (Laurie Jorgensen); Ward Bond

(Captain Reverend Samuel Clayton); Natalie Wood (Debbie Edwards); John Qualen (Lars Jorgensen); Olive Carey (Mrs. Jorgensen); Henry Brandon (Chief Scar); Ken Curtis (Charlie McCorry); Harry Carey, Jr. (Brad Jorgensen); Antonio Moreno (Emilio Figueroa); Hank Worden (Mose Harper); Lana Wood (Debbie as a Child); Walter Coy (Aaron Edwards); Dorothy Jordan (Martha Edwards); Pippa Scott (Lucy Edwards); Pat Wayne (Lieutenant Greenhill); Beulah Archuleta (Look); Jack Pennick (Private); Peter Mamakos (Futterman); Chuck Roberson (Lawrence, a Texas Ranger); Nacho Galindo (Mexican Bartender); Robert Lyden (Ben); Chief Thundercloud (Indian Chief); Cliff Lyons (Col. Greenhill); Billy Cartledge, Chuck Hayward, Slim Hightower, Fred Kennedy, Frank McGrath, Chuck Roberson, Dale van Sickel, Henry Wills, Terry Wilson (Stunt Men); Away Lulna, Billy Yellow, Bob Many Mules, Exactly Sonnie Betsuie, Feather Hat, Jr., Harry Black Horse, Jack Tin Horn, Many Mules Son, Percy Shooting Star, Pete Grey Eyes, Pipe Line Begishe, Smile White Sheep (Comanches); Mae Marsh, Dan Borsage (Bits). ¶Location shooting in Monument Valley, Utah-Arizona; Gunnison, Colorado; Alberta, Canada. ¶Filmed June–August, 1955; released March 13, 1956.

The Wings of Eagles (Metro-Goldenn-Mayer, 1957), Metrocolor, 110 min. ¶*Director* John Ford; *producer* Charles Schnee; *associate producer* James E. Newcom; *scenarists* Frank Fenton, William Wister Haines, *based on life and writings of* Commander Frank W. Wead, USN *and the biography, Wings of Men; cinematographer* Paul C. Vogel; *art directors* William A. Horning, Malcolm Brown; *set decorators* Edwin B. Willis, Keogh Gleason; *costumes* Walter Plunkett; *music* Jeff Alexander; *editor* Gene Ruggiero; *aerial stunts* Paul Mantz; *assistant director* Wingate

Smith. ¶**John Wayne** (Frank W. "Spig" Wead); Maureen O'Hara (Minnie Wead); Dan Dailey (Jughead Carson); Ward Bond (John Dodge); Ken Curtis (John Dale Price); Edmund Lowe (Adm. Moffett); Kenneth Tobey (Capt. Herbert Allen Hazard); James Todd (Jack Travis); Barry Kelley (Capt. Jock Clark); Sig Ruman (Party Manager); Henry O'Neill (Capt. Spear); Willis Bouchey (Barton); Dorothy Jordan (Rose Brentmann); Peter Ortiz (Lt. Charles Dexter); Louis Jean Heydt (Dr. John Deye); Tige Andrews ("Arizona" Pincus); Dan Borzage (Pete); William Tracy (Air Force Officer); Harlan Warde (Executive Officer); Jack Pennick (Joe McGuffey); Bill Henry (Naval Aide); Alberto Morin (Second Manager); Mimi Gibson (Lila Wead); Evelyn Rudie (Doris Wead); Charles Trowbridge (Adm. Crown); Mae Marsh (Nurse Crumley); Janet Lake (Nurse); Fred Graham (Officer in Brawl); Stuart Holmes (Producer); Olive Carey (Bridy O'Faolain); Maj. Sam Harris (Patient); May McEvoy (Nurse); William Paul Lowery (Wead's Baby, "Commodore"); Chuck Roberson (Officer); James Flavin (M.P. at Garden Party); Cliff Lyons, Veda Ann Borg, Christopher James. ¶Filmed July–October, 1956; released February 22, 1957.

Jet Pilot (Howard Hughes-RKO Radio/Universal International, 1957), Technicolor, RKO-Scope, 112 min. ¶*Director* Josef von Sternberg; *writer* Jules Furthman; *cinematographer* Winton C. Hoch; *art directors* Albert S. D'Agostino, Field Gray; *editorial supervisor* James Wilkinson; *editors* Michael R. McAdam, Harry Marker, William M. Moore; *music* Bronislau Kaper; *Technicolor color consultant* Francis Cugat; *assistant to producer* Brig. Gen. Clarence A. Shoop; *supervision of aerial sequences* Philip A. Cochran; *project pilot* Captain J.S. Nash; *editorial supervision* Jim Wilkinson; *set decorations* Darrell Silvera, Harley Miller; *sound*

Earl Wolcott, Terry Kellum; *music con-ducted by* C. Bakaleinikoff; *unit production manager* Edward Killy; *assistant director* Fred A. Fleck; *gowns* Michael Woulfe; *make-up supervision* Mel Burns; *hair stylist* Larry Germain; *producer* Jules Furthman. ¶**John Wayne** (Colonel Shannon); Janet Leigh (Anna); Jay C. Flippen (Maj. Gen. Black); Paul Fix (Maj. Rexford); Richard Rober (George Rivers); Roland Winters (Col. Sokolov); Hans Conreid (Col. Matoff); Ivan Triesauault (Gen. Langrad); John Bishop (Maj. Sinclair); Perdita Chandler (Georgia Rexford); Joyce Compton (Mrs. Simpson); Denver Pyle (Mr. Simpson); Jack Overman, Gene Roth, Don Haggery, Carleton Young; "And the United States Air Force." ¶Filmed principally December, 1949–May, 1950; released October, 1957.

Legend of the Lost (Batjac-Rogert Hagging-Dear Film/United Artists, 1957), Technicolor, Technirama, 109 min. ¶*Director* Henry Hathaway; *writers* Robert Presnell, Jr., Ben Hecht; *cinematographer* Jack Cardiff; *art director* Alfred Ybarra; *editor* Bert Bates; *music* A.F. Lavagnino; *producer* Henry Hathaway. ¶**John Wayne** (Joe January); Sophia Loren (Dita); Rossano Brazzi (Paul Bonnard); Kurt Kasznar (Prefect Dukas); Sonia Moser (Girl); Angela Portaluri (Girl); Ibrahim El Hadish (Galli Galli). ¶Location filming in Lybian Desert. ¶Released December 17.

I Married a Woman (Universal-International, for RKO Radio, 1958), Technicolor Sequence, RKO-Scope, 85 min. ¶*Director* Hal Kanter; *writer* Goodman Ace; *cinematographer* Lucien Ballard; *art directors* Albert S. D'Agostino, Walter E. Keller; *editor* Otto Ludwig; *music* Cyril Mockridge; *producer* William Bloom. ¶George Gobel (Marshal Briggs); Diana Dors (Jancie Blake); Adolphe Menjo (Sutton); Jessie Royce Landis (Mother-in-Law); Nita Talbot (Miss Anderson);

William Redfield (Eddie); Steve Dunne (Bob); John McGiver (Girard); Steve Pendleton (Photographer); Cheerio Meredith (Mrs. Wilkins); Kay Buckley (Camera Girl); Angie Dickinson (Wife of Wayne in Film); **John Wayne** (Himself). ¶Filmed July–August, 1956; released March, 1958.

The Barbarian and the Geisha (20th Century-Fox, 1958), Eastman Color, Cinemascope, 105 min. ¶*Director* John Huston; *writers* Charles Grayson, Alfred Hayes (uncredited), Nigel Balchin (uncredited), *from a screen story by* Ellis St. Joseph; *cinematographer* Charles G. Clarke; *art directors* Lyle R. Wheeler, Jack Martin Smith; *editor* Stuart Gilmore; *music* Hugo Friedhofer; *set decorations* Walter M. Scott, Don B. Greenwood; *executive wardrobe designer* Charles LeMaire; *makeup* Webb [for Web?] Overlander; *assistant director* Joseph E. Rickards; *sound* W.D. Flick, Warren B. Delaplain; *cinemascope lenses by* Bausch and Lomb; *script supervisor* Teinosuke Kinugasa; *dialogue coach* Mindru Inuzuka; *technical supervisor* Mitsuo Hirotsu; *technical art adviser* Kibaku Itoh; *Japanese technical adviser* Kampo Yoshikawa; *assistant to producer* Paul Nakaoka; *producer* Eugene Frenke. ¶**John Wayne** (Townsend Harris); Eiko Ando (Okichi); Sam Jaffe (Henry Heusken); So Yamamura (Baron Tamura); Norman Thomson (Capt. Edmunds); James Robbins (Lt. Fisher); Morita (Prime Minister); Kodaya Ichikawa (Daimyo); Hiroshi Yamato (The Shogun); Tokujiro Iketaniuchi (Harusha); Fuji Kasai (Lord Hotta); Takeshi Kumagai (Chamberlain). ¶Filmed entirely in Japan. Filmed December 1957–February 1958, as **The Townsend Harris Story**; released September 30.

Rio Bravo (Armada/Warner Brothers, 1959), Technicolor, 141 min. ¶*Producer-director* Howard Hawks;

based on a short story by Barara Hawks McCampbell *(and, uncredited,* Howard Hawks); *screenplay* Jules Furthman, Leigh Brackett; *music-music conductor* Dimitri Tiomkin; *songs* Tiomkin and Paul Francis Webster—*"Rio Bravo," "My Rifle, My Pony and Me"; art director* Leo K. Kuter; *set decorator* Ralph S. Hurst; *costumes* Marjorie Best; *makeup* Gordon Bau; *assistant director* Paul Helmick; *sound* Robert B. Lee; *camera* Russell Harlan; *editor* Folmar Blangsted. ¶John Wayne (John T. Chance); Dean Martin (Dude); Ricky Nelson (Colorado); Angie Dickinson (Feathers); Walter Brennan (Stumpy); Ward Bond (Pat Wheeler); John Russell (Nathan Burdette); Pedro Gonzales-Gonzales (Carlos); Estelita Rodriguez (Consuela); Claude Akins (Joe Burdette); Malcolm Atterbury (Jake); Harry Carey, Jr. (Harold); Bob Steele (Matt Harris); Bob Terhune (Nesdon Booth); George Bruggeman (Ted White); Myron Healey (Barfly); Tom Monroe (Henchman); Riley Hill (Messenger); Bing Russell (Cowboy Murdered In Saloon); Eugene Iglesias (1st Burdette Man in Shootout); Fred Graham (2nd Burdette Man in Shootout). ¶Location filming at Old Tucson, near Tucson, Arizona. ¶Filmed May–July, 1958; released April.

The Horse Soldiers (Mahin-Rackin/Mirisch Company-United Artists, 1959), Color by DeLuxe, 119 min. ¶*Director* John Ford; *based on the novel by* Harold Sinclair; *screenplay* Mahin, Martin Rackin; *art director* Frank Hotaling; *set decorator* Victor Gangelin; *makeup* Webb Overlander; *wardrobe* Frank Beetson, Ann Peck; *assistant directors* Wingate Smith, Ray Gosnell, Jr.; *music* David Buttolph; *song, "I Left My Love,"* Stan Jones; *sound* Jack Solomon; *special effects* Augie Lohman; *camera* William Clothier; *editor* Jack Murray; *production manager* Allen K. Wood; *producers* John Lee Mahin, Martin Rackin. ¶John Wayne (Colonel

John Marlowe); William Holden (Major Hank Kendall); Constance Towers (Hannah Hunter); Althea Gibson (Lukey); Hoot Gibson (Brown); Anna Lee (Mrs. Buford); Russell Simpson (Henry Goodbody, the Sheriff); Stan Jones (General U.S. Grant); Carleton Young (Colonel Jonathan Miles); Basil Ruysdael (Boys' School, Jefferson Military Academy, Commandant [The Reverend]); Willis Bouchey (Colonel Phil Secord); Ken Curtis (Wilkie); O.Z. Whitehead (Hoppy Hopkins); Judson Pratt (Sergeant Major Kirby); Denver Pyle (Jagger Jo); Strother Martin (Virgil); Hank Worden (Deacon); Walter Reed (Union Officer); Jack Pennick (Sergeant Major Mitchell); Fred Graham (Union Soldier); Chuck Hayward (Union Captain); Donald Foster (Dr. Marvin); Charles Seel (Newton Station Bartender); Major Sam Harris, Stuart Holmes (Passengers to Newton Station); Richard Cutting (General Sherman); Bing Russell (Dunker); William Forrest (General Hurlbut); William Leslie (Major Gray, Confederate Artillery); Ron Hagerthy (Bugler); Bill Henry (Confederate Lieutenant); Chuck Lyons (Sergeant); Fred Kennedy (Cavalryman); William Wellman, Jr. (Bugler); Jan Stine (Dying Man); Dan Borsage. ¶Location filming in Louisiana. ¶Filmed October 1958–January 1959; released June 12.

The Alamo (Batjac/United Artists, 1960), Technicolor, Todd-AO, 192 min. (originally; then 167 min.; then 140 min.) ¶*Producer-director* John Wayne; *screenplay* James Edward Grant; *art director* Alfred Ybarra; *set decorator* Victor A. Gangelin; *technical supervisors* Frank Beetson, Jack Pennick; *assistant directors* Robert E. Relyea, Robert Saunders; *costumes* Beetson, Ann Peck; *music, music director* Dimitri Tiomkin; *songs* Tiomkin and Paul Francis Webster—*"The Green Leaves of Summer" and "Lisa"; sound* Jack Solomon, Gordon Sawyer, Fred Hynes,

Don Hall, Jr.; *special effects* Lee Zavitz; *make-up* Webb Overlander; *camera* William Clothier; *editor* Stuart Gilmore; *2nd unit director* Cliff Lyons; *some sequences directed, without credits, by* John Ford; *associate producer* James Edward Grant; *production manager* Nate Edwards; *assistant to the producer* Michael Wayne. ¶**John Wayne** (Colonel David Crockett); Richard Widmark (Colonel James Bowie); Laurence Harvey (Colonel William Travis); Richard Boone (General Sam Houston); Frankie Avalon (Smitty); Linda Cristal (Flaca); Patrick Wayne (Captain James Bonham); Joan O'Brien (Mrs. Dickinson); Chill Wills (Beekeeper); Joseph Calleia (Juan Seguin); Ken Curtis (Captain Dickinson); Carlos Arruza (Lieutenant Reyes); Jester Hairston (Jethro); Veda Ann Borg (Blind Nell); John Dierkes (Jocko Robertson); Denver Pyle (Gambler); Aissa Wayne (Lisa Dickinson); Bill Henry (Dr. Sutherland); Hank Worden (Parson); Bill Daniel (Colonel Neill); Wesley Lau (Emil Sande); Chuck Roberson (A Tennessean); Guinn "Big Boy" Williams (Lieutenant Finn); Olive Carey (Mrs. Dennison); Ruben Padilla (General Santa Anna); Carol Baxter (Texan, a Teenager); Jack Pennick (Sgt. Lightfoot), Red Morgan (A Tennessean); Julian Trevino (Silvero Sequin); Tom Hennesssey (Bull); Cy Malis (Pete); Fred Graham (Bearded Volunteer); Le Jeanne Guye (Woman). ¶Location filming at Bracketville, Texas. ¶Filmed September–December 1959; released October 24, 1960.

North to Alaska (20th Century Fox, 1960), DeLuxe Color, CinemaScope, 122 min. ¶*Director* Henry Hathaway; *writers* John Lee Mahin, Martin Rackin, Claude Binyon, Wendell Mayes *(uncredited), from the play Birthday Gift, by* Laszlo Fodor, *from an idea by* John Kafka; *2nd unit director* Richard Talmadge; *cinematographer* Leon Shamroy; *art directors* Duncan Cramer, Jack Martin Smith; *editor* Dorothy Spencer; *music* Lionel Newman; *orchestration* Urban Thielmann, Bernard Mayers; *costumes* Bill Thomas; *choreography* Josephine Earl; *assistant director* Stanley Hough; *special effects* L.B. Abbott, Emil Kosa, Jr.; *song, "If You Knew," by* Russell Faith, Robert P. Marcucci, Peter DeAngelis; *producer* Henry Hathaway. ¶**John Wayne** (Sam McCord); Stewart Granger (George Pratt); Ernie Kovacs (Frankie Canon); Fabian (Billy Pratt); Capucine (Michelle [Angel]); Mickey Shaughnessy (Peter Boggs); Karl Swenson (Lars Nordquist); Joe Sawyer (Commissioner); Kathleen Freeman (Lena Nordquist); John Qualen (Logger); Stanley Adams (Breezy); Stephen Courtleigh (Duggan); Douglas Dick (Lieutenant); Jerry O'Sullivan (Sergeant); Ollie O'Toole (Mack); Tudor Owen (Boat Captain); Lilyan Chauvin (Jenny Lamont); Marcel Hillaire (Jenny's Husband, the Butler); Richard Deacon (Angus, the Desk Clerk); James Griffith (Salvationist); Max Hellinger (Bish, the Waiter — Everett Bishop); Richard Collier (Skinny Sourdough); Esther Dale (Woman at Picnic); Fortune Gordien, Roy Jensen (Loggers); Charles Seel, Rayford Barnes (Gold Buyers); Fred Graham (Ole); Alan Carney (Bartender); Peter Bourne (Olaf); Tom Dillon (Barber); Arlene Harris (Queen Lil); Pamela Raymond (Pony Dancer); Maurice Delamore (Bartender); Patty Wharton (Specialty Dancer); Johnny Lee (Coachman); James Griffith (Speaker); Kermit Maynard, Paul Maxey, Oscar Beregi, Joel Faye. ¶Filmed, as **Go North,** May–August; released November 7.

The Comancheros (Twentieth Century-Fox, 1961), DeLuxe Color, CinemaScope, 107 min. ¶*Director* Michael Curtiz, **John Wayne** *(uncredited); based on the novel by* Paul I. Wellman *screenplay* James Edward

Grant, Clair Huffaker; *action sequences director* Cliff Lyons; *art directors* Jack Martin Smith, Alfred Ybarra; *set decorators* Walter M. Scott, Robert Priestly; *costumes* Marjorie Best; *music* Elmer Bernstein; *orchestrators* Leo Shuken, Jack Hayes; *assistant director* Jack R. Berne; *sound* Alfred Bruzlin, Sarren DeLaplain; *camera* William H. Clothier; *editor* Louis Loeffler; *producer* George Sherman. ¶John Wayne (Jake Cutter); Stuart Whitman (Paul Regret); Ina Balin (Pilar); Nehemiah Persoff (Graile); Lee Marvin (Tully Crow); Michael Ansara (Amelung); Pat Wayne (Tobe); Bruce Cabot (Major Henry); Joan O'Brien (Melinda Marshall); Edgar Buchanan (Judge Thaddeus Jackson Breen); Guinn "Big" Boy Williams (Ed McBain); Jack Elam (Horseface); Henry Daniell (Gireaux); Richard Devon (Estevan); Steve Baylor (Comanchero); John Dierkes (Bill); Roger Mobley (Bub Schofield); Bob Steele (Pa Schofield); Aissa Wayne (Bessie Marshall); Tom Hennessy (Graile's Bodyguard); Jackie Cubat, Leigh Snowden (Hotel Girls); Luisa Triana (Spanish Dancer); Iphigenie Castiglioni (Josefina); George Lewis (Iron Shirt); Greg Palmer (Duel Opponent); John Lormer (Elderly Man on Riverboat); Don Brodie (Card Dealer); Phil Arnold (Nervous Man); Alan Carney (Bartender); Ralph Volkie (Steward on Riverboat); Dennis Cole. ¶Filmed June–August; released October.

The Man Who Shot Liberty Valance (Ford Productions/Paramount, 1962), 122 min. ¶*Director* John Ford; *producer* Willis Goldbeck; *scenarists* Goldbeck, James Warner Bellah, *from story by* Dorothy M. Johnson; *photography* William H. Clothier; *art directors* Hal Pereira, Eddie Imazu; *set decorators* Sam Comer, Darrell Silvera; *costumes* Edith Head; *music* Cyril J. Mockridge: *theme from Young Mr. Lincoln, by* Alfred Newman; *editor* Otho Lovering;

assistant director Wingate Smith. ¶James Stewart (Ransom Stoddard); John Wayne (Tom Doniphon); Vera Miles (Hallie Stoddard); Lee Marvin (Liberty Valance); Edmond O'Brien (Dutton Peabody); Andy Devine (Link Appleyard); Ken Murray (Doc Willoughby); John Carradine (Major Cassius Starbuckle); Jeanette Nolan (Nora Ericson); John Qualen (Peter Ericson); Willis Bouchey (Jason Tully); Carleton Young (Maxwell Scott); Woody Strode (Pompey); Denver Pyle (Amos Carruthers); Strother Martin (Floyd); Lee Van Cleef (Reese); Robert F. Simon (Handy Strong); O.Z. Whitehead (Herbert Carruthers); Paul Birch (Mayor Winder); Joseph Hoover (Hasbrouck); Jack Pennick (Barman); Anna Lee (Widow in Stage Holdup); Charles Seel (President, Election Council); Shug Fisher (Drunk); Earle Hodgins (Clue Dumphries); Stuart Holmes, Dorothy Phillips, Buddy Roosevelt, Gertrude Astor, Eva Novak, Slim Talbot, Monty Montana, Bill Henry, John B. Whiteford, Helen Gibson, Maj. Sam Harris, Ted Mapes, Jack Kenny. ¶Filmed September–November, 1961; released April 22, 1962.

Hatari! (Malabar/Paramount, 1962), Technicolor, 155 min. ¶*Director* Howard Hawks; *associate producer and 2nd unit director* Paul Helmick; *assistant directors* Tom Connors, Russ Saunders; *screenplay* Leigh Brackett; *story* Hary Kurnitz; *camera* Russell Harlan, Joseph Brun; *art directors* Hal Pereira, Carl Anderson; *sets* Sam Comer, Claude Carpenter; *music* Henry Mancini; *song, "Just for Tonight," by* Johnny Mercer and Hoagy Carmichael; *editor* Stuart Gilmore; *special effects* John P. Fulton; *special mechanical effects* Richard Parker; *technical advisor* Willy DeBeer; *producer* Howard Hawks. ¶John Wayne (Sean Mercer); Elsa Martinelli ("Dallas," Anna Maria D'Allesandro); Hardy Kruger (Kurt Mueller); Gerard Blain (Chips

Chalmoy); Red Buttons (Pockets); Michele Girardon ("Brandy," de la Corte); Bruce Cabot (Indian); Valentin de Vargas (Luis Francisco Garcia Lopez); Eduard Franz (Dr. Sanderson). ¶Filmed in Tanganyika; released May 24.

The Longest Day (20th Century-Fox, 1963), CinemaScope, 180 min. ¶*Directors* Ken Annakin (British exterior episodes), Andrew Marton (American exterior episodes), Bernhard Wicki (German episodes), Darryl F. Zanuck (American interior episodes), Gerd Oswald (Parachute drops on Ste. Mere Eglise); *writers* Cornelius Ryan, *from his book, with additional episodes by* Romain Gary, Jack Jones, David Pursall, Jack Seddon; *cinematographers* Jean Burgoin, Henri Persin, Walter Wottitz, Guy Tabary, Pierre Levent; *art directors* Ted Haworth, Leon Barsacq, Vincent Korda; *editor* Samuel E. Beetley; *music* Maurice Jarre; *coordinator of battle episodes/associate producer* Elmo Williams; *producer* Darryl F. Zanuck. ¶Eddie Albert (Col. Tom Newton); Paul Anka (U.S. Ranger); Areltty (Mme. Barrault); Jean-Louis Barrault (Father Roulland); Richard Beymeer (Pvt. Schulz); Bourvil (Mayor of Colleville); Richard Burton (R.A.F. Pilot); Red Buttons (Pvt. John Steele); Sean Connery (Pvt. Flanagan); Ray Danton (Capt. Frank); Irina Demich (Janine Boitard); Fabian (U.S. Ranger); Mel Ferrer (Maj. Gen. Robert Haines); Henry Fonda (Brig. Gen. Theodore Roosevelt); Steve Forrest (Capt. Harding); Gert Frobe (Sgt. Kaffeeklatsch); Leo Genn (Brig. Gen. Parker); Henry Grace (Gen. Dwight D. Eisenhower); John Gregson (British Padre); Paul Hartmann (Field-Marshal Gerd Von Rundstedt); Werner Hinz (Field-Marshal Erwin Rommel); Jeffrey Hunter (Sgt. Fuller); Curt Jurgens (Maj. Gen. Gunther Blumontritt); Alexander Knox (Maj. Gen. Walter Bedell Smith); Peter Lawford (Lord Lovat); Christian Marquand (Comm. Philippe Kieffer);

Roddy McDowall (Pvt. Morris); Sal Mineo (Pvt. Martini); Robert Mitchum (Brig. Gen. Norman Cota); Kenneth More (Capt. Colin Maud); Edmond O'Brien (Gen. Raymond O. Barton); Ron Randell (Joe Williams); Madeleine Renaud (Mother Superior); Robert Ryan (Brig. Gen. James M. Gavin); Tommy Sands (U.S. Ranger); Rod Steiger (Destroyer Commander); Richard Todd (Maj. John Howard); Tom Tryon (Lt. Wilson); Peter Van Eyck (Lt. Col. Ocker); Robert Wagner (U.S. Ranger); Stuart Whitman (Lt. Sheen); **John Wayne** (Lt. Col. Benjamin Vandervoort); Michael Medwin (Pvt. Watney); Norman Rossington (Pvt. Clough); John Robinson (Admiral Sir Bertram Ramsey); Parick Barr (Group Capt. J.N. Stagg); Leslie Phillips (R.A.F. Officer); Donald Houston (R.A.F. Pilot); Frank Finlay (Pvt. Coke); Lyndon Brook (Lt. Walsh); Bryan Coleman (Ronald Callen); Trevor Reid (Gen. Sir Bernard L. Montgomery); Simon Lack (Air Chief Marshal Sir Trafford Leigh-Mallory); Louis Mounier (Air Chief Marshal Sir Arthur William Tedder); Sian Phillips (Wren); Howard Marion Crawford (Doctor); Richard Wattis (British Soldier); George Wilson (Alexandre Renaud); Fernand Ledoux (Louis); Hans Christian Blech (Maj. Werner Pluskat); Wolfgang Preiss (Maj. Gen. Max Pemsel); Heinze Reincke (Col. Josef "Pips" Priller); Richard Munch (Gen. Erich Marcks); Ernst Schroeder (Gen. Hans von Salmuth); Kurt Meisel (Capt. Ernst During); Heinz Spitzner (Lt. Col. Hellmuth Meyer); Robert Freytag (Meyer's Aide); Wolfgang Luckschy (Col. Gen. Alfred Jodl); Til Kiwe (Capt. Hellmuth Lang); Wolfgang Buttner (Maj. Gen. Dr. Hans Speidel); Ruth Hausmeister (Frau Rommel); Michael Hinz (Manfred Rommel); Paul Roth (Col. Schiller); Harmut Rock (Sgt. Bergsdorf); Karl John (Luftwaffe General); Deitmar Schonherr (Luftwaffe Major); Reiner Penkert (Lt. Frit Theen); Kurt

Pechner (German Commander); Serge Tolstoy (German Officer); Eugene Deckers (Nazi Soldier); Mark Damon (Pvt. Harris); Dewey Martin (Pvt. Wilder); John Crawford (Col. Caffey); Nicholas Stuart (Lt. Gen. Omar N. Bradley); John Meillon (Rear Admiral Alan G. Kirk); Jack Hedley (Briefing Officer); Fred Dur (Rangers Major); George Segal (1st Commando Up the Cliff); Georges Riviere (Sgt. Guy de Montlaur); Jean Servais (Rear Admiral Janjard); Maurice Poli (Jean); Alice Tissot (Housekeeper); Jo D'Avra (Naval Captain); Bill Nagy, Harold Goodwin, Michael Beint, Harry Fowler, Peter Helm, Pauline Carton, Neil McCallum, Christopher Lee. ¶Filmed August 1961–March 1962; world premiere in Paris, September 1962; general release, October 1963.

How the West Was Won (Cinerama-Metro-Goldwyn-Mayer, 1962), Metro-color, Cinerama and Ultra Panavision, Westrex Recording System, 162 min. ¶*Directors* John Ford *(The Civil War)*, George Marshall *(The Railroad)*, Henry Hathaway *(The Rivers, The Plains, The Outlaws)*; Richard Thorpe *(uncredited; transitional historical sequences); suggested by the series appearing in Life magazine; writers* James R. Webb, John Gay *(uncredited); cinematographers* Joseph LaShelle *(The Civil War, The Railroad)*, William H. Daniels *(The Plains)*, Charles Lang, Jr. *(The Rivers)*, Milton Krasner *(The Outlaws); overall production supervising cinematography* Milton Krasner; *producer* Bernard Smith; *scenarist* James R. Webb, *suggested by series in Life; art directors* George W. Davis, William Ferrari, Addison Hehr; *set decorators* Henry Grace, Don Greenwood, Jr., Jack Mills; *color consultant* Charles K. Hagedorn; *music* Alfred Newman, Ken Darby; *editors* Harold F. Kress, Margaret Booth; *2nd unit cinematographers* Harold E. Wellman, Dale Deverman, Robert L. Surtees, Peter Gibbons; *assis-*

tant directors George Marshall, Jr., William McGarry, Robert Saunders, William Shanks, Wingate Smith; *production supervisor for Cinerama, Inc.,* Coleman Thomas Conroy, Jr.; *special effects* Glenn E. Robinson; *special visual effects* A. Arnold Gillespie, Robert R. Hoag; *costume designer* Walter Plunkett; *hair styles* Sydney Guilaroff, Mary K. Keats; *makeup creator* William Tuttle; *music* Alfred Newman conducting the MGM Studio Symphony Orchestra; *music associate* Ken Darby; *music coordinator* Robert Emmett Dolan; *recording supervisor* Franklin E. Milton; *sound recording* Fred Bosch, Ray Sharples, Harold V. Moss, William Steinkamp; *sound consultant* Douglas Shearer; *2nd unit directors* Yakima Canutt, Richard Talmadge; *cinerama visual consultant* Peter Gibbons; *cinerama technical consultant* Walter Gibbons-Fly; *process photography* Harold E. Wellman; *music editor* Richard C. Harris; *sound editor* Milo Lory; *historical technical adviser* David Humphreys Miller; *The Civil War technical adviser* Jack Pennick; *livestock supervisors* Richard Webb and Vernon Mouce; *location manager* Howard "Dutch" Horton; *"How the West Was Won" music* Alfred Newman; *lyrics* Ken Darby; *"Home in the Meadow," music adaptation* Robert Emmett Dolan; *lyric adaptation* Sammy Cahn; *conductor* Robert Arbruster; *"Raise a Ruckus" music adaptation* Robert Emmett Dolan; *lyric adaptation* Johnny Mercer; *"Wait for the Hoedown," "What Was Your Name in the States" lyric adaptation* Johnny Mercer; *solo singer* Debbie Reynolds; *folk singing* Dave Gard and The Whiskeyhill Singers, The Ken Darby Chorus; *accordian solos* Carl Fortina; *narrator* Spencer Tracy. ¶*Civil War Episode* ¶**John Wayne** (Gen. William T. Sherman); George Peppard (Zeb Rawlings); Carroll Baker (Eve Prescott); Henry (Harry) Morgan (Gen. U.S. Grant); Andy Devine (Cpl. Peterson); Russ Tamblyn

(Confederate Deserter from Texas); Willis Bouchey (Surgeon); Claude Johnson (Jeremiah Rawlings); Ken Curtis (Ben, Union Corporal); Walter Reed, Carleton Young. ¶*Rest of the Cast* ¶Lee J. Cobb (Marshal Lou Ramsey); Henry Fonda (Jethro Stuart); Carolyn Jones (Julie Rawlings); Karl Malden (Zebulon Prescott); Gregory Peck (Cleve Van Valen); Robert Preston (Roger Morgan); Debbie Reynolds (Lilith Prescott); James Stewart (Linus Rawlings); Eli Wallach (Charley Gant); Richard Widmark (Mike King); Brigid Bazlen (Dora); Walter Brennan (Col. Hawkins); David Brian (Lilith's Lawyer); Raymond Massey (Abraham Lincoln); Agnes Moorehead (Rebecca Prescott); Thelma Ritter (Aggie Clegg); Mickey Shaughnessy (Deputy Stover); Rodolfo Acosta (Outlaw in Gant Gang); Dean Stanton (Outlaw); Lee Van Cleef (Marty); Kim Charney (Sam Prescott); Bryan Russell (Zeke Prescott); Karl Swenson (Train Conductor); Jack Lambert (Gant Henchman); Christopher Dark (Poker Player); Jay C. Flippen (Huggins); Gene Roth (Poker Player on Riverboat); Joe Sawyer (Ship's Officer); Clinton Sundberg (Hylan Seabury); James Griffith (Poker Player); Walter Burke (Poker Player on Wagon); John Larch (Grimes); Edward J. McKinley (Auctioneer); Barry Harvey (Angus); Jamie Ross (Bruce); Mark Allen (Colin); Craig Duncan (James Marshall); Charles Briggs (Barker); Paul Bryar (Auctioneer's Assistant); Tudor Owen (Parson Harvey); Beulah Archuletta, Chuck Roberson, Boyd "Red" Morgan, Jack Pennick. ¶Filmed at MGM Studios and on location in Custer State Park, Black Hills and Rapid City, South Dakota; Uncompaghre National Forest, Rocky Mountains, Montrose, Durango and Silverton, Colorado; on the Ohio and Cumberland rivers and in Paducah, Kentucky; Oatman, Perkinsville, Superior and Canyon de Chelly, Arizona; Monument Valley, Utah; Eugene and Grand Pass, Oregon; San Francisco, Lone Pine, Bishop, Simi and Scotia, California; Tonto National Forest and Inyo National Forest. ¶Filmed May–November, 1961; world premiere in London, November, 1962; general release, February–March, 1963.

Donovan's Reef (Ford Productions/ Paramount, 1963), Technicolor, 106 min. ¶*Director-producer* John Ford; *scenarists* Frank S. Nugent, James Edward Grant, *from a screen story by* Edmund Beloin; *cinematographer* William H. Clothier; *art directors* Hal Pereira, Eddie Imazu; *set decorators* Sam Comer, Darrell Silvera; *costumes* Edith Head; *music* Cyril J. Mockridge; *conductor* Irvin Talbot; *editor* Otho Lovering; *special photographic effects* Paul K. Lerpae; *process photography* Farciot Edouart; *orchestration* Leo Shuken, Jack Hayes; *Technicolor color consultant* Richard Mueller; *makeup supervisor* Wally Westmore; *hair style supervisor* Nellie Manley; *sound recording* Hugo Grenzbach, Charles Grenzbach; *assistant director* Wingate Smith. ¶John Wayne (Michael Patrick "Guns" Donovan); Lee Marvin (Thomas Aloysius "Boats" Gilhooley); Elizabeth Allen (Amelia Sarah Dedham); Jack Warden (Dr. William Dedham); Cesar Romero (Marquis Andre De Lage); Dorothy Lamour (Miss Lafleur); Jacqueline Malouf (Lelani Dedham); Mike Mazurki (Sgt. Menkowicz); Marcel Dalio (Father Cluzeot); Jon Fong (Mister Eu); Cheryline Lee (Sally Dedham); Tim Stafford (Luki Dedham); Carmen Estrabeau (Sister Gabrielle); Yvonne Peattie (Sister Matthew); Frank Baker (Capt. Martin); Edgar Buchanan (Boston Notary); Pat Wayne (Navy Lieutenant); Charles Seel (Grand Uncle Sedley Atterbury); Chuck Roberson (Festus); Mae Marsh, Maj. Sam Harris (Members of the Family Counsel in Boston); Dick Foran (Irish Officer); Cliff Lyons (Officer); Aissa Wayne (Native girl in Pool Scene).

¶Location filming on island of Lauai, Hawaii. ¶Filmed July–September, 1962; released July, 1963.

McLintock! (Batjac/United Artists, 1963), Technicolor, Panavision, 127 min. ¶*Director* Andrew V. McLaglen; *screenplay* James Edward Grant; *music* Frank De Vol; *songs* De Vol and By Dunham; *art directors* Hal Pereira, Eddie Imazu; *set decorators* Sam Comer, Darrell Silvera; *costumes* Frank C. Beetson, Jr.; *ladies costumes* Sam B. Peck; *assistant director* Frank Parmenter; *sound* Jack Solomon; *cinematographer* William H. Clothier; *editors* Otho Lovering, Bill Lewis; *consultant for fight sequences* Cliff Lyons; *assistant director* Frank Parmenter; *makeup* Webb Overlander; *song*, "Love in the Country," *sung by* The Lifetimers; *production supervisor* Robert E. Morrison; *producer* Michael Wayne. ¶**John Wayne** (George Washington McLintock); Maureen O'Hara (Katherine McLintock); Yvonne De Carlo (Louise Warren); Patrick Wayne (Devlin Warren); Stefanie Powers (Becky McLintock); Jack Kruschen (Birnbaum); Chill Wills (Drago); Jerry Van Dyke (Matt Douglas, Jr.); Edgar Buchanan (Bunny Dull); Bruce Cabot (Ben Sage); Perry Lopez (Davey Elk); Michael Pate (Puma); Strother Martin (Agard); Gordon Jones (Matt Douglas); Robert Lowery (Governor Cuthbert H. Humphrey); Ed Faulkner (Young Ben Sage); H.W. Gim (Ching); Aissa Wayne (Alice Warren); Chuck Roberson (Sheriff Lord); Hal Needham (Carter); Pedro Gonzales, Jr. (Carlos); Hank Worden (Curly Butler); Leo Gordon (Jones); Mary Patterson (Beth); John Hamilton (Fauntleroy); Ralph Volkie (Loafer); Kari Noven (Millie); John Stanley (Running Buffalo); Mari Blanchard (Camille); Bob Steele (Train Conductor); Dan Borgaze (Loafer); Big John Hamilton (Fauntelroy); Ralph Volkie (Old Timer in Saloon). ¶Filmed October, 1962–January, 1963; released November.

Circus World (British title, **The Magnificent Showman**, Bronston-Midway/Paramount, 1964), Technicolor, 70mm Super Technirama, 135 min. ¶*Director* Henry Hathaway; *writers* Ben Hecht, Julian Halevy, James Edward Grant, *from a screen story by* Philip Yordan, Nicholas Ray; *2nd unit director* Richard Talmadge; *cinematographer* Jack Hildyard; *2nd unit cinematographer* Claude Renoir; *production designer* John DeCuir; *editor* Dorothy Spencer; *music* Dimitri Tiomkin; *2nd unit production manager* C.O. Erickson; *assistant director* Jose Lopez Rodero; *sound mixer* David Hildyard; *sound re-recorded by* Gordon K. McCallum; *costumes designed by* Renie; *makeup* Mario Van Riel; *hairdressing* Grazin de Rossi; *continuity* Elaine Schreyeck; *song*, "Circus World," *music by* Dimitri Timkin, *lyrics by* Ned Washington; *executive associate producer* Michael Waszynski; *producer* Samuel Bronston. ¶**John Wayne** (Matt Masters); Claudia Cardinale (Toni Alfredo); Rita Hayworth (Lili Alfredo); Lloyd Nolan (Cap Carson); Richard Conte (Aldo Alfredo); John Smith (Steve McCabe); Henri Dantes (Emile Schuman); Wanda Rotha (Mrs. Schuman); Katharyna (Giovana); Kay Walsh (Flo Hunt); Margaret MacGrath (Anna); Katherine Ellison (Molly); Miles Malleson (Billy Hennigan); Katharine Kath (Hilda); Moustache (Bartender); George Tyne (Bartender in Madrid); Franz Alotoff and His Circus; Robert Cunningham. ¶Filmed at Bronston Studios, Madrid, Spain, September 1963–February 1964; released July.

The Greatest Story Ever Told (George Stevens Production Company/United Artists, 1965), Technicolor, Ultra Panavision 70, originally presented in Cinerama, 260 min. (later, 238 min.; then 190 min.; then 147 min.) ¶*Director* George Stevens; *writers* James Lee Barrett, George Stevens, *from the Bible, other ancient writings,*

the book, The Greatest Story Ever Told,
by Fulton Oursler, *and writings by*
Henry Denker; *creative associate* Carl
Sandburg; *additional direction (un-*
credited) David Lean, Jean Negulesco;
2nd unit direction Richard Talmadge,
William Hale; *cinematographers* Wil-
liam C. Mellor, Loyal Griggs; *assistant*
directors Ridgeway Callow, John
Veitch; *art directors* Richard Day,
William Creber, David Hall; *costumes*
Vittorio Nino, Novarese; *editors* Harold
F. Kress, Argyle Nelson, Frank O'Neill;
music Alfred Newman; *choral supervi-*
sion Ken Darby; *executive producer*
Frank I. Davis; *associate producers*
George Stevens, Jr., Antonio Vellani;
producer George Stevens. ¶Max Von
Sydow (Jesus); Michael Anderson, Jr.
(James the Younger); Carroll Baker
(Veronica); Ina Balin (Martha of Be-
thany); Pat Boone (Young Man at the
Tomb); Victor Buono (Sorak); Richard
Conte (Barabbas); Joanna Dunham
(Mary Magdalene); Jose Ferrer (Herod
Antipas); Van Heflin (Bar Amand);
Charlton Heston (John the Baptist);
Martin Landau (Caiaphas); Angela
Lansbury (Claudia); Janet Margolin
(Mary of Bethany); David McCallum
(Judas Iscariot); Roddy McDowall
(Matthew); Dorothy McGuire (Mary);
Sal Mineo (Uriah); Nehemiah Persoff
(Shemiah); Donald Pleasance (The
Dark Hermit); Sidney Poitier (Simon of
Cyrene); Claude Rains (Herod the
Great); Gary Raymond (Peter); Telly
Savalas (Pontius Pilate); Joseph
Schildkraut (Nicodemus); Paul Stewart
(Questor); **John Wayne** (The Cen-
turion); Shelley Winters (Woman of No
Name); Ed Wynn (Old Aram); Robert
Loggia (Joseph); Robert Blake (Simon
the Zealot); Burt Brinckerhoff (An-
drew); John Considine (John); Jamie
Farr (Thaddaeus); David Hedison
(Philip); Peter Mann (Nathanael); Tom
Reese (Thomas); David Sheiner (James
the Elder); Michal Tolan (Pilate's Aide);
Harold J. Stone (General Varus); Robert
Busch (Emissary); John Crawford

(Alexander); Russell Johnson (Scribe);
John Lupton (Speaker of Capernaum);
Abraham Sofaer (Joseph of Arim-
athaea); Chet Stratton (Theophilus);
Ron Whelan (Annas); John Abbott
(Aben); Rodolfo Acosta (Captain of
Lancers); Michael Ansara (Herod's
Commander); Philip Coolidge (Chuza);
Dal Jenkins (Philip); Joe Perry (Ar-
chelaus); Marian Seldes (Herodias);
Frank De Kova (The Tormentor);
Joseph Sirola (Dumah); Cyril Delevanti
(Melchior); Frank Silvera (Caspar);
John Pickard (Peter's 2nd Accuser);
Celia Lovsky (Woman Behind Rail-
ings); Mickey Simpson (Rabble Rou-
ser); Richard Bakalyan (Good Thief on
Cross); Marc Cavell (Bad Thief on
Cross); Renata Vanni (Weeping Wo-
man); Frank Richards, Harry Wilson,
Dorothy Neumann, Inbal Dance
Theatre of Israel. ¶Filmed in Utah.
Filmed October 1962–July 1963;
released February 1965.

In Harm's Way (Sigma/Paramount,
1965), Panavision, 167 min. ¶*Director*
Otto Preminger; *writer* Wendell
Mayes, *from the novel by* James Bassett;
cinematographer Loyal Griggs; *2nd unit*
cinematographer Philip Lathrop; *spe-*
cial photography Farciot Edouart; *as-*
sistant directors Daniel McCauley,
Howard Joslin, Michael Daves; *produc-*
tion designer Lyle Wheeler; *camera*
operator George Nagle; *chief gaffer*
Homer Plannette; *construction* Elmer
C. Rodgers; *key grip* Carl Gibson, Morris Rosen; *painter* Eugene Acker; *pro-*
perty master Wallace Oliver; *assistant*
editor James Wells; *sound effects editor*
Don Hall, Jr.; *music editor* Richad Car-
ruth; *negative cutter* Connie Roese;
special effects Lawrence W. Butler;
script supervisor Kathleen Fagan; *set*
decorator Morris Hoffman; *associate*
art director Al Roelofs; *executive assis-*
tant to the producer Nat Block; *dialogue*
coach Max Slater; *casting* Bill Barnes;
costume coordinator Hope Bryce; *make-*
up Del Armstrong, Webb Overlander,

David Grayson; *hairdressing* Frederic James; *production managers* Eva Manley, Stanley N. Goldsmith; *wardrobe* Eric Seelig, Alan Levine, Gordon Dawson, Grace M. Harris, Aldo Scareno; *art director* Al Roelofs; *editors* George Tomasini, Hugh S. Fowler; *music* Jerry Goldsmith; *titles* Saul Bass; *producer* Otto Preminger. Captain Blake M. Bath, USN, project officer; Captain Colin J. Mackenzie, USN (Ret.), technical advisor. ¶John Wayne (Capt. Rockwell Torrey); Kirk Douglas (Cdr. Paul Eddington); Patricia Neal (Maggie Haynes); Tom Tryon (Lt. William McConnel); Paula Prentiss (Bev McConnel); Brandon de Wilde (Jeremiah Torrey); Jill Haworth (Annalee Dorne); Dana Andrews (Admiral "Blackjack" Broderick); Stanley Holloway (Clayton Canfil); Burgess Meredith (Cdr. Egan Powell); Franchot Tone (Cinpac I Admiral); Henry Fonda (Cinpac II Admiral); Patrick O'Neal (Cdr. Neal Owynn); Carroll O'Connor (Lt. Cdr. Burke); Slim Pickens (C.P.O. Culpepper); James Mitchum (Ensign Griggs); George Kennedy (Col. Gregory); Bruce Cabot (Quartermaster Quoddy); Barbara Bouchet (Liz Eddington); Hugh O'Brian (Liz's Officer Friend, Air Force Major); Tod Andrews (Capt. Tuthill); Larry Hagman (Lt. Cline); Stewart Moss (Ensign Balch); Richard Le Pore (Lt. Tom Agar); Chet Stratton (Ship's Doctor); Soo Young (Tearful Woman); Dort Clark (Boston); Phil Mattingly (PT-Boat Skipper); Christopher George. ¶Location filming in Hawaii; San Francisco, San Diego, California. Filming aboard USS Brane, USS Captaine, USS O'Bannon, USS Walker, USS Saint Paul. ¶Filmed June–September, 1964; world premiere in Cannes, May; general release, June.

The Sons of Katie Elder (Hal Wallis Production/Paramount, 1965), Technicolor, Panavision, 122 min. ¶*Director* Henry Hathaway; *story* Talbot Jennings;

screenplay William H. Wright, Allan Weis, Harry Essex; *music* Elmer Bernstein; *costumes* Edith Head; *assistant director* D. Michael Moore; *set decorators* Sam Comer, Ray Moyer; *makeup* Loren Cossand, Webb Overlander; *hair stylist* Dorothy White; *sound recording* Harold Lewis, Charles Grenebach; *unit production manager* William W. Gray; *art directors* Hal Pereira, Walter Tyler; *cinematogrpaher* Lucien Ballard; *editor* Warren Low; *producer* Hal B. Wallis; *associate producer* Paul Nathan. ¶John Wayne (John Elder); Dean Martin (Tom Elder); Martha Hyer (Mary Gordon); Michael Anderson, Jr. (Bud Elder); Earl Holliman (Matt Elder); James Gregory (Morgan Hastings); Paul Fix (Sheriff Billy Wilson); Jeremy Slate (Deputy Sheriff Ben Latta); George Kennedy (Curley); Dennis Hopper (Dave Hastings); Sheldon Allman (Judge Harry Evers); John Litel (Minister); John Doucette (Undertaker Hyselman); James Westerfield (Banker Vennar); Rhys Williams (Charlie Bob Striker); John Qualen (Charlie Biller); Rodolfo Acosta (Bondie Adams); Strother Martin (Jeb Ross); Percy Helton (Storekeeper Peevey); Karl Swenson (Doc Isdell/Bartender); Harvey Grant (Jeb, the Blacksmith's Son); Jerry Gatlin (Amboy); Loren James (Ned Reese); Red Morgan (Burr Sandeman); Charles Roberson (Townsman); Ralph Volkie (Bit Man); Jack Williams (Andy Sharp); Henry Wills (Gus Dolly); Joseph Yrigoyen (Buck Mason). ¶Filmed on the Northern Plateau of Mexico, near Durango, at El Saltito, Chupaderos, Casa Blanca, etc.; and at the Churubusco Studios in Mexico City. ¶Filmed January–March; released July 1.

Cast a Giant Shadow (Mirisch-Llenroc-Batjac/United Artists, 1966), Technicolor, Panavision, 141 min. ¶*Director/ Writer* Melville Shavelson, *from the biography of* Col. David Marcus, *by*

Ted Berkman; *2nd unit direction* Jack Reddish; *cinematographer* Aldo Tonti; *production designer* Michael Stringer; *art director* Arrigo Equini; *editors* Bert Bates, Gene Ruggiero; *music* Elmer Bernstein; *producers* Melville Shavelson, Michael Wayne. ¶Kirk Douglas (Col. David "Mickey" Marcus); Yul Brynner (Asher Gonen); Senta Berger (Magda Simon); Frank Sinatra (Spence Talmadge); John Wayne (General Mike Randolph); Angie Dickinson (Emma Marcus); Luther Adler (Jacob Zion); Stathis Giallelis (Ram Oren); James Donald (Major Safir); Gordon Jackson (James MacAfee); Haym Topol (Abou Ibn Kadir); Ruth White (Mrs. Chaison); Michael Shilo (Andre Simon); Shlomo Hermon (Yussuf); Rina Gaynor (Rona); Michael Hordern (British Ambassador); Gary Merrill (Pentagon Chief of Staff); Allan Cuthbertson (Immigration Officer); Jeremy Kemp (Senior British Officer); Sean Barrett (Junior British Officer); Roland Bartrop (Bert Harrison); Vera Dolen (Mrs. Martinson); Robert Gardett (General Walsh); Michael Balston (1st Sentry); Claude Aliotti (2nd Sentry); Samra Dedes (Belly Dancer); Michael Shagrir (Truck Driver); Frank Latimore, Ken Buckle (U.N. Officers); Rodd Dana (Aide to Randolph); Robert Ross (Aide to Chief of Staff); Arthur Hansell (Officer); Don Sturkie (Parachute Sgt.); Hillel Rave (Yaakov). ¶John Wayne's scenes filmed in Rome, July–August, 1965. ¶Released April, 1966.

The War Wagon (Marvin Schwartz-Batjac/Universal, 1967), Technicolor, Panavision, 101 min. ¶*Director* Burt Kennedy; *writer* Clair Huffaker, *from his novel, Badman; 2nd unit director* Cliff Lyons; *cinematographer* William H. Clothier; *art director* Alfred Sweeney; *editor* Harry Gerstad; *music* Dimitri Tiomkin; *song, "Ballad of the War Wagon,"* Dimitri Tiomkin, Ned Washington; *ballad sung by* Ed Ames; *assistant directors* Al Jennings, H.A.

Silverman; *wardrobe* Robert Chiniquy, Donald Wolz; *sound* Waldon O. Watson, Robert R. Bertrand; *set decoration* Ray Moyer; *re-recording* Clem Portman; *sound effects* Edit-Rite, Inc.; *unit production manager* Joseph Behm; *assistant director* Al Jennings; *makeup* Donald W. Roberson, Dave Grayson; *costumes* Oscar Rodriguez; *script supervisor* Marshall T. Wolins; *property* Julius Rosenkrantz; *mattes* Albert Whitlock; *titles* Cinefx; *producer* Marvin Schwartz. ¶John Wayne (Taw Jackson); Kirk Douglas (Lomax); Howard Keel (Levi Walking Bear); Robert Walker (Billy Hyatt); Keenan Wynn (Wes Catlin); Bruce Cabot (Frank Pierce); Valora Noland (Kate); Gene Evans (Hoag); Bruce Dern (Hammond); Terry Wilson (Sheriff Strike); Joanna Barnes (Lola); Don Collier (Shack); Sheb Woolley (Dan Snyder); Ann McCrea (Felicia); Emilio Fernandez (Calito); Frank McGrath (Bartender); Chuck Roberson (Brown); Red Morgan (Early); Hal Needham (Hite); Marco Antonio Arzate (Wild Horse); Perla Walter (Rosita); Miko Mayama, Midori, Margarite Luna (Oriental Women); Jose Trinidad Villa (Townsman at Bar). ¶Location filming at Durango, Mexico. ¶Filmed September–December, 1966; released June 1967.

El Dorado (Laurel/Paramount, 1967), Technicolor, 127 min. ¶*Director* Howard Hawks; *assistant director* Andrew J. Durkas; *screenplay* Leigh Brackett, *from the novel The Stars in Their Courses, by* Harry Brown; *cinematographer* Harold Rosson; *art directors* Hal Pereira, Carl Anderson; *music* Nelson Riddle; *makeup* Wally Westmore; *editor* John Woodcock; *special photographic effects* Paul K. Lerpae; *set decoration* Robert Benton, Ray Moyer; *unit production manager* John Coonan; *assistant director* Andrew J. Durkus; *property master* Earl Olan; *makeup supervision* Wally Westmore; *hair style supervisor* Nellie

Manley; *costumes* Edith Head; *original
paintings of* Olaf Wieghorst; *special
photographic effects* Paul K. Lerpae;
process photography Farciot Edouart;
sound recording John Carter, Charles
Grenzbach; *orchestration* Gil Grau;
script supervisor Charlsie Bryant; *song,
"El Dorado,"* lyrics by John Gabriel,
music by Nelson Riddle, *sung by* George
Alexander, *accompanied by the* Mello-
men; *associate producer* Paul Helmick;
producer Howard Hawks. ¶John
Wayne (Cole Thornton); Robert Mit-
chum (J.P. Harrah); James Caan (Alan
Bourdillon Traherne/Mississippi); Char-
lene Holt (Maudie); Michele Carey
(Joey MacDonald); Arthur Hunnicutt
(Bull Harris); Christopher George
(Nelse McLeod); R.G. Armstrong
(Kevin MacDonald); Edward Asner
(Bart Jason); Paul Fix (Doc Miller);
Robert Donner (Milt); John Gabriel
(Pedro); Jim Davis (Jim Purvis, Jason's
Foreman); Marina Ghane (Maria);
Anne Newman (Saul MacDonald's
Wife); Johnny Crawford (Luke Mac-
Donald); Olaf Wieghorst (Swedish
Gunsmith); Robert Rothwell (Saul
MacDonald); Adam Roarke (Matt Mac-
Donald); Charles Courtney (Jared
MacDonald); Diane Strom (Matt's
Wife); Victoria George (Jared's Wife);
Anthony Rogers (Dr. Donavan); Wil-
liam (Bill) Henry (Sheriff Tod Draper);
Nacho Galindo (Mexican Saloon
Keeper); John Mitchum (Bartender in
Jason's Saloon). ¶Location filming in
Arizona. ¶Filmed October 1965–Feb-
ruary 1966; premiered Denver, De-
cember 31, 1966; released June 7, 1967.

The Green Berets (Batjac/Warner
Bros.—Seven Arts, 1968), Technicolor,
Panavision, 141 min. ¶*Directors* John
Wayne, Ray Kellogg; *writer* James Lee
Barrett, *from the novel by* Robin Moore;
2nd unit director Cliff Lyons; *adviser*
Mervyn LeRoy *(uncredited); cinematog-
rapher* Winton C. Hoch; *production
designer* Walter M. Simonds; *editor*
Otho Lovering; *music* Miklos Rozsa; *set

decorations* Ray Moyer; *sound* Stanley
Jones; *special effects* Sass Bedic; *unit
production manager* Lee W. Lukather;
assistant director Joe L. Cramer; *transportation coordinator* George Coleman; *Department of Defense Project
Officer* Lt. Col. William G. Byrns,
U.S.A.; *Special Forces Advisor* Major
Jerald R. Dobbs, U.S.A.; *Fort Benning
Prefect Officer* Capt. August Schow-
bulg, Jr.; *make-up* Dave Grayson; *cos-
tumes* Jerry Alpert; *script supervisor*
Crayton Smith; *property* "Red" Turner;
construction coordinator "Hank" Wil-
liams; *title designed by* Wayne Fitz-
gerald; *producer* Michael Wayne. ¶John
Wayne (Col. Mike Kirby); David Jans-
sen (George Beckworth); Jim Hutton
(Sgt. Petersen); Aldo Ray (Sgt. Mul-
doon); Raymond St. Jacques (Doc Mc-
Gee); Jack Soo (Col. Cai); Bruce Cabot
(Col. Morgan); George Takei (Capt.
Nim); Patrick Wayne (Lt. Jamison);
Luke Askew (Sgt. Provo); Irene Tsu
(Lin); Edward Faulkner (Capt. Mac-
Daniel); Jason Evers (Capt. Coleman);
Mike Henry (Sgt. Kowalski); Craig Jue
(Hamchunk); Chuck Roberson (Sgt.
Griffin); Eddy Donno (Sgt. Watson);
Rudy Robins (Sgt. Parks); Richard
"Cactus" Pryor (Collier); William Olds
(Phan Son Ti); Bach Yen, Frank Koo-
men. ¶Location filming at Fort Ben-
ning, Georgia. ¶Filmed August–De-
cember, 1967; released July.

Hellfighters (Universal, 1969),
Technicolor, Panavision, 121 min.
¶*Director* Andrew V. McLaglen; *writer*
Clair Huffaker; *cinematographer* Wil-
liam H. Clothier; *art directors* Alex-
ander Golitzen, Frank Arrigo; *editor*
Folmar Blangsted; *music* Leonard
Rosenman; *set decorators* John McCar-
thy, James S. Redd; *sound* Waldon O.
Watson, Lyle Cain, Ronald Pearce;
makeup Bud Westmore; *hair stylist*
Larry German; *dialogue coach* Robert
Forrest; *matte supervisor* Albert Whit-
tock; *stunt coordinator* Hal Needham;
cosmetics by Cinematique; *assistant

director Terry Morse, Jr.; *special effects* Fred Knoth, Whitey McMahan, Herman Townsley; *titles by* Universal Title; *technical advisors* "Red" Adair, "Boots" Hansen, "Boots" Matthews, of the Red Adair Wild Well Control Company; *costumes* Edith Head; *producer* Robert Arthur. ¶John Wayne (Chance Buckman); Katharine Ross (Tish Buckman); Jim Hutton (Greg Parker); Vera Miles (Madelyn Buckman); Jay C. Flippen (Jack Lomax); Bruce Cabot (Joe Horn); Edward Faulkner (George Harris); Barbara Stuart (Irene Foster); Edmund Hashim (Col. Valdez); Valentin De Vargas (Amal Bokru); Frances Fong (Madame Loo); Alberto Morin (Gen. Lopez); Alan Caillou (Harry York); Laraine Stephens (Helen Meadows); John Alderson (Jim Hatch); Lal Chand Mehra (Dr. Songla); Rudy Diaz (Zamora); Bebe Louie (Gumdrop); Pedro Gonzales Gonzales (Hernando, the House Boy); Edward Colmans (Senor Caldez); Chuck Roberson (Firefighter in Airplane). ¶Location filming at Houston, Texas, and Wyoming. ¶Filmed March–June, 1968; released December.

True Grit (Hal Wallis Production/ Paramount, 1969), Technicolor, 128 min. ¶*Director* Henry Hathaway; *based on the novel by* Charles Portis; *screenplay* Marguerite Roberts; *music* Elmer Bernstein; *song* Bernstein and Don Black; *production designer* Walter Tyler; *set decorators* Ray Moyer, John Burton; *sound recording* Roy Meadows; Elder Ruberg; *costumes* Dorothy Jenkins; *makeup* Jack Wilson; *assistant director* William W. Gray; *cinematographer* Lucien Ballard; *editor* Warren Low; *hair stylist* Carol Meikle; *production manager* Frank Beetson; *associate producer* Paul Nathan; *producer* Hal B. Wallis. ¶John Wayne (Reuben J. "Rooster" Cogburn); Glen Campbell (La Boeuf); Kim Darby (Mattie Ross); Jeremy Slate (Emmett Quincy); Robert Duvall (Ned Pepper); Dennis Hopper

(Moon); Alfred Ryder (Goudy); Strother Martin (Colonel G. Stonehill); Jeff Corey (Tom Chaney); Ron Soble (Captain Boots Finch); John Fiedler (Lawyer J. Noble Daggett); James Westefield (Judge Parker); John Doucette (Sheriff); Donald Woods (Barlow); Edith Atwater (Mrs. Floyd); Carlos Rivas (Dirty Bob); Isabel Boniface (Mrs. Bagby); H.W. Gim (Chen Lee); John Pickard (Frank Ross); Elizabeth Harrower (Mrs. Ross); Ken Renard (Yarnell); Jay Ripley (Harold Parmalee); Kenneth Becker (Farrell Parmalee); Myron Healey (A Deputy); Hank Worden (Undertaker); Guy Wilkerson (The Hangman); Red Morgan (Red, the Ferryman); Robin Morse. ¶Location filming around Montrose, Colorado, and Mammoth Lakes, California. ¶Filmed September– December, 1968; released July.

The Undefeated (20th Century Fox, 1969), Deluxe Color, Panavision, 118 min. ¶*Director* Andrew V. McLaglen; *writer* James Lee Barrett, *from a screen story by* Stanley L. Hough; *cinematographer* William Clothier; *art director* Carl Anderson; *editor* Robert Simpson; *music* Hugo Montenegro; *costumes* Bill Thomas; *stunt coordinator* Hal Needham; *set decorations* Walter M. Scott, Chester L. Bohym; *orchestration* Herbert Spencer; *unit production manager* Clarence Euris; *assistant director* Jack Cunningham; *sound* Leland Overton, David Dockendorf; *special photographic effects* L.B. Abbott, Art Cruickshank; *makeup supervisor* Dan Strlepek; *makeup artist* Leo Lotita; *hairstyling* Edith Lindon; *producer* Robert L. Jacks. ¶John Wayne (Col. John Henry Thomas); Rock Hudson (Col. James Langdon); Tony Aguilar (Gen. Rojas); Roman Gabriel (Blue Boy); Marian McCargo (Ann Langdon); Lee Meriwether (Margaret Langdon); Merlin Olsen (Big George); Melissa Newman (Charlotte Langdon); Bruce Cabot (Jeff Newby); Michael Vincent

(Bubba Wilkes); Ben Johnson (Short Grub); Edward Faulkner (Anderson); Harry Carey, Jr. (Webster); Paul Fix (Gen. Joe Masters); Royal Dano (Major Sanders); Richard Mulligan (Dan Morse); Carlos Rivas (Diaz); John Agar (Christian); Guy Raymond (Giles); Don Collier (Goodyear); Big John Hamilton (Mudlow); Dub Taylor (McCartney, the Cook); Henry Beckman (Thad Benedict); Victor Junco (Major Tapia); Robert Donner (Judd Mailer); Pedro Armendariz, Jr. (Escalante); James Dobson (Jamison); Rudy Diaz (Sanchez); Richard Angarola (Petain); James McEachin (Jimmy Collins); Gregg Palmer (Parker); Juan Garcia (Col. Gomez); Kiel Martin (Union Runner); Bob Gravage (Joe Hicks); Chuck Roberson (Yankee Officer at River Crossing). ¶Location filming at Durango, Mexico, and near Baton Rouge, Louisiana. ¶Filmed February–March, 1969; released November.

Chisum (Batjac/Warner Bros., 1970), Technicolor, Panavision, 110 min. ¶*Director* Andrew V. McLaglen; *writer* Andrew J. Fenady; *cinematographer* William H. Clothier; *art director* Carl Anderson; *set decorator* Ray Moyer; *editor* Robert Simpson; *music* Dominic Frontiere; *music supervisor* Sonny Burke; Merle Haggard *sings, "Turn Me Around," lyrics by* Norman Gimbel, *music by* Dominic Frontiere, *and "Ballad of John Chisum," lyrics by* Andrew J. Fernody, *music by* Dominic Frontiere; *paintings* Russ Vickers; *special effects* Howard Jensen; *unit production manager* Joseph G. Behm; *assistant director* Fred R. Simpson; *property* Ray Thompson; *transportation coordinator* George Coleman; *makeup* Dave Grayson; *wardrobe* Michael Harte, Luster Bayless; *grip supervisor* Marshall J. Wolins; *stills* Dave Sutton; *main titles designed by* Larry Bees, Art Shinko; *producer* Andrew J. Fenady; *executive producer*

Michael A. Wayne. ¶**John Wayne** (John Chisum); Forrest Tucker (Lawrence Murphy); Christopher George (Dan Nodeen); Pamela McMyler (Sally Chisum); Geoffrey Deuel (William Bonney, "Billy The Kid"); Ben Johnson (James Pepper); Glenn Corbett (Pat Garrett); Bruce Cabot (Sheriff Brady); Andrew Prine (Alex McSween); Patric Knowles (John Tunstall); Richard Jaeckel (Jess Evans); Lynda Day (Sue McSween); John Agar (Patton); Lloyd Battista (Neemo); Robert Donner (Morton); Ray Teal (Justice Wilson); Edward Faulkner (Dolan); Ron Soble (Bowdre); John Mitchum (Baker); Glenn Langan (Dudley); Alan Baxter (Governor Axtell); Alberto Morin (Delgado); William Bryant (Jeff); Pedro Armendariz, Jr. (Ben); Christopher Mitchum (O'Folliard); Abraham Sofaer (White Buffalo); Gregg Palmer (Riker); Chuck Roberson (A Trail Herder); Hank Worden (Stage Depot Clerk); Ralph Volkie (Blacksmith); Pedro Gonzales Gonzales (Mexican Rancher); John Pickard (Aggressive Sergeant). ¶Location filming at Durango, Mexico. ¶Filmed October–December, 1969; released July.

Rio Lobo (Malabar/Cinema Center, 1970), Technicolor, 114 min. ¶*Director* Howard Hawks; *assistant director* Mike Moder; *story* Burton Wohl; *screenplay* Leigh Brackett, Wohl; *production designer* Robert Smith; *art director* William Kiernan; *set decorator* William Kiernan; *2nd unit director* Yakima Canutt; *music* Jerry Goldsmith; *technical adviser* William Byrne; *sound* John Carter; *special effects* A.D. Flowers, Clifford P. Wenger; *cinematographer* William Clothier; *editor* John Woodcock; *unit production manager* Robert M. Becke; *property* Ray E. Mercer, Jr.; *recording sound editors* Jack Finley, Gene Feldman; *casting* Bott Bowers; *makeup* Monty Westmore; *hair stylist* Jean Austen; *key grip* Harry R. Joses; *costumes supervisor*

William J. Dodds; *associate producer* Paul Helmick; *producer* Howard Hawks. ¶John Wayne (Cord McNally); Jorge Rivero (Pierre Cordona); Jennifer O'Neill (Shasta); Jack Elam (Phillips); Victor French (Ketcham); Chris Mitchum (Tuscarora); Susana Dosamantes (Maria Carmen); Mike Henry (Sheriff Hendricks); David Huddleston (Dr. Jones, the Dentist); Bill Williams (Sheriff Cronin); Edward Faulkner (Lieutenant Harris); Sherry Lansing (Amelita); Dean Smith (Bitey); Robert Donner (Whitey Carter); Jim Davis (Riley); Peter Jason (Lieutenant Forsythe); Robert Rothwell, Chuck Courtney, George Plimpton (Whitey's Henchmen); Bob Steele (Henchman); Donald "Red" Barry (Bartender); Chuck Roberson (Soldier in Baggage Car; also Guard at Ranch); Red Morgan (Train Engineer); Hank Worden (Hank, the Hotel Clerk); John Ethan Wayne. ¶Location filming at Old Tucson, Arizona and Cuernavaca, Mexico. ¶Filmed, under title **San Timoteo,** March–June, 1970; premiered Chicago, November 6; released December 16.

Chesty: A Tribute to a Legend (1970). ¶A dramatized documentary of the life of Ford's friend, Lieutenant General Lewis Puller. ¶*Director* John Ford; *producer* James Ellsworth; *photography* Brick Marquard. ¶John Wayne.

Big Jake (Batjac/National General, for Cinema Center, 1971), Technicolor, Panavision, 110 min. ¶*Director* George Sherman; *writers* Harry Julian Fink, R.M. Fink; *2nd unit director* Cliff Lyons; *cinematographer* William Clothier; *art director* Carl Anderson; *editor* Harry Gerstad; *music* Elmer Bernstein; *main title design* Wayne Fitzgerald; *set decorator* Ray Moyer; *assistant director* Newton Arnold; *property* Ray Thompson; *production manager* Lee Luckather; *unit manager* Joseph C. Behm; *special effects* Howard Jensen; *special*

photographic effects Albert Whitlock; *makeup* David Grayson; *wardrobe* Luster Bayless; *script supervisor* Charlsie Bryant; *casting* Hoyt Bowers; *stills* Dave Sutton; *transportation coordinator* George Coleman; *producer* Michael A. Wayne. ¶John Wayne (Jacob McCandles); Richard Boone (John Fain); Maureen O'Hara (Martha McCandles); Patrick Wayne (James McCandles); Chris Mitchum (Michael McCandles); Bobby Vinton (Jeff McCandles); Bruce Cabot (Sam Sharpnose); Glenn Corbett (O'Brien); Harry Carey, Jr. (Pop Dawson); John Doucette (Buck Dugan); Jim Davis (Head of Lynching Party); John Agar (Bert Ryan); Gregg Palmer (John Goodfellow); Robert Warner (Will Fain); Jim Burke (Trooper); Dean Smith (James William "Kid" Duffy); John Ethan Wayne (Little Jack McCandles); Virginia Capers (Delilah); William Walker (Moses Brown); Jerry Gatlin (Stubby); Tom Hennesy (Saloon Brawler); Don Epperson (Saloon Bully); Everett Creach (Walt Devries); Jeff Wingfield (Billy Devries); Hank Worden (Hank); Jerry Summers (Hotel Desk Clerk); Chuck Roberson (One of Dugan's Men); Bernard Fox (Scots Sheepfarmer); Roy Jenson (Gunman in Bath House). ¶Location filming at Durango, Mexico. ¶Filmed, as **The Million Dollar Kidnapping,** October–December, 1970; released June, 1971.

The Cowboys (Sanford/Warner Bros., 1972), Technicolor, Panavision 70, 128 min. ¶*Director* Mark Rydell; *based on the novel by* William Dale Jennings; *screenplay* Irving Ravetch, Harriet Frank, Jr., William Dale Jennings; *assistant director* Tom Zinnemann; *2nd unit director* Robert "Buzz" Henry; *production designer* Philip Jefferies; *set decorator* William Kiernan; *music* John Williams; *titles* Phill Norman; *makeup* Emile La Vigne, Dave Grayson; *costumes* Anthea Sylbert; *sound* Kay Rose, Jack Solomon, Richard Portman;

cinematographer Robert Surtees; *editors* Robert Swink, Neil Travis; *production manager* Kate M. Edwards; *unit production manager* Rick Moder; *assistant director* Jim Zinnemann; *property master* Robert Schultz; *hair stylist* Patricia Abbott; *key grip* Don Lambert; *gaffer* Glen Bird; *script supervisor* Bob Forrest; *casting* Lynn Stalmaster; *associate producer* Tom Zinnemann; *producer* Mark Rydell. ¶John Wayne (Will Andersen); Roscoe Lee Browne (Jebediah Nightlinger); Bruce Dern (Long Hair); Colleen Dewhurst (Kate); Slim Pickens (Anse); Lonny Chapman (Preacher); Charles Tyner (Mr. Jenkins); A. Martinez (Cimarron); Alfred Barker, Jr. (Singing Fats); Nicolas Beauvy (Four Eyes); Steve Benedict (Steve); Robert Carradine (Slim Honneycutt); Norman Howell, Jr. (Weedy); Stephen Hudis (Charlie Schwartz); Sean Kelly (Stuttering Bob); Mike Pyeatt (Homer Weems); Clay O'Brien (Hardy Fimps); Sam O'Brien (Jimmy Phillips); Sarah Cunningham (Annie Andersen); Allyn Ann McLerie (Ellen Price); Wallace Brooks (Red Tucker); Jim Bruke (Pete); Maggie Costain (Phoebe); Walter Scott (Okay); Dick Farnsworth (Henry Williams); Matt Clark (Smiley); Larry Finley (Jake); Jerry Gatlin (Howdy); Charise Cullin (Elizabeth); Collette Poeppel (Rosemary); Norman Howell (Jim's Father); Margaret Kelly (Bob's Mother); Larry Randles (Ben); Fred Brookfield, Tap Canutt, Chuck Courtney, Gary Epper, Henry Wills, Kent Hays, J.R. Randall, Joe Yrigoyen (Rustlers). ¶Filmed around San Cristobel ranch, near Santa Fe, New Mexico. ¶Filmed April–July, 1971; released January 1972.

Cancel My Reservation (Naho/Warner Bros., 1972), Technicolor, 99 min. ¶*Director* Paul Bogart; *writers* Arhur Marx, Robert Fisher, *from the novel, The Broken Gun, by* Louis L'Amour; *executive producer* Bob Hope; *producer* Gordon Oliver. ¶Bob Hope, Eva Marie Saint, Ralph Bellay, Forrest Tucker, Anne Archer, Keenan Wynn. **John Wayne,** in cameo with Bing Crosby and Flip Wilson, as smiling figure in (Bob Hope's) nightmare sequence involving a lynching.

The Train Robbers (Batjac/Warner Bros., 1973), Technicolor, Panavision, 92 min. ¶*Director* Burt Kennedy; *writer* Burt Kennedy; *cinematographer* William Clothier; *art director* Al Sweeney; *editor* Frank Santillo; *stunt coordinator* Cliff Lyons; *music* Dominic Frontiere; *set decorator* Ray Moyer; *special effects* Howard Jensen; *production manager* Kate H. Edwards; *assistant director* Fred Simpson; *script supervisor* Marshall Wolins; *property* Jerry Graham; *stills* Dave Sutton; *wardrobe* Luster Bayless; *main title* Wayne Fitzgerald; *special photographic effects* Albert Whitlock; *makeup* David Grayson, Joe Di Bella; *transportation coordinator* George Coleman; *Anne-Margaret's hairstyling and makeup created by* George Masters; *producer* Michael Wayne. ¶John Wayne (Lane); Ann-Margret (Mrs. Lowe); Rod Taylor (Grady); Ben Johnson (Jesse); Chris George (Calhoun); Bobby Vinton (Ben); Jerry Gatlin (Sam); Ricardo Montalban (Pinkerton Man). ¶Location filming at Durango, Mexico. ¶Filmed March–June, 1972; released February, 1973.

Cahill, United States Marshal (British Title, **Cahill;** Batjac/Warner Bros., 1973), Technicolor, Panavision, 103 min. ¶*Director* Andrew V. McLaglen; *writers* Harry Julian Fink, Rita M. Fink, *from a story by* Barney Slater; *cinematographer* Joseph Biroc; *production designer* Walter Simonds; *editor* Robert L. Simpson; *music* Elmer Bernstein; *set decorator* Ray Moyer; *script supervisor* Marshall Wolins; *makeup* David Grayson; *production manager* William C. Davidson; *assistant director* Fred B. Simpson; *special effects* Howard Jensen; *property* Jerry

Graham; *wardrobe* Luster Bayless; *special photographic effects* Albert Whitlock; *main title* Wayne Fitzgerald; *transportation coordinator* James Brubaker; *stills* David Sutton; *2nd assistant director* Joe Florence; *stunt coordinator* Chuck Roberson; *song, "A Man Gets To Thinkin'," music by* Elmer Bernstein, *lyrics by* Don Black, *sung by* Charlie Rich; *producer* Michael A. Wayne. ¶John Wayne (J.D. Cahill); George Kennedy (Abe Fraser); Gary Grimes (Danny Cahill); Neville Brand (Lightfoot); Clay O'Brien (Billy Joe Cahill); Marie Windsor (Mrs. Green [Hetty]); Morgan Paull (Struther); Dan Vadis (Brownie); Royal Dano (MacDonald); Scott Walker (Ben Tildy); Denver Pyle (Denver); Jackie Coogan (Charlie Smith); Rayford Barnes (Pee Wee Simser); Dan Kemp (Joe Meehan); Harry Carey, Jr. (Hank); Walter Barnes (Sheriff Grady); Paul Fix (Old Man); Pepper Martin (Hard Case); Vance Davis (Negro); Chuck Roberson (Leader of Bunch); Ken Wolger (Boy); Hank Worden (Albert); James Nusser (Doctor); Murray MacLeod (Deputy Gordine); Hunter Von Leer (Deputy Jim Kane). ¶Location filming at Durango, Mexico. ¶Filmed, as **Wednesday Morning**, November–December, 1972; released July 1973.

McQ (Batjac, Levy-Gardner/Warner Bros., 1974), Technicolor, Panavision, 111 min. ¶*Director* John Sturges; *writer* Lawrence Roman; *2nd unit director* Ron R. Rondell; *cinematographer* Harry Stradling. Jr.; *production designer* Walter Simonds; *editor* Bill Ziegler; *music* Elmer Bernstein; *sound* Charles Wilborn; *set decorator* Tony Montanero; *re-recording* Tex Rudloff; *1st assistant director* Ric Fondell; *makeup* David Grayson, Joe DiBella; *property master* Jerry Graham; *wardrobe* Luster Bayless; *special effects* Howard Jensen; *2nd assistant director* Jerry Grandey; *script supervisor* John Franco; *transportation coordinator*

James Brubaker; *production coordinator* Robert Levy; *assistant to the producers* Thomas J. Kane; *casting* Ness Hyams; *titles* Wayne Fitzgerald; *special weapon* Military Armament Corporation; *unit production manager* Michael S. Glick; *producers* Jules Levy, Arthur Gardner, Lawrence Roman; *executive producer* Michael Wayne. ¶John Wayne (Detective Lieutenant Lon McQ); Eddie Albert (Captain Ed Kosterman); Diana Muldaur (Lois Boyle); Colleen Dewhurst (Myra); Clu Gulager (Franklin Toms); David Huddleston (Edward M. "Pinky" Farrow); Jim Watkins (J.C. Davis); Al Lettieri (Manny Santiago); Julie Adams (Elaine Forrester); Roger E. Mosley (Rosey); William Bryant (Sgt. Stan Boyle); Joe Tornatore (LaSalle); Kim Sanford (Ginger); Richard Kelton (Radical); Richard Eastham (Walter Forrester); Dick Friel (Bob Mahoney); Fred Waugh (Bodyguard); Chuck Roberson (Bodyguard). ¶Location filming in Seattle. ¶Filmed June–August, 1973; released February 6, 1974.

Brannigan (Wellborn/United Artists, 1975), Deluxe Color, Panavision, 111 min. ¶*Director* Douglas Hickox; *writers* Christopher Trumbo, Michael Butler, William P. McGivern, William Norton, *from a screen story by* Christopher Trumbo, Michael Butler; *cinematographer* Gerry Fisher; *art director* Ted Marshall; *editor* Malcolm Cooke; *music* Dominic Frontiere; *production manager* Geoffrey Haine; *location manager* Arnold Ross; *sound* Simon Kaye; *dubbing mixer* Gerry Humphries; *titles* G.S.E. Limited; *dubbing editor* Less Wiggins; *set decorator* Josie Mac Avin; *costume designer* Emma Porteous; *makeup* Dave Grayson, Alan Brownie; *continuity* Angela Allen; *camera operator* Freddie Cooper; *assistant director* Ted Sturges; *stunt co-ordinator* Peter Brayham; *casting* Miriam Brickman; *assistant to the producers* Sara Romilly; *production assistant*

Robert Levy; *executive producer*
Michael Wayne; *producers* Jules Levy,
Arthur Gardner. ¶John Wayne (Branni-
gan); Richard Attenborough (Com-
mander Sir Charles Swann); Mel Ferrer
(Mel Fields); Judy Geeson (Det.-Sgt.
Jennifer Thatcher); John Vernon (Ben
Larkin); Daniel Pilon (Gorman); James
Booth (Charlie the Handle); John
Stride (Det.-Inspector Traven); An-
thony Booth (Freddy); Del Henney
(Drexel); Don Henderson (Geef);
Ralph Meeker (Capt. Moretti). ¶Studio
work at Shepperton; location filming in
the London area. ¶Filmed, as **Joe Bat-
tle,** June–August, 1974; released
March, 1975.

Rooster Cogburn (Hal B. Wallis/Uni-
versal, 1975), Technicolor, Panavision,
108 min. ¶*Director* Stuart Millar; *sug-
gested by the character created by*
Charles Portis *in the novel, True Grit;*
screenplay Martin Julien; *art director*
Preston Ames; *set decorator* George
Robert Nelson; *music* Laurence Rosen-
thal; *2nd unit director* Michael Moore;
assistant directors Pepi Lenzi, Richard
Hashimoto; *stunt coordinator* Jerry
Gatlin; *men's costumes* Luster Bayless;
Miss Hepburn's wardrobe Edith Head;
sound John Carter; *special effects* Jack
McMasters; *cinematographer* Harry
Stradling; *2nd unit cinematographer*
Rexford Metz; *editor* Robert Swink;
associate producer Paul Nathan; *pro-
ducer* Hal B. Wallis. ¶John Wayne
(Rooster Cogburn); Katharine Hep-
burn (Eula Goodnight); Anthony Zerbe
(Breed); Richard Jordan (Hawk); John
McIntire (Judge Isaac C. Parker); Paul
Koslo (Luke); Jack Colvin (Red); Jon
Lormer (Reverend Goodnight); Richard
Romancito (Wolf); Lane Smith (Leroy);
Warren Vanders (Bagby); Jerry Gatlin
(Nose); Strother Martin (McCoy); Mic-
key Gilbert (Hambone); Chuck Hay-
ward (Jerry); Gary McLarty (Emmett);
Tommy Lee (Chen Lee). ¶Location
filming in the Deschutes National
Forest and Rogue River area of

Oregon. ¶Filmed September–November, 1974; released November, 1975.

The Shootist (Dino De Laurentiis/
Paramount, 1976), Technicolor, 100
min. ¶*Director* Don Siegel; *writers*
Miles Hood Swarthout, Scott Hale,
from the novel by Glendon Swarthout;
cinematographer Bruce Surtees; *production designer* Robert Boyle; *editor*
Douglas Stewart; *music* Elmer Bernstein; *executive production manager*
Russell Saunders; *assistant director* Joe
Cawalier; *script supervisor* Betsy Nor-
ton; *2nd assistant director* Joe Flo-
rence; *sound mixer* Alfred J. Overton;
sound re-recording Arthur Piantadosi,
Les Fresholtz, Michael Minkler; *camera
operator* Tom Del Ruth; *camera
assistants* Timothy E. Wade, Rick Men-
tion; *property master* Bill Dietz; *gaffer*
Chuck Holmes; *key grip* Kenneth
Adams; *construction coordinator*
Joseph M. LeBaron; *special effects*
Angie Lohman; *Miss Bacall's costumes*
Moss Mabry; *set decorator* Arthur
Parker; *assistant art decoration* Richard
Lawrence; *hair stylist* Vivienne
Walker; *makeup* Dave Grayson, Joe Di
Bella; *public relations* Al Howits;
publicity Jack Casey; *men's costumes*
Luster Bayless; *ladies' costumes* Edna
Taylor; *casting* Polifroni/Sabba; *produc-
tion coordinator* Eudie Charnes; *assis-
tant editor* Jerrold L. Ludwig; *music
editing* D. Harris Music Service; *sound
effects* Burbank Editorials Service, Inc.;
titles and optical effects Universal Op-
tical; *producers* M.J. Frankovich,
William Self. ¶John Wayne (John Ber-
nard Books); Lauren Bacall (Bond
Rogers); Ron Howard (Gillom Rogers);
James Stewart (Dr. Hostetler); Richard
Boone (Mike Sweney); Hugh O'Brian
(Pulford); Bill McKinney (Cobb); Harry
Morgan (Marshal Thibido); John Carradine (Beckum); Sheree North (Se-
repta); Richard Lenz (Sam Dobkins);
Scatman Crothers (Moses); Gregg
Palmer (Burly Man); Alfred Dennis
(Barber); Dick Winslow (Streetcar

Driver); Melody Thomas (Girl on Streetcar); Kathleen O'Malley (School-teacher). ¶Location filming at Carson City, Nevada. ¶Filmed January–March, 1976; released August.

Sources

Carpozi, George, Jr. *The John Wayne Story*. New York: Dell Publishing Co., Inc., 1972, 1979.

Eyles, Allen. *John Wayne*. Introduction by Louise Brooks. Memorial Edition. South Brunswick and New York: A.S. Barnes, 1976, 1979.

Garbicz, Adam, and Klinowski, Jacek. *Cinema, the Magic Vehicle: A Guide to Its Achievement. Journey One: The Cinema Through 1949*. New York: Schocken Books, 1983.

Katz, Ephraim. *The Film Encyclopedia*. New York: Thomas Y. Crowell, 1979.

Michael, Paul, Editor-in-Chief. *The American Movies Reference Book: The Sound Era*. Associate editor, James Robert Parish; contributing editors John Robert Cocchi, Ray Hagen, Jack Edmund Nolan. Englewood Cliffs, N.J.: Prentice-Hall, 1970.

Parish, James Robert, and Pitts, Michael R. *The Great Western Pictures*. Editor, T. Allan Taylor. Research Associates: John Robert Cocchi, Edward Connor, Richard Picchiarini, Florence Solomon, Vince Terrace. Metuchen, N.J.: Scarecrow, 1976.

Shaw, Sam. *John Wayne in the Camera Eye*. New York: Exeter Books, 1979.

Shepherd, Donald, and Slatzer, Robert, with Dave Grayson. *Duke: The Life and Times of John Wayne*. New York: Zebra Books, Kensington Publishing, 1985.

Sinclair, Andrew. *John Ford*. New York: Dial Press/James Wade, 1979.

Zolotow, Maurice. *Shooting Star: A Biography of John Wayne*. New York: Simon and Schuster, 1974.

Notes

1. Eric Bentley, "The Political Theatre of John Wayne," pp. 306–312, *Theatre of War: Comments on 32 Occasions*. New York: The Viking Press, 1972, p. 308.

2. Ron Kovic, *Born on the Fourth of July*. New York: McGraw-Hill Book Company, 1976, pp. 43, 158.

3. Joan Didion, "John Wayne: A Love Song," pp. 29–41, *Slouching Towards Bethlehem*. New York: Farrar, Straus, & Giroux, 1968, pp. 30, 30–31, 41.

4. Northrop Frye, "Myth, Fiction, and Displacement," pp. 21–38, *Fables of Identity: Studies in Poetic Mythology*. A Harbinger Book. New York: Harcourt, Brace & World, Inc., 1963, p. 27. First published in *Daedalus*, Summer 1961.

5. Northrop Frye, *The Secular Scripture: A Study of the Structure of Romance*. Cambridge, Massachusetts: Harvard University Press, 1976, p. 15.

6. Ralph Waldo Emerson, "Nature" (1836) pp. 3–42, *The Selected Writings of Ralph Waldo Emerson*. Modern Library College Editions. New York: Random House, Inc., 1940, 1950, p. 6.

7. Emerson, "Self Reliance" (1841), pp. 145–69, *Selected Writings*, Ibid., p. 159.

8. H.L. Mencken, "The Hallmarks of America," Chapter 1 of Part II, as revised in enlarged edition published in 1936. Pp. 1146–1151, *The American Tradition in Literature*, Third Edition. Edited by Sculley Bradley, Richmond Croom Beatty, and E. Hudson Long. Volume 2. New York: W.W. Norton & Company, Inc., 1967. Page 1149.

9. Quoted by Dumas Malone, *Jefferson and the Rights of Man*. Volume Two of *Jefferson and His Time*. Boston: Little, Brown and Company, 1951. Page 4.

10. Lionel Trilling, "Art and Neurosis," (1945) pp. 155–175, *The Liberal Imagination: Essays on Literature and Society*. Anchor Books. Garden City, New York: Doubleday & Company, Inc., 1953. Originally published by the Viking Press, Inc., in 1950. Page 174.

11. See Gerald Mast, *The Comic Mind: Comedy and the Movies*. Second

Edition. Chicago and London: The University of Chicago Press, 1979. First
Edition, 1973. This is an invaluable discussion of the subject.

12. Francis MacDonald Cornford, *The Origin of Attic Comedy*. Edited
with Foreword and Additional Notes by Theodor H. Taster. Anchor Books.
Garden City, New York: Doubleday & Company, Inc., 1961. Originally
published 1914 (?). Page 173. This is an important source of ideas about comedy which I have used in my discussion of Wayne's comic talent.

13. Suzanne K. Langer, *Feeling and Form: A Theory of Art*, Chapter 18,
"The Great Dramatic Forms: The Comic Rhythm," pp. 326–350. New York:
Charles Scribner's Sons, 1953. Pages 328, 331. Another important source of
ideas about comedy.

14. Emerson, "Circles" (1841), pp. 279–291, *Selected Writings*. Pages
279, 280, 283.

15. Emerson, "Circles," pages 281, 283.

16. Joseph Campbell, *The Hero with a Thousand Faces*. Second Edi-
tion. Bollingen Series XVII. Princeton, New Jersey: Princeton University
Press, 1968. (First edition, 1949; Bollingen Paperback Printing, 1972; Third
Printing, 1973).

17. Northrop Frye, *Anatomy of Criticism: Four Essays*. Princeton, New
Jersey: Princeton University Press, 1957. See particularly the third essay,
"Archetypal Criticism: Theory of Myths," pp. 131–239. A fundamental
source of ideas for my discussion of Wayne's films.

18. Northrop Frye, *Anatomy of Criticism*, page 220.

19. Northrop Frye, *Anatomy of Criticism*, page 214.

20. Northrop Frye, *Anatomy of Criticism*, page 226.

21. Northrop Frye, *Anatomy of Criticism*, page 228.

22. D.H. Lawrence, *Studies in Classic American Literature*. New York:
The Viking Press, 1961. Originally published in 1923 by Thomas Seltzer Inc.
Pages 4, 5.

23. D.H. Lawrence, *Studies*, page 36.

24. Ralph Waldo Emerson, "Self Reliance," pages 145, 149.

25. Clare Boothe Luce, "Woman: A Technological Castaway," pp.
24–29, *1973 Britannica Book of the Year*. Chicago: Encyclopaedia Britannica, Inc., 1973. Page 24.

26. See Stanley Cavell, *Pursuits of Happiness: The Hollywood Comedy
of Remarriage*. Cambridge, Massachusetts: Harvard University Press, 1981.

Index

All entries in boldface indicate photographs.